Whiptail Ruin (AZ BB:10:3 [ASM]): A Classic Period Community in the Northeastern Tucson Basin

edited by
Linda M. Gregonis
Gayle Harrison Hartmann

with contributions by

Jenny L. Adams
Carl F. Aten
Lane Anderson Beck
Lisa W. Huckell
James P. Lombard
Laural Myers
Sharon F. Urban

In Collaboration with the
Arizona Archaeological and Historical Society
Tucson

Arizona State Museum Archaeological Series 203

Arizona State Museum
The University of Arizona
Tucson, Arizona 85721-0026

Printed in the United States of America

ISBN (paper): 978-1-889747-88-0
Library of Congress Control Number: 2011906328

ARIZONA STATE MUSEUM ARCHAEOLOGICAL SERIES

The *Archaeological Series* of the Arizona State Museum, The University of Arizona, publishes the results of research in archaeology and related disciplines conducted in the Greater Southwest. Original, monograph-length manuscripts are considered for publication, provided they deal with appropriate subject matter. Information regarding procedures or manuscript submission and review is given under Research Publications on the Arizona State Museum website: *www.statemuseum.arizona.edu/research/pubs.* Information may be also obtained from the General Editor, *Archaeological Series*, Arizona State Museum, P.O. Box 210026, The University of Arizona, Tucson, Arizona, 85721-0026; Email: langer@email.arizona.edu. Electronic publications and previous volumes in the Arizona State Museum Library or available from the University of Arizona Press are listed on the website noted above.

The Arizona State Museum *Archaeological Series* is grateful to the many donors and supporters who continue to make this publication possible, particularly those who supported the 200th volume of the *Archaeological Series*.

The publication of this volume is made possible by the Arizona Archaeological and Historical Society Haury Fund. Cover image is Figure 1.10 in the text.

Distributed by The University of Arizona Press, P.O. Box 210055, The University of Arizona, Tucson, Arizona, 85721-0055.

Contents

Figures

Figures, continued

Tables

Tables, continued

Foreword

A lot has happened in archaeology in the 40-plus years that have passed since I was first shown the site that would become known as Whiptail Ruin. We have passed from a focus on culture history, through processualism and post-modernism, beyond any imaginings of us as new undergraduate students.

I was in my second year of university in Tucson and was keen to start 'doing' archaeology. At the time, the policy of the Anthropology Department was that fieldwork should only be done after the undergraduate degree had been completed. It was also a time when there was little interest in Tucson Basin archaeology. It was apparent that the more interesting research was in areas to the north, whether it was the Hohokam heartland of the Phoenix Basin or the massive Pueblo sites of the Mogollon rim. Since there was little chance of digging in my courses, I found the opportunity to investigate the archaeological remains near the Agua Caliente Springs. I was first shown the site by an anthropology graduate student whose family was renting the houses at the springs. What made the remains so evident wasn't only the scatter of pot sherds and flakes but the numerous holes that had already been dug, seemingly randomly, across the site. Many of these had exposed adobe wall segments and evidence of burning. The stone outlines of the buried houses excited my imagination. For me this was the dawn of what has become a life-long fascination with the hidden past.

I enquired into who owned the land and made contact with Dr. Otis Miller. He had recently purchased the land as a development investment and gave me written permission to excavate. This I did, and I freely admit that I had no idea how to go about it. After a few weekends of poking into one partly exposed house, Larry Hammack came out to the site and gave me a crash course on not only how to excavate but on the importance of keeping notes, records, photos, etc. and how to go about it. It wasn't long before I was joined in my efforts by classmates who were also anxious to get field experience. Through time the project morphed in a number of different ways and became a major training ground for aspiring archaeologists as well as an opportunity for amateurs to get practical experience. One only has to read the extensive list of names in Table 1.1 to get a sense of the impact this project had on individuals. There are quite a few who have become senior archaeologists over the years.

The history of what transpired at the site is well documented in this report but what it meant to, and the impact it had on individuals, is incalculable. As I read the list of participants, memories of people and events long forgotten come back. One name in particular, Lisbet

Nillsen, reminded me of a non-archaeological consequence of our weekend forays into the desert; even though she only dug at the site once or twice. In the late 1960s a newly identified disease, coccidioidomycosis (valley fever), was being studied by a group of medical scientists in Tucson. Somehow they became aware of a high infection rate amongst a particular cadre of student archaeologists—the Whiptail crew. We became the focus of one of the first studies of this disease and it was found that, up to the point of the study, all participants tested positive. While not a great outcome for some of us, Lisbet had to give up her year abroad and others of us had medical complications, the study did pioneer research into this affliction.

While the sort of independent digging we did is not generally accepted as a valid approach to archaeology or preservation, I rationalized what we were doing by the argument that if we didn't do something the site would be destroyed. This was a time when Tucson development was expanding at an incredible rate and the profession stood by as sites such as Hodges and St. Mary's, amongst many others, fell to construction. While my primary motivation was probably more acquisitive than altruistic, this rationale has been born out. Had we not investigated the site much of it would have been lost to development. Because of the disjointed history and nature of the work at Whiptail and subsequent analyses and use of the collection for teaching, quite a bit of information was either not recorded or lost through time. Nevertheless, this report does show what can be done with old information; albeit with massive effort and perseverance, and even in cases like Whiptail much can be learned.

I believe that one very positive effect of the Whiptail investigations was a growing interest in and acknowledgment of the importance of the early human experiences in the Tucson Basin. This is especially the case for the principal authors and contributors to this book. Another very positive effect of this project was the involvement of the amateurs and the impact it had on the people who lived in the area and those who eventually built houses on the property. While we didn't know it at the time, through our willingness and enthusiasm to share, we were pioneering what has become a standard procedure in Southwestern archaeology: public education. I'm sure that it was this early experience that influenced some of us to spend much of our careers in public archaeology.

On a personal note, I am extremely grateful for the herculean effort of all those who have contributed to this book and for the honor and opportunity to say a few words. Whiptail has too long been a skeleton in my professional closet. While my career has seen me involved in research from the Paleolithic in Eurasia, horse domestication in Central Asia, Paleoindian in North America, experimental archaeology and not least Ancestral Pueblo in the Southwest, it was the work at Whiptail in those halcyon days of discovery that has had the greatest impact on my career and is a vibrant lasting memory.

Bruce Bradley
University of Exeter

Preface and Acknowledgments

The archaeological history of the Southwest is replete with field projects that are begun with the best of intentions, directed with diligence and conducted with enthusiasm, but not published in a timely manner. This is especially true when the projects are volunteer efforts, lacking the discipline of a deadline imposed by a contract or grant. The work reported here, the excavations at the Whiptail Ruin, is a case in point.

Lengthy "prepublication" periods used to be relatively common in excavation projects, especially in cases where the individuals in charge moved on to other institutions or where, as noted above, the work was conducted by volunteers. A notorious example close to home was the pioneering work conducted by Carl Miller and Isabel Kelly at the Hodges Ruin, a large, long-lived Hohokam community located near the confluence of Rillito Creek and the Santa Cruz River. The results of excavations that began in 1936 and ended in 1938 were not published for 40 years (Kelly 1978). Fortunately, this lackadaisical approach to publication is almost a thing of the past. Now, most fieldwork is a product of the world of contract archaeology, which imposes strict deadlines that result in timely publications – at least most of the time. This publication, which reports the results of excavations that were completed 33 years ago, represents, we believe the next to last Arizona Archaeological and Historical Society (AAHS) field project from the Tucson Basin with a lengthy prepublication period. Final analysis has just begun on the one remaining unpublished project, excavations at the Redtail site, which is on the northwest side of Tucson near the north end of the Tucson Mountains.

Excavations at the Whiptail Ruin, located in the northeast corner of the Tucson Basin immediately south of Agua Caliente Park, began in 1966 when Bruce Bradley, then an undergraduate at the University of Arizona, dug a single Tanque Verde phase structure on property owned by Dr. Otis B. Miller. Excavations continued as a volunteer effort under the auspices of the Arizona Archaeological and Historical Society from 1967 to 1971 and then again in 1973, 1974, 1977, and 1978, with a Pima Community College field program conducted on the site in 1970 and 1971. Efforts at analyzing and reporting these excavations occurred in the 1980s. (Details of the history of the project are reported in Chapter 1). Our work on this project began in 1996 when Mark Slaughter, then president of the Arizona Archaeological and Historical

Society, asked if we would prepare the results of the excavation for publication. Working as volunteers, we (and others who have volunteered their time) have not moved any too quickly, taking 14 years to finish this project. During the course of the analysis, Paul Grebinger returned some long-held artifacts to the Arizona State Museum for curation and Bruce Bradley donated collections from the site that he had held in his Museum of Primitive Technology. Phil Lord, who ran the Pima College excavation, has recently given his slides to Pima College, and we are in the process of getting them archived into the Arizona State Museum Library and Archives, Photographic Collections Section.

Because the data available to us were somewhat uneven, although substantial, this report focuses on a straight-forward presentation of the architectural remains and artifactual material from the site, including a discussion of the site's chronology as determined from tree-ring dates. In addition to the editors, who are the primary authors of the chapters on architecture, ceramics, animal remains, plant remains, and the conclusions, other archaeologists with expertise in specific aspects of material culture graciously volunteered their time to report on a variety of site attributes: Laural Myers, chipped stone; Jenny L. Adams, ground stone; and Lane A. Beck, human remains. Lisa W. Huckell analyzed botanical materials, in some cases reexamining samples that Vorsila Bohrer looked at in the 1970s. Sharon F. Urban analyzed the shell artifacts and some of the miscellaneous artifacts.

The Whiptail Ruin has several interesting attributes that deserve attention, and may be better understood today than they might have been had the report been completed in the 1970s. It was a short-lived community of the early Classic period, one of very few in the northeast corner of the basin. As reported in Chapter 11, tree-ring samples (collected during the excavations but not dated until the 1990s), provide occupation dates from the A.D. 1230s to the A.D. 1250s. Researchers working in the San Pedro Valley and Safford area have confirmed that migrants from the Mogollon highlands were present in those areas in the A.D. 1200s. The significant percentages of locally made corrugated wares found at Whiptail indicate that some of those migrants came over Redington Pass into the northeast part of the Tucson Basin. Other indicators of migrants at Whiptail include the use of conifers in house construction and the presence of obsidian from the Mule Creek source of western New Mexico, pieces of which can be found in the Gila River alluvium in the Safford Valley. Whiptail, representing something of an outlying contact zone between the Tucson Basin and regions to the north and east, thus sheds light on the relationship between Classic period sites west of Whiptail along the Santa Cruz and contemporaneous sites in the San Pedro Basin. Interesting artifactual arrays found on some of the structure floors and in roof contexts were used to hypothesize that Whiptail Ruin was the home to hunting specialists, that some structures were used for ritual, and that several houses were ritually abandoned.

We were both involved, to varying degrees, as volunteers in the original excavations. In the last 15 years, working as analysts, writers, and editors, we have worked with the Whiptail field notes and materials to assemble a publishable account of the Whiptail excavations. We have tried our best to come to reasonable conclusions with the available material, which was sometimes internally inconsistent. We hope that this report will be useful to future researchers and will fill a gap in the record of Classic period Hohokam communities in the Tucson Basin.

Many individuals have been helpful in bringing this report to fruition. All the field workers, both with AAHS and Pima Community College, are listed in Chapter 1. We thank them for their notes and excavation records, which were, on the whole, clear and detailed. We thank all those who helped curate the artifacts and ready the basic data for analysis (also listed in Chapter 1). We appreciate the space provided by the Arizona State Museum for our project. Arthur Vokes was most helpful during the curation process. Thanks go to Jeff Jones and Sue Pereza for their help with data entry; mapmakers Austin Lenhart, Elizabeth Vinson, and Helen O'Brien; illustrators Gerry Crouse and Christine Lange; and photographer Helga Teiwes. Thanks also to Karen Adams, Suzanne Fish, Jeffery Clark, Jane Sliva, John McClelland, Barbara Murphy, James Ayres, and Phil Lord for answering "last minute" questions about various pieces of data. Through the auspices of Jeff Clark and the Center for Desert Archaeology, Steve Shackley sourced several pieces of obsidian for us. Bruce Bradley provided his memories of the excavation and cogent comments about the manuscript, as well as the Foreword to this volume. Thanks are also due Jeff Clark, Henry Wallace, and Doug Craig, who provided helpful reviews of our manuscript. We are pleased that Rich Lange thought that this volume should be in the Arizona State Museum Archaeological Series. We appreciate the work done by Elizabeth May and Laura Burghardt to prepare the manuscript for publication. Last, but not least, we thank Mark Slaughter, former AAHS president, who started us down this long road. Had we known how long it would take we probably wouldn't have accepted his challenge. But, we are glad we did and very glad that the report of this excavation has finally achieved publication.

Linda M. Gregonis
Gayle Harrison Hartmann

Abstract

In the 1960s and 1970s, Arizona Archaeological and Historical Society volunteers, University of Arizona students, and Pima Community College students excavated Whiptail Ruin, a mid- to late A.D. 1200s village in the northeastern Tucson Basin. This volume presents the results of analyses of the notes and artifacts from work at that site. The village may have been home to hunting specialists. Artiodactyl remains were "stored" in structures in a manner similar to that described for historic O'odham hunting practices. Pottery and lithics from the site show that its residents had strong ties to the Tucson area, as well as to migrants from the Mogollon highlands who moved into the San Pedro Valley in the thirteenth century. And, of interest to chronologists of the region, Whiptail Ruin is one of the first sites in the Tucson Basin to be tree-ring dated. In addition to providing scholars with usable data, the research detailed in this volume shows that information mined from old, archived projects can be relevant and important to today's archaeological questions.

Resumen

En las décadas de 1960 y 1970 los voluntarios de la Sociedad Arqueológica e Histórica de Arizona, los estudiantes de la Universidad de Arizona y también los de Pima Community College excavaron las ruinas de Whiptail, un pueblo ubicado en el noreste de la Cuenca de Tucson a mediados y finales del siglo XIII. Este tomo contiene los resultados del análsis de los apuntes y artefactos del trabajo que hicieron al sitio. El pueblo podría haber sido el lugar donde habitaban cazadores. Los restos del artiodactyl fueron almacenados en una manera semejante a los que venían por medio del estilo de cazar de los O'odham en la época histórica. Céramica y líticos del sitio muestran que sus habitantes tenían lazos fuertes a Tucson, así como también a los migrantes de las tierras altas de Mogollón quienes se radicaron al Valle de San Pedro durante el siglo XIII. De interés a las cronistas de la región, las ruinas de Whiptail son uno de los sitios de la Cuenca de Tucson que han sido datados por medio de los anillos de árboles. Además de proporcionar información útil a los investigadores, las investigaciones divulgadas en este tomo demuestran que los datos que vienen de proyectos antiguos todavía son relevantes e importantes a las cuestiones arqueológicas en la actualidad.

Chapter 1

Introduction

Linda M. Gregonis, Sharon F. Urban, and
Gayle Harrison Hartmann

Tucked along a bedrock pediment at the base of the Santa Catalina Mountains in the northeastern corner of the Tucson Basin are a series of perennial springs. These springs have provided water for thousands of years, creating small oases where birds, mammals, and other animals could always find a drink. The springs attracted humans, too. Beginning around 2,000 B.C., Archaic-era people hunted game at these watering holes and left behind stone points and other tools. Later, the Hohokam used the springs as hunting sites. In some locations they also used the springs for farming and built villages nearby.

Whiptail Ruin is one of the villages established near these springs. It is situated within and just south of Agua Caliente Park, which is east of Soldier Trail (Figure 1.1). Roger Road bisects the site, which is named for western whiptail lizards (*Cnemidophus tigris*) that were hibernating on the site when Bruce Bradley started excavation in the mid-1960s (Bradley, personal communication 2001). The excavated portion of the village was occupied from about A.D. 1150 possibly up to A.D. 1300; this corresponds to the Tanque Verde phase of the Classic period in the Tucson Basin Hohokam chronology. Whiptail Ruin may have been used occasionally after the A.D. 1300s by people who were hunting and gathering and processing wild plants. Because archaeological work at the site focused on the Tanque Verde phase features, it is not clear whether there was an earlier habitation at the site. Pre-Classic sherds were found in the excavated portion of the site and there are several artifact concentrations near the springs in Agua Caliente Park that remain untested. A nearby sherd and lithic scatter, AZ BB:10:16 (ASM), that has Snaketown through Rincon phase ceramics, indicates occupation of the area, if not Whiptail itself. It is situated just west of Agua Caliente Wash and south of Roger Road.

Historically, the Agua Caliente area was first recorded in 1872 by Tucsonans who were exploring the warm springs with an eye toward development. The first formal claim to the property was made in 1873 by Peter B. Bain, a local photographer. In 1875, he sold the property to James P. Fuller, who first used

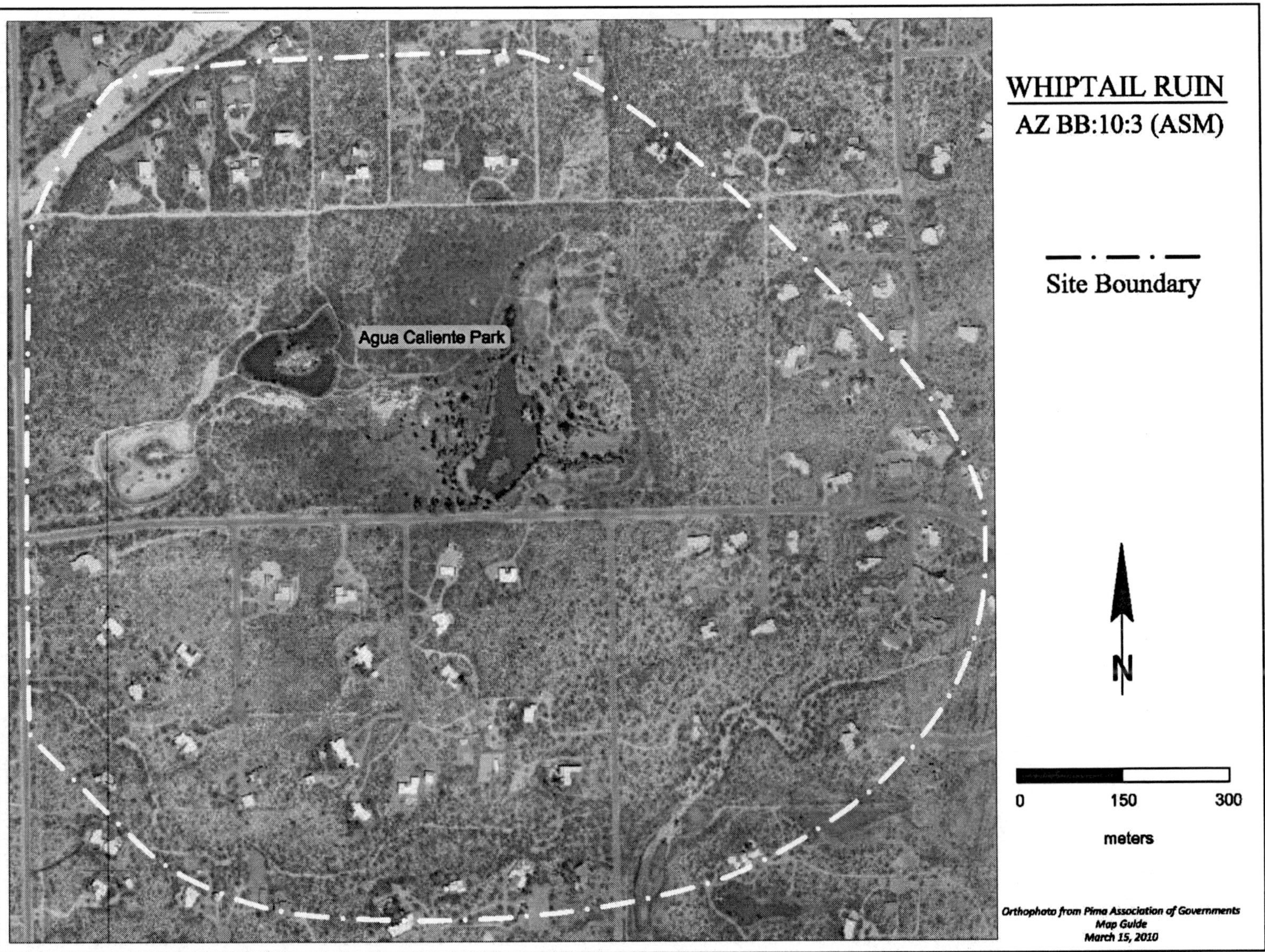

Figure 1.1. Map showing location and boundaries of Whiptail Ruin (prepared by Helen L. O'Brien).

the property to run livestock. In 1878, Fuller began to develop the hot springs as a health resort and orchard. The resort was variously known as Fuller's Springs, Agua Caliente, or Mountain Park Thermal Spring. The ranch passed through a series of owners, some of whom tried to promote the hot springs, others who raised livestock there. The orchard survived into the 1960s and the ranch was often used as guest quarters for various visitors. Pima County purchased the springs in the 1980s and has since developed the northern half of the Whiptail Ruin as the Roy P. Drachman Agua Caliente Regional Park (Ayres 2001).

Environment

The springs that attracted the prehistoric people to the site come to the surface along the low-angle Catalina Fault. At Agua Caliente Park, spring temperatures at this spot are 87°F and flow at 40 to 50 gallons per minute depending on seasonal precipitation. Historically, flow was estimated at 150 gallons per minute. The current single warm spring is a result of a dynamiting operation (probably in the early 1900s) that combined a hot spring and a cold spring. Water quality is poor as a result of dissolved solids including magnesium, iron, sulphur, and calcium. Currently, the springs feed three ponds that were used historically to serve a bathhouse and five other, now dry, ponds on the county park property (Huckleberry 2001:6). The ponds and spring area support an extensive cattail thicket as well as large date palm, Aleppo pine, and other non-native trees. Velvet mesquites, some quite large, are also abundant in the park. The park attracts a variety of birds including ducks, coots, grebes, herons, blackbirds, and flycatchers. Other animals seen in the area include deer, javelina, cottontail, jackrabbit, bobcat, and mountain lion.

Outside of Agua Caliente Park, the vegetation is typical Arizona Upland Sonoran desert scrub, characterized by saguaro, cholla, and prickly pear interspersed with mesquite, paloverde, acacia, creosote bush, bursage, and other shrubs. The site is situated on alluvial fan gravels and gravelly sands with poor soil development (Huckleberry 2001:5–6). The gravels and sands consist primarily of gneiss, other granitic rocks, and their components—quartz, feldspar, and mica.

History of Archaeological Work

Adolph Bandelier may have been the first scholar to become aware of Whiptail Ruin. According to Lange and Riley (1970:207), Bandelier toured sites in the northeastern part of the Tucson Basin in 1883 and described a site that may have been the University Indian Ruin. While visiting Fort Lowell (also the site of a prehistoric Hohokam village), Bandelier made a painting of "a canteen of corrugated pottery, painted red, which was found at the estanque, nine miles east-northeast of here. This is a permanent water pool belonging to the Riito [Rillito] system. There are evidently ruins there" (Lange and Riley 1970:206). He may have been describing a pool associated with the springs at what is now Agua Caliente Park.

In 1960, museum archaeologist Alfred E. Johnson gave Whiptail its Arizona State Museum (ASM) site number, AZ BB:10:3. At the time he prepared the ASM site card, Johnson noted that the site had been "partially excavated," with "well done" trenches that did "not appear to be the usual run of pothunting." Johnson also noted that the site had been located by Fred Porfley of the USGS groundwater branch. Rumor has it that in 1950 some scientific excavations were conducted at the site, but whoever was doing the work had a falling out with the Department of Anthropology at the University of Arizona, and the excavations were abandoned. We were unable to locate any record of this early excavation.

By the early 1960s, Dr. Otis B. Miller had acquired the property on which much of Whiptail is located. He bought the land with the intention of subdividing it. In 1966, Dr. Miller gave Bruce Bradley, then an undergraduate in anthropology at the University of Arizona, permission to excavate the site. Working with a few friends (Figure 1.2), Bradley recognized the importance of the site and brought it to the attention of the Arizona Archaeological and Historical Society (AAHS).

By fall 1967 AAHS had begun excavating in earnest, and in January 1968 Dr. Miller signed an agreement with the society to formalize permission to excavate at the site. The Arizona Archaeological and Historical Society

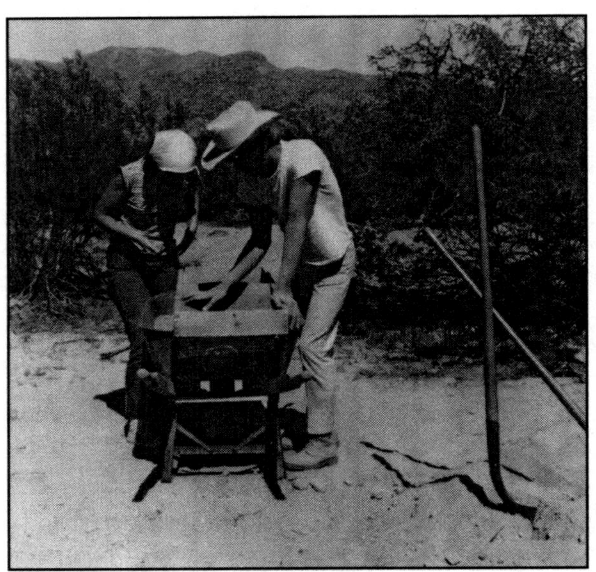

Figure 1.2. Bruce Bradley at right, Donna LaRocca at left, screening fill from Structure 4 (Catalog Number 106569, Arizona State Museum, University of Arizona).

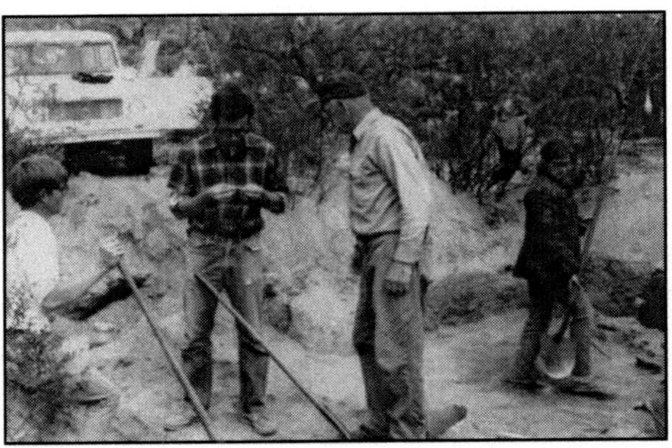

Figure 1.3. Excavation of Structure 15, left to right: Bruce Bradley, Paul Grebinger, Mr. Anderson, and Donna LaRocca (uncatalogued, Arizona State Museum, University of Arizona).

work continued for two more years (1968–1969) under the direction of Paul Grebinger, then a graduate student at the Department of Anthropology at the University of Arizona and member of the society (Figure 1.3). Excavation took place on Sundays throughout the fall, winter, and spring, with an all-volunteer crew including society members and University of Arizona students (Table 1.1). Work was concentrated in and around the structures at the site, most of which were visible on the ground's surface. During this time researchers also used the site to test a new dating method—archaeomagnetic dating. The limited success of archaeomagnetic sampling at the site is described in Chapter 11.

During the summer of 1970, Pima Community College's fledgling archaeology program was invited to participate in the excavation, while AAHS continued to work at the site. In 1970 Sharon Urban (then a graduate student at the university and AAHS member), Joyce Rehm (then a recent university graduate and AAHS member), and Dick Dannels (a retired engineer and AAHS member) took over as the directors of the project. Work continued as it had in the past with Sunday dig

Table 1.1. Individuals Who Have Worked on the Whiptail Project

Arizona Archaeological and Historical Society and Bruce Bradley's Efforts

Linda Allen (1968, 1969, 1970)
Olivia Arrieta (1968)
Aileen (Carpenter) Ayers (1968, 69)
David Banks (1969)
Ruth Baran (1968, 1969)
Holly (Woelke) Barnes (1968)
Tim Blank (1969, 1970)
Bruce Bradley (1966–69, 74, 77–78)
Cindy Bradley (1977–1978)
Jim Bradley
Melody Brancott (1968)
Donald Brannaman (1968, 1969)
Robert E. Brehaut II (1969)
Jill Bright (1969)
Bruce Brockhagen (1968)
Mary Louise Cameron (1968)
Eleanor Carney (1969)
Tony Celeya (1968, 1969, 1970)
Arlyene Charlip (1969)
Annetta (Long) Cheek (1968, 1969)
Charles Cheek (1968, 1969)
Charles Cheshire (1969, 1970)
Herta-Dana Cox (1968)
Kenneth Crumbacker (1969)
Ellen Cummings (1968–1971)
Eloise Cushing (1968)
Jon Czaplicki (1968, 1969)
Richard Dannells (1968–1971)
Elsie Darmer (1968)
Peggy Davis (1968)
Becky Dunton (1969, 1970)
Cindy Edgil (1968)
A. E. Eldridge (1968, 1969)
D. Y. Eldridge (1968, 1969)
C. Wes Ferguson (1968)
Eileen Ferguson (1968)
Erica Ferguson (1968)
Rick Fish (1969, 1970)
Nancy Flint (1968)
John Francisco (1968, 1969)
Lee Fuller (1969, 1970)
Roger Fuller (1968)
Chris Gidden (1969)
Joe Gordon (1977, 1978)
Mark Gordon (1977, 1978)
Stanley Gordon (1977, 1978)
Frederick Gorman (1968)
Ellen (Richardson) Grebinger (68, 69)
Paul Grebinger (1968, 1969)
Cameron Greenleaf (1968)
Phillip Greenleaf (1968)
Linda Gregonis (1970, 1971)
George Gumerman (1968)
Sheila Gumerman (1968)
Pam Haas (1968, 1969)
Laurens Hammack (1968)
Nancy Hammack (1968)
Jessica Harrison (1968)
Gayle (Harrison) Hartmann (1968)
Joe Hatch (1968)
Julian Hayden (1968)
Michael Hays (1968)
Caryl Holden (1968)
Zelpha Holden (1968)
Nancy Horn (1968)
Bruce Huckell (1968–1970, 1974)
Lisa (Washbon) Huckell (1969, 1974)
Ann Hudacek (1969)
Madeline Irell (1968)
Nancy Jacobus (1968)
Linda Jo Jensen (1969)
E. Wes Jernigan (1968)
Joey, Juniper, and Jake (dogs)(77–78)
Wilma Kaemlein (1968)
Susanne (Rothstein) Katz (1968)
Marsha (Schlicht) Kelley (1968)
Meade Kemrer (1968)
Lyn Knapp (1968)
Donald Kucera (1969)
Mary Kuegle (1968)
Barbara Kurcinell (1969, 1970)
Andy La Master (1968)
Donna La Rocca (1968–1971)
Allan Lester (1969, 1970)
Ernest Lewis (1968, 1969)
Joseph Lischka (1968)
Leslie Lischka (1968)
Frank Lobo (1968)
Sue Lobo (1968)
Jan Lockett (1968)
Larry Lusk (1968)
David McLeod (1969)
Linda McConnell (1968)
Craig McPail (1969)
Ellie Manire (1968)
Larry Manire (1968)
David Mastler (1969)
Ellen Milner (1968)
George Milner (1968)
Milton Milner (1968)
David Mogul (1969)
Pat Mogul (1969)
Geene Moore (1969)
Alan Mottolo (1969–1971)
James Mueller (1968)
Cindy Naylor (1968)
Eileen Nicholas (1968–1970)
Lisbet Deeger Nillsen (1968)
Bob Nurin (1968)
Larry Ott (1968, 1969)
Vivian Ott (1968, 1969)
Lucile Paddock (1969)
Sherry Pagel (1968)
Richard Polhemus (1968, 1969)
Dana Potts (1968)
Sandy Rayl (1968)
Joyce Rehm (1968–1970)
Kelley Rehm (1968)
Thomas Rehm (1968)
Barry Richards (1974)
Joyce Rinehart (1968–1971)
Frank Runnel (1968)
Rene Sage (1968, 1969)
Lenny Schloss (1969)
Mary Scott (1968)
Andy Segale (1969, 1970)
Tim Seagle (1968–1970)
Myra Sidowski (1968)
Gary Skinner (1969, 1970)
Lois Smith (1968, 1969)
Heather Sowls (1968)
Alan Spaulding (1968)
Sheila Spellman
Lisa Spray (1968)
Susan Summers (1968)
Larry Sweet (1968)
George Thomas (1968)
Carol Tolaski (1968, 1969)
Janet Tolaski (1968)
Albert Turner (1968)
Catherine Ungar (1969)
Sharon Urban (1968–1972)
Dick Vandemark (1968, 1969)
Melva Vandemak (1968, 1969)
Sue Walker (1969, 1970)
Christine Walsh (1969)
Steve Watson (1968)
Carol Weed (1969–1971)
Richard White (1968, 1969)
Pat Wiener (1969)
Susan (Furer) Wilcox (1969)
Jennifer Wiley (1969)
Cavin Willis (1968)
Jan Winfield (1968)
Fred Wiseman (1968)
Dick Witzens (1969, 1970)
Don Wood (1969)

Table 1.1. Individuals Who Have Worked on the Whiptail Project, cont'd.

Visitors		
Mary (Fordyce) Andersen (1971)	Chip Lockwood (1968)	Cathy Moser (1968)
Agnese (Lockwood) Haury (1968)	Becky Moser (1968)	William Robinson and son (1968)
Helen Hayden (1968)	Ed Moser (1968)	Richard Sense (1968)
Dick Hsu (1968)		
Pima College Class, Summer 1971 (taught by Phil Lord)		
Lee Coley	Rusty McInroy	Adele Taylor
Garrett Cook	Michael D. Mauer	Beth Welman
Sharon Hargrave	John Molfese	Margaret Wilke
Robert Jones	Tim Seagle	Julie Wizorek
Alice Knapp	Pauline Spurgiesz	Debby Zubow
Mary McCutcheon		
University of Arizona Laboratory Techniques Class, Spring 1973 (taught by R. Gwinn Vivian)		
Hugh S. Ball	Doug Herrick	Tim Murphy
John Beezley	Robert Jones	Misty Murray
Richard Burchim	Nancy Kays	Shirley Pettengill
Peter Coston	William Kessel	Barry Richards
Gordon Fritz	Pamela Magers	Tim Seagle
Linda Gregonis	W. Bruce Masse	Stephen Small
Sharon Hargrave	Glenn Miller	David Stahle
Andrew Harvey	Alan Mottolo	Julie Wizorek
Eisenhower College Classes, 1974–1975 (taught by Paul Grebinger)		
"B.E.B"	Alan B. Hamor	Brenda Prince
Melanie Gehen	Elizabeth Mayer	Harry Rosenberg
Emmie Hamilton	Glenn Page	Kathryn A. Youngs
Eisenhower Survey Crew, 1979 (taught by Paul Grebinger)		
Lisa Bain	Helen Linden	Barbie Parry
Vicki Blondine	Michael McCrosser	Linda Pawlik
Mary Nona Brophy	Jean McBride	Tina Reitz
Cindy Brower	Mann Masiak	Angela Sweet
Joanne Carney	Chris Niehoff	Emily Wiggin
Debbie Darby		
Arizona State Museum Laboratory Analysis, 1980s (William Hohmann, Supervisor)		
Eric Abbott	Mildred Garrettson	Phil Perry
Becky Allen	Fran Goodwin	Joan Pettit
Jack Barbie	Anne Hay	Lucy Potter
Louis Blackwater	Sandy Hayes	Nancy Rockoff
Harry Bowers	Gordon Jacobsen	Jo Rogers
Gwen Brown	Bob Jones	Sarah Rosenberg
Laura Burkart	Frank Kenney	Kay Rosenow
Sharon Cox	Kent Larson	Lisa Sierra
Lydia Cza	Judith Modarasy	Jim Vint
John Earl	Gordon Newton	Barbara Teso
Sheri Fernley	Tim Oldenberg	Russ Wilde
Max Fogleman	Lita Oldham	Lisa Young
Ed Garrettson	Inez Pannella	
Efforts 1995 to Present		
Briggs Ackert	Linda Gregonis	Patricia Montgomery
Jenny Adams	Gayle Harrison Hartmann	Laural Myers
Lane Beck	Lisa Huckell	Helen O'Brien
Debbie Carroll	Jeffrey Jones	Sue Pereza
Gerry Crouse	Dolores Kazantzis	Sharon Urban
Lee Fratt	Christine Lange	Marta Wallace
Mary Andersen	Austin Lenhart	

Note: Over the years a large number of volunteers contributed untold hours to the excavation, analysis, and write up of this project. We hope that we have listed everyone who participated in this project, but we are sure that we've missed a few. Our apologies to anyone we've left out, and our thanks to one and all.

days throughout much of the year (Figures 1.4–1.10). The Arizona State Museum provided most of the equipment used at the site, and Julian Hayden provided a backhoe that was used to trench the compound and spare the crew the onerous task of backfilling the site (Figure 1.11). As part of the excavation process, Jamie Lytle-Webb collected pollen samples from various features. She used those samples in her master's thesis (Lytle 1971).

In the summer of 1971 Pima Community College again conducted a field school at the site. That year, Phil Lord and Chief Assistant Mary McCutcheon directed the work. During both years, the Pima Community College crew kept notes, drew sketch maps, and took photographs. Artifacts were processed in a lab class and subsequently, by mid-1972, were turned over to the Arizona State Museum for curation. On November 15, 1971, Sharon Urban and Phil Lord gave individual reports at the Arizona Archaeological and Historical Society's monthly meeting.

During the spring semester of 1973 R. Gwinn Vivian taught a laboratory analysis course at the University of Arizona, Department of Anthropology, using materials from Whiptail. Dr. Vivian had at least 21 students and a teaching assistant (Table 1.1). The class consisted of visits to the site including limited fieldwork, laboratory sorting and analysis, and discussion sessions. Materials used in the class included structure notes, photographs, sketch maps, and artifacts. The class produced "house reports," which collected and summarized the information known about various structures at the site. The class was considered a type of salvage project, with the ultimate goal of publishing a report on the site. Unfortunately this did not come to pass, although we made good use of the house reports during our preparation of this report.

In 1973 and 1974 and again in 1977 and 1978, Bruce Bradley, Bruce and Lisa Huckell, and other volunteers excavated several structures on private property in the northeastern corner of the site. Bradley prepared descriptive reports on each structure, which were filed in the ASM archives on Whiptail. Copies of the reports were given to the property owners and the artifacts found in each of the structures were returned to those owners.

The next work at the site occurred in 1978, when Paul Grebinger, then on the faculty at Eisenhower College in Seneca Falls, New York, thought that one of his classes could do some surveying in the Whiptail area with the goal of completing the Whiptail project. Materials were shipped to Dr. Grebinger, and in January 1979 he and 16 students came to Tucson to conduct an archaeological survey of the Whiptail area. Between January 16 and February 2, 1979, Grebinger and his crew conducted a reconnaissance survey of Whiptail Ruin and the surrounding area. This survey had a three-pronged focus: The first was to determine the site boundary for Whiptail (shown in Figure 1.1). The second was to survey the area between the site and the Agua Caliente Wash to the west and northwest, and the third was to collect clay samples for chemical analysis for comparison with pottery from the ruin. Appendix A reports the results of the chemical analysis. Much of Grebinger's Eisenhower College project was successful, but his goal of preparing a site report was not met.

Grebinger used the original datum at the site for the starting place for survey transects. (The exact location of that datum is no longer known.) He and his crew found that the greatest concentration of artifacts occurred within the first 33 to 66 meters (100 to 200 feet) of the datum, and that the site boundary occurred 370 meters (1100 feet) to the northeast, about 240 meters (720 feet) to the east-northeast, and at 160 meters (470 feet) to the west. On the northwest margin of the site was a dense stand of four-wing salt bush (*Atriplex canescens*);

surveyors noted that artifacts did not occur in that area. Finally, the surveyors found no evidence of habitation on the southeast side of a wash that borders the site to the south and southeast.

During their survey of the upper bajada to the north of Whiptail as well as the area west of the site, Grebinger and his students identified three additional sites. Two of the sites—AZ BB:10:16 (ASM) and AZ BB:10:35(ASM)—had been recorded previously. Site AZ BB:10:16 is a large sherd and lithic scatter with pottery dating from the Snaketown through the Rincon phases. Site AZ BB:10:35 is a trash mound that dates to the Tanque Verde phase. The location and character of the third site is not known. AZ BB:10:35 (ASM) may actually be within the boundaries of Whiptail Ruin as shown in Figure 1.1.

Beginning in 1985 William Hohmann (then a university graduate student who later served as president of the Arizona Archaeological and Historical Society) gathered several volunteers to again attempt to analyze the Whiptail materials and prepare a report. Many individuals helped with the processing of materials (Table 1.1). Others took on the task of analyzing specific artifact classes. Margaret Ross examined corrugated wares from the site; Gail Brown, Loraine Yoshikawa, and Carol Rosenow analyzed the faunal material; Maxwell Fogleman worked on the cremations and inhumations at the site; James Lombard performed a petrographic analysis of sherd temper (Appendix B); Phil Perry prepared a report on the site's formation processes; and Carol Rosenow drew Tanque Verde Red-on-brown pottery designs for a stylistic analysis. The Arizona Archaeological and Historical Society volunteers worked diligently on the project, but were eventually lured away from it by an opportunity to excavate at the Redtail site on the west side of the Tucson Basin. The Whiptail project once again went back on the shelf.

In the mid-1990s, two archaeological projects in the Whiptail area brought renewed interest to the old Whiptail Ruin project. The first was the 1993 excavation of the nearby Gibbon Springs site, a Tanque Verde phase village located around a series of springs about 3 miles northwest of Whiptail (Slaughter and Roberts 1996b) (Figure 1.12). Wood from this project yielded tree-ring dates, a first for the Tucson Basin. In the process of dating the wood from Gibbon Springs, the Laboratory of Tree-Ring Research reexamined wood from Whiptail and found that some of it, too, was datable. The dates indicate that the Whiptail villagers procured wood for construction during the A.D. 1230s and A.D. 1240s. The dates from Gibbon Springs are similar, indicating that at least portions of both sites were occupied at the same time (Dean et al. 1996).

Between 1995 and 2002 a series of small projects were conducted in conjunction with improvements to Agua Caliente Park, which includes the northern end of the Whiptail Ruin. Work in the park included a monitoring project (Slaughter et al. 1995), excavations related to construction of parking and other facilities (Wellman and Slaughter 2001), and an inventory of prehistoric and historical features and artifacts visible on the surface (Twilling et al. 2002). Although the excavations in the park were limited, the presence of roasting pits, ash deposits, and clusters of fire-cracked rock indicated that this portion of the Whiptail Ruin was used for resource processing by the Hohokam and for a variety of ranch-related activities by Agua Caliente Ranch inhabitants (Wellman and Slaughter 2001).

As part of the excavation project, James Ayres (2001) prepared a history of the Agua Caliente Ranch, construction of which began in the 1870s. Ranch buildings and activities were

Figure 1.4. Mapping Structure 2, Joyce Rehm in foreground with tape, Nancy Hammack at the plane table (Catalog Number 106580, Arizona State Museum, University of Arizona).

Figure 1.6. Structure 6, Gayle Harrison Hartmann on left, Charles Cheek on right (uncatalogued, Arizona State Museum, University of Arizona).

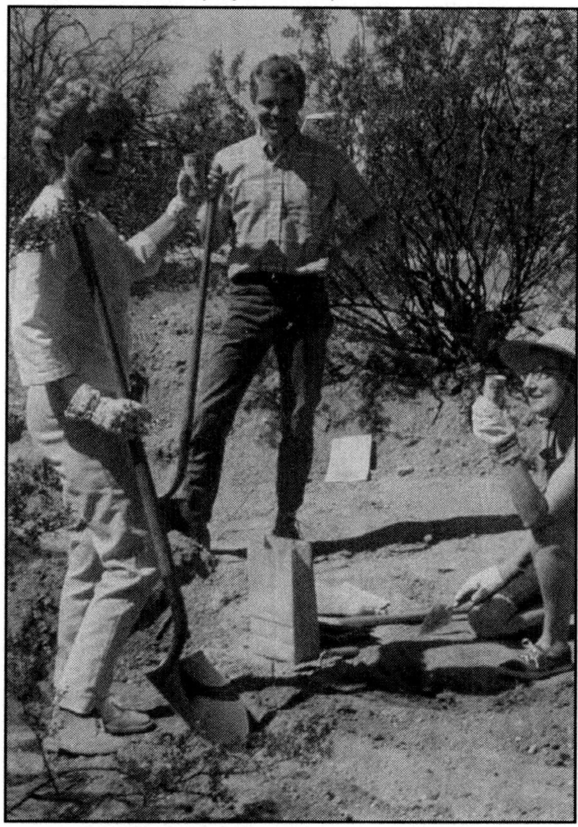

Figure 1.5. Structure 5 excavation: left to right, Aileen Carpenter, George Thomas, and Joyce Reinhart (Catalog Number C-41053, Arizona State Museum, University of Arizona).

Figure 1.7. Mapping Structure 2, Steve Watson [?] and Joyce Rehm (Catalog Number C-41030, Arizona State Museum, University of Arizona).

Figure 1.8. Excavations in western half of Structure 13; people unidentified (Catalog Number C-41094, Arizona State Museum, University of Arizona).

Figure 1.9. Structure 2 mapping; Joyce Rehm at left, Steve Watson [?] at right (Catalog Number 106543, Arizona State Museum, University of Arizona).

Figure 1.10. Excavation of Structure 16, looking west. Clockwise from left: Richard Polhemus, unidentified, Richard White, Donna La Rocca, Bruce Bradley (Catalog Number 106642, Arizona State Museum, University of Arizona).

Figure 1.11. Backfilling operation, spring 1968, Pete Muñiz on front end loader (Catalog Number 106548, Arizona State Museum, University of Arizona).

concentrated around the springs, but several historical trash deposits can still be seen on the south side of Roger Road among the prehistoric structures in the excavated portion of Whiptail. According to Bruce Bradley (e-mail communication, 2009), student Dale Berge excavated one of the historical trash middens at the site. Otherwise, the historical ranch and its features and artifacts were ignored by the archaeologists who worked on the prehistoric site.

In 1998, Jeffrey Jones, then with Old Pueblo Archaeology, surveyed an area just east of Whiptail Ruin and discovered an archaeological site consisting of bedrock mortars and a grinding slick situated on granitic bedrock along a wash. In January 1999, Jones mapped the site, which was recorded as AZ BB:10:52 (ASM). The survey and recording was done as part of a private land assessment (Jones 1999).

The most recent effort to produce a Whiptail Ruin report began with Mark Slaughter, who worked on the Gibbon Springs and Agua Caliente Park projects for SWCA. He was elected president of the Arizona Archaeological and Historical Society in 1995 and asked Linda Gregonis to consider preparing a site report for the Whiptail project. She enlisted the help of Gayle Hartmann and Sharon Urban. Along with a number of other volunteers (Table 1.1), the three inventoried the collection, analyzed or assigned for analysis various materials, and prepared various chapters for this report. When possible, older analyses (e.g., the 1980s faunal analysis, the 1970s ceramic analyses, and the 1970s house reports) were used as the basis for writing various chapters. Other analyses in this volume were the result of much-appreciated new work by volunteers (e.g., the ground and chipped stone, shell, plant, and human remains chapters).

Site Structure

As mentioned previously, although there is evidence of Archaic and earlier Hohokam (Rillito and Rincon phase) use of the site, the excavated features date no earlier than the early Classic period. The lack of earlier habitation features may be illusory. Excavation at the site concentrated on features that were visible on the surface, so anything that was completely buried would not have been found. And, although the Agua Caliente Park portion of the site has been surveyed, very little of it has been excavated (Wellman and Slaughter 2001).

The artifact concentrations and features in Agua Caliente Park should be considered a locus of the Whiptail site, although they are not discussed here. Several roasting pits were found in the park. Most of them date to the Classic period, although one yielded radiocarbon dates of A.D. 160 to A.D. 530, which puts it in the Pioneer period (Wellman and Grimm 2001:68). To date, no structural features have been found in the Agua Caliente portion of the park; it is probable that, like the area near the springs at Gibbon Springs, the Agua Caliente portion was used for agricultural and other subsistence pursuits.

The Tanque Verde phase component of Whiptail described in this report includes at least 40 structures (most of which were probably houses or segments of houses), a compound, two cemeteries, and a few low trash mounds. We chose to use the term "structure," when describing the architectural features because contiguous-walled buildings (presumably parts of a single household) were assigned separate "house" numbers (e.g., Structures 27a, 27b, and 28 or 31a, 31b, and 31c). The term "feature" was also not suitable, as excavators assigned separate feature numbers to the few non-architectural features that were recorded, as well as features within structures.

The excavated features were broadly distributed (Figure 1.13) across an area of approximately 500 meters (north-south) by 800 meters (east-west). The features were numbered as they were excavated or identified, so there is no logical grouping in the numbering of the structures. For organizational purposes, we defined six loci within the site: Compound, Southwestern, Northern, Central, Southern, and Northeastern. When possible, these locus designations have been followed throughout this report.

Definition of the loci was partially subjective and partially based on the physical layout of Whiptail. As shown in Figure 1.13, the Compound, Central, Southwestern, and Northern loci are clustered in the center of the site, and in some cases are only a few meters apart. We made the subjective judgment to separate compound-associated features from features in the Southwestern and Central loci. A shallow dip or drainage between the Central and Northern loci formed a natural boundary between the two loci.

True physical distances and distinctions exist between the Northeastern and Southern loci and the central cluster of loci at the site. The Southern Locus consists of two houses (Structures 14 and 19) situated within the southern bank of a shallow wash that forms the southern border of the site. The two features are below the rim of the wash on a low rise and would not have been visible from the rest of the site. Structure 19 was excavated and recorded as two structures: 19a and 19b. The earlier structure, 19b, was a rectangular house with rounded corners. Structure 19a, a square-cornered rectangular house with sturdy puddled adobe and rock walls, was built directly over the top of Structure 19b. The setting of Structures 14 and 19 is peculiar, in that the wash they are situated in has been stable, with little erosion, for at least 800 years. The lack of runoff and erosion in the northeast-southwest running wash may indicate that the wash is part of the earthquake fault structure that created the Agua Caliente spring system. This geological activity formed a series of parallel faults that carry into the Tanque Verde Ridge area (Spencer 2000). The wash direction matches the direction of those faults.

The Northeastern Locus (Structures 1, 22, 40, 41, and 42) is several hundred feet east of the Northern Locus and is separated by an area that today contains trash from the historical Agua Caliente Ranch. Two structures in this area (41 and 42) are contiguous walled structures, attached to each other by a shared wall.

The decision to separate the Northern, Central, Compound, and Southwestern loci from one another was based on the proximity of features relative to one another, but the divisions among the loci are somewhat arbitrary. The Compound Locus includes the puddled-adobe, rock-reinforced compound that encloses three structures (6, 7, and 17), and two structures (4 and 8) that are physically closer to

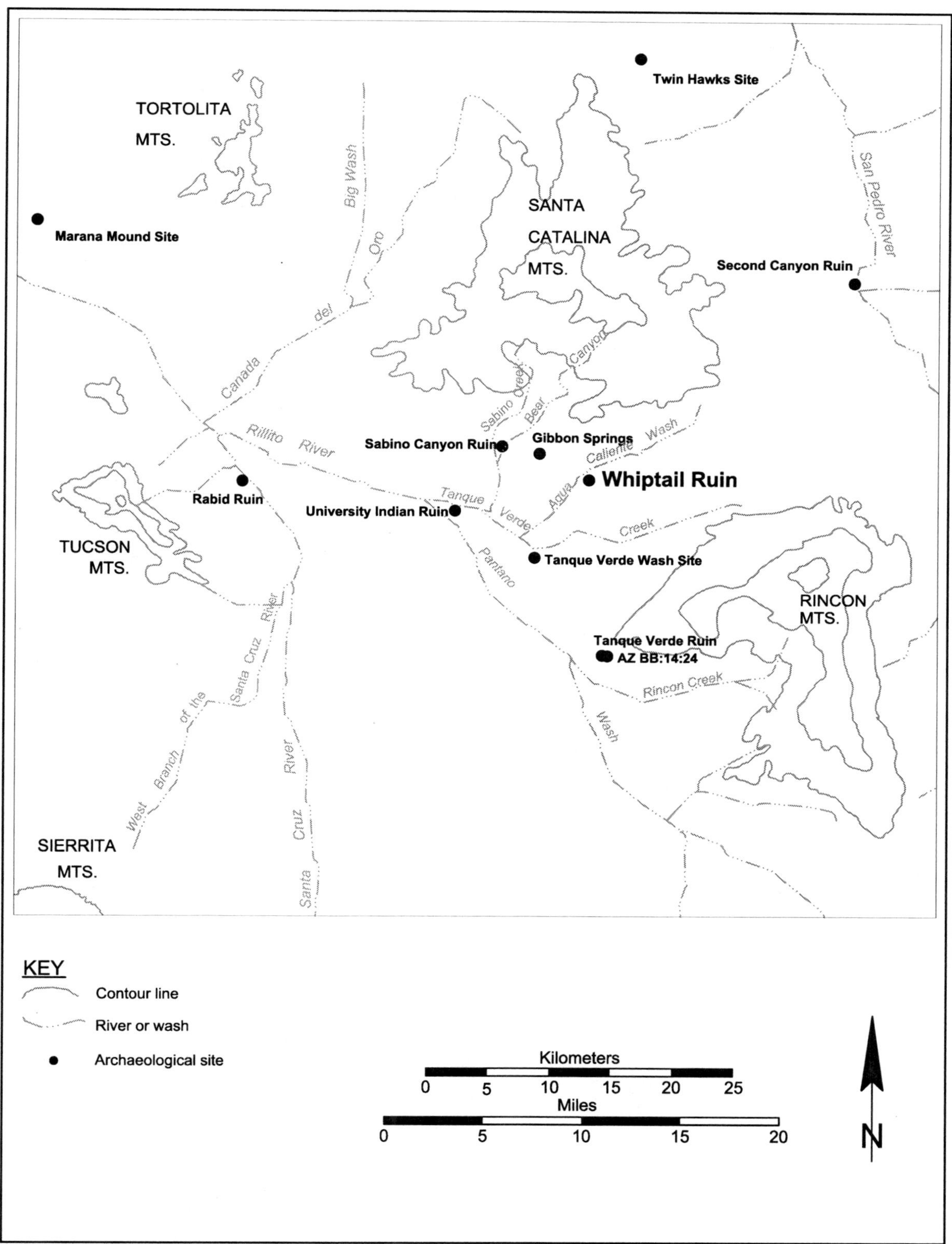

Figure 1.12. Locations of some sites discussed in this volume (prepared by Helen L. O'Brien).

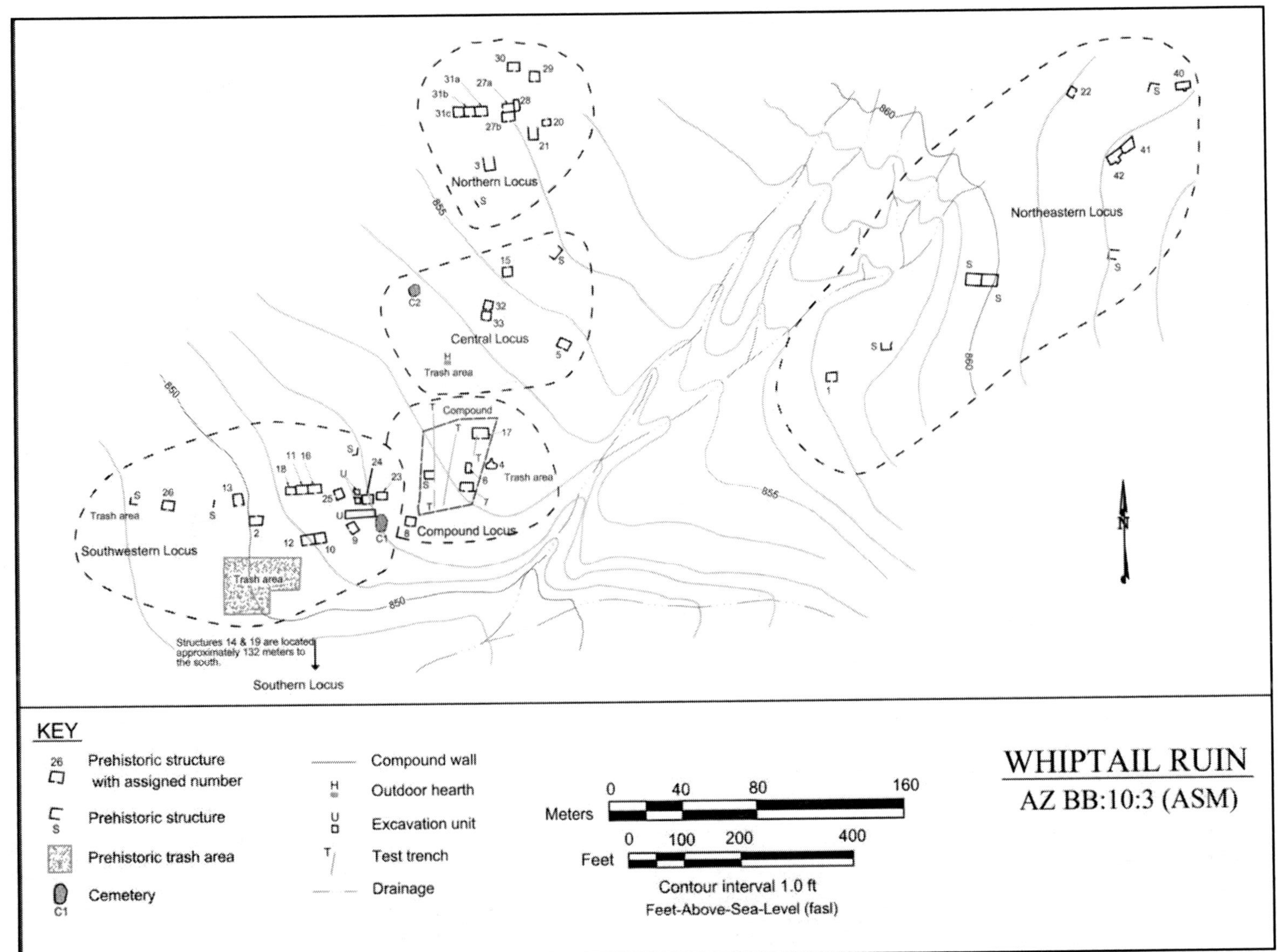

Figure 1.13. Map showing loci and excavated features (prepared by Austin Lenhart, Elizabeth Vinson, and Helen L. O'Brien).

the compound than to other features. Structure 4 may be the oldest structure on the site. It is stratigraphically lower than the compound. Artifacts were recovered from the compound, but neither a detailed map of the compound nor notes about excavation of the compound could be located. A visit to the site in 2002 confirmed that at least part of the compound is still intact and is being protected by the landowner. It now is partially within a horse corral.

The Southwestern Locus of the site, situated west and south of the Compound Locus, includes Cemetery 1, a contiguous walled structure with three rooms (Structures 11, 16, and 18), and two Structures—10 and 12—that are nearly contiguous. Seven other structures (2, 9, 13, 23, 24, 25, and 26), all detached, were excavated in this section. At one point, excavators surface-stripped an area in this segment, but no other features were found.

The Central Locus is north of the Compound Locus. It includes five features—Structures 5, 15, 32, and 33, and Cemetery 2.

The Northern Locus is separated from the Central Locus by a few meters. It contains five single-unit structures (Structures 3, 20, 21, 29, and 30) and two sets of contiguous walled structures, each with three rooms (designated as separate features). These are Structures 31a-b-c, and 27a-27b-28.

About 40 structures and parts of two cemeteries were excavated during the 1960s and 1970s. We now turn to an in-depth description of Whiptail's architecture.

Chapter 2

Architectural Structures

Gayle Harrison Hartmann and Linda M. Gregonis

The description of structures that follows is condensed from several sources: excavation forms titled "Pithouse Excavation Records" that were completed at the time of excavation, field notes written by a member of the excavating team, field notes written by the supervising archaeologist, student reports written for a class instructed by R. Gwinn Vivian at the University of Arizona, and student reports written for a class instructed by Paul Grebinger at Eisenhower College in New York state. These various sources are generally, but not always, in agreement. When the sources disagree, the "Pithouse Excavation Records" (when available) and notes written at the time of excavation were given preference. All of these documents can be found in the Whiptail files in the Arizona State Museum Archives.

The available architectural information is uneven. Some structures were described clearly and in detail, while others were described sparsely. Thus, the site descriptions must be considered a "best effort" at summarizing available data. Plan and profile maps of structures were frequently, but not always, available. Maps that were well drawn and that illustrate either common structural characteristics or interesting structural details are included with the architectural descriptions.

The structures were spread over an area approximately 500 m north-south by 800 m east-west. As discussed in Chapter 1, we organized the structures into six loci: Compound, Central, Southwestern, Southern, Northern, and Northeastern. Two of the loci—the Southern and Northeastern—were separated from the rest of the site (Figure 1.13). Features in the Southern Locus were on a low rise just above the bottom of a shallow wash that defined the southern edge of the site. The Northeastern Locus was at the northeastern edge of the site, separated from the main part of the site by an area of historical trash scatters that were likely associated with the Agua Caliente Ranch (Ayres 2001). Excavation information is available for 40 structures (counting Structure 19a and the structure immediately below it, 19b, as two structures), but what portion of the Whiptail community these represent is uncertain. On a sketch map of the site drawn in

February 1973 and updated in 1974-1975, what may be 14 additional structures are shown, but nothing more is known about them. For the 40 excavated structures described in this chapter, as much structural detail is presented as could be extracted from the available information. Mention is always made of characteristics that differentiate structures from each other, such as the configuration of entries, post hole patterns that suggest bench supports, the presence of buttresses, stone steps, an adobe collar around a post hole, and so on. Also included are names of all excavators and student reporters. Tables 2.1 through 2.5 summarize the characteristics of the 40 structures. They provide details on structure shape, size, and mode of abandonment; wall measurements; entry characteristics; floor features and artifacts; and samples taken from structures.

There were two basic structure types, slant-walled pit structures and adobe-walled structures. The earlier, slant-walled structures can be considered "true" pit houses, in that the pit formed the lower walls of the house and upper walls were formed outside of the pit. The pit walls slanted inward from top to bottom. These structures were subrectangular and had appended, bulbous entryways. Structure 4 in the Compound Locus is an example of this house and, by shape, Structure 19b in the Southwestern Locus is inferred to be one as well, although its presumed pit walls were demolished when Structure 19a was constructed over the top of it. Structure 23 in the Northern Locus had a pit-structure shape, but had thick adobe walls and was, as a result, classified as an adobe-walled structure.

Adobe-walled structures were constructed in pits. In this type, rock-reinforced puddled adobe walls were most often constructed inside the pit walls and extended above the pit walls from the floor of the structure. Like the earlier pit structures, most of the adobe-walled structures were single units that were detached from other rooms; others at the site (e.g., Structures 27a, 27b, and 28) were attached to one another by common or immediately adjacent walls and were typed as "contiguous."

Artifact assemblages from floors are described briefly. Information on the floor assemblages is based on field notes compared with the results of various artifact analyses (ceramics, lithics, etc.). Artifacts noticed by excavators in the fill or in roof fill may also be noted here. More detailed information on various artifact classes can be found in Chapters 3 through 9.

Description of Structures by Locus

Compound Locus

The Compound Locus included five structures—4, 6, 7, 8, and 17— not counting the compound itself. The two largest free-standing structures at the site (Structures 7 and 17) occurred in this locus, as did one of the two earliest structures identified (Structure 4). Structure 4 was located just outside and below the east wall of the compound, and Structure 8 was located just off the southwest corner of the compound. Structures 6, 7, and 17 were all inside the compound walls, as was an unexcavated structure along the west wall of the compound (Figure 1.13).

Structure 4

Structure 4 (Figure 2.1) was located just outside the compound wall on the east side. It was a detached, subrectangular, slant-walled pit structure. The walls were made of puddled adobe and at one time were all probably 48 cm high, though now they vary from 33 cm to 48 cm. Along the neck of the entryway, the walls were between 10 cm and 18 cm thick. They were in excellent condition where they were

Table 2.1. Shape, Size, and Mode of Abandonment.

Structure No.	Type & Nature of Attachment	Shape	Depth Below Surface (m)	Length (m)	Width (m)	Floor Area (square m)	Mode of Abandonment and Post-habitation Use	Comments
						Compound Locus		
4	Pit structure; detached	Subrectangular	0.67	5.0	4.5	22.5	Burned, trash filled	Figurine in post hole
6	Adobe walled; detached	Rectangular	0.60	4.9	3.6	17.6	Burned; trash filled	Possible "ledges" along wall; probable staged floor assemblage including artiodactyl bone, tabular tool, pestle, turquoise piece
7	Adobe walled; detached	Rectangular	1.00	8.1	5.5	45	Burned	
8	Adobe walled; detached	Rectangular	0.45-0.55	5.6	4.7	26	Ritually staged and burned	Staged floor assemblage including ceramic vessels and artiodactyl bone; impressions of wood roofing poles in adobe chunks.
17	Adobe walled; detached	Rectangular	0.30-0.50	8.2	5.0	41	Probably not burned; not trash filled	Prepared surface outside of structure.
						Central Locus		
5	Adobe walled; detached	Rectangular	0.55	6.2	4.6	28.6	Unknown	Seriously vandalized
15	Adobe walled; detached	Rectangular	0.50-0.70	7.0	5	35	Burned	Probable storage room with at least 19 vessels with plant materials on floor
32	Adobe walled; detached	Rectangular	Unknown	5.1-5.4	4.2-4.5	22.6	Unknown	
33	Adobe walled; detached	Subrectangular	Unknown	Unknown	Unknown	Unknown	Burned; craft production in structure after abandonment, perhaps before burning.	Six post holes may be bench supports
						Southwestern Locus		
2	Adobe walled; detached	Rectangular	0.50-0.70	7.0	5.0	35	Unknown (charcoal on floor)	
9	Adobe walled; detached	Rectangular	0.6	5.6	3.8-4.7	approx. 23.5	No evidence of burning	Horizontal grooves along both sides of entry
10	Adobe walled; detached but nearly contiguous with 12	Rectangular	0.6	6.0	5	30	Burned	
11	Adobe walled; contiguous with 16 & 18	Rectangular	0.71	6.1	4.3	26.2	Burned	
12	Adobe walled; detached but nearly contiguous with 10	Rectangular	0.40-0.50	6.5	4.6	30	Ritually staged and burned	Staged floor assemblage of pottery making materials; north entry plugged
13	Adobe walled; detached	Rectangular	0.6	5.0	4.0	20	Burned	
16	Adobe walled; contiguous with 11	Rectangular	0.60-0.70	6.0	4.5	27	Burned	
18	Adobe walled; contiguous with 11 & 16	Rectangular	0.40	8.0	5	40	Burned	
23	Adobe walled; detached	Subrectangular	0.95	5.3	3.9	20.6	Burned; lithic production after abandonment	Two floors
24	Adobe walled; detached	Rectangular	Unknown	5.8-6.6	4.5-5.0	29	Burned; lithic production after abandonment; storage of ground stone artifacts	Buttress along interior of east wall
25	Adobe walled; detached	Rectangular	Unknown	5.1-5.7	4.1-4.4	22	Burned; lithic production after abandonment	Two floors; lower floor artifacts staged on floor and upper floor laid on top
26	Adobe walled; detached	Rectangular	Unknown	6.3	4.7	30	Probably not burned	Seriously vandalized

Table 2.1. Shape, Size, and Mode of Abandonment, cont'd.

Structure No.	Type & Nature of Attachment	Shape	Depth Below Surface (m)	Length (m)	Width (m)	Floor Area (square m)	Mode of Abandonment and Post-habitation Use	Comments
Northern Locus								
3	Adobe walled; detached	Rectangular	0.39	6.9	5.4	36	Unknown; trash filled	
20	Adobe walled; detached	Rectangular	0.50-0.70	4.2	3.5	14.7	Probably not burned, cleaned out?	North entry plugged
21	Adobe walled; detached	3-sided rectangle	0.18-0.36	Unknown	Unknown	Unknown	Probably not burned, cleaned out?	
27a	Adobe walled; contiguous with 27b & 28	Rectangular	0.50-0.80	7.8	5	39	Possibly not burned, attached to burned house	
27b	Adobe walled; contiguous with 27a & 28	Rectangular	Unknown	6.0	4.4-4.7	27	Burned as part of burial ritual	One burial on floor, along with numerous artiodactyl bones and vessels; external buttresses
28	Adobe walled; contiguous with 27a & 27b	Rectangular	1.1	6.0	1.5-3.5	15	Burned; possibly cleaned out; possible use as cooking area prior to burial being placed in fill	Two floors; burial in fill
29	Adobe walled; detached	Rectangular	0.7	6.1	5.0	30.5	Burned, probably with burial in it; possible use for storage, food processing, or lithic production after abandonment	Seriously vandalized; 1 burial
30	Adobe walled; detached	Rectangular	Unknown	6.6	4.1	27	Ritually staged and burned	Adobe collar around one post hole
31a	Adobe walled; contiguous with 31b	Rectangular	0.85	6.1	4.3	26	Possibly cleaned out prior to burning; trash filled	Some post holes may be bench supports
31b	Adobe walled; contiguous with 31a & 31c	Rectangular	0.7	5.8-6.0	4.7	27.7	Burned, trash deposit on floor	
31c	Adobe walled; contiguous with 31b	Rectangular	0.9	5.1-5.5	4.8-5.5	26	Possibly cleared out prior to burning; trash filled	
Southern Locus								
14	Adobe walled; detached	Nearly square	0.60-0.90	4 .7	4.1	19.3	Ritually staged and burned	
19a	Adobe walled; detached	Rectangular	0.79	6.0	4.7	28.2	Ritually staged and burned	Staged artifacts include ceramic vessels and artiodactyl bones including a pronghorn skull
19b	Pit structure; detached	Subrectangular	Unknown	5.0	3.5-3.9	18.5	Unknown; Structure 19a built directly on top.	Six post holes may be bench supports
Northeastern Locus								
1	Adobe walled; detached	Subrectangular	0.56	4.2	3.6	15	Unknown (some charcoal in fill)	
22	Adobe walled; detached	Rectangular	Unknown	Unknown	Unknown	Unknown	Probably burned	Exceedingly well-made floor
40	Adobe walled; detached	Rectangular	0.5	6.0	3.5	21	Burned	
41	Adobe walled; contiguous with 42	Rectangular	Unknown	Unknown	Unknown	Unknown	Unknown	Seriously vandalized
42	Adobe walled; contiguous with 41	Rectangular	0.6	6.0	4.5	27	Burned	Tanque Verde Red-on-brown bowl sunk into hearth depression

still standing with some plaster preserved from 2 cm to 3 cm thick.

The entry, which was centered in the north wall, was 1.5 m from the east wall and 1.6 m from the west wall. The entry was bulbous in shape, with a narrow neck that connected the bulbous portion to the house proper. This was the only structure with post holes noted in association with the entry, indicating that the entry was roofed. The entryway was 1.7 m from the northern tip to the point where it attached to house and it was 0.73 m wide at its widest point. An adobe step was puddled into the northern tip of the entry.

The floor was prepared and apparently was used and then replastered. There were at least two levels, each not more than 1 cm to 2 cm thick, with replastering evident around the hearth.

The hearth was a round, basin type, of prepared clay. It was located directly south of the entrance and had been partially destroyed by pot hunters.

Two postholes were noted in the approximate center of the north-south axis of the structure. The western hole was 23 cm by 21 cm in cross section and 46 cm deep; the eastern hole was also 23 cm by 21 cm in cross section and was 49 cm deep. Both post holes were plugged with adobe at floor level. The western hole was also plugged at approximately two-thirds of the distance down from the top. The eastern post hole contained an unfired adobe figurine at 32 cm below the floor's surface (Figure 2.1). Two more possible post holes were just outside the entryway at its point of greatest width.

No pits were associated with this structure, and evidence for the roof was missing or was not noted by excavators.

Profiles drawn of the fill in this structure revealed some wall slumpage onto the floor near the west wall and a dark, ashy lens above. The eastern part of the structure included a pot hunter's hole, which destroyed a portion of the wall in the northwest corner of the house.

Four pollen samples were taken—from the upper fill, lower fill, adobe layer, and floor. All were taken from a stratigraphic column left intact for this purpose along the north wall east of the entry. According to the 1974 room report, bags of bone were set aside for special analysis as well as a bag of sherds of an unusual type "not native to the site." We believe that the pottery sherds "not native to the site," may refer to 353 sherds of corrugated and incised pottery found in the structure.

Pottery found in the fill and on the floor consisted of Tanque Verde Red-on-brown, obliterated indented corrugated and plain ware. One half of a suprahemispherical Tanque Verde Red-on-brown bowl was found in the house. Half of a perforated disk (a probable spindle whorl), a whole unperforated disk, and a sherd that may have been used as a pottery scraper were found in the upper fill. All of the worked sherds are plain wares. Also found in the upper fill was worked shell including possible bracelet fragments. More than 1,100 flakes and 10 projectile points (both Classic period and Archaic types) were found in the fill and on the floor of the structure. Field notes indicate that 17 hammerstones were also found, although they were not analyzed. Groundstone artifacts found in the house included a pestle, five manos, two polishing stones, a spindle whorl, and five tabular tools. As noted above, a human figurine was found in the eastern posthole, and an animal figurine was found in the lower fill of the structure. Burned bones from a cottontail rabbit and a white-tailed deer were also found in the structure.

According to field notes, the floor of Structure 4 was clearly evident and contained dark patches indicating burning. The walls consisted of a thin veneer, perhaps only 3 cm of adobe, laid against the pit excavation. A

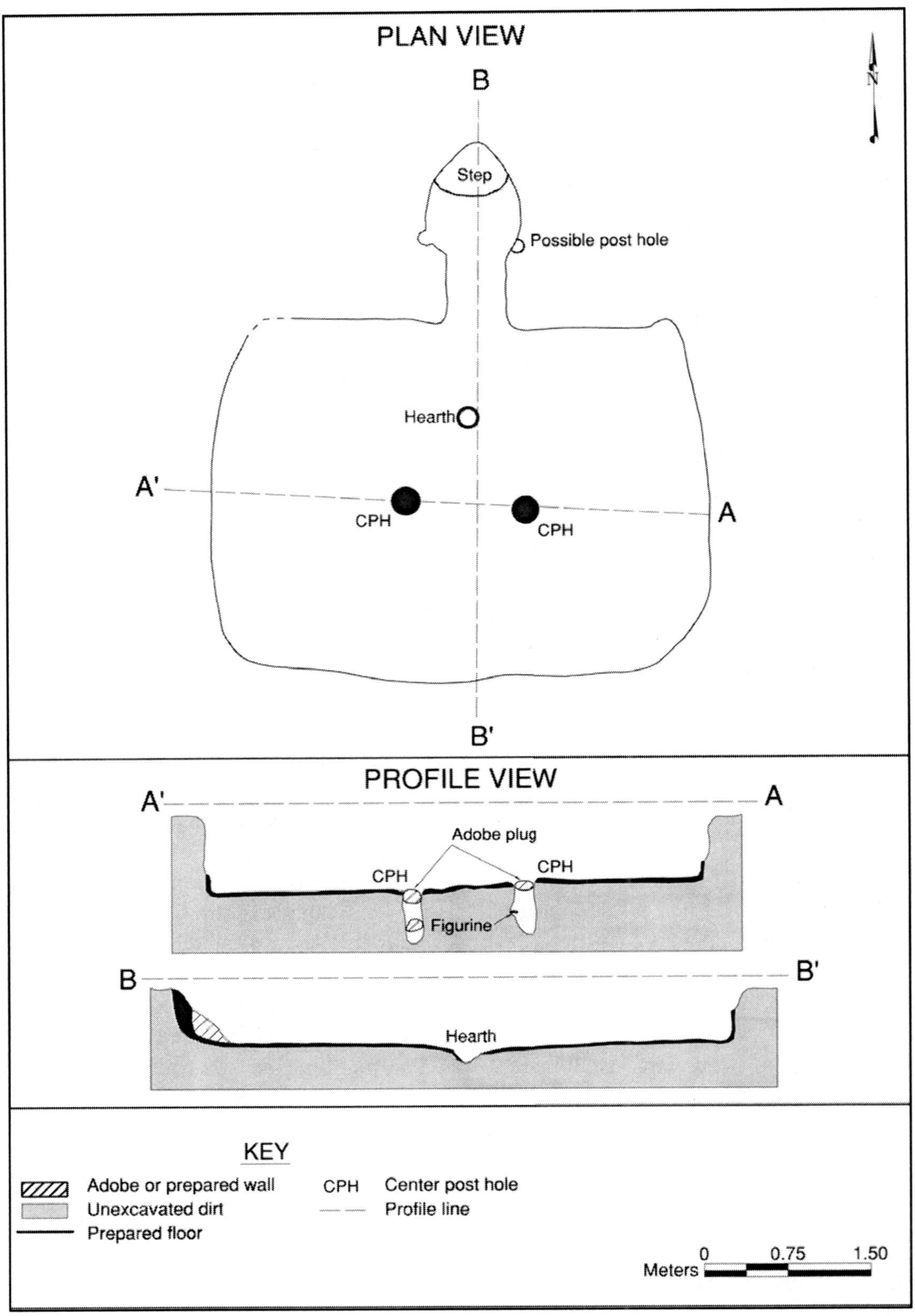

Figure 2.1. Structure 4, plan view and profiles (prepared by Austin Lenhart and Elizabeth Vinson).

pot hunter's hole took out most of the northwestern corner of the structure. This structure was stratigraphically earlier than the nearly adjacent compound. A test trench that extended from Structure 4 to the compound revealed that the bottom of the compound wall was on the same level as the top of the pit house wall. The numerous artifacts relating to flaked stone tool manufacture indicate that the feature may have been used for flint knapping after it was abandoned.

Structure 4 was excavated by Bruce Bradley, Richard Polhemus, and others in the spring of 1968. Bruce Bradley and Paul Grebinger recorded the structure in March of 1968 and wrote the field notes. Kathryn A. Youngs, a student in a class taught by Paul Grebinger of Eisenhower College, Seneca Falls, New York, wrote a student report on the structure in January 1974.

Structure 6

Structure 6 (Figure 2.2) was located inside the compound, near its eastern wall. It was an adobe walled, detached, rectangular structure. The walls were apparently cobble-constructed according to information shown on the plan with some plaster visible on the walls that may have been reworked in places. The walls were between 30 cm and 50 cm tall and 10 cm to 30 cm thick.

The entry of Structure 6 was in the center of the east wall and was apparently appended with parallel walls. A vertical, stone slab was located at the outer edge of the entry.

Apparently two floors were present in this structure, but much of the floor evidence was destroyed by pot hunting. The more recent floor rose in elevation from the center of the structure to the north and south walls. There apparently were ledges at the base of the wall slightly above the floor level. Small patches of the floor(s) were burned.

Two hearths were present. The upper hearth was a conical to rounded pit scooped out of the sterile soil and was definitely associated with the more recent floor. The lower hearth was a prepared, adobe-lined basin with a plastered area of floor surrounding it. Its location was not indicated on the profile view.

Two pits along the width of the central axis of the structure were identified as post holes. Seven additional pits were present, four of which were identified as storage pits and three as post holes. A large, shallow pit adjacent to the south wall contained a number of sherds, flakes, and a drill. A conical pit was overlain with a stone that may have been intended as a cap.

We could locate no information on the roof of Structure 6.

The upper level of fill consisted of loose sand and gravel similar to that from all houses previously excavated. Below that layer was a hard layer that had the feeling, but not the appearance, of adobe. Below this, and just above the floors, was a layer of loose silt and gravels apparently blown in by wind and washed in by water. No samples were taken from the fill.

A deer jaw, a worked piece of turquoise, a tabular tool, a pestle, and two projectile points were recovered from the floor. In addition to pottery and some flaked stone debitage, four tabular tools, three manos, a handstone, a polishing stone, and a metate fragment were found in the fill. Jackrabbit and cottontail bones were also found in the house.

Information on this structure was extrapolated from a plan, profiles, and field notes. No excavation form could be located. According to the field notes, this was the last house excavated in the spring of 1968, though it is unknown who excavated or recorded it. The field notes were written by Paul Grebinger. Although it appears that the house had been remodeled (with two floors and two hearths), it was difficult to be

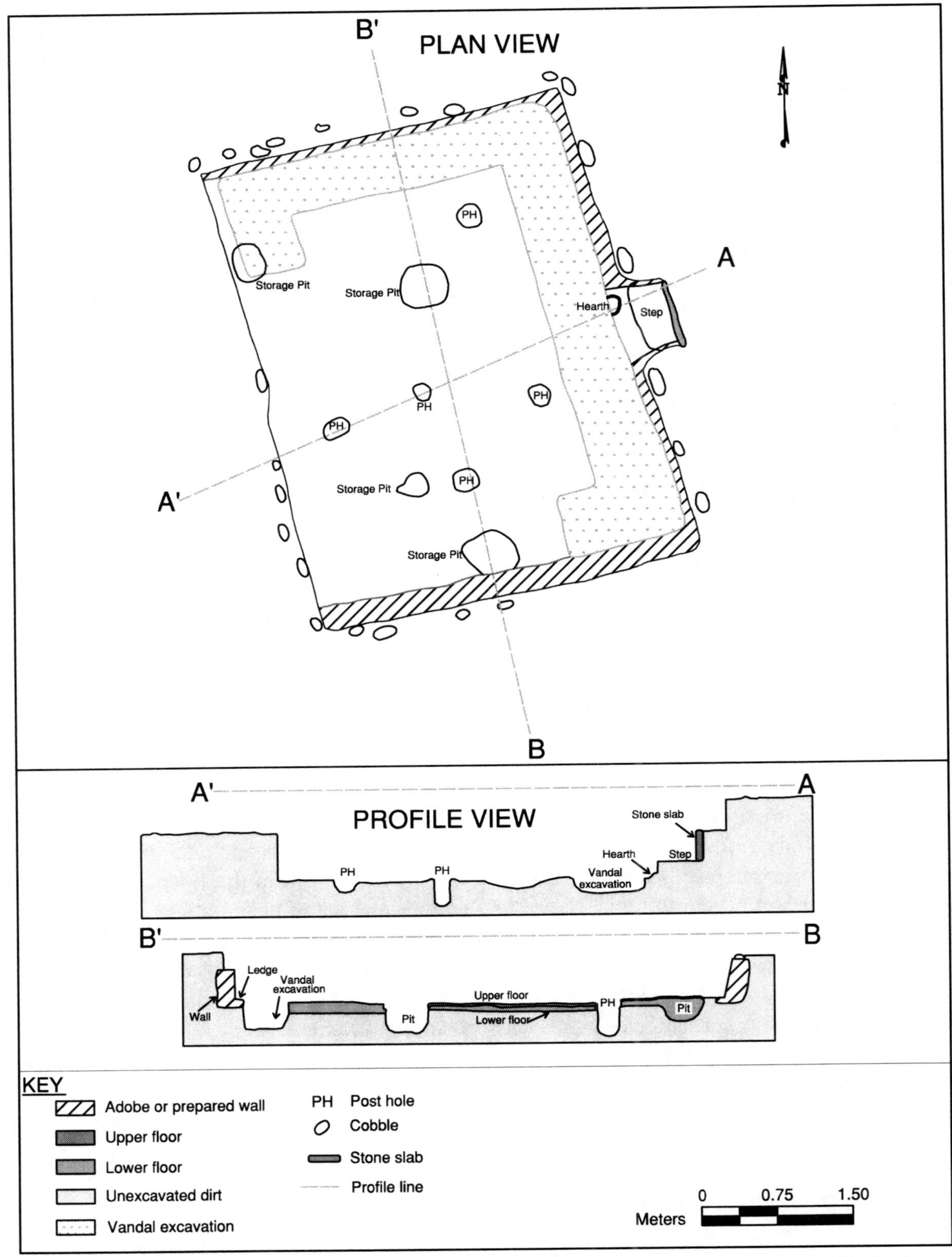

Figure 2.2. Structure 6, plan view and profiles (prepared by Austin Lenhart, Elizabeth Vinson, and Helen L. O'Brien).

certain because the structure was severely pot hunted. A long trench had been dug along the east wall, and shallow holes had been dug along the outside of all the other walls. Most evidence for the two floors was destroyed. In addition, during excavation the floors in the center of the house were not identified, and the excavators dug through them. A layer of dark, charcoal-like material in the profile, in combination with evidence of burning on other parts of the lower floor, suggested that the earlier structure must have burned.

Structure 7

Structure 7 (Figures 2.3, 2.4) was a detached, adobe walled structure located inside the compound near its east wall, immediately south of Structure 6. The walls were made of puddled, coursed adobe inset with cobbles. The cobbles tied the lower wall to the superstructure. Numerous small (pebble-size) stones were embedded in the adobe, surrounding the larger cobbles. On the east wall thin layers of adobe were present, either as the remains of plaster or as a patch. The walls were between 60 cm and 80 cm in height, and varied in thickness. The northern wall was 45 cm thick, the southern wall 51 cm thick, the eastern wall 40 cm thick and the western wall 45 cm thick. Vertical grooves in the western wall suggested that the roof was pole-reinforced.

The entry, which was 78 cm wide, was centered in the south wall, 3.4 m from the east wall and 3.1 m from the west wall. It was apparently appended to the structure by a low threshold, about 10 cm wide and 15 cm tall.

The floor was prepared and fire-hardened with the plastering rising in a steep curve to meet all four walls. The floor's surface was disturbed by root activity in the northeast corner. A very irregular pit dug into sterile soil was located inside the entry in the usual hearth location. It may never have been prepared. Two main post holes were along the east-west central axis of the structure. A number of small pits were present, especially in the southwest corner; these may have held posts, probably for a bench rather than providing roof support. Nineteen pits (post holes and storage pits) were located; several of these were prepared pits.

Evidence for the roof included large north-south cross beams as well as adobe chunks in the fill with reed impressions.

The fill consisted of three layers: an upper washed-in layer, a second layer of two parts (a dark, loose organic layer and a tan layer of a tougher consistency like the fallen adobe found in other houses) and a lower burned layer.

Six tree-ring samples were taken from the house; five of mesquite and one of juniper. None could be dated. Two pollen samples were taken from under Sherd clusters 4 and 5 on the floor. Macrobotanical samples from the roof fall area yielded reeds (*Phragmites*), saguaro wood and callus material, and an agave or yucca stalk.

Several Cibola White Ware sherds, pieces from a San Carlos Red bowl, a bone awl or hair-pin fragment, a polishing stone, and a stone pot lid were found in the dark, loose gravelly fill. Nine projectile points were found in the fill and on the floor of the feature including one Cortaro point, one Cienega point, three San Pedro points, and four Classic period points. Some large plain ware jar sherds were found in the fill above the house's hearth; a mano from the roof fill was also near the hearth. On the floor in the center of the house near the hearth and the entry were a number of sherds, a core, and a mano. Most of a suprahemisperical Tanque Verde Red-on-brown bowl and a metate were also found on the floor. A piece of a deer pelvis, and bones from a jackrabbit and cottontail were also found in the house.

According to field notes, the fill did not contain much cultural material. Concentrations of artifacts on the floor were located near the

Figure 2.3. Structure 7, looking west (uncatalogued, Arizona State Museum, University of Arizona).

north wall of the structure as well as to the west of the entry. Level 3, the level above the floor, was burned.

Structure 7 was excavated by Charles and Annetta (Long) Cheek from the fall of 1968 to the spring of 1969. Paul Grebinger recorded the structure and the field notes were written by Charles Creek and Paul Grebinger. Two students, Melanie Gehen and Glenn Page, wrote reports on the structure in January 1975 while attending a class taught by Paul Grebinger at Eisenhower College, Seneca Falls, New York.

Structure 8

Structure 8 (Figure 2.5) was located immediately southwest and outside of the compound. It was an adobe walled, detached, rectangular structure. Walls were of puddled adobe with stones inset in the lower wall to bind with the superstructure. What appeared to be grooves in the east and west walls suggested a pole-reinforced superstructure. A large area of smoothed plaster was found on the south portion of the east wall. It is not known how tall the walls were, although a fallen section of wall to the west of the entry suggested they were higher than the standing walls. All four walls were about 30 cm thick. Two possible post holes were located in the center of the wall on either side of the entry.

The entry was located in the center of the south wall. Apparently appended, it was almost square with a probable threshold. The thin wall of the entry extended around the inside edge of the house wall. The entry was 40 cm from north to south and 30 cm from east to west.

The floor was well prepared and fire hardened and rose in a sharp curve to meet the

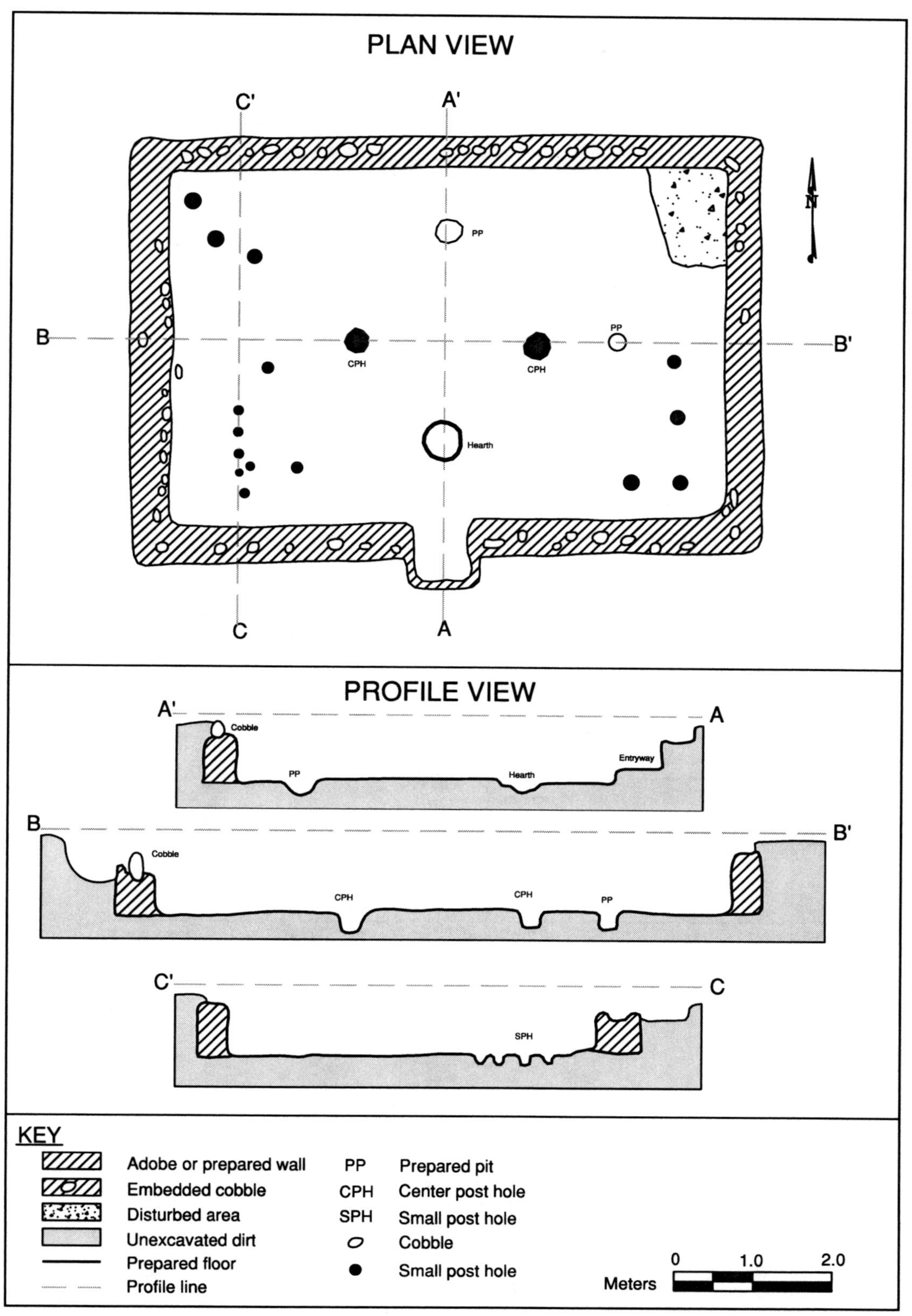

Figure 2.4. Structure 7, plan view and profiles (prepared by Austin Lenhart, Elizabeth Vinson, and Helen L. O'Brien).

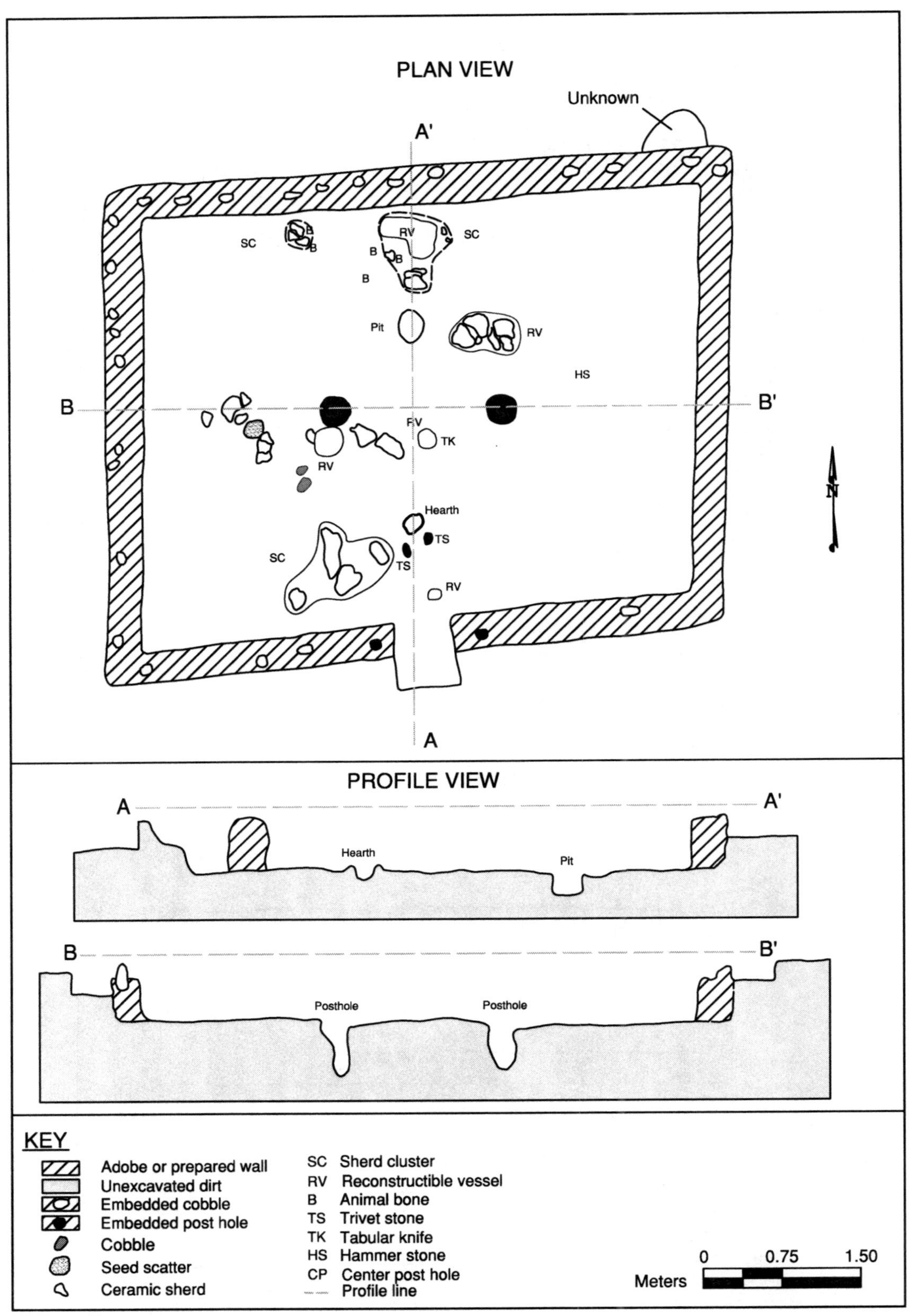

Figure 2.5. Structure 8, plan view and profiles (prepared by Austin Lenhart, Elizabeth Vinson, and Helen L. O'Brien).

walls. The hearth was round, 20 cm in diameter, and basin-shaped (about 12 cm deep). It was adobe-lined and located about 1 meter north of the entry. Two post holes were located along the central axis of the structure, each about 25 cm in diameter and between 40 cm and 50 cm deep. One possible storage pit or post hole was located in the center of the house, north of the hearth. The pit was 22 cm by 32 cm in diameter and about 20 cm deep.

Chunks of burned adobe were evidence of the roof; each had one flat smooth surface and looked as if it had fallen from the superstructure. The remains of beams were found that probably were laid from north to south to form the roof.

The fill consisted of a burned layer just above the floor.

Both tree ring and pollen samples were taken. The tree-ring samples, 10 in all, were identified as ponderosa pine (n = 5), pinyon pine (n = 3), juniper (n = 1), and mesquite (n = 1). One of the pinyon pine samples (WTR-32) was dated to A.D. 1242 (Dean et al. 1996). Because outer rings were missing from the sample, the date was not considered to be a cutting date.

Structure 8 contained pieces from six corrugated vessels including two bowls and four jars. The sherds represent between 50 percent and 90 percent of each vessel; four of the vessels (two jars and two bowls) were found on the floor. Sherds representing about 90 percent of a plain ware bowl were found in the fill of the house. Also recovered from the floor were a number of burned bones from mule deer, white-tailed deer, pronghorn, and bighorn sheep. One handstone, two trivet stones, and a tabular tool were found on the floor. Other groundstone artifacts including four manos, a metate, two pecking stones, a pestle, and a tabular tool were found in the fill.

Excavators made note of a great deal of wall fall and slump along the north and east walls as well as along the south wall west of the entry. They also noted that the floor of this structure was littered with pottery and that on the floor were some adobe chunks with impressions of wood roofing poles. A probable adobe-mixing basin was located outside the north wall at the northeast corner of the structure.

Structure 8 was excavated by Meade Kemrer, Dick Dannells, and Bruce Bradley in the fall of 1968. Paul Grebinger took the field notes and recorded the site along with Bruce Bradley.

Structure 17

Structure 17 was an adobe-walled, detached structure located in the northeastern corner of the compound. It was rectangular in shape and the walls were made of puddled adobe. No wall cobbles were visible on the ground surface; thus, the structure was not visible until backhoe trenching revealed it. The interior walls of the structure ranged between 10 cm and 30 cm in thickness, while the exterior walls measured between 20 cm and 50 cm in thickness. The thickest portion of the wall was in the southeast corner and was 61 cm thick. The north, east, and west walls were thin and no plaster was observed on any of the walls. The eroded condition of the wall may explain the lack of wall cobbles. This structure seems to have had double walls on at least portions of the east, west and north sides. On these sides a thin, interior wall was constructed, with the area between the walls containing loose fill. The top was filled with or capped by adobe.

The entry of Structure 17 was in the center of the south side. It was appended, short and rounded in plan view. It was 78 cm wide from north to south and 65 cm wide from east to west.

The floor consisted of prepared adobe hardened by the burning of the house and curved up to meet the wall in many places.

The hearth was 25 cm in diameter and 15 cm deep and was prepared and adobe-lined with a relatively flat bottom. Two post holes were located along the central axis of the structure; in addition, one large and several small pits were present in the floor. According to the field notes, the large pit, located in the northeast corner, was "prepared." With the exception of two small, nearly contiguous pits in the southeast corner, the other small pits were probably rodent holes.

The only evidence of the roof was chunks of adobe recovered in the fill. Some cobbles were encountered in the fill, but not a lot, suggesting that stones may not have been an important part of the wall construction.

Pollen samples were taken from two jars that were in pits just outside the southeast corner of the structure. Twelve charcoal samples were retrieved from the house, with all being ponderosa pine; none could be dated.

The artifact assemblage includes pieces from four vessels—one McDonald Corrugated and three Tanque Verde Red-on-brown bowls, all of which were found on the floor. Other artifacts on the floor included two nether stones, an abrader, and an arrowshaft straightener. A lapstone was found in the roof fall level and three handstones and a tabular tool were found in the fill. A polishing stone was found in one subsurface pit. Remains of two additional vessels—one Tanque Verde Red-on-brown and one corrugated jar—were recovered from extramural pits. A triangular piece of turquoise was found in the lower fill.

According to the field notes, the jars located outside the structure were associated with a hard-packed floor that lay about 10 cm below the surface between the eastern wall of the structure and the eastern wall of the compound about 1 m to 2 m away. This may have been a roofed work area.

Structure 17 was excavated by Paul Grebinger, Bruce Bradley and Dick Dannells in the fall of 1968; Paul Grebinger took the field notes. The recorders were Paul Grebinger and Sharon Urban.

Central Locus

The Central Locus was located between the Compound Locus and the Northern Locus (Figure 1.13). Four excavated structures (5, 15, 32, and 33), one unexcavated structure, and Cemetery 2 were in the Central Locus. The architecture of the structures suggests that Structure 32 was built prior to Structure 33 because the entry to Structure 32 opens directly into the back of Structure 33. Structure 15 has been interpreted as a store room because of the botanical remains and large numbers jars found in the house.

Structure 5

Structure 5 was a rectangular, adobe-walled, detached structure located approximately 100 feet northeast of the compound. The average depth of the floor below ground surface was 55 cm and the average depth of the floor below the top of the wall was 22 cm.

The walls stood approximately 30 cm above the floor and were made of a mixture of caliche, gravel and mud. Originally, stones had apparently been set in the top level of the wall; however, most had been removed by a pot hunter. Numerous stones were lying around the exterior of the house. The walls were in good condition although there was no plaster on the walls. There were vertical, column-like grooves in the northeast, southeast, and southwest corners from the top to the bottom of the wall; these were identified as "probably rodent burrows."

The entry was in the center of the south wall. It was appended, with curved walls and was apparently semicircular in plan. It was approximately 70 cm wide and 22 cm deep.

It had been previously uncovered by pot hunters.

The floor was in excellent condition where it was still preserved. Pot hunters had dug through the floor along the entire length of the northern wall. The hearth, which was directly north of the entry, was circular, 50 cm to 55 cm in diameter, and 8 cm deep in the center. There were two post holes along the central axis of the structure. The western hole was badly disturbed by pot hunters; the eastern hole was 40 cm by 34.5 cm in diameter and 59.5 cm deep with a narrow, lower hole that was 22.5 cm in diameter. There were no additional pits.

The condition or construction of the roof was difficult to determine as this structure had been extensively pot hunted. The only materials that may have been from the roof were two chunks of earth on either side of the hearth.

Associates of Robert DuBois attempted to sample the hearth for archaeomagnetic dating, but concluded it was too badly damaged, thus no samples were taken. Two metates were recovered from the northwest corner of the structure, at the bottom of the pot hunter's hole. They were probably used in wall construction.

The excavators commented that this structure had been seriously vandalized before excavation began, although the floor, associated sherds, and features such as the hearth and two post holes were intact. This structure was very similar to Structures 1 and 2. It was close to Structure 1 in size, but lacked an adobe pad in the entry, and the hearth was not as well prepared. It was excavated in March of 1968; the names of the excavators were not recorded. The structure was recorded by Joyce Rehm, Nancy Jacobus, and Paul Grebinger, who also took the field notes.

Structure 15

Structure 15 was a rectangular, adobe-walled, detached structure 100–150 feet [30–45 m] north of northeast corner of compound. (The original dimensions were given in feet and inches). The walls were made of puddled adobe. Stones remained inset in the north and south walls at the point where the upper and lower walls joined. There was no observable plaster. The walls were between 40 cm and 60 cm high and 20 cm to 40 cm thick.

Except for portions near the entry, the walls were relatively thin.

The entry was in the center of the north wall. It was appended and short and rectangular in plan. It was 90 cm wide from east to west and 60 cm long from north to south.

The floor consisted of a thick layer of adobe on top of caliche. Where it was present it sloped up to meet the wall. The floor was badly damaged in the eastern half of the structure as a result of root activity and pot hunting. There was no hearth. Two probable post holes were located along the central axis of the structure. They were not well defined as they occurred in areas disturbed by root activity. Some fragments of charcoal were observed in the west hole. There were no pits, although three shallow depressions served as vessel rests for large, round-bottomed storage jars.

The remains of charred beams were evidence of the roof of this structure. Twelve samples were taken, consisting of three of juniper, six of pinyon pine, one of mesquite, and two of ponderosa pine. Tree-ring dates were derived from four of the pinyon pine samples. One sample from a large beam (WTR-56, 57, 63) was dated to A.D. 1226, although an unknown number of rings may be missing. Sample WTR-60 dated to A.D. 1229; it is missing one or two rings from the end of the sequence. Sample WTR-62, which has been dated to A.D. 1232, is missing an unknown number of rings, and Sample WTR-64, which has been dated to A.D. 1239, is missing one or two rings (Dean et al. 1996). Macrobotanical samples taken from the house include hackberry, corn, beans, cholla buds, and reed. A pollen sample taken from the house has not been analyzed.

According to field notes, portions of 4 large plain ware jars, 11 corrugated vessels, 8 painted vessels (probably Tanque Verde Red-on-brown), and 1 complete jar were encountered in this structure. We should note that the complete jar has not been relocated; 8,686 sherds in the research collection represent the vessels just described plus up to 11 more for a minimum of 34 vessels found in this house. Corn and beans were found in the fill and one vessel contained cholla buds. In addition, a tabular tool was found in the fill and one of greenish slate or shale was recorded as being found on the floor. We should note that the tabular tool from the floor was not identified in the analyzed collection. Two shell pendants and portions of two shell frogs were also located on the floor, and two sherds with ground edges were located in the fill.

Two pot hunters dug in this structure. When archaeologists came upon them they had completely destroyed the northeast quarter of the structure, although almost all of the remainder of the structure was salvageable. The student report concluded that this structure was used for storage, based on the presence of a number of large plain ware and corrugated jars. The report also noted that the structure had a wider door than other structures, perhaps to accommodate the very large jars.

Paul Grebinger and Bruce Bradley excavated and recorded the structure in the spring of 1969. Brenda Prince, Alan B. Hamor, and Harry Rosenberg wrote papers on this structure in January 1975 when they were students in a class taught by Paul Grebinger, Eisenhower College, Seneca Falls, New York.

Structure 32

Structure 32 was a rectangular, adobe-walled, detached structure. The walls were made of puddled adobe with stones in the north and east walls. They stood approximately 3 ft. (36 cm) high; as with Structure 15, the original measurements were given in feet and inches. The entry was appended in the center of the south wall. It consisted of two, short wall segments perpendicular to the south wall, the longest being 2 ft (0.6 m).

There was no information as to the condition of the floor. The hearth was inside the entryway and was 6 in (15cm) in diameter and 4 in (10cm) deep. Two post holes were located along the central long axis of the structure; the western hole was 28 cm in diameter and 48 cm deep; the eastern hole was 46 cm in diameter and 58 cm deep. One pit was found in the northwest quadrangle of the structure. It was 19 in (48 cm) in diameter and 10 in (25 cm) deep.

From the floor or just above the floor a slate spindle whorl, two projectile points, two shell bracelet fragments, and sherds were recovered. These artifacts are not included in the analyses for this report. A piece of turquoise or chrysocolla was found in the western central-axis posthole of this feature. No samples were taken.

This structure was recorded by Bruce Bradley and was excavated by him in December 1972. No field notes or student reports exist for the structure.

Structure 33

Structure 33 was a detached subrectangular, adobe-walled structure. The walls were made of puddled adobe with stones set at a standard interval. The walls stood 40 cm high, with an approximate reconstructed height of the east wall of 1.6 m to 2 m high. The walls were in poor condition; they sloped out and were thin (approximately 5 cm). An opening in the west wall was thought to be a window; originally, it would have been about 1 m above the floor.

The entry was appended onto the center of the south wall and consisted of two short walls perpendicular to the structure. There is no information on the condition of the floor, though a hearth was discovered inside the entryway. Eleven post holes were noted on a sketch map. One post hole was along the central long axis of the structure. There was a burned area in the location where a second major post hole would be expected. A group of six post holes in the southeast quadrant of the structure could have provided support for a bench or other raised structure. There were no pits.

There was no direct evidence of the roof, though lumps of burned adobe could have been roof or wall remains. The upper portion of the fill was gray in color and sandy and gravelly in consistency; the middle portion was brown and gravelly; the lower portion was ashy and gray. All levels of the fill contained chunks of adobe and stones that were apparently part of the east and west walls. Soil samples were taken of the fill at 10 cm intervals.

The following artifacts were recovered from the floor or immediately above the floor: two shell beads, one bone awl, a stone sphere, a slate knife, a ground stone knife, a piece of worked slate with red pigment, a metate fragment, a "microcardium" bead, a fragment of a deer mandible, one projectile point, hammerstones, a metate fragment, sherds, and bone. Two rock clusters, largely of unmodified rocks, were noted on the floor; each contained one or more hammerstones.

Although fairly detailed notes exist for this feature, with the exception of two projectile points, the artifacts were not analyzed and are not in the ASM research collections.

Excavators concluded that the structure had been abandoned, then burned, eroded, and collapsed. Supporting evidence includes (1) the large quantity of potsherds and other artifactual material in the fill, as well as (2) a "talus" wedge of reddish-orange sandy gravel that apparently was the result of the erosion of the wall by natural forces after the structure burned.

The structure was excavated by Bruce Huckell, Lisa (Washbon) Huckell, and Al [last name unknown] from January to May of 1973. Bruce Huckell recorded the structure and wrote the field notes.

Southwestern Locus

Twelve structures were excavated in the Southwestern Locus, which was situated immediately west of the Compound Locus (Figure 1.13). Among the structures excavated were two sets of contiguous-walled structures: 16-11-18 and 10-12. Structures 2, 9, 13, 23, 24, 25, and 26; three unexcavated structures; and Cemetery 1 were all located in the Southwestern Locus.

Structure 2

Structure 2 (Figure 2.6) was an adobe-walled and detached rectangular structure located 150 to 200 feet (60 m) west of the compound. Again, we should note that the original measurements were given in feet and inches. The walls were made of puddled adobe mixed with caliche and gravel with cobbles set into the top of the walls. The north wall was plastered east of the entry. The walls were in excellent condition and stood 26 cm to 35 cm above the floor. They were at least 41 cm to 56 cm thick along the north wall east of the entry. Some wall stones were noted in the fill along the west wall.

The entry was centered in the north wall and was little more than a niche that was lower than the rest of the wall. It was 0.55 m in length and 0.55 m in width. There was no step or adobe pad.

The floor was in good to excellent condition. The hearth was located directly south of

Figure 2.6. Structure 2, looking west (Catalog Number 106528, Arizona State Museum, University of Arizona).

the entrance and was round with a prepared lip on the eastern edge. The inside diameter was 0.32 cm and the outside diameter was 0.43 cm. The hearth was dug into sterile soil. Two post holes were located along the central axis of the structure. The western hole was 27 cm in diameter; the eastern hole was 37 cm in diameter. There were no pits in the floor.

A layer of adobe-like fill was noted above the floor; it may or may not have been roof fall. There was no information on the fill itself.

Archaeomagnetic samples were taken from the hearth by Robert DuBois with the assistance of Tom Hemmings and Cameron Greenleaf on March 27, 1968.

A striking number of ground-stone artifacts were found in this structure including nine fragmentary tabular tools (one from the floor, others from the fill), three manos (one whole from the floor, two fragmentary from the fill), a mortar found in the roof fall level, a quartz polishing stone from the floor, two metate fragments (one from the floor, one from the fill), and a fragmentary nether stone found in the fill. A shell pendant in the form of a toad or lizard and chalcedony and jasper flakes were found in a cluster on the floor near the southwest corner of the house. An overturned metate with chipped edges was found to the right of the doorway. It apparently was not recovered. A large number of Tanque Verde Red-on-brown bowl fragments were found on the floor near the hearth and entryway. A number of projectile points, a piece of turquoise, a faceted stone with a hematite coating, a sherd with a ground edge, an oval-shaped sherd, and a bone piece from an awl or hairpin were also found in the house.

According to the field notes, several cobbles were noted in the fill within two to three feet from the inside of the west wall. They were "strung out" in a north-south direction and were probably "wall slabs." Fire-reddened areas as well as extensive quantities of charcoal were noted on the floor near the entry. At the end of the excavation, as the exterior of the walls were being clearly defined, two horizontal grooves were noted at the level of the original ground surface along the exterior of the north wall east of the entry. They may represent wall repair or more likely were intended for poles set upright, forming part of the wall above the ground surface.

From the fall of 1967 to March 24, 1968, Bruce Bradley, Eileen and Wes Ferguson, Cameron Greenleaf, Albert Turner, and Joyce Rinehart excavated the structure while Annetta Long (Cheek) excavated and recorded the hearth. Paul Grebinger and Bruce Bradley took the field notes. The recorder of the structure is unknown.

Structure 9

Structure 9 (Figure 2.7) was a roughly rectangular, adobe-walled detached structure approximately 10 m east of Structure 10. Cemetery 1 was approximately 4 m east of the east wall of the house. The walls were made of puddled adobe with cobbles set along the

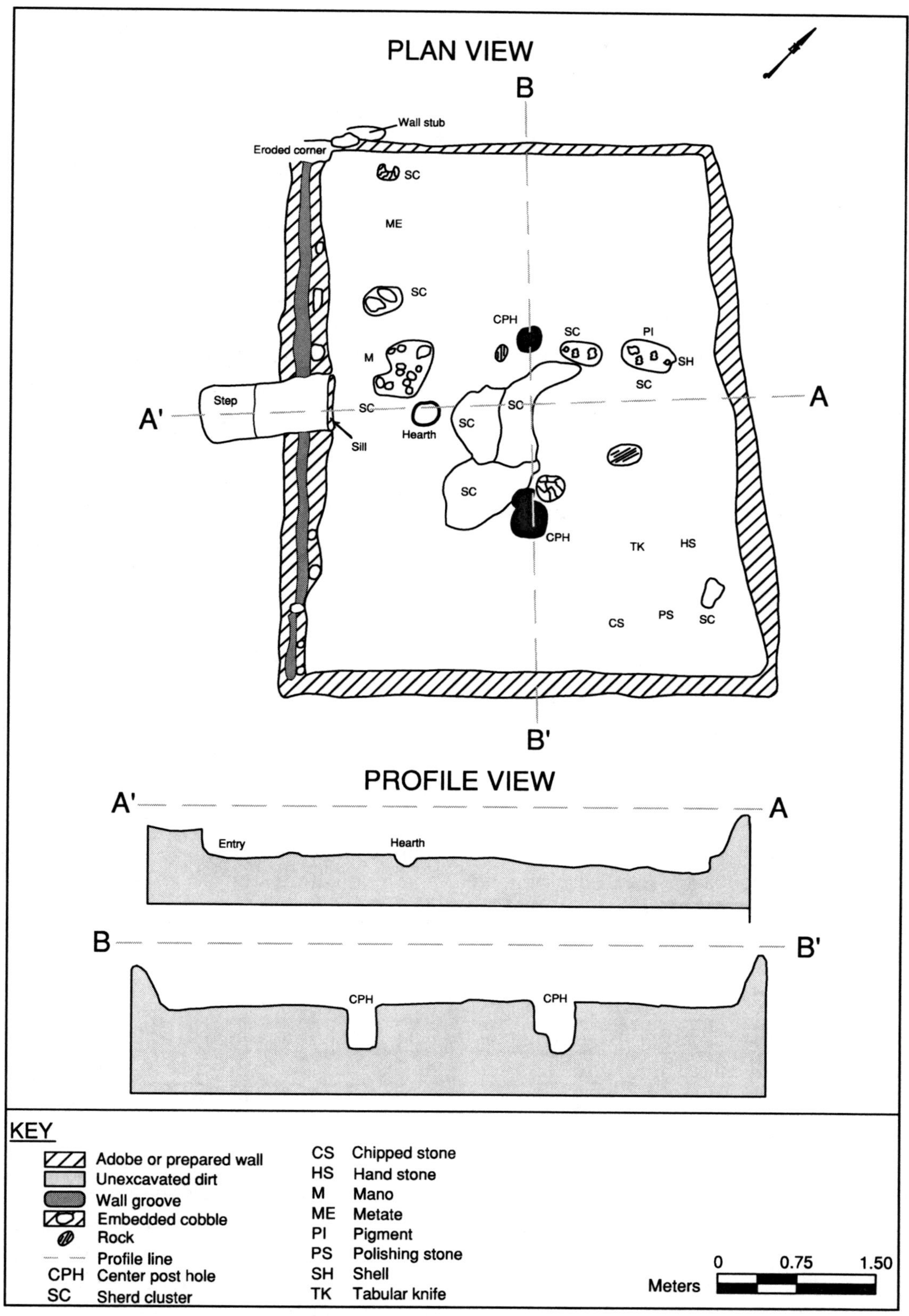

Figure 2.7. Structure 9, plan view and profiles (prepared by Austin Lenhart, Elizabeth Vinson, and Helen L. O'Brien).

top of the west wall; one cobble remained on top of the north wall. Evidence of a groove for possible post reinforcement was found in the west wall. The north wall was thin and heavily eroded. The walls stood between 40 cm and 60 cm high and were of variable thickness. The west wall was thickest and measured between 30 cm and 55 cm. The north wall was the thinnest, measuring only 10 cm. The walls were in good condition except for the north wall and the southeast and southwest corners. There were horizontal grooves in the west wall along both sides of the entry.

The entry was located in the center of the west wall. It was appended with parallel walls, and had a slight threshold 10 cm in width that separated the entry from the structure interior. There was an adobe step in the outer portion of the entry.

The floor was in good condition. It was very smooth in spots and sloped to the east; the floor had been replastered several times. There was evidence in the southern half of the structure that there were two floors vertically separated by about 4 cm. The hearth was to the east of the entry and was approximately 20 cm in diameter and 10 cm deep; the bottom of the hearth was crumbly.

Two post holes were located along the central axis of the structure. The northern hole measured 30 cm in diameter and was 35 cm deep. The southern hole measured 15 cm to 40 cm in diameter and was 50 cm deep. A large rim sherd from a Tanque Verde Red-on-brown bowl was found adhering to the side of the northern hole approximately 15 cm to 25 cm below the floor. A sherd and a piece of *Glycymeris* shell that had been ground to a point at one end were recovered from the base of the southern hole. There were no pits, and no information was recorded about the roof.

The upper fill contained dense adobe-like material, but few artifacts. The lower fill was sandier and had no burned material.

Eleven pollen samples were taken from the floor including samples from under the mano and the metate fragment. In the fill of the entryway a perforated *Conus* shell tinkler and a shaped piece of mica were recovered along with other cultural debris. Three large sherd clusters were located on the floor in the center of the house, approximately in the area between the two post holes. The largest cluster consisted of 424 plain ware sherds. The pottery was largely identified as Tanque Verde Red-on-brown, indented obliterated corrugated, and "local plain ware." The ceramic inventory also included a single sherd each of Snowflake Black-on-white, Reserve Black-on-white, and Wingate Black-on-red.

The remaining floor inventory consists of smaller sherd clusters, one metate fragment, one mano, a tabular tool, a pecking stone, one flake, a piece of juvenile *Glycymeris* shell with a perforated umbo, and pieces of malachite that may have been used as a green pigment. According to the field notes, the metate fragment (located in the northwest corner of the structure) may have been set in the top of the wall. It was apparently left in the field. A piece of worked mica, two tabular tools (one fragmentary), three pecking stones, a handstone, and a polishing stone were found in the fill of the house.

According to field notes, the structure was identified on the surface by a north-south line of rocks assumed to be the east wall and an east-west line assumed to be the south wall. The house was quite irregular in shape, especially along the east wall, which was badly deteriorated. All the walls suffered from erosion. The house walls may not all have been constructed according to the same technique. The west wall, in which the entry was located, seems to have had a groove between the inner and outer walls with the wall stones set into the innermost part of this wall. Perhaps the groove allowed for poles to be set in it as reinforcement. The east wall appears to have been of similar construction. The north wall was barely more than a thin layer of adobe that slanted away from the house interior so that it was not very vertical. There was no evidence that the house burned.

Sharon Urban, Frank Lobo, Sue Lobo, Lisa Spray, Jon Czaplicki, Larry Lusk, Catherine Unger, Linda Allen, and Ilene Nicholas excavated the house from October 27 to December 1, 1968. The structure was recorded by Sharon Urban and Catherine Unger on November 3, 1968 and by Paul Grebinger in the fall of 1968. Both Paul Grebinger and Sharon Urban took the field notes. Emmie Hamilton, a student in a class taught by Paul Grebinger at Eisenhower College, Seneca Falls, New York, wrote a report on the structure in January of 1975. Richard Burchim, a student in a class taught by Gwinn Vivian at the University of Arizona, Tucson, wrote a report in the spring of 1973.

Structure 10

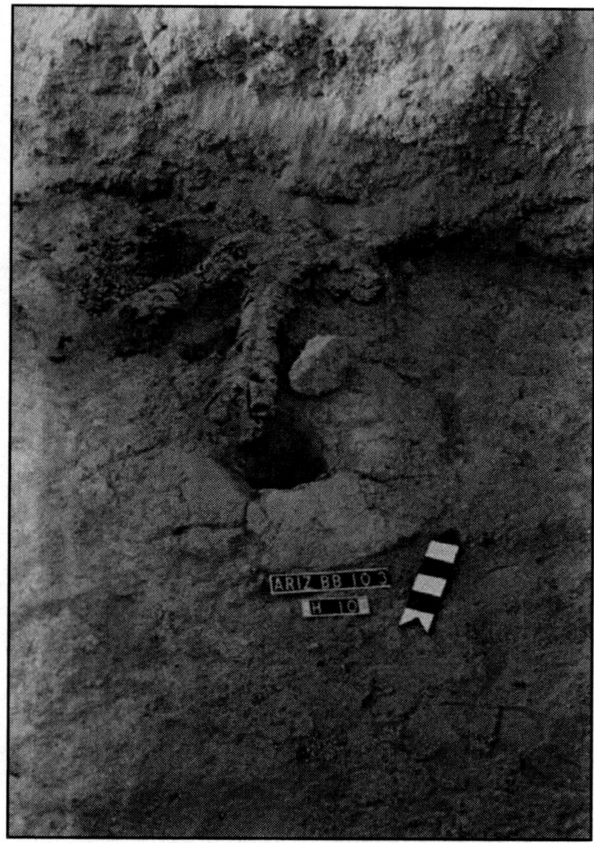

Figure 2.8. Structure 10, showing wide collar of hearth and beams on floor (Catalog Number 106374, Arizona State Museum, University of Arizona).

Structure 10 (Figure 2.8) was approximately 50 m due west of the west wall of the compound. The west wall of Structure 10 was about 26 cm east of the east wall of Structure 12. It was a rectangular adobe-walled house and was detached, but nearly contiguous with Structure 12.

The walls were made of puddled adobe, and the considerable wall fall and cobbles outside of the south wall suggested that the wall was constructed using alternating stone and adobe courses. The south wall had two deep grooves indicating reinforcement with vertical poles. Wall stones had toppled into the structure along the inside edge of the north wall. In general, the walls stood between 40 cm and 50 cm high, although the thickest wall segment stood only about 20 cm. The east wall was very thin; there was no apparent plaster on any of the walls. Depressions in the wall indicated the locations of stones, although no stones were still in position.

The entry was in the center of the south wall and was apparently a simple opening. It measured approximately 50 cm from north to south and 60 cm from east to west. There may have been an adobe threshold outlining the entry.

The floor was well preserved as a result of burning. The hearth was deep and straight sided with a rounded bottom; it was clay lined and very well smoothed. A ring or apron of prepared clay surrounded the hearth making it very similar to the south hearth in Structure 12 (Figure 2.8). Two post holes were found along the central axis of the structure. One large deep pit was found near the southwest corner; it may have been used for storage.

Evidence for the roof included burned beams that lay approximately north-south; there was also considerable adobe in the fill. The upper fill was yellowish and sandy while the lower fill was gray and ashy.

Twelve tree-ring samples were taken from Structure 10. They included beams and posts of ponderosa pine (n = 8) and juniper (n = 4). Three of the ponderosa pine beams yielded dates of A.D. 1234 (WTR-1), A.D. 1237 (WTR-9), and A.D. 1231 (WTR-35) (Dean et al. 1996). The A.D. 1231 and A.D. 1234 dates are not cutting dates, as outer rings are missing from the samples. The outer ring is present on sample WTR-9, making A.D. 1237 a cutting date. Pollen samples were taken from the hearth and beneath a couple of beams. An archaeomagnetic sample was taken from the hearth though a date could not be obtained from it.

The floor of Structure 10 contained numerous groundstone artifacts including seven tabular tools, one handstone, one polishing stone, an open trough metate, and seven manos. The manos were made of varieties of gneiss—a locally available material (Norman Meader, Department of Geology, University of Arizona, personal communication 1998). Also found on the floor was a small perforated piece of quartzite worked in the shape of a bird, a stone bead, and a schist spindle whorl. A large, thin stone slab with a small depression in at least one surface (which may have been used for grinding) was found on the floor about midway between the post holes.

One partially reconstructible plain ware handled jar and a turquoise pendant were found in the fill of this house. A completely reconstructible, reworked Tanque Verde Red-on-brown bowl was found on the floor.

According to field notes, numerous charred beams were encountered in the lower fill of the south half of the structure. These were lying generally in a north-south direction, with some variance. Samples taken from these beams yielded tree-ring dates (see above). The metate was uncovered inside of the structure, slightly west of the entrance and apparently resting on an ashy layer. The low end of the metate rested on two hammerstones that were on the floor. The high end was set on two manos that were stacked on top of each other.

It is unknown who excavated the structure, though it was dug between October 13, 1968 and January 26, 1969. It was recorded by Bob Nurin and Paul Grebinger, who also took the field notes. Misty Murray wrote a report on Structure 10 in the spring of 1973 while a student in a class taught by Gwinn Vivian at the University of Arizona, Tucson.

Structure 11

Structure 11 (Figures 2.9, 2.10) was immediately to the west of Structure 16 and to the east of Structure 18, and to the north of Structures 10 and 12. It was rectangular and adobe walled and stood between and was contiguous with Structures 16 and 18. Rocks joining the upper and lower walls were evident in all of the walls. The north and east walls had evidence of grooves, presumably for vertical poles. This house apparently shared a wall with Structure 18 to the west as well as a wall with Structure 16 to the east. Well-smoothed plaster was definitely visible around the interior corners of the entry. Also, some plaster remained on the western half of the south wall. The walls were generally 40 cm to 60 cm thick although the northeast corner was thin, about 20 cm.

The entry was in the center of the south wall and was 70 cm by 60 cm. It was appended with short parallel walls. The remains of two posts were visible against the sides of the entry (Figure 2.11). A single stone was set in an adobe step similar to Structure 16 and an upper step was probably also present.

The floor was well preserved as a result

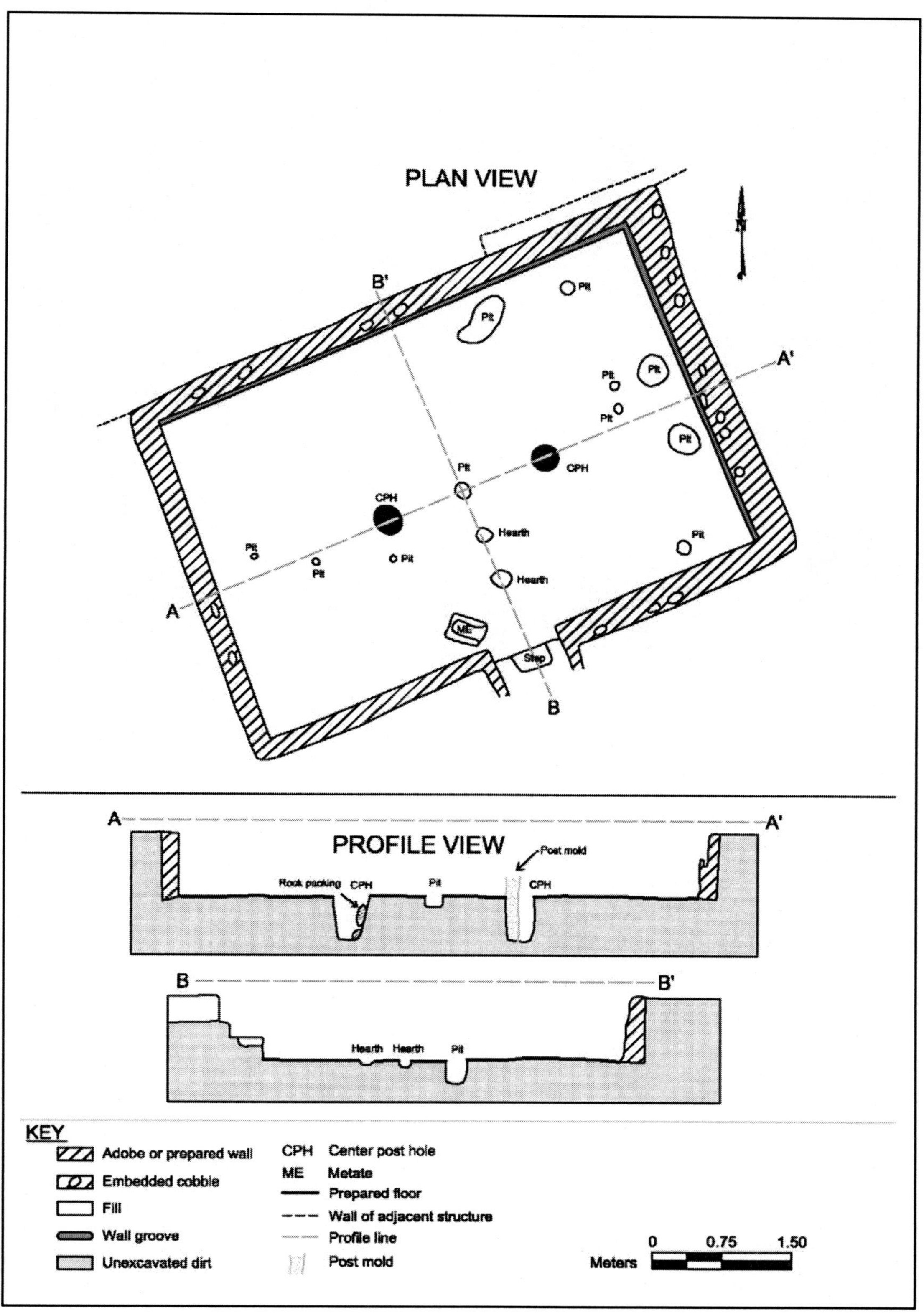

Figure 2.9. Structure 11, plan view and profiles (prepared by Austin Lenhart, Elizabeth Vinson, and Helen L. O'Brien).

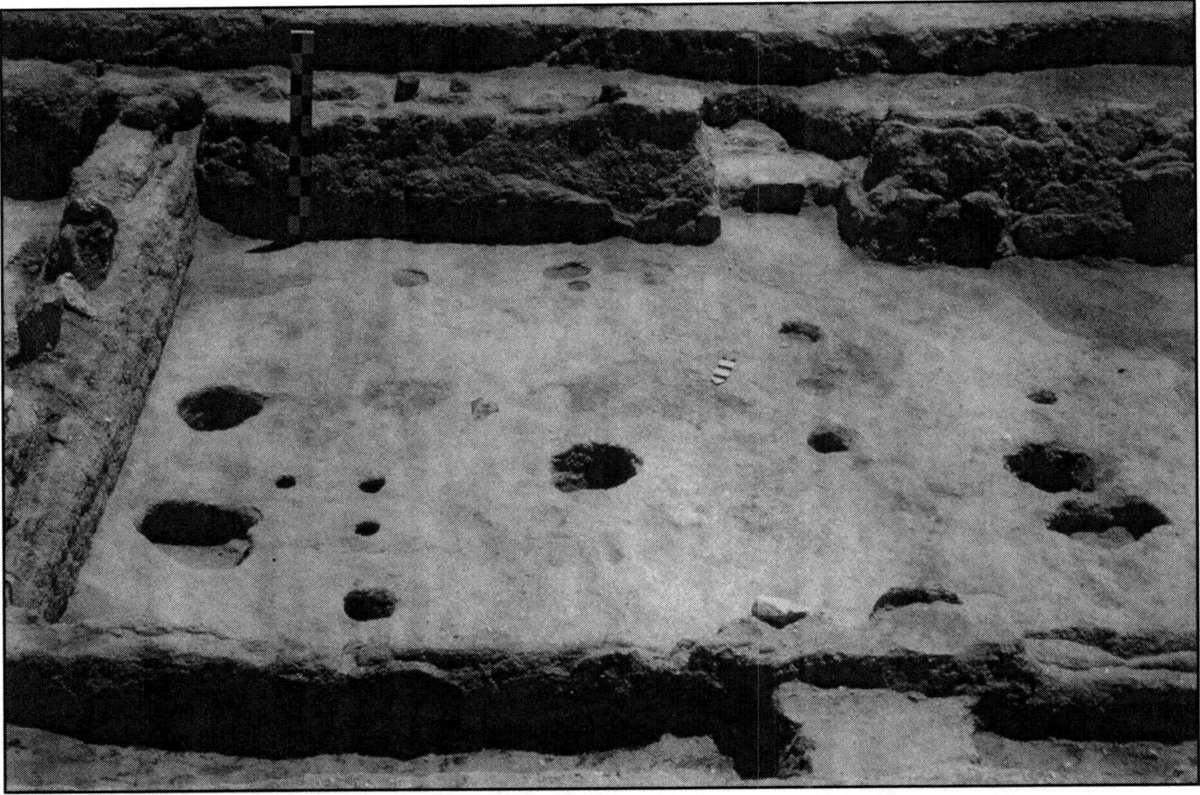

Figure 2.10. Structure 11, looking south (Catalog Number 106465, Arizona State Museum, University of Arizona).

of burning and it curved up to meet the wall. There was considerable rodent damage in the northeast, southeast, and southwest corners. Two hearths were present, both in line with the entry. Each was approximately 20 cm in diameter while one was 10 cm deep and the other was 7 cm deep. Both hearths were surrounded by an oval area of floor that had either slumped or been worn away.

Two post holes were located along the central axis of the structure. One contained the post mold (very soft soil surrounded by hard-packed fill) of the original post against the west wall of hole; the mold protruded 20 cm above the floor. The other contained four rocks (one a mano) stacked against the east wall of the hole. These are identified on the original map as "rock packing." The hole with the post mold was 38 cm in diameter and 50 cm deep; the hole with four rocks was oval in outline (40 cm by 25 cm) and 51 cm deep.

Two large pits were found along the east wall, and there were also several smaller ones in the house. One pit contained a layer of sherds at a depth of 28 cm, all from one large sherd placed in the pit with the outer surface down. This pit also contained a stone spindle whorl. A pollen sample was taken from the other pit, which was in the southeast quarter of the structure and had a conical shape.

Evidence for the roof included burned beams that were found on the floor and considerable adobe found in the fill. Addition evidence for the roof may have been reed fragments found in the house.

The upper fill was hard and contained adobe chunks (presumably from the roof), as well as a considerable quantity of gravel. The lower fill contained less gravel and was softer.

About 10 tree-ring samples were taken from burned beams. Two of those samples, from ponderosa pine, were accessioned by the Laboratory of Tree-Ring Research at the University of Arizona, but have not yielded dates. Pollen samples were taken from the locus of significant artifacts, from two stratigraphic profiles and from two floor pits.

A trough metate was located on the floor to the west of the door in this structure (Figure 2.11), in approximately the same position as the one in Structure 10. Also on the floor were part of a Tanque Verde Red-on-brown bowl, two small turquoise artifacts, a tabular tool, a pestle, a pot anvil, a lapstone, five manos and a mano fragment, a shell ring, and a fragment of a shell animal, perhaps a frog. A small black-on-white sherd came from the lower fill, and a stone spindle whorl and a polishing stone came from a floor pit. A large, ground quartz crystal came from a post hole for one of the two main roof supports. Unfortunately, the spindle whorl and quartz crystal have not been located for analysis. In 1998, Norman Meader, Department of Geology, University of Arizona, identified the material from which two of the manos from this structure are made—one is a fine-grained volcanic material, the other is a coarse-grained quartzite from the Santa Catalina Mountains. A handstone found between Structures 11 and 13 was made of quartzite derived from feldspathic sandstone. A charred deer ischium was also found in the structure.

According to field notes, the entry of this house was constructed with attention to detail. The place where the house wall met the entry wall was carefully molded and sloped gently down to the floor. The floor in Structure 11 was slightly lower (by about 4 inches) than the floor in Structure 16, which adjoined Structure 11. Many charred beams and a heavily burned area around the hearth indicated that Structure 11 burned.

Richard Polhemus, Richard S. White, and others excavated the structure between October and December of 1968. Paul Grebinger, Richard S. White, and Pam Haas recorded the structure while Paul Grebinger and Richard S. White wrote the field notes. In 1974, Elizabeth Mayer, a student in class taught by Paul Grebinger at Eisenhower College, Seneca Falls, New York, wrote a report on the structure.

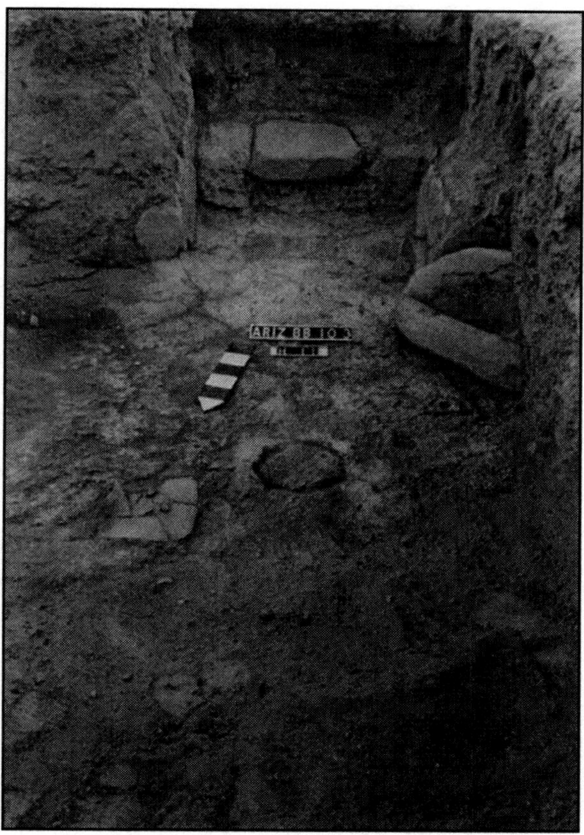

Figure 2.11.Structure 11 entryway, showing one hearth with eroded area in front of it and metate against wall at right (Catalog Number 106388, Arizona State Museum, University of Arizona).

Structure 12

Structure 12 was an adobe-walled, detached, rectangular structure west of the compound and just south of contiguous Structures, 11, 16, and 18. Structure 12 was the western structure of a pair of nearly contiguous structures. Structure 10 was about 26 cm east of the east wall of

Structure 12.

The walls were made of puddled adobe that as a result of erosion, were thin, especially in the southeast corner. Stones were present between the upper and lower walls. There was no evidence of plaster; it was probably destroyed by salt erosion. The walls were approximately 40 cm tall and between 20cm and 30cm thick. They were eroded, especially at the southeast corner where the wall was very thin.

Two entrances were present and both were appended. They were short and rectangular in plan; one was in the center of north wall, the other in the center of the south wall. The south entry was 60 cm by 35 cm; the north entry was 58 cm by 49 cm. The south entry had an adobe step that sloped down toward the interior of the house. The north entry was plugged by two puddled adobe chunks.

The floor was in excellent condition as a result of burning and it was well smoothed. There were two hearths, each in line with the entry. The north hearth was about 20 cm deep and was straight-sided, with a flat bottom. The south hearth was also 20 cm deep and straight-sided, but had a rounded bottom. Two post holes were located along the central axis of the house. The west post hole contained charred and rotted wood. No definite storage pits were found. Only one pit was found (in the southeast corner) that was not a result of rodent activity.

Evidence of the roof included beam (Figure 2.12) and saguaro rib impressions (Figure 2.13) that were found at right angles to each other in large, well-fired chunks of adobe. The remains of long, burned beams occurred in the lower fill. The upper fill was defined as all material above the burned layer; the burned layer was defined as lower fill.

Two beam samples were taken from this structure. One was mesquite and one was juniper. Although identified by the Laboratory of Tree-Ring Research, they apparently were not kept or assigned sample numbers. A large number of artifacts came from this room including one complete Tanque Verde Red-on-brown bowl, about 90 percent of a plain ware jar, and an unfired Tanque Verde Red-on-brown jar (Figure 2.14). Pieces of red ocher and hematite were also found, as was a piece of white kaolin clay with ground facets, and a lump of clay set on a plain ware sherd that had been reworked into a plate. Some pieces of ocher were found in a burned vessel. Also on the floor were eight tabular tools and one tabular tool fragment, three manos and a mano fragment, three polishing stones, a metate fragment, a plane, a nether stone, and two perforated disks (spindle

Figure 2.12. Structure 12, showing thick adobe with beam impressions (Catalog Number 106443, Arizona State Museum, University of Arizona).

Figure 2.13. Saguaro rib impressions in adobe in Structure 12 (Catalog Number 106391, Arizona State Museum, University of Arizona).

Figure 2.14. Unfired Tanque Verde Red-on-brown jar on floor of Structure 12 (photography by Bruce Bradley).

whorls). A burned fragment of deer metacarpal with a groove and a plain ware sherd with ground edges were found in the lower fill.

The use of the house for pottery making is supported by the unfired Tanque Verde Red-on-brown jar, the polishing stones, the hematite, ocher, and kaolin. In addition, a possible scraper made from a potsherd was found during analysis.

Structure 12 was excavated in the fall of 1968. Paul Grebinger took the field notes; the excavators and recorders are unknown.

Structure 13

Structure 13 was a rectangular, adobe-walled, detached structure north of Structure 2 and west of contiguous Structures 18, 11, and 16. The walls were made of puddled adobe with stones inset between the superstructure and the lower wall. Grooves were clearly visible in the south, west, and east walls and may have been present in the north wall. The east wall was definitely coursed stone and adobe as revealed from wall fall in the fill, and the wall had well-rounded corners. Some portions of the walls were very flat and smooth, but did not seem to be plastered. The walls were about 35 cm high and 30 cm thick.

The entry was appended in the center of the south wall. It was short and rounded in plan (Figure 2.15). The floor was present in the entry and it sloped down slightly into the house; it was not in good condition. It was defined more by associated sherds than by a hard surface. Apparently two floors were present, with the upper floor 5 cm to 10 cm above the lower floor. The upper floor hearth was ill-defined and had nearly been destroyed by pot hunters. All that remained was a slight depression reddened by fire, unlined, and containing ash and pebbles. The lower hearth had a double shape, as if one hearth had been placed inside another.

Two post holes were along the central axis of the structure. One contained a modeled spindle whorl. One small pit was noted adjacent to the lower hearth.

Essentially two natural layers were present. The upper fill was defined as the ground surface to the bottom of the wall fall. The lower layer consisted of the wall fall to the floor. The house burned, although only a very thin layer of burned material was present.

Charcoal samples were taken for species identification. The Laboratory of Tree-Ring Research identified two (WTR-22 and WTR-26) as mesquite. The WTR-22 sample crumbled and was discarded.

Very few artifacts were encountered on

Figure 2.15. Entryway of Structure 13, looking south (Catalog Number C-41097, Arizona State Museum, University of Arizona).

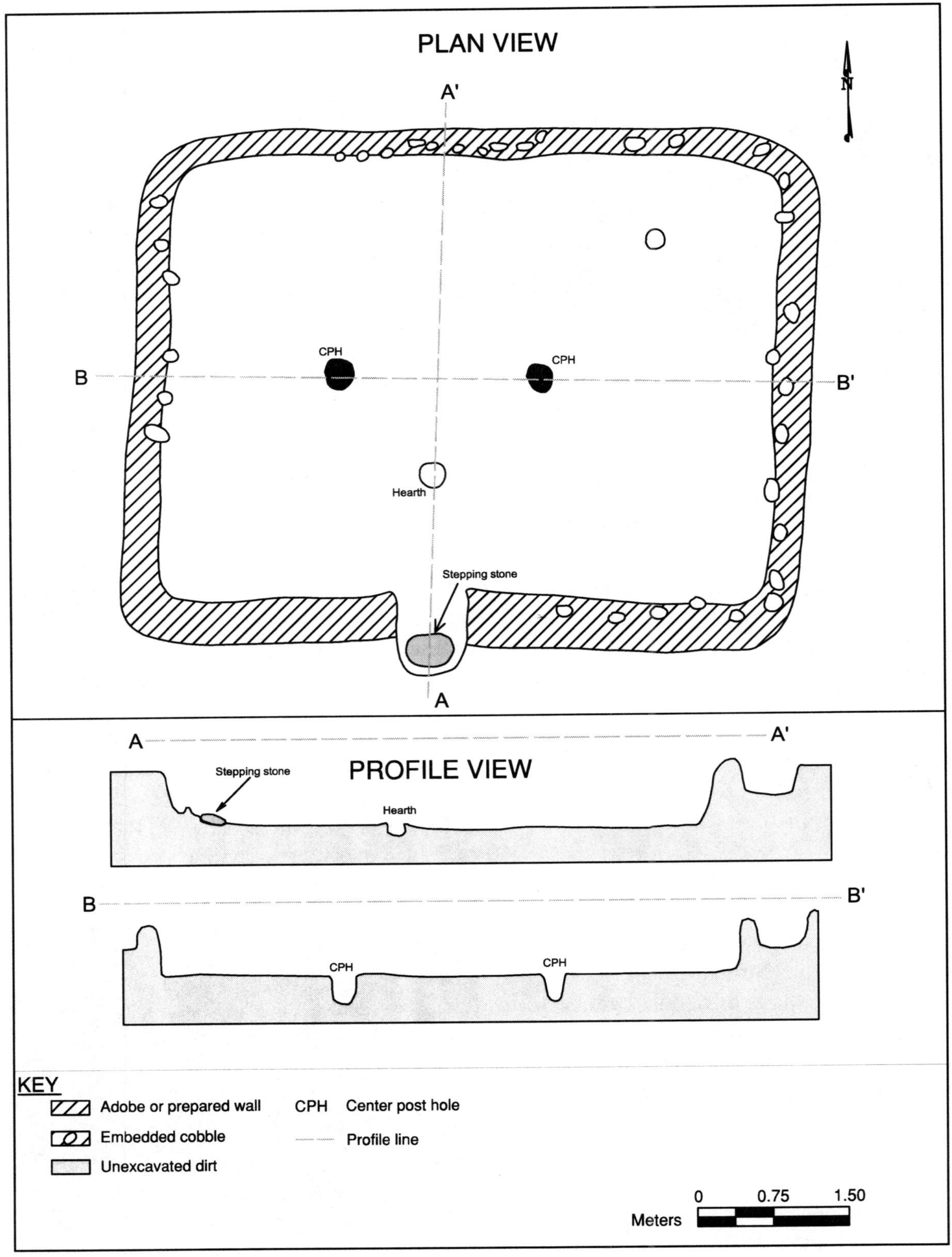

Figure 2.16. Structure 16, plan view and profiles (prepared by Austin Lenhart, Elizabeth Vinson, and Helen O'Brien).

the floor other than sherds, two manos (one whole, one fragment), and occasional pieces of chipped stone. Two lapstones and a mano fragment were found in the fill. Evidence of pot hunting was found in the form of two pieces from a glazed stoneware jar.

A late season effort to clean-up this structure for a map revealed that there were definitely two floors. Overall, this structure was similar to Structures 7 and 9.

Structure 13 was excavated by Richard White, Aileen Carpenter, Joyce Rinehart, and Ruth Baron from the fall of 1968 to the spring of 1969. Paul Grebinger and Richard White recorded the structure and Paul Grebinger took the field notes.

Structure 16

Structure 16 (Figure 2.16) was the easternmost of three houses that were attached to each other; the other two were Structures 11 and 18 (Figures 2.17, 2.18). Structure 16 was rectangular and adobe-walled and was either attached to or within a few centimeters of Structure 11.

The walls were made of puddled adobe with stones set into the walls at the point where the upper and lower walls joined. The walls were in excellent condition except for some erosion of the upper portion with some plaster remaining on most walls near the floor. Rather than being a separately applied substance, however, the "plaster" seemed to be the result of an attempt to smooth the adobe. The walls were in excellent condition except for some erosion in the upper portions.

The entry was appended in the center of the south wall and was short and rounded in plan. There was a single stone set in an adobe step, similar to Structure 11.

The floor was well smoothed and was in excellent condition except where it was slightly disturbed by rodents in the southwest corner. The floor curved up to meet the walls; it was

Figure 2.17. Structure 16, looking west; note large beams on floor (Catalog Number 106454, Arizona State Museum, University of Arizona).

baked hard when the house burned. The hearth was about 20 cm in diameter and 15 cm deep. Most of the bottom was missing; an apron was present. Two post holes were present along the east-west central axis of the structure.

Evidence for the roof included a fair amount of adobe that was found in the house, as well as portions of four burned beams that were oriented primarily north-south. Two sets of reed impressions were also encountered in the fill.

An archaeomagnetic sample was taken from the hearth, but it did not yield dates. Seven samples of charred beams were collected: six of pinyon pine and one of ponderosa. Two pinyon beams (WTR-17 and WTR-67) yielded outer

Figure 2.18. Structures 16, 11, and 18, looking west (Catalog Number 106610, courtesy Arizona State Museum, University of Arizona).

ring dates of A.D.1246 (Dean et al. 1996).

Artifacts encountered in the fill include part of a clay human figurine, a cylindrical clay bead, a basalt phallus-shaped stone, a schist adze, three manos (two fragments, one whole), two tabular fragments, two polishing stones, one handstone, one handstone fragment, a lapstone fragment, four hammerstones, five choppers, and one bowl. A corrugated jar, in pieces, was found on the floor. The hammerstones and choppers were not analyzed for this report. Pieces from a burned artiodactyl innominate and a long bone fragment that may have been a rasp were also found in Structure 16.

Structure 16 was excavated by Bruce Bradley, Donna LaRocca, Richard Polhemus, Richard White, and Bruce Huckell in the spring of 1969. Recorders are unknown, and no field notes were located.

Structure 18

Structure 18 was a rectangular, adobe-walled room that was contiguous with Structures 11 and 16. The walls were made of puddled adobe. Rocks, many of which are metate fragments, were inset into the lower wall. One section of interior wall (the southeast portion of the east wall) may have been grooved to hold upright poles. Part of this grooved section was probably removed by a pot hunter. The walls were between 30 cm and 40 cm high and 10 cm to 20 cm thick, and there was no evidence of plastering. The walls of the room seemed thinner and less substantial than those of either Structure 11 or Structure 16.

The entry was appended onto the center of the south wall. It was short and rounded in plan. Little can be determined about the entry as a result of extensive rodent activity although a small slate slab was recovered from the probable entry that could have been part of a step.

Except for a patch between the hearth and the post holes, the floor was in poor condition. What remained was fairly well smoothed and hardened from burning. The western half had been disturbed, probably by rodents, and the eastern half by pot hunters. A hearth was present but it was either not well prepared or was badly disturbed; it measured approximately 30 cm in diameter and 10 cm in depth. There were two post holes along the central axis of the structure. One medium-sized, possibly prepared pit was located in the northeast quadrant of the floor. A small opening, either bell shaped or indeterminate in form was located near the western post hole.

The structure had burned and contained some charcoal; other than that there was little evidence of roof construction.

Two juniper samples were recovered from Structure 18 but did not yield any tree-ring dates. Two pinyon samples from the floor of Structure 16, which was contiguous with Structures 11 and 18, yielded outer ring dates of A.D. 1246.

Objects recovered from the floor of Structure 18 included two complete Tanque Verde Red-on-brown bowls, four manos, and two tabular tools. A spear-point shaped sherd was found in the fill. At least eight metate fragments were used in wall construction. They were apparently not collected from the field. The slate slab identified previously as an entry step may be a lapstone that was analyzed by Jenny Adams (Chapter 5). A large river cobble of magnetite with hematite, apparently used as a hammerstone, was also found on the floor.

The eastern half of this structure had been heavily pot hunted. Also, a saguaro stood at the western edge of the structure, making it impossible to conduct complete excavation for fear that it would fall.

Structure 18 was excavated by Donna LaRocca, Bruce Bradley, Richard White, and Bruce Huckell in the spring of 1969. It was recorded by Paul Grebinger; no field notes were located.

Structure 23

Structure 23 (Figure 2.19) was a detached, rectangular room with adobe walls. The walls were made of puddled adobe with stone visible in the east wall only. There was evidence of two or three plastering episodes. The walls stood at a maximum of 75 cm high and were between 20 cm and 50 cm thick. The north and east walls were well preserved, as was the eastern portion of the south wall.

The appended entry was in the center of the south wall; it was short, rounded, and triangular in plan. There was a rectangular step, measuring 50 cm by 25 cm, and raised 6 cm above the floor of the entry. The upper floor was in poor condition with disintegrated plaster and rodent activity. The lower floor was in variable condition (good in the eastern half, poor in the western and central portions) with much rodent activity around the hearth. One hearth was present. It was in line with the entry and 40 cm in diameter; its depth was unknown. Field notes suggested that the hearth has a "figure-eight" shape, indicating that it was remodeled at some point. Two post holes were situated approximately along the east-west (central) axis of the house; a third post was found in the northeast corner. One ash pit in poor condition was found near the center of the house; it measured 80 cm by 25 cm. Two small storage pits, approximately 45 cm in diameter, were found in the west-central portion of the house.

Evidence of the roof included a large quantity of adobe lumps in the bottom of the upper fill. Several chunks of charcoal were found scattered throughout the house, presumably from charred beams.

The upper fill was very compacted, dark brown in color, gravelly, and probably derived from decomposed adobe. The lower fill, just above the floor, was ashy, fairly compacted, and gray in color. Several charcoal chunks were saved for tree-ring samples; at least one pollen sample was taken from the fill.

A large boulder metate was found in the fill, and three projectile points were found on the lower floor. Other projectile points, 6 hammerstones, 336 pieces of debitage, 2 handstones and 2 handstone fragments, 9 mano fragments, 2 whole manos, 1 tabular tool and 1 fragment, 2 metate fragments, a slate pendant fragment, a piece of chrysocolla or turquoise, 3 pieces of mica, and a sherd with 2 ground edges were also found in the floor fill and upper fill of the structure. A burned white-tailed deer mandible and burned jackrabbit and cottontail bones were found in the structure, as was a bone fragment of an awl or hairpin.

Structure 23 was excavated by Bruce Huckell, Alan Mottolo, Linda Gregonis, Barbara Harty, Gary Skinner, Lisa Washbon (Huckell), and Susie Faludi in the winter of 1970 and the spring and fall of 1971. Lisa Washbon (Huckell), Bruce Huckell, and Alan Mottolo recorded the structure and Sharon Urban took the field notes.

Structure 24

Structure 24 was an adobe-walled, detached, rectangular room. The walls were made of adobe with no mention of stones. A secondary reinforcing buttress-type wall was found along the interior of the east wall. Two layers of plaster were evident along the interior of the north, south, and east walls and the walls were between 55 cm and 80 cm high. They were in good condition, though there was some root disturbance and erosion.

The entry was appended in the center of the south wall. A step was present with blocks of adobe forming the back edge.

The floor was present and hard packed, but was not well defined. A section in the northeast corner showed signs of plastering. The hearth was present in the east side of the

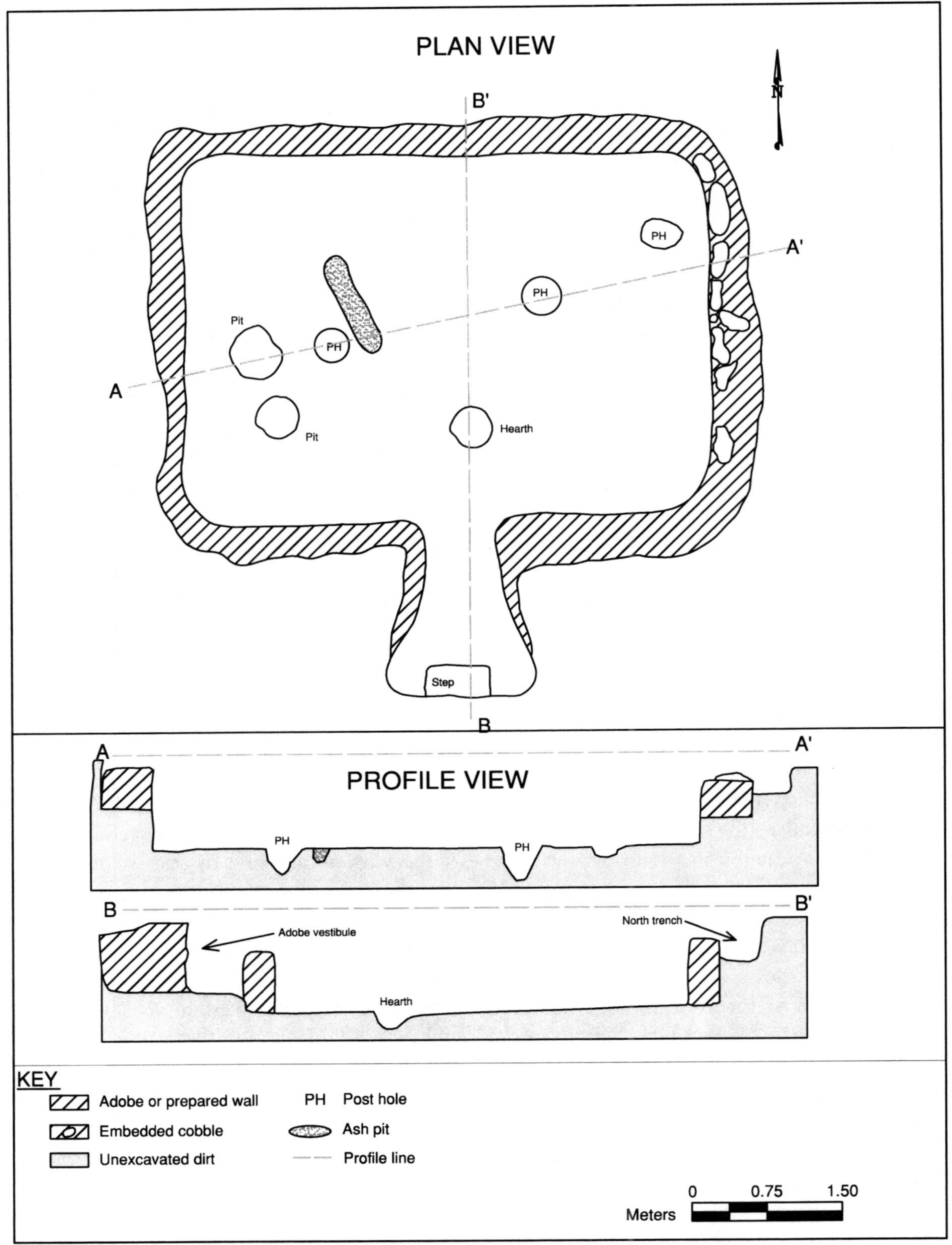

Figure 2.19. Structure 23, plan view and profiles (prepared by Austin Lenhart and Elizabeth Vinson).

southwest quadrant and was roughly circular in shape, 25 cm in diameter, and 15 cm deep. It was lined with very hard baked adobe, was gray in color, and was filled with rocks and sherds. Four post holes, non-lined, formed a rectangle toward the interior of the structure.

A well-defined burned, reddish-brown layer about 20 cm above the floor probably represented roof fall. Large rocks and pieces of adobe were scattered throughout the fill; a fine, sandy, windblown layer occurred just above the floor.

Included in the artifact assemblage are *Glycymeris* shell bracelet fragments, a broken pendant, hammerstones, manos, and a metate fragment. Analysts recorded 101 pieces of debitage and 15 hammerstones in floor fill and floor contexts, which may indicate that the house was used for stone tool manufacture after it was abandoned. Other artifacts found in the structure included an axe fragment, 10 mano fragments, 1 mano, 2 polishing stones, 3 handstones and 1 handstone fragment, 2 pestles, 2 tabular tool fragments, an abrader, a phyllite pendant fragment, and a sherd with two ground edges. Pieces from 18 vessels were also found in the fill and floor of the house.

Alan Mottolo, Jill Bright, Ilene Nicholas, Linda Allen, Kelly Rehm, Carol Weed, Ellen Cummings, Jim Tallmadge, Jon Czaplicki, James Hill, Dick Dannells, and Joyce Rehm excavated the structure between December 6, 1970 and June 5, 1971. Ellen Cummings and Carol Weed recorded the structure. The field notes were taken by Sharon Urban and Alan Mottolo.

Structure 25

Structure 25 was a detached, rectangular, adobe-walled room. Though there was no information as to the construction or dimensions of the walls, the north wall was described as being in especially good condition. The entry was in the center of the southwest side of the structure. It was possibly appended, though the shape is unknown.

There were two floors, approximately 5 cm apart. Two post holes were found, with the one in the northeast quadrant of the structure almost twice as big as the one in the southwest quadrant.

A layer of burned beams in association with sherds, the base of a vessel, and 13 manos apparently represented the remains of the roof. The fill was mostly fine, gray-brown soil; a consolidated, faintly orange layer occurred just above the floor. Wall fall and burned reeds were also found. Charcoal samples were taken from the upper fill, and pollen samples were taken from under a sherd cluster in the entry, as well as from under other sherd clusters, and from under a T-shaped stone. A "mesquite post" was removed from the southwest quad, close to the south wall; a "juniper post" was removed from the southeast quad. No additional information was provided regarding the two wood posts; they apparently were not sent to the Laboratory of Tree-Ring Research.

A broken jar and seven shell beads were recorded as being in the fill and a Tanque Verde Red-on-brown sherd with ground edges came from a test pit. A fragment of a clay human figurine was found in the upper fill. Pot sherds, manos, a pestle, a mortar, a lapstone and a tabular tool were all found at roughly the 40-cm level. On the floor were parts of a painted bowl, three whole or partial manos, and two tabular tools (one fragmentary). The base of a large corrugated, stuccoed jar was also found on the floor, although it was not recorded in the field notes. A burned mule deer sacrum was also found in the house. A T-shaped stone was found under the upper floor; and a stone spindle whorl and shell pendant were on the lower floor.

Donna LaRocca, Emil Witzens, Tom Rehm, Joyce Rehm, Kelly Rehm, Patricia Witzens, Robert Brehart, Ellen Cummings, Ilene

Nicholas, Lewis McNaught, Gary Skinner, and Alan Mottolo excavated the structure from December 6, 1970 to November 7, 1971 (not including summer months). Donna LaRocca recorded the structure, and Sharon Urban, Donna LaRocca, Ellen Cummings, and Emil Witzens took the field notes.

Structure 26

Structure 26 was a detached, rectangular, adobe-walled room that had been heavily pot hunted prior to excavation. The walls were made of puddled adobe with some cobbles in the east, west, and south walls. In addition, some plaster was visible on the south wall. The walls were approximately 50 cm tall. The entry was a simple opening in the center of the south wall about 1 meter wide; the entry also featured a step.

The floor was in fair shape in spite of pot hunting activities. There may have been two floors about 5 cm apart. The hearth was inside the entry and was 23 cm in diameter and 9.2 cm deep. There were no post holes or pits in the floor.

Adobe chunks in the fill presumably were from the roof. There was no evidence of burned beams. The fill consisted of much adobe, presumably from the roof and the walls. One pollen sample was taken from underneath a sherd on the floor; a second one was taken from the bottom of the hearth. Three manos, three projectile points, a hammerstone, a shell ring, and shell bracelet fragments were recorded in floor and floor fill contexts.

Richard Dannells, Robert Brehart, Joyce Rinehart, Aileen Carpenter, and Thomas Alexander excavated the structure from February 7, 1971 to May 24, 1971. Richard Dannells recorded the structure. Sharon Urban, Richard Dannells, and Joyce Rinehart took the field notes.

Northern Locus

Eleven structures were excavated in the Northern Locus, which was situated north of the Central Locus (Figure 1.13). Two contiguous-walled features—Structures 31a-31b-31c and Structures 27a-27b-28 were located in this locus, as were detached Structures 3, 20, 21, 29, and 30. An unexcavated structure, three inhumations (found in Structures 27b, 28, and 28), and one cremation (found outside of Structure 27a) occurred in this locus. Two of the structures in the Northern Locus were three sided (Structures 3 and 21), perhaps indicating that the structures were "sheds" or three-walled ramadas rather than rooms or houses.

Structure 3

Structure 3 (Figure 2.20) was a detached, rectangular, adobe-walled room without a north wall. The east wall was 6.9 m long; the south wall was 5.4 m long; and the west wall was 6.9 m long. The walls were made of adobe with stones set in at intervals. One of the wall stones in the east wall was a broken metate fragment; very little plaster was present on the walls. The east wall was 20 cm high, the south wall 31 cm, and the west wall 40 cm at its highest point. The height from the floor to the top of the wall cobbles was variable; the height of the east wall was 45 cm, the south wall 47 cm, and the west wall 50 cm. The walls were in fair condition, although there were many rodent holes. No entry was discovered in any of the three surviving walls and no prepared floor was located. The surface assumed to be floor consisted of natural, claylike soil mixed with caliche. It was in poor condition and very uneven. There was no hearth, but two post holes were present. The south post hole was 44 cm deep and 24 cm in diameter. The north post hole was 37 cm deep and 25 cm in diameter.

Figure 2.20. Structure 3, looking south (uncatalogued, Arizona State Museum, University of Arizona).

There was no positive evidence of a roof. A layer of sherds and other artifacts (manos, chipped stone) was recovered from the fill at an average of 5 cm to 10 cm above what was definitely the lowest (red clay) level.

The fill was exceptionally dark and must have contained a large amount of organic material. A large chunk of wood was retrieved from the north post hole and a pollen sample was taken from under a number of contiguous sherds just above the floor.

Three manos (one of vesicular basalt; none was analyzed), one phallus-shaped stone of quartzite, and two pieces of unworked shell were recovered from the fill, as was a sherd with a ground edge. In addition, a large number of sherds were found in a level just above what was believed to be the floor. An open trough metate and a tabular tool fragment were found in the roof fall level. A small bird-like quartzite effigy was also found in the roof fall level.

According to the field notes, there was a layer heavily laden with sherds just above the floor. Locations where whole vessels had been sitting were visible. This may represent roof fall; that is, it seems that the vessels were resting on the roof and were smashed in place when the roof collapsed. This structure had no clearly discernible floor, only a reddish zone that was uneven, very hard, and full of stones. No artifacts were recovered from this level. This structure may have been used for storage, or perhaps the structure was never completed and the fill just above the floor level represented use of the depression for trash deposition. Jeffery Clark (personal communication 2009), who reviewed this manuscript, suggests that this structure may have been a "shed" similar to those found at sites in the Tonto Basin that date to approximately the same time period.

In those structures, floors were difficult to distinguish and, like Structure 3, material had accumulated in them as if they had not been swept regularly.

Nancy Hammack, Albert Turner, Annetta Long (Cheek), Charles Cheek, and Bruce Bradley excavated the structure in the spring of 1968. Larry Hammack and Paul Grebinger recorded the structure on March 3, 1968. The field notes were taken by Paul Grebinger and Bruce Bradley.

Structure 20

Structure 20 was a rectangular, adobe-walled, detached room. Its walls were made of puddled adobe, with stones placed randomly in the adobe at approximately the present ground surface. The walls were between 20 cm and 60 cm thick, and no plaster was observed. A layer of adobe wall fall was encountered inside the east and west walls. The layers in both walls were vertical and probably represented the upper portions of the walls that had slid away.

A plugged entry was identified in the center of the north wall. It consisted of stones placed between adobe blocks. The useable entry was probably simple, though its shape was uncertain. It was appended onto the center of the south wall. A large tabular stone supported by a series of smaller stones and surrounded by a thin adobe wall (?) was found in the entry. [Editorial note: The question mark regarding the thin adobe wall is the original author's.]

There was no information about the floor of this structure; there were, however, some details about the hearth. About 25 cm in diameter and 10 cm deep, the hearth was small and irregularly shaped. It was located on the north side of the house in line with a probable plugged entry. A single post hole was located along the west side of the central axis of the structure (20 cm diameter, 60 cm deep). One small, circular subfloor pit was located in the northeast corner.

The gravelly reddish-brown fill noted below may have been the remains of roof fall. The upper fill was a gravelly reddish-brown; it looked like decomposed adobe and was up to 18 cm deep. The upper fill contained a large number of unassociated sherds and what appeared to be general trash. The lower fill was extremely ashy—gray to white in color and powdery. It contained a greater abundance of sherds and other artifacts, but also seemed to be a trash deposit.

Four pollen samples were taken: one from the upper fill, one from the lower fill, one from the floor, and one from the south hearth. Artifacts recovered from the lower fill included a perforated disk made from a White Mountain Red Ware sherd, a shell bracelet fragment, a plain ware sherd disk, a piece of specular hematite with one ground surface, and a projectile point of chalky blue-gray chert that was roughly triangular with a concave base. At least three manos and one cluster of hammerstones were found on the floor. The flaked stone and ground stone artifacts from this feature have not been analyzed.

Structure 20 was excavated by Bruce Bradley, Bruce Huckell, Dick Dannells, Donna LaRocca, and Bob Brehaut from February to April 1970. It was recorded by Bruce Bradley. Doug Herrick, a student in a class taught by Gwinn Vivian at the University of Arizona, Tucson, wrote a report on the structure in the spring of 1973.

Structure 21

Structure 21 was a detached, three-sided rectangular structure with adobe walls. There was no evidence of a northern wall. The walls were made of puddled adobe with stones in the three existing walls. There was no entry.

A prepared adobe floor was noted in the

southern three-quarters of the structure. Neither a hearth nor post holes were present. A roughly circular concentration of fire-cracked rock was located in the northern half of the house along its north-south axis. It measured 80 cm in diameter and 35 cm in depth. It was identical to some stone concentrations that were found outside of some of the structures. The fill among the rocks in the upper part of the pit was sandy with numerous sherds. The lower fill was ashy and contained charcoal. A pollen sample was taken below the sherds in the upper part of the pit. Chunks of adobe were noted 40 cm below the surface in the southwest corner of the house and might have been evidence of the roof.

Pollen samples were taken from the rock-filled pit in the floor, and from the floor under two manos and under plain ware jar sherds. A partial storage jar, sherd clusters, and a cluster of manos were noted on the floor. The manos have not been analyzed.

Sketches of the structure showing wall stones, location of the hearth, and two test pits were provided in the field notes.

Dick Dannells, Bruce Huckell, and Donna LaRocca excavated the structure in the spring of 1970. It is not known who recorded it or took the field notes.

Structure 27a

Structure 27a was a rectangular adobe-walled room that was contiguous with Structures 27b and 28. The walls were made of puddled adobe with wall rocks noted in all four walls. There was caliche plastering on the eastern half of the south wall. The walls stood between 40 cm and 50 cm high and between 40 cm and 60 cm thick. Possible internal adobe wall buttresses were situated midway on the south and north walls; they were about 2 m long and were approximately 20 cm above floor level.

The entry was appended onto the center of the west wall. It was 75 cm wide and flanked by standing wall rocks. A 10-cm-high, crescent-shaped adobe step was located directly outside the entrance.

The floor consisted of hard-packed dirt or adobe with traces of caliche plastering except around the hearth. The hearth was approximately 1.75 m inside (east) of the entrance; it was made of caliche or hardened adobe, and was an irregular oval in shape. The hearth was roughly 60 cm in diameter and 20 cm deep; there were no pits or post holes.

Evidence for the roof consisted of the remnants of two or three roof beams and some adobe chunks. The upper fill was "undefined" and gray-brown in color. A layer of ash and plaster separated the upper fill from a hard, reddish lower layer. At least four soil samples were taken; one was identified specifically as a pollen sample.

Numerous flakes, cores, hammerstones, a mano and a mano fragment, one spindle whorl, and a shell bracelet fragment were found in the fill. One large metate, a mano and a mano fragment, a tabular tool fragment, half of a Tanque Verde Red-on-brown bowl, and two hammerstones were found on the floor. A fragment of an awl or hairpin and another long bone fragment with a groove and polish were also found on the floor.

The report by Hugh Ball and Barry Richards suggested that this structure may have been a store room and that it was built after Structure 27b and before Structure 28.

Adele Taylor and Lee Coley excavated the structure as part of the Pima Community College Summer Field Program, directed by Phil Lord from in the summer of 1971. Adele Taylor and Lee Coley also recorded the structure and took the field notes. In addition to field notes, a report was prepared by Taylor and Coley summarizing the excavation of Structures 27a and 27b.

Hugh G. Ball and Barry Richards, students in Anthropology 215L taught by Gwinn

Vivian at the University of Arizona, Tucson, wrote a student report during the spring of 1973.

Structure 27b

Structure 27b (Figure 2.21) was rectangular and adobe walled and was contiguous with Structure 27a. It was made of puddled adobe, with an occasional stone present. The northwest corner was bonded to the southwest corner of Structure 27a; the northeast corner abutted the southeast corner of Structure 27a. The north wall of Structure 27b was the south wall of Structure 27a, and Structure 27a shared its eastern wall with Structure 28. The eastern wall of Structure 27b abutted the wall shared by Structures 27a and 28, indicating that the southeastern corner of Structure 27b was built after Structures 27a and 28. This may indicate that Structure 27b was originally a three-sided structure (perhaps a ramada), and that the southeastern corner was added to make the structure a room. There were well-plastered areas on the north wall. The walls were less than 75 cm above the highest occupation surface. The lower portions were approximately 30 cm to 50 cm thick and external wall buttresses occurred at the east and west walls.

The entry was a simple opening at the center of the south wall. The entry was disturbed, but there was apparently no step.

The burned floor was hard-packed clay mixed with sand and caliche. The hearth was a circular, clay-lined depression inside the entry. Two post holes (33 cm and 35 cm in diameter) were located along the central axis of the structure. A third post hole a few cm below the western post hole suggested a lower occupational surface. There was also a small, circular, clay-lined depression in the northeast corner that was 14 cm in diameter and 8 cm deep.

Adobe and reed impressions in the plaster were evidence of the structure's roof. An ashy layer above the floor was darker and finer textured than the remainder of fill. Charcoal samples were collected from the fill.

Numerous artifacts were found on the floor including a cluster of four vessels, a metate, artiodactyl bones, projectile points, three tabular tool fragments, an ax, two manos, a lapstone, a handstone, and an engraved shell bracelet fragment. The artiodactyl bones, which included foot, leg, pelvic, and skull elements from pronghorn, white-tailed deer, mule deer, and bighorn sheep, were associated with human skeletal remains. Flaked stone tools and numerous flakes were found in two of the vessels, along with four faceted and scratched rocks that were imbedded with hematite. Field notes state that the artifacts in one of the vessels were in a leather bag; unfortunately, we have been unable to locate the bag. A small turquoise pendant was found in association with the artiodactyl bones and human remains.

A single human skeleton was found in association with the numerous artiodactyl bones on the floor of the house. Like the animal bone in the house, the human skeletal remains were charred.

Adele Taylor and Lee Coley excavated the structure as part of the Pima Community College Summer Field Program, directed by Phil Lord during the summer of 1971. Adele Taylor and Lee Coley also recorded the structure and took the field notes. In addition to field notes, a report was prepared by Taylor and Coley summarizing the excavation of Structures 27a and 27b. Gordon Fritz, Peter Coston, and Barry Richards, students in Anthropology 215L taught by Gwinn Vivian in the spring of 1973 at the University of Arizona, Tucson, wrote a student report.

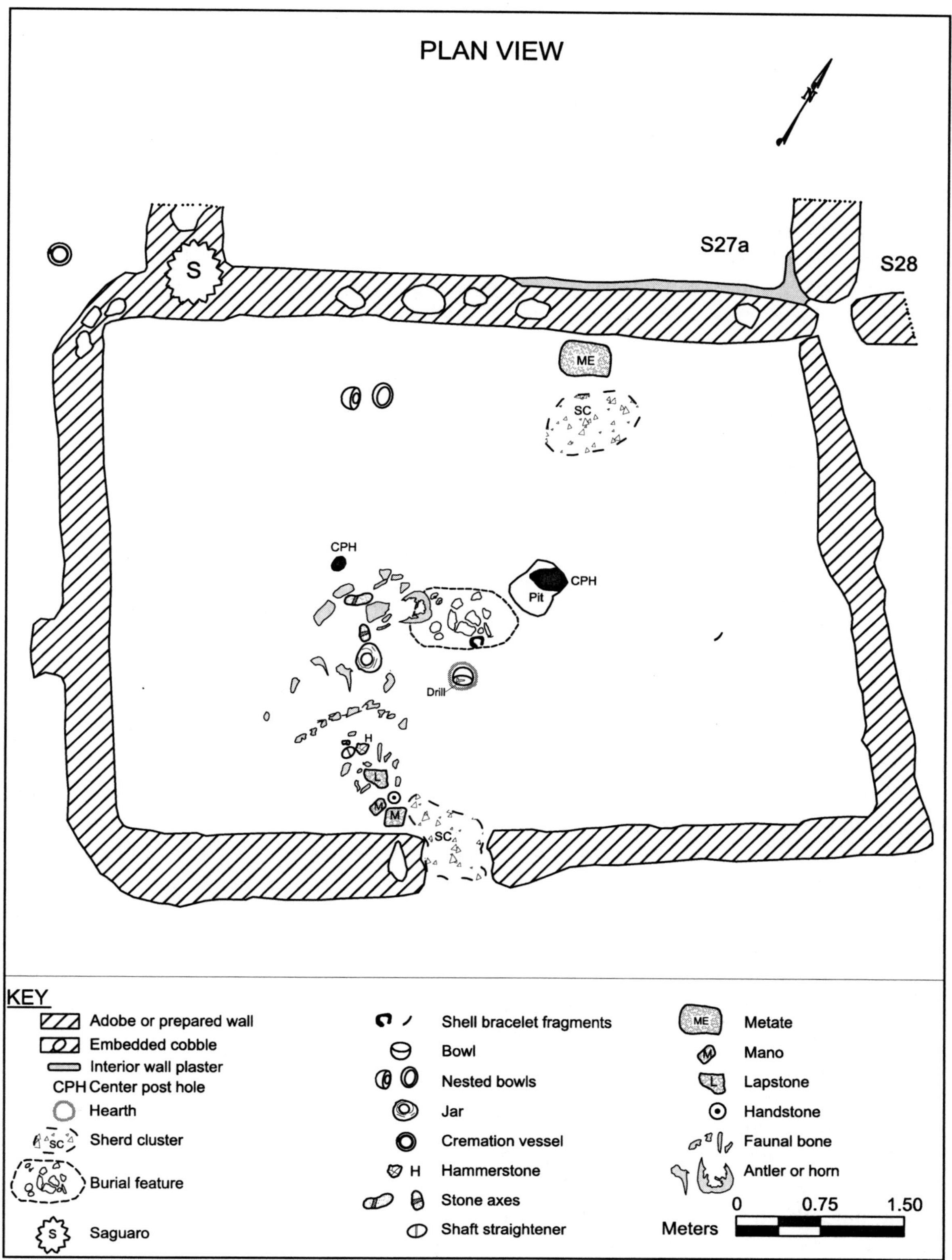

Figure 2.21. Structure 27b, plan view reconstructed from notes and sketch maps (prepared by Helen L. O'Brien).

Structure 28

Structure 28 was a rectangular and adobe-walled room that was contiguous with Structure 27a. It was constructed from puddled adobe with stones at intervals of about 45 cm in the east and west walls. The west wall abutted the northeast corner of Structure 27a; the south wall abutted the intersection of Structure 27a (southeast corner) and Structure 27b (northeast corner). The 1973 report concluded that, because the west wall abutted Structure 27, it postdated that structure. All of the walls showed signs of plastering and replastering. They were about 62 cm high and 38 cm to 100 cm thick and there was a buttress extending from the southeast corner.

The entry was a simple opening in the south wall, about 1 m from the west wall. The north wall may have had a blocked entry in the north wall. This "blocked doorway," defined by vertical cracks in the wall, was interpreted in the 1973 report as evidence that the north wall was built in sections.

There was an upper floor and a lower floor. The upper floor was plastered in the east-central portion of the structure; the lower floor was thick and hard and made of the same material as the wall plaster. An ash pit in the upper floor was 20 cm in diameter and 7 cm deep. A possible post hole in the floor was 3 cm in diameter and 5 cm deep. A depression in the lower floor contained three manos; it was 45 cm in diameter and 10 cm deep. A circle of rocks in the northwest corner at a depth of 60 cm was identified as a cooking feature. Two burned logs may have been remains of the roof.

Excavators attributed the upper level of debris to erosion and natural decay (0 to 35 cm). The middle level consisted of ashy, red soil with burned roof fall (35 to 55 cm). The lower level consisted of soft red, ashy soil (55 to 70 cm). No artifacts were found on the upper floor. A circle of rocks and a pit containing three mano fragments were found on the lower floor; in addition, numerous artifacts were recorded from the fill.

A burial was found in the fill of this structure. The burial was flexed, with the head to the east; no definite burial pit was noted. A projectile point that had been ground, a shell fragment, and a bracelet fragment were associated with the burial. This structure was interpreted in the 1973 report as a shaded summer work area for Structure 27a.

Alice Knapp and Margaret Wilkie recorded and excavated the structure with the Pima Community College Summer Field Program directed by Phil Lord in the summer of 1971. Alice Knapp, Margaret Wilkie, and Phil Lord took field notes. Hugh S. Ball, Pamela Magers, and Linda Gregonis, students in Anthropology 215L, taught by Gwinn Vivian in the spring of 1973 at the University of Arizona, Tucson, wrote the report on this structure.

Structure 29

Structure 29 was a rectangular, detached, adobe-walled structure that apparently had been severely damaged by pot hunting prior to excavation. It was made of puddled adobe with stones noted in all four walls. The plaster on the south wall was in excellent condition.

The short, rectangular entry was apparently appended in the center of the south wall. It was 1 m long by 1.2 m wide. The doorway was not cut completely to the floor, so the lower part of the wall remained.

Although there may have been as many as three floors in the structure (identified only in the southeast quad), the actual floor level was not well defined. The first floor, overlain by charcoal, was found at 62 cm below the surface. The second floor was at 69–72 cm and was also overlain by charcoal. The third floor was at 77 cm. In the northeast quadrant a floor was noted at 85 to 90 cm. The hearth was inside the entry and was circular. There were nine possible post holes and two possible subfloor pits.

An ash layer probably represented roof fall. A large, whole metate was found on top of the ash layer and may have been on the roof. The remains of a large log and adobe chunks may also have been roof materials. Numerous fill levels were described with the upper levels consisting of sandy, loose soil containing some gravel and the lower levels containing more ash.

Soil samples and charcoal samples were taken from post holes. Samples of charred material that appeared to be pine needles were taken from the floor and a sample of a log was also retrieved. Neither the possible pine needles nor the log were analyzed.

Artifacts mentioned in the field notes for this structure included one metate fragment, four manos, an obsidian flake, a knife blank, flakes of chipped stone, and three sherd clusters on the floor in the northwest quadrangle. A black-on-white sherd (possibly Pinedale Black-on-white) was found in the southwest quadrant near the floor, and a plain ware sherd with two ground edges was found in the fill. Laural Myers and Linda Gregonis (Chapter 4) identified 28 hammerstones, 74 pieces of debitage, 2 cores, 1 projectile point and 2 unifaces in floor and floor fill contexts. Jenny Adams (Chapter 5) identified 1 stone disk fragment, 3 lapstones, 1 lapstone fragment, 2 mano fragments, 5 mano fragments, 1 hammerstone and 1 hammerstone fragment, 2 tabular tools, 2 tabular tool fragments, 2 polishing stones, and 1 nether stone fragment in the fill and on the floor of the house. Three bone awl fragments were found in the fill and a piece of pigment was found in a sealed pit in the floor of the house. It was not clear which, if any, of the artifacts were associated with the burial.

One human burial was found in a 24- by 75-cm pit in the northwest quadrant of the structure.

The structure was excavated by John Molfese and Debby Zubow with the Pima Community College Summer Field Program directed by Phil Lord in the summer of 1971. It was recorded by Sharon Hargrave, and the field notes were taken by John Molfese, Debby Zubow, and Phil Lord. Sharon Hargrave and Andrew Harvey, students in Anthropology 215L taught by Gwinn Vivian in the spring of 1973 at the University of Arizona, Tucson, wrote the student report on this structure.

Structure 30

Structure 30 was adobe-walled, rectangular, and detached. The walls were made of puddled adobe with a few wall stones. The northwest corner was eroded. The northeast and southeast corners were bonded and the southwest corner had abutting walls. Some plaster was present on the walls, and the entryway was also plastered. The walls were 90 cm tall and they varied in thickness with the east wall measured as 31 cm thick and the south wall as 65 cm thick.

The entry was a simple opening in the center of the south wall. It was 67 cm wide and had an adobe step, 21 cm in height. A slight adobe rise connecting to the outside of the entry may have been a "rain stop."

A 4-cm-thick adobe floor was reported at a depth of 70 to 96 cm. The hearth was inside the entryway and was 21 cm in diameter and 11 cm deep. It had an adobe collar and/or "cap," and ashy content. Two post holes were located along the central axis of the structure, both containing charred wood. The western post hole had an adobe collar. Eight additional small post holes (about 5 cm in diameter) were shown on the original map; no pits were identified.

Roof and wall fall were identified as being "very hard." Six levels of fill were identified. From the surface, the first level was sandy and 10 cm thick; the second level had soft soil and was 20 cm thick; the third level (17 cm thick) consisted of roof and wall fall and was very hard; the fourth level was relatively soft and 12 cm thick; the fifth level (8 cm thick) was dark orange and adobe like; and the sixth level was a 5-cm-thick very dark, soft ashy layer.

Charcoal, pollen, and soil samples were collected during excavation. Floor artifacts included potsherds, a tabular tool, a tabular tool fragment, and 75 bone and antler fragments. An obliterated corrugated bowl was also found in the structure. Burned bones from a pronghorn, white-tailed deer, and bighorn sheep were found in the feature. Two metapodial awl or hairpin fragments (one from a white-tailed deer, one from an unknown artiodactyl) were found, as was a flaking tool made from an antler tine.

Structure 30 was excavated by Rusty McInroy and Pauline Spurgiesz with the Pima Community College Field Program directed by Phil Lord from in the summer of 1971. The structure was recorded by Robert Jones and Michael D. Mauer. The field notes were taken by Rusty McInroy, Pauline Spurgiesz, and Phil Lord.

A student report was written by Robert Jones and William Kessel when they were students in Anthropology 215L taught by Gwinn Vivian in the spring of 1973 at the University of Arizona, Tucson.

Structure 31a

Structure 31a was a rectangular, adobe-walled room that was contiguous with Structure 31b. The walls were made of puddled adobe. No stones were evident in the walls. The southwest corner of the structure abutted the southeast corner of Structure 31b. This suggested that Structure 31b was built prior to Structure 31a. Plaster was visible near the entryway on the east side of the south wall.

The entry was a simple opening in the center of the south wall and was 80 cm wide. There was a caliche step at the interior edge of the entry. Stone slabs were found at the exterior (south edge) of the entry, one on top of the other.

A single floor was present, ranging from 105 cm to 112 cm in depth. The hearth was inside the entryway; it was 68 cm by 48 cm in diameter and 12 cm to 22 cm deep. Two major post holes were found along the central axis of the structure. The west hole was 58 cm by 44 cm in diameter and 37 cm deep; the east hole was 48 cm in diameter and 54 cm deep. Twenty-one additional post holes were found; they ranged in diameter from 13 cm to 32 cm and in depth from 14 cm to 47 cm. Four possible post holes ranged in diameter from 13 cm to 17 cm and in depth from 13 to 18 cm. Several of these post holes were arranged both in rows and around the interior perimeter of the structure in a way that suggested bench supports. A single oval subfloor pit measured 46 cm by 40 cm in diameter and 37 cm in depth.

From the roof, five recognizable beam fragments were noted, three of which were oriented north-south. The 1973 student report noted that "it seems logical that the major beams rested in an East-West orientation on top of the major support posts and that the North-South beams Pima College noticed were secondary, cross beams." Evidence for charred reeds was also noted.

The upper level of fill was described as "loose fill." The middle level was gray and compacted and contained caliche, rubble, and plaster. The lower level had fine, ashy soil and contained burned wall plaster and burned reeds. Burned wall plaster, ash and rubble found directly on the floor suggested that this structure burned.

There was 1 sample of adobe plaster, 13 of charcoal, 3 of soil, and 3 of bone fragments. Artifacts recorded for this feature included 9 whole or partial manos, 1 metate, 2 spindle whorls, 1 drilled sherd, 1 shell object, and 1 turquoise pebble, as well as pottery and numerous artifacts of chipped stone.

Structure 31a was excavated by Phil Lord, Pauline Spurgiesz, Mike Mauer, and others with the Pima Community College Field Program directed by Phil Lord in the summer of 1971. Nancy Kays and Shirley Pettengill recorded the structure and Phil Lord took the field notes. A student report was written by Glenn Miller, John Beezley, Nancy Kays, and Shirley Pettengill, students in Anthropology 215L taught by Gwinn Vivian in the spring of 1973 at the University of Arizona, Tucson.

Structure 31b

Structure 31b was an adobe-walled rectangular room that was contiguous with Structures 31a and c. The walls were made of puddled adobe, with stones in the fill that may have been part of the construction. The southeast corner of Structure 31b abutted the south wall of 31a; the southwest corner of Structure 31b abutted the south wall of 31c; the northeast corner of Structure 31b may have abutted the north wall of Structure 31a.

The entry was a simple 61 cm wide opening in the center of the south wall.

There was a single floor of compact dark gray soil. The hearth was inside the entryway and was approximately 37 cm in diameter and 8 cm deep. It was identified by a reddish, burned clay lining.

Two major post holes were found along the central axis of the structure. The west post hole was 19 cm in diameter and 62 cm deep; the east post hole was 23 cm in diameter and 40 cm deep. Two possible small post holes were near the west wall. A pit in the southeast corner of the structure was probably a rodent burrow.

Adobe chunks in the fill and at least one piece on the floor were probably from the roof as well as an adobe chunk with a burned reed impression. Numerous soil and charcoal samples were taken including a portion of a charred beam. More than 4,000 potsherds and pieces of chipped stone were recovered including ceramic vessels resting on the floor. Animal bone was also collected. Burned beams on floor indicate that the structure burned.

The structure was excavated by Lee Coley, Garrett Cook, Beth Welman, and Phil Lord with the Pima Community College Field Program directed by Phil Lord in the fall of 1971. Phil Lord and Tim Seagle recorded the structure. Phil Lord and others wrote the field notes.

John A. Beezley, Bruce Masse, Glenn A. Miller, Tim Murphy, and Tim Seagle wrote a report as students in Anthropology 215L taught by Gwinn Vivian in the spring of 1973 at the University of Arizona, Tucson.

Structure 31c

Structure 31c was a rectangular, adobe-walled room that was contiguous with Structure 31b. The walls were made of puddled adobe with stones in the fill that may have been part of wall construction. Analysis by the Anthropology 215L class suggested that the northeast and southeast corners of Structure 31c abutted 31b, thus they inferred that 31c was built after 31b. They also noted that the southwest and northwest corners were bonded to the west wall.

The entry was a simple 67 cm-wide opening in the center of the south wall.

Neither a floor nor a hearth was identified. One possible post hole, approximately 11 cm deep, was identified in the northwest quadrant by the original excavators of the structure. The Anthropology 215L class identified three additional holes, all in the southeast quadrant. Two of these were 16 cm deep; one was 21 cm deep. These may have been post holes, storage holes, or post-excavational disturbance. No definite large post holes along the central axis of the structure were identified.

The only evidence of a roof was reference to an ash layer.

Three basic layers were identified in the fill: a top layer of light brown or reddish ash, a middle layer of light or dark ash, and a lower layer of red stony soil. Phil Lord, the Pima Community College field director, noted that the red stony layer probably represented a sterile level.

Large numbers of sherds were found in the fill including one sherd of Sahuarita Polychrome. A drilled pendant fragment was also found.

The structure was excavated by Margaret Wilkie and Alice Knapp during the summer of 1971. Margaret Wilkie and Julie Wizorek recorded the structure while Phil Lord and others took the field notes. A student report was written by Julie Wizorek, Alan Mottolo, Stephen Small, and David Stahle while they were students in Anthropology 215L taught by Gwinn Vivian in the spring of 1973 at the University of Arizona, Tucson.

Southern Locus

Three structures–14, 19a, and 19b–occurred in the Southern Locus. This locus was approximately 132 meters south of the Southwestern Locus. The features were on small rises within the banks of a roughly northeast-southwest trending wash at the southern edge of the site. The outline of Structure 19b was entirely within and below Structure 19a. Structure 14 was about 30 meters northeast of Structures 19a-19b. The isolated and somewhat hidden location of these structures suggests that their use was ritual in nature.

Structure 14

Structure 14 (Figures 2.22, 2.23) was a nearly square adobe-walled detached room about 200 yards (183 m) south of Structures 10 and 12. It was made of puddled adobe with stones inset between the lower and upper walls. The adobe contained a large amount of very small, weathered pieces of stone. There was no plaster, and the walls were thick and had no grooves.

Because this structure was located on a low rise in a wash, it was estimated that some erosion of the walls has occurred. The wash bank is above the remains of the east wall of the structure. During excavation it was noted that the east wall was higher and less eroded than the west wall.

There was a 70 cm break in the center of the west wall that was probably the remains of a simple opening entry.

The floor consisted of gravelly material similar to the walls, but was not nearly as hard or as smooth as other floors excavated at this site. The floor did not slope up to meet the walls; rather it met them abruptly at nearly a right angle. The hearth was located directly east of the entry and was 30 cm in diameter and about 10 cm deep. Two post holes were located along the central axis of the structure. The northern hole measured 25 cm in diameter and 45 cm in depth; the southern hole measured 11 cm in diameter and 25 cm in depth. There were no pits inside the structure, although a basin-shaped pit containing charcoal and fire-cracked rock was located just outside the entry.

Evidence for the roof consisted of burned beams and very hard, heavily weathered fill that was probably adobe.

Eighteen charcoal samples were collected from Structure 14. Seventeen were ponderosa pine; the eighteenth was a juniper specimen. None could be dated. Reed fragments were also recovered from the structure. Floor-associated artifacts consisted of a deer mandible, four hammerstones, one mano, a handstone fragment, a red ware bowl with a smudged interior, and a handle from a plain ware vessel. Pot hunters had excavated a cone-shaped pit into

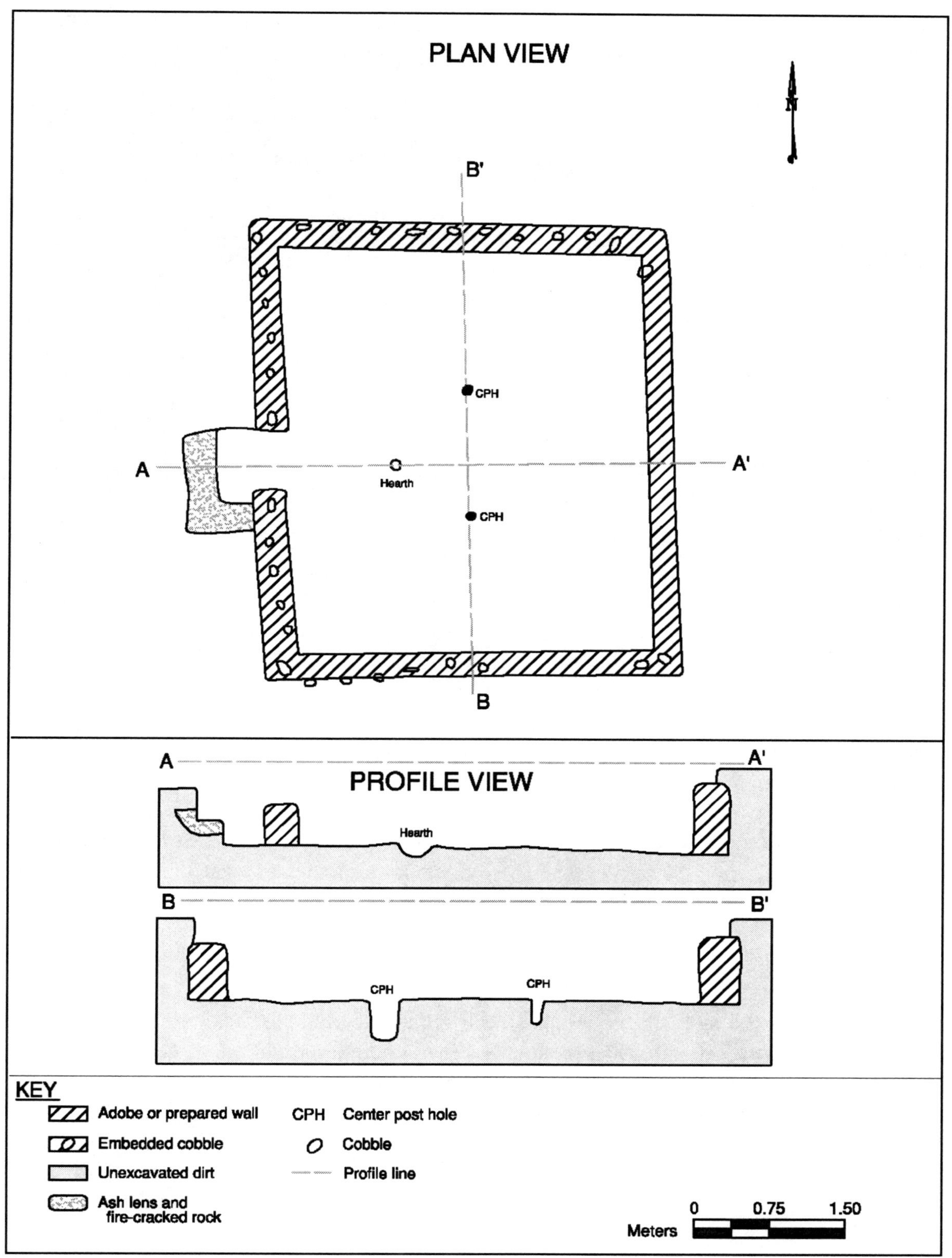

Figure 2.22. Structure 14, plan view and profiles (prepared by Austin Lenhart, Elizabeth Vinson, and Helen L. O'Brien).

Figure 2.23. Structure 14, looking east (Catalog Number 106618, Arizona State Museum, University of Arizona).

the northwest quadrant near the north wall. The pit went through the floor, disturbing about two square feet of area.

The structure was excavated in the spring of 1969. Paul Grebinger recorded it and took the field notes.

Structure 19a

Structure 19a (Figure 2.24) was the southernmost house in the site, on the south side of a wash and about (30 m) 100 feet southwest of Structure 14. It was adobe-walled, detached, and rectangular in shape. Structure 19a was located directly over Structure 19b. The walls were made of puddled adobe. No specific information could be found regarding construction.

The entry was appended in the center of the north side of the structure. It was short and rectangular in plan. There were two steps; the first was 40 cm above the floor, the second, made of stone, was 5 cm above the floor.

In some areas the floor had been replastered several times; it measured 5 cm in thickness. The hearth was located between and about 1 m north of the post holes. The hearth was 35 cm in diameter and 8 cm deep. Two main post holes were found along the central axis of the structure. The east hole measured 22–27 cm in diameter and the west hole measured 25 cm in diameter. In addition, three pits were listed. No information was available on the function of the other holes shown in Figure 2.24.

Structure 19a had burned. Evidence for the roof consisted of reed and charcoal bits in an ashy lens. Fill Levels A through E were mapped but not described. Forty-four pollen samples were taken from a variety of locations including wall profiles, floor locations, inside

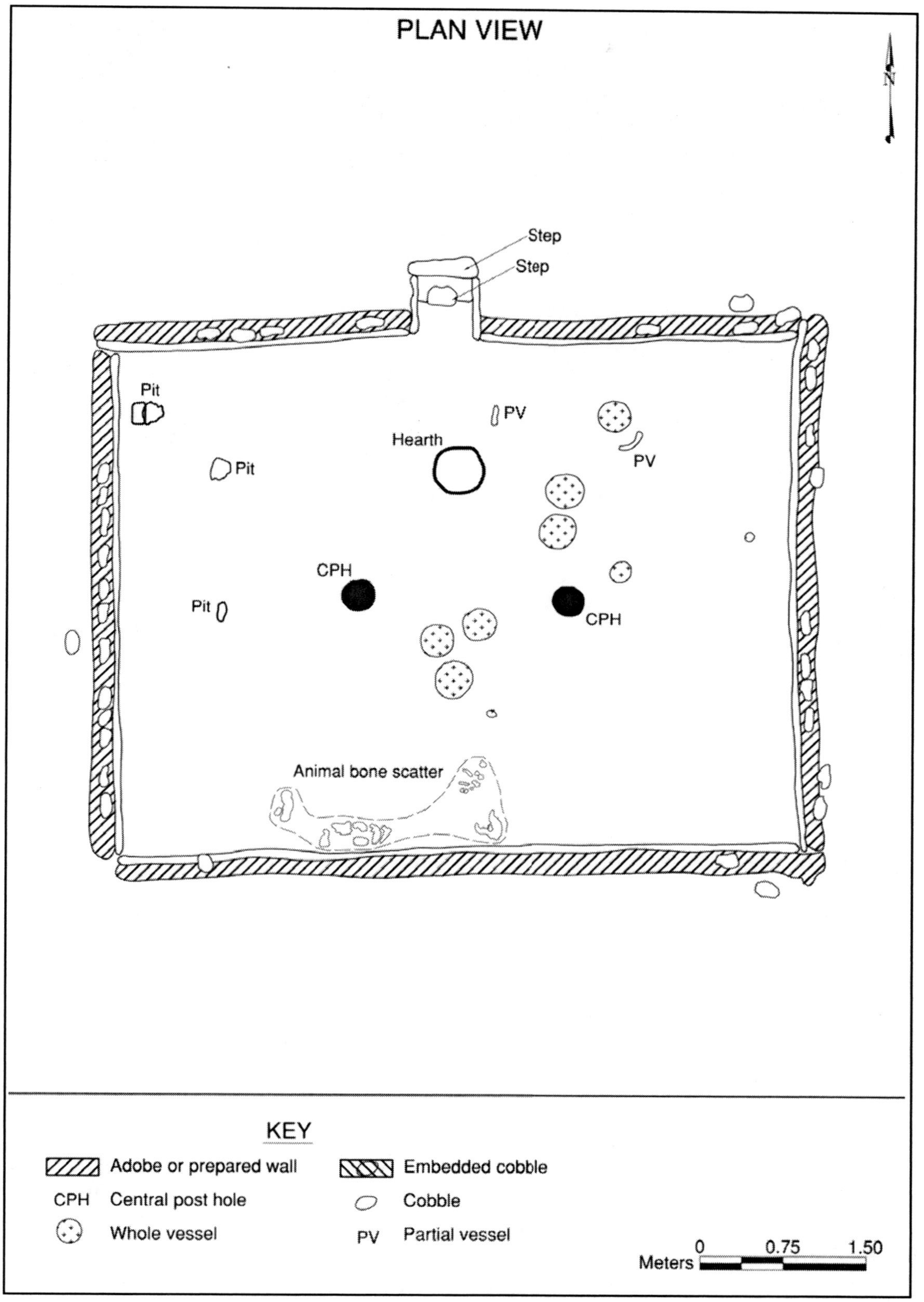

Figure 2.24. Structure 19a, plan view (prepared by Austin Lenhart and Elizabeth Vinson).

Figure 2.25. Restored pottery assemblage on floor of Structure 19a (photograph by Bruce Bradley).

vessels, below vessels, and from the center of the hearth. Charred seeds were collected from the lower fill; they have not been analyzed. Six ponderosa pine beams were sampled. All of them yielded dates: WTR-94 dated to A.D. 1236; WTR-96 dated to A.D. 1210; WTR-100 dated to A.D. 1234, WTR-101 dated to A.D. 1245, WTR-112 dated to A.D. 1233; and WTR-114 yielded a date of A.D. 1239. All but Sample WTR-101 are missing an unknown number of outer rings. Although missing diagnostic attributes of an outer ring, Dean thought that the A.D. 1245 date from Sample WTR-101 is the cutting date for that beam (Dean 1969; Dean et al. 1996).

The floor assemblage from this house was substantial, consisting of eight reconstructible and whole bowls, about one-third of another bowl, several projectile points, an ax fragment, a mano, an abrader, a lapstone, a pestle, two bone awls (one-double ended), a number of obsidian flakes, a polishing stone with red coloring on it, a piece of red quartzite with a ground corner, an igneous stone with polishing facets and striations, a piece of red ocher, and clusters of flakes. In addition, there were three and one-half deer or pronghorn mandibles as well as four antlers, a scapula, teeth, a skull, and assorted other bones of deer, pronghorn, and rabbit that may have been on a shelf or bench just above the floor. The floor assemblage appeared to have been staged, possibly as a part of a ritual to "close" the house. Some but not all of these artifacts are shown in Figure 2.25.

Bruce Bradley (personal communication 2009) remembers a wall niche at floor level to the left of the doorway as one enters the structure, although this was not noted in the room description or on the map.

Bruce Bradley, Bruce Huckell, Dick Dannells, Donna LaRocca, Rich White, and Nancy Horn excavated the structure from October 1969 to January 1970. Donna LaRocca took the field notes and, along with Bruce Huckell, recorded the structure. There is a student report written by "B.E.B," probably in 1974 or 1975 as part of a class taught by Paul Grebinger, Eisenhower College, Seneca Falls, New York.

Structure 19b

Structure 19b (Figures 2.26, 2.27) was a subrectangular, detached pit structure located directly under Structure 19a. There was no information on its construction or walls. The entry was appended in the center of the north side of the structure. It was bulbous with a narrow neck and was destroyed during the excavation of Structure 19a.

There was no information about the floor. The hearth was located directly south of the entry and was 14.5 cm deep and 30 cm in diameter. There were two major post holes in approximately the same location as those in Structure 19a. The east post hole was 37 cm in diameter; the west post hole was 35 cm in diameter; their depths were unknown. Eight small post holes were located in the western portion of the floor. Six of these occurred in two rows of three each, near the front and back walls, suggesting use as bench supports (Figure 2.26). Others may have been rodent holes.

There was no information about the roof or fill of this structure.

Some of the 44 pollen samples and charred seeds from Structure 19a may have come from 19b. Because the floor of Structure 19a was constructed directly on top of Structure 19b, few artifacts could be directly associated with Structure 19b.

Information on this structure was extrapolated from a plan and field notes. No excavation form could be located. It was excavated by Bruce Bradley, Bruce Huckell, Dick Dannells, Donna LaRocca, Rich White, and Nancy Horn in January of 1970. Donna LaRocca and Bruce Huckell recorded it. A student report by "B.E.B," was written, probably in 1974 or 1975, as part of a class taught by Paul Grebinger, Eisenhower College, Seneca Falls, New York.

Northeastern Locus

The Northeastern Locus included several widely separated structures, five of which were excavated as part of the Whiptail project (Figure 1.13). The excavated structures included three free-standing rooms (Structures 1, 22, and 40) and one set of contiguous-walled rooms (Structures 41 and 42). At least five other unexcavated structures occurred in the Northeastern Locus.

Structure 1

Structure 1 (Figure 2.28) was a subrectangular, adobe-walled, detached room. The walls were made of puddled adobe with cobbles set into the top of the wall courses. In some places the walls seemed to be smoothed, but not plastered. All the walls were intact, but all showed some erosion. A small hole, at floor level, extended into the north wall at the northeast corner. It did not appear to be a rodent hole, but contained nothing.

The entry was appended to the south wall in its center, 1.98 m from the east wall. It had short, curved walls and was semicircular in plan. It was 56 cm across the front and 56 cm deep. An adobe step set in the entry was 18 cm in height above the floor.

The floor was well plastered and smoothed. It was also heavily cracked and there was some damage from vandalism. The round, fired clay hearth had a slightly raised rim. The hearth was

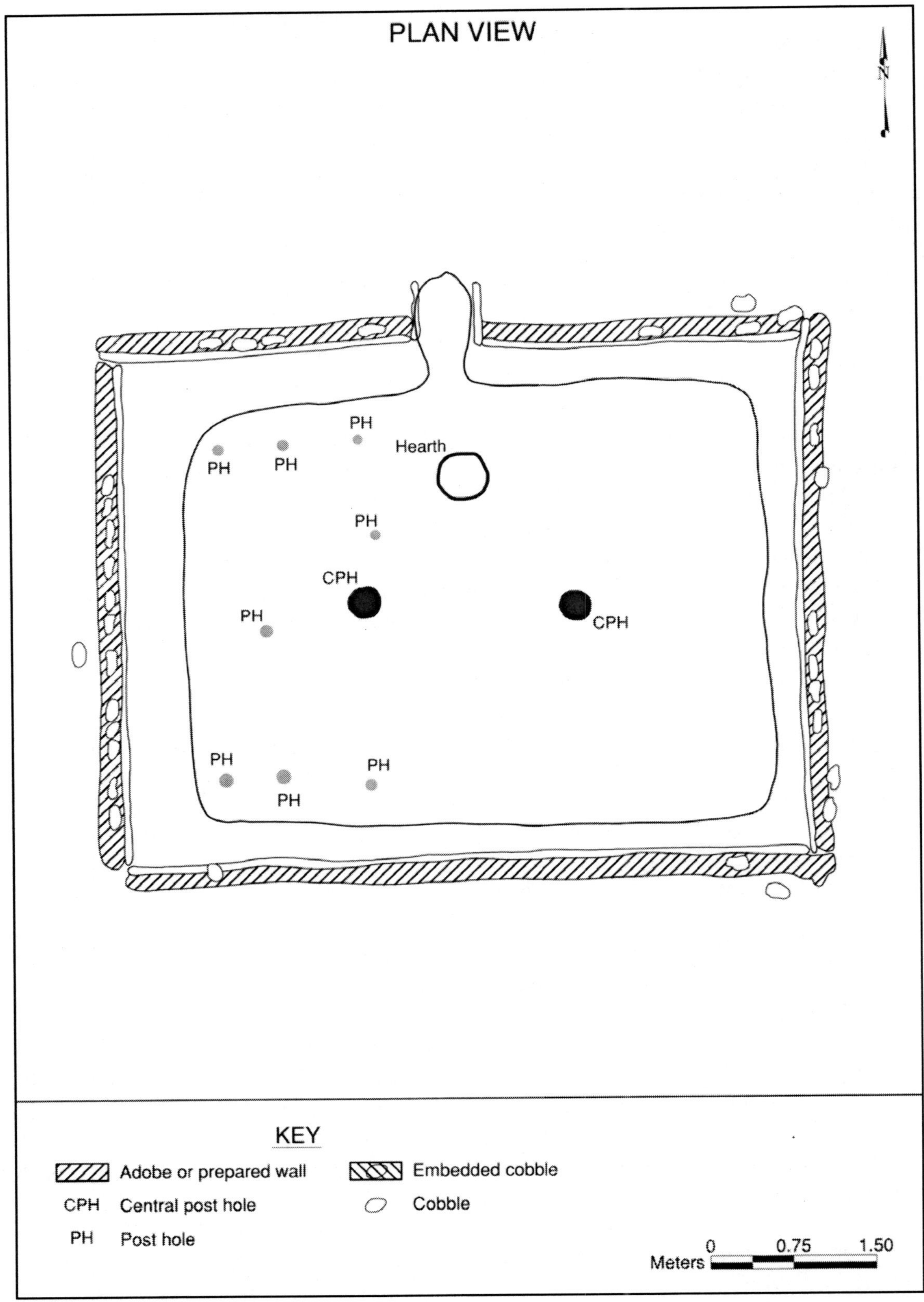

Figure 2.26. Structure 19b, plan view (prepared by Austin Lenhart and Elizabeth Vinson).

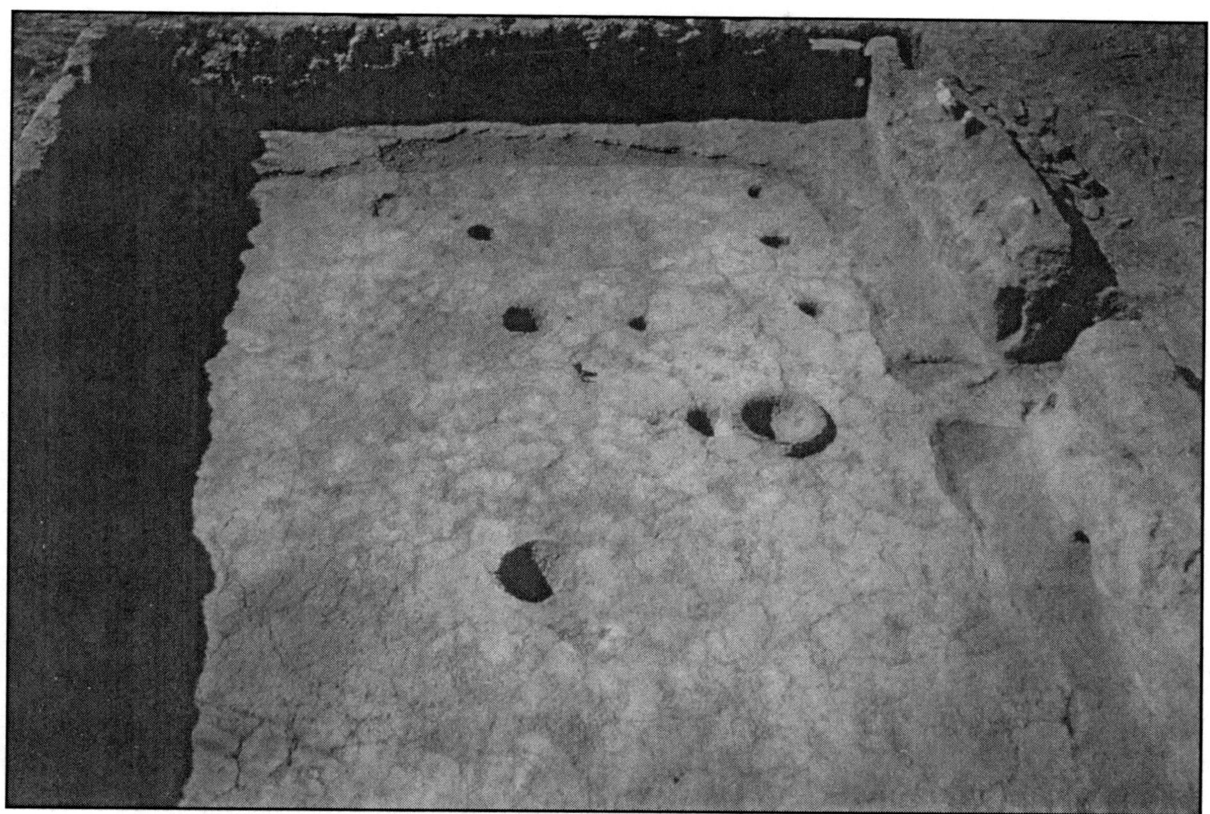

Figure 2.27. Structure 19, showing superimposed structures (photograph by Bruce Bradley).

20 cm in diameter, 23 cm deep and was located 93 cm north of the entrance. One possible post hole was found in the center of the floor. It had been destroyed by vandalism.

Small chunks of adobe scattered throughout the house on top of the floor fill may have been roof or wall fall. The fill was trashy, but not black, though it did contain some charcoal. No samples were taken.

A small piece of slate was recovered from the fill that may be a mescal knife fragment. Also in the fill were three pieces of unmodified shell; two were *Pecten* and one was *Glycymeris*. A gray, slate spindle whorl was recovered from the floor east of the firepit.

Bruce Bradley excavated and recorded the structure from August 1966 to April 1967. He also wrote the field notes and the report.

Structure 22

Structure 22 was rectangular, adobe-walled, and detached. It was made of puddled adobe with stones set into the walls. Many places showed evidence of several layers of plaster. Courses could be identified in the southeast corner of the structure. The lowest course (Course 1) protruded, ledge-like, below Course 2. Course 1 was completely plastered from the floor to the top of the course. Course 2 was not as thick as Course 1. On the east wall close to the southeast corner the second course was finished with a rounded end, with what appears to have been a plug set in place to fill the corner and join the south and east walls. Coursing cracks were apparent in two places. Figure 2.29 illustrates construction detail of the southeast

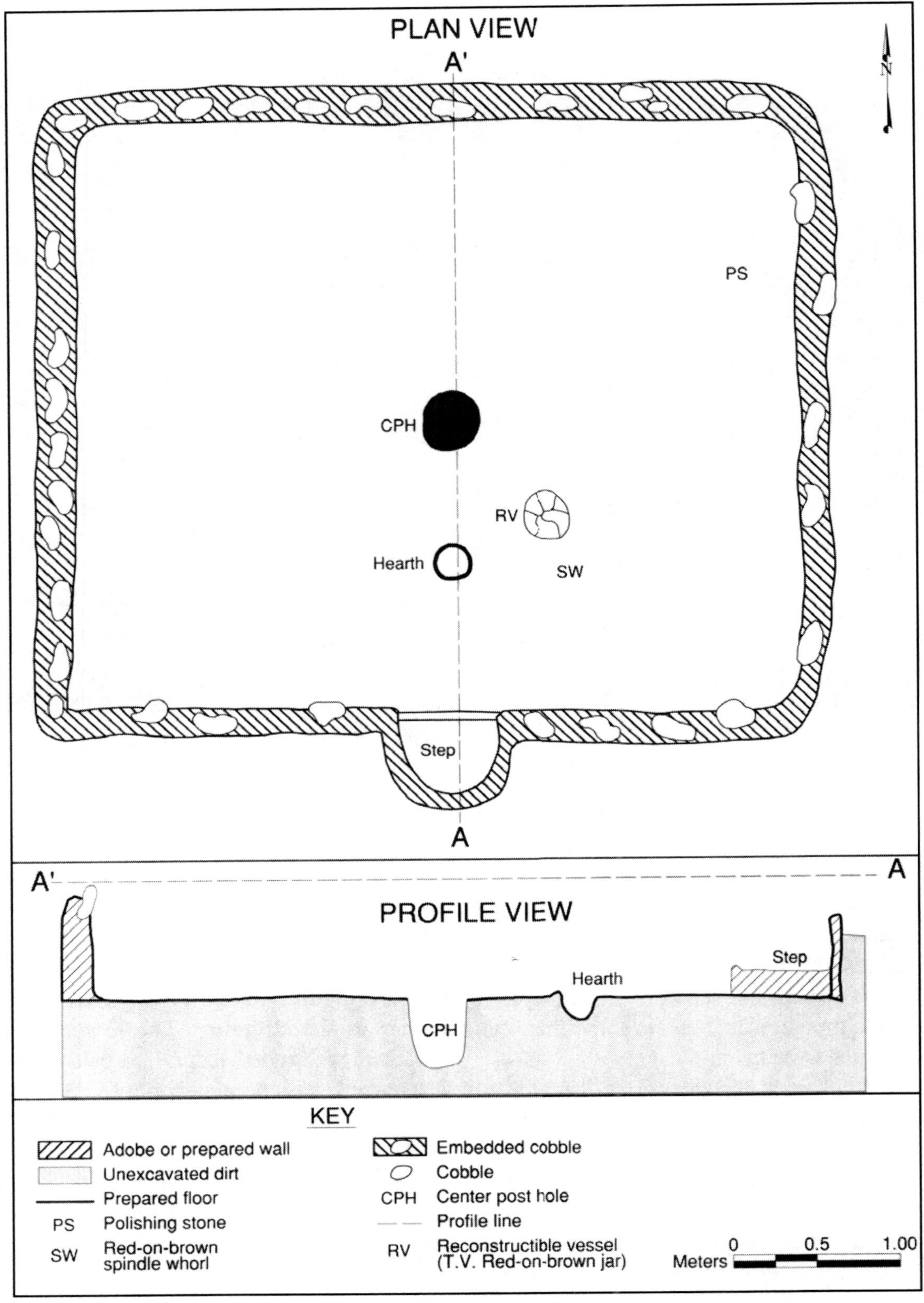

Figure 2.28. Structure 1, plan view and profiles (prepared by Austin Lenhart and Elizabeth Vinson).

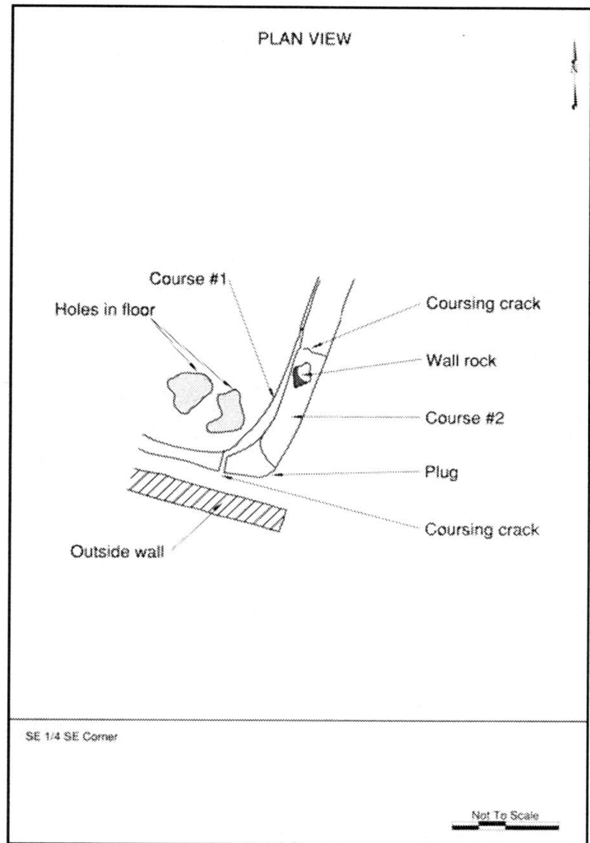

Figure 2.29. Plan view of courses in southeast corner of Structure 22 (prepared by Austin Lenhart and Elizabeth Vinson).

corner of the structure.

The entry was appended in the center of the east wall. It was short and rectangular in plan.

The floor was exceedingly well made. A burned layer was evident on and just above the floor. The hearth was oval in shape and measured 70 cm by 30 cm. Two post holes, 25 cm and 15 cm in diameter, were found along the long axis of the structure. Two subfloor pits were noted. Both were irregular in shape; one was immediately below the hearth.

Evidence for the roof consisted of some adobe that was noted in the fill. The fill was divided into three layers. The upper layer consisted of gray, gravelly sand and included stones that may have been part of the walls. The middle layer was similar to the upper but included chunks of adobe that may have been part of the roof. The lower fill was dark gray and ashy and included some adobe.

A partial bowl, a sherd cluster, a handstone, a polishing stone, and a knife were recorded as occurring in this feature. Except for the pottery and polishing stone, artifacts from this feature have not been analyzed.

It is unknown who excavated or recorded the structure, but it was probably done in the winter of 1970.

Structure 40

Information on Structure 40 was extrapolated from a plan, profile, and field notes. No excavation form could be located. The structure was rectangular, adobe-walled, and detached. The walls were made of puddled adobe with wall stones present in the north and west walls. Walls were built in a trench that had been cut into sterile caliche. Double plaster or a replastering event was evident on all but the north wall.

The short, rectangular entry was appended in the center of the south wall.

The floor was puddled adobe poured onto the sterile caliche level. There were two hearths inside the entryway. The lower hearth was level with the floor and made of finely fired clay. The upper hearth was built directly into the lower hearth and thus was slightly elevated above floor level. The lower hearth was apparently completely cleaned out, and the upper hearth was built into it as there was no ash or fill between the two hearths. No replastering of the floor was visible. Two large post holes were situated along the central axis of the structure. Three smaller holes were shown on a map of the house. One was in the southwest corner, one in the southeast corner, and one near the north wall in the center of structure. No mention was made of their possible function.

Heavily burned adobe with reed impressions in the fill were probably evidence of the roof. The upper fill contained orange-red angular, gravelly soil suggesting the structure burned. The middle fill was similar in texture, but had dark, burned soil. It also contained pieces of heavily burned adobe, some with reed impressions. Sherds were evenly distributed throughout with some sherd concentrations, primarily from the same vessel.

Sherds and a sherd spindle whorl were mentioned in field notes and on the field specimen sheet. The artifacts are in possession of the landowners and have not been analyzed.

According to the field notes, wall stones found outside of the west wall suggested this wall fell outward, as did the north wall. There was no evidence of wall fall from the east wall inside the house. The south wall fell into the house, as seen by the melted adobe washed into the structure and by numerous wall stones in the upper fill in a line parallel to the wall.

Structure 40 was excavated by Bruce Huckell, Lisa Washbon (Huckell), Bruce Bradley, Jim Bradley, and Berry [last name unknown] from February 1 to 3 [year unknown]. Bruce Bradley recorded the structure and took the field notes.

Structure 41

Structure 41 was adobe-walled and rectangular. It was contiguous with Structure 42 and was made of puddled adobe with stones in the south and east walls. The north and west walls were still solid during excavation.

An entry was apparently present, but its location and shape are unknown. The floor was very badly disturbed. There was no information on a hearth, post holes, pits, or the roof.

The upper fill was light-brown sandy gravel, extremely loose and uncompacted. The middle fill was a dark brown sandy soil containing chunks and flecks of charcoal.

A worked slab of green slate and a jasper biface rested on the floor. The artifacts are in possession of the landowners and have not been analyzed.

This structure had been badly vandalized prior to excavation as indicated by a plastic bag and some flash cubes in the middle fill, as well as a recently cut bone from a cut of meat just above the floor and a shotgun shell butt on the floor.

Bruce Huckell, Lisa Washbon (Huckell), and Barry Richards excavated the structure on February 16, 1974. Bruce Huckell wrote the field notes. No excavation record has been located.

Structure 42

Structure 42 was rectangular and adobe-walled. It was contiguous with Structure 41. The walls were made of puddled adobe with wall stones present in all four walls. The method of construction consisted of overlapping sections of puddled adobe in courses approximately 40 cm in height, 25 cm thick, and 75 cm long. Small boulders were embedded in the top of the first course at more or less regular intervals. These were left protruding upward so that they would be embedded into the bottom of the next level of puddled adobe. The walls were abutted at the corners with an additional thin layer of adobe applied to the interior thus creating rounded interior corners. Although no remnants of wall foundation trenches were located, it is thought that the first course of wall adobe was puddled into a foundation trench. After the adobe hardened, the builders of the structure would have excavated the interior to the bottom of the walls. This construction scenario is based on the rounded nature of the base of the walls. At least two episodes of plastering occurred. The walls were between 20 cm and 50 cm high. It was estimated that originally the walls stood at least 2 m above the floor level; they were in good condition.

The entry was appended in the center of the southeast-facing wall. It was short and rounded in plan. The entry was constructed by the application of a layer of adobe 3 cm to 5 cm thick to a shallow excavation into the native soil. This adobe layer was laid down like wall and floor plaster; it was not puddled. The wall opening was about 70 cm wide and the entryway protruded about 60 cm measured from the interior wall of the structure. A single step of puddled adobe was present.

The floor was smoothed adobe, 2 cm to 5 cm thick, burned gray in color and very level. The hearth was constructed by burying a Tanque Verde Red-on-brown bowl into the floor so that the rim was even with the floor. The hearth bowl showed some signs of pre-hearth use, but was not burned on the interior indicating that it saw little or no use as a hearth. It is probable that the bowl replaced the normal clay-lined firepit during the final refurbishing of the structure. Two post holes existed along the central long axis of the structure. The west post hole retained the native caliche as a base for the post, while a flat cobble was added to the bottom of the east post hole as a base for the post. After the east post was placed in the hole, adobe was poured in around it to fill up the empty area; then the floor adobe was applied right up to the post. Construction information is lacking for the west post because of extensive rodent and/or root disturbance. There were no pits.

Ash and adobe chunks in the middle and lower fill were thought to represent roof fall. Upper fill (0–15 cm) was defined as sterile and gravelly; middle fill (15–35 cm) as gray in color, sandy and gravelly in consistency; lower fill (35 cm to 5 cm above floor) as dark gray and ashy with distinct burned adobe chunks. There were occasional chunks of charcoal in the lower fill. One bowl rim sherd from the upper fill fit into the bowl that was buried in the floor as a hearth, demonstrating the amount of artifact displacement that occurred in this structure.

Samples of soil and charcoal were taken, as well as samples of burned roofing adobe that contained impressions of perishable material. One soil sample was taken from inside a Tanque Verde Red-on-brown jar. A red siltstone "nose plug" and a biface with heavy dulling along one edge were collected from the surface about 20 m south of Structure 42; one projectile point was collected from a flat surface outside the northeast corner of the structure. Three whole or restorable vessels—a Tanque Verde Red-on-brown bowl, a Tanque Verde Red-on-brown jar, a plain ware jar, and a plain obliterated corrugated jar—were found on the floor, as was a metate. A Tanque Verde Red-on-brown bowl was also found imbedded in the floor and used as a hearth. Most artifacts were recovered from the middle and lower fill (probably roof fall). They consist of 1 vesicular basalt "doughnut" stone, 1 slate slab, 1 three quarter-grooved maul, 1 partial schist spindle whorl, 2 fragmentary manos, 1 complete mano, 1 restorable Tanque Verde Red-on-brown bowl, 3 sherds of an incised ware, 677 additional sherds, and an assortment of chipped stone.

The structure was excavated from December 22, 1977 to January 29, 1978 by Bruce Bradley, Joe Gordon, Mark Gordon, Stanley Gordon, Bruce Huckell, Cindy Bradley, and Joey, Juniper, and Jake (dogs belonging to Bruce Bradley). Bruce Bradley recorded it and wrote the field notes.

Architectural Overview

In this concluding section we synthesize architectural characteristics and make comparisons to the nearby community of Gibbon Springs (Slaughter and Roberts 1996b). Gibbon Springs is located approximately 4 miles west of Whiptail in very similar surroundings (Figure 1.12).

Whiptail and Gibbon Springs (AZ BB:9:50 [ASM]) are both early Classic period sites and are contemporary or very nearly contemporary. Recent tree-ring analyses from a single structure at Gibbon Springs (Feature 106) provide dates that

> range from A.D. 1209 to A.D. 1249 with a tight cluster of two cutting dates and one noncutting date at A.D. 1247 to 1249. This clustering indicates that the house was built or, perhaps, remodeled in or shortly after A.D. 1249 with at least one timber procured in A.D. 1247. . . . The evidence is definite, . . . that this structure was in use as late as the summer of 1249 and that the fill and floor assemblages postdate that year (Dean et al. 1996:17)

Tree-ring analyses from six structures at Whiptail provide strikingly similar dates. These dates

> range from A.D. 1210 to 1246, with all but one falling in the 20-year period between A.D. 1226 and 1246. . . . This date distribution places extensive wood procurement in the A.D. 1230s and A.D. 1240s, at least partly contemporaneously with that at the Gibbon Springs Site (Dean et al. 1996:19).

Thus, from the available tree-ring evidence, both communities appear to have been occupied from at least the 1230s into the 1250s. Other evidence—primarily ceramic—indicates occupation into at least the A.D. 1270s (Chapter 3; Chapter 11).

In many ways the layout and architecture at the sites were also strikingly similar. In both cases the sites covered large areas and structures were dispersed. Including the Agua Caliente Park segment, Whiptail was about 500 m by 1000 m in size and Gibbon Springs extended about 400 m on a side. (The southern part of Gibbon Springs was destroyed before excavation, so it may have been the same size as Whiptail Ruin.) At both sites structures were organized into loci. At Whiptail we defined six loci including a compound that contained the largest structure at the site. At Gibbon Springs six loci were also identified including a compound, which also contained the site's largest structure (Slaughter 1996a:70, 71). At Gibbon Springs agricultural fields were identified by the presence of check dams, rock piles terraces, and drainages (Roberts 1996b:166); no agricultural fields were identified at Whiptail, but it seems probable that they existed. It is likely that they were destroyed during the construction of the historical Agua Caliente Ranch and the pond and marsh system that can currently be seen at Agua Caliente Park.

At both sites all structures were semi-subterranean with the shallow pits averaging virtually the same depth—38 cm below surface at Gibbon Springs and 40 cm below surface at Whiptail. Also at both sites the majority of the structures were rectangular with adobe walls while the minority were true pit structures. At Whiptail all were described as rectangular or nearly rectangular in shape. Structures 4 and 19b at Whiptail were described as pit structures—subrectangular in shape and with bulbous, narrow-necked entries. At Gibbon Springs 24 definite architectural structures were excavated. Of these, 18 were described as semi-subterranean with adobe walls and 6 as pit structures (Slaughter 1996a:69).

In all but one case at both sites, where the construction technique can be determined, the preferred material was puddled adobe. Generally, the adobe was mixed with caliche and gravel, with cobbles visible in the tops of exposed portions of walls. At Whiptail there were seven cases (Structures 2, 8, 9, 10, 11, 13, and 18) in which walls contained grooves or remnants of grooves presumably intended for vertical poles used as part of upper wall construction. At Feature 112 at Gibbon Springs, a pit structure, the presence of a large amount of burned daub suggested a wattle-and-daub technique (Slaughter 1996a:129). In a few cases at Whiptail walls were buttressed, either on the interior or exterior of the structures. There was no definitive evidence for poles as part of wall construction or buttresses at Gibbon Springs.

Based on the presence of vertical grooves at several Whiptail structures and the abundance of adobe chunks in the fill, as well as the amount of "burned daub" at Feature 112 at Gibbon Springs, we surmise that many if not all of the adobe structures at both sites were reinforced with poles embedded in the walls. At both sites the roofs were generally supported similarly, with two posts aligned along the central axis of the structure. In many cases at both sites, post holes provided evidence of other posts both large and small. There was one example of an adobe collar around a post hole, at Structure 30 at Whiptail. In a few cases post holes probably contained posts that provided support for benches or other raised structures, for example, a pit structure at Whiptail (Structure 19b) (see Figure 2.25).

At both sites horizontal beams were apparently a common component of roof construction, and adobe and wood chunks, impressions of beams, and remnants of burned beams were found in numerous structures. At both sites many structures burned (26 at Whiptail and 16 at Gibbon Springs [Slaughter 1996a:70]), with charcoal from the burned beams providing the tree-ring dates.

The interior walls of most of the structures were plastered. Archaeological evidence showed that roofs were commonly adobe covered and supported by two posts along the central, long axis of the houses. Wood used as beams and posts in the structures included mesquite, juniper, pinyon pine, and ponderosa pine. Ceiling and wall materials included reeds, saguaro ribs, and agave stalks (Chapter 9).

At Whiptail all but three structures were interpreted as houses by the excavators. Structure 15, located in the Central Locus, was interpreted as a storage room because of a wide entryway and the large vessels found inside; Structure 3 was interpreted as a possible storage structure; and Structure 28 was interpreted as a shaded summer work area for Structure 27a. Structure 7 at Whiptail, based on its large size and location within the compound, could be interpreted as having a communal function. And Structures 14 and 19a, the two structures in the wash on the south edge of the site, may have been ritual buildings.

At Gibbon Springs two structures, both within the compound, may have been used for storage (Slaughter and Roberts 1996a:504, 507), while one (Feature 8) was interpreted as a possible meeting room, based on its large size, the presence of two hearths, and a possible bench around its interior perimeter (Slaughter 1996a:525). All others, for which sufficient evidence was available, suggested residential use.

Of the 40 structures at Whiptail, 27 were detached, 13 were contiguous (3 groups of 3, and 2 groups of 2) and 2 were nearly contiguous (the walls were immediately adjacent to one another). In two of the contiguous groups of three (Structures 11, 16, and 18 and Structures 31a-b-c), rooms were attached on the short side producing lines of rooms. It should be noted that Structures 11 and 18 definitely shared a wall, while information for Structures 11 and 16 is conflicting—they may have shared a wall or they may have been a few centimeters apart. Structures 27a and 27b were attached along their long sides with Structure 28 jutting out of the northeast corner of 27a. The excavation records note that Structure 28 abutted Structure 27a and was, therefore, more recent. For the

Structure 31a-b-c room block, information indicates that each structure abutted the next, suggesting that each was built separately. Structures 11-16-18 were in the Southwestern Locus; Structures 27a-27b-28 and 31a-b-c were in the Northern Locus. Structures 10 and 12, in the Southwestern Locus, were separated by about 26 cm. Structures 41 and 42, in the Northeastern Locus, were contiguous.

At Gibbon Springs the only definitely contiguous structures were Features 45 and 46, with Feature 45 abutting Feature 46; that is, the two structures shared one common wall. Feature 100, a pit structure, apparently abutted Feature 149, which was not excavated. In describing Feature 149, Slaughter (1996a:138) remarks that this structure "was an adobe wall ...that touched, but did not overlap, Feature 100." He goes on to comment, "if this proposed structure is real, then it likely was attached to the compound wall."

At Whiptail, with the exception of Structures 27a and b, the entries of contiguous structures faced south. The entries of Features 45 and 46 at Gibbon Springs faced in opposite directions—north and south.

A single case of superposition was found at Whiptail with Structure 19a (a detached, rectangular structure) located directly over Structure 19b (a pit structure). These were the southernmost structures at the site, situated in a wash and located about 30 m southwest of the nearest structure, Structure 14. The ceramic assemblage from the structures includes Tanque Verde Red-on-brown, obliterated indented corrugated, two sherds of Roosevelt Black-on-white, and plain ware. Unfortunately, which structure the artifacts are associated with cannot be determined, as artifacts are identified only as being from Structure 19, not 19a or 19b. We assume all artifacts are associated with Structure 19a because there was very little space between the two floors. At Gibbon Springs, there were no examples of superposition.

Structure 4, the other pit structure at Whiptail, was defined as "slant-wall" and, according to the field notes, seems to be stratigraphically earlier than the nearly adjacent compound. A test trench showed that the bottom of the compound wall was on the same level as the top of the pit house. Pottery from this structure included Tanque Verde Red-on-brown, obliterated indented corrugated, and plain ware.

At both sites, there was considerable range in structure size, with those at Whiptail being, on the whole, slightly larger. At Whiptail, the smallest structure (Structure 20) had a 14.7-meter-square floor area, while the largest two (Structures 7 and 17) had 45- and 41.7-meter-square floor areas respectively. The two largest structures were located within the compound. In terms of floor area, if adobe-walled structures and the two pit structures are averaged separately, the adobe-walled structures average just over 27 meters square and the pit structures, 20.5 meters square.

At Gibbon Springs the smallest structure was 11.6 meters square while the largest was 36.7 meters square. Again, the largest structure (Feature 8) was within the compound. The adobe-walled structures averaged 21.6 meters square while pit structures averaged 19 meters square (Slaughter 1996a:70, Table 4.1).

At both sites, most entryways were either appended and outlined by low walls or sills, or they were simple openings in walls. Whiptail entryways were generally appended; that is, there was some kind of enclosed vestibule. It is, however, not possible from the available information to precisely understand the characteristics of all the entryways. At Whiptail 21, structures apparently had some kind of appended entry—typically they were short in length, and either rectangular/square or rounded in plan. In 10 structures, 5 of which were contiguous, the entries were simple openings in one of the walls. At Gibbon Springs, only one adobe-walled structure had evidence of an enclosed entryway (Feature 46); in all others the entry was apparently a simple break in the wall.

Both pit structures at Whiptail had bulbous entryways with narrow necks; one of these (at Structure 4) had evidence for postholes that likely supported a roofed vestibule. This was the only entryway at the site with evidence of postholes. Of the six pit structures at Gibbon Springs, four provided entry information, with two of these exhibiting the most interesting entries at the site. Feature 100 had a long (2.5 m), ramped, adobe-lined entryway with a single step while, at Feature 125, an entry antechamber was connected to the structure by a narrow passageway (Slaughter 1996a:120,134).

At both sites elaboration of entryways centered primarily around step construction. In two cases at Whiptail (Structures 11 and 16, which were contiguous) a single stone was set in an adobe step, while at Structure 20 the step consisted of a large tabular stone supported by a series of smaller stones and surrounded by a thin adobe "wall" (probably a threshold). Structure 31a, which had a simple opening as an entryway, had a caliche step on the interior of the wall opening and two stone slabs on top of each other on the exterior.

At Gibbon Springs a few structures had steps; one (Feature 15) incorporated a stone riser and stone step into the entry. Several incorporated adobe pads into the entryway.

Of the 39 entries recorded at Whiptail, by far the largest number (25) faced south with two facing southwest and one facing southeast. Seven faced north, two faced east, and two faced west. At Gibbons Springs, of the 20 structures with probable entries, south was also the dominant direction. Fourteen of the 20 faced south, southeast, or southwest (Slaughter 1996a: 70, Table 4.1).

At Gibbon Springs, Slaughter and Roberts (1996a:509) identified between two and five courtyard groups based largely on entries facing each other, as well as roasting pits and trash middens that may have been used communally. At Whiptail, although structures were located in clusters, entries generally did not face each other and extramural features such as roasting pits and middens were not identified. Even in the compound, the entries of the three structures faced away from each other. Thus, courtyard groups do not seem to be part of the Whiptail architectural layout. It is worth noting that, at the Tucson phase portion of Second Canyon Ruin in the San Pedro valley, Franklin (1980:13) notes that, "entry ways [to the surface rooms] always face toward the closest plaza," which means they generally face east or west, while the Tanque Verde phase and earlier pit structures generally face east (Figure 1.12).

Overall, these two small foothills communities that are nearby and contemporary, or nearly so, are remarkably similar in most architectural attributes. They share overall site layout, a compound that contains the largest structure, construction techniques, structural characteristics, and probably site size. The possible significance of these similarities is discussed in the final chapter of this report.

Table 2.2. Wall Characteristics.

Structure No.	Structure Description	Wall Characteristics: Construction	Plaster	Height	Thickness	Condition	Other Features
Compound Locus							
4	Subrectangular detached pit	Puddled adobe	Present, 2- to 3-cm thick	33 to 48 cm, all were probably 48 cm high at one time	10 to 18 cm (thickest along entryway neck)	Excellent were still standing	None noted
6	Rectangular, detached adobe-walled	Cobble, based on information shown on plan	Some, walls have been reworked in some areas	30 to 50 cm	10 to 30 cm	No information	None noted
7	Rectangular detached, adobe-walled	Puddled, coursed adobe inset with cobbles; cobbles tied lower wall to superstructure. Numerous pebble-sized stones were embedded in adobe, surrounding the larger cobbles	Present in thin layers on east wall, either as remains of plaster or as patch	60 to 80 cm	North 45 cm; south 51 cm; east 40 cm; west 45 cm	No information	Vertical grooves in west wall suggest that roof was pole-reinforced.
8	Rectangular, detached, adobe- walled	Puddled adobe with stones inset in lower wall to bind with superstructure.	Large area of smoothed plaster found on south portion of east wall	Unknown, although fallen section to west of entry suggests at least two feet above presently standing walls.	About 30 cm	No information	Grooves in east and west walls suggest a pole-reinforced superstructure. Two possible post holes were located in the center of the wall on either side of the entry.
17	Rectangular, detached adobe-walled	Puddled adobe; no wall cobbles were visible on the ground surface so structure was not visible until backhoe trenching revealed it.	None observed	Interior walls 10 to 30 cm; exterior walls about 50 cm.	Interior walls, 10 cm; exterior walls 20 to 50 cm. Thickest portion (in southeast corner) was 61 cm.	North, east, and west walls were thin. The eroded condition of the wall may explain the lack of wall cobbles.	The structure seems to have had double walls on at least portions of the east, west, and north sides. On these sides a thin, interior wall had been constructed with the area between the walls containing loose fill. The top was filled with or capped by adobe.
Central Locus							
5	Rectangular, detached, adobe- walled	Mixture of caliche, gravel, and mud. Originally stones had apparently been set in top level of wall, most of which had been removed by a pot hunter. Numerous stones were lying around the exterior of the house.	None	Approximately 30 cm above floor.	Unknown	Good	Vertical, column-like grooves in northeast, southeast, and southwest corners from the top to the bottom of the wall were identified as "probably rodent burrows."

Table 2.2. Wall Characteristics, cont'd.

Structure No.	Structure Description	Wall Characteristics: Construction	Plaster	Height	Thickness	Condition	Other Features
15	Rectangular, detached, adobe- walled	Puddled adobe; stones remain inset in north and south walls at point were upper and lower wall join.	None observed	40 to 60 cm	20 to 40 cm	Except for portions near the entry, the walls were relatively thin.	None
32	Rectangular, detached, adobe- walled	Puddled adobe with stones in north and east walls	No information	Approximately 36 cm	No information	No information	No information
33	Subrectangular, detached, adobe- walled	Puddled adobe with stones set at a standard level	No information	40 cm, approximate reconstructed height of east wall is 1.6 to 2 m	Thin (approximately 5 cm), sloping out	Poor	An opening in the west wall was thought to be a window.
Southwestern Locus							
2	Rectangular, detached, adobe- walled	Puddled adobe mixed with caliche and gravel with cobbles set into tops of walls	Plastered along north wall, east of entry	26 to 35 cm above floor	At least 41 to 56 cm thick along north wall east of entry	Excellent	Some wall stones noted in fill along west wall.
9	Rectangular, detached, adobe- walled	Puddled adobe with cobbles set along the top of the west wall; one cobble remained on top of the north wall. Evidence of a groove for possible post reinforcement was found in the west wall.	None	40 to 60 cm	Variable; west wall was thickest measuring 30 to 55 cm; north wall was thinnest, measuring 10 cm.	North wall was thin and heavily eroded. Southeast and southwest corners were also in poor shape.	Horizontal grooves along both sides of entry.
10	Rectangular adobe-walled, nearly contiguous with Structure 12	Puddled adobe. Considerable wall fall and cobbles outside of the south wall suggest that the wall was constructed using alternating stone and adobe courses. The south wall had two deep grooves indicating reinforcement with vertical poles.	None apparent	Between 40 and 50 cm	Thickest wall segment about 20 cm.	Wall stones had toppled into structure along inside edge of north wall. East wall was very thin.	Depressions in wall indicated locations of stones, although no stones were present
11	Rectangular adobe-walled, contiguous with Structures 16 & 18	Rocks joining the upper and lower walls were evident in all walls. The north and east walls had evidence of grooves for vertical poles. Structure shared walls with Structure 18 to the west and Structure 16 to the east.	Definitely visible around interior corners of entry; well smoothed. Some plaster also remained on western half of south wall.	No information	Generally 40 to 60 cm; northeast corner is thin, about 20 cm.	No information	None

Table 2.2. Wall Characteristics, cont'd.

Structure No.	Structure Description	Construction	Plaster	Wall Characteristics Height	Thickness	Condition	Other Features
12	Rectangular, adobe-walled; nearly contiguous with Structure 10	Puddled adobe. Stones were present between the upper and lower walls.	No evidence; probably destroyed by salt erosion	Approximately 40 cm	20 to 30 cm.	Eroded, especially in southeast corner.	None
13	Rectangular, detached, adobe-walled	Puddled adobe with stones inset between superstructure and lower wall. Grooves are visible in south, west, and east walls and may have been present in the north wall. The east wall was coursed stone and adobe as revealed by wall fall. Corners were well rounded.	Some portions of walls are very flat and smooth but do not appear to be plastered.	About 35 cm	About 30 cm	No information	None
16	Rectangular, adobe-walled; contiguous with Structure 11	Puddled adobe; stones set into walls at point where upper and lower walls join.	Some on most walls near the floor. Rather than being a separately applied substance, however, the "plaster" seemed to be the result of an attempt to smooth the adobe.	40 to 60 cm	10 to 50 cm. The south wall was the thickest.	Excellent except for erosion of the upper portion.	None
18	Rectangular, adobe-walled; contiguous with Structures 11 & 16	Puddled adobe. Rocks and numerous metate fragments were inset into the lower wall. One section of the interior wall (the southeast portion of the east wall) may have been grooved to hold upright poles.	None observed	30 to 40 cm	10 to 20 cm	Part of the grooved section of wall was removed by a pothunter.	None
23	Subrectangular, detached, adobe- walled	Puddled adobe with stones visible in east wall only.	Evidence of two or three plastering episodes	75 cm (maximum)	20 to 50 cm	The north and east walls are well preserved, as was the eastern portion of the south wall.	None
24	Rectangular, detached, adobe- walled	Puddled adobe. A secondary reinforcing buttress-type wall was found along the interior of the east wall.	Two layers of plaster were evident along the interior of the north, south, and east walls.	Maximum 80 cm; minimum 55 cm.	Unknown.	Good; some root disturbance and erosion	None
25	Rectangular, detached, adobe- walled	No information	No information	No information	No information	North wall was in especially good condition	No information
26	Rectangular, detached, adobe- walled	Puddled adobe with some cobbles in east, west, and south walls.	Some visible on south wall	Approximately 50 cm	No information	No information	No information

Table 2.2. Wall Characteristics, cont'd.

Structure No.	Structure Description	Construction	Plaster	Wall Characteristics Height	Thickness	Condition	Other Features
				Northern Locus			
3	Rectangular, detached, adobe- walled	Puddled adobe with stones set in at intervals. One of the wall stones in the east wall was a broken metate fragment.	Very little	The east wall was 20 cm high, the south wall 31 cm, and the west wall 40 cm at highest point. Height from floor to top of wall cobbles was variable; East wall was 45 cm, south wall 47 cm, west wall 50 cm.	28 cm	Fair; many rodent holes	None
20	Rectangular, detached, adobe- walled	Puddled adobe, with stones placed randomly in the adobe at approximately the present ground surface.	None	No information	20 to 60 cm	A layer of adobe wall fall was encountered inside the east and west walls. The layers in both walls were vertical and probably represented upper portions of the walls that had slid down.	None
21	Three-sided rectangle, adobe walled; detached	Puddled adobe with stones in the three existing walls	No information	No information	No information	No information	No information
27a	Rectangular, adobe-walled; contiguous with Structures 27b & 28	Puddled adobe with rocks in all four walls.	Caliche plaster on eastern half of south wall	40 to 50 cm	40 to 60 cm	No information	Possible internal adobe wall buttresses were situated midway on south and north walls. They were about 2 m long and approximately 20 cm above floor level.
27b	Rectangular, adobe-walled; contiguous with Structures 27b & 28	Puddled adobe, with an occasional stone present. The northwest corner was bonded to the southwest corner of Structure 27a; the northeast corner abutted the southeast corner of Structure 27a.	Well-plastered areas on north wall.	Less than 75 cm above highest occupation surface.	The lower portions were thick, approximately 30 to 50 cm	No information	External wall buttresses occurred at the east and west walls.

Table 2.2. Wall Characteristics, cont'd.

Structure No.	Structure Description	Wall Characteristics: Construction	Plaster	Height	Thickness	Condition	Other Features
28	Rectangular, adobe-walled; contiguous with Structures 27b & 27b	Puddled adobe with stones at intervals of about 45 cm in east and west walls. The west wall abutted the northeast corner of Structure 27a; the south wall abutted the intersection of Structure 27a (southwest corner) and Structure 27b (northeast corner).	All walls showed signs of plastering and replastering	About 62 cm	38 to 100 cm	No information	Buttress extending from southeast corner.
29	Rectangular, detached, adobe- walled	Puddled adobe with stones in all four walls.	Plaster on south wall in excellent condition.	No information	No information	No information	No information
30	Rectangular, detached, adobe- walled	Puddled adobe, with a few walls tones. The northwest corner was eroded. The northeast and southeast corners were bonded and the southwest corner had abutting walls.	Plaster was mentioned in field notes. The entryway was also plastered.	90 cm	31 cm (east wall) to 65 cm (south wall)	No information.	No information
31a	Rectangular, adobe-walled; contiguous with Structure 31b	Puddled adobe; no stones were evident in walls. The southwest corner of the structure abutted the southeast corner of Structure 31b.	Visible near entryway on east side of south wall.	No information	North and west walls were 45 cm; east and south walls were 80 cm.	No information	No information
31b	Rectangular, adobe-walled; contiguous with Structures 31a & 31c	Puddled adobe, with stones in fill that may have been part of construction. The southeast corner of Structure 31b abutted the south wall of 31a; the southwest corner of Structure 31b abutted the south wall of 31c; the northeast corner of Structure 31b may have abutted the north wall of Structure 31a	No information	No information	North wall was 36 cm; east wall 45 cm, south wall 57 cm, west wall 35 cm	No information	No information
31c	Rectangular, adobe-walled; contiguous with Structure 31b	Puddled adobe with stones in fill that may have been part of wall construction. Southwest and northwest corners are bonded to west wall.	None noted	Average height is 58 cm above floor	East wall is 40 cm; south wall is 27 cm; north and west wall thicknesses unknown	No information	No information

Table 2.2. Wall Characteristics, cont'd.

Structure No.	Structure Description	Wall Characteristics Construction	Plaster	Height	Thickness	Condition	Other Features
				Southern Locus			
14	Nearly squar, detached, adobe- walled	Puddled adobe with stones inset between lower and upper walls. The adobe contained a large amount of very small, weathered pieces of stone. The thick walls had no grooves	None	40 to 70 cm	About 40 cm.	Some erosion probably occurred; ths structure is on a low rise in the wash.	No information
19a	Rectangular, detached, adobe- walled	Puddled adobe.	None	No information	25 cm	No information	None.
19b	Subrectangular, detached pit	No information	No information	No information	No information	No information	No information
				Northeastern Locus			
1	Subrectangu-lar, detached, adobe- walled	Puddled adobe with cobbles set into top of wall courses	In some places walls seemed to be smoothed, but not plastered	46 cm on average	23 cm at southeast corner	Some erosion of walls	A small hole at floor level extended into the north wall at the northeast corner. It did not appear to be a rodent hole, but was not otherwise defined.
22	Rectangular, detached, adobe- walled	Puddled adobe with stones set into walls. Courses were identified in the southeast corner. The lowest course was completely plastered from floor to top of course. Second course was thinner. Second course was finished with a rounded end and what appears to b e a plug set to fill the corner and join the south and east walls (Figure 2.29).	Many places had evidence of several layers of plaster	No information	No information	No information	None
40	Rectangular, detached, adobe- walled	Puddled adobe with wall stones in north and west walls. Walls were built in a trench cut into sterile caliche	Double wall or replastering on all but north wall.	No information	No information	No information	
41	Rectangular, adobe-walled; contiguous with Structure 42	Puddled adobe with stones in south and east walls.	No information	No information	No information	North and west walls were still solid.	No information

Table 2.3. Entry Characteristics.

Structure Number	Size	Shape and location	Features
		Compound Locus	
4	1.7 m long; 0.73 m wide	Bulbous with narrow neck, centered in north wall.	Post holes were associated with entry, indicating it was roofed. An adobe step occurs at the outer edge.
6	No information	Center of east wall	A vertical stone slab was located at the outer edge of the entry.
7	78 cm wide	Appended to center of south wall	Adobe threshold is 10 cm wide, 15 cm high.
8	40 cm wide, 30 cm deep	Appended to center of south wall.	Low threshold
17	65 cm wide, 78 cm deep	Short, round area appended to center of south wall	
		Central Locus	
5	70 cm wide, 22 cm deep	Semicircle appended to center of south wall	Curved walls
15	90 cm wide, 60 cm deep	Short, rectangular, appended to center of north wall.	
32	70 cm wide, 60 cm deep	Two short wall segments perpendicular to and appended to center of south wall	
33	No information	Two short wall segments perpendicular and appended to center of south wall.	
		Southwestern Locus	
2	55 cm wide, 55 cm deep	Niche centered in north wall that was lower than the rest of the wall.	
9	55 to 60 cm wide, 122 cm deep	Parallel walls appended to center of west wall	Slight (10 cm wide) threshold separating entry from structure interior.
10	60 cm wide, 50 cm deep	Simple opening in center of south wall	
11	70 cm wide, 60 cm deep	Short parallel walls appended to center of south wall.	Remains of two posts were visible against sides of the entry. A single stone was set in an adobe step. An upper step was probably also present.
12	North entry: 58 by 49 cm South entry: 60 cm wide, 35 cm deep.	Two entrances were present, both appended, short, and rectangular. One was in the center of the north wall and one in the center of the south wall.	The south entry had an adobe step that sloped down toward the interior of the house. The north entry was plugged by two puddled adobe chunks.
13	53 cm wide, 60 cm deep	Short and round, appended to center of south wall	Floor plaster continued into entry, which sloped down into house.
16	50 to 6 cm wide, 80 to 90 cm deep	Short and round, appended to center of south wall.	A single stone was set in an adobe step.
18	64 cm wide	Short and round, appended to center of south wall.	Rodent damaged. A small slate slab recovered from the probable entry may have been a step.
23	1.88 m long, 70 cm wide at house wall, 1.5 m at end	Short, rounded triangle appended to center of south wall	A 6cm high, 50 by 25 cm rectangular (adobe?) step.
24	66 cm wide, 60 cm deep	Appended to center of south wall, shape unknown.	
25	No information	Center of southwest side of structure, possibly appended.	
26	1 m wide	Simple opening in center of south wall	One step.

Table 2.3. Entry Characteristics, cont'd.

Structure Number	Size	Shape and location	Features
		Northern Locus	
3		Missing fourth wall is presumed entrance	
20	Plugged entry was 100 cm wide, 60 cm deep; South wall entry was 80 cm wide, 50 cm deep	Plugged entry identified in center of north wall; appended entry in center of south wall.	A large, tabular stone supported by smaller stones and surrounded by a thin adobe wall (?) Was found in the south wall entry. [Editorial note: The question mark regarding the thin adobe wall was in the original report.]
21		None	
27a	75 cm wide	Center of west wall, probably appended.	Entry flanked by standing wall rocks. Crescentic, 10-cm-high adobe step located directly outside of the entrance.
27b	66 cm wide	Simple opening in center of south wall.	Entry disturbed.
28	90 cm wide	Simple opening in south wall, 1 m from west wall. The north wall may have had a blocked entry.	
29	1.2 m wide, 1 m deep	Short, rectangular, appended to center of south wall.	Doorway was not cut completely to floor, so the lower part of the wall formed a threshold.
30	67 cm wide	Simple opening in center of south wall	The entry had a 21-cm-high adobe step. A slight adobe rise connected to the outside of the entry may have been a "rain stop."
31a	80 cm wide	Simple opening in center of south wall	Caliche step at interior edge of the entry. Stone slabs were found at the exterior (south edge) f the entry, one on top of the other.
31b	61 cm wide	Simple opening in center of south wall	No information
31C	67 cm wide	Simple opening in center of south wall	
		Southern Locus	
14	70 cm wide	Probably simple opening in center of west wall	
19a	65 cm wide	Short, rectangular, appended to center of north wall.	The entry had two steps, the first (adobe) 40 cm above the floor, the second (stone), 5 cm above the floor.
19b	Unknown, destroyed during excavation of 19a	Bulbous with a narrow neck in center of north wall	
		Northeastern Locus	
1	56 cm wide, 56 cm deep	Short, semicircular, appended to center of south wall.	An 18-cm-high adobe step was in the entry.
22	No information	Short, rectangular, appended to center of east wall	
40	70 cm wide, 50 cm deep	Short, rectangular, appended to center of south wall	
41	No information	Unknown	No information
42	70 cm wide, 60 cm deep.	Short, round, appended to southeast-facing wall	The entry was constructed by the application of a layer of adobe 3 to 5 cm thick to a shallow excavation into the native soil. The adobe layer was laid down like wall and floor plaster; it was not puddled. A single step of puddled adobe was present.

Table 2.4. Floor Features and Artifacts.

Structure	Floor Features				
No.	Hearth	Post Holes	Pits	Artifacts on Floor	Comments
			Compound Locus		
4	Round, basin type of prepared clay. Located directly south of the entrance. It had been partly destroyed by pot hunters.	Two in the center of the north-south axis of the structure. The western hole was 21 by 23 cm in diameter and 46 cm deep; the eastern hole was also 21 by 23 cm in diameter and 49 cm deep. Both post holes were plugged with adobe at the floor level. The western hole was also plugged about two-thirds of the distance below the top. The eastern hole contained an unfired adobe figurine at 32 cm below the floor. Two more possible post holes were outside the entry at its greatest width.	None	Tanque Verde Red-on-brown, corrugated, and plain ware sherds.	The floor was prepared, used, and replastered. There were at least two levels, each not more than 1 to 2 cm thick. Replastering was evident around the hearth.
6	Two hearths were present. The upper hearth was a conical to rounded pit scooped out of sterile soil. It was associated with the more recent floor. The lower hearth was a prepared, adobe-lined basin with a plastered area of floor surrounding it. Its location was not noted on the profile view.	Two pits along the central axis were identified as post holes. Three additional post holes were also noted.	Four storage pits were identified. A large, shallow pit adjacent to the south wall contained sherds, flakes, and a drill. A conical pit was overlain by a stone that may have been a cap.	Floor artifacts consisted of a deer jaw, a worked piece of turquoise, a tabular tool, a pestle, and two projectile points.	Two floors were present in this structure, although much of the floor was destroyed by pot hunting. Ledges at the base of the wall, slightly above the floor, were noted. Small patches of the floor were burned.
7	An irregular pit dug into sterile soil was located inside the entry in the usual hearth location. It may never have been prepared.	Two main post holes were identified along the east-west central axis of the structure. A number of small pits, especially in the southwest corner, may have held pots, but probably not for roof support.	Nineteen pits (post holes and storage pits) were found.	Most of a suprahemispherical Tanque Verde Red-on-brown bowl, a metate, a number of sherds, a core, a mano, and an undetermined number of projectile points were found on the floor.	The floor was prepared and fire-hardened. Plastering rose in a steep curve to meet all four walls. The floor was disturbed by roots in the northeast corner.
8	The round, basin-shaped, adobe-lined hearth was located about 1 m north of the entry; it was 20 cm in diameter and 12 cm deep.	Two post holes occurred along the central axis of the structure. Each was about 25 cm in diameter and between 40 and 50 cm deep.	One possible storage pit (or post hole) was found in the center of the house, north of the hearth. The pit was 22 by 32 cm in diameter and 20 cm deep.	Four reconstructible corrugated vessels (two jars and two bowls); burned bones from a mule deer, white-tailed deer, pronghorn, and bighorn sheep; a handstone, two trivet stones, and a tabular tool were found on the floor.	Well-prepared, fire-hardened. The floor rose in a sharp curve to meet the walls.

Table 2.4. Floor Features and Artifacts, cont'd.

Structure	Floor Features				
No.	Hearth	Post Holes	Pits	Artifacts on Floor	Comments
17	The hearth was a prepared, basin-shape with a relatively flat bottom. It was adobe-lined, 25 cm in diameter and 15 cm deep.	One large and several small pits were found. The large pit, in the northeast corner, had been "prepared." With the exception of two small, nearly contiguous pits in the southeast corner, the other pits were probably rodent holes.	Two post holes were located along the central axis of the structure. A polishing stone was found in one of the pits.	Pieces from a McDonald Corrugated bowl and three Tanque Verde Red-on-brown bowls were found on the floor, along with two nether stones, an abrader, and an arrowshaft straightener.	The floor was prepared adobe that curved up to meet the walls.
			Central Locus		
5	The hearth was directly north of the entry. It was circular, 50 to 55 cm in diameter and 8 cm deep.	Two post holes were found along the central axis of the structure. The western hole was disturbed by pot hunters. The eastern hole was 34.5 by 40 cm in diameter and 59.6 cm deep, with a narrow, lower hole that was 22.5 cm in diameter.	No pits were found	None recorded.	The floor was in excellent condition where preserved. Pot hunters had dug through the floor along the entire length of the northern wall.
15	None found.	Two probable post holes were located along the central axis of the structure. They were in the area of root damage and not well defined. Some charcoal fragments were observed in the west hole.	None, although three shallow depressions served as rests for large, round-bottomed storage jars.	Field notes describe portions of 4 large plain ware jars, 11 corrugated vessels, 8 painted vessels (probably Tanque Verde Red-on-brown) and 1 complete jar on the floor. A tabular tool of greenish slate or shale was recorded as being on the floor, as were two shell pendants and portions of two shell frogs.	The floor was a thick layer of adobe on top of caliche. It sloped up to meet the wall. It was badly damaged in the eastern half due to root activity and pot hunting.
32	The hearth was inside the entry; it was 15 cm in diameter and 10 cm deep.	Two post holes were located along the central long axis of the structure. The western hole was 28 cm in diameter and 48 cm deep; the eastern hole was 46 cm in diameter and 58 cm deep.	One pit was found in the northwest quadrangle of the structure. It was 48 cm in diameter and 25 cm deep.	A slate spindle whorl, two projectile points, two shell bracelet fragments, and sherds were found either on or just above the floor.	No information.
33	Inside entryway	Eleven post holes were noted on a sketch map. One post hole was along the central long axis of the structure. There was a burned are in the location where a second major post hole would be expected. Six post holes in the southeastern quadrant could have provided support for a bench or other raised structure.	None	These artifacts were recovered from the floor or immediately above the floor: two shell beads, one bone awl, a stone sphere, a slate knife, a ground stone knife, a piece of worked slate with red pigment, a metate fragment, a "microcardium" bead, a deer mandible fragment, a projectile point, hammerstones, a m, sherds and bones.	Two rock clusters were noted as being on the floor. Each contained one or more hammerstones as well as unmodified rocks.

Table 2.4. Floor Features and Artifacts, cont'd.

Structure No.	Floor Features: Hearth	Floor Features: Post Holes	Floor Features: Pits	Artifacts on Floor	Comments
			Southwestern Locus		
2	Round with prepared lip on eastern edge, directly south of entrance. The inside diameter was 0.32 cm, outside diameter is 0.43 cm. Hearth was dug into sterile soil.	Two post holes along central axis of structure. The western hole was 27 cm in diameter, the eastern hole 37 cm diameter	None	One whole mano; quartz polishing stone; 1 metate fragment; cluster of chalcedony and jasper flakes and shell pendant; overturned metate with chipped edges; Tanque Verde Red-on-brown bowl fragments.	Fire-reddened areas and extensive quantities of charcoal were found on the floor near the entry.
9	Hearth was east of entry, approximately 20 cm in diameter, 10 cm deep; bottom was crumbly.	Two post holes were located along central axis of structure. Northern hole was 30 cm in diameter and was 35 cm deep; southern hole was 15 to 40 cm diameter and 50 cm deep. A large rim sherd from a Tanque Verde Red-on-brown bowl was found in northern hole approximately 15 to 25 cm below floor. Sherd and piece of *Glycymeris* shell ground to a point at one end found in base of southern post hole.	None	Three large sherd clusters on floor in center of house, between the two post holes. Largest cluster consisted of 424 plain ware sherds. Other pottery identified as Tanque Verde Red-on-brown and obliterated corrugated, plus two sherds of Cibola White wares. Also found on floor were smaller sherd clusters,, a mano, a tabular tool, a pecking stone, a flake, a juvenile *Glycymeris* fragment with perforated umbo; and pieces of malachite.	Two floors were evident, separated by 4 cm; replastered several times.
10	Deep, straight-sided with round bottom. The hearth was clay-lined and well smoothed with an apron of prepared clay around the hearth. It is similar to the south hearth in Structure 12.	Two post holes were found along the central axis of the structure	One large, deep pit was found near the southwest corner, possibly used for storage	Numerous ground stone artifacts including two hammerstones; 7 tabular tools, 1 handstone, 1 polishing stone, 1 open trough metate, 7 manos. In addition a small, perforated pie of quartzite in the shape of a bird, a stone bead, and a schist spindle whorl were found. A large, thin stone slab with a small depression on one surface was found between the two post holes. A reworked Tanque Verde Red-on-brown bowl was also found.	The metate found on the floor rested on an ashy layer. The lower end rested on two hammerstones that were on the floor; the high end was set on two manos stacked on one another.

Table 2.4. Floor Features and Artifacts, cont'd.

Structure	Floor Features				
No.	Hearth	Post Holes	Pits	Artifacts on Floor	Comments
11	Two hearths were present, both in line with the entry. Each was about 20 cm in diameter. One was 10 cm deep, the other 7 cm deep. Both were surrounded by an oval area of floor that had either slumped or was worn away.	Two post holes occur along the central axis of the structure. One contained the post mold of the original post The mold consisted of soft soil surrounded by hard-packed fill. It extended 20 cm above the floor. The other post hole contained 4 rocks (one a mano) stacked against the eastern wall of the hole. The post hole with the mold was 38 cm in diameter and 50 cm deep; the hole with rocks was oval, 40 by 25 cm in size and 51 cm deep. A quartz crystal reportedly came from one post hole	Two large pits occurred on the east wall; several smaller ones were also found. One pit had a layer of sherds at 28 cm depth from a large sherd placed in the pit with the outer surface down. The pit also contained a spindle whorl.	Trough metate to the west of the door, in approximately the same location as the metate in Structure 10. Other floor artifacts included part of a Tanque Verde Red-on-brown bowl, two small turquoise artifacts, a tabular tool, a pestle, a pot anvil, a lapstone, 5 manos, a mao fragment, a shell ring, a fragment of a shell animal.	The floor curved up to the wall; considerable rodent damage in the northeast, southeast, and southwest corners.
12	Two hearths, each in line with entry. The north heath was 20 cm deep, straight-sided, with a flat bottom. The southern hearth was 20 cm deep, straight-sided, with a rounded bottom	Two post holes were located along the central axis of the house. The western post hole contained charred and rotted wood.	One pit in southeastern corner; use unknown.	One complete Tanque Verde Red-on-brown bowl; 90 % of a plain ware jar; an unfired Tanque Verde Red-on-brown jar (Figure 2.14); pieces of red ocher and hematite; a piece of kaoline with ground facets; a lump of clay on a plain ware sherd that had been reworked into a plate. Eight tabular tools, one tabular tool fragment, 3 manos, 1 mano fragment, 3 polishing stones, a metate fragment, a plane, a nether stone, and two spindle whorls were also found.	Well smoothed floor. Pottery making is indicated by the assemblage found in this house.
13	Two hearths. Upper hearth was Ill-defined and nearly destroyed by pot hunters. A reddened, unlined depression with ash and pebbles was all that was left. Lower hearth had double shape as if one hearth had been placed inside the other.	Two post holes occur along the central axis of structure. One contained a modeled spindle whorl.	One small pit was noted adjacent to the lower hearth.	Sherds, 1 whole mano, 1 mano fragment; a few pieces of chipped stone; two pieces of glazed stoneware jar left by pot hunters.	Floor identified by associated sherds rather than a hard surface. Two floors apparently with upper floor 5 to 10 cm higher than lower floor.
16	One hearth, 20 cm in diameter, 15 cm deep, most of bottom was missing; Apron was present.	Two post holes were present along the east-west central axis of the structure.	None	A reconstructible corrugated jar is the only piece listed as on the floor.	Floor well-smoothed and in excellent condition except where slightly disturbed by rodents in the southwest corner.

Table 2.4. Floor Features and Artifacts, cont'd.

Structure No.	Floor Features: Hearth	Post Holes	Pits	Artifacts on Floor	Comments
18	Badly preserved or disturbed hearth was 30 cm diameter, 10 cm deep	Two post holes were found along central axis of structure	1 medium-sized, possibly prepared pit in northeast quadrant. A small hole, possibly bell-shaped in form was near the western post hole	Two complete Tanque Verde Red-on-brown bowls; 4 manos, 2 tabular tools; and a large magnetite and hematite cobble used as a hammer stone.	Floor in poor condition except for area around hearth and the post holes; western half disturbed by rodents; eastern half by pot hunters.
23	One hearth in line with entry; 40 cm diameter, depth unknown. May have had a figure-eight shape, indicating remodeling.	Two post holes along east-west axis of house, a third posthole was in the northeast corner.	One ash pit in poor condition near the center of the house, measuring 80 by 25 cm. Two small storage pits, approximately 45 cm in diameter, were found in the west-central portion of the house.	Three projectile points found on the lower floor.	Two floors, upper one in poor condition, with disintegrated plaster and rodent activity. Lower floor was in variable condition.
24	One hearth in the east side of the southwest quad. The hearth was roughly circular, 25 cm in diameter and 15 cm deep; lined with adobe.	Four post holes formed a rectangle toward the interior of the structure	None	Debitage, 15 hammerstones, pieces from 18 vessels in floor fill and on floor.	Hard-packed earth; one section in the northeast corner showed signs of plastering.
25	No information	Two postholes, one in northeast quadrant, one in southwest. The one in the northeast 1/4 was twice the size of the one in the southwest.	No information	Parts of a painted bowl, base of a large corrugated, stuccoed jar. three whole or partial manos, and two tabular tools. A T-shaped stone was found under the upper floor and a stone spindle whorl and shell pendant were on the lower floor.	Two floors about 5 cm apart.
26	One hearth inside entry, 23 cm diameter, 9.2 cm deep	None recorded	None.	3 manos, 3 projectile points, 1 hammer stone, 1 shell ring, shell bracelet fragment sin floor and floor fill contexts.	Possibly 2 floors about 5 cm apart
			Northern Locus		
3	None	Two post holes. South post was 44 cm deep and 24 cm in diameter; north post was 37 cm deep and 25 cm in diameter	None	Nothing directly associated with level thought to be floor.	No prepared floor was found; floor area was clay-like soil mixed with caliche, uneven.
20	Located on north side of house in line with plugged entry, hearth was irregularly shaped; about 25 cm in diameter and 10 cm deep	A single post hole found on west side of central axis of structure; 20 cm diameter, 60 cm deep.	One small, circular subfloor pit in the northeast corner	At least 3 manos and one cluster of hammerstones found on floor (not analyzed)	

Table 2.4. Floor Features and Artifacts, cont'd.

Structure	Floor Features				
No.	Hearth	Post Holes	Pits	Artifacts on Floor	Comments
21	None	None	Roughly circular concentration of fire-cracked rock in northern half, 80 cm diameter, 35 cm deep; upper fill sandy with artifacts, lower ashy with charcoal	One partial storage jar, sherd clusters, and a cluster of manos were noted on the floor.	Prepared adobe floor in southern 3/4 of structure
27a	Approximately 1.75 m inside (east) of entrance; irregular oval shape, caliche or hardened adobe; Hearth was 60 cm diameter and 20 cm deep.	None	None	One large metate, 1 mano, 1 mano fragment, 1 tabular tool fragment, ½ of a Tanque Verde Red-on-brown bowl, 2 hammer stones, bone awl or hairpin fragment, long bone fragment with groove and polish.	Hard-packed dirt/adobe with some caliche plastering
27b	Circular, clay-lined depression inside entry	Two post holes along central axis of structure; 33 and 35 cm in diameter. A third post hole was a few cm below the western post hole, suggesting a lower occupation surface.	1 small, circular clay-line depression in northeast corner, 14 cm diameter, 8 cm deep	1 human burial, artiodactyl skulls and bones, 4 vessel with flakes and polishing stones, 2 manos, 3 tabular tool fragments, 1 stone ax, 1 lapstone; 1 handstone, 1 engraved shell bracelet, turquoise pendant. fragment	Hard-packed clay mixed with sand and caliche.
28	Upper floor: ash pit 20 cm in diameter, 7 cm deep; lower hearth not noted.	1 possible post hole 3 cm in diameter, 5 cm deep	One depression in lower floor, 45 cm diameter, 10 cm deep.	No artifacts on upper floor. Circle of rocks and pit with 3 mano fragments on lower floor.	Two floors: Upper floor plastered in east-central portion; lower floor thick and plastered.
29	Circular, inside entry	9 possible post holes	Two possible subfloor pits	1 metate fragment, 4 manos, 1 obsidian flake, 1 "knife blank," chipped stone flakes; 3 sherd clusters. Artifacts recorded as "floor and floor fill" include 29 hammerstones, 1 hammer stone fragment, 74 pieces debitage, 2 cores, 1 projectile point, 2 unifaces, 1 stone disk fragment, 3 lapstones, 1 loadstone fragment, 7 mano fragments, 2 polishing stones, 1 netherstone fragment.	Floor level not well defined, although it may have made as many as 3 floors. First and second floors were overlain by charcoal.
30	Inside entryway, 21 cm diameter, 11 cm deep with adobe collar and ash.	Two post holes were located along the central axis; western post hole had adobe collar; both had charred wood. Eight additional post holes (5 cm in diameter) also occurred.	None	Potsherds, 1 tabular tool, 1 tabular tool fragment, 75 bone and antler fragments.	4-cm thick adobe floor

Table 2.4. Floor Features and Artifacts, cont'd.

Structure	Floor Features				
No.	Hearth	Post Holes	Pits	Artifacts on Floor	Comments
31a	Inside entryway, 48 by 68 cm diameter, 12 to 22 cm deep	Two major post holes along central axis; west hole was 58 by 44 cm in diameter, 37 cm deep; east hole was 48 cm diameter, 54 cm deep. Twenty-one additional post holes from 13 to 32 cm diameter and 14 to 47 cm deep. Several were arranged in rows and around interior perimeter, suggesting bench supports.	1 oval pit, 40 by 46 cm in diameter, 37 cm deep.	Not clear if artifacts were on floor or in fill.	
31b	Inside entryway, 37 cm diameter, 8 cm deep; burned clay lining.	Two major post holes along central axis of structure, west post hole 19 cm diameter and 62 cm deep; east post hole 23 cm diameter and 40 cm deep. Two possible small post holes near west wall.	Possible pit in southeast corner, may be a rodent burrow	Sherds from vessels that were resting on floor.	Compact dark, gray soil.
31C	None identified	One possible post hole, about 11 cm deep in northwest quadrangle plus 3 holes in southeast quadrangle; two of these were 16 cm deep, one 21 cm deep.	Holes in southeast quadrant may be pits rather than post holes.		Not identified
			Southern Locus		
14	Directly east of entry, 30 cm diameter and 10 cm deep.	Two post holes along central axis of structure; northern hole is 25 cm diameter and 45 cm deep; southern hole is 11 cm diameter and 25 cm deep.	None inside structure. A basin-shaped pit with charcoal and fire-cracked rock was located just outside entry.	Deer mandible, 4 hammerstones, 1 mano, 1 handstone fragment, 1 red ware bowl with smudged interior, 1 handle from plain ware vessel.	Gravelly material similar to walls
19a	Hearth was about 1 m north of central post holes; 35 cm diameter, 8 cm deep.	Two main post holes along central axis; east hole was 22 to 27 cm diameter, west hole 25 cm diameter	Three listed, no further information; see Figure 2.23 for other holes shown in figure.	8 reconstructible and whole (Tanque Verde Red-on-brown and corrugated) bowls, 1/3 of another bowl; several projectile points, 1 ax fragment, 1 mano, 1 abrader, 1 loadstone, 1 pestle, 2 bone awls, obsidian flakes, polishing stone with red coloring, red quartzite piece with ground corner, igneous stone with polishing facets, red ocher, flake clusters; 3 ½ pronghorn or deer mandibles, 4 antlers, 1 scapula, teeth, pronghorn skull, "string" of rabbit innominates, other assorted artiodactyl bone. (Bones not analyzed as part of Faunal analysis because they were not available.)	Floor was replastered several times; 5 cm thick; floor assemblage appears to have been staged.

Table 2.4. Floor Features and Artifacts, cont'd.

Structure	Floor Features				
No.	Hearth	Post Holes	Pits	Artifacts on Floor	Comments
19b	Directly south of entry, 14.5 cm deep, 30 cm diameter	Two major post holes in approximately same location as 19a. East post hole was 37 cm diameter, west hole was 35 cm diameter; 8 small post holes in western part of floor, 6 in two rows of three near front and back walls suggesting use as benches.	None found	None found	
			Northeastern Locus		
1	Round with a slightly raised rim, 20 cm diameter, 23 cm deep, 93 cm north of entrance	One possible post hole in center of floor	One small hole at floor level extended into north wall of northeast corner	1 slate spindle whorl.	Well plastered ans smoothed, heavily cracked. House was vandalized.
22	Oval, 30 by 20 cm	Two post holes, 25 and 15 cm diameter along long axis of structure	Two irregular pits, one immediately below hearth.	No information on whether artifacts were on floor.	Well made
40	Inside entryway, 2 hearths. Lower hearth was level with floor and made of finely fired clay. Upper hearth was built directly in lower hearth and slightly elevated above floor.	Two large post holes along central axis of structure	Three small holes shown on map of house, one in southwest corner, one in southeast, one near north wall in center of structure.	No information on whether artifacts were on floor.	Puddled adobe poured onto sterile caliche.
41	No information	No information	No information	One worked slab of green slate; 1 jasper biface.	Badly disturbed
42	Constructed by burying a Tanque Verde Red-on-brown bowl into the floor so rim was even with floor. Vessel was not burned on interior, indicating little or no use as hearth.	Two post holes along central long axis. West hole has caliche at bottom; east hole has flat cobble as base. Adobe was poured around post in east hole. Rodent disturbed	None	One Tanque Verde Red-on-brown bowl, 1 Tanque Verde Red-on-brown jar, 1 plain ware jar, 1 plain obliterated corrugated jar; 1 metate.	Smoothed adobe, 2 to 5 cm thick.

Table 2.5. Samples from Structures.

Structure Number	Type of Sample: Pollen	Ethnobotanical	Archaeomagnetic	Tree-ring	Other
			Compound Locus		
4	Four from stratigraphic column: One each from upper fill, lower fill, adobe layer, and floor	None noted	None noted	None noted	None noted
6	None noted	None noted	Adjacent to entry step = A.D. 1245 +/- 33	None noted	None noted
7	Two: one each from under sherd clusters 4 and 5 on floor	Roof area: reeds, saguaro callus material and wood, agave or yucca stalk.	None noted	Six: 5 mesquite, 1 juniper; none dateable	None noted
8	Unknown number taken	None noted	None noted	Ten: 5 ponderosa pine, 3 pinyon pine, 1 juniper, 1 mesquite. One pinyon sample (WTR-32) dated to A.D. 1242 vv	None noted
17	Samples taken from two jars in pits just outside southeastern corner of structure.	Twelve ponderosa pine charcoal, none dateable	None noted	None noted	None noted
			Central Locus		
5	None noted	None noted	Hearth = A.D. 1350 +/- 44	None noted	None noted
15	One sample, not analyzed.	Samples from jars and from house fill include hackberry, corn, beans, cholla buds, and reeds. Material may have been in jars, but house had been vandalized.	None noted.	Twelve samples: 3 juniper, 6 pinyon pine; 2 ponderosa pine, 1 mesquite. Combined sample from one beam WTR-56, 57, 63 =A.D. 1226++ vv; WTR-62 = A.D. 1232 vv; WTR-64 = A.D. 1239 +vv	None noted
32	None noted	None noted	None noted	None noted	None noted
33	None noted	None noted	None noted	None noted	Soil samples taken at 10-cm intervals
			Southwestern Locus		
2	None noted	None noted	Hearth = A.D. 1250 +/- 45	None noted	None noted
9	Eleven samples from floor including from under a mano and a metate fragment.	None noted	None noted	None noted	None noted
10	From hearth and beneath a couple of beams.	None noted	Hearth = A.D. 1250 +/- 17	Twelve samples: 8 ponderosa pine, 4 juniper. Three ponderosa pine dates: WTR-1 = A.D. 1234vv; WTR-9 = A.D. 1237r; WTR-35 = A.D. 1231vv	None noted
11	Samples from "locus of significant artifacts," from 2 stratigraphic profiles, and from 2 floor pits.	None noted	None noted	Ten samples: 2 ponderosa pine accessioned by Tree-Ring Lab, not dated. Pinyon pine =A.D. 1246r	None noted

Table 2.5. Samples from Structures, cont'd.

Structure Number	Type of Sample: Pollen	Ethnobotanical	Archaeomagnetic	Tree-ring	Other
12	None noted	None noted	South entry = A.D. 1235 +/1 13 Unspecified = A.D. 1225 +/- 18	Two: 1 mesquite, 1 juniper. Identified by Tree-Ring Lab, but not accessioned or kept.	None noted
13	None noted	Charcoal samples for species identification. Tree-Ring Lab identified both (WTR-22 and WTR-26) as mesquite. WTR-22 sample crumbled and was discarded.	None noted	None noted	None noted
16	None noted	None noted	Hearth = A.D. 1250 +/15	Seven samples: 6 pinyon,1 ponderosa. One pinyon samples: WTR-67 = A.D. 1246r	None noted
18	None noted	None noted	None noted	Two juniper samples, not dated	None noted
23	At least one sample from fill	None noted	None noted	Several charcoal chunks, none dated	None noted
24	None noted	None noted	None noted	None noted	None noted
25	Samples from under sherd clusters (one in entry) and from under T-shaped stone.	Charcoal from upper fill; mesquite post from southwest quad, juniper post from southeast quad; samples were apparently not sent to Tree-Ring Lab; location of specimens not known.			
26	One sample from beneath sherd on floor; 1 from bottom of hearth.	None noted	None noted	None noted	None noted
			Northern Locus		
3	"Pollen Sample 3" from sherd cluster just above floor.	One chunk of wood from north post hole.	None noted	None noted	None noted.
20	Four: 1 from upper fill, 1 from lower fill, 1 from floor, 1 from south hearth.	None noted.	None noted	None noted	None noted
21	Samples from rock-filed pit in floor, from under two manos on floor and from under plain ware jar sherds.	None noted	None noted	None noted	None noted
27a	One: location not specified.	None noted	None noted	None noted	Three soil samples.
27b	None noted	Charcoal samples	None noted	None noted	None noted
28	None noted	None noted	None noted	None noted	None noted
29	None noted	Charcoal samples from post holes; possible charred pine needles from floor; log sample. None analyzed.	None noted	None noted	Soil samples from post holes

Table 2.5. Samples from Structures, cont'd.

Structure Number	Type of Sample: Pollen	Ethnobotanical	Archaeomagnetic	Tree-ring	Other
30	Samples taken, location not specified.	Charcoal samples	None noted	None noted	Soil samples
31a	None noted	Thirteen charcoal samples	None noted	None noted	Adobe plaster; 3 soil samples, 3 pieces of bone.
31b	None noted	Numerous charcoal samples.	None noted	One beam sampled, not analyzed or submitted to Tree-Ring Lab.	Numerous soil samples, not analyzed.
31C	None noted	None noted	None noted	None noted	None noted
			Southern Locus		
14	None noted	Reed fragments	None noted	Eighteen: 17 ponderosa pine, 1 juniper, none datable.	None noted
19a	Forty-four samples: locations included wall profiles, floor, inside vessels, below vessels, and center of hearth.	Charred seeds from lower fill (not analyzed)	None noted	Six ponderosa pine beams: WTR-94 = A.D. 1236vv; WTR-96: A.D. 1210vv; WTR-100 = A.D. 1234vv; WTR-101 = A.D. 1245v; WTR-112 = A.D. 1233vv; WTR-114 = A.D. 1239vv. WTR-101 thought to be cutting date.	None noted
19b	None noted	None noted	None noted	None noted	None noted
			Northeastern Locus		
1	None noted	None noted	None noted	None noted	None noted
22	None noted	None noted	None noted	None noted	None noted
40	None noted	None noted	None noted	None noted	None noted
41	None noted	None noted	None noted	None noted	None noted
42	None noted	Charcoal samples	None noted	None noted	Soil samples, one from inside a Tanque Verde Red-on-brown jar; roofing adobe samples

Note: Archaeomagnetic dates are considered tentative. See Chapter 11 for further explanation.

Key: + = one or two rings missing near the end of the ring series.

++ = Ring count near the end of the ring series; unknown number of rings missing.

vv = Sample lacks the attributes of cutting date; unknown number of rings missing.

v = Considered to be cutting date but lacking diagnostic attributes.

r = Cutting date; outer ring is consistent around arc of circumference of sample.

Chapter 3

Ceramics

Linda M. Gregonis

Ceramics were the most common artifacts found at Whiptail Ruin. More than 90,000 potsherds and 63 whole or partial vessels were collected during excavations at the site. Table 3.1 lists the types of pottery recovered. As a whole, the assemblage is characteristic of sites in the northeastern Tucson Basin and the adjacent San Pedro Valley that date to the A.D. 1200s. At Whiptail, corrugated and other textured sherds make up 13 percent of the assemblage and decorated wares make up 25.6 percent. Most of the decorated sherds (25.3%) are Tanque Verde Red-on-brown (including black paint and white-slipped variants). These percentages are similar to those found at the nearby Gibbon Springs site, which also contains a high percentage (15.5%) of corrugated and textured sherds and 26 percent decorated wares (Gregonis 1996:239). In addition to locally manufactured Tanque Verde Red-on-brown pottery, the ceramic assemblage from Whiptail Ruin contains trade wares that date to the A.D. 1200s including black-on-white sherds and vessels from above the Mogollon Rim and polychromes from the middle and upper Santa Cruz Valley. A few pre-Classic (pre-A.D. 1150) sherds were also found, as were some late Classic (post-A.D. 1300) polychromes and black-on-red sherds. Worked sherds recovered from the site include perforated and unperforated disks, sherds from large vessels that were reworked into plates or bowls, and an assortment of sherds with one or more ground edges. Five figurine fragments, three modeled spindle whorls, a cylindrical bead, and a cone-shaped object round out the ceramic assemblage.

Analytic Methods

The information in this chapter was compiled from several inventories and analyses that have been done over the years. During the 1960s and 1970s whole and diagnostic artifacts were routinely catalogued into the Arizona State Museum system. I used information from the museum's catalog cards in various tables in this chapter.

The first sorting and analysis of ceram-

Table 3.1. Summary of Pottery Types and Wares: Sherds and Minimum Number of Vessels.

Pottery Types and Wares	Sherds		Minimum Number of Vessels	
	Number of Sherds	% of Assemblage	Number of Vessels	% of Assemblage
Tucson Basin Decorated Wares				
Rillito Red-on-brown	3	< 0.01	2	0.4
Rincon Red-on-brown	99	0.1	27	5.0
Late Rincon or Early Tanque Verde Red-on-brown	0	0	1	0.2
Tanque Verde Red-on-brown	24194	24.8	105	19.8
Tanque Verde Red-on-brown with white slip	415	0.4	39	7.4
Tanque Verde Black-on-brown	143	0.1	25	4.7
Tanque Verde Black-on-white	9	<0.01	3	0.6
Rincon Polychrome	3	<0.01	3	0.6
Tanque Verde Polychrome	15	0.02	1	0.2
Total, Tucson Basin Decorated Wares	*24881*	*25.5*	*206*	*38.9*
Other Southern Arizona Decorated Wares				
Topawa Red-on-brown	2	<0.01	1	0.2
Trincheras Purple-on-red	1	<0.01	1	0.2
San Carlos Red-on-brown	23	0.02	5	1.0
Casa Grande Red-on-buff	5	<0.01	3	0.6
Possible Nogales Polychrome	1	<0.01	1	0.2
Sahuarita Polychrome	2	<0.01	3	0.6
Santa Cruz Polychrome	3	<0.01	1	0.2
Pinto Polychrome	2	<0.01	1	0.2
Gila Polychrome	3	<0.01	1	0.2
Total, Other Southern Arizona Decorated Wares	*42*	*0.04*	*17*	*3.4*
Central and Northeastern Arizona Decorated Wares				
Wingate Black-on-red	1	<0.01	1	0.2
St. Johns Black-on-red	3	<0.01	1	0.2
St. John's Polychrome	1	<0.01	1	0.2
Roosevelt Black-on-white	3	<0.01	2	0.4
Cibola Whiteware	29	0.03	14	2.6
Puerco Black-on-white	2	<0.01	1	0.2
Tularosa Black-on-white	0	0	3	0.6
Reserve-Tularosa Black-on-white	25	0.03	3	0.6
Pinedale Black-on-white	0	0	1	0.2
Snowflake or Tularosa Black-on-white	4	<0.01	2	0.4
Unclassified black-on-white	3	<0.01	2	0.4
Total, Central and Northeastern Arizona Decorated Wares	*71*	*0.07*	*31*	*6*

Table 3.1. Summary of Pottery Types and Wares: Sherds and Minimum Number of Vessels, cont'd.

Pottery Types and Wares	Sherds		Minimum Number of Vessels	
	Number of Sherds	% of Assemblage	Number of Vessels	% of Assemblage
	Red Wares			
Rincon Red	1	<0.01	1	0.2
Gila Red	55	0.06	5	0.9
Sells Red	11	0.01	1	0.2
San Carlos Red	86	0.09	15	2.8
Local San Carlos Red	1	<0.01	1	0.2
Indeterminate red ware	0	0	1	0.2
Total, Red Wares	*154*	*1.5*	*24*	*4.5*
	Textured Wares			
MacDonald Corrugated	2	<0.01	3	0.6
Mogollon Corrugated	5	<0.01	4	0.7
Corrugated	12559	12.9	91	17.2
Corrugated with red slipped interior	1	<0.01	1	0.2
Incised	15	0.02	4	0.7
Corrugated and incised	30	0.03	6	1.0
Tooled	1	< 0.01	1	0.2
Corrugated and tooled	3	<0.01	1	0.2
Possible Playas Red incised	15	0.02	6	1.0
Incised red ware	1	<0.01	1	0.2
Stuccoed plain	3	<0.01	1	0.2
Total, Textured Wares	*12635*	*12.9*	*119*	*22.2*
	Plain Wares			
San Carlos Brown	514	0.53	31	5.9
Micaceous plain	171	0.17	18	3.4
Plain ware	59206	60.6	81	15.3
Total Plain Wares	*59891*	*61.3*	*130*	*24.6*
	Miscellaneous Other Wares			
Possible Mexican ware	1	<0.01	1	0.2
Possible Palomas Buff	1	<0.01	1	0.2
White slipped ware	10	0.01	--	0
Total, Miscellaneous Other Wares	*12*	*0.01*	*2*	*0.4*
Grand Total	**97686**	**100**	**529**	**100**

Note: The minimum number of vessels includes 63 whole or partial vessels, many of which were catalogued. The other 466 "vessels" were identified on the basis of sherd counts found in distinct proveniences (see Table 3.14 and Appendix 3.A). The total differs from that listed in Table 3.14 because surface-collected sherds and those not associated with features were not included in the counts for Table 3.14.

ics was done as part of a laboratory analysis class taught at the University of Arizona in the spring of 1973. As part of the class, students rough sorted and inventoried the pottery from the features they analyzed. Summaries of their analyses can be found in the Arizona State Museum archives files for Whiptail.

Bruce Bradley prepared brief "site" reports for features that he dug before he turned material back to various land owners. Information on the pottery from Structure 42 was extrapolated from one of these reports.

During the analysis efforts in the 1980s, Arizona Archaeological and Historical Society volunteers prepared forms that included information on pottery type or ware and vessel shape. With Sue Pereza's help, I used information from these forms to compile a computerized database.

Standardized Southwestern types were used for decorated and red wares where possible. If they could not be assigned to a type, a descriptive category was used. Plain, corrugated, and other textured wares were classified descriptively unless a particular type (e.g., McDonald Corrugated) could be assigned. Tanque Verde Red-on-brown pottery was subdivided into several styles, according to the color of the paint and presence or absence of a white to cream-colored slip. These styles are red-on-brown, red-on-brown with white slip, black-on-brown, and black-on-white (obviously not a true white ware, but a style with black paint on a white-slipped background). Brief descriptions of each pottery type or ware used are provided in Table 3.2.

Using the catalog card information and the information compiled on the database, I estimated the minimum number of vessels represented in the assemblage. The procedure follows one I used in analysis of the Gibbon Springs pottery (Gregonis 1996), where I assigned a minimum number of one vessel for each different pottery type or ware in a particular feature, adding to that number if more than one vessel form of a particular type was represented, and then accounted for the number of partially reconstructible or whole vessels from that feature. Sherds from different strata in a given feature were lumped together for the minimum count, unless it was very clear that the vessels from the upper levels represented different vessels from those in the floor and floor fill. For example, 1,991 sherds were recovered from Structure 3. They consist of four identifiable pottery types or wares (Tanque Verde Red-on-brown, Tanque Verde Red-on-brown with a white slip, corrugated, and plain ware) and three different vessel forms (bowl, jar, and indeterminate vessel forms) for a minimum of eight vessels: a Tanque Verde Red-on-brown bowl, a Tanque Verde Red-on-brown jar, one white-slipped Tanque Verde Red-on-brown bowl, a white-slipped Tanque Verde Red-on-brown jar, a corrugated bowl, a corrugated jar, a plain ware bowl, and one plain ware jar. The "indeterminate" category was not used in the minimum vessel count unless it represented the only occurrence of a pottery type or ware in a feature.

Due to the nature of the excavation and sometimes haphazard analysis afterwards, many vessels recognized in the field were not later catalogued as such. In those instances, if field notes and structure reports (as described in Chapter 2, this volume) seemed reliable, I adjusted the numbers of vessels accordingly. For example, according to sherd counts, Structure 15 contained a minimum of 14 vessels. The structure description states that the adobe-walled store room contained at least 23 vessels (including some with botanical remains). Comparison between the vessels described in the field and the types found in the sherd collection indicates that at least 11 more vessels were represented by the sherds, for a minimum total of 34 vessels.

In addition to the simple morphological

Table 3.2. Brief Descriptions of Pottery Types and Wares Used in This Report.

Pottery Type or Ware and References	Description
	Tucson Basin Decorated Wares
Rillito Red-on-brown (Kelly 1978)	This brown ware has surface colors ranging from gray-buff to buff and tends to be more muddy (i.e., less clearly fired) than Rincon Red-on-brown. Rillito Red-on-brown pieces tend to have a micaceous surface. Designs are fine lined and well controlled. The paint used is evenly mixed and tends to blend into the surface of the vessel more than later types. Overall or banded designs include repeated geometric elements, zoomorphs, and anthropomorphs, squiggly or zig-zag lines, line and stagger (alternating straight and squiggly or zig-zag line), curvilinear scrolls, and interlocking scrolls. Fringed lines are common. Vessels tend to be thin-walled; shapes include squat-bodied jars, flare-rim bowls with trailing lines, subhemispherical bowls, and scoops.
Rincon Red-on-brown (Kelly 1978)	Rincon Red-on-brown has an orange brown paste, usually with granitic or volcanic sand temper. The paste color tends to be less "muddy" than Rillito Red-on-brown and vessel walls tend to be thicker. The hematite paint used is sometimes thick and may be boldly or sloppily applied. Bowl interiors may be smudged. Vessels may have a white to cream slip in addition to the paint. Designs include curvilinear and rectilinear scrolls, parallel and squiggly lines, bold bull's eyes, and other elements. Some slightly flare-rimmed bowls have paired trailing lines and vessel rims are usually painted. Design layouts include quartering, offset quartering, banding, panels, and plaiting. Bowls are usually painted on the interior. Jars, especially during the Middle Rincon, may have sharply recurved (Gila) shoulders. Vessel forms include hemispherical bowls, scoops, large platters, jars with recurved shoulders and short, recurved necks, and miniature vessels.
Rincon or Tanque Verde Red-on-brown	Pottery identified in this intermediate category has characteristics of both Rincon and Tanque Verde Red-on-brown. The sherds are too small or the design area incomplete, so that they cannot clearly be assigned to Late Rincon or to Tanque Verde Red-on-brown.
Tanque Verde Red-on-brown (Kelly 1978)	This brown ware has a dull dark tan to bright orange paste with granitic or granitic-volcanic temper. The hematite paint is bright red to dark red and sometimes applied so thickly that it flakes off. Designs tend to be rectilinear and laid out in quartering or panels that are often offset 45 degrees to the rim of the vessel, giving a plaited or woven appearance. Bowls may be painted on the interior and exterior and jar necks are often painted with a separate design from the body of the vessel. Bowl forms include hemispherical, platter-like, or suprahemispherical with a slight restriction and outcurved neck at the top. Jars may be high necked, many have a low shoulder that angles into the base in a way that looks like the base was built separately from the top or that a puki-like form was used for the base. Vessel bases are sometimes flat or indented. Effigy forms are more common than in earlier periods.
Tanque Verde Red-on-brown with white slip	This pottery has a creamy colored to white slip. The slip can be watery and thin to thick. Except for the slip, the pottery has all of the characteristics of Tanque Verde Red-on-brown.

Table 3.2. Brief Descriptions of Pottery Types and Wares Used in This Report, cont'd.

Pottery Type or Ware and References	Description
	Tucson Basin Decorated Wares, cont'd.
Tanque Verde Black-on-brown	This pottery has a black (magnetite?) paint but is similar in all other ways to Tanque Verde Red-on-brown.
Tanque Verde Black-on-white	This pottery has black (magnetite?) paint and thin creamy to white slip that gives it the appearance of a northern Arizona black-on-white. The black-on-white effect is seen most often on the neck area of vessels. In other ways, the pottery is similar to Tanque Verde Red-on-brown.
Rincon Polychrome (Greenleaf 1975; Wallace 1986a, 1986b)	This red-slipped brown ware pottery is thought to have been manufactured primarily at the West Branch site in Tucson. Rincon Polychrome vessels have a thick red slip that may be fugitive, with chalky white paint used to define blocks of space. The white spaces have black paint that sometimes fades. Vessel shapes are primarily neckless jars and tall bowls with insloping sides. The paneled designs have elements similar to other Rincon phase pottery, but simplified. The use of hachuring is unusual for this time period.
Tanque Verde Polychrome (DiPeso 1956; Heidke 1995)	Like Tanque Verde Red-on-brown in most respects, Tanque Verde Polychrome incorporates red and black paint, often on a white-slipped background. The interiors may be scraped and smudged.
	Other Southern Arizona Decorated Wares
Topawa Red-on-brown (Withers 1941: 32-33)	This Papaguerian equivalent of Tanque Verde Red-on-brown has reddish brown to yellowish brown paste and polished surfaces. Temper includes granitic material and volcanic tuff particles. Design layouts resemble Tanque Verde Red-on-brown but are looser than and not as elaborate as Tucson Basin wares.
Trincheras Purple-on-red (Sauer and Brand 1931; Heckman 2000)	This pottery is characterized by a dense brown paste, often with a carbon core, dark red slips, and the use of red or purple paints. The purple paints are a deep blackish purple and sometimes have a glittery appearance due to use of specular hematite. The surface finish is often an even and uniform polish, sometimes with dimpling or a hammered appearance. Scoring using stiff grass stems on vessel interiors is also a distinctive trait.
San Carlos Red-on-brown (Hawley 1936)	This brown ware made in eastern central and southeastern Arizona is of coil and scrape manufacture. It is thin walled, well polished or burnished, often with smudged interiors. San Carlos Red-on-brown can be phyllite or sand tempered. The designs, usually on exterior, are panels set at an angle from the rim and include plaited panels similar to Tanque Verde Red-on-brown, but more finely executed and busier. Hemispherical and suprahemispherical bowls are the most common form.

Table 3.2. Brief Descriptions of Pottery Types and Wares Used in This Report, cont'd.

Pottery Type or Ware and References	Description
	Other Southern Arizona Decorated Wares, cont'd.
Casa Grande Red-on-buff (Gladwin and Gladwin 1933; Haury 1945)	This Gila Basin buff ware has vessel forms that are more limited than earlier Gila Basin types. They include hemispherical bowls, handled jugs or pitchers, tall-necked jars, and effigy vessels. Painted bowls are rare. The vessels are decorated with hematite paint over a white to cream slip. Designs include rectilinear geometric designs, often giving the effect of plaiting or weaving. The designs and elements, which are similar to Tanque Verde Red-on-brown, are usually smaller than elements found on Sacaton Red-on-buff. The paint is thin and yellowish compared to the hematite used in Sacaton Red-on-buff.
Nogales Polychrome (Heckman 2000: McGuire and Villalpando 1993:39)	This brown ware from northern Sonora and the upper Santa Cruz drainage has brown to yellow-brown or red-brown paste with a cream to white slip and purple and red paint. The paint and slip are not as chalky looking or feeling as on Babocomari Polychrome. Bowl forms predominate; these are painted primarily on the interior surface. The banded or quartered designs sometimes have a nested appearance. Curvilinear scrolls, bands or panels of diamond shapes (as found in Babocomari wares) are also common.
Sahuarita Polychrome (Deaver 1984:328)	This brown ware pottery resembles Rincon Red-on-brown on the exterior, but has a red-slipped interior. The red slip resembles that found on Rincon Red and Rincon Polychrome. Bowl forms predominate.
Santa Cruz Polychrome (Sauer and Brand 1931; McGuire and Villalpando 1993:41; Whittlesey and Heckman 2000:110)	This pottery resembles Babocomari and Nogales Polychrome, but has black and red designs painted over a thick white slip. Motifs are similar to Tanque Verde Red-on-brown. The slip on this pottery is often crazed.
Pinto Polychrome (Gladwin and Gladwin 1933; DiPeso 1958; Whittlesey and Heckman 2000:112)	Pinto Polychrome is characterized by a raspberry slip on the exterior surface of bowls and a chalky white slip with black paint on the interior. The black paint often appears gray and has blurred edges from being polished over, so that the black blends into the white slip in some instances. Design styles can be banded or quartered layouts with opposed solid and hachured scrolls and keys. The designs extend to the rim without an encircling rim band like that found in Gila Polychrome; framing lines and hachure are the same width.
Gila Polychrome (Haury 1945; DiPeso 1958)	This brown ware pottery has a red-slipped exterior. Bowls have interiors slipped white with bold black paint. Jars have a field of white slip with black paint—the black-on-white design is not integrated with the red slip on the exterior. The white paint is crisp and often crackled. Designs are broader lined than Pinto Polychrome. Interior bands at the rim are common in bowls.

Table 3.2. Brief Descriptions of Pottery Types and Wares Used in This Report, cont'd..

Pottery Type or Ware and References	Description
	Northern Arizona Decorated Wares
Wingate Black-on-red (Hays-Gilpin 1998:164)	This pottery has orange to pinkish paste, and a thick light to dark red or maroon slip that is often polished. The slip is soft and weathers to a chalky finish. It often exfoliates. The paint may be organic or mineral; edges are often fuzzy and the color varies from black to thin and brownish. Designs include opposed solid and oblique hachured elements, with hachured element larger than solid.
St. Johns Black-on-red (Hays-Gilpin 1998:168)	St. Johns Black-on-red has orange to red paste (when well oxidized) and an orange to red slip. It is sand tempered with occasional hematite and magnetite particles. Designs include opposed solid and hatched elements with hachured area being larger than the solid. Line work is finer and neater than Wingate Black-on-red; designs often resemble Tularosa Black-on-white.
St. John's Polychrome (Hays-Gilpin 1998:170)	This pottery has brown to brownish red (when underfired) to orange red paste and a thick polished orange to red slip. Designs include solid and oblique hachured designs on the inside with the hachured element larger than solid. The line work is finer and neater than Wingate Black-on-red; designs resemble Tularosa Black-on-white. Bowl exteriors have broad, white-lined designs. The black paint is a mineral-organic combination or mineral subglaze; the white paint is probably an iron-free clay.
Roosevelt Black-on-white (Gladwin and Gladwin 1931; Pomeroy 1962)	This black-on-white pottery is often found in association with Roosevelt Red wares. It is often found in jug form, has solid black elements and paste similar to black-on-white pottery from the Show Low area.
Cibola Whiteware (Hays-Gilpin 1998:59)	This black-on-white pottery has a mineral paint and sand or sherd temper. The paste may have a carbon streak. Early types have no slip; later types have slips that may be washy or thick.
Puerco Black-on-white (Hays-Gilpin 1998:77)	This white ware has a hard paste with a fine to medium texture. It has sherd and sand temper (sometimes black sand) and a light gray to white paste. Designs are drawn with black to dark brown, iron-based mineral paints. Designs include sets of vertical parallel lines or checkerboards used to divide panels of solid elements; negative lightning, dot-filled squares, and bold triangles also occur.
Tularosa Black-on-white (Hays-Gilpin 1998:89)	Tularosa Black-on-white has a hard paste and a vitrified, shattering fracture. The temper is fine and often nearly invisible crushed sherd or quartz sand. Sherd temper is often of a dark-paste white ware that looks gray against the white paste. The pottery is slipped and polished and has a matte black to brown, iron-based mineral paint. Motifs include curvilinear and rectilinear opposed bands of sold and hachured elements. Hatching is oblique with finer line widths and spacing than Reserve or Wingate Black-on-white. Where hatching meets at a corner, lines often cross to form small squares or diamonds. Tularosa Black-on-white has a thicker slip, better polish, and finer line work than Reserve Black-on-white.

Table 3.2. Brief Descriptions of Pottery Types and Wares Used in This Report, cont'd..

Pottery Type or Ware and References	Description
	Central and Northeastern Arizona Decorated Wares, cont'd.
Reserve-Tularosa Black-on-white (Hays-Gilpin 1998)	This white ware has a hard paste, coarse to vitrified fracture, white to light gray paste, and opposed solid and hachured elements. The framing lines usually have the same weight as hachure. There is not enough of the design to distinguish between fine-lined (Tularosa) and thicker-lined (Reserve) style
Pinedale Black-on-white (Hays-Gilpin 1998:98)	Pinedale Black-on-white has crushed sherd temper, a thick white slip, and a light gray to white paste. It has iron-based mineral black paint that contains other minerals and may resemble a flat glaze. Decorative motifs include solid elements or balanced solid and hatched elements, usually angular. Longitudinal hatching is frequent; cross-hatching also occurs.
Snowflake or Tularosa Black-on-white (Hays-Gilpin 1998)	This white ware has crushed sherd temper and fine sand. Sherds have solid stepped elements but not enough to determine if elements are opposed by solids (Snowflake) or hachure (Tularosa).
Unclassified black-on-white	These include white ware pottery with black paint that are too small or otherwise undistinguished to type any further.
	Red Wares
Rincon Red (Kelly 1978)	This Sedentary period red ware is found in the Tucson Basin and vicinity. It is characterized by a clear red slip that may become powdery and fugitive in weathering. The surface tends to pit and flake. Patterned polishing is common on the interior of deep, outcurved or hemispherical bowls (the characteristic form).The temper is most commonly granitic or granitic-volcanic sand particles.
Gila Red (Haury 1945, 1976)	Gila Red is a micaceous (schistose), thin-walled ware with a thin wash or slip. It is polished so that striations appear on the surface.
Sells Red (Scantling 1940)	Sells Red has a dark, reddish brown clay body with angular sand temper. The paste is generally coarse and it has a thick, brick red slip. Fire clouding is common. The finely spaced striated polishing marks run slightly oblique to vertical on the interior and exterior of bowls and horizontally around the rim. Vertical polishing marks are common on jars. Forms include deep flare- or outcurved-rim bowls, shallow bowls with thickened rims, short-necked globular jars with outflared, straight, or slightly insloping necks; neckless or "seed" jars. Bases are commonly indented, and shallow bowls may have lugs on the rim (making them a "bean pot" form).
San Carlos Red (Steen et al. 1962)	This red-slipped brown ware may have phyllite temper. Vessels are thin-walled and well polished (sometimes to a burnish). Vessels commonly have smudged interiors. In Tucson, some may be locally made, with granitic temper and a more red-orange color to paste.

Table 3.2. Brief Descriptions of Pottery Types and Wares Used in This Report, cont'd..	
Pottery Type or Ware and References	Description
	Red Wares, cont'd.
Local San Carlos Red	This variant has a brown ware paste with bright orangey red slip that sometimes has small dots of darker color in it. It is thin-walled and highly polished. It resembles San Carlos Red, but has granitic rather than phyllite temper.
	Textured Wares
MacDonald Corrugated (Bettison 1998; Colton and Hargrave 1937)	This brown ware is typically made in the Point of Pines region. It is usually tempered with quartz sand. Surface finishes can include clapboard and patterned indentations. The pottery is painted white with geometric designs in the patterned indentations on the vessel exterior. Bowl interiors are usually highly polished and smudged. Late McDonald Corrugated may have a brick-red slip on its exterior.
Corrugated (Gregonis 1996; Franklin 1980)	This brown ware pottery is coil-and-scrape manufactured, with outside surfaces manipulated to resemble corrugation. The corrugated lines may be simple horizontal lines (plain corrugation) or have indentations impressed at an angle to those lines (indented). Most of the corrugated pottery at Whiptail was locally manufactured and often paddled over its surface, which obscures the corrugation. This ware resembles Mogollon-area corrugated wares such as Reserve Corrugated.
Corrugated, red-slipped interior	This refers to corrugated pottery with a thick red slip on its interior. The slip may be polished over or smoothed, with a chalky feel.
Incised (includes Playas types) (Gregonis 1996, 2001a)	Incised pieces are created by drawing lines through the surface of the clay before it becomes leather hard. Lines may be carefully patterned, as in Playas Incised, or more random, with less even spacing or line width. The latter can be found on the upper bodies of small jars from the Tucson Basin and Upper Santa Cruz Valley.
Corrugated and incised	Corrugated and incised refers to corrugated pieces that have also been incised, either to emphasize a corrugated pattern or in a separate part of the vessel from the corrugation.
Tooled	Tooled pottery refers to pieces with punctation with a stick or other pointed tool.
Corrugated and tooled	These pieces have corrugation with punctate, finger-nail impressed, or other tooling in addition to the corrugation.
Incised red ware	These sherds have red slips and incisions that resemble Playas Red Incised or Reserve-style incised and corrugated pieces. They appear to be a local variant of those styles.
Stuccoed plain (Heidke and Elson 1988)	Stuccoed pieces have an uneven coating of clay brushed over an already fired surface. It is thought to keep a pot from cracking or exfoliating when heated.

Table 3.2. Brief Descriptions of Pottery Types and Wares Used in This Report, cont'd..

Pottery Type or Ware and References	Description
Plain Wares	
San Carlos Brown (DiPeso 1956)	San Carlos Brown is thought to have been made in the San Pedro Valley or slightly farther east. It is of coil and scrape manufacture and has a well-polished to burnished finish. Interiors of vessels are often smudged and usually occur as small bowl forms found in this area. The paste is a dark yellow brown, with fine sand or phyllite temper.
Micaceous plain ware	Micaceous plain ware has a brown ware paste that most often contains quartz-feldspar-mica or granitic temper. Mica is abundant on the surface of the vessel, but it may or may not be as abundant in the paste. Sherds may exhibit patterned polishing, but the temper does not appear to be different from other local plain wares except for the apparent amount of mica. Plain wares with micaceous surfaces are common in the northern and northeastern Tucson Basin.
Plain ware	Plain wares in the Tucson Basin have a brown ware paste and temper that ranges from quartz-feldspar-mica particles to granitic, to granitic-volcanic sands. The surface finish may be polished or hand smoothed and the surface color variable.
Miscellaneous Other Wares	
Mexican	One sherd of possible Mexican origin found at the site appears to have a red background with black paint and fine quartz, feldspar, and mica temper. It is harder fired and has a higher polish than pottery more commonly found in the area, but is too small to classify further.
Palomas Buff (Waters 1982:568)	This Patayan pottery has a yellowish-beige clay body with fine, rounded to subangular granitic sand temper. It has a soft, crumbly fracture and roughly smoothed surfaces that may or may not be wiped (Waters calls this a mopped finish). The pottery may have a scum-like slip. Forms include jars with outcurved (recurved) necks and globular bodies; jars with narrow, canteen-like necks; hemispherical and shallow bowls that may have outcurved tops or angled, low shoulders. Scoops also occur. Rim finishes may be round, square, or folded (reinforced or coiled).
White slipped ware	This category refers to unpainted brown ware that is slipped with a cream to white slip. Sherds with these characteristics may be an unpainted part of a decorated vessel.

analyses just described, samples of the pottery from Whiptail were used to perform one chemical analysis and one petrographic analysis. The chemical analysis was performed in the early 1980s by Carl F. Aten of Hobart and William Smith College (Appendix A). The goal of the analysis was to determine the similarities and differences among the pottery's clay bodies. The petrographic analysis was performed in the 1980s by James Lombard (Appendix B). His goal was to determine if the pottery could have been made on or near the Whiptail site. The results of their analyses are described briefly later in this chapter and can be read in full in Appendices A and B.

The Assemblage

Site Chronology and Distribution of Pottery

Pottery is often used to indicate the length of occupation at a site. At Whiptail, although the majority of the pottery dates to the early Classic period (ca. A.D. 1200 to 1300), sherds from earlier and later periods were also found. Tables 3.3 through 3.11 show the distribution of various pottery types and wares by feature.

A small amount of Sedentary period pottery, dating from A.D. 900 to A.D. 1150, occurs throughout the site (Table 3.3). A few sherds from the middle and upper Santa Cruz Valley also hint at use or occupation of the site during the Sedentary period (Table 3.4). One Trincheras Purple-on-red sherd was found on the surface of the site; a Sahuarita Polychrome sherd was found in the fill of Structure 25; three Santa Cruz Polychrome sherds occurred in Structure 2; and one Nogales Polychrome sherd was found in Structure 4. In addition, a few pre-Classic sherds have also been found in the portion of the site underlying Agua Caliente Park (Gregonis 2001b). The numbers of Rincon Red-on-brown sherds (n = 99) may indicate an actual occupation of the site during the Sedentary period rather than temporary use of the area for hunting and gathering. At the excavated portion of Whiptail, Sedentary period sherds occur primarily in the Compound and Southwestern Loci.

Based on their architecture, Pit Structures 4 and 19b might date to the Late Rincon subphase (A.D. 1100 to 1150), but they contained few sherds (one each) that date before the Tanque Verde phase. Later reuse of the structures may have obscured their original dates. For example, Structure 4, which is part of the compound, was filled with trash including numerous Classic period sherds, half of a Tanque Verde Red-on-brown bowl, 17 hammerstones, 18 projectile points (including one San Pedro point), and other lithic debris. One Nogales Polychrome sherd was found in the fill of the structure. The only other object found in Structure 4 that might date it to the Sedentary period was a figurine found in the eastern post hole. It has characteristics of earlier figurines, but is also similar to pieces found in Classic period contexts. In contrast, Structure 19b had few artifacts in its fill because a later structure (19a) was built directly over the top of it. Structure 19 is one of two structures at the southern edge of the site.

Like pre-A.D. 1200s pottery, ceramics representing post-A.D. 1300 activity at the site are present but scarce. Table 3.4 lists the few pieces of Salado polychromes found at the site: two in nonfeature contexts, the others in the Compound and Southwestern Loci of the site. Limited use of the site after A.D. 1300 may also be indicated by the presence of "F" frets and parallel dash motifs on a few Tanque Verde Red-on-brown sherds. About one-third of a white-slipped bowl with the parallel dash motif was found in the fill of Structure 13. And one sherd with a parallel dash motif was found in Structure 8, where one Pinto Polychrome sherd, four San Carlos Red-on-brown sherds, and 15 San Carlos Brown sherds were also found (Table 3.5). A Roosevelt Black-on-white sherd was identified from the work at Agua Caliente Park (Gregonis 2001b:Table F.3). Although the pottery assemblage includes a number of types (such as the poorly dated San Carlos wares and the nonlocal Hohokam types) that could date into the A.D. 1300s, the scarcity of Roosevelt Red Wares (Salado Polychromes) and lack of any Hopi or Zuni trade wares indicate that the site was not occupied to any extent during the late Classic period.

Nonlocal types that help to place the occupation of the site in the A.D. 1200s include Cibola White Ware and White Mountain Red Ware sherds (Table 3.6) as well as incised sherds (Table 3.7), nonlocal corrugated sherds (Table 3.6), and Hohokam pottery from outside of the Tucson Basin (Casa Grande Red-on-buff, Topawa Red-on-brown, Sells Red, and Gila Red [Table 3.8]). The Cibola White Ware, White Mountain Red Ware, and nonlocal corrugated ware sherds were found primarily in the Compound, Southwestern, and Northern loci of the site. In addition to sherds, two Cibola black-on-white vessels were recovered, both from cremation areas (Figures 3.1 and 3.2). One of these, a Tularosa Black-on-white jar (Figure 3.1), was found in association with Cremation 8. The other, a Pinedale Black-on-white jar (Figure 3.2), was found in association with Cremation 23.

The A.D. 1200s occupation is well represented by local wares. Tanque Verde Red-on-brown pottery, corrugated wares, and plain wares make up the bulk of the collection (Tables 3.9–3.11). The Tanque Verde Red-on-brown pottery (Figures 3.3 and 3.4) includes white-slipped and black paint variants, as well as a polychrome variant and one with black paint on a white background (listed as "black-on-white" in Table 3.9). The nine Tanque Verde Black-on-white sherds found at the site all came from the Compound Locus. The polychrome sherds (Figure 3.4), which came from the Southwestern Locus, have red and black paint on a brown or white background. Tanque Verde Red-on-brown and polychrome sherds make up 25 percent of the overall assemblage, with nearly half (n = 10,173) coming from the Southwestern Locus of the site. Fifty-six percent of the whole and reconstructible vessels (n = 35 out of 63) recovered from the site are Tanque Verde Red-on-brown.

It has often struck me that Tanque Verde Red-on-brown designs resemble weaving patterns, with their rectilinear patterns, use of off-set quartering or (in weaving parlance) rotated symmetry, and repeated interlocking elements and motifs. In her volume on prehistoric south-western textiles, Lynn Teague (1998:146-49) made note of the similar use of elements on pottery, carved rock artifacts, and textiles. I asked her to evaluate several Tanque Verde Red-on-brown sherds with an eye to possible

Figure 3.1. Tularosa Black-on-white jar with missing handle, which held Cremation No. 8. The handle may have been an animal form. The jar is 17.5 cm high (drawing by Christine H. Lange from a photograph by Helga Teiwes).

Table 3.3. Distribution of Pre-Classic Tucson Basin Pottery.

Provenience	Pottery Types*				Total No. of Sherds
	Rillito R/B	Rincon R/B	Rincon Red	Rincon Poly	
Compound Locus					
Structure 6		12			12
Structure 7		9		1	10
Structure 8	2	13			15
Structure 17		2			2
Total, Compound Locus	2	36	0	1	39
Central Locus					
Structure 15		2			2
Structure 32		1			1
Total, Central Locus		3			3
Southwestern Locus					
Structure 2	1	8			9
Structure 9		5			5
Structure 10		1			1
Between Structures 10 and 12		2			2
Structure 11		3			3
Structure 12		4			4
Structure 24		8		1	9
Structure 25		8		1	9
Grid squares		1			1
Total, Southwestern Locus	1	43		2	43
Northern Locus					
Structure 21		1			1
Structure 27a			1		1
Structure 27b		4			4
Structure 29		5			5
Structure 30		3			3
Structure 31a		2			2
Structure 31b		2			2
Total, Northern Locus		17	1		18
Southern Locus					
Structure 14		2			2
Structure 19		1			1
Total, Southern Locus		3			3
Grand Total	3	99	1	3	106

*Note: Rillito R/B= Rillito Red-on-brown; Rincon R/B= Rincon Red-on-brown; Rincon Poly=Rincon Polychrome

Table 3.4. Distribution of Middle and Upper Santa Cruz and Salado Types and Wares.

	Middle and Upper Santa Cruz Wares				Salado Polychromes		
Provenience	Trincheras Purple-on-red	Sahuarita Polychrome	Santa Cruz Polychrome	Nogales Polychrome	Pinto	Gila	Total No. of Sherds
Surface	1					1	2
Compound Locus							
Structure 4				1			1
Structure 8					1		1
Total, Compound Locus				1	1		2
Southwestern Locus							
Structure 2			3				3
Structure 24						1	1
Structure 25		1					1
grid square					1	1	2
Total, Southwestern Locus		1	3		1	2	7
Northern Locus							
Structure 31c		1					1
Total, Northern Locus		1					1
Grand Total	**1**	**2**	**3**	**1**	**2**	**3**	**12**

Table 3.5. Distribution of San Carlos Wares.

Provenience	Pottery Type or Ware				
	San Carlos Red-on-brown	San Carlos Red	Local San Carlos Red	San Carlos Brown	Total No. of Sherds
	Compound Locus				
Structure 6				12	12
Structure 7		2		36	38
Structure 8	4	1		15	20
Structure 17	7	7		2	16
Total, Compound Locus	11	10		65	86
	Central Locus				
Structure 15				146	146
Structure 32				10	10
Total, Central Locus				156	156
	Southwestern Locus				
Structure 2		2		63	65
Structure 9				9	9
Structure 10				10	10
Structure 11		7		7	14
Structure 12	4	2		48	54
Structure 13		2		5	7
Structure 16				20	20
Structure 18		5		12	17
Structure 24	4	26		8	38
Structure 25				20	20
Structure 26		2		9	11
Total, Southwestern Locus	8	46		211	265
	Northern Locus				
Structure 21		3			3
Structure 27a		2		20	22
Structure 27b		3		2	5
Structure 28				1	1
Structure 29	4		1	26	31
Structure 30		18			18
Structure 31a		4		1	5
Structure 31b				20	20
Structure 31c				6	6
Total, Northern Locus	4	30	1	76	111
	Northeastern Locus				
Structure 22				2	2
Structure 42				4	4
Total, Northeastern Locus				6	6
Grand Total	**23**	**86**	**1**	**514**	**624**

Table 3.6. Distribution of White Mountain Red Ware, Cibola White Ware, and Nonlocal Corrugated Wares.

Provenience	Pottery Types and Wares										Total No. of Sherds
	St. John's Polychrome	Cibola Black -on- white	Roosevelt Black -on- white	Reserve-Tularosa Black -on- white	Snowflake Black -on- white	Wingate Black -on- red	Puerco Black -on- white	Black -on- white	Mogollon corrugated	McDonald Corrugated	
Surface	3			17	1						21
Compound Locus											
Structure 4		2									2
Structure 6		2									2
Structure 7		4									4
Structure 8				2							2
Total, Compound Locus		8		2							10
Southwestern Locus											
Structure 2		2	2								4
Structure 9				2	1	1		1			5
Structure 11				2					1	1	4
Structure 12		4					2			1	7
Structure 16				1							1
Structure 24		1						2			3
Structure 25		1									1
grid squares	1	2									3
Total, Southwestern Locus	1	10	2	5	1	1	2	3	1	2	28
Northern Locus											
Structure 20			1								1
Structure 27b		2									2
Structure 29		1							3		4
Structure 31a		1									1
Structure 31b		6		1					1		8
Structure 31c		1									1
Total, Northern Locus		11	1	1					4		17
Southern Locus											
Structure 19					2						2
Total, Southern Locus					2						2
Grand Total	4	29	3	25	4	1	2	3	5	2	78

Table 3.7. Distribution of Other Pottery Wares and Types.

Provenience	Incised	Tooled	Incised red ware	White	Palomas Buff	Mexican	Total No. of Sherds
	Pottery Types and Wares						
Surface					1		1
Compound Locus							
Structure 7	2			1			3
Structure 8	2						2
Structure 17	2			1			3
Total, Compound Locus	6			2			8
Central Locus							
Structure 15	2						2
Total, Central Locus	2						2
Southwestern Locus							
Structure 2						1	1
Structure 11	1		1				2
Structure 12				5			5
Structure 13				3			3
Structure 18	1						1
Total, Southwestern Locus	2		1	8		1	12
Northern Locus							
Structure 21	1						1
Total, Northern Locus	1						1
Northeastern Locus							
Structure 22	1						1
Structure 42	3						3
Total, Northeastern Locus	4						4
Southern Locus							
Structure 19		1					1
Total, Southern Locus		1					1
Grand Total	15	1	1	10	1	1	29

Table 3.8. Distribution of Other Hohokam Pottery.

Provenience	Pottery Types: Topawa Red-on-brown	Casa Grande Red-on-buff	Gila Red	Sells Red	Total No. of Sherds
Surface			1		1
Southwestern Locus					
Structure 2	2				2
Structure 10				1	1
Structure 11		2	40		42
Structure 12		2	6		8
Total, Southwestern Locus	2	4	46	1	53
Northern Locus					
Structure 28				4	4
Structure 29		1	1	2	4
Structure 30			2		2
Structure 31b				2	2
Structure 31c			5	2	7
Total, Northern Locus		1	8	10	19
Grand Total	**2**	**5**	**55**	**11**	**73**

Table 3.9. Distribution of Tanque Verde Red-on-brown and Variants.

Provenience	Tanque Verde Red-on-brown	Tanque Verde Red-on-brown Variants				Total No. of Sherds
		White slip	Black paint	Black-on-white	Polychrome	
Compound						
Structure 4	385	1				386
Structure 6	375	2				377
Structure 7	1697	100	8			1805
Structure 8	856		15	8		879
Structure 17	827	4		1		832
Total, Compound	4140	107	23	9		4279
Central Locus						
Structure 5	277	20				297
Structure 15	1618	38	4			1660
Structure 32	421					421
Total, Central Locus	2316	58	4			2378
Southwestern Locus						
Structure 2	1969	6				1975
Structure 9	465		37			502
Structure 10	428	3	1			432
Between Structures 10 and 12	130					130
Structure 11	866					866
Structure 12	1892	12	11		14	1929
Structure 13	442	31	2			475
Structure 16	983	10	37			1030
Structure 18	398	4	2		1	405
Structure 24	850	8	3			861
Structure 25	1336	16	1			1353
Structure 26	205		4			209
Cremation 96/1	6					6
Total, Southwestern Locus	9970	90	98		15	10173
Northern Locus						
Structure 3	772	2				774
Structure 20	313	2				315
Structure 21	146	1				147
Structure 27a	384	13	1			398
Structure 27b	481	15	4			500
Structure 28	238	5	1			244
Structure 29	1026	1	2			1029
Structure 30	498	19	2			519
Structure 31a	618	10	2			630
Structure 31b	1303	78	2			1383
Structure 31c	885	13	3			901
Total, Northern Locus	6664	159	17			6840
Southern Locus						
Structure 14	380					380
Structure 19	398	1	1			400
Total, Southern Locus	778	1	1			780
Northeastern Locus						
Structure 22	171					171
Structure 42	155					155
Total, Northern Locus	326					326
Grand Total	24194	415	143	9	15	24776

Table 3.10. Distribution of Locally Made Corrugated Wares.

Provenience	Corrugated	Corrugated Variants: Incised	Tooled	Slipped	Total No. of Sherds
Surface	1	1			2
Compound Locus					
Structure 4	353				353
Structure 6	128				128
Structure 7	868				868
Structure 8	655	1			656
Structure 17	87	1			88
Total, CompoundLocus	2091	2			2093
Central Locus					
Structure 5	100				100
Structure 15	2623	10			2633
Structure 32	68	1			69
Total, Central Locus	2791	11			2802
Southwestern Locus					
Structure 2	323				323
Structure 9	51				51
Structure 10	63				63
Between Structures 10 and 12	8				8
Structure 11	537	1			538
Structure 12	436	6			442
Structure 13	220				220
Structure 16	303		2		305
Structure 18	69				69
Structure 24	406				406
Structure 25	394	1		1	396
Structure 26	34	1			35
Total, Southwestern Locus	2844	9	2	1	2856
Northern Locus					
Structure 3	241				241
Structure 20	200				200
Structure 21	89	1			90
Structure 27a	280				280
Structure 27b	300				300
Structure 28	135				135
Structure 29	578				578
Structure 30	306				306
Structure 31a	529				529
Structure 31b	1033				1033
Structure 31c	500				500
Total, Northern Locus	4191	1			4192
Southern Locus					
Structure 14	120				120
Structure 19	170				170
Total, Southern Locus	290				290
Northeastern Locus					
Structure 22	234				234
Structure 42	117	6			123
Total, Northeastern Locus	351	6			357
Grand Total	**12559**	**30**	**2**	**1**	**12591**

Table 3.11. Distribution of Plain Wares.

Provenience	Pottery Types: Micaceous plain	Pottery Types: Plain ware	Pottery Types: Stuccoed	Total No. of Sherds
Surface		2		2
Compound Locus				
Structure 4		512		512
Structure 6		1208		1208
Structure 7		3957		3957
Structure 8		4967		4967
Structure 17		647		647
Total, Compound Locus		11291		11291
Central Locus				
Structure 5		453		453
Structure 15	12	4231		4243
Structure 32		1162		1162
Total, Central Locus	12	5846		5858
Southwestern Locus				
Structure 2		2113		2113
Structure 9		1451	2	1453
Structure 10	2	1074		1076
Between Structures 10 and 12		394		394
Structure 11	79	1777		1856
Structure 12	1	5217		5218
Structure 13	16	1361		1377
Structure 16	12	2116		2128
Structure 18	19	1124		1143
Structure 24		2264		2264
Structure 25		4474		4474
Structure 26		517		517
Total, Southwestern Locus	129	23882	2	24013
Northern Locus				
Structure 3		976		976
Structure 20		712		712
Structure 21	4	463		467
Structure 27a	1	879		880
Structure 27b	2	1039		1041
Structure 28		385		385
Structure 29		2230		2230
Structure 30		1594		1594
Structure 31a		1405		1405
Structure 31b		2931		2931
Structure 31c		2381		2381
Total, Northern Locus	7	14995		15002
Southern Locus				
Structure 14		1324	1	1325
Structure 19		1016		1016
Total, Southern Locus		2340	1	2341
Northeastern Locus				
Structure 22	23	451		474
House 42		399		399
Total, Northeastern Locus	23	850		873
Grand Total	**171**	**59206**	**3**	**59380**

Table 3.12. Descriptions of Whole and Reconstructible Vessels.

Provenience	Pottery Type or Ware	Vessel Shape	Description
		Compound Locus	
Structure 4	Tanque Verde Red-on-brown	suprahemispherical bowl	Just over half of this bowl was found. When whole the bowl was 30.6 cm in diameter and 16.2 cm high. The interior has a painted line below the rim. Between the rim and the painted line are individual red "Hs" or "Is" in no apparent pattern. The exterior has been smoothed and polished with a painted design consisting of running nested chevrons. The rim has a square finish. The vessel is thinnest at the rim, thickening to 1.1 cm at the base (in ASM research collection).
Structure 7 fill	San Carlos Red	hemispherical bowl	Five sherds representing an unknown percentage of a San Carlos Red bowl were found (in ASM research collection).
Structure 7 floor	Tanque Verde Red-on-brown	suprahemispherical bowl	More than 90% of this vessel was found and reconstructed. The bowl has a round base, with slightly flaring sides and a direct rim. It is decorated on the interior with a band of three parallel lines that break at intervals with ends interlocked; at the rim are long and narrow solid triangles. The exterior design goes from the rim to near the base. The paneled design is divided into triangular areas by narrow lines; each panel has a wide, cross-hatched panel, ticked lines, and interlocking rectilinear scrolls or single scrolls. The interior is fire clouded and has visible polishing or scraping marks. The bowl has fairly coarse temper that contains mica. The bowl is 17.8 cm in diameter and 9 cm high (ASM Catalog Number A-38,121).
Structure 8 fill	Plain ware	hemispherical bowl	Ninety percent of this bowl was found in Structure 8. Most of the bowl's rim is missing. The vessel has a round base and steep walls. The interior is smudged. The bowl has coarse temper that includes mica. The bowl's exterior is weathered and the bowl is pitted on the interior and exterior. The bowl is 13.7 cm in diameter and 7.8 cm high (ASM Catalog Number A-38,126).
	Corrugated	jar	Three-quarters of this squat wide-mouthed vessel were found. The jar has an almost flat base that is indented in the center; the sides are low and rounded and the rim is slightly everted. The corrugations are in an obliterated indented pattern. The interior of the jar is smudged and has an eroded surface (probably due to cooking) and the exterior is sooted. The vessel is 18.5 cm diameter in its body and 15.8 cm high (ASM Catalog Number A-38,130).
	Obliterated corrugated	jar	Two pieces representing one half of this vessel were found. It has a weathered exterior with rounded sides and a short neck with a slightly everted rim. The jar has coarse temper and a small hole chipped through the base from the inside. When whole, the jar was 28 cm diameter and 28 cm high (ASM Catalog Number A-38,145).
Structure 8 floor	Corrugated	subhemispherical bowl	Ninety percent of this smudged, shallow bowl was found and reconstructed. It has a flat base and smoothed over indented corrugations. The vessel is 20.1 cm in diameter and 6.9 cm high (ASM Catalog Number A-38,143).

Table 3.12. Descriptions of Whole and Reconstructible Vessels. cont'd.

Provenience	Pottery Type or Ware	Vessel Shape	Description
Structure 8 floor	Corrugated	jar	Ninety-nine percent of this obliterated corrugated jar was found and reconstructed from sherds. The jar has a straight neck with a slightly everted rim. Its fine corrugations are indented and smoothed over. The interior is blackened near the base, possibly from material that was in it when the house burned around it. The jar is 24.7 cm in diameter and 22 cm high. The base is slightly weathered (ASM Catalog Number A-38,137).
Structure 8 floor	Corrugated	hemispherical bowl	Sherds making up three-quarters of this bowl were found. The bowl has a flat base and straight sides that slope out to the rim. The interior of the vessel was smudged; it has obliterated indented corrugations. When whole, the vessel was 33.4 cm in diameter and 14.5 cm high (ASM Catalog Number A-38, 125).
Structure 8 floor	Corrugated	jar	About 90 percent of this pear-shaped, obliterated corrugated jar was found and reconstructed from sherds. The jar has a round base and sides, with a sloping shoulder, tapering neck, and a slightly everted rim. The last couple of coils below the rim are completely smoothed. The jar is 33.5 cm in diameter and is 31.5 cm high (ASM Catalog Number A-38,129).
Structure 17 floor	Tanque Verde Red-on-brown	suprahemispherical bowl	About 3/4 of this bowl was found on the floor of Structure 17. The rounded base of the vessel is weathered. It has outsloping walls. The interior decoration is a series of nested Vs around the rim; the design is almost obscured by large fire clouds. On the exterior, a wide band goes from the rim to near the base. It consists of five rows of short, diagonal lines that are joined at tips with interlocking rectilinear scrolls. There is one ticked line and one plain line around base. The exterior is fire clouded. The bowl is 17.1 cm in diameter and 10.8 cm high (ASM Catalog Number A-38,116).
Structure 17 floor	Tanque Verde Red-on-brown	suprahemispherical bowl	About 2/3 of this bowl was found on the floor of Structure 17. The bowl has a slightly rounded base and steep, slightly rounded sides. The decoration consists of a band of solid red triangles around the rim on the interior; on the exterior it has a plaited design of lines of opposed pendant triangles and parallel lines separating triangular and irregular areas that have interlocking rectilinear scrolls surrounded by solid triangles. The reconstructed bowl is 24.7 cm in diameter and is 13.4 cm high (ASM Catalog Number A-38,133).
Structure 17 floor	Tanque Verde Red-on-brown	hemispherical bowl	Sherds from half of this mended bowl were found. The vessel is decorated on the interior by a band of small triangles with interlocking rectilinear hooks and on the exterior by a plaited layout with alternating net designs and parallel rows of opposed pendant triangles separated by parallel lines. When whole, the bowl was 26 cm in diameter and 11.5 cm high (ASM Catalog Number A-38,134).
Structure 17 floor	McDonald Corrugated	hemispherical bowl	About 3/4 of this bowl was found on the floor of Structure 17. The bowl has a flat base and slightly rounded, steep sides. It is heat crackled, with a smudged interior. Unlike many McDonald Corrugated vessels, the polishing and scraping marks are still visible. The exterior of the vessel appears to have been red slipped before the white design was painted on. Much of the slip and design have been burned off. When whole, the bowl was 23.2 cm in diameter and 14.3 cm high (ASM Catalog Number A-38,142).

Table 3.12. Descriptions of Whole and Reconstructible Vessels. cont'd.

Provenience	Pottery Type or Ware	Vessel Shape	Description
Structure 17, outside use surface	Tanque Verde Red-on-brown	jar	The top of this large jar is missing and the vessel has an eroded exterior. The jar has a low base and low shoulder with rounded sides. It has coarse temper that contains mica. The design is laid out in a band that goes from the base of the neck to the shoulder. The plaited design consists of parallel lines drawn diagonally from the neck base, alternating with rectilinear interlocking scrolls. Solid triangular areas at the base have interlocking rectilinear scrolls. The jar is 13.1 cm in diameter and 21.5 cm high to the broken neck (ASM Catalog Number A-38,119).
Structure 17, outside east wall	Corrugated	jar	About 3/4 of this obliterated corrugated jar has been reconstructed from sherds found outside of Structure 17. The jar is globular in shape, with a slightly rounded base. The neck is missing. The jar is lumpy and egg shaped; paddle and anvil marks are evident and there is a diagonal scratch on the lower part of the vessel that was made when the clay was wet. The interior of the base is eroded. The jar is 22.6 cm in diameter and 22.0 cm high to the broken neck (ASM Catalog Number A-38,132).
Inside NE 1/4 of compound	Tanque Verde Red-on-brown	jar	The upper portion of this jar is missing. The vessel has a rounded base with a low shoulder. It has a plaited design with lines of opposed pendant triangles offset by parallel lines. The exterior is heavily weathered, especially around the base (ASM Catalog Number A-38,138).
Central Locus			
Structure 15			Although 24 whole and partial vessels were found in Structure 15, they were not included in the collections at ASM and are not described here. The vessels likely were given to the land owners.
Southwestern Locus			
Structure 10 upper fill	Plain ware	handled jar	About 3/4 of this handled jar was found in the fill of Structure 10. It has a spherical body and a slightly everted rim that includes the upper part of the handle. The interior and exterior of the base is badly weathered. When whole, the jar was 18.5 cm in diameter and 18.8 cm high (ASM Catalog Number A-38,135).
Structure 10 floor	Tanque Verde Red-on-brown	subhemispherical bowl	This mended, complete vessel has been formed by grinding it down from a larger bowl. Most of the rim is missing; the bowl has a slightly rounded base, flared sides, and an uneven rim. The interior of the rim has a band with a series of parallel lines forming triangular or V-shaped areas. On the exterior, a plaited design includes parallel lines with lines of opposed pendant triangles and triangles with rectilinear scrolls. The vessel has a repair hole on one side. The bowl is 28 cm in diameter and 11 cm high (ASM Catalog Number A-38,127).
Structure 11 floor	Tanque Verde Red-on-brown	hemispherical bowl	Twenty percent of this bowl was found on the floor of Structure 11. The rim is slightly narrower than the rest of the bowl. Its interior design has four identical narrow bands of opposed small triangles with hook projections. The exterior design begins at the rim and has large angular areas outlined with heavy lines and filled with fine cross-hatching. The lines are plaited. When whole, the vessel was approximately 30 cm in diameter (ASM Catalog Number A-38,181).

Table 3.12. Descriptions of Whole and Reconstructible Vessels. cont'd.

Provenience	Pottery Type or Ware	Vessel Shape	Description
Structure 12 floor	Tanque Verde Red-on-brown	suprahemispherical bowl	This complete vessel is 24.6 cm in diameter and 15.5 cm high. It is fire clouded on the interior and exterior and is slightly indented just below the rim. The interior has a band of opposed solid triangles; each triangle has a short line extending out from one edge. The exterior has a diagonally plaited design with offset pendant triangles and parallel lines (ASM Catalog Number A-38,118).
Structure 12 floor	Plain ware	jar	Ninety percent of this large-mouthed globular jar was found on the floor of Structure 12. The vessel has vertical polishing or scraping marks on its body and horizontal marks around the exterior of the outflared rim. A small hole has been chipped in the base, starting in the interior. Reconstructed, the jar is 16.5 cm in diameter and 14.7 cm high. It is weathered on the interior and the base of the exterior (ASM Catalog Number A-38,131).
Structure 12 floor	Tanque Verde Red-on-brown	jar	This vessel was unfired and was found with a group of pottery making artifacts. The jar is rather squat-bodied and thick-walled in comparison to most Tanque Verde Red-on-brown vessels. The structure it was in burned, thus preserving the shape of the jar (ASM A-38,284). Figure 2.14.
Structure 16, floor	Plain obliterated corrugated	jar	Ninety-nine percent of this restored, wide-mouthed jar is represented. Its exterior is soot blackened. It has coarse temper that contains mica. The interior of the base is weathered; the base exterior is extensively pitted. The jar is 25.4 cm in diameter and 24 cm high (ASM Catalog Number A-38,136).
Structure 18, floor Vessel 2	Tanque Verde Red-on-brown	hemispherical bowl	This bowl is whole. It has a rim that is slightly thicker than the rest of the bowl. The design on the interior is a band of small solid triangles and interlocking rectilinear scrolls. An exterior band design consists of triangular areas of varying sizes; each has opposed barbed lines with interlocking rectilinear scrolls. The bowl is extensively fire clouded over its interior and exterior and has some pitting and weathering on its exterior. The bowl is 19.5 cm in diameter and 9.5 cm high (ASM Catalog Number A-38,122).
Structure 18 floor	Tanque Verde Red-on-brown	suprahemispherical bowl	This whole vessel has a smudged interior and weathered and pitted exterior. Its exterior design consists of triangular areas with barbed lines and interlocking rectilinear scrolls. The bowl is 24.7 cm in diameter and 12.2 cm high (ASM Catalog Number A-38,123).
Structure 18, floor	Tanque Verde Red-on-brown	incurved bowl	One-third of a badly weathered bowl was found on the northwest corner of the floor in Structure 18. The vessel has a rounded base and steep sides. Its interior design consists of two horizontal rows of opposed solid triangles with interlocking rectilinear scroll hooks. Its exterior design starts at the rim and is a plaited design of triangular areas bounded by narrow lines and opposed pendant fringe. The design is very hard to distinguish due to the weathering (Catalog Number A-38,182).
Structure 25 floor	Obliterated corrugated	jar	This artifact is the base of a large vessel. The base measures 15 cm by 21 cm and is 5.5 cm high. The interior of the jar has a mottled dark gray color and traces of hematite. The exterior of the jar is stuccoed (in ASM research collection).

Table 3.12. Descriptions of Whole and Reconstructible Vessels. cont'd.

Provenience	Pottery Type or Ware	Vessel Shape	Description
		Southern Locus	
Structure 14 floor	Red ware	subhemispherical bowl	Two-thirds of this bowl with a burnished, smudged interior was found on the floor of Structure 14. The bowl has thin, even walls; polishing marks on the inside go from rim to base at slight diagonal. The paste is micaceous. The bowl is 22.1 cm in diameter and 9.7 cm high. The exterior base is worn (ASM Catalog Number A-38,146).
Structure 19a	Tanque Verde Red-on-brown	hemispherical bowl	About one-third of the vessel is represented. It has an interior design of solid pendant triangles with angled lines that work into interlocking rectilinear scrolls. The exterior has the same pattern. The bowl is 20.3 cm in diameter and 14.6 cm high (in ASM research collection).
Structure 19a floor	Tanque Verde Red-on-brown	suprahemispherical bowl	This nearly complete bowl has an exterior design of solid triangles at its rim and base with two lines of parallel plaited lines between. It is 18.7 cm in diameter and 12.4 cm high. The rim outflares slightly (in ASM research collection).
Structure 19a	Tanque Verde Red-on-brown	suprahemispherical bowl	This whole vessel has a banded design on the interior that consists of pendant triangles with fringe on the edges opposing another line of fringe. The polished exterior has diagonal pendant triangles with square frets on the end and triangles of checkerboard patterns. The vessel is straight sided and has a worn base. It is 30.4 cm in diameter and 16.1 cm high (in ASM research collection).
Structure 19a floor Vessel 1	Tanque Verde Red-on-brown	suprahemispherical bowl	The interior of this bowl was smoothed but not polished. The exterior is lightly polished. The base is worn. The faded exterior design has a band of opposed triangles and parallel lines. The complete bowl is 23.5 cm in diameter and 10.5 cm high (in ASM research collection).
Structure 19a floor	Tanque Verde Red-on-brown	bowl	One-third of a bowl is represented by this artifact. The interior has a half-band of hachured pendant triangles. The exterior design consists of plaited opposed pendant triangles separated by parallel lines. It has granitic temper and is 14.3 cm high, with 5-mm-thick walls; the diameter could not be determined (in ASM research collection).
Structure 19a	Tanque Verde Red-on-brown	suprahemispherical bowl	This large, complete bowl has large triangles containing interlocking rectilinear scrolls and two parallel lines of opposed pendant triangles. It has a worn base and 5-mm-thick walls. The bowl is 30.4 cm in diameter and is 17.8 cm high.
Structure 19a floor	Tanque Verde Red-on-brown	bowl	This complete vessel has squat, rounded sides that curve in, then straighten to the rim. It has a plaited design of opposed pendant triangles and parallel lines with large rectangular open spaces. The base is flat and worn, with sand temper. It is 31.7 cm in diameter and 19 cm high (in ASM research collection).
Structure 19 floor	Obliterated indented corrugated	outflared, hemispherical bowl	This nicely fired bowl has a flat bottom. The interior is well smudged and polished. Reconstructed, the bowl is 22 cm in diameter and 10 cm high, with 5-mm-diameter walls.
Structure 19 floor	Obliterated corrugated	suprahemispherical bowl	This vessel has a polished exterior and smudged interior, with slightly outflaring walls. It has sand temper and a worn base. The bowl is 27 cm in diameter and 12 cm high (in ASM research collection).

Table 3.12. Descriptions of Whole and Reconstructible Vessels. cont'd.

Provenience	Pottery Type or Ware	Vessel Shape	Description
		Northern Locus	
Structure 27b floor NE 1/4	Tanque Verde Red-on-brown	suprahemispherical bowl	This nearly complete vessel is missing its base. It is slightly incurved, with a straight "neck" and squared rim finish. It has thin walls and a smudged interior. The interior rim has a row of interlocked hooked pendant triangles. The exterior is weathered and most of design is gone; the visible portions show a typical Tanque Verde plaited layout with designs that include pendant triangles and interlocking rectilinear scrolls in some segments; another segment includes a wide line band with fine line pendants separated by fine parallel lines ending in rectilinear scrolls that are in opposition to one another. The vessels are 24.3 cm in diameter and 15.2 cm high.
Structure 27b floor, subfeature 6	Indented obliterated corrugated	handled jar	This globular bodied vessel has a short neck with an 11-cm-diameter opening.
Structure 27b or 28	Tanque Verde Red-on-brown	jar	This large vessel has a Classic period shoulder and paint that is eroding from the surface of the vessel. The neck design consists of long bands of parallel lines with solid opposing rectilinear scrolls that have ticked edges. The body design consists of long bands of netting and parallel lines of pendant triangles that end in a hook. The jar is 22.7 cm in diameter and 25.5 cm high. The vessel walls are 8 mm thick.
Structure 27b and Structure 28	Tanque Verde Red-on-brown	jar	This globular vessel is 20.0 cm high with 6-mm-thick walls. The neck is missing, but looks as if it was short and outflared. The base is irregular and slightly flattened. The jar has been mended.
Structure 30, Level 3, SW 1/4 (subfeature 1)	Obliterated corrugated	incurved bowl	About half of the vessel is represented; interior is smudged and spalling; rim has wide band where coils have been flattened and smoothed in the Reserve style; coil construction is partially obliterated (probably by paddling); base is missing; rim has rounded and beveled rim finish; 30.6 cm diameter, 17.1 cm high. (Mended)
		Northeastern Section	
Structure 42, replaces floor in hearth	Tanque Verde Red-on-brown	hemispherical bowl	This slightly incurved bowl has mica and quartz sand temper. The base is heavily eroded through use. Its paint is rubbed off in some areas. The exterior plaited design includes netting, opposed pendant triangles with slight extensions on triangles, and rectilinear interlocking scrolls with solid triangles. The interior banded design consists of rectilinear interlocking scrolls with triangles separated by rows of opposed fringe. The bowl is 24.5 cm in diameter and 15 cm high, with 5 to 8-mm-thick walls (in possession of land owner).
Structure 42	Tanque Verde Red-on-brown	hemispherical bowl	The exterior design on this vessel consists of triangular areas separated by open areas. The design is offset from the rim at a 45-degree angle; each design unit includes 1 interlocking rectilinear scroll with a triangle motif, a line of opposed interlocking hooked pendant triangles, and a line of free-floating "x" or "+" symbols, bounded by a segment of netting. The interior band consists of pendant triangles along the rim, with interlocking rectilinear scrolls and a zig-zag solid line. The vessel is about 30 cm and about 15 cm high, with 6-mm-thick walls at the rim (in possession of land owner).

Table 3.12. Descriptions of Whole and Reconstructible Vessels. cont'd.

Provenience	Pottery Type or Ware	Vessel Shape	Description
Structure 42 floor	Tanque Verde Red-on-brown	jar	This whole, medium-sized vessel has a straight, 6-cm-high neck with a round rim finish. The vessel is 16.5 cm in diameter at the rim and is 36 cm high. It has a 38-cm-maximum diameter body. Its vessel walls vary from 5 mm thick at the rim to 6.5 mm in the body, and 10 mm thick at the base. The design includes an exterior rim band of triangles with a line below it that has tick marks coming off of a triangular base. The body design includes triangular units offset from the base of the neck and shoulder. The design in each unit includes an interlocking rectilinear scroll with a solid triangle and rows of diamond-like patterns with ticks on the ends made by blending two rows of opposed pendant triangle. The exterior is well smoothed but not highly polished (vessel in possession of land owner).
Structure 42 floor	Plain ware	jar	This restored, globular-bodied jar has a short (3.5 cm high), slightly outcurved neck. The rim is 20 cm in diameter and the vessel is approximately 37.5 cm high. The jar has 8-mm-thick walls. its exterior has a light, irregular polish (in possession of land owner).
Structure 42 floor	Plain obliterated corrugated	jar	Reconstructed, this jar is 27 cm high, 32 cm in maximum diameter and 15.5 cm diameter at the room. It has a 3.5-cm-high, slightly outflared neck and 6-mm-thick vessel walls. The jar is tempered with crushed quartz sand with very little mica. It has spalled on the exterior and interior, probably from use (in possession of land owner).
			Cremation-Associated Vessels
Cemetery 1	Tanque Verde Red-on-brown	bowl	This 1/4 to 1/3 of a bowl is twice as thick at the base as at rim. The interior design consists of opposed solid triangles with a narrow line on the lower side of the band. the exterior design consists of narrow triangular panels with two pairs of opposed pendant triangles that delineate small triangular areas with rectilinear scrolls. The interior is smudged. The bowl is 26 cm in diameter and 15 cm high (ASM Catalog Number A-38,183).
Cemetery 1	Tanque Verde Red-on-brown	subhemispherical bowl	This mended bowl is 99 percent complete. It has a slightly rounded base with sides that out slope to the rim. It has coarse white temper and uneven interior and exterior surfaces. The interior has a large fire cloud that has nearly obscured the design. That design consists of pairs of wavy lines running from the rim to the base line, with small crosses between the pairs. The bowl is 13.2 cm in diameter and 4.8 cm high (ASM Catalog Number A-38,115).
Cemetery 1 Cremation 4	Tanque Verde Red-on-brown	jar	This whole, globular vessel has a nearly pointed base that has no apparent wear. It has a straight, 5-cm-high neck with an outcurving rim. The interior of the neck is polished and the rim is painted. The exterior neck design consists of a band of opposed triangles between which are fine zig-zag lines that frame the triangles with one heavy zig-zag through the center. The body of the vessel has a repeated pattern of opposed solid triangles that extend into interlocking rectilinear scrolls alternating with widely spaced opposed barbed lines. The jar is 23 cm in diameter at the neck and is 22.1 cm high (in ASM research collection).

Table 3.12. Descriptions of Whole and Reconstructible Vessels. cont'd.

Provenience	Pottery Type or Ware	Vessel Shape	Description
Cemetery 1 Cremation 7	Plain ware	jar	Ninety percent of this reconstructed vessel is represented; about half of the neck and rim are missing. The vessel is globular with a slightly rounded base. It is elongated and lopsided in shape: one side of the vessel is rounded, the other more straight. The jar has a short, squat neck with a rounded rim. The vessel is 24.6 cm in diameter and 24.5 cm high with 6-mm-thick walls. The vessel apparently held the cremated remains, which left a reddish ring around the inside of the vessel. The exterior is slightly spalled, perhaps indicating exposure to a crematory fire (in ASM research collections).
Cemetery 1 Cremation 8	Tularosa Black-on-white	handled jar	This globular-bodied vessel had a three-dimensional animal formed on its handle, which is now missing. The rim of the jar is painted; the body has a series of triangular scrolls that end in pendant triangles as well as opposed and hatchured pendant triangles. The jar has a 7.5-cm-diameter neck and is 17.5 cm high, with an 18.9 cm maximum diameter. The neck 5.8 cm high and straight (Figure 3.1).
Cemetery 1 Cremation 10	Plain ware	jar	Large jar covered with Tanque Verde Red-on-brown sherd; contained a San Carlos Red bowl sherd. Sketch of cemetery area shows globular jar with short straight neck. No other information available.
Cemetery 1 Cremation 12	Plain ware	jar	This low-bodied jar has a Late Rincon shape. It is cracked and slightly heat warped. It has a low, slightly squared shoulder. The 2.9-cm-high neck is outcurved. The vessel is 24 cm high and 24.3 cm diameter (in ASM research collection).
Cemetery 1 Cremation 12	Late Rincon or early Tanque Verde Red-on-brown	bowl	Less than 1/4 of this bowl was found. It has a very busy design of hook-like frets along with parallel lines, fringed lines, and interlocking rectilinear motifs (in ASM research collection).
Cemetery 1 Cremation 12	Tanque Verde Red-on-brown	suprahemispherical bowl	About half of this deep, steep-sided vessel is represented. Its weathered interior makes the design on the interior hard to see. The interior design is quartered or offset quartered and has parallel lines with sawtooth or pendant triangle lines. The interior is heavily fire clouded and has fine micaceous temper. It is 18 cm in diameter and 9.7 cm high (ASM Catalog Number A-38,128).
Cemetery 1 Cremation 12	Tanque Verde Red-on-brown	bowl	One quarter of the vessel is represented. It is 16.6 cm in diameter and 10.6 cm high, with 7-mm-thick vessel walls. The rim has a rounded finish and both interior and exterior are polished to a high gloss; the interior is also smudged. The paste is sandy. The exterior design is faint and difficult to see but includes parallel fringed lines and an area with spaced, solid blocks of color, perhaps a checkerboard pattern. It served as the cremation's cover vessel (in ASM research collection).
Cemetery 2? Cremation 14	Tanque Verde Red-on-brown	suprahemispherical bowl	This whole vessel is 14.5 cm in diameter and 9.3 cm high. The exterior design is laid out in bands that are parallel to the rim. The band of opposed thick solid pendant triangles near rim emphasizes the negative space; below that is a band of rectilinear interlocking scrolls that have fringe on the outside edges. The exterior base is worn (ASM Catalog Number A-38,124).

Table 3.12. Descriptions of Whole and Reconstructible Vessels. cont'd.

Provenience	Pottery Type or Ware	Vessel Shape	Description
Cemetery 2? Cremation 14	Tanque Verde Red-on-brown	hemispherical bowl	This whole vessel held the cremains. The bowl has an interior design that has been nearly obliterated by fire clouds. The design is quartered and consists of opposed pendant triangle lines and a narrow panel bounded by two parallel lines. The bowl has a rounded base. The bowl is 15.5 cm diameter and 7.8 cm high (ASM Catalog Number A-38,120).
Cemetery 2? Cremation 15	Tanque Verde Red-on-brown	suprahemispherical bowl	This bowl, used to cover the cremains, is broken but mended and nearly complete except for a few sherds. It has slightly rounded sides and a slightly rounded base. The vessel's exterior is weathered or worn, especially the base. Its exterior design goes from rim to base and consists of a series of narrow diagonal panels that meet at the rim and near the base to form a zig-zag pattern; each panel has two parallel wavy lines that run the length of the panel. Triangular areas between the diagonal panels contain interlocking rectilinear scrolls and solid triangles. The bowl is 19 cm in diameter and 12.5 cm high (ASM Catalog Number A-38,117).
Cemetery 2? Cremation 16	Plain ware	suprahemispherical bowl	This bowl has straight sides, one of which is slightly warped, either through the firing process or the result of being in a crematory fire. Size was not recorded; no other information is available (Bradley n.d.).
Cemetery 2? Cremation 23	Pinedale Black-on-white	jar	This vessel has a straight neck and globular body. The base is worn. The rim has a band of stepped triangles descending vertically from rim. The design on the body consists of interlocking stepped triangles—one solid, one hatchured. The jar is 13.75 cm in diameter at the base and 10.4 cm diameter elsewhere. It is 7 cm diameter at the mouth. The vessel is 14 cm high. Information from Bradley (n.d.) (Figure 3.2).
Cremation outside of Structure 27a	Plain ware	handled jar	This small vessel is 12.4 cm from the base to the top of the handle, and is 12.4 cm in maximum diameter with a 10-cm-diameter mouth and 7-mm-thick walls. Its flat bottom is off center, and it has a polished surface and fire clouds (in ASM research collection).
Probable cremation, location not known	Tanque Verde Red-on-brown	jar	This poorly mended jar is squat and has a sharp shoulder. The body and neck are decorated. The neck design is contained between the rim and a fine line at base of neck and consists of grouped, parallel vertical lines associated with solid triangles and interlocked, rectilinear scrolls. The vessel body is painted in diagonal bands of broad areas of cross-hatching and a broad band created by two widely spaced parallel lines; inside the two lines are squat solid triangles with the apex angle extended into a rectilinear hook. The neck of the vessel is 13 cms in diameter; the vessel body is 28.1 cm diameter. The jar is 20.0 cm high and has 6-mm-thick walls (in ASM research collection).
Other Proveniences			
No provenience information	Plain ware	jar	This jar has a globular shape and granitic temper. It has a 27.2-cm-diameter body and a 2.5-cm-high straight neck. It is 24.3 cm high in total and has 6-mm-diameter vessel walls. The base is unworn.

Figure 3.2. Pinedale Black-on-white jar found in a cemetery (not specified), possibly in association with Cremation 23. The jar is 14 cm high and 13.75 cm in diameter at the base (drawing by Christine H. Lange from a photograph by Helga Teiwes).

weaving patterns. The sherds in Figures 3.5 and 3.6 illustrate some of the patterns she discerned. She noted possible examples of interlacing and oblique interlacing (Figure 3.5b, d), simple interlocked frets (also referred to as interlocking rectilinear scrolls) illustrative of brocade (Figure 3.5c), lines seen on bands or sashes found at Tonto National Monument (Figure 3.5a), a 1/1 interlaced plain weave design found in basketry (Figure 3.6a), and brocade with rotated symmetry (Figure 3.5b). Teague noted that brocade designs with rotated symmetry (Figure 3.5b) are common from Chihuahua to the Tonto Basin (see also King 1974). Teague also mentioned that she thought the pottery designs were more characteristic of basketry or braiding patterns, not warp-and-weft loom weaving (Teague, personal communication 1998). The interlocked fret elements illustrated in Figure 3.5b, c and d, along with the pendant triangles shown in Figure 3.5b are among the most common elements seen on Tanque Verde Red-on-brown pottery.

The 1/1 weaving pattern illustrated in Figure 3.6a is on a bilobed or gourd-shaped jar, a shape that seems to be a marker for the Classic period. The vessel was found in Structure 16. Figure 3.6b is part of a pumpkin or squash-shaped vessel, another Classic period shape. It was found on the floor of Structure 27b.

The plain wares from Whiptail are typical of those found in the Tucson Basin: brown wares made with local clays and tempers that are finished using paddle and anvil technology. Although only 171 sherds were identified as "micaceous plain" (i.e., plain ware with substantial amounts of mica), many of the sherds contained mica, which is not surprising considering that washes in and around the site contain gneiss. Overall, the plain wares make up 61 percent of the sherd assemblage at the site. Eight of the reconstructible or whole vessels found at the site were plain ware (Table 3.12).

Surface textured sherds include corrugated, incised, and tooled pieces (Figure 3.7). Most of the textured wares from Whiptail are obliterated corrugated sherds and vessels. They make up 13 percent of the overall sherd assemblage (Table 3.10). The highest numbers of corrugated and other textured sherds (n = 4,192) came from the Northern Locus of the site and the lowest (n = 290) from the Southern Locus of the site. Fifteen of the reconstructible vessels were corrugated wares (Table 3.12). Six of these vessels came from Structure 8, which was adjacent to the compound. Another corrugated vessel came from Structure 17, which was inside the compound. (A McDonald Corrugated vessel was also found in Structure 17.) The other corrugated vessels were found throughout the site: two in the Southwestern Locus (one each in Structures 16 and 25), the Northern Locus (one each in Structures 27b and 30), one in the Northeastern Locus (Structure

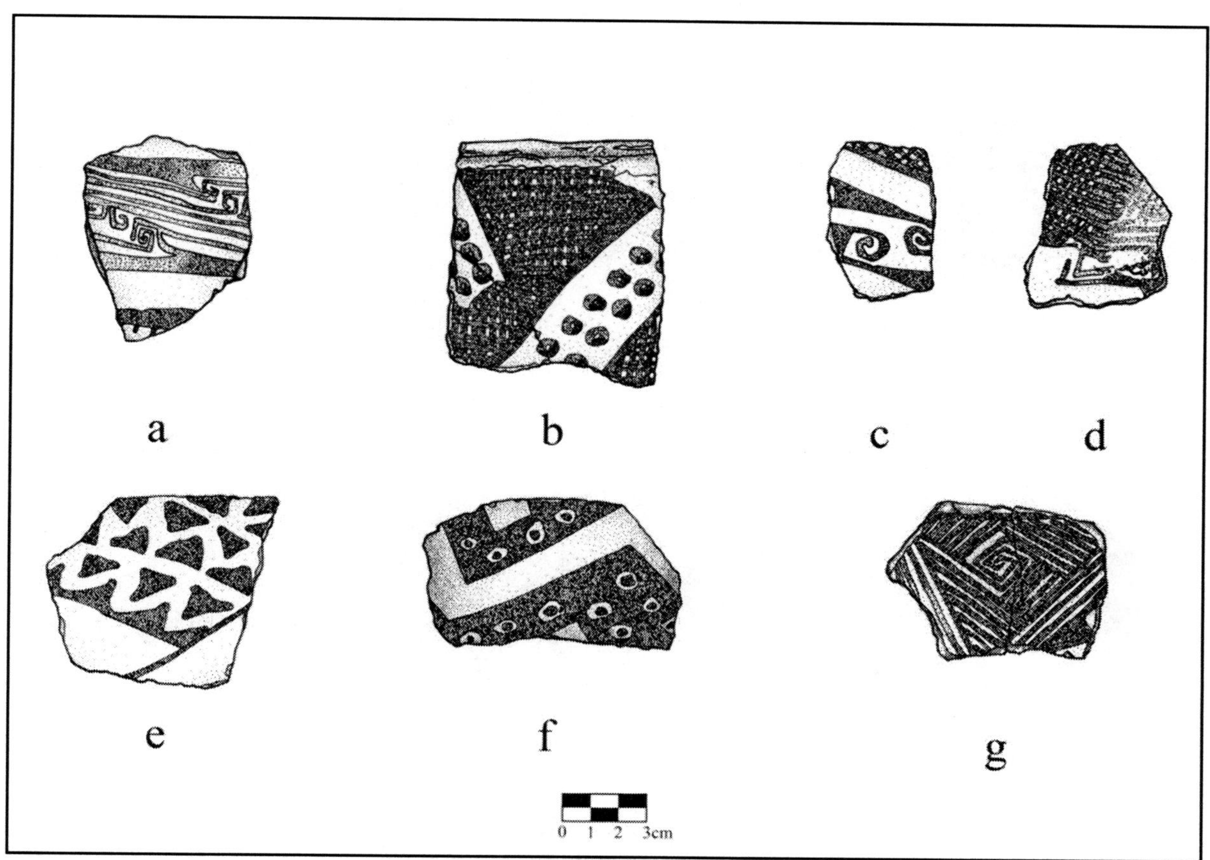

Figure 3.3. Assorted Tanque Verde Red-on-brown sherds: (a) interlocking frets; (b) oblique interlacing and bull's-eye designs that resemble tie-dyed cloth; (c) curvilinear frets; (d) rectilinear frets and oblique interlacing; (e) free-floating triangles that appear to be missing framing lines, paint is very thick; (f) bull's-eye pattern; and (g) complex interlocking rectilinear scrolls (drawing by Gerry Crouse).

42), and two in the Southern Locus (Structure 19). The percentage of corrugated wares relative to other types at Whiptail is comparable to that found at the nearby Gibbon Springs site, where 15.3 percent (n = 2,559 out of 16,743) of the sherds found at the site were corrugated wares (Gregonis 1996:184, Table 6.1).

Table 3.13 shows the relative percentages of pottery wares as they occur across the site. Corrugated wares appear to have the most variation in their relative distribution across the site, with a high of 25 percent in the Central Locus and a low of 7.6 percent in the Southwestern Locus. Four structures, Features 4, 15, 22, and 31a, have the highest percentage of corrugated sherds (20% or greater).

Twenty-eight percent of the sherds from Structure 4, the pit structure just east of the compound, were corrugated and textured wares (n = 353 out of 1,254 sherds); 38.8 percent (n = 386) were Classic period Tucson Basin decorated wares. As mentioned previously, the sherds found in Structure 4 likely represent trash dumping rather than vessels left behind in the house.

Ninety-four percent of the corrugated and other textured sherds found in the Central Locus (n = 2,633 out of 2,802) came from one feature, Structure 15. Corrugated and textured sherds outnumbered Tucson Basin decorated sherds (n = 1,660) in that same feature. According to the description of the structure (Chapter

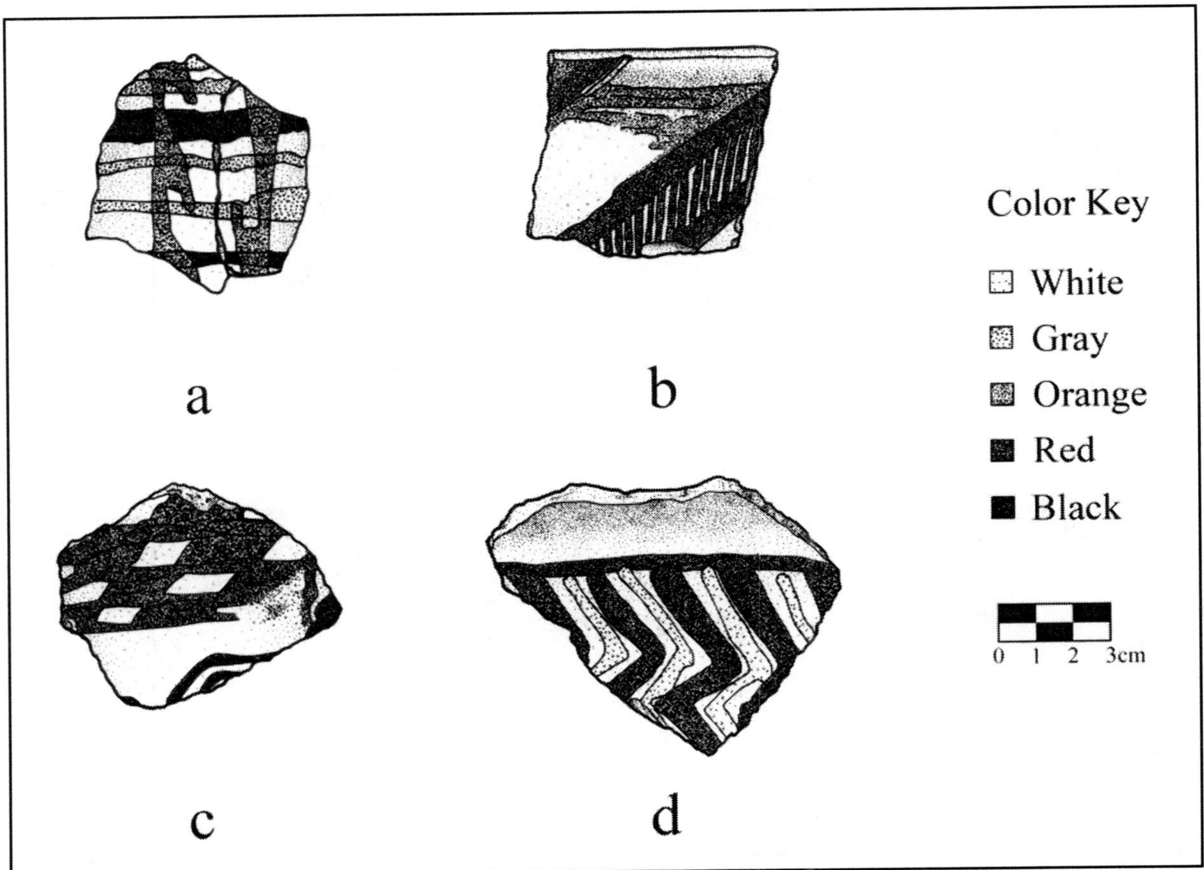

Figure 3.4. Assorted polychrome variants of Tanque Verde Red-on-brown: (a) Black and gray (faded black) parallel lines are underneath the overpainted red pendant hooks or triangles; the black paint appears to be organic; the red design was painted after the pot was fired. (b) Although difficult to see, the white lines outline the red painted areas in a manner similar to White Mountain Red wares; the interior also has white paint used to highlight red design. (c) This sherd has both red and black paint. (d) The paint on this vessel is bright; the red paint is thick and white heightens impact of red design. (drawing by Gerry Crouse).

2), portions of 4 large plain ware jars, 11 corrugated vessels (primarily jars), 8 painted vessels (probably Tanque Verde Red-on-brown) including 5 whole or partial bowls and 1 complete jar were found (Chapter 2; Appendices 3.A and 3B). Three plain ware sherds recovered from the feature are handle segments that may have come from small jugs. The number and types of vessels and presence of cholla buds, corn, and beans indicate that the house was a store room. None of the vessels was catalogued in the ASM collection as a partial or complete vessel but undoubtedly the large numbers of sherds (n = 8,686), most of which are big, are the remnants of those jars and bowls.

Corrugated sherds also outnumbered Tucson Basin decorated sherds in Structure 22, which is in the Northeastern Locus. In that feature, one Playas incised and 233 corrugated sherds were found, representing a minimum of two vessels. The corrugated wares make up 27 percent of the total number of sherds (n = 883) found in the feature. Tanque Verde Red-on-brown sherds make up 19 percent of the sherds from the structure (n = 171), representing a minimum of two vessels (Appendices 3.A and 3.B).

Corrugated sherds make up 20.6 percent

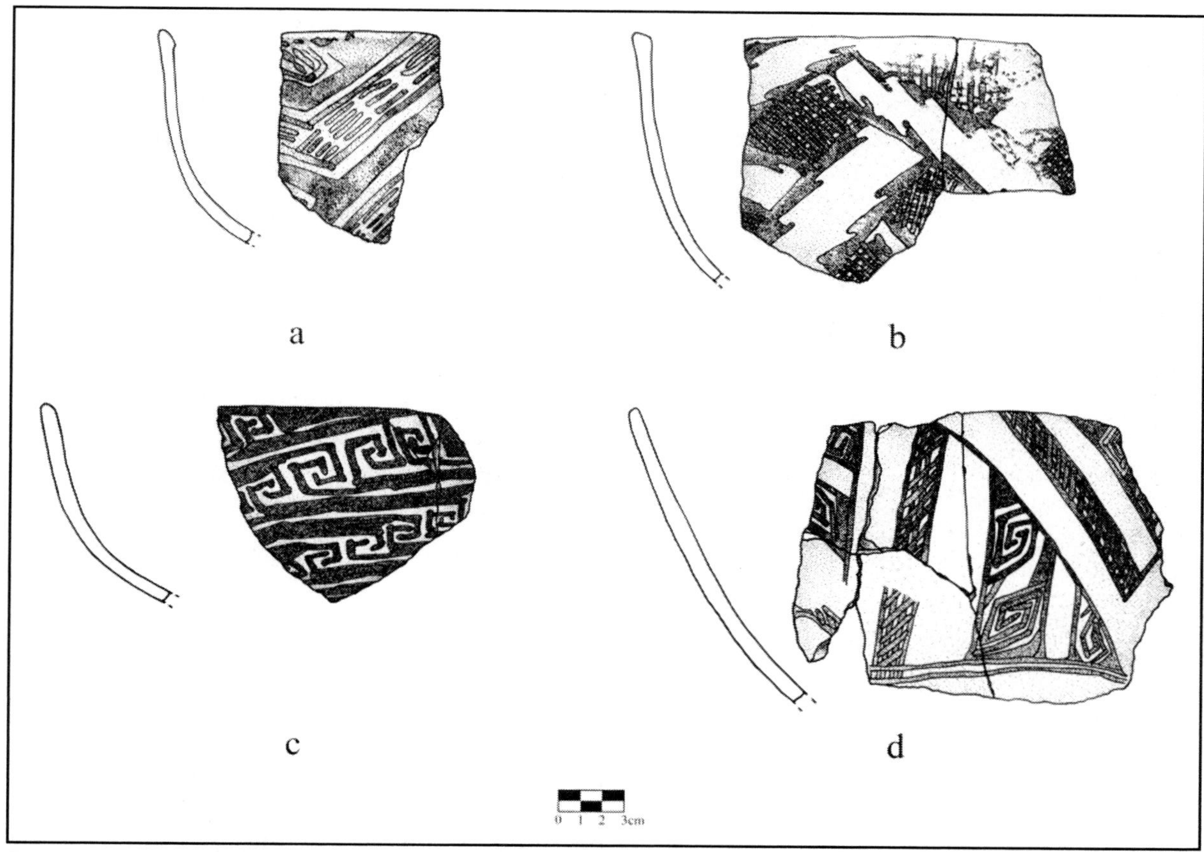

Figure 3.5. Tanque Verde Red-on-brown sherds with possible weaving or braiding designs: (a) parallel dash motif similar to designs on sashes found at Tonto National Monument; (b) brocade design with rotated symmetry and oblique interlaced weave; (c) design with simple interlocked frets illustrating brocade; and (d) design showing oblique interlacing and brocade (drawing by Gerry Crouse).

(n = 529 out of 2,572) of the sherds found in Structure 31a. The corrugated sherds represent a minimum of two vessels. In contrast, the 630 Tanque Verde Red-on-brown sherds including the black paint and white-slipped variants (24.5% of the collection from the feature) represent a minimum of five vessels (Appendices 3.A).

Although much of the pottery in structures appears to represent trash fill, several structures had intact floor assemblages that contained whole or reconstructible pots. Houses 8, 17, and 19 are examples of such houses.

As mentioned previously, excavators found six corrugated vessels in Structure 8, which is just outside the southwest corner of the compound. Four of these—two jars and two bowls—were found on the floor of the structure. Two partial corrugated jars were found in the fill of the feature, along with 90 percent of a hemispherical plain ware bowl. All of the vessels are of medium size (about 13 cm to 34 cm in diameter and 8 cm to 32 cm high), about right for serving or cooking, but not for storage. Skull fragments from mule deer and bighorn sheep were also found on the floor of the structure, as were a mano and a pestle. The floor assemblage may have been part of

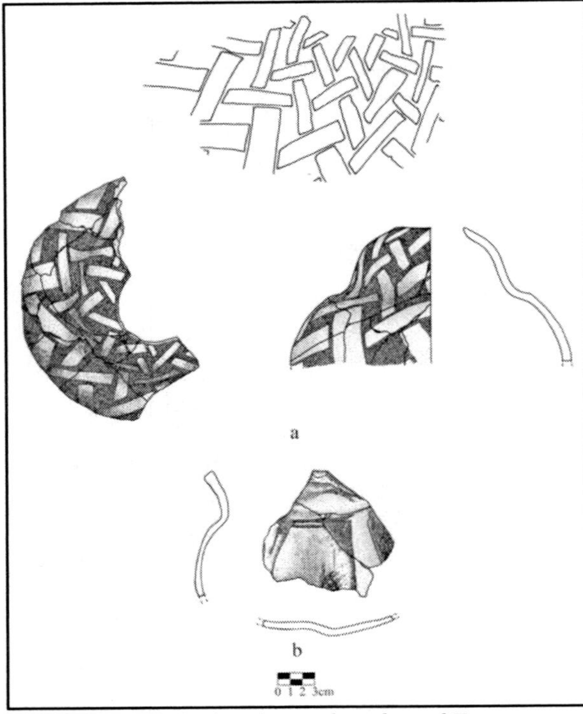

Figure 3.6. Bilobed and pumpkin-shaped Tanque Verde Red-on-brown vessels: (a) bilobed gourd-shaped jar from Structure 16 showing 1/1 interlacing, plain weave design found in basketry; (b) squash or pumpkin-shaped vessel fragments from floor of Structure 27b (drawing by Gerry Crouse).

a formal abandonment or retirement ritual, as the house was subsequently burned and filled with trash.

The floor assemblage of Structure 17 included three Tanque Verde Red-on-brown bowls, and one McDonald Corrugated bowl. Sherds in the fill included pieces of at least three Tanque Verde Red-on-brown bowls and one Tanque Verde Red-on-brown jar. A mano and an arrow shaft straightener were also found on the floor. In addition to the pottery and other artifacts inside the house, a Tanque Verde Red-on-brown jar and a corrugated jar were found on a working surface just outside of the structure. This house was also burned, but it contains very little trash.

Structure 19 is one of two houses built in the wash on the south side of the site. On its upper floor (19a), excavators found six whole or partial Tanque Verde Red-on-brown bowls and two obliterated corrugated bowls (Figure 3.8; see also Figure 2.25). The bowls range in size from 18.7 cm in diameter and 12.4 cm high to 31.7 cm in diameter and 19 cm high. Like those in Structure 8, the bowls seem to be of a serving size rather than storage size. In addition to the pottery, several projectile points, an ax fragment, a mano, an abrader, a lapstone, a pestle, two bone awls (one-double ended that may be a weaving heddle), a number of obsidian flakes, a polishing stone with red coloring on it, a piece of red quartzite with a ground corner, an igneous stone with polishing facets and striations, a piece of red ocher, and clusters of flakes were found on the floor. Also found on the floor were three and a half pronghorn or deer mandibles, a pronghorn skull, four antlers, other artiodactyl bones, and at least 16 rabbit or hare innominates that had been laid out as if they were strung together (Figures 8.1–8.4). The amount of material on the floor and the positioning of artifacts seems to reflect a purposeful (i.e., ritual) rather than incidental placement of the materials. I think that this structure also reflects a retirement or abandonment ritual—this house was also burned and there was very little trash in the layers above the burned roof and wall materials (see Chapter 11 for a discussion of ritual abandonment of houses).

Pottery Manufacture

Archaeologists who have worked with Whiptail Ruin pottery have tried to determine whether the ceramics were made on site or were imported from elsewhere in the Tucson Basin or points east. The most direct evidence for manufacture of Tanque Verde Red-on-brown pottery is an unfired jar found on the floor of Structure 12 (Figure 2.14). The crudely finished medium-sized jar has coarse sand temper.

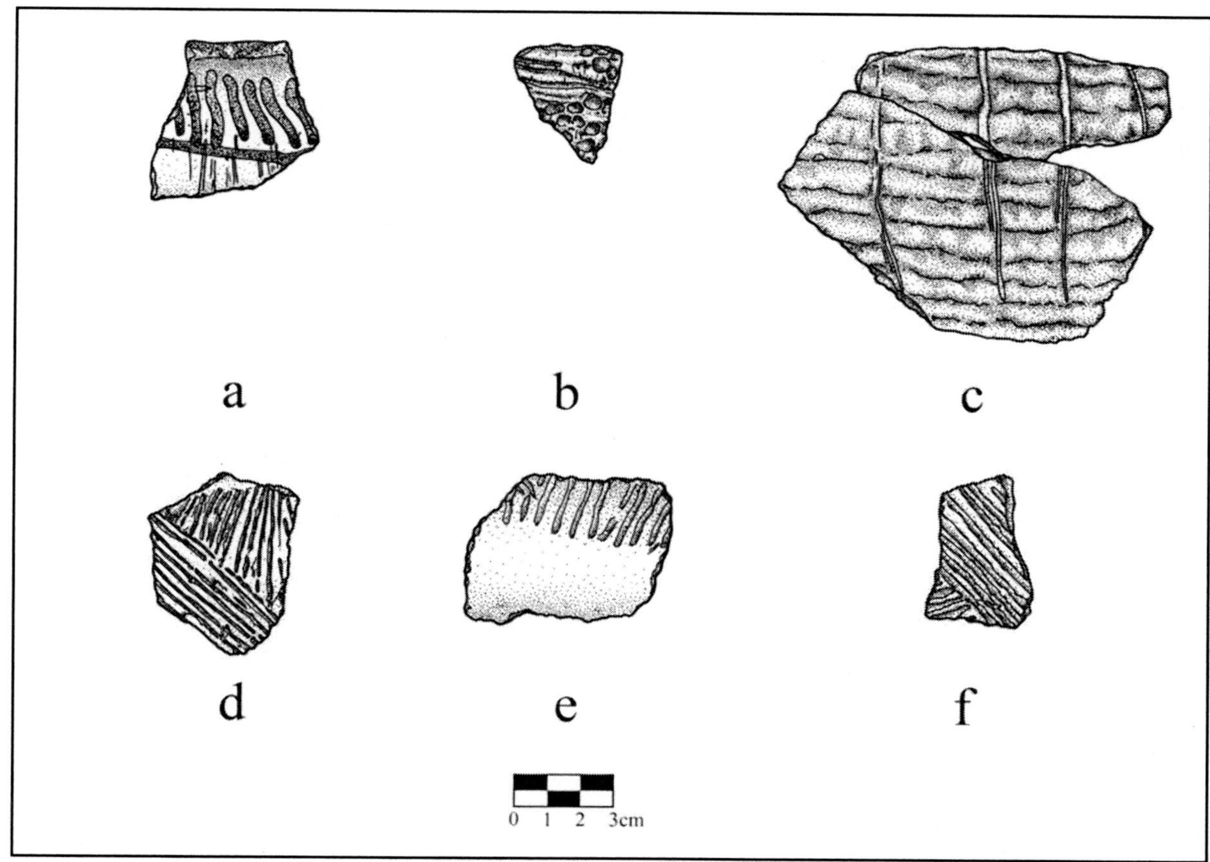

Figure 3.7. Assorted scored, incised, and tooled sherds: (a) Tanque Verde Red-on-brown jar with scoring (scratch-like marks) over the painted design; (b) clapboard corrugated and tooled jar sherd with red-slipped interior and nonlocal dark volcanic temper; (c) locally made obliterated indented corrugated sherd with incised lines; (d) Reserve-style incised jar sherd that was polished after incising; (e) incised sherd possibly from the San Pedro Valley; and (f) Playas Incised (drawing by Gerry Crouse).

Other evidence of pottery making was found in that room. A pile of unfired clay was found in association with a plain ware sherd that had been made into plate or, perhaps, a puki that was used support the base of a pot. Another large, plain ware sherd found on the floor had also been made into a plate or puki. A piece of kaolin clay with ground facets, several chunks of ocher and a hematite-coated rock were also found (Figure 7.1). Kaolin clay, usually associated with potters above the Mogollon Rim or in southwestern New Mexico, is uncommon in southern Arizona. It may have been used to make the slips on the white-slipped and black-on-white variants of Tanque Verde Red-on-brown. Three of the ocher chunks were found inside of a pottery vessel. The hematite-coated rock has faceted edges and scratch marks. The hematite appears to have been mixed with clay and packed into the rock for use in applying pigment (although perhaps not on ceramics; see Chapter 7). These pigmented rocks were also found in Structure 27b (Table 7.2). The assemblage of artifacts in Structure 12 appears to have been staged. The fire that destroyed the structure must have been slow and smoldering because it was not hot enough to fire the unfired jar or the pile of unfired clay on the floor.

The tempering material used in the pottery and the clay itself provide clues in regard

Table 3.13. Distribution of Wares by Locus and Feature, Showing Relative Percentages.

Provenience	Pre-Classic Tucson Basin Wares	Tucson Basin Classic Decorated Wares	Local Corrugated, Tooled, Incised Wares	Hohokam Plain Ware	Other Hohokam Wares	San Carlos Wares	Middle and Upper Santa Cruz Wares	Mogollon and Western Pueblo Wares	Salado Polychromes	Other	Total Number of Sherds
Surface			2 (7%)	2 (7%)	1 (3.4%)		1 (3.4%)	21 (72.4%)	1 (3.4%)	1 (3.4%)	29
Compound Locus											
Structure 4	0	386 (38.8%)	353 (28.1%)	512 (40.8%)	0	0	1 (0.1%)	2 (0.2%)	0	0	1254
Structure 6	12 (0.7%)	377 (22%)	128 (7%)	1208 (69.5%)	0	12 (0.7%)	0	2 (0.1%)	0	0	1739
Structure 7	10 (0.1%)	1805 (27%)	868 (13%)	3957 (59.2%)	0	38 (0.6%)	0	4 (0.1%)	0	3 (< 0.1%)	6685
Structure 8	15 (0.2%)	879 (13.4%)	656 (10%)	4967 (76%)	0	20 (0.3%)	0	2 (< 0.1%)	1 (<0.1%)	2 (< 0.1%)	6542
Structure 17	2 (0.1%)	832 (52.4%)	88 (5.5%)	647 (40.7%)	0	16 (1%)	0	0	0	3 (0.2%)	1588
Total, Compound Locus	39 (0.2%)	4279 (24%)	2093 (11.7%)	11291 (63.4%)	0	86 (0.5%)	1 (< 0.1%)	10 (0.1%)	1 (< 0.1%)	8 (< 0.1%)	17808
Central Locus											
Structure 5	0	297 (35%)	100 (12%)	453 (53%)	0	0	0	0	0	0	850
Structure 15	2 (< 0.1%)	1660 (19%)	2633 (30.3%)	4243 (49%)	0	146 (1.7%)	0	0	0	2 (< 0.1%)	8686
Structure 32	1 (0.1%)	421 (25.3%)	69 (4%)	1162 (70%)	0	10 (0.6%)	0	0	0	0	1663
Total, Central Locus	3 (< 0.1%)	2378 (21.2%)	2802 (25%)	5858 (52.3%)	0	156 (1.4%)	0	0	0	2 (< 0.1%)	11199
Southwestern Locus											
Structure 2	9 (0.2%)	1975 (44%)	323 (7.2%)	2113 (47%)	2 (< 0.1%)	65 (1.4%)	3 (0.1%)	4 (0.1%)	0	1 (< 0.1%)	4495
Structure 9	5 (0.2%)	502 (25%)	51 (2.5%)	1453 (71.7%)	0	9 (0.4%)	0	5 (0.2%)	0	0	2025
Structure 10	1 (0.1%)	432 (27.3%)	63 (4%)	1076 (68%)	1 (0.1%)	10 (0.6%)	0	0	0	0	1583
Between Structures 10 and 12	2 (0.4%)	130 (24.3%)	8 (1.5%)	394 (73.8%)	0	0	0	0	0	0	534
Structure 11	3 (0.1%)	866 (26%)	538 (16.2%)	1856 (55.8%)	42 (1.2%)	14 (0.4%)	0	4 (0.1%)	0	2 (0.1%)	3325
Structure 12	4 (0.1%)	1929 (25.1%)	442 (5.8%)	5218 (68%)	8 (0.1%)	54 (0.7%)	0	7 (0.1%)	0	5 (0.1%)	7667
Structure 13	0	475 (23%)	220 (10.5%)	1377 (66.1%)	0	7 (0.3%)	0	0	0	3 (0.1%)	2082
Structure 16	0	1030 (29.5%)	305 (9%)	2128 (61%)	0	20 (0.5%)	0	1 (< 0.1%)	0	0	3484
Structure 18	0	405 (25%)	69 (4%)	1143 (69.9%)	0	17 (1%)	0	0	0	1 (0.1%)	1635
Structure 24	9 (0.3%)	861 (24%)	406 (11.3%)	2264 (63.2%)	0	38 (1%)	0	3 (0.1%)	1 (< 0.1%)	0	3582
Structure 25	9 (0.1%)	1353 (22%)	396 (6%)	4474 (71.5%)	0	20 (0.3%)	1 (< 0.1%)	1 (< 0.1%)	0	0	6254
Structure 26	0	209 (27%)	35 (5%)	517 (67%)	0	11 (1%)	0	0	0	0	772
Cremation 96/1	0	6 (100%)	0	0	0	0	0	0	0	0	6
grid squares	1 (17%)	0	0	0	0	0	0	3 (50%)	2 (33%)	0	6
Total, Southwestern Locus	43 (0.1%)	10173 (27%)	2856 (7.6%)	24013 (64%)	53 (0.1%)	265 (1%)	4 (< 0.1%)	28 (0.1%)	3 (< 0.1%)	12 (< 0.1%)	37450

Table 3.13. Distribution of Wares by Locus and Feature, Showing Relative Percentages, cont'd.

Provenience	Pre-Classic Tucson Basin Wares	Tucson Basin Classic Decorated Wares	Local Corrugated, Tooled, Incised Wares	Hohokam Plain Ware	Other Hohokam Wares	San Carlos Wares	Middle and Upper Santa Cruz Wares	Mogollon and Western Pueblo Wares	Salado Polychromes	Other	Total Number of Sherds
					Northern Locus						
Structure 3	0	774 (39%)	241 (12%)	976 (49%)	0	0	0	0	0	0	1991
Structure 20	0	315 (25.6%)	200 (16.3%)	712 (58%)	0	0	0	1 (0.1%)	0	0	1228
Structure 21	1 (0.1%)	147 (20.7%)	90 (12.7%)	467 (66%)	0	3 (0.4%)	0	0	0	1 (0.1%)	709
Structure 27a	1 (0.1%)	398 (25.1%)	280 (17.7%)	880 (55.7%)	0	22 (1.4%)	0	0	0	0	1581
Structure 27b	4 (0.2%)	500 (27%)	300 (16.2%)	1041 (56.2%)	0	5 (0.3%)	0	2 (0.1%)	0	0	1852
Structure 28	0	244 (31.7%)	135 (17.6%)	385 (50%)	4 (0.5%)	1 (0.1%)	0	0	0	0	769
Structure 29	5 (0.1%)	1029 (26.5%)	578 (14.9%)	2230 (57.5%)	4 (0.1%)	31 (0.8%)	0	4 (0.1%)	0	0	3881
Structure 30	3 (0.1%)	519 (21.2%)	306 (12.5%)	1594 (65.3%)	2 (0.1%)	18 (0.7%)	0	0	0	0	2442
Structure 31a	2 (0.1%)	630 (24.5%)	529 (20.6%)	1405 (54.6%)	0	5 (0.2%)	0	1 (< 0.1%)	0	0	2572
Structure 31b	2 (<0.1%)	1383 (25.7%)	1033 (19.2%)	2931 (54.5%)	2 (< 0.1%)	20 (0.4%)	0	8 (0.1%)	0	0	5379
Structure 31c	0	901 (23.7%)	500 (13.2%)	2381 (62.7%)	7 (0.2%)	6 (0.2%)	1 (< 0.1%)	1 (<0.1%)	0	0	3797
Total, Northern Locus	18 (0.1%)	6840 (26%)	4192 (16%)	15002 (57.3%)	19 (0.1%)	111 (0.4%)	1 (<0.1%)	17 (0.1%)	0	1 (<0.1%)	26201
					Southern Locus						
Structure 14	2 (0.1%)	380 (20.8%)	120 (6.6%)	1325 (72.5%)	0	0	0	0	0	0	1827
Structure 19	1 (0.1%)	400 (25%)	171 (10.8%)	1016 (64%)	0	0	0	2 (0.1%)	0	0	1590
Total, Southern locus	3 (0.1%)	780 (22.8%)	291 (8.5%)	2341 (68.5%)	0	0	0	2 (0.1%)	0	0	3417
					Northeastern Locus						
Structure 22		171 (19%)	234 (27%)	474 (53.7%)	0	2 (0.2%)	0	0	0	1 (0.1%)	883
Structure 42		155 (23%)	123 (18%)	399 (58%)	0	4 (0.6%)	0	0	0	3 (0.4%)	684
Total, Northeastern Locus	0	326 (20.8%)	357 (22.8%)	873 (55.7%)	0	6 (0.4%)	0	0	0	4 (0.3%)	1566
Grand Totals	**106 (0.1%)**	**24776 (25%)**	**12593 (13%)**	**59380 (61%)**	**73 (0.1%)**	**624 (0.6%)**	**7 (<0.1%)**	**78 (0.1%)**	**5 (<0.1%)**	**28 (<0.1%)**	**97670**

to where vessels were manufactured. As mentioned previously, a chemical study of the clay and a petrographic analysis of tempering material were conducted.

The clay study was conducted by Carl F. Aten (Appendix A). He dissolved pottery samples and used an inductively coupled plasma spectrometer to determine the chemical spectrum of the resulting solution. He looked at 14 elements in particular—aluminum, calcium, iron, magnesium, strontium, barium, titanium, manganese, potassium, zirconium, boron, zinc, vanadium, and copper. The concentrations of barium, boron, zinc, and copper proved to be too low and agreement between duplicate samples poor, so the final analysis dealt with the remaining 10 elements.

The 13 sherds sampled included plain ware and Tanque Verde Red-on-brown. Three of the samples were taken from Tanque Verde Red-on-brown bowls found in Structure 27b and a fourth sample was taken from a plain ware vessel found in that feature. The other sherds came from various other features. Aten also processed and analyzed two locally collected clays. One of the clays came from a "saltbush flat northwest of Whiptail Ruin" (Appendix A). This was likely the dried spring area west of the existing ponds at Agua Caliente Park. The second sample came from the north bank of the wash on the south side of the site, that is, the wash that contains Structures 14 and 19.

Aten was able to cluster the samples into two groups. Seven of the plain ware samples came from a single clay source, although that clay source was not determined. Two samples, from two Tanque Verde Red-on-brown bowls found in Structure 27b, came from one clay source. The samples from the plain ware vessel and the other Tanque Verde Red-on-brown vessel from Structure 27b came from other clay sources. One sample, a plain ware rim sherd (provenience unspecified), matched the clay from the saltbush flat. None of the samples could be correlated with the clay from the wash. The results of this study indicate that at least some of the pottery was made using materials available on or near the site and that particular clay sources were used to make more than one vessel at a time.

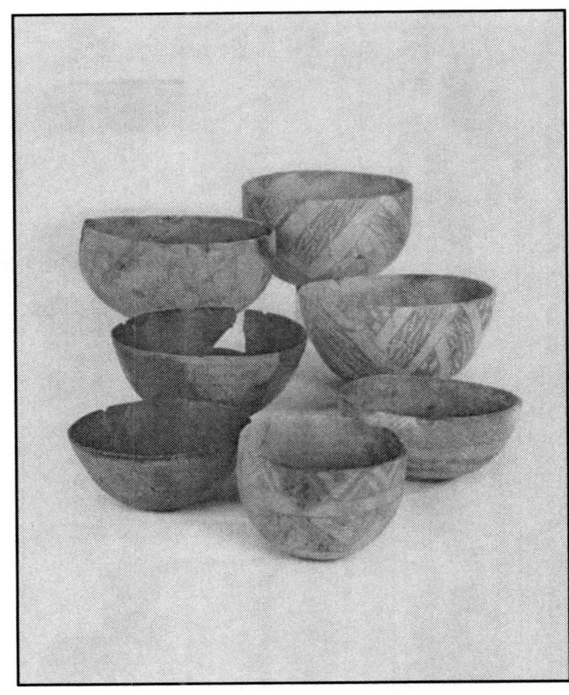

Figure 3.8. Corrugated and Tanque Verde Red-on-brown bowls found on the floor of Structure 19a (photograph by Helga Teiwes).

James Lombard's petrographic study (Appendix B) consisted of preparing thin sections of 12 sherds: three Tanque Verde Red-on-brown, three plain ware, and six corrugated. He found that the temper compositions among the 12 samples are nearly identical, consisting of granitic sands with an abundance of quartz, biotite mica, and granitic plutonic rock fragments. Lombard did not collect any local wash sands, but thought that the high frequency of plutonic rocks and low frequency of mylonitic particles (derived from the metamorphic granitic terranes that are common in and around the site) implied that wash sands were not used in the pottery sampled for the study. Instead, Lombard suggests that the potters collected clays that were naturally mixed with nonmylonitic sand in the vicinity of the Agua Caliente Hills and Milagrosa Canyon area, or the Rillito I Beds that outcrop "less than 1 kilometer south of the site" (Appendix B).

Lombard's study has two main implications. First, the pottery sampled was made using clays and tempers that were available in the immediate vicinity of the site. Second, corrugated pottery was made using locally available materials. Tucson Basin manufacture of corrugated pottery was confirmed in a petrographic analysis done by James Heidke for the Gibbon Springs site. Ninety-one percent of the corrugated wares he sampled were tempered with Catalina Petrofacies sands (Heidke 1996:264). Of interest to this study is that Lombard's results seem to imply a more restricted local temper source than the area circumscribed as contributing to the Catalina Petrofacies. This may mean that at least some of the Whiptail potters used a specific temper (and possibly clay) source that was distinct from the temper sources used by potters from Gibbon Springs and other sites in the area.

Migration Implications

The presence of locally manufactured corrugated pottery in the northeastern portion of the Tucson Basin strongly indicates that the people in the area were part of the migration from the Mogollon highlands in the early to mid-A.D. 1200s. This migration presaged the Kayenta Anasazi movement to southeastern Arizona that occurred in the late A.D. 1200s (Clark and Lengyel 2002).

Corrugated ceramics are not associated with the Hohokam pottery tradition and they do not predate the early Classic period in the Hohokam culture area. In the Tucson Basin, they are rare outside of the area east of Pantano Wash and north of Rincon Creek. But in the northeastern part of the basin, only a few sites—Whiptail Ruin, Gibbon Springs, and possibly Sabino/Bear Canyon Ruin—contain relatively high percentages of the wares (13% at Whiptail and 15.3% at Gibbon Springs; materials from Sabino/Bear Canyon have yet to be analyzed).

Moving away from these three sites, the numbers and relative percentages of corrugated wares drop off precipitously. At the Classic period component of the Tanque Verde Wash site, which is about four miles southwest of Whiptail, only three corrugated sherds (out of 17,299) were recovered. Heidke and Lavayen's (2009) petrographic analysis of those three sherds showed that two were made using local Catalina petrofacies sands and the third was produced in the San Pedro Valley.

South of Whiptail, along the bajadas coming out of the Rincon Mountains in Saguaro National Park East, corrugated sherds were found in small numbers. At the cluster of sites around the Tanque Verde Ruin and AZ BB:14:24(ASM), five percent of the sherds recorded during a survey were corrugated, and corrugated sherds make up two percent of the sherds recovered from excavations at AZ BB:14:24(ASM) (Zahniser 1966). Zahniser (1970) found one site—AZ BB:14:42—where seven percent (16 out of 236) of the sherds he collected were corrugated. In a later survey, Simpson and Wells (1983:57) found 61 sites with Classic period components. Forty-four of the sites had small numbers of corrugated sherds. At site SAGU 83A-101, they collected 11 corrugated sherds in their sample of 3,000 pieces (Simpson and Wells 1983:59). And in the 1990s, Kevin Wellman (1994) found two sites with corrugated pottery in a survey of a land acquisition for the park.

Clark and Lengyel (2002) mapped the distribution of corrugated wares in east-central and southeastern Arizona and discovered a gradation that ranges from 80 percent of utilitarian assemblages (i.e., nonpainted wares) in the Silver Creek area north of Showlow to 30 percent near San Manuel in the lower San Pedro Valley to between 10 and 20 percent in the northeastern Tucson Basin. Moving west into the Tucson Basin, corrugated pottery becomes very rare; only a few sherds are ever found on Classic period sites. If the presence of locally made corrugated ware implies the presence of Mogollon Highland migrants in the Tucson Basin, as I think it does, then the precipitous drop-off in corrugated pottery outside of the northeastern basin implies that the migration may have stopped in the vicinity of Whiptail, Gibbon Springs, and Sabino/Bear Canyon. The migration issue is discussed more thoroughly in Chapter 11.

Pottery Use at the Site

As migrants introduced, distributed, and manufactured corrugated wares in new areas, they adapted the technology to local vessel shapes and sizes. Before A.D. 1200, above the Mogollon Rim and especially in Anasazi country where corrugated pottery seems to have originated, corrugated wares are thought to have been used primarily as cooking pots. As the technology spread south, potters began to increase the sizes of the jars and to make more bowls. By the time corrugated pottery reached the northeastern Tucson Basin, corrugated wares were being used for storage, serving, and, probably, personal eating vessels. I have seen little to suggest that the corrugated vessels found at either Whiptail or Gibbon Springs (Gregonis 1996) were used for cooking. Instead, the corrugated wares include jars of varying sizes (Figures 3.9 and 3.10), bowls ranging from about two cups in size (including at least one with a red-slipped interior) to large McDonald Corrugated bowls that may have been used in feasting. Although the provenience information is sketchy, the handled jar illustrated in Figure 3.10 was probably used to hold a cremation that was found outside of structure 27a.

Out of the minimum of 102 corrugated vessels of various types (including McDonald Corrugated and corrugated and incised wares) identified in the Whiptail collection, 45 were bowl forms, 46 were jars, and the shapes of 11 could not be determined. The nearly even ratio of bowls to jars suggests that they were used for a range of activities at the site. The corrugated ware ratio contrasts with plain wares, which have a ratio of 1.2 jars to every bowl (n = 45 bowl forms and 53 jar forms), and Tanque Verde Red-on-brown and Polychrome vessels, which have a ratio of 1.5 bowls to every jar (n = 99 bowl forms and 63 jar forms). The site as a whole has a ratio of 1.4 bowls to 1 jar (n = 280 bowl forms including scoops and 199 jar forms) (Appendix 3.A).

The general ratio of more bowls than jars holds for most of the features at the site, including two of the three features that excavators described as "storage rooms," where more jars than bowls might be expected. Structure 15 contained a minimum of 11 bowls and 9 jars (a 1.2 to 1 ratio). Structure 27a contained a minimum of seven bowls and five jars (a 1.8 to 1 ratio). Structure 3, the other possible storage structure contained four bowls and four jars (a 1 to 1 ratio). Structure 19 contained the highest bowl:jar ratio with 3.75 bowls recovered for every jar (n = 15 bowls and 4 jars).

Structures that contained slightly more jars than bowls were compound Structures 4 (1.3 jars to 1 bowl) and 6 (1.25 jars to 1 bowl); Southwestern Locus Structures 9 (1.2 jars to 1 bowl), 10 (1.3 jars to 1 bowl), and 16 (1.1 jars to 1 bowl); and Northeastern Locus Structure 42 (2 jars to 1 bowl). Structures 4 and 6 were trash filled; the vessel ratios in those houses probably reflect activities in and around the compound rather than use of the structures. Structure 9 had an intact floor assemblage that may have

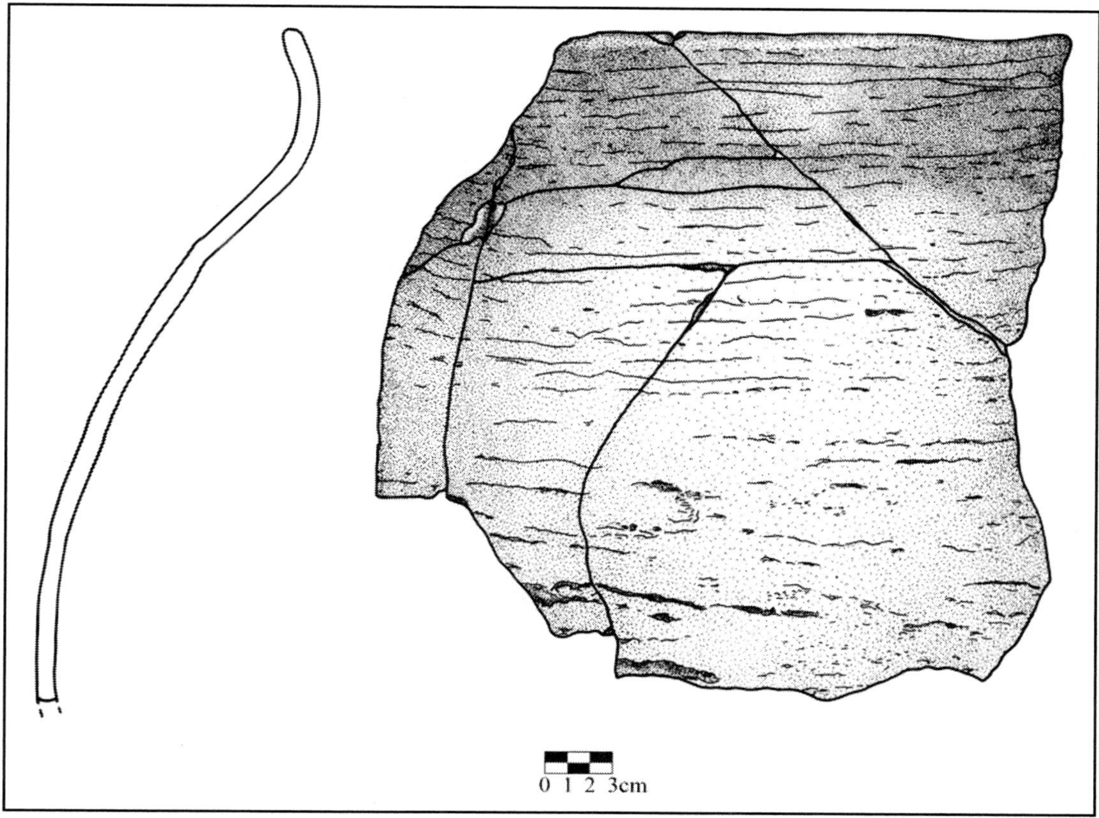

Figure 3.9. Large obliterated corrugated jar found in Structure 11. The jar has a 4.5 cm high straight neck with a 24 cm diameter orifice. The whole vessel was at least 4 gallons in size. It has Catalina petrofacies temper (drawing by Gerry Crouse).

included storage jars; the association of the pottery found in Structure 10 is uncertain; and a possible corrugated storage jar was found on the floor of Structure 16. Three medium to large jars (one plain, one corrugated, one Tanque Verde Red-on-brown) and a Tanque Verde Red-on-brown bowl were found on the floor of Feature 42. It appears from the architectural descriptions (Chapter 2) that medium to large jars occur in a number of features at the site. This may imply that each household kept one or more jars in each of their rooms for storage rather than dedicating one room in their household group of rooms to storage. Or, it may mean that an assortment of bowls and jars was placed on the floors of various structures as part of a formal retirement ceremony.

Recycled Vessels, Worked Sherds, and Modeled Spindle Whorls

At most Hohokam sites, broken pots and sherds were reused in various ways (Table 3.14; Figure 3.11). The Whiptail Ruin is no exception. For example, the hearth in Feature 42 was constructed by burying a Tanque Verde Red-on-brown bowl into the floor so that the rim was even with the floor. Another recycled Tanque Verde Red-on-brown bowl was found on the floor of Structure 10 (Table 3.14). A shallow plate found in Structure 7 had been made out of a Tanque Verde Red-on-brown jar. The flat base of a large obliterated corrugated jar was found on the floor of Structure 5 and about one quarter of a plate made from a large plain ware sherd was found in Structure 27. Figure 3.11e

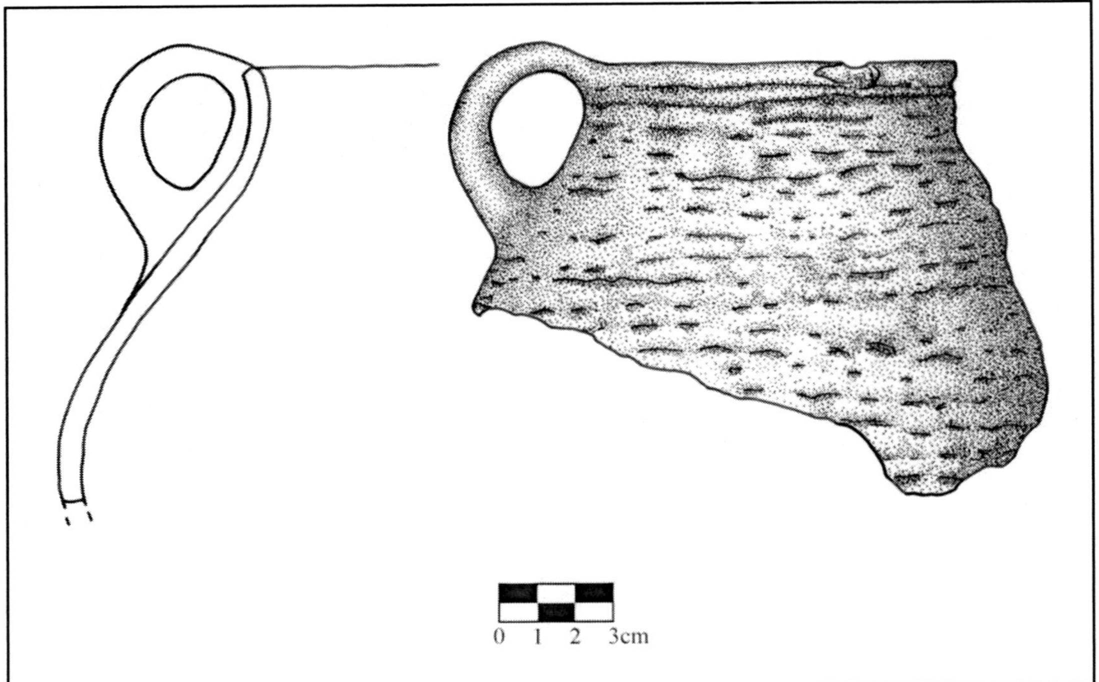

Figure 3.10. Handled corrugated jar, probably vessel holding cremation found outside of Structure 27a. The jar has a 10-cm-diameter neck and was about quart-sized when whole (drawing by Gerry Crouse).

illustrates a piece of a large Tanque Verde Red-on-brown bowl or platter that was reworked into a plate.

Structure 12 contained several recycled vessels and worked sherds. In addition to the previously mentioned plain ware plate that was found under a pile of unfired clay, a plate made from a plain ware jar, and a corrugated bowl made from a jar were found on the floor of the structure. A trapezoidal plain ware sherd with ground edges was found in the structure. Three perforated disks were also found in Structure 12, one in the fill and two on the floor (Table 3.14).

Thirteen other perforated disks, which are generally thought to be spindle whorls, were found at the site. Two were found in Structure 3, two in Structure 8, three in Structure 10, two in Structure 11, one west of Structure 6 (Figure 3.11a), and one each in Structures 4, 9, and 20. The perforated disk found in Structure 20 was made from a White Mountain Red Ware sherd. Five disks with partially drilled holes were also found—one in Structure 9, one in Structure 10, one in Structure 19, one in Structure 23, and one in Structure 27a (Table 3.14).

Three modeled clay spindle whorls were also found at the site. One was found in the fill of Structure 10. It has one flat surface and one convex surface that has a raised lump in its center. The artifact is 3.3 cm in diameter and 1.7 cm thick. Another was found in Structure 20. The whorl is made out of local clay with mica inclusions; it is rain-drop or top shaped, with wear on the pointed end. The whorl is 3.5 cm wide, 3 cm high, and 1.5 cm in diameter at its tip. The third spindle whorl was found in a post hole in Structure 13. It is wider at one end than the other and resembles a rounded door knob. It has a hole through the center that is slightly indented. The whorl is 2.1 cm long, 1.7 cm in diameter at its smallest diameter and 3.5 cm in diameter at its widest.

Eleven unperforated disks were found in

features and on the surface of the site: two were in Structures 3 and 23 and one each in Structures 4, 18, 20, 24, 27a, 29, and the surface of the site (Figure 3.11b, c; Table 3.14). Although such disks are found on most Hohokam sites, their uses are unknown. The same is true of the many sherds with one or two ground edges that occur in Hohokam sites. Some of these may be pottery scraping and polishing tools; others may simply be sherds that had one edge exposed to heavy foot traffic that wore that edge down. Twelve sherds with ground edges were found at Whiptail: one each in Structures 2, 3, 4, 8, 9, 23, 24, 25, 29, and the compound; two in the fill of Structure 15 (Table 3.14).

Still other worked sherds found at the site had odd shapes. One roughly oval sherd made from a red-slipped corrugated ware was found in Structure 2. A spearpoint-shaped sherd from Structure 8 was made from a plain or red ware sherd, and a roughly finished rectangular Tanque Verde Red-on-brown sherd from Structure 31 had the start of an off-center hole on one side. Six sherds had what appeared to be repair holes in them. One each was found in Structures 7, 10, 30, and Cemetery 2 in the Southwestern Locus; two were found in Structure 25 (Table 3.14). A large plain ware jar sherd with whittled edges was also found (Figure 3.11d); its provenience is unknown.

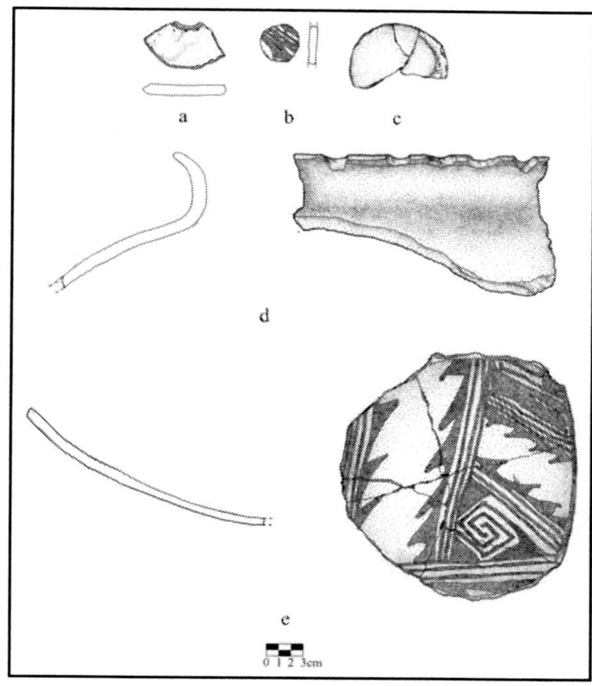

Figure 3.11. Worked sherds: (a) about 1/3 of a perforated disk with a large diameter hole; (b) unperforated disk with ground edges; (c) plain ware sherd with ground edges made from near the base of a vessel with a Classic shoulder; (d) rim from a large plain ware jar with whittled edge; (e) large plate made from a Tanque Verde Red-on-brown bowl (drawing by Gerry Crouse).

Other Clay Objects

In addition to the modeled spindle whorls described in the previous section, figurine fragments and other clay objects were found. Fragments of five figurines were found at Whiptail. Two of these—one human and one animal figurine fragment—were found in Structure 4. The human figurine fragment was found in the eastern post hole. The artifact is roughly cylindrical and made of brown clay with coarse sand temper. It has a flat face and slight indentations for the eyes. It has a typical, ridge-like nose. Areas where the arms should be have been broken off. The figurine is 7.5 cm long and 3.7 cm in diameter. The artifact was catalogued as ASM Number A-38,197.

A fragment from an animal figurine was found in the lower fill of Structure 4. The artifact has an irregular, ill-defined shape. It is made of a reddish brown clay with sand temper. It has a nose-like projection with a lump above it. It might be classified as a deer or dog. The figurine is 22.2 cm long (not including the nose) and 2.9 cm high. The figurine fragment has been catalogued as ASM A-38,195.

A human figurine head and torso was found in the lower fill of Structure 16. The figurine has a cylindrical body and micaceous temper. The head is flattened with a large nose

Table 3.14. Recycled Vessels and Worked Sherds.

Provenience	Description
	Plates and Other Dishes
Structure 5 floor	This is the flat base of what once was a large obliterated corrugated jar. The edge is rough and uneven with no attempt to smooth or otherwise alter it. The interior is smoothed but not polished. Part of the interior has some sooting or smoking that has produced a dark gray, mottled area. There appear to be traces of hematite on the lighter potion of the inside. The exterior has been stuccoed. It is 15 by 21.9 cm and 5.5 cm high.
Structure 7	This artifact consists of about 3/4 of a plate or shallow bowl made by grinding the edges of a Tanque Verde Red-on-brown jar fragment. It is 32 cm by 24 cm and is 8 cm high (ASM Catalog Number A-38,139).
Structure 8, floor	Twelve sherds make up this plate made from the base of an obliterated corrugated jar. The edges of the plate have been ground. The interior is smudged except for small area along one edge. The exterior of the plate is worn. Reconstructed from 12 sherds, it is 21.8 cm in diameter and curves to a height of 5 cm (ASM Catalog Number A-38,143).
Structure 10 floor	This mended, complete Tanque Verde Red-on-brown bowl has been formed by grinding down the upper portion of a larger bowl. Most of the rim is missing; the bowl has a slightly rounded base, flared sides, and an uneven rim. The interior of the rim has a band with a series of parallel lines forming triangular or V-shaped areas. On the exterior, a plated design includes parallel lines with lines of opposed pendant triangles and triangles with rectilinear scrolls. The vessel has a repair hole on one side. The bowl is 28 cm in diameter and 11 cm high (ASM Catalog Number A-38,127).
Structure 12 floor, under pile of unfired mud or clay	This small plate is made from a plain ware vessel. It has uneven edges and is roughly round in plan view. It has blackened exterior. The plate is 17.4 cm in diameter and is 2.1 cm high (ASM Catalog Number A-38,184).
Structure 12 floor	This plate is made from a large, plain ware jar sherd. The edges of the plate have been ground. It has a slightly rounded base and low sides that flare out to the rim. The sherd is thicker in the center than on the edges. The interior of the plate is pitted and weathered. The plate is 29.4 cm in diameter and 4.8 cm high.
Structure 12 floor	This obliterated corrugated bowl was made from the lower portion of a jar. It has a flat base and an uneven rim created by grinding down the top of a coil. The interior of the vessel is fire blackened. The bowl is 28 cm in diameter and 8.5 cm to 15.5 cm high (ASM Catalog Number A-38,144).
Structure 27, top of south wall	This is about one quarter of a disk or plate made from a large plain ware sherd. When whole, it was about 12 cm in diameter.
Structure 30, SW 1/4 floor contact	A large Tanque Verde Red-on-brown bowl or platter sherd made into a roughly round to oblong plate. The sherd is 19.4 cm from the rim to one ground edge and 20.5 cm from one ground edge to another (Figure 3.11e).
	Perforated Disks
Structure 3 fill	Half of a perforated red ware disk was found in the fill of Structure 3. It is 3.3 by 2.1 cm in size (ASM Catalog No. A-38,267 x-2).
Structure 3 fill	One quarter of a perforated plain ware disk was found in Structure 3. The complete disk was about 6 cm in diameter; the hole is about 6 mm in diameter.
Structure 4 fill	This half of a perforated disk was made from a plain ware sherd. The disk has ground edges; it is 3.3 cm in diameter and has a 3-mm-diameter hole.
West of Structure 6	This artifact consists of about 1/3 of a perforated disk with a large diameter hole, made on a plain ware sherd. The sherd is 3.5 cm in radius, has a beveled, ground center hole and chipped and ground edged (Figure 3.11a).
Structure 8 fill	This perforated disk fragment made from a plain ware sherd is roughly circular in shape; it is 4.9 cm in diameter and 7 mm thick (ASM Catalog No. A-38,055).
Structure 8 fill	This perforated disk fragment was made from a plain ware sherd with a fire cloud. The artifact is 4.7 cm in diameter an 8 mm thick (ASM Catalog No. A-38,064).
Structure 9 fill	This perforated disk fragment (about 1/4 represented) was made from a red ware. It has ground edges and a 2-cm radius.
Structure 10	This perforated disk is red-slipped on its concave surface and has a fire cloud on its exterior. The sherd is 4.6 cm in diameter and has 5-mm-thick vessel walls (ASM Catalog No. A-38,052).

Table 3.14. Recycled Vessels and Worked Sherds, cont'd.

Provenience	Description
Structure 10	This perforated disk was made from a red ware sherd with a smudged interior. The disk is 4.3 cm in diameter and 4 mm thick (ASM Catalog No. A-38,053).
Structure 10 floor	This perforated disk is roughly circular, with one flat and one irregular surface. The disk is 5.2 cm in diameter and 5 mm thick (ASM Catalog No. A-38,063).
Structure 11 floor fill	This perforated sherd disk has slightly irregular surfaces. It is 5 cm in diameter and 6-mm-thick walls (ASM Catalog No. A-38,062).
Structure 11, pit 16	This perforated sherd disk is roughly circular and has a biconically drilled center hole. The disk is 4.7 cm in diameter and 3-mm-thick walls (ASM Catalog No. A-38,059).
Structure 12 fill	This perforated disk fragment is roughly circular. It is 3.6 cm in diameter and 7 mm thick (ASM Catalog No. A-38,056).
Structure 12 floor	This perforated disk is roughly circular and has two flat surfaces. The sherd is 6.3 cm in diameter and 4 mm thick (ASM Catalog No. A-38,060).
Structure 12 floor	This perforated sherd disk is roughly circular. It is 4.8 cm in diameter and 5 mm thick (ASM Catalog No. A-38,061).
Structure 20	This is a whole perforated disk with ground edges made from a black-on-red White Mountain Red ware bowl. It is 4.5 cm in diameter and 4 mm thick.
Partially Perforated Disks	
Structure 9 fill	This Tanque Verde Red-on-brown sherd disk has the start of a drill hole on one side. The disk is 6 by 5.2 cm and 9 mm thick (ASM Catalog No. A-38,110).
Structure 10 fill	This disk fragment made from a piece of plain ware has an unfinished drill hole. It was probably about 4.1 cm in diameter and has 8 mm thick (ASM Catalog No. A-38,057).
Structure 19	This sherd disk with chipped edges has the start of a drill hole on one side. It was made from a micaceous plain ware; it is 3.3 cm in diameter and 7 mm thick.
Structure 23 fill	This complete plain ware disk with chipped edges has the start of a drill hole near its center. It is 6.5 cm in diameter.
Structure 27a fill	This plain ware disk has chipped edges and is 3.2 cm diameter. It has the start of a drill hole on its interior surface.
Unperforated Disks	
Structure 3 fill	This whole plain ware disk is 4.4 cm in diameter (ASM Catalog No. A-38,267 x-2).
Structure 3 roof fall	This whole disk made from a plain ware sherd has smoothed and rounded edges. It is 5.3 cm in diameter and 1.1 cm thick (ASM Catalog No. A-38,108).
Structure 4 fill	This whole disk made from a plain ware sherd has ground edges. It is 3 cm in diameter and is unperforated.
Structure 18 fill	About 1/4 of a plain ware disk was found in the fill of Structure 18. It is 3 cm by 2 cm in size and has ground edges. It does not appear to have been ground.
Structure 20	This sherd disk with ground edges is made from a micaceous plain ware. It has beveled edges and is 4.5 cm on one side and 4 cm in diameter on the other. It is 1 cm thick.
Structure 23 floor b	This disk with ground edges was made from a Late Rincon Red-on-brown or Tanque Verde Red-on-brown sherd. It is 3 cm in diameter (Figure 3.11b).
Structure 23 floor b	This disk with ground edges was made from a micaceous plain ware jar sherd. It is about 8 cm in diameter. Four pieces of the disk were found.
Structure 24 fill	This whole plain ware sherd disk has ground edges; it is 4.4 by 5 cm in diameter.
Structure 27a fill	This micaceous plain ware sherd was made into a disk with ground edges. It is 5.5 by 4.2 cm in size; about 3/4 of the sherd is represented. The sherd was made from near the base of a vessel with a Classic shoulder (Figure 3.11c).
Structure 29 fill	This complete plain ware disk has chipped edges. It is 5 cm in diameter.
General Site	This whole sherd disk has slightly ground edges. It is made from a plain ware and is 5 by 4.6 cm. It is 9 mm thick (ASM Catalog No. A-38,113).

Table 3.14. Recycled Vessels and Worked Sherds, cont'd.

Provenience	Description
	Sherds with Ground Edges
Structure 2	This possible scraper was made from a plain ware sherd. It is roughly rectangular and has two parallel edges that are smoothed and finished. Reconstructed from two pieces, it is 6.5 by 4.5 cm and 8 mm thick (ASM Catalog No. A-38,111).
Structure 3 fill	This triangular plain ware sherd has one ground edge. It is 3 by 3 by 4 cm; one of 3-cm edges is ground.
Structure 4 fill	This possible pottery scraper was made from a plain ware sherd. It has a curved, ground edge and is 3.1 by 2.2 cm in size and 5 mm thick (ASM Catalog No. 38,266).
Structure 8 outside S wall and entry	This obliterated corrugated sherd has one curved, ground edge. The sherd is 5 by 8 cm.
Structure 9 fill	This plain ware sherd was made into a possible scraper. It is roughly square, with two edges and one corner ground smooth and rounded. It is 4.2 by 3.6 cm and is 6 mm thick (ASM Cat No. A-38,112).
Structure 12 fill	This trapezoidally shaped plain ware sherd has ground edges and is roughly 4 by 4.5 to 5 cm.
Structure 15	This roughly triangular red ware sherd may have been a scraper. It is 3 by 2.1 cm and 5 mm thick. The edges of the short side and one long side have been worked smoothed (ASM Catalog No. A-38,054).
Structure 15 fill	This plain ware sherd has one ground edge and one chipped edge. It may have been half of a disk and is 5 by 9 cm in size.
Structure 23 fill	This Tanque Verde Red-on-brown sherd has two ground edges--one straight and one curved. The sherd is 3.5 by 2.6 cm in size.
Structure 24 fill	This Tanque Verde Red-on-brown sherd has two ground edges. It is 3.4 by 5 cm in size.
Structure 25 test pit	This 4 by 6 cm Tanque Verde Red-on-brown sherd has ground edges.
Structure 29, fill	This broken plain ware sherd has two ground edges. It measures 4 by 3.7 cm.
Compound Trench, along North wall	This Cibola Black-on-white bowl sherd has one ground edge. It is 3.5 by 2 cm.
	Other Shapes
Structure 2	This whole, roughly oval sherd was made from a red corrugated ware. Its edges are rough and unfinished. The artifact is 3.7 by 3 cm and has 7-mm-thick walls (ASM Catalog No. A-38,109).
Structure 18 fill	This spearpoint-shaped sherd was made from a plain or red ware sherd. It is 2 by 4.5 cm in size.
Structure 31 fill	This Tanque Verde Red-on-brown sherd has chipped edges and an off-center hole started on one side. The sherd is 6.2 by 5.5 cm in size and is 5 mm thick.
Unknown provenience	This rim from a large jar has five semicircular chips taken out of the edge, making it look as if it were whittled (Figure 3.11d).
	Repair Holes
Structure 7 fill	One Tanque Verde Red-on-brown sherd has a repair hole.
Structure 10 lower fill	This worked sherd is a San Carlos Brown with a repair hole. The shape of the vessel that the sherd came from is unknown.
Structure 25, floor fill, SW 1/4	A plain ware bowl sherd with a repair hole was found on the floor of Structure 25.
Structure 25, below floor 1	This plain ware sherd has a 4-mm diameter drill hole that is 9 mm below the rim of the vessel.
Structure 30, SW 1/4, level 3	This obliterated corrugated sherd has a repair hole. The rim on this sherd is folded.
Cemetery (not further specified)	This sherd has a drill hole on one edge.

ridge that has been broken off. The artifact was catalogued as ASM Number A-38,215.

A figurine arm or leg fragment was found in the upper fill of Structure 25. It is 0.75 cm in diameter and 2.5 cm in length.

A human figurine fragment was found in a sherd concentration directly west of Structure 6. The head of the figurine has been broken off; the bottom of the torso and legs are also missing. The figurine has rounded, flattened, pinched out arms or shoulders.

A modeled, cylindrical clay bead was found in the fill of Structure 16. It has slightly rounded ends and is 2.7 cm long and 1.9 cm in diameter. The bead has been catalogued as ASM A-38,194.

A 3-cm-diameter, 1.9-cm-high broken pottery cone was found in Structure 9. The cone has an irregular oval base and the artifact is lumpy and rough. Its use is uncertain; it may have been part of an oddly shaped handle on a vessel or, perhaps, a paho (feather shrine) stand or other type of support. The artifact has been catalogued as ASM A-38,193.

Summary

Information gleaned from the Whiptail ceramic assemblage can be used to address issues of chronology, site and feature use, cultural contacts, migration, and feature abandonment. The ceramics found at the site date primarily to the A.D. 1200s, a time when the Hohokam culture was changing in response to contact with migrants from the Mogollon highlands. The pottery reflects that interaction from the presence of Cibola White Ware trade vessels used in cremation burials to the local manufacture of corrugated ware, which is usually associated with Mogollon and Anasazi peoples. The corrugated wares at Whiptail appear to have been used for storage, serving, or as personal dishes rather than for cooking.

Observations made during excavation and analyses done in the 1980s suggest that the inhabitants of Whiptail made at least some of their own pottery including the corrugated wares. A pile of unfired clay and an unfired jar in Structure 12, along with an assemblage of pottery-making tools and materials in that house are indicative of manufacture. Petrographic and clay analyses indicate that local clays and tempering materials were used in the manufacture of some of the pottery found at the site.

Features that were thought to have been storerooms did not, as expected, have larger numbers of jars than bowls, but they did have intact floor or roof artifact assemblages. Rather than indicating that the features were store rooms, the artifact assemblages may indicate that Whiptail's inhabitants used formal rituals when abandoning a structure (more about this in Chapter 11). The presence of one or two large corrugated or plain ware jars in most of the structures indicates that storage may have been accomplished at an individual household level, not a courtyard group or more communal level.

The ceramic assemblage from Whiptail fits well within a broader southeastern Arizona pattern for the A.D. 1200s. It is most similar to the ceramic assemblage from the nearby Gibbon Springs site and has affinities with assemblages from the San Pedro Valley as well as the western Tucson Basin. The relatively high percentages of corrugated wares, however, indicate a cultural difference between the Whiptail and Gibbon Springs sites and the rest of the Tucson Basin. The ceramics are, perhaps, the strongest indicator that migrants from the Mogollon highlands moved over Redington Pass into the northeastern Tucson Basin in the early to mid-A.D.1200s.

Appendix 3.A. Minimum Number of Vessels in Features, Determined from Partial and Whole Vessels and Sherds.

Provenience	Pottery Type or Ware	Vessel Shape					Total No. of Sherds
		Bowl	Effigy	Scoop	Jar	Indeterminate	
	Compound Locus						
Structure 4	Tanque Verde Red-on-brown	1			1		2
	Tanque Verde Red-on-brown, white slip variant					1	1
	Nogales Polychrome					1	1
	Cibola White Ware					1	1
	Corrugated	1			1		2
	Corrugated and incised				1		1
	Plain ware	1			1		2
Total, Structure 4		*3*			*4*	*3*	*10*
Structure 6	Rincon Red-on-brown	1			1		2
	Tanque Verde Red-on-brown	1			1		2
	Tanque Verde Red-on-brown, white slip variant					1	1
	Cibola Black-on-white					1	1
	Corrugated	1			1		2
	San Carlos Brown				1		1
	Plain ware	1			1		2
Total, Structure 6		*4*			*5*	*2*	*11*
Structure 7	Rincon Red-on-brown	1			1		2
	Tanque Verde Red-on-brown	2			1		3
	Tanque Verde Black-on-brown	1			1		2
	Tanque Verde Red-on-brown, white slip variant	1			1		2
	Rincon Polychrome	1					1
	Cibola Black-on-white	1			1		2
	San Carlos Red	1					1
	Corrugated	1			1		2
	Playas Incised				1		1
	San Carlos Brown	1					1
	Plain ware	1			1		2
Total, Structure 7		*11*			*8*		*19*
Structure 8	Rillito Red-on-brown	1					1
	Rincon Red-on-brown	1			1		2
	Tanque Verde Red-on-brown	1			1		2
	Tanque Verde Black-on-brown	1			1		2
	Tanque Verde Black-on-white					1	1
	San Carlos Red-on-brown	1					1
	San Carlos Red	1					1
	Reserve-Tularosa Black-on-white				1		1
	Pinto Polychrome	1					1
	Playas incised					1	1
	Incised and corrugated	1					1
	Corrugated	3			5		8
	San Carlos Brown	1					1
	Plain ware	2	1		1		4
Total, Structure 8		*14*	*1*		*10*	*2*	*27*
Structure 17	Rincon Red-on-brown	*1*			1		2
	Tanque Verde Red-on-brown	*1*			1		2
	Tanque Verde Red-on-brown, white slip variant	*1*					1
	Tanque Verde black-on-white	*1*					1
	San Carlos Red-on-brown	*1*					1
	San Carlos Red	*1*					1
	Playas incised				1		1
	Incised				1		1
	Corrugated	*1*			1		2
	San Carlos Brown	*1*					1
	Plain ware	*1*			1		2
Total, Structure 17		*9*			*6*		*15*
Inside Compound, Northeast Quarter					1		1

Appendix 3.A. Minimum Number of Vessels in Features, Determined from Partial and Whole Vessels and Sherds, cont'd.

Provenience	Pottery Type or Ware	Vessel Shape					Total No. of Sherds
		Bowl	Effigy	Scoop	Jar	Indeterminate	
	Central Locus						
Structure 5	Tanque Verde Red-on-brown	1			1		2
	Tanque Verde Red-on-brown, white slip variant	1			1		2
	Corrugated	1			1		2
	Plain ware	1			1		2
Total, Structure 5		*4*			*4*		*8*
Structure 15	Rincon Red-on-brown				1		1
	Tanque Verde Red-on-brown	5			1	2	8
	Tanque Verde Red-on-brown, white slip variant	1					1
	Tanque Verde Black-on-brown	1					1
	Playas Incised					1	1
	Corrugated and incised				1		1
	Corrugated	1			1	11	13
	San Carlos Brown	1					1
	Micaceous plain	1			1		2
	Plain ware	1			4		5
Total, Structure 15		*11*			*9*	*14*	*34*
Structure 32	Rincon Red-on-brown	1					1
	Tanque Verde Red-on-brown	1			1		2
	San Carlos Brown	1					1
	Incised and corrugated	1					1
	Corrugated	1			1		2
	Plain ware	1			1		2
Total, Structure 32		*6*			*3*		*9*
	Southwestern Locus						
Structure 2	Rillito Red-on-brown	1					1
	Rincon Red-on-brown	1					1
	Tanque Verde Red-on-brown	1			1		2
	Tanque Verde Red-on-brown, white slip variant	1					1
	Topawa Red-on-brown	1					1
	Cibola Black-on-whit	1					1
	Roosevelt Black-on-white	1					1
	Santa Cruz Polychrome				1		1
	San Carlos Red	1					1
	Unidentified Mexican ware	1					1
	Corrugated	1			1		2
	San Carlos Brown	1			1		2
	Plain ware	1			1		2
Total, Structure 2		*12*			*5*		*17*
Structure 9	Rincon Red-on-brown				1		1
	Tanque Verde Red-on-brown	1			1		2
	Tanque Verde Black-on-brown	1			1		2
	Reserve Black-on-white					1	1
	Snowflake Black-on-white					1	1
	Unidentified black-on-white					1	1
	Wingate Black-on-red					1	1
	Corrugated	1			1		2
	San Carlos Brown	1					1
	Stuccoed plain				1		1
	Plain ware	1			1		2
Total, Structure 9		*5*			*6*	*4*	*15*
Structure 10	Rincon Red-on-brown					1	1
	Tanque Verde Red-on-brown	2			1		3
	Tanque Verde Black-on-brown	1					1
	Tanque Verde Red-on-brown, white slip variant	1					1
	Sells Red	1					1
	Corrugated	1			1		2
	San Carlos Brown	1			1		2

Appendix 3.A. Minimum Number of Vessels in Features, Determined from Partial and Whole Vessels and Sherds, cont'd.

Provenience	Pottery Type or Ware	Vessel Shape					Total No. of Sherds
		Bowl	Effigy	Scoop	Jar	Indeterminate	
	Micaceous plain				1		1
	Plain ware	1			2		3
Total, Structure 10		*8*			*6*	*1*	*15*
Between 10 & 12	Rincon Red-on-brown	1					1
	Tanque Verde Red-on-brown	1			1		2
	Corrugated	1			1		2
	Plain ware	1			1		2
Total, between Structures 10 and 12		*4*			*3*		*7*
Structure 11	Rincon Red-on-brown	1					1
	Tanque Verde Red-on-brown	2			2		4
	Casa Grande Red-on-buff				1		1
	Reserve-Tularosa Black-on-white				1		1
	Gila Red	1					1
	San Carlos Red	1					1
	Incised					1	1
	MacDonald Corrugated	1					1
	Mogollon corrugated	1					1
	Corrugated	1			1		2
	San Carlos Brown	1			1		2
	Micaceous plain				1		1
	Plain ware	1			2		3
Total, Structure 11		*10*			*9*	*1*	*20*
Structure 12	Rincon Red-on-brown	1					1
	Tanque Verde Red-on-brown	1			1		2
	Tanque Verde Red-on-brown with slip	1			1		2
	Tanque Verde Black-on-brown	1					1
	Tanque Verde Black-on-white				1		1
	San Carlos Red-on-brown	1					1
	Sahuarita Polychrome				1		1
	Casa Grande Red-on-buff					1	1
	Puerco Black-on-white	1					1
	Cibola Black-on-white				1		1
	MacDonald Corrugated	1					1
	Gila Red	1					1
	San Carlos Red					1	1
	Corrugated and incised	1			1		2
	Corrugated	1			1		2
	Micaceous Plain	1					1
	San Carlos Brown	1					1
	Plain ware	1			1		2
Total, Structure 12		*13*			*8*	*2*	*23*
Structure 13	Tanque Verde Red-on-brown	1			1		2
	Tanque Verde Red-on-brown, white slip	1				1	2
	Tanque Verde Black-on-brown	1					1
	San Carlos Red	1					1
	Corrugated	1			1		2
	San Carlos Brown	1					1
	Micaceous plain				1		1
	Plain ware	1			1		2
Total, Structure 13		*7*			*4*	*1*	*12*
Structure 16	Tanque Verde Red-on-brown	1			1		2
	Tanque Verde Black-on-brown	1			1		2
	Tanque Verde Red-on-brown, white slip variant	1			1		2
	Tularosa Black-on-white					1	1
	Corrugated and tooled				1		1
	Corrugated	1			2		3
	Micaceous plain	1			1		2
	San Carlos Brown	1					1
	Plain ware	1			1		2
Total, Structure 16		*7*			*8*	*1*	*16*

Appendix 3.A. Minimum Number of Vessels in Features, Determined from Partial and Whole Vessels and Sherds, cont'd.

Provenience	Pottery Type or Ware	Vessel Shape					Total No. of
		Bowl	Effigy	Scoop	Jar	Indeterminate	Sherds
Structure 18	Tanque Verde Red-on-brown	4			2		6
	Tanque Verde Black-on-brown	1					1
	Tanque Verde Red-on-brown, white slip variant	1					1
	Tanque Verde Polychrome				1		1
	San Carlos Red	1					1
	Playa incised				1		1
	McDonald Corrugated	1					1
	Corrugated	1			2		3
	San Carlos Brown					1	1
	Micaceous plain	1					1
	Plain ware	1			1		2
Total, Structure 18		*11*			*7*	*1*	*19*
Structure 24	Rincon Red-on-brown	1			1		2
	Rincon Polychrome					1	1
	Tanque Verde Red-on-brown	1			1		2
	Tanque Verde Black-on-brown				1		1
	Tanque Verde Red-on-brown, white slip variant	1					1
	San Carlos Red-on-brown	1					1
	Cibola White Ware				1		1
	Unidentified black-on-white					1	1
	Gila Polychrome				1		1
	San Carlos Red	1					1
	Corrugated	1			1		2
	San Carlos Brown	1			1		2
	Plain ware	1			1		2
Total, Structure 24		*8*			*8*	*2*	*18*
Structure 25	Rincon Red-on-brown	1					1
	Rincon Polychrome	1					1
	Tanque Verde Red-on-brown	1			1		2
	Tanque Verde Black-on-brown					1	1
	Tanque Verde Red-on-brown, white slip variant	1			1		2
	Sahuarita Polychrome					1	1
	Cibola black-on-white	1					1
	Incised and corrugated					1	1
	Corrugated	1			1		2
	San Carlos Brown	1					1
	Plain ware	1			1		2
Total, Structure 25		*8*			*4*	*3*	*15*
Structure 26	Tanque Verde Red-on-brown	1			1		2
	Tanque Verde Black-on-brown				1		1
	San Carlos Red	1					1
	Incised and Corrugation				1		1
	Corrugated	1					1
	San Carlos Brown	1					1
	Plain ware	1			1		2
Total, Structure 26		*5*			*4*		*9*
Cremation Area 1	Late Rincon or Tanque Verde Red-on-brown	1					1
	Tanque Verde Red-on-brown	7			2		9
	Pinedale Black-on-white				1		1
	Tularosa Black-on-white				1		
	Plain ware				3		3
Total, Cremation Area 1		*8*			*7*		*15*
	Northern Locus						
Structure 3	Tanque Verde Red-on-brown	1			1		2
	Tanque Verde Red-on-brown, white slip variant	1			1		2
	Corrugated	1			1		2
	Plain ware	1			1		2
Total, Structure 3		*4*			*4*		*8*
Structure 20	Roosevelt Black-on-white					1	1
	Tanque Verde Re-on-brown	1			1		2

Appendix 3.A. Minimum Number of Vessels in Features, Determined from Partial and Whole Vessels and Sherds, cont'd.

Provenience	Pottery Type or Ware	Vessel Shape					Total No. of Sherds
		Bowl	Effigy	Scoop	Jar	Indeterminate	
	Tanque Verde Red-on-brown, white slip variant	1					1
	Corrugated	1			1		2
	Plain ware	1			1		2
Total, Structure 20		*4*			*3*	*1*	*8*
Structure 21	Rincon Red-on-brown	1					1
	Tanque Verde Red-on-brown	1			1		2
	Tanque Verde Red-on-brown, white slip variant	1					1
	San Carlos Red	1					1
	Incised	1					1
	Corrugated	1			1		2
	Micaceous plain	1					1
	Plain ware	1			1		2
Total, Structure 21		*8*			*3*		*11*
Structure 27a	Tanque Verde Red-on-brown	1			1		2
	Tanque Verde Black-on-brown					1	1
	Tanque Verde Red-on-brown, white slip variant	1			1		2
	Rincon Red	1					1
	San Carlos Red	1					1
	Corrugated	1			1		2
	San Carlos Brown	1					1
	Micaceous plain				1		1
	Plain ware	1			1		2
Total, Structure 27a		*7*			*5*	*1*	*13*
Structure 27b	Rincon Red-on-brown	1					1
	Tanque Verde Red-on-brown	3			1		4
	Tanque Verde Black-on-brown				1		1
	Tanque Verde Red-on-brown, white slip variant	1			1		2
	Cibola Black-on-white				1		1
	San Carlos Red	1					1
	Corrugated	1			2		3
	San Carlos Brown	1					1
	Micaceous plain	1					1
	Plain ware	1			1		2
Total, Structure 27b		*10*			*7*		*17*
Structure 28	Tanque Verde Red-on-brown	1			2		3
	Tanque Verde Black-on-brown	1					1
	Tanque Verde Red-on-brown, white slip variant	1					1
	Corrugated	1			1		2
	Micaceous plain				1		1
	San Carlos Brown	1					1
	Plain ware	1			1		2
Total, Structure 28		*6*			*5*		*11*
Structure 29	Rincon Red-on-brown	1					1
	Tanque Verde Red-on-brown	1			1		2
	Tanque Verde Black-on-brown	1					1
	Tanque Verde Red-on-brown, white slip	1					1
	Casa Grande Red-on-buff					1	1
	San Carlos Red-on-brown	1					1
	Cibola black-on-white				1		1
	Local San Carlos Red					1	1
	Gila Red					1	1
	Mogollon corrugated	1			1		2
	Corrugated	1			1		2
	San Carlos Brown	1					1
	Micaceous plain	1					1
	Plain ware	1			1		2
Total, Structure 29		*10*			*5*	*3*	*18*
Structure 30	Rincon Red-on-brown	1					1
	Tanque Verde Red-on-brown	1			1		2
	Tanque Verde Black-on-brown	1					1

Appendix 3.A. Minimum Number of Vessels in Features, Determined from Partial and Whole Vessels and Sherds, cont'd.

Provenience	Pottery Type or Ware	Vessel Shape					Total No. of
		Bowl	Effigy	Scoop	Jar	Indeterminate	Sherds
	Tanque Verde Red-on-brown, white slip variant	1			1		2
	Gila Red	1					1
	San Carlos Red	1					1
	Corrugated	1			1		2
	Plain ware	1			1		2
Total, Structure 30		*8*			*4*		*12*
Structure 31a	Rincon Red-on-brown	1					1
	Tanque Verde Red-on-brown	1			1		2
	Tanque Verde Black-on-brown				1		1
	Tanque Verde Red-on-brown, white slip variant	1			1		2
	Cibola black-on-white				1		1
	San Carlos Red	1					1
	Corrugated	1			1		2
	San Carlos Brown	1					1
	Plain ware	1			1		2
Total, Structure 31a		*7*			*6*		*13*
Structure 31b	Rincon Red-on-brown	1					1
	Tanque Verde Red-on-brown	1			1		2
	Tanque Verde Black-on-brown				1		1
	Tanque Verde Red-on-brown, white slip variant	1			1		2
	Tularosa Black-on-white				1		1
	Cibola Black-on-white	1			1		2
	Mogollon corrugated	1					1
	Corrugated	1			1		2
	San Carlos Brown	1				1	2
	Micaceous plain	1					1
	Plain ware	1			1		2
Total, Structure 31b		*9*			*7*	*1*	*17*
Structure 31c	Tanque Verde Red-on-brown	1		1	1		3
	Tanque Verde Black-on-brown	1					1
	Tanque Verde Red-on-brown, white slip variant	1			1		2
	Sahuarita Polychrome	1					1
	Cibola Black-on-white	1					1
	Corrugated	1			1		2
	Gila Red	1					1
	San Carlos Brown	1					1
	Micaceous plain				1		1
	Plain ware	1		1	1		3
Total, Structure 31c		*9*		*2*	*5*		*16*
Southern Locus							
Structure 14	Rincon Red-on-brown	1					1
	Tanque Verde Red-on-brown	1			1		2
	Corrugated	1			1		2
	Indeterminate red ware	1					1
	Plain ware	1			1		2
Total, Structure 14		*5*			*3*		*8*
Structure 19a	Rincon Red-on-brown	1					1
	Tanque Verde Red-on-brown	8			1		9
	Tanque Verde Black-on-brown	1					1
	Tanque Verde Red-on-brown, white slip variant					1	1
	Snowflake or Tularosa Black-on-white				1		1
	Tooled	1					1
	Corrugated	3			1		4
	Plain ware	1			1		2
Total, Structure 19a		*15*			*4*	*1*	*20*
Northeastern Locus							
Structure 22	Tanque Verde Red-on-brown	1			1		2
	Playas Incised	1					1

Appendix 3.A. Minimum Number of Vessels in Features, Determined from Partial and Whole Vessels and Sherds, cont'd.

Provenience	Pottery Type or Ware	Vessel Shape					Total No. of Sherds
		Bowl	Effigy	Scoop	Jar	Indeterminate	
	Corrugated	1			1		2
	San Carlos Brown	1					1
	Micaceous plain	1			1		2
	Plain ware	1			1		2
Total, Structure 22		*6*			*4*		*10*
Structure 42	Tanque Verde Red-on-brown	2			1		3
Structure 42	Incised				1		1
	Corrugated				1		1
	San Carlos Brown					1	1
	Plainware				1		
Total, Structure 42		*2*			*4*	*1*	*7*
No Provenience	Plainware				1		1
	Grand Total	**275**	**1**	**2**	**199**	**45**	**524**

Note: This number does not include sherds collected from the surface or from grid squares not associated with a feature but does include whole or partial vessels from nonfeature contexts.

Appendix 3.B. Vessel Shapes Determined by Sherds.

Provenience	Pottery Type or Ware	Bowl	Effigy	Scoop	Jar	Vessel Shape Indeterminate	Total No. of Sherds
	Compound Locus						
Structure 4	Tanque Verde Red-on-brown	226			157	2	385
	Tanque Verde Red-on-brown, white slip variant					1	1
	Nogales Polychrome					1	1
	Cibola White Ware					2	2
	Corrugated	19			333		352
	Corrugated and incised				1		1
	Plain ware	43			469		512
Structure 6	Rincon Red-on-brown	2			10		12
	Tanque Verde Red-on-brown	141			87	147	375
	Tanque Verde Red-on-brown, white slip variant					2	2
	Cibola Black-on-white					2	2
	Corrugated	35			37	56	128
	San Carlos Brown				12		12
	Plain ware	166			294	748	1208
Structure 7	Rincon Red-on-brown	7			2		9
	Tanque Verde Red-on-brown	742			399	556	1697
	Tanque Verde Black-on-brown	1			7		8
	Tanque Verde Red-on-brown, white slip variant	94			2	4	100
	Rincon Polychrome	1					1
	Cibola Black-on-white	2			2		4
	San Carlos Red	2					2
	Corrugated	140			234	494	868
	Playas Incised				2		2
	San Carlos Brown	36					36
	Plain ware	436			801	2720	3957
Structure 8	Rillito Red-on-brown	2					2
	Rincon Red-on-brown	4			9		13
	Tanque Verde Red-on-brown	382			203	271	856
	Tanque Verde Black-on-brown	9			1	5	15
	Tanque Verde Black-on-white					8	8
	San Carlos Red-on-brown	4					4
	San Carlos Red	1					1
	Reserve-Tularosa Black-on-white				2		2
	Pinto Polychrome	1					1
	Playas incised					2	2
	Incised and corrugated	1					1
	Corrugated	203			304	148	655
	San Carlos Brown	14				1	15
	Plain ware	532	1		1088	3346	4967
Structure 17	Rincon Red-on-brown	1			1		2
	Tanque Verde Red-on-brown	239			213	375	827
	Tanque Verde Red-on-brown, white slip variant	4					4
	Tanque Verde black-on-white	1					1
	San Carlos Red-on-brown	7					7
	San Carlos Red	4				3	7
	Playas incised				1		1
	Incised				1		1
	Corrugated	36			18	33	87
	San Carlos Brown	2					2
	Plain ware	108			191	348	647
	Central Locus						
Structure 5 fill	Tanque Verde Red-on-brown	128			32	117	277
	Tanque Verde Red-on-brown, white slip variant	2			12	6	20
	Corrugated	18			5	77	100

Appendix 3.B. Vessel Shapes Determined by Sherds, cont'd.

Provenience	Pottery Type or Ware	Bowl	Effigy	Scoop	Jar	Vessel Shape Indeterminate	Total No. of Sherds
	Plain ware	27			84	342	453
Structure 15	Rincon Red-on-brown				2		2
	Tanque Verde Red-on-brown	1004			308	306	1618
	Tanque Verde Red-on-brown, white slip variant	38					38
	Tanque Verde Black-on-brown	4					4
	Playas Incised					2	2
	Corrugated and incised				10		10
	Corrugated	355			2186	82	2623
	San Carlos Brown	146					146
	Micaceous plain	4			8		12
	Plain ware	99			3340	792	4231
Structure 32	Rincon Red-on-brown	1					1
	Tanque Verde Red-on-brown	228			150	43	421
	San Carlos Brown	10					10
	Incised and corrugated	1					1
	Corrugated	31			27	10	68
	Plain ware	139			376	647	1162
	Southwestern Locus						
Structure 2	Rillito Red-on-brown	1					1
	Rincon Red-on-brown	8					8
	Tanque Verde Red-on-brown	739			203	1027	1969
	Tanque Verde Red-on-brown, white slip variant	6					6
	Topawa Red-on-brown	2					2
	Cibola Black-on-whit	2					2
	Roosevelt Black-on-white	2					2
	Santa Cruz Polychrome				3		3
	San Carlos Red	2					2
	Unidentified Mexican ware	1					1
	Corrugated	45			145	133	323
	San Carlos Brown	62				1	63
	Plain ware	215			504	1394	2113
Structure 9	Rincon Red-on-brown				1	4	5
	Tanque Verde Red-on-brown	227			35	203	465
	Tanque Verde Black-on-brown	5			17	15	37
	Reserve Black-on-white					2	2
	Snowflake Black-on-white					1	1
	Unidentified black-on-white					1	1
	Wingate Black-on-red					1	1
	Corrugated	12			18	16	46
	San Carlos Brown	6				3	9
	Stuccoed plain				2		2
	Plain ware	70			344	1042	1456
Structure 10	Rincon Red-on-brown					1	1
	Tanque Verde Red-on-brown	247			51	130	428
	Tanque Verde Black-on-brown	1					1
	Tanque Verde Red-on-brown, white slip variant	1				2	3
	Sells Red	1					1
	Corrugated	25			16	22	63
	San Carlos Brown	9			1		10
	Micaceous plain				2		2
	Plain ware	180			202	692	1074
Between 10 & 12	Rincon Red-on-brown	2					2
	Tanque Verde Red-on-brown	120			6	4	130
	Corrugated	4			2	2	8
	Plain ware	48			65	281	394
Structure 11	Rincon Red-on-brown	3					3
	Tanque Verde Red-on-brown	597			106	163	866
	Casa Grande Red-on-buff				2		2

Appendix 3.B. Vessel Shapes Determined by Sherds, cont'd.

Provenience	Pottery Type or Ware	Bowl	Effigy	Scoop	Jar	Vessel Shape Indeterminate	Total No. of Sherds
	Reserve-Tularosa Black-on-white				1		1
	Gila Red	40					40
	San Carlos Red	6				1	7
	Incised					1	1
	MacDonald Corrugated	1					1
	Nonlocal corrugated	1					1
	Corrugated	42			400	95	537
	San Carlos Brown	4			3		7
	Micaceous plain				79		79
	Plain ware	306			478	993	1777
Structure 12	Rincon Red-on-brown	4					4
	Tanque Verde Red-on-brown	1066			338	488	1892
	Tanque Verde Red-on-brown with slip	5			2	5	12
	Tanque Verde Black-on-brown	5				2	7
	Tanque Verde Black-on-white				4		4
	San Carlos Red-on-brown	4					4
	Sahuarita Polychrome				14		14
	Casa Grande Red-on-buff					2	2
	Puerco Black-on-white	2					2
	Cibola black-on-white				2	2	4
	MacDonald Corrugated	1					1
	Gila Red	6					6
	San Carlos Red					2	2
	Corrugated and incised	2			2	2	6
	Corrugated	119			223	94	436
	Micaceous Plain	1					1
	San Carlos Brown	48					48
	Plain ware	820			1532	2865	5217
Structure 13	Tanque Verde Red-on-brown	318			31	93	442
	Tanque Verde Red-on-brown, white slip	28				3	31
	Tanque Verde Black-on-brown	2					2
	San Carlos Red	2					2
	Corrugated	52			93	75	220
	San Carlos Brown	5					5
	Micaceous plain				16		16
	Plain ware	351			276	734	1361
Structure 16	Tanque Verde Red-on-brown	580			138	265	983
	Tanque Verde Black-on-brown	26			1	10	37
	Tanque Verde Red-on-brown, white slip variant	7			3		10
	Tularosa Black-on-white					1	1
	Corrugated and tooled				2		2
	Corrugated	79			81	143	303
	Micaceous plain	2			6	4	12
	San Carlos Brown	18				2	20
	Plain ware	406			569	1141	2116
Structure 18	Tanque Verde Red-on-brown	251			55	92	398
	Tanque Verde Black-on-brown	1				1	2
	Tanque Verde Red-on-brown, white slip variant	3				1	4
	Tanque Verde Polychrome				1		1
	San Carlos Red	11					11
	Playa incised				1		1
	Corrugated	22			14	33	69
	San Carlos Brown					6	6
	Micaceous plain	19					19
	Plain ware	136			401	587	1124
Structure 24	Rincon Red-on-brown	4			1	3	8
	Rincon Polychrome					1	1
	Tanque Verde Red-on-brown	468			234	148	850

Appendix 3.B. Vessel Shapes Determined by Sherds, cont'd..

Provenience	Pottery Type or Ware	Bowl	Effigy	Scoop	Jar	Vessel Shape Indeterminate	Total No. of Sherds
	Tanque Verde Black-on-brown				1	2	3
	Tanque Verde Red-on-brown, white slip variant	3				5	8
	San Carlos Red-on-brown	4					4
	Cibola White Ware				1		1
	Unidentified black-on-white					2	2
	Gila Polychrome				1		1
	San Carlos Red	17				9	26
	Corrugated	178			132	96	406
	San Carlos Brown	7			1		8
	Plain ware	396			850	1018	2264
Structure 25	Rincon Red-on-brown	8					8
	Rincon Polychrome	1					1
	Tanque Verde Red-on-brown	864			191	288	1343
	Tanque Verde Black-on-brown					1	1
	Tanque Verde Red-on-brown, white slip variant	14			2		16
	Sahuarita Polychrome					1	1
	Cibola black-on-white	1					1
	Incised and corrugated					1	1
	Corrugated	88			160	150	398
	San Carlos Brown	20					20
	Plain ware	472			1760	2242	4474
Structure 26	Tanque Verde Red-on-brown	117			22	66	205
	Tanque Verde Black-on-brown				2	2	4
	San Carlos Red	2					2
	Incised and Corrugation				1		1
	Corrugated	3				21	24
	San Carlos Brown	1				8	9
	Plain ware	54			103	360	517
Cremation 1	Tanque Verde Red-on-brown	6					6
	Northern Locus						
Structure 3	Tanque Verde Red-on-brown	232			118	422	772
	Tanque Verde white slip	1			1		2
	Corrugated	28			39	174	241
	Plain ware	185			266	525	976
Structure 20	Roosevelt Black-on-white					1	1
	Tanque Verde Red-on-brown	72			120	121	313
	Tanque Verde Red-on-brown, white slip variant	1				1	2
	Corrugated	32			54	114	200
	Plain ware	62			413	237	712
Structure 21	Rincon Red-on-brown	1					1
	Tanque Verde Red-on-brown	88			26	32	146
	Tanque Verde Red-on-brown, white slip variant	1					1
	San Carlos Red	3					3
	Incised	1					1
	Corrugated	21			30	38	89
	Micaceous plain	4					4
	Plain ware	45			119	299	463
Structure 27a	Tanque Verde Red-on-brown	208			66	110	384
	Tanque Verde Black-on-brown					1	1
	Tanque Verde Red-on-brown, white slip variant	9			4		13
	Rincon Red	1					1
	San Carlos Red	2					2
	Corrugated	67			91	122	280
	San Carlos Brown	17				3	20
	Micaceous plain				1		1
	Plain ware	126			206	547	879
Structure 27b	Rincon Red-on-brown	4					4
	Tanque Verde Red-on-brown	258			72	151	481

Appendix 3.B. Vessel Shapes Determined by Sherds, cont'd.

Provenience	Pottery Type or Ware	Bowl	Effigy	Scoop	Jar	Vessel Shape Indeterminate	Total No. of Sherds
	Tanque Verde Black-on-brown				4		4
	Tanque Verde Red-on-brown, white slip variant	12			2	1	15
	Cibola black-on-white				1	1	2
	San Carlos Red	3					3
	Corrugated	29			120	151	300
	San Carlos Brown	2					2
	Micaceous plain	2					2
	Plain ware	119			419	501	1039
Structure 28	Tanque Verde Red-on-brown	117			42	79	238
	Tanque Verde Black-on-brown	1					1
	Tanque Verde Red-on-brown, white slip variant	4				1	5
	Corrugated	32			27	76	135
	Micaceous plain				3	1	4
	San Carlos Brown	1					1
	Plain ware	78			120	187	385
Structure 29	Rincon Red-on-brown	5					5
	Tanque Verde Red-on-brown	468			352	206	1026
	Tanque Verde Black-on-brown	1				1	2
	Tanque Verde Red-on-brown, white slip	1					1
	Casa Grande Red-on-buff					1	1
	San Carlos Red-on-brown	4					4
	Cibola black-on-white				1		1
	Local San Carlos Red					1	1
	Gila Red					1	1
	Mogollon corrugated	2			1		3
	Corrugated	81			91	141	313
	San Carlos Brown	22				4	26
	Micaceous plain	2					2
	Plain ware	353			809	1333	2495
Structure 30	Rincon Red-on-brown	1				2	3
	Tanque Verde Red-on-brown	333			88	77	498
	Tanque Verde Black-on-brown	2					2
	Tanque Verde Red-on-brown, white slip variant	8			10	1	19
	Gila Red	2					2
	San Carlos Red	18					18
	Corrugated	106			134	66	306
	Plain ware	191			848	555	1594
Structure 31a	Rincon Red-on-brown	2					2
	Tanque Verde Red-on-brown	380			82	156	618
	Tanque Verde Black-on-brown				1	1	2
	Tanque Verde Red-on-brown, white slip variant	4			4	2	10
	Cibola black-on-white				1		1
	San Carlos Red	4					4
	Corrugated	88			71	142	301
	San Carlos Brown	1					1
	Plain ware	298			501	834	1633
Structure 31b	Rincon Red-on-brown	2					2
	Tanque Verde Red-on-brown	671			252	380	1303
	Tanque Verde Black-on-brown				2		2
	Tanque Verde Red-on-brown, white slip variant	58			8	12	78
	Tularosa black-on-white				1		1
	Cibola black-on-white	4			2		6
	Mogollon corrugated	1					1
	Corrugated	222			374	437	1033
	San Carlos Brown	19				1	20
	Micaceous plain	2					2
	Plain ware	318			938	1696	2952

Appendix 3.B. Vessel Shapes Determined by Sherds, cont'd.

Provenience	Pottery Type or Ware	Bowl	Effigy	Scoop	Jar	Vessel Shape Indeterminate	Total No. of Sherds
Structure 31c	Tanque Verde Red-on-brown	485		2	242	156	885
	Tanque Verde Black-on-brown	3					3
	Tanque Verde Red-on-brown, white slip variant	6			5	2	13
	Sahuarita Polychrome	1					1
	Cibola black-on-white	1					1
	Corrugated	100			247	153	500
	Gila Red	5					5
	San Carlos Brown	6					6
	Micaceous plain				2		2
	Plain ware	440		1	1017	902	2360
	Northeastern Locus						
Structure 22	Tanque Verde Red-on-brown	88			32	51	171
	Playas Incised	1					1
	Corrugated	71			83	80	234
	San Carlos Brown	2					2
	Micaceous plain	17			2	4	23
	Plain ware	39			201	211	451
Structure 42	Incised				3		3
	San Carlos Brown					2	2
	Southern Locus						
Structure 14	Rincon Red-on-brown	2					2
	Tanque Verde Red-on-brown	214			68	98	380
	Corrugated	49			29	42	120
	Plain ware	150			518	657	1325
Structure 19	Rincon Red-on-brown	1					1
	Tanque Verde Red-on-brown	213			43	142	398
	Tanque Verde Black-on-brown	1					1
	Tanque Verde Red-on-brown, white slip variant					1	1
	Snowflake or Tularosa Black-on-white				2		2
	Tooled	1					1
	Corrugated	60			55	55	170
	Plain ware	126			222	668	1016
	Grand Total	**23681**	**1**	**3**	**31080**	**42176**	**96941**

Note: Total numbers do not include surface-collected sherds.

Chapter 4

Flaked Stone Artifacts

Laural Myers and Linda M. Gregonis

The nearly 9,000 flaked stone artifacts recovered during the 1960s and 1970s excavations of Whiptail include 7,645 pieces of debitage and 887 flaked stone tools. In this chapter we present an analysis of these artifacts. Comparisons are made to the flaked stone artifact assemblage from the Gibbon Springs site (AZ BB:9:50 [ASM]), a nearby Classic period village that has been extensively excavated. Gibbon Springs is contemporaneous with the bulk of the prehistoric remains from Whiptail, and is also located near a spring in the northeastern Tucson Basin.

Flaked stone artifacts from 26 structures, the compound, unspecified nonfeature contexts, and random surface finds are represented in this analysis. Flaked stone artifacts from structures in the Northeastern Locus and several other structures were not available to the analyst (Laural Myers) and are not represented in this sample.

Analytic Methods

The flaked stone artifacts were analyzed using a two-step process that included a rough sort to categorize specific attributes. All flaked stone artifacts were assigned to either the debitage or tool categories. Both categories of artifacts were analyzed further, but data on tools were recorded in greater detail.

Debitage Analysis

The debitage analysis focused on raw material selection and use, flaked stone reduction techniques, and completeness of each artifact. Each piece of debitage was analyzed using a coding system that recorded seven variables, along with comments. The variables were: (1) provenience (2) flake size, (3) raw material, (4) platform type, (5) flake type, (6) percentage of cortex remaining, and (7) flake completeness. A brief discussion of each variable follows.

Provenience

Provenience information includes feature number and level (floor fill, surface, floor). Flaked stone artifacts found in floor or roof contexts were not point-provenienced, but on rare occasions, specific locational information was available and was recorded.

Flake Size

Flakes were size-graded using a template; that is, artifacts were placed at the center of a series of concentric rings and were classified according to the size of the smallest ring into which the artifact fit. The ring sizes are: 0 = 0.5 cm in diameter; 1 = 1.5 cm in diameter; 2 = 2.5 cm in diameter; 3 = 3.5 cm in diameter; 4 = 4.5 cm in diameter; 5 = 5.5 cm in diameter; 6 = 6.5 cm in diameter; 7 = 7.5 cm in diameter; 8 = 8.5 cm in diameter; and 9 = > 9.5 cm in diameter.

Experimental evidence indicates the frequency distribution of flake size classes reflects flaked stone reduction stages. Some experimental research indicates that smaller flakes are more numerous than larger flakes when biface production is represented in a chipped-stone assemblage (Patterson 1979, 1982). If the flake size distribution is not indicative of biface reduction, then other flaked stone production strategies such as core reduction may be indicated in the assemblage (Patterson 1990).

Raw Material

Raw material type was determined solely on visual attributes. Information about raw materials can be useful for evaluating flaked stone procurement and trading mechanisms. In addition, correlations between material and morphological types can be useful for investigating how flaked stone technology was organized.

Platform Type

Platform type was recorded to help categorize the flaked stone reduction techniques employed at the site. With bifacial reduction, as well as some other technologies, platform remnants indicate the stages of reduction through which an artifact has passed (Callahan 1979). In core technologies, platform faceting increases with progressive reduction of the core. In this analysis, five distinctive platform types were recognized: cortical, single-faceted, multi-faceted, bifacial, and crushed. The remaining types were indeterminate

Flake Type

Flake type was recorded to help determine the reduction method employed by occupants of the site. Large quantities of a particular flake type can indicate an emphasis on a specific reduction method. Flake types recorded were primary, secondary, tertiary, shattered, and bifacial, with indeterminate types being recorded as a separate class.

Percentage of Cortex Remaining

Cortical variation has been linked to understanding procurement patterns and flaked stone reduction sequences (Callahan 1979; Hoffman 1988). All artifacts classified as debitage were examined for the presence of cortex. Each piece of debitage was subsequently assigned to a cortex class based on the percent of cortex present on the dorsal surface. The cortical classes are defined as follows: (1) none, (2)1 to 24 percent, (3) 25 to 49 percent, (4) 50 to 74 percent, and (5) 75 to 100 percent.

Flake Completeness

Flake completeness can be used to indicate post-depositional modification, physical qualities of raw materials, and reduction stage of the artifacts. Categories include complete/almost complete, proximal fragment, distal fragment, midsection, and spall, as well as indeterminate.

Tool Analysis

The flaked stone tool analysis was designed to capture information concerning tool type and function. Functional variables such as edge angle, wear pattern, and edge shape were analyzed to determine if correlations existed between tool function and morphology. Along with comments, 14 variables were recorded for each of the tool types: (1) provenience, (2) raw material, (3) fracture type, (4) weight, (5) length, (6) width, (7) thickness, (8) artifact morphological category, (9) artifact functional category, (10) previous functional category if reused, (11) use-wear patterns, (12) edge angle, (13) edge shape, (14) percentage of cortex remaining, and (15) comments. A discussion of these variables follows, with the exception of variables (5), (6), and (7), which are self-explanatory and variables (1), (2), and (14), which were explained in the preceding section.

Fracture Type

Flaked stone artifacts frequently exhibit manufacturing errors. Artifacts displaying errors were likely removed from production as a result of some fault in the raw material or workmanship (Johnson 1981). Most irretrievable errors are made during the final preparation of tools. As part of the current analysis artifacts whose production was aborted because fractures prevented conformity with mechanical or stylistic canons were identified and classified according to their defect. Johnson (1981) suggests that production failures can be divided into two broad categories: direct fracture and indirect fracture. Direct fractures originated from a point of force, whereas indirect fractures occur from force applied elsewhere to the artifact. Direct fracture types are hinge, perverse, reverse, longitudinal, and impact. Indirect fracture types are lateral snap, crenated, and haft snap. Appendix 4.A, at the end of this chapter, defines the various fracture types (or see Johnson 1981:43–52).

Weight

All tools were weighed to the nearest 0.1 g using an Ohaus triple-beam scale, and were measured with a caliper. Tools exhibiting edge-wear modifications were examined using a low-power binocular microscope.

Morphological-Functional Categories (Variables 8, 9, and 10)

Each flaked tool was classified by morphological or functional type, that is, general shape or assumed use. Morphological-functional categories for tools included cores, hammerstones, unifaces, bifaces, informal unifaces (utilized flakes), and projectile points. Unifaces and bifaces were further coded according to their presumed function. For flaked stone tools that appeared to have been reworked from earlier tools, the original function was also recorded, if it was identifiable. An example of this type of artifact would be a hammerstone that was reworked as a core.

Use-Wear Patterns

The analysis of use-wear patterns can provide information on the function of flaked stone implements (Ahler 1979; Keeley 1980; Odell 1981). Use-wear analysis is done using a low magnification binocular microscope with 1.8 to 110x magnification to physically inspect the edges of a tool. Evidence of use comes in many forms, such as dulling or rounding of the tool edges, use-removal of tiny flakes from along utilized edges, the presence of striations, retouch and utilization (both unifacial and bifacial), and assorted other indicators that can be associated with specific tool functions.

See Appendix 4.B at the end of this chapter, as well as Keeley (1980) and Odell (1981) for use wear definitions.

Edge Angle

Edge angles were recorded using a goniometer. Edge-angle measurements were taken from representative spots on the used edges. These measurements were averaged and then recorded to the nearest degree. Wilmsen (1970) suggests that the angle formed by the working edges of a tool may directly correlate with the tool's function. He states that edge angles can be used to define three broad functional categories. Cutting operations require tools with the most acute angles (26 to 35 degrees). Angles between 45 and 55 degrees are appropriate for applications such as skinning and hide scraping, sinew and plant-fiber shredding, heavy wood cutting, and bone or horn working. Steep angles of between 66 and 75 degrees are associated with wood and bone working and heavy shredding. Thomas (1971) suggests that the very sharpest edges, those measuring less than 20 degrees, would have been used for shaping wood.

Edge Shape

Ethnographic examples of stone tool use suggest there is a relationship between edge shape and tool function (Carr 1982). In this analysis, edge shape is not automatically equated with a particular function. Instead, edge shape is examined in conjunction with morphological and use-wear data.

Edge shapes reflect a variety of processes in the use-life of the tool. Prolonged use and tool-maintenance techniques, such as resharpening or reshaping of tool edges, may lead to changes in the shape of the tool edges through attrition of the mass of the edge (Frison 1968; Hoffman 1985). For example, a straight edge may become convex when there is attrition of the central portion of an edge relative to the end portion of that edge.

Edge shape may reflect tool function (that is, slicers tend to have convex or straight edges and wood shavers will have concave edges), but edge shapes may not be specific to a single task. Certain edge shapes are more suitable for some tasks than for others. For example, for butchering, corners and straight-to-convex edges are preferred while concave edges are most appropriate for wood working (Gould et al. 1971).

A Note on Heat Treatment

Ethnographic evidence exists to suggest that heat treating was widely practiced by Native Americans on chert and other siliceous materials (Gregg and Greybush 1976; Hester 1972). Crabtree and Butler (1964) state that heating siliceous materials slowly to the proper temperature and then slowly cooling them improves their flaking characteristics. After heat treating, the flaked surface of the materials often reflects more light and appears more lustrous than untreated materials. It is on the basis of this altered appearance that artifacts were judged to have been heat treated during the current analysis. Many others have done further work with heat treatment since Crabtree and Butler's initial experiment (Collins and Fenwick 1974; Flenniken and Garrison 1975; Mandeville and Flenniken 1974; Purdy 1974).

The phenomenon of heat treating is rare in Tucson Basin sites and, thus, was not included as a separate variable in the analysis system. Instead, any indications of heat treating were noted in comments.

Table 4.1 Raw Material by Flake Type.

Material Type	Flake Type						Total No. of Flakes	% of Flakes
	Primary	Secondary	Shatter	Tertiary	Bifacial	Indeterminate		
Andesite	3	13	-	25	-	-	41	.05
Basalt	119	557	43	941	-	28	1688	23.00
Chalcedony	1	15	-	34	-	1	51	.05
Chert	15	113	19	741	16	19	923	13.00
Dacite	1	3	-	4	-	-	8	.05
Obsidian	3	3	-	4	-	3	13	.05
Granite	2	1	-	3	-	-	6	.05
Igneous, NFS[a]	7	19	1	35	-	-	62	05
Indeterminate	1	1	-	8	-	1	11	.05
Jasper	11	109	39	424	5	14	602	9.00
Limestone	6	34	3	165	-	1	209	3.00
Olivine Basalt	3	7	-	16	-	-	26	.05
Other[b]	1	3	-	5	1	1	11	.05
Quartzite/Basalt	-	10	-	7	-	-	17	.05
Quartz	143	303	27	534	-	5	1012	12.00
Quartzite	146	732	40	1243	1	20	2182	29.00
Rhyolite	18	114	9	276	1	1	419	5.00
Sandstone	21	128	13	192	-	3	357	5.00
Siltstone	-	2	1	4	-	-	7	.05
Total No. Pieces	501	2167	195	4661	24	97	7645	100

Key: a. NFS = not further specified;
b. Other = 3 dolomite, 3 schist, 2 sedimentary, 1 slate, 1 steatite, and 1 diorite.

Debitage

The most abundant flaked stone artifact type recovered from Whiptail Ruin is debitage. The debitage assemblage includes a wide variety of raw materials, the vast majority of which are available locally. Table 4.1 lists the debitage recovered from this site by material type and flake type. The majority of the raw materials identified were fine-grained (n = 6,391; 84%), followed by medium-grained (n = 993; 13%), and coarse-grained (n = 261; 3%). The most common material types, in order of frequency, were quartzite, basalt, quartz, chert, jasper, and rhyolite. Less than one percent of the debitage pieces show evidence of thermal alteration. This may be because the raw materials available were of sufficient quality that no such alteration was necessary or because the Hohokam peoples used an expedient technology and did not require high-quality tools that warranted pretreating of raw materials.

Technologically, the debitage assemblage reflects a flake-core reduction and use system typically identified as "expedient." Haury (1976) has described this common Hohokam system as acquiring the nearest suitable rock, removing flakes by direct percussion, discarding the core, and then using and discarding the flakes with little attention to modification of the original form.

Tertiary flakes comprised most of the debitage (n = 4,664; 61%), followed by secondary flakes (n = 2,167; 28%), primary flakes (n = 501; 7%), and shatter (n = 195; 3%). The remaining 118 pieces of debitage are bifacial flakes of indeterminate category. Table 4.2 presents the distribution of flakes of each type found at the site. The distribution pattern is a reflection of the field methods used to collect the debitage, the technology used to produce stone tools, and the natural and cultural processes that formed the site's deposits.

As is the case in most Hohokam flaked

Table 4.2. Distribution of Flakes.

Provenience	Flake Type: Primary	Secondary	Shatter	Tertiary	Bifacial	Indeterminate	Total No. of Flakes
Surface and nonfeature contexts	110	534	53	1536	10	23	2266
Compound Locus							
Compound	19	73	-	118	-	-	210
Structure 4	74	293	5	750	2	25	1149
Structure 6	4	9	1	35	-	2	51
Structure 7	25	81	3	175	-	4	288
Structure 8	4	32	1	66	-	1	104
Structure 17	7	28	6	53	-	-	94
Totals, Compound Locus	133	516	16	1197	2	32	1896
Central Locus							
Structure 5	2	4	2	3	-	-	11
Structure 15	6	29	6	52	1	-	94
Totals, Central Locus	8	33	8	55	1	--	105
Northern Locus							
Structure 3	10	35	8	65	-	3	121
Structure 27 (a and b)	5	22	2	31	-	-	60
Structure 27a	3	-	-	9	-	-	12
Structure 27b	7	29	2	50	2	1	91
Structure 27b bowl C	-	14	-	21	1	3	39
Structure 27b pot A	-	11	-	35	1	-	47
Structure 28	2	7	-	3	-	-	12
Structure 29	20	86	8	124	1	1	240
Structure 30	2	7	1	21	-	-	31
Totals, Northern Locus	49	211	21	359	5	8	653
Southwestern Locus							
Structure 2	31	73	21	219	-	7	351
Structure 9	4	26	7	31	-	-	68
Structure 10	16	77	1	132	1	14	241
Structure 11	27	116	7	158	2	3	313
Structure 12	31	149	39	310	4	2	535
Structure 13	8	43	2	59	-	-	112
Structure 16	9	30	3	51	-	2	95
Structure 18	10	39	1	94	-	-	144
Structure 23	19	120	7	186	4	-	336
Structure 24	30	76	6	99	1	-	212
Structure 25	12	86	1	171	1	3	274
Structure 26	2	10	-	14	-	-	26
Totals, Southwestern Locus	199	845	95	1524	13	31	2707
Southern Locus							
Structure 14	1	6	2	9	-	-	18
Total No. of Flakes	500	2145	195	4680	31	94	7645

Note: Flaked stone from features in the Northeastern Locus (Structures 22, 40, 41, and 42) were not analyzed, nor were flaked stone artifacts from Structures 1, 19, 20, 21, 31a, 31b, 31c, or 33.

stone assemblages, flake size is skewed toward smaller flakes, although none is smaller than 1.5 cm. This is probably a reflection of the use of quarter-inch wire mesh screens in the field rather than use of a smaller mesh, but it may also reflect a paucity of tool modification and finishing at the site. Flake sizes of 3.5 cm or smaller account for 70 percent of the assemblage; those between 3.6 and 6.5 cm account for 28 percent of the assemblage. The small percentage of remaining flakes is larger than 6.5 cm (Table 4.3).

Sixty-four percent of the debitage pieces (n = 4,874) had dorsal cortex. As expected,

Table 4.3. Flake Type by Flake Size.

Flake Type	Flake Size (in centimeters)									Total No. of Flakes
	1.5	1.6-2.5	2.6-3.5	3.6-4.5	4.6-5.5	5.6-6.5	6.6-7.5	7.6-8.5	>8.5	
Primary	14	104	151	92	79	31	19	8	3	501
Secondary	41	433	587	507	329	169	71	23	7	2167
Tertiary	466	1994	1289	527	266	88	29	5	-	4664
Shatter	25	73	51	24	14	7	1	-	-	195
Bifacial	3	12	9	-	-	-	-	-	-	24
Indeterminate	22	46	16	6	2	1	1	-	-	94
Total No.	571	2662	2103	1156	690	296	121	36	10	7645
% of Flakes	7	35	28	15	9	4	2	.05	.01	100.06

most of the primary flakes had 50 to 100 percent dorsal cortex; cortex on secondary flakes ranged from 1 to 74 percent. This suggests that the debitage was primarily produced during core reduction. The smaller flakes conform to expectations for flakes produced during the latter stages of the reduction sequence. Eighty-seven percent of the debitage pieces (n = 6,666) are complete flakes. Nine percent of the assemblage are distal fragments, one percent are proximal fragments, two percent are midsections, and fewer than one percent are indeterminate fragments (Table 4.4).

In the Whiptail flake sample, it appears that platforms were most commonly prepared by the removal of a single flake (n = 3,790; 49%). Seventeen percent of the debitage (n = 1,295) had crushed platforms, and platform type could not be determined on another 17 percent (n = 1,295). Cortical platforms accounted for 14 percent of the sample and less than one percent was bifacial platforms. The platform types observed suggest that hard-hammer percussion was the principal reduction technique employed, and core reduction was the primary flaked stone-production activity at this site.

Flaked Stone Tools

Eight hundred and eighty-six flaked stone tools were examined for this study. Most were made of chert, quartz, or quartzite (Table 4.5). These tools included high labor-input items such as projectile points, as well as expedient tools, such as informal unifaces (also known as utilized flakes). A few tools (n = 25) showed signs of thermal alteration, which was identified by color change, luster change, or, in a few instances, crazing. The majority of the tools in the sample analyzed are complete (80.9%). The remaining 17.3 percent represent different kinds of manufacturing errors including lateral snap (13.1%), followed by hinging (4.2%). The

Table 4.4. Flake Portion Represented.

Flake Type	Flake Portion					Totals
	Complete	Distal	Midsection	Proximal	Indeterminate	
Bifacial	24	--	--	--	--	24
Indeterminate	27	19	30	3	15	94
Primary	451	43	4	3	--	501
Secondary	1981	114	13	29	30	2167
Shatter	195	--	--	--	--	195
Tertiary	3988	514	96	59	7	4664
Totals	6666	690	143	94	52	7645

Table 4.5. Tool Type or Morphological Category by Raw Material.

Raw Material	Formal Unifaces	Informal Unifaces	Thick Bifaces	Thin Bifaces	Projectile Points	Cores	Hammer-stones	Total No. of Tools
Andesite	—	—	—	1	—	—	1	2
Basalt	7	42	6	3	—	26	30	114
Granite	—	1	—	—	—	—	3	4
Igneous, not further specified	—	1	—	1	1	—	—	3
Chalcedony	—	2	—	2	25	—	—	29
Chert	18	72	9	54	74	5	—	232
Indeterminate	—	1	1	—	1	—	4	7
Jasper	5	15	1	6	10	8	—	45
Limestone	—	—	—	—	—	2	5	7
Metamorphosed limestone	—	—	—	—	2	—	—	2
Obsidian	1	1	2	2	14	1	—	21
Quartz	—	15	1		3	4	179	202
Quartzite	3	46	10	3	3	29	72	166
Rhyolite	—	5	1	1	5	3	11	26
Sandstone	1	8	—	—	—	4	4	17
Sedimentary, not further specified	—	—	—	—	3	—	—	3
Siltstone	—	1	—	—	—	—	—	1
Tuff	—	1	1	—	—	—	3	5
Total No. of Tools	35	211	32	73	141	82	312	886

remaining 1.8 percent of broken tools show evidence of impact fractures or crenellated or hinge or lateral snaps.

Unifacial Tools

A uniface is a tool that exhibits modifications to one surface. For this analysis, the uniface category was divided into two subclasses, formal and informal.

Formal Unifaces

Thirty-five formal unifaces, representing 3.9 percent of the tool count, were recovered from Whiptail. Formally shaped unifaces were distinguished by the amount of modification to the tool blank, creating task-specific tools such as side and end scrapers, gravers, and spoke shaves.

Seven unifacial gravers were recovered: one each from the fill of Structures 2, 4, and 16; two from the floor of Structure 23, one from the floor of Structure 27b, and one from the site's surface. These artifacts are complete tools made of chert (n = 6), and basalt (n = 1). Use wear on them consists of three examples of rounding and bidirectional retouch, and two each of bidirectional retouch and unidirectional retouch. Edge angles range from 25 to 60 degrees. The gravers range in size from 12.4 mm to 33.9 mm in length; 10.4 mm to 22.9 mm in width, and weigh from 0.06 g to 18.6 g. All seven of the gravers had concave-convex working edges.

One denticulate tool made of chert was recovered from floor fill of Structure 7. This tool had a lateral snap fracture and weighed 16.5 g. No use wear could be determined.

Five end scrapers were recovered from the site's surface, the fill of Structure 12, the floor of Structure 23, and inside a pot in Structure 27b. Three are of jasper, one is basalt, and one is chert. These tools measure from 11.9 mm to 67.8 mm in length; 7.9 mm to 74.8 mm in width, and weigh 0.20 g to 59.2 g. Two tools display unidirectional retouch, one has bidirectional retouch, and one has rounding or bidirectional retouch. The use wear on one end scraper could not be determined. Two of the end scrapers had straight working edges, two had convex working edges, and the remaining tool had a concave-convex working edge.

Nine complete side scrapers were recovered from the site's surface, the fill of Structures 11, 23, and 24, 29, and the floor of Structure 10. These tools are made of chert (n = 3), quartzite (n = 2), and one of each jasper, basalt, sandstone, and obsidian. The use wear consists of three each of bidirectional retouch, unidirectional retouch, and rounding; five examples of unidirectional retouch along straight working edges, and two each along concave-convex working edges and convex working edges. These tools range in size from 22.3 mm to 67.4 mm in length and 11.6 mm to 36.9 mm in width; weights range from 2.3 g to 140.8 g. The edge angles range from 35 to 70 degrees.

Five side/end scrapers were recovered: three from the site's surface, and one each from the fill of Structures 17 and 28. These tools are complete; two are basalt and one each is chert, jasper, and quartzite. Two examples have rounding/unidirectional retouch and three have unidirectional retouch use wear. Three edge shapes are concave-convex, one is convex, and one is straight. Edge angles range from 45 to 75 degrees. These tools measured 35.7 mm to 53.6 mm in length, 28.0 mm to 45.4 mm in width, and weigh from 3.4 g to 43.5 g.

Eight unifaces are indeterminate fragments with lateral snap fractures; they are made of basalt (n = 2) and chert (n = 6). Seven have unidirectional retouch caused by use and one has rounding and bidirectional retouch. Edge angles range from 25 to 70 degrees with edges that are straight (n = 3), concave (n = 2), concave-convex (n = 2), and convex (n = 1). These artifacts were recovered from the fill of Structures 2, 4, 7, 10, 12, and 16.

Informal Unifaces

Informally shaped unifaces were identified when the overall morphology of the flake or tool blade had not been significantly restructured by patterned development of a retouched edge. Utilization of unmodified flakes on resistant materials often alters the edge of a flake by detachment of microflakes. Incidental edge damage could have been caused by a variety of postdepositional factors. Informal unifaces can exhibit large flake scars, but these occur in a more irregular pattern than with retouch and occur in conjunction with edge nibbling.

Informal unifaces were the second most common tool type recovered from the Whiptail site (n = 211). Informal unifaces—also known as utilized flakes—were recovered from the site's surface, the compound, and the fill and floors of structures; in addition, many came from unknown proveniences. These tools account for 23.8 percent of the tool assemblage. The most common raw material used for these tools is chert (34.5%), followed by quartzite (21.8%), basalt (19.9%), and jasper and quartz (both at 7.1 %); the remaining 9.6 percent belong to nine other material types. These tools vary considerably in size; lengths range from 3.0 mm to 162.0 mm, widths from 7.0 mm to 98.0 mm, and weights from 0.30 g to 602.3 g. These tools exhibit a mixture of use-wear patterns with various edge shapes. The edge angles of these tools range from 30 to 90 degrees.

Bifacial Tools

Not including projectile points, 105 bifaces were recovered from the site, comprising 11.9 percent of the flaked tool assemblage. Most were made of chert (n = 63; 59.4%) and all of them were bifacially shaped to a general outline, size and thickness. Flake scars were usually broad and irregular and occurred on both faces of the artifact. The edges were often sinuous, the result of the removal of large, irregular flakes. These irregularities generally occurred as the artifact neared its final production stage. The flake scars on tool surfaces exhibited irregular patterns and unsuccessful flake removals, for example, step and hinge terminations.

The thick and thin bifaces discussed here designate different morphological stages in the reduction trajectory (Callahan 1979). These categories were useful in determining the level of effort put into the manufacture of these tools.

Thick bifaces recovered from the site include identifiable tools, shaped pieces, and fragments of indeterminate use and shape. Identifiable tools include three choppers, two complete drills (Figure 4.1k, v), a drill tip (Figure 4.1l), and one drill base. The thick bifaces show signs of minor, intentional shape modification and have sinuous to slightly sinuous edges. The artifacts are knapped on all margins and exhibit thick, mostly irregular, cross sections. The faces retain 50 percent or less of the cortex.

Eleven thick bifaces are indeterminate fragments with lateral snap fractures. These tool fragments are made of chert (n = 3), quartzite (n = 6), basalt (n = 1), and jasper (n = 1); they range in weight from 2.3 g to 165 g. The edge angles of these items range from 60 to 85 degrees with convex-concave edge shapes. No use wear could be determined.

The choppers were recovered from the fill of Structures 2, 7, and 16. One made of quartzite measures 59.4 mm in length, 59.4 mm in width, and weighs 109.1 g. The use wear is bidirectional along a straight working edge, with an edge angle of 78 degrees. The second chopper is made of tuff, measures 81.6 mm in length and 70.0 mm in width, and weighs 250 g. The use wear consists of bidirectional utilization along a convex working edge. The edge angle is 90 degrees. The wear patterns on these tools suggest that they were used to cut soft to medium materials. The third chopper is a miniature piece of an indeterminate rock type measuring 18 mm in length by 10 mm in width. The use wear consists of rounding along a concave-straight working edge. This tool was used to pound material of medium hardness; it was recovered from the feature fill of Structure 7.

Two drills made from chert flakes were found in the sample. One, which was heat-treated, exhibits polish and rounding along a straight working edge. This tool measures 23.2 mm in length by 10 mm in width and weighs 1.2 g. The other tool measures 29.3 mm in length by 23.6 mm in width and weighs 9.2 g. This tool has a concave-convex working edge with unidirectional utilization. One tool was recovered from a pot on the floor of Structure 27b (Figure 4.2u); the other is from an unknown provenience.

One flake-base drill made of chert exhibits polish and rounding along a concave-straight working edge, has an edge angle of 70 degrees, and was heat-treated. This tool measures 21.1 mm in length by 13.0 mm in width, and weighs 1.1 g. It was also recovered from Pot A on the floor of Structure 27b (Figure 4.2.aa)

Three thick bifaces—made of basalt, obsidian, and quartz—are elongated in shape. These tools measure between 15.9 mm to 55.3 mm in length, 12.0 mm to 36.9 mm in width, and weigh 5.1 g to 33.2 g. Use wear consists of one example each of rounding, bidirectional retouch, and rounding with bidirectional utilization. The edge angles range from 60 to 80 degrees along convex working edges. These tools were recovered from the site's surface and from the floor fill of Structure 25.

Eight thick bifaces are ovate in shape. Three are quartzite, two are basalt, and one each is chert, obsidian, and rhyolite. The tools range from 15.6 mm to 52.0 mm in length, 14.0 mm to 46.7 mm in width, and 1.6 g to 74.2 g in weight. Use wear consists of rounding (n = 2), unidirectional utilization (n = 4), bidirectional utilization (n = 1), and rounding with unidirectional retouch (n = 1). These tools were

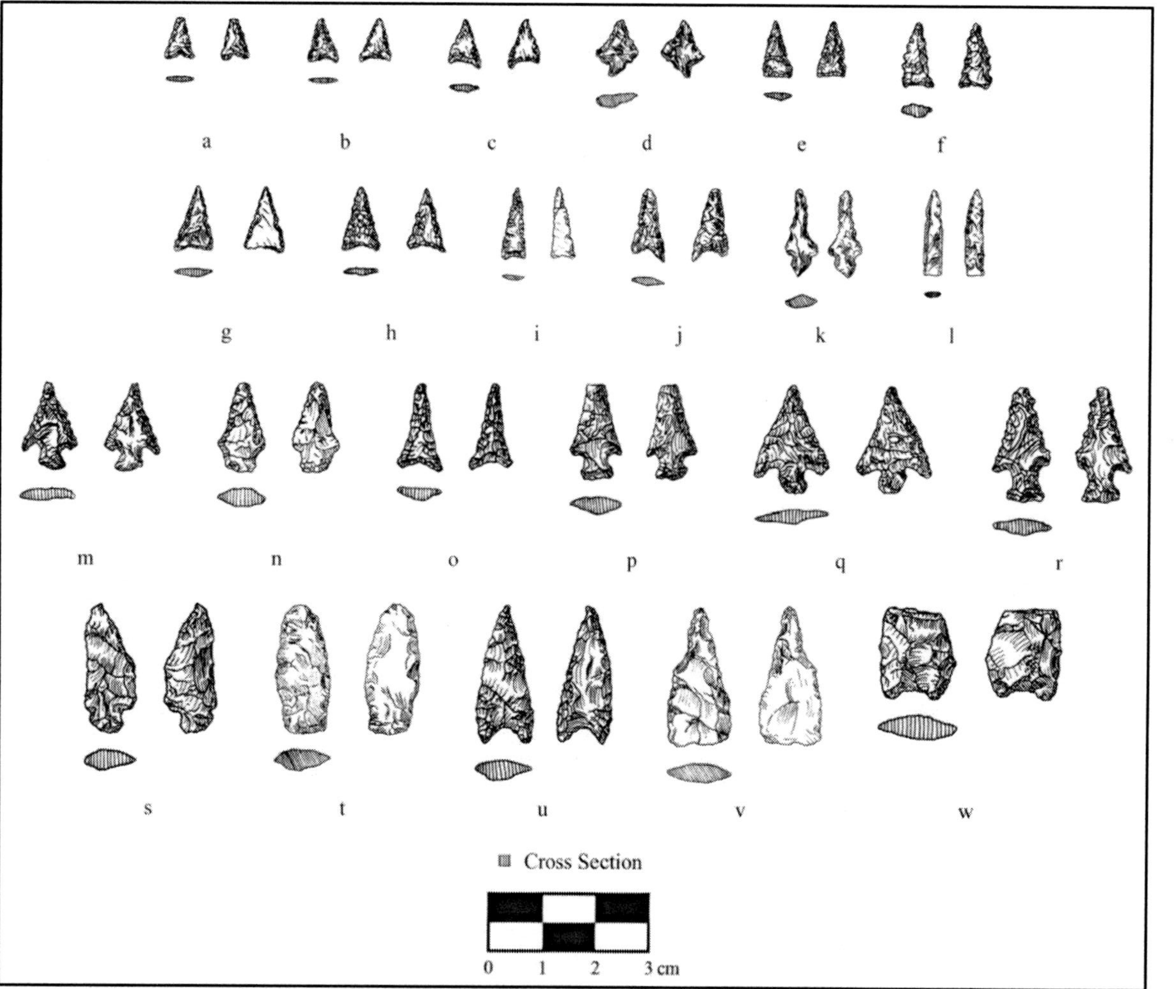

Figure 4.1. Points and bifaces found at the site: (a, b) obsidian Classic period Type 1 points; (c) chalcedony Type 1 point, (d) jasper biface, possibly reworked from Cienega point; (e, f, g) chalcedony Classic period Type 2 points; (h) obsidian Type 1 point; (i) chert Type 2 point; (j) chalcedony Type 2 point); (k) chalcedony drill; (l) chert drill tip; (m) Cienega point of unidentified sedimentary material; (n) jasper San Pedro point; (o) chalcedony drill; (p) Cienega point of unidentified sedimentary material; (q) jasper Cienega point; (r) Cienega point of unidentified fine-grained stone; (s) biface of unidentified fine-grained stone; (t) rhyolite San Pedro point, reworked and used as a biface; (u) chert Cortaro point; (v) chert drill; and (w) quartzite Cortaro point (drawing by Gerry Crouse). Three obsidian points, Figures 4.1a, b, and h, are from the Mule Creek, New Mexico, source (Shackley 2009).

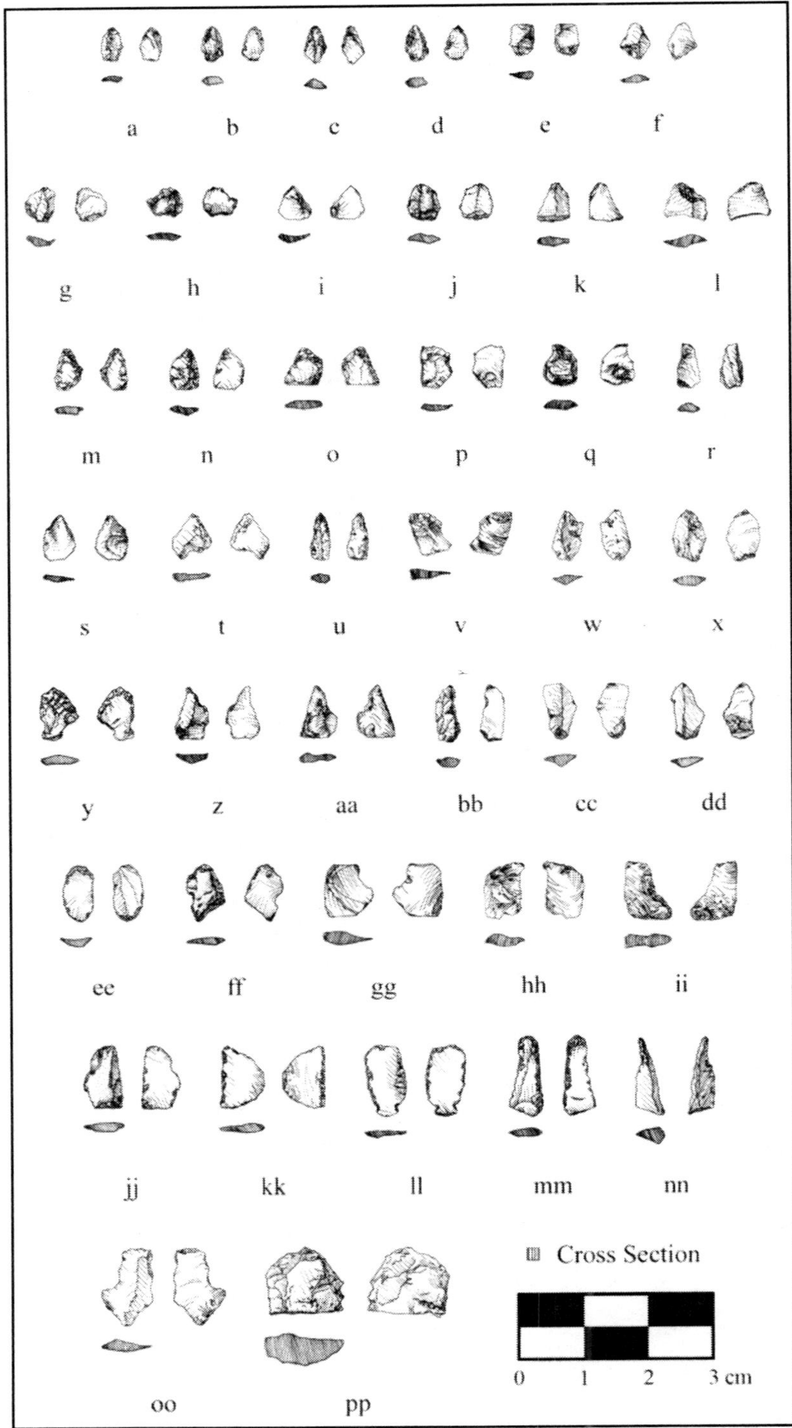

Figure 4.2. Assemblage of material from pot A, found on the floor of Structure 27b: (a, b, e, f, g, h, k, l, p, q, r, s, v, x, z, aa, bb, cc, ff, gg, hh, ii, jj) chert flakes; (c, d, j, t, w, oo) jasper flakes; (i) chalcedony flake; (m) retouched chert flake; (n) chert biface, perhaps used as a graver; (o) broken chert biface, perhaps used as a graver); (u) heat-treated chert drill point; (y) retouched chert flake; (dd) chert biface fragment; (ee) retouched chalcedony flake; (kk) retouched chert flake; (ll) jasper knife; (mm) retouched jasper flake; (nn) jasper drill; (pp) jasper core.

recovered from the site's surface, the fill of Structures 10, 12, and 25, the floor of Structure 2, and the floor fill of Structure 24.

One thick biface, of chert, is triangular in shape. This tool measures 27.9 mm in length, 26.7 mm in width, and weighs 6.8 g. Use wear on the biface consists of bidirectional retouch along a concave-convex working edge. This artifact was recovered from the fill of Structure 23.

Seventy-six thin bifaces were identified. These artifacts exhibit uniformally thinned cross sections, refined shaping, and predominately small flake scars. The edges tend to be straightened, regular, or refined by retouch. Cross sections are symmetrical, biconvex, or planoconvex. Twenty-four are thin biface fragments made of chert (n = 13), jasper (n = 3), obsidian (n = 2), quartzite (n = 2), chalcedony (n = 1), basalt (n = 1), and rhyolite (n = 1). Twenty-one of these tools have lateral snap fractures, two have hinge fractures, and one has a hinging and lateral snap fracture. The edge angles range from 30 to 65 degrees. Three are elongated bifaces with no visible use wear. These items range from 30.1 mm to 44.9 mm in length, with weights ranging from 0.80 g to 6.8 g.

Nineteen thin bifaces are triangular in shape. Raw materials include chert (n = 11), igneous (not further specified) (n = 2), basalt (n = 1), chalcedony (n = 1), quartzite (n = 1), rhyolite (n = 1), andesite (n = 1), and jasper (n = 1). Thirteen of these artifacts have lateral snap fractures; only one displayed hinging. Only four of these tools are complete. Use wear could not be determined on 16 of these artifacts. The three with use wear consist of one each of polish with rounding, unidirectional utilization, and rounding with bidirectional retouch along straight modified working edges. Weights range from 0.50 g to 6.0 g and edge angles from 30 to 67 degrees. Eight of these artifacts came from unknown proveniences; the remaining 11 were associated with structures.

One thin biface graver was recovered from bowl C in Structure 27b (Figure 4.3d) and one came from the fill of Structure 12. One basalt graver measures 34.5 mm in length and 16.5 mm in width and weighs 3.5 g. Use wear on this tool consists of rounding with unidirectional utilization along a concave-convex working edge. The other graver is made of chert; it measures 35.6 mm in length and 17.9 mm in width and weighs 3.5 g. Both of these tools have a 45° edge angle.

One thin jasper knife was recovered from the pot on the floor of Structure 27b. The tool, which was made to be hafted, measures 35.3 mm in length by 19.4 mm in width and weighs 2.1 g. The working edge is straight and serrated with a 40 degree edge angle. This tool shows evidence of heat treating.

Three preforms occur in the sample analyzed. One made of chalcedony is 36 mm long, 14.4 mm wide, and weighs 29 g. Use wear on this artifact consists of rounding with bidirectional retouch along a straight working edge; it has a 35-degree edge angle. Another preform is made of chert; it measures 42.2 mm in length and 20.5 mm in width and weighs 29 g. This tool exhibits bidirectional retouch along a straight working edge and has a 40° edge angle. Both of these tools show evidence of heat treating. The third preform is made of chert; it measures 26.8 mm in length by 15.3 mm in width and weighs 1.2 g. It has an edge angle of 67 degrees along a straight edge. No use wear could be determined. These tools were recovered from the fill of Structures 7 and 16, and from the floor of Structure 2.

Twenty bifacial drills of the following types were recovered: T-drills (n = 2), point drills (n = 2), flake base drills (n = 8), and drill tips (n = 8). Seventeen are made of chert, and one each is made of quartzite, jasper, and basalt. The drill tips all have lateral snap fractures with use wear consisting of round-

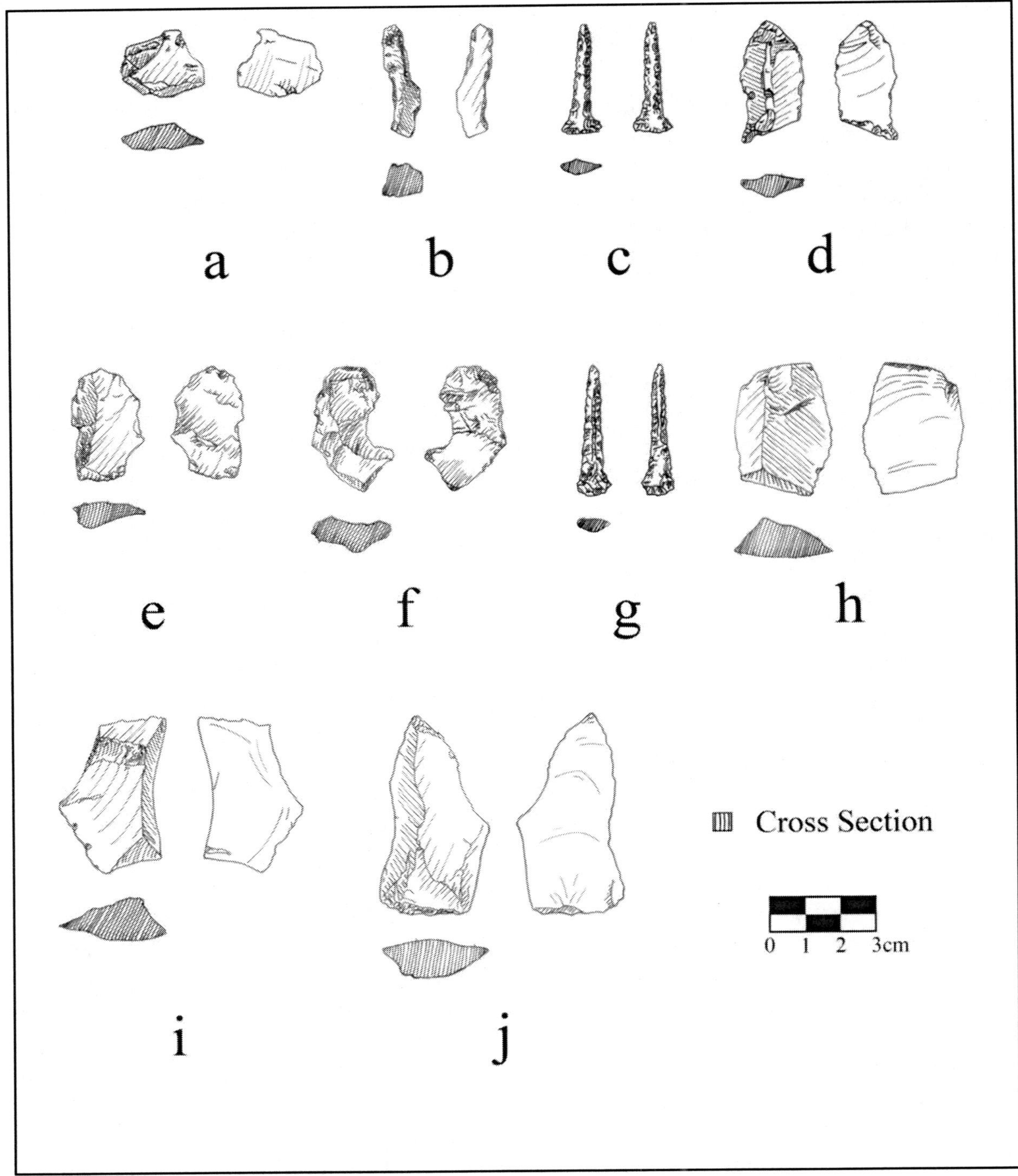

Figure 4.3. Flaked stone tools and flakes from pot C, found on the floor of Structure 27b: (a, b) jasper flakes; (c) chalcedony drill; (d) chert graver; (e) chert flake; (f) jasper flake; (g) chert or chalcedony drill; (h, i, j) fine-grained basalt flakes (drawing by Gerry Crouse).

ing, rounding and bidirectional utilization, and rounding with polish. Edge angles range from 45 to 80 degrees. The two T-drills are both complete and have convex-straight edges that show rounding and bidirectional retouch. One of these artifacts measures 37.5 mm in length and 8.4 mm in width; it weighs 1.2 g; the other is 31.2 mm long, 10.6 mm wide, and 0.80 g in weight. The flake base drills are all made of chert, with only two being complete tools; the remaining six display lateral snaps. The weights of these tools range from 2.1 g to 5.6 g with edge angles from 50 to 80 degrees. The two point drills measure 35.1 mm and 37.5 mm in length, 12.5 mm and 8.4 mm in width, and weigh 2.1 g and 1.2 g, respectively. Both these tools display rounding and bidirectional retouch. Two of the tools came from unknown proveniences; the remaining 18 came from various structures.

Projectile Points

Projectile points found at the Whiptail site include Classic period Hohokam, Middle to Late Archaic period, and Late Archaic/Early Ceramic period arrow heads and dart tips. Table 4.6 lists the provenience of the projectile points and fragments found at the site as well their measurements and material type. Figure 4.1 illustrates a number of the points found at the site.

Archaic Points

The Archaic points include Cortaro, San Pedro, and Cienega types. They occur throughout the site including the portions in Agua Caliente Park (Myers 2001) and are the best evidence for use of the area during the Late Archaic-Early Agricultural period.

The earliest point type found at the site is the Cortaro point (Figure 4.1u, w), which dates from the late Middle Archaic through the Late Archaic period (Roth and Huckell 1992). Five Cortaro points were recovered: from Structures 7 and 26, and from unknown proveniences at the site. The Cortaro points are made of quartz, quartzite, rhyolite, and a fine-grained sedimentary material (Table 4.6).

Cienega points date to the Late Archaic-Early Agricultural period (Figure 4.1m, p, q, r). Found throughout southern Arizona, they exhibit a wide range of morphological variability, with triangular blades, corner notching, expanded or convex bases (Sliva 1996, 1997, 1999). Because of their morphological variability, Sliva (1999) suggests that some Cienega points were used as arrowheads rather than dart points. Thirteen Cienega points were recovered from Structures 4, 7, 11, and 12, from a pot in Structure 27b, and from unknown proveniences. The points are made of chert, chalcedony, jasper, rhyolite, obsidian, and an undefined sedimentary material.

Sixteen San Pedro points (Figure 4.1n, t) made of chert, jasper, rhyolite, an undefined igneous rock, a fine-grained metamorphic limestone, and sedimentary rock were recovered from Structures 4, 7, 24, 28, and 30, from the site's surface, and from unknown proveniences within the main village area. San Pedro points are among the most common Late Archaic-Early Agricultural point styles found in southern Arizona; they date from approximately 1500 B.C. to as late as A.D. 650 (Huckell 1988b; Sliva 1999, 2001). One feature in the Agua Caliente Park portion of the site, an ash stain (Feature 73), was radiocarbon-dated to A.D. 160 to A.D. 530 (Wellman and Grimm 2001:59). It is possible that some of the San Pedro points were associated with an Early Ceramic to early Pioneer period use of the site.

Table 4.6. Projectile Points, Organized by Material Type and Provenience.

Material	Provenience	Weight (grams)	Length (mm)	Width (mm)	Thickness (mm)	Number of points
Cortaro Points						
Quartz	Structure 26 fill	--	30.46	18.13	7.86	1
Rhyolite	Unknown provenience	3.1	--	17.70	7.40	1
Sedimentary, NFS	Structure 7 feature fill	3.8	39.50	18.10	6.00	1
Quartzite	Unknown provenience	4.3	45.40	18.70	6.60	1
Quartzite	Unknown provenience	6.3	--	26.00	8.10	1
			Total Cortaro Points			5
San Pedro Points						
Chert	Structure 4 feature fill	0.4	--	12.50	3.10	1
Chert	Structure 7 feature fill	0.4	20.00	12.00	1.50	1
Chert	Structure 7 feature fill	1.8	26.60	14.00	4.50	1
Chert	Structure 28 fill	--	46.96	20.52	5.74	1
Chert	Structure 28 fill	--	48.43	16.17	4.19	1
Chert	Unknown provenience	4.2	31.10	17.00	7.20	1
Jasper	Surface	3.6	39.40	15.50	6.00	1
Jasper	Structure 4 floor	1.3	32.30	20.60	4.90	1
Jasper	Unknown provenience	3.5	24.00	17.90	8.10	1
Rhyolite	Structure 7 feature fill	7.9	58.00	25.00	6.00	1
Rhyolite	Unknown provenience	6.5	43.40	19.40	6.80	1
Rhyolite	Unknown provenience	6.9	--	26.10	6.10	1
Fine-grained igneous	Structure 28 fill	--	53.61	23.87	5.20	1
Metamorphic limestone	Structure 24 fill	--	40.24	16.89	6.19	1
Metamorphic limestone	Structure 30 fill	--	--	19.25	6.61	1
Sedimentary, NFS	Unknown provenience	2.7	--	19.20	5.90	1
			Total San Pedro Points			16
Cienega Points						
Obsidian	Unknown provenience	3.3	38.6	18.70	6.00	1
Chalcedony	Structure 27b, in pot	--	24.37 to break	19.45	4.97	1
Chert	Structure 7 feature fll	4.1	43.4	16.20	7.40	1
Chert	Structure 11 feature fill	1.9	33.2	14.20	4.70	1
Chert	Structure 12 feature fill	3.2	35.4	18.30	4.80	1
Chert	Unknown provenience	0.5	--	12.30	2.50	1
Chert	Unknown provenience	1.8	29.6	18.30	4.30	1
Chert	Unknown provenience	2.3	--	17.30	5.00	1
Jasper	Structure 4 feature fill	1.4	31.0	9.00	6.00	1
Jasper	Unknown provenience	0.7	--	13.70	3.10	1
Jasper	Unknown provenience	2.6	35.2	25.70	4.60	1
Rhyolite	Unknown provenience	4.4	42.1	16.50	7.20	1
Sedimentary, NFS	Unknown provenience	2.5	29.3	15.70	6.10	1
			Total Cienega Points			13
Type 1, Classic Period Points						
Quartz	Structure 17 feature fill	1.10	18.70	14.80	4.60	1
Quartz	Unknown provenience	0.60	20.90	10.00	4.50	1
Obsidian	Surface	0.30	15.90	10.50	2.30	1
Obsidian	Surface	0.40	12.40	7.50	3.70	1
Obsidian	Compound surface	0.40	17.50	1.80	3.00	1
Obsidian	Structure 2 floor fill	0.10	--	8.10	2.20	1

Table 4.6. Projectile Points, Organized by Material Type and Provenience, cont'd.

Material	Provenience	Weight (grams)	Length (mm)	Width (mm)	Thickness (mm)	Number of points
		Type 1, Classic Period Points, cont'd.				
Obsidian	Structure 2 floor	0.20	15.20	--	1.90	1
Obsidian	Structure 7 feature fill	0.40	19.50	--	3.80	1
Obsidian	Structure 17 feature fill	0.20	--	10.10	2.00	1
Obsidian	Structure 25 floor	0.10	12.80	9.00	.80	1
Obsidian	Structure 4 feature fill	0.60	17.20	8.90	2.90	1
Obsidian	Unknown provenience	0.40	20.40	12.30	2.80	1
Obsidian	Unknown provenience	0.10	--	9.70	1.70	1
Chalcedony	Surface	0.60	--	13.50	2.30	1
Chalcedony	Surface	0.60	20.90	10.0	1.70	1
Chalcedony	Surface	0.40	16.30	9.40	5.00	1
Chalcedony	Structure 2 feature fill	0.20	18.20	7.90	2.00	1
Chalcedony	Structure 2 feature fill	0.10	11.50	9.10	1.30	1
Chalcedony	Structure 2 floor	0.30	2.19	10.80	3.10	1
Chalcedony	Structure 17 surface	0.40	21.10	8.10	2.00	1
Chalcedony	Structure 17 feature fill	0.90	24.20	9.80	3.50	1
Chalcedony	Structure 23 fill	--	16.73	13.94	3.35	1
Chalcedony	Structure 23 fill	--	11.70	9.67	2.57	1
Chalcedony	Structure 23 post hole fill	--	23.55	11.74	1.85	1
Chalcedony	Structure 25 floor	--	--	12.20	3.96	1
Chalcedony	Structure 26 fill	--	19.48	13.98	3.41	1
Chalcedony	Structure 27b fill	--	22.72	12.00	3.23	1
Chalcedony	Structure 27b in Pot A	--	24.53	14.07	4.87	1
Chalcedony	Structure 29 fill	--	23.79	14.51	3.91	1
Chalcedony	Structure 31a	--	22.84	16.64	4.76	1
Chalcedony	Structure 31b	--	27.30	17.28	4.54	1
Chert	Surface	0.20	--	12.10	2.70	1
Chert	Surface	0.70	--	10.50	7.00	1
Chert	Surface	0.20	--	10.70	2.20	1
Chert	Structure 2 floor fill	0.20	18.20	8.60	2.20	1
Chert	Structure 4 feature fill	0.40	23.80	11.70	2.30	1
Chert	Structure 4 feature fill	0.10	--	7.50	0.20	1
Chert	Structure 6 feature fill	0.20	10.50	6.50	1.20	1
Chert	Structure 6 feature fill	0.10	9.00	5.20	1.10	1
Chert	Structure 7 floor	0.90	32.30	14.00	3.50	1
Chert	Structure 10 feature fill	0.30	17.40	10.40	2.70	1
Chert	Structure 10 feature fill	0.20	16.50	9.70	2.30	1
Chert	Structure 11 subfeature fill	0.30	15.50	8.00	1.30	1
Chert	Structure 11b feature fill	0.30	13.50	6.90	2.10	1
Chert	Structure 11b feature fill	0.50	12.60	12.70	2.70	1
Chert	Structure 12 feature fill	0.40	16.00	8.60	1.50	1
Chert	Structure 13 surface	0.40	23.20	10.40	1.70	1
Chert	Structure 18 feature fill	0.80	--	10.00	2.10	1
Chert	Structure 23 fill	--	19.83	8.86	1.70	1
Chert	Structure 27b Pot A	1.40	20.80	13.70	4.10	1
Chert	Unknown provenience	0.60	--	10.00	1.30	1
Chert	Unknown provenience	1.10	28.80	14.40	4.60	1
Chert	Unknown provenience	0.50	21.00	10.00	2.80	1
Chert	Unknown provenience	0.40	--	10.40	2.10	1
Chert	Unknown provenience	0.30	--	14.00	2.80	1
Chert	Unknown provenience	0.20	19.50	10.60	1.70	1
Chert	Unknown provenience	0.20	15.40	10.80	2.90	1
Chert	Unknown provenience	0.30	14.60	10.10	3.00	1
Chert	Unknown provenience	0.40	15.40	10.50	2.80	1
Chert	Unknown provenience	0.20	17.80	9.30	2.40	1
Chert	Unknown provenience	0.20	--	9.20	2.50	1

Table 4.6. Projectile Points, Organized by Material Type and Provenience, cont'd.

Material	Provenience	Weight (grams)	Length (mm)	Width (mm)	Thickness (mm)	Number of points
Chert	Unknown provenience	0.10	--	10.10	1.70	1
Chert	Unknown provenience	0.60	21.50	13.20	2.50	1
Jasper	Structure 33 floor fill	--	15.02	9.29	2.65	1
Jasper	Unknown provenience	0.40	--	--	2.80	1
unknown	Structure 27 fill	--	26.92	18.02	3.93	1
				Total Type 1 Points		66
		Type 2 Classic Period Points				
Obsidian	Structure 10 feature fill	0.20	15.70	10.20	2.20	1
Obsidian	Structure 16 feature fill	0.50	--	9.20	2.00	1
Chalcedony	Compound surface	0.30	25.40	10.20	2.80	1
Chalcedony	Structure 2 floor fill	0.30	17.50	10.50	3.00	1
Chalcedony	Structure 3 floor fill	--	21.95	10.36	2.84	1
Chalcedony	Structure 23	--	15.10	11.40	1.91	1
Chalcedony	Structure 26	--	27.05	9.82	2.40	1
Chalcedony	Structure 23	--	20.84	10.12	2.55	1
Chert	Compound surface	0.20	--	10.00	2.00	1
Chert	Surface	0.30	22.60	9.40	2.60	1
Chert	Surface	0.20	14.50	9.80	1.70	1
Chert	Surface	0.10	--	--	1.90	1
Chert	Surface	0.50	--	11.70	2.00	1
Chert	Surface	0.50	14.10	8.40	1.50	1
Chert	Structure 2 floor fill	0.10	10.70	9.10	1.90	1
Chert	Structure 2 floor fill	0.20	--	10.00	2.30	1
Chert	Structure 4 feature fill	0.20	--	9.50	2.50	1
Chert	Structure 4 feature fill	0.50	21.10	10.60	2.40	1
Chert	Structure 4 feature fill	0.20	--	10.60	1.80	1
Chert	Structure 7 feature fill	0.40	17.90	9.00	2.00	1
Chert	Structure 10 feature fill	0.20	--	--	2.60	1
Chert	Structure 17 feature fill	0.30	--	10.00	2.40	1
Chert	Structure 17 feature fill	0.30	--	9.70	2.00	1
Chert	Structure 23 fill	--	7.54 to break	12.52	1.89	1
Chert	Structure 25 fill	--	10.82	9.91	1.57	1
Chert	Structure 33 fill	--	21.24	11.27	3.53	1
Chert	Cremation No. 4	--	29.98	11.96	2.46	1
Chert	Cremation No. 4	--	25.76	12.59	2.56	1
Chert	Cremation No. 4	--	24.13	12.85	2.26	1
Chert	Cremation No. 4	--	21.86	10.59	1.79	1
Chert	Cremation No. 4	--	15.49	13.38	--	1
Chert	Unknown provenience	0.60	--	10.00	1.30	1
Chert	Unknown provenience	0.40	--	10.40	2.10	1
Chert	Unknown provenience	0.10	--	11.40	1.60	1
Chert	Unknown provenience	0.70	18.70	13.00	3.20	1
Chert	Unknown provenience	0.10	23.60	8.10	1.60	1
Chert	Unknown provenience	0.30	--	--	2.10	1
Chert	Unknown provenience	0.30	18.50	9.50	2.50	1
Jasper	Structure 4 feature fill	0.50	21.20	11.20	2.30	1
Jasper	Structure 7 feature fill	0.20	14.20	11.60	1.50	1
Quartzite	Structure 10 feature fill	0.20	--	13.00	2.30	1
						41
				Total Type 2 Points		
				Grand Total		141

Key: NFS = not further specified
Note: Obsidian point from Structure 19a was not part of this analysis.

Classic Period Points

The Classic period types are small and can be sorted into two basic forms. Type 1 points are small, triangular, bifacially flaked, and are nonserrated with straight to slightly convex lateral margins and concave bases (Figure 4.1 a, b, c, h). Sixty-six of them were recovered from the site (Table 4.6). The points are made of obsidian (n = 11), quartz (n = 2), chalcedony (n = 18), chert (n = 32), jasper (n = 2), and an unknown material (n = 2). Type 1 points are common in Classic period and earlier contexts in the Tucson area (Huckell 1988a; Myers 1996; Steere 1987; Yarborough 1986).

Type 2 points are small, triangular, concave-based, and side notched (Figure 4.1e, f, g, i, j). Forty-one of these points were found in various contexts at Whiptail (Table 4.6). The Type 2 points were made of obsidian (n = 2), chalcedony (n = 6), chert (n = 30), jasper (n=2), and quartzite (n = 1). They occur primarily in Classic period contexts (Franklin 1980; Hayden 1957; Kelly 1978).

Cores

The flaked stone sample analyzed includes 82 cores, which make up 9.3 percent of the analyzed tool assemblage (Table 4.5). Six core types were identified: bidirectional (n = 10, 12.2%), indeterminate (exhausted) fragments (n = 21, 25.6%), multidirectional (n = 24, 29.3%), unidirectional (n = 24, 29.3%), and tested cores (n = 3, 3.6%). Most of the cores (88.8%) had concave-convex edge shapes, followed by convex (7.4%), concave (2.4%), and one concave-straight edge. Measurements for these tools range from 17.2 mm to 180.2 mm in length and 16.7 mm to 133.8 mm in width; weights range from 3.2 g to 1250.6 g. Edge angles range from 65 to 90 degrees.

Quartzite (n = 29; 35.3%) and basalt (n = 26; 31.7%) make up the majority of the cores. Not surprisingly, these two materials were the most common types of flakes identified in the collection. The remaining 33 percent of cores are made of jasper (n = 8), chert (n = 5), sandstone (n = 4), quartz (n = 4), rhyolite (n = 3), limestone (n = 2), and obsidian (n = 1). Use wear on the cores consists of edge grinding (edge preparation for flake removal), whether unidirectional, bidirectional, or multidirectional. Only 11.1 percent of the cores exhibit no use wear.

Hammerstones

Although hammerstones may or may not be flaked stone per se (i.e., they are not necessarily formed by percussion or pressure flaking), the tools are often included in the general flaked stone category. At Whiptail, 312 hammerstones were identified, constituting 35 percent of the flaked stone tool assemblage. This artifact class includes 179 quartz and 72 quartzite hammerstones, which together comprise 80.4 percent of the total hammerstone collection. Other raw materials include andesite, basalt, granite, rhyolite, limestone, sandstone, and tuff (Table 4.5). Tuff and sandstone do not seem to be sufficiently sturdy to be used as hammerstones. Tools made of those materials may have had a specialized use.

Two hundred and eighty-eight of these tools are cobble hammerstones; 302 have multidirectional use wear; eight have bidirectional wear; and two have been used on only one surface. Only five hammerstones were made from multidirectional cores. Most of the hammerstones have convex edge shapes (n = 264, 84.6%), followed by convex-straight (n = 30, 9.6%), convex-concave (n = 17, 5.4%), and straight (n = 1, 0.3%). One multidirectional hammerstone was also used for grinding. Three hammerstones display scattered pecking and one had an area of concentrated pecking that created a concave impression. Hammerstone artifacts varied in size. The lengths of these artifacts ranged from 37 mm to 141 mm by 27.3 mm to 104.7 mm in width; weights range from 49 g to 3411.8 g. The different weights and sizes suggest use for different tasks. The working edge angles range from 70 to 90 degrees. Many of these hammerstones were probably used for something other than flaked stone production. They likely served in a variety of tasks including the pecking or battering of plant fibers, ground-stone shaping, removal and roughening of grinding surfaces, and preparation of food stuffs (e.g., Gregonis and Slaughter 1993).

The majority of hammerstones (n = 232) were located in the upper fill of structures or in general surface contexts. Eighty hammerstones were found in the floor fill or on the floor of various features (Table 4.7). Two houses, Structures 24 and 29, had exceptional numbers of hammerstones in the floor fill or on the floor (n = 15 in Structure 24, n = 28 in Structure 29). These numbers may indicate that after abandonment the two features were used for processing a particular resource or that the hammerstones were stored in those features.

Obsidian Artifacts

Out of the prime flaking materials—chert, jasper, obsidian—used for tools at Whiptail, obsidian was the rarest, making up only 0.05 percent (n = 13 of 7,645) of the flakes analyzed in the sample and only two percent (n = 21 of 886) of the tools (Tables 4.1 and 4.5). More than half (n = 14 of 21) of the obsidian tools are projectile points. The obsidian tools were found in 13 structures, as well as on the site's surface (Table 4.8). Structure 25, in the Southwestern Locus, had the most obsidian artifacts, with one point found on the floor, and a thin biface and two flakes found in the fill of the feature.

The rarity of obsidian artifacts was not unexpected as items made from that material are never common in Tucson Basin sites, but it is interesting that so few pieces of debitage were found in relation to the number of finished tools. There is a ratio of 1.6 obsidian tools to 1 piece of debitage. That is not to say, however, that none of the obsidian tools were made on the site. The few obsidian flakes recovered were found in seven structures and on the surface of the site (Table 4.8), indicating manufacture and retouch of at least a few artifacts in more than one location at Whiptail. Only one obsidian core (included in the tool count) is represented in the sample. It was found on the surface of the site.

In contrast to the high obsidian tool-to-debitage ratio and single core, the 45 jasper tools, which make up five percent of the total number of tools, include eight cores. Jasper flakes are also more common, making up nine percent (n = 602) of the debitage totals, for a ratio of one tool to 13.4 flakes. Chert flakes make up 13 percent of the total pieces of debitage (n = 923), while chert tools account for 26 percent (n = 232) of the total number of tools including five cores. The ratio for chert artifacts is 3.9 flakes to 1 tool.

Part of the reason for the differences in the tool-to-debitage ratios between obsidian, jasper, and chert is that jasper and chert were probably collected locally, while obsidian was imported from outside of the Tucson Basin. As part of a Center for Desert Archaeology project, Jeffery Clark offered us the opportunity to submit three of our obsidian projectile points for sourcing. Steven Shackley, director of the Berkeley Archaeological XRF Laboratory, analyzed the points using X-ray fluorescence. His

Table 4.7. Distribution of Flaked Stone Artifacts in Floor Fill and Floor Contexts in Various Structures.

Structure Number	Artifact Types							Totals
	Debitage	Uniface-informal	Uniface-formal	Bifaces	Projectile points	Cores	Hammer stones	
Compound Locus								
4	13	1			1			15
6					2			2
7			1		9	1	4	15
8							4	4
17	1				6	1	2	10
Southwestern Locus								
2	24	1	--	2	9	1	--	37
9		1					1	2
10	44	7	1		5			57
11	13			1	4	1	1	20
12	44	1			2	1		48
13	18	4			1	1	4	28
16					1			1
18	10	1			1	2	3	17
23	55		2		7		6	70
24	101	9		1	1	1	15	128
25	25	1		1	3		1	31
26					3		1	4
Central Locus								
15							1	1
33					2			2
Northern Locus								
3	3				1		1	5
27a	2			1			1	4
27b	6	1			5	1	1	14
28					3			3
29	74	1	1		1	2	28	107
30		1			1			2
31a					1			1
31b					1			1
Southern Locus								
14							6	6
Totals	**433**	**29**	**5**	**6**	**70**	**12**	**80**	**635**

Table 4.8. Types and Distribution of Obsidian Artifacts.

Provenience	Cienega Point	Classic Period Point	Informal Uniface	Side Scraper	Thick Biface	Thin Biface	Core	Flakes	Total No. Artifacts
Surface or Unknown Provenience	1	4			1	1	1	5	13
Compound Locus									
Compound surface		1							1
Structure 4 fill		1	1						2
Structure 4 floor								1	1
Structure 7 fill		1							1
Structure 17 fill		1							1
Southwestern Locus									
Structure 2 floor fill		1							1
Structure 2 floor		1							1
Structure 10 fill		1							1
Structure 12 fill					1				1
Structure 16 fill		1							1
Structure 18 pit								1	1
Structure 25 fill						1		2	3
Structure 25 floor		1							1
Structure 26 fill								1	1
Central Locus									
Structure 15 fill								1	1
Northern Locus									
Structure 29 fill				1				2	3
Southern Locus									
Structure 19a floor		1						several	1
Total No. of Artifacts	1	14	1	1	2	2	1	13	35

Note: Flakes and projectile point from Structure 19a were not part of the analysis discussed elsewhere in this chapter; field notes describe "several" obsidian flakes being found on the floor of the structure. The projectile point from Structure 19a is illustrated in Figure 4.1h. Tools are described as "edge prepared" and "from flake, not Apache tear."

letter report (Shackley 2009) is quoted here:

> Although not that unusual, all the artifacts were produced from the Mule Creek (Antelope Creek/Mule Mountains) source. While the primary source is in western New Mexico, secondary deposits are readily available in the Gila River alluvium in the Safford Valley, Arizona. Indeed, the elemental concentrations are so similar; these points could have been made all from the same nodule. The samples were analyzed with a Thermo Scientific Quant'X EDXRF spectrometer in the Geoarchaeological XRF Laboratory. Specific instrumental methods can be found at http://www.swxrflab.net/anlysis.htm, and Shackley (2005). Source assignment was made by comparison to source standard data at Berkeley and Shackley (1995, 2005). Analysis of the USGS RGM-1 standard indicates high machine precision for the elements of interest (Govindaraju 1994; Table 4.9).

Because of Shackley's comment that the artifacts were so similar that they could have come from the same nodule, Clark had flaked-stone analyst Jane Sliva look at the points. In a July 24, 2009, email to Clark, she stated that, on the basis of edge treatment and flaking angle, the two more translucent points (Figure 4.1a and

Table 4.9. Elemental Concentrations for the Obsidian Samples. All measurements in parts per million (ppm).

	Elements (in parts per million)								
Sample No.	Ti	Mn	Fe	Rb	Sr	Y	Zr	Nb	Source
25-138	853	429	10004	276	18	44	115	27	Mule Cr/AC-MM
No provenience	825	438	9903	265	20	40	110	27	Mule Cr/AC-MM
19-129	735	410	9189	256	16	42	105	23	Mule Cr/AC-MM
RGM1-S4	1649	309	13009	156	108	25	212	9	standard

Source: Shackley 2009.

4.1h) were made by the same person, while the more opaque point (Figure 4.1b) was likely made by someone else. The two translucent points come from the floor of Structure 19a (Figure 4.1h) and from the site's surface (Figure 4.1a). The more opaque point (Figure 4.1b) is from the floor of Structure 25.

If the points were made from the same nodule, Sliva's observations imply that two people shared a single piece of obsidian. The occurrence of two of the points on the floors of two different structures is also interesting in the implication that the two structures may have been contemporary and that their inhabitants were socially connected or the two structures were socially or ritually tied. That 3 of 13 Classic period obsidian points found at the site may have been made from the same nodule and by two different people further implies that the acquisition of obsidian was a rare event at Whiptail, perhaps happening only once or twice during the Classic period occupation of the site.

Discussion and Conclusion

Intrasite Comparison

Of the 8,532 flaked stone items analyzed for this project, 7.4 percent (n = 635) came from floor-contact and floor fill of structures (Table 4.10). Of those, 433 artifacts (68%) were pieces of debitage and 202 (32%) were tools including informal unifaces (n = 29), formal unifaces (n = 5), projectile points (n = 70), cores (n = 12), and hammerstones (n = 80). Keep in mind that this sample is incomplete and does not include

Table 4.10. Comparison of Flaked Stone Categories between Whiptail and Gibbon Springs.

	Whiptail			Gibbon Springs		
Artifact Category	No. of Artifacts	Percentage of Total Assemblage	Percentage of Tools	No. of Artifacts	Percentage of Total Assemblage	Percentage of Tools
Flakes	7645	89.6	--	3868	90.9	--
Bifaces	106	1.2	12	49	1.2	12.7
Cores	82	1.0	9.3	48	1.1	12.5
Hammerstones	312	3.6	34.9	71	1.7	18.4
Projectile Points	141	1.7	16	48	1.1	12.5
Formal Unifaces	35	0.4	3.9	20	0.5	5.2
Informal Unifaces (Utilized flakes)	211	2.5	23.9	149	3.5	38.7
Totals	8532	100	100	4253	100	100

flaked stone material from all of the structures that were excavated.

Table 4.7 shows the distribution of artifacts with floor or floor fill context of structures. Structures 9, 15, 26, and 30 contained very few flaked stone artifacts in the lower levels. Debitage was not recovered from 13 of the 28 houses in the sample, but it is unclear from field notes as to how much of the fill in any of the houses was screened, so it is likely that a fair number of small artifacts were not recovered. Structure 24 had the largest number of flaked stone artifacts on the floor (n = 128), consisting of hammerstones, cores, a projectile point, a biface, nine informal unifaces, and numerous pieces of debitage. The high percentage of debitage and tool-making equipment indicates that people may have been making tools in the structure (probably after the house had been abandoned for habitation).

Two other structures—14 and 29—also had relatively high numbers of tool-manufacturing equipment and debris associated with tool manufacture. Structure 14 contained six hammerstones. Structure 29 contained 74 pieces of debitage, two cores, 28 hammerstones, a projectile point, a formal uniface, and an informal uniface. The number of hammerstones in the lower fill and floor of Feature 29 indicate that, like Structure 24, the structure was used as a workshop area or as a storage area for the hammerstones and cores.

The largest sample of lithic artifacts in floor-fill and floor contexts (n = 443, 69.7%) came from the Southwestern Locus (Structures 2, 9–13, and 23–26). Almost one-third of those artifacts came from Structure 24. Structures in the Southwest Locus contained the most projectile points (n = 37) and the highest number of hammerstones (n = 32). This area also has the most cores and informal unifaces. The next highest number of artifacts came from the Northern Locus (Structures 3, 27a, 27b, 28, 29, and 30, 31a, and 31b), where 137 artifacts (21.6%) were found. Eighty-eight percent of those artifacts came from Structure 29.

The structures associated with the Compound, 4, 7, 8, and 17, comprise only 7.2 percent (n = 46) of the artifacts associated with floor and floor-fill contexts. As mentioned previously, the only lithic artifacts analyzed from the Southern Locus came from Structure 14; they consisted of six hammerstones. Finally, the Central Locus yielded one hammerstone (from Structure 15) and two projectile points (Structure 33).

One of the most peculiar assemblages of flaked stone tools were the scraper, drills, bifaces, and utilized and other flakes found inside of two pots on the floor of Structure 27b (Figures 4.2 and 4.3). These pots also contained faceted and scratched igneous stones that were coated or impregnated with hematite (Chapter 7) and what appeared to be the burned remains of a leather bag. The cluster of flaked stone and associated hematite-impregnated stones may have been a kit of some kind, perhaps for working hide or wood. The pots were part of a burial of an adult male between the ages of 35 and 50 when he died (Chapter 10). The man may have been an important hunter. In addition to the interesting stone artifact assemblage, he was also buried with the remains of a bighorn sheep, white-tailed deer, and mule deer (Chapter 8).

As discussed previously, obsidian artifacts were uncommon at the site. Thirty-seven percent of the obsidian pieces (n = 13 of 35) were found on the surface of the site. The remainder were found primarily in structures in the Southwestern and Compound Loci (Table 4.8) and nearly half of those artifacts (n = 10 of 22) were projectile points.

Intersite Comparison

The Whiptail flaked stone assemblage was compared with the assemblage from the nearby

Gibbon Springs site, an early Classic period village in the eastern Tucson Basin that is similar in many ways to Whiptail (Slaughter and Roberts 1996b). Information on the Gibbon Springs flaked stone assemblage comes from Myers (1996).

Debitage from the two sites are similar; the collections from both sites were comprised primarily of whole flakes, few of which were platform bearing, and most of which were smaller than 4.5 cm in size. There seems to have been more intensive reduction activity at Whiptail, where 61 percent of the debitage (n = 4,664) consisted of tertiary flakes. At Gibbon Springs, tertiary flakes comprised 48 percent (n = 1,849) of the debitage. Secondary flakes made up 35 percent (n = 1,366) of the collection from Gibbon Springs; at Whiptail, secondary flakes constituted only 28 percent (n = 2,167) of the collection. Primary flakes from each site formed less than 10 percent of the collection (n = 290 from Gibbon Springs; n = 501 from Whiptail).

Tool frequencies from both sites are remarkably similar, with a few notable differences (Table 4.10). Both sites have similar percentages of bifaces. The Whiptail assemblage, however, has almost twice the percentage of hammerstones as the Gibbon Springs assemblage (34.9% of the tools from Whiptail compared to 18.4% from Gibbon Springs). The Whiptail assemblage also has higher percentages of projectile points (16% at Whiptail compared to 12.5% at Gibbon Springs). In contrast, the Gibbon Springs assemblage contains higher percentages of informal unifaces (38.7% at Gibbon Springs compared to 23.9% from Whiptail), cores (12.5% compared to 9.3%), and formal unifaces (5.2% compared to 3.9%). The high percentage of hammerstones from Whiptail skews the perceived distribution of tools somewhat, but when hammerstones are removed from the counts at both sites, the Whiptail assemblage still retains a higher percentage of projectile points than the Gibbon Springs assemblage (24.5% from Whiptail, 15% from Gibbon Springs) and the Gibbon Springs assemblage retains a higher percentage of informal unifaces (47% from Gibbon Springs, 37% from Whiptail). If hammerstones are eliminated, the relative percentages for formal unifaces are the same for each site and the Whiptail assemblage has a slightly higher percentage of bifaces (18%) compared to the Gibbon Springs assemblage (16%).

The similarities in tool debitage frequency from the two sites suggest that tool preparation and use were similar. The higher percentage of projectile points at Whiptail may relate to a slightly higher rate of hunting at that site through time, but more likely reflects a penchant by the Whiptail site owners and excavators for collecting projectile points from the surface of the site that was not replicated at Gibbon Springs.

It is interesting that the higher numbers (and relative percentages) of hammerstones occurred at Whiptail, where excavations focused on structures, rather than Gibbon Springs, where excavations covered the entire site including pits and agricultural features.

Conclusion

In general, the inhabitants of Whiptail relied primarily on an expedient core reduction technology that is characteristic of Hohokam flint knapping. This technology has been described (Haury 1976) as one in which the simple tasks of cutting, scraping, crushing, and the like were done with the nearest rock at hand, modified as needed, and then discarded. Formal tools are relatively rare and when present appear to reflect fairly standardized forms such as projectile points, bifaces, and unifaces. Expedient technologies have a low tool-to-debitage ratio and intensive core reduction with little or no modification to flakes before use (Chapman

1977, Sullivan and Rozen 1985). At Whiptail, the tool-to-debitage ratio for the artifacts analyzed is 1:8.6 (883 tools to 7,645 pieces of debitage).

The most common raw materials found in the flaked stone assemblage are quartzite and basalt. These materials show up primarily in debitage and in informal unifaces (utilized flakes), thus supporting the idea that lithic procurement and use was expedient. With the exception of obsidian, all of the raw materials recovered from Whiptail are available locally within the Tucson Basin. Raw materials available on site or in nearby local drainages or in the adjacent Santa Catalina and Tanque Verde Mountains were used in tool manufacture.

At least some of the obsidian found at Whiptail came from the Mule Creek (Antelope Creek/Mule Mountains) source in west-central New Mexico. As Shackley (2009) stated, nodules from this source are found in the Gila Valley in the Safford area; that may have been the source for the obsidian found at Whiptail. Shackley's analysis and Sliva's (email communication 2009) observations of three projectile points suggest that nodules were shared among people and locales at the site and that acquisition of obsidian was a rare occurrence.

The diversity of tool categories and morphological variety indicates that the inhabitants of Whiptail used flaked stone technology to perform a wide range of activities. Projectile points are, of course, indicative of hunting activities. The points, which include late Middle and Late Archaic dart points as well as Classic period arrowheads, were found throughout the site. As mentioned previously, the collection of flakes, bifaces, drills, and unifaces found in two pots in Structure 27b may have been a kit of some kind, perhaps used for working with hide or wood. Flakes of granite and sandstone may indicate that the inhabitants of Whiptail were manufacturing or reshaping ground stone tools on the site. The hammerstones on the site may have been used for processing plant material such as agave or for preparing stone tools. The provenience of many of the hammerstones in abandoned structures could indicate that use of the site for plant collecting and hunting continued long after Whiptail was abandoned for habitation.

Appendix 4.A. Definitions of Fracture Types

The following definitions are based on Johnson (1981).

Hinge Fracture.
Hinge fractures display an abruptly outcurving, right-angle termination to the thinning flake. As the name implies, the termination on the distal end of a flake looks like a hinge; a matching scar is found on the core or tool that was being reduced.

Perverse Fracture.
This type of fracture occurs when the fracture plane twists on an axis of rotation corresponding with the direction of force. As a result, the tool is truncated.

Reverse Fracture.
These fractures occur when a bifacial thinning flake that curves back through the body of the tool is struck, removing the bifacial edge opposite the point of origin. Other names for this type of fracture are overshot fracture, plunged flake, and outrepassè.

Longitudinal Fracture.
Longitudinal fractures occur when a flake terminates abnormally by reversing through the biface. This is considered a subtype of a reverse fracture.

Impact Fracture.
Impact fractures occur when the tool or flake strikes another object. Impact fractures usually have a crushed point of contact and abnormal termination (i.e., step, hinge).

Lateral Snap.
This type of transverse fracture bisects an artifact in a relatively straight line and forms an obtuse angle with the longitudinal axis. In profile, the fracture forms a gentle "S" curve. The fracture occurs when the force of a thinning blow exceeds the elastic properties of the raw material.

Crenellated Snap.
This type of failure is caused by improper thermal treatment. The fracture forms a sinuous line across the face of the tool, giving it the appearance of having been cut with a jigsaw.

Haft Snap.
This type of fracture is seen as a transverse break across the stem of a projectile point; it occurs through use.

Incipient Fracture Plane.
This type of fracture is caused by the presence of pre-existing fracture planes within a piece of raw material. These cracks are often discontinuous and hard to detect. Artifacts can be destroyed by fractures along these fault lines.

Expansion Fracture.
This type of fracture occurs in the early stages of thermal failure. The fracture causes a piece to separate from the artifact like a lid being removed from a pot, truncating the artifact.

Appendix 4.B. Use-wear Definitions

The following definitions are derived from Keeley (1980) and Odell (1981).

Unidirectional Utilization.
Utilization occurs along a single edge. Types of wear patterns are feathers, steps, and scallops. Odell (1981) suggests that such wear patterns result from moving a cutting tool in a single direction across a surface during use. Scarring is generally continuous; its development is dependent upon the angle at which the tool is held in relation to the object cut during use.

Bidirectional Utilization.
Wear patterns occur along opposing surfaces of a tool's edge. Characteristic types of wear patterns are feathers, steps, and scallops. This wear is caused by the use of bidirectional (i.e., back-and-forth) cutting and sawing motions in use (Odell 1981). The exact wear patterns produced depend on the angle at which the tool is held during use.

Rounding or Dulling.
Abrasion causes the rounding or dulling of use edges. This type of wear occurs as a polish along the edge margin. Hammerstones frequently exhibit this kind of wear pattern because the use of these tools requires direct impact and pressure contact.

Striations.
These are "tracks" of use, indicators of the direction of tool use (Keeley 1980). Striations are rarely noted on flake tools, with the exception of flake scrapers and unifaces, both informal and formal. Striations usually form perpendicular to the working edge. They result from abrasive contact, either with the material being processed or with foreign matter introduced during the course of work. Striations may also be produced during the preparation of a tool by grinding under mechanical pressure.

Chapter 5

Ground Stone Artifacts

Jenny L. Adams

The ground stone assemblage from Whiptail (AZ BB:10:3) discussed in this chapter consists of a sample of 553 artifacts collected from six loci of adobe-walled structures. Of these, 105 were too fragmentary for identification, leaving 448 pieces that were analyzed. The artifacts were classified into 27 types (Table 5.1). Definitions for the types can be found in Adams (2002). The artifacts were analyzed to assess design, the activity for which the artifact was designed (food processing, pottery manufacture, pigment processing, etc.), the possibility of secondary use, and its location in the archaeological record (Appendix 5.A). Through such an analysis it is possible to track the "life history" of an artifact (Adams 1994, 1995, 1996; Schiffer 1987; Schlanger 1990). The life history framework questions whether morphological variations among tools of the same type result from differences in their life histories or differences in their original design (Adams 1994, 1995, 1996).

Artifact design was assessed in terms of complexity (Adams 1994:23–26, 1996:2–3). If the natural shape of the rock was altered only through use, the artifact was expediently designed. Modifications that made the tool easier to hold, or to achieve a specific shape, indicate that it was strategically designed. This distinction allows us to explore whether strategically designed tools were used or curated differently than those of expedient design.

Tool use was categorized as single, reuse, redesign, multiple use, or recycling (Adams 1994:41–42, 1996:3–4). Single-use artifacts were employed only in the task for which they were designed. Reused artifacts were designed for a specific primary task, but employed in a second without altering the artifact design (e.g., food-grinding mano reused to grind pigment). Multiple-use tools were designed for one task, but have another area or surface employed in a second task. Use in one would not preclude use in the other task, even if tool configuration was slightly altered. For example, the nonworking surface of a food-grinding mano may have been used as a lapstone to shape stone or shell ornaments. Such examples were considered to have had a concomitant secondary use (Adams 1994:41, 1996:4). Concomitant use broadened the range of accomplishable activities without increasing the number of tools, and also

Table 5.1. Ground Stone Artifact Types Recovered from Architectural Loci.

Artifact	Northern Locus		Central Locus		Compound		Southwestern Locus		Southern Locus		Northeastern Locus		Unassigned		Totals
	N.	%	N.	%	N.	%	N.	%	N.	%	N.	%	N.	%	
Abraders	2	2	-	-	1	2	3	1	1	8	-	-	-	-	7
Adzes	-	-	-	-	-	-	1	1	-	-	-	-	-	-	1
Axes	2	2	-	-	-	-	2	1	1	8	-	-	-	-	5
Choppers	-	-	-	-	2	3	3	1	-	-	-	-	-	-	5
T-shaped stones	1	1	-	-	-	-	-	-	-	-	-	-	-	-	1
Disks	1	1	-	-	1	2	1	1	-	-	-	-	-	-	3
Griddles	-	-	-	-	-	-	2	1	-	-	-	-	-	-	2
Handstones	4	5	1	7	5	8	24	10	1	8	1	100	9	29	45
Lapstones	5	6	-	-	1	2	10	4	2	15	-	-	-	-	18
Manos	33	38	1	8	14	23	94	38	4	31	-	-	6	20	152
Metates	4	5	3	23	3	5	7	3	1	8	-	-	2	8	20
Mortars	-	-	-	-	-	-	2	1	-	-	-	-	-	-	2
Nether stones	4	5	-	-	3	5	3	2	-	-	-	-	1	4	11
Pecking stones	-	-	-	-	3	5	4	2	1	8	-	-	-	-	8
Pestles	1	1	-	-	5	8	11	4	2	15	-	-	1	4	20
Pigment	1	1	-	-	-	-	1	1	-	-	-	-	-	-	2
Planes	-	-	-	-	-	-	1	1	-	-	-	-	-	-	1
Polishing stones	6	7	-	-	6	10	15	6	-	-	-	-	3	10	30
Pot lids	-	-	-	-	1	2	-	-	-	-	-	-	-	-	1
Pot rests	-	-	-	-	1	2	-	-	-	-	-	-	-	-	1
Pottery anvils	-	-	-	-	-	-	1	1	-	-	-	-	-	-	1
Pulping stones	-	-	-	-	-	-	-	-	-	-	-	-	1	4	2
Roasting rocks	1	1	-	-	-	-	2	1	-	-	-	-	-	-	3
Shaped	3	3	1	8	-	-	7	3	-	-	-	-	-	-	11
Slabs	-	-	-	-	1	2	-	-	-	-	-	-	-	-	1
Tabular tools	18	21	6	46	12	20	51	20	-	-	-	-	6	19	93
Temper	-	-	-	-	-	-	1	1	-	-	-	-	-	-	2
Total No. Artifacts	86	-	12	-	60	-	246	-	13	-	1	-	30	-	448

conserved raw material. The original designer and user were likely to have been the same person who reused the tool without affecting its original function.

Redesigned tools were designed for a primary task and either remanufactured or altered through use in a second task to the extent that the tool could no longer function in the first. Such redesign might involve placing a groove across the working surface of a mano. Recycled tools were designed and used in one task, but were ultimately employed in a completely different context that may or may not have physically altered the tool (Adams 1994:41–42, 1996:4). Manos and metates used as building stones or as roasting rocks are examples of recycled tools. Such tools are considered to have been involved in sequential secondary use (Adams 1994:41–42, 1996:4). The user of the redesigned or recycled tools may or may not have been the same person as the original designer and user, who did not care to maintain original tool function.

The activity for which a tool was used can be determined with some confidence through macroscopic techniques; however, more confidence is achievable with the use of a microscope (Adams 1993, 1995:45). Microscopic examinations were not conducted on the Whiptail assemblage. Macroscopically, use wear patterns help identify motor habits involved in tool manufacture and use. Tool design may

Table 5.2. Nature of Ground Stone Artifacts from Whiptail.

Variable	Typeable N.	Typeable %	Totals N.	Totals %
Locus				
Central	13	3	14	2.0
Compound	61	14	71	13.0
Northeastern	1	< 1	1	< 1.0
Northern	86	19	120	22.0
Southwestern	250	56	297	54.0
Southern	13	3	15	3.0
Unassigned	24	5	35	6.0
Context				
Disturbed	23	5.0	31	6.0
Fill	195	44.0	258	47.0
Floor fill	11	2.5	15	3.0
Floor	121	27.0	134	24.0
Pit fill	11	2.5	11	2.0
Unknown	87	19.0	104	19.0
Condition				
Fragments	237	53.0	340	61.0
Whole	211	48.0	213	39.0
Burn				
Heat cracked	19	5.0	40	8.0
Indeterminate	51	-	52	-
No	309	78.0	389	78.0
Yes	69	17.0	72	3.0
Design				
Expedient	107	35.0	113	36.0
Indeterminate	139	-	231	-
Strategic	202	65.0	209	64.0
Use				
Destroyed	2	1.0	3	1.0
Indeterminate	194	-	279	-
Secondary	99	39.0	117	43.0
Primary	138	55.0	139	51.0
Unused	14	6.0	14	5.0
Sequence				
Concomitant	37	38.0	37	32.0
Indeterminate	120	-	143	-
Not applicable	231	-	294	-
Sequential	60	62.0	79	68.0
Activity/Process				
Food	133	30.0	133	24.0
Pottery	33	7.0	33	6.0
Pigment	25	6.0	25	4.5
Wood	6	1.0	6	1.1
Ritual	13	3.0	13	2.5
Percussion	30	7.0	30	5.4
Grinding	57	13.0	57	10.3
Abrading	6	1.0	6	1.1
Scraping	91	20.0	91	16.5
Other	4	1.0	3	0.5
Multiple	50	11.0	56	10.1
Unidentified	-	-	100	18.0
Totals	448		553	

indicate the intended use of the tool. A tool designed with special comfort features, such as finger grips, may have been intended for longer term or more intense use than a similar one made without such features.

An assessment of design can also help determine the one or more activities in which a tool was used. For example, manos and metates and some mortars and pestles were designed for use in food processing activities. A food-grinding mano with remnants of pigment was used in multiple activities, both food and pigment processing. Activities and wear processes represented among the Whiptail ground stone assemblage are shown in Table 5.2. Some were not identifiable and were lumped into an eighth "other" category.

In combination, assessments of design, activities represented, and primary and secondary use, allow reconstruction of an artifact's life history including how and why it was made and how it was used. With the addition of an assessment of its location in the archaeological record, these interpretations are used to infer similarities and differences in technological behavior among the inhabitants of Whiptail.

Analysis Approach

The ground stone assemblage has been partitioned into categories that reflect certain activities, such as the processing of food, pottery production, pigment processing and others (Table 5.2). Some artifacts are generic enough that the activity in which they were used cannot be identified more specifically than that they were used in general grinding, abrading, or percussion activities. Ground stone artifacts from Whiptail can be categorized as follows: food processing tools include manos, metates, griddles, and pot rests; pottery processing tools include pottery anvils, pottery polishing stones, and temper sources; pigment processing includes raw pieces of pigment and tools with remnants of pigment on them; percussion includes axes, choppers, mortars, pestles, pecking stones, and pulping stones; grinding includes handstones, lapstones, and nether stones; abrading includes abraders; scraping includes adzes, planes, and tabular tools; other includes all those items not in the above categories, such as disks, T-shaped stones, pot lids, roasting rocks, shaped, and slabs. The counts of items involved in pigment processing are low because most of the tools with pigment on them were classified into the other categories and pigment processing was a secondary use (see Chapter 7 for a description of some pigment processing artifacts).

By assessing the activities in which the ground stone artifacts were used it is possible to make inferences about occupation strategy. Settlements with occupations of longer duration should have relatively higher percentages of each of these activity types than settlements of shorter duration. Limited activity sites may be missing some activity types altogether. People who continuously occupied a location over a long period of time or returned to the same location for repeated short-term occupations have more of an opportunity to scavenge artifacts from abandoned features or trash deposits than people who occupied a location for a short time. Scavenged artifacts may have continued in use at the task for which they were designed, thereby making it impossible to determine if they were used secondarily. In specific cases, however, it is possible to determine if they were used in ways other than those for which they were originally designed. Evidence for this behavior exists as tools that were redesigned in such a manner as to make them no longer useable as originally designed, for example, manos that were modified by flaking into choppers. Because they could no longer be used as manos they had sequential secondary use. If, however, the tools were modified in such a way as to make them useful in more than one activity they had concomitant secondary use, such as manos modified with abrader grooves across the sides that did not contact the metates. A tool useable in more than one activity saves raw material—something that might be important to sedentary populations who have limited access to sources—and it lowers the number of tools that need to be stored, transported, and accounted for. Thus, it seems reasonable to infer that settlements with relatively high percentages of secondarily used artifacts were either occupied continuously for a long time, or were repeatedly reoccupied.

Conversely, people who occupied a location for a short time probably used their tools only as they were originally designed. This is primary use. Comparisons among assemblages may highlight relative differences in percentages of primary and secondary use artifacts, which should be useful in understanding the duration and continuity of settlement occupation. It is expected that among the continuous range of site categories from permanent settlements to single-use campsites there would be predictable differences in the design and use of artifacts as well as the range of activities in which they were used, as mentioned above. For example, permanent settlements would have the highest percentages of strategically designed artifacts, secondarily used tools, and items used in a wider range of activities. Distinguishing the nature of the sites within the continuum will be more of a challenge.

Nature of the Assemblage

The ground stone artifacts recovered from Whiptail were sorted according to the architectural locus from which they were recovered (Table 5.2). Most (54 %) were recovered from the Southwestern Locus. The Northern and the Compound Loci have assemblages large enough for some discussion. Those from the Central, Southern, and Northeastern Loci are too small for comparison. A few artifacts were not associated with any particular locus. More than half (60 %) of the artifacts are broken, but few of them became that way through burning or heat-cracking. Most (78 %) are unburned. The largest percentage of artifacts were recovered from fill contexts (47 %); however, enough were recovered from floor contexts (24 %) for some evaluation of the activities associated with certain structures. [Editoral note: It is clear from the field notes and photographs that metates were commonly reused as architectural elements at Whiptail. It is not clear, however, whether the metates and metate fragments were recovered or left in the field.]

Most of the loci comparisons are at a general level. One guiding assumption is that the fill within structures is from the sequential occupation of structures within each locus. Comparisons among loci will include the artifact context, condition, design, and how and in what activities the artifacts were used. The goals are to identify the technological evidence of occupation nature and duration for each locus and assess the similarities and differences among loci.

Loci Assemblages

Northern Locus

Slightly more than half of the artifacts from the Northern Locus were recovered from fill contexts (Table 5.3). The next largest percentage was recovered from floor contexts and it is these artifacts that are the most useful for understanding what activities occurred within specific structures. Those found in the fill will be used to postulate on a more general level the activities that occurred in this area of the site. Most of the artifacts are broken and unburned (Table 5.3), a pattern that holds for those recovered from structure floors as well (Table 5.4; Figure 5.1). Similarly, with those artifacts for which it is possible to determine design, more were of strategic than expedient design both on floors and in general (Tables 5.3 and 5.4).

A higher percentage of artifacts found on structure floors in the Northern Locus were used only in the activity for which they were primarily designed (Tables 5.3 and 5.4). More were used in food processing and general scraping activities than any others. Of those floor artifacts secondarily used, substantially more were concomitantly than sequentially used (Table 5.4). This hints at the possibility that some artifacts were used or stored in structures because they were usable in more than one activity serving as an efficient use of perhaps scarce or difficult to acquire materials. Including those artifacts from other contexts, secondary use was more often sequential than concomitant. Perhaps sequentially used artifacts were more apt to be deposited as discarded tools in fill and other contexts than on floors.

In general, those artifacts recovered from the Northern Locus were more commonly used in food processing than any other activity. General grinding and scraping activities were also well represented by artifacts from all contexts. Among floor artifacts, pigment processing is better represented than in other contexts. Ritual artifacts were missing from structure floors in the Northern Locus. Thus, the floor assemblages from the Northern Locus do not seem to represent all of the activities that probably occurred there, suggesting that many of the structures were probably cleaned of many important artifacts upon their abandonment.

Compound Locus

As with those recovered from the Northern Locus, slightly more than half of the artifacts recovered from the Compound Locus were

Table 5.3. Nature of Ground Stone Artifacts from Selected Groups.

	Locus					
	Northern		Compound		Southwestern	
Variable	N	%	N	%	N	%
Context						
Disturbed	4	5	1	2	8	3
Fill	46	53	31	52	99	40
Floor Fill	2	2	-	-	8	3
Floor	26	30	12	20	73	30
Pit Fill	3	4	1	2	4	2
Unknown	5	6	15	25	54	22
Condition						
Fragments	47	55	34	57	116	47
Whole	39	45	26	43	130	53
Burning						
Heat Cracked	7	8	1	2	7	3
Indeterminate	-	-	5	-	44	-
No	55	64	52	95	158	78
Yes	24	28	3	5	37	19
Design						
Expedient	19	27	14	34	65	40
Indeterminate	16	-	19	-	84	-
Strategic	51	73	27	66	99	60
Use						
Destroyed	-	-	2	6	-	-
Indeterminate	27	-	25	-	118	-
Secondary	24	41	11	32	48	38
Primary	33	56	20	59	70	55
Unused	2	3	1	3	10	8
Sequence						
Concomitant	9	38	9	69	14	33
Indeterminate	1	-	24	-	87	-
Not Applicable	61	-	24	-	116	-
Sequential	15	63	4	13	29	67
Processing						
Food	31	36	11	18	79	32
Pottery	6	7	7	12	17	7
Pigment	6	7	3	5	14	6
Wood	2	2	-	-	4	2
Ritual	4	5	-	-	8	3
Percussion	1	1	6	10	8	3
Grinding	9	10	9	15	29	12
Abrading	2	2	1	2	3	1
Scraping	17	20	12	20	50	20
Other	1	1	3	5	10	4
Multiple	7	8	8	13	24	10
Total	86		60		246	

Table 5.4. Nature of Floor Artifacts from Selected Loci.

	Locus					
	Northern		Compound		Southwestern	
Variable	N	%	N	%	N	%
Condition						
Fragments	13	50	1	8	29	37
Whole	13	50	12	92	49	63
Burning						
Heat Cracked	1	4	-	-	-	-
Indeterminate	-	-	3	-	22	-
No	14	54	8	89	47	82
Yes	11	42	1	11	10	18
Design						
Expedient	6	25	1	13	9	21
Indeterminate	2	-	4	-	27	-
Strategic	18	75	7	88	33	79
Use						
Indeterminate	7	-	3	-	44	-
Secondary	6	32	2	22	12	34
Primary	13	68	7	78	18	51
Unused	-	-	-	-	5	14
Sequence						
Concomitant	4	67	1	11	6	46
Indeterminate	-	-	5	-	33	-
Not Applicable	20	-	7	78	31	-
Sequential	2	33	1	11	7	54
Processing						
Food	9	31	3	25	24	33
Pottery	2	8	1	8	4	6
Pigment	3	12	1	8	4	6
Wood	1	4	-	-	2	3
Ritual	-	-	1	8	2	3
Percussion	-	-	1	8	3	4
Grinding	-	-	2	17	3	4
Abrading	1	4	1	8	-	-
Scraping	9	35	-	-	24	33
Other	1	4	-	-	-	-
Multiple	-	-	2	17	7	10
Totals	26	-	12	-	79	-

in fill contexts. Fewer were on Compound Locus structure floors than were on floors in the Northern Locus (Table 5.3). However, some of the differences in distribution may be a factor of a smaller sample recovered from the Compound Locus. Whereas a considerable percentage of artifacts were recovered from floors in Compound Locus structures, this was a larger percentage than from floors in the Northern Locus. Also considerably more were from unknown contexts within the Compound Locus than the Northern Locus (Table 5.3). The

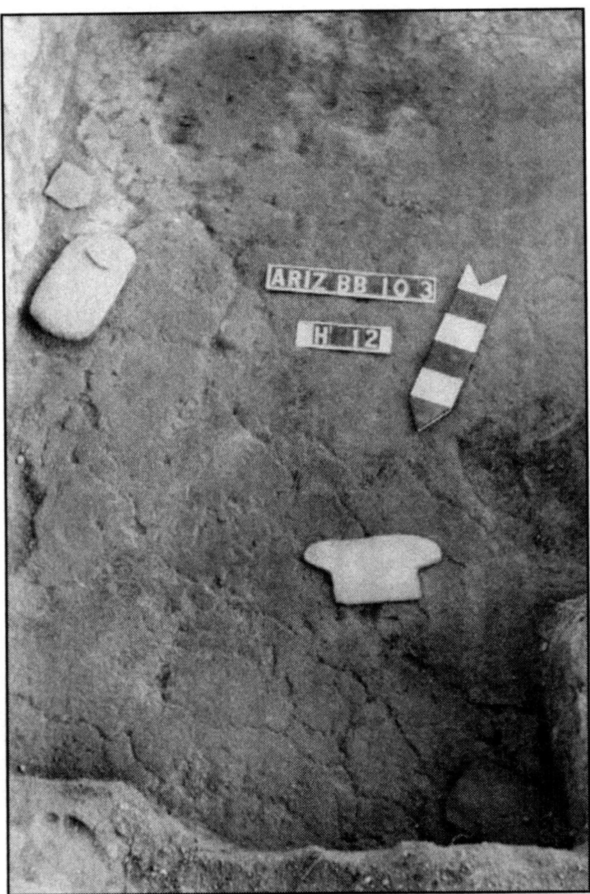

Figure 5.1. Ground stone on the floor of Structure 12 (ASM Negative No. 106438).

assemblage from the Compound Locus had relatively more complete artifacts and fewer were burned than the artifacts from the Northern Locus. Perhaps less trash accumulated among Compound Locus structures.

Compound Locus artifacts were mostly of strategic design and more than half were used only in the activity for which they were designed. Relatively fewer were secondarily used than those from the Northern Locus (Table 5.3). Considerably more of those on Compound Locus feature floors were strategically designed than those found in other contexts and more on the floor were used only in the activity for which they were designed. Of those used secondarily, the few on the floors were equally concomitantly and sequentially used (Table 5.4). Those in other contexts were much more apt to have been used concomitantly. This is a different pattern than was noticed for floor and other contexts in the Northern Locus; however, the small sample size of Compound Locus structure floor artifacts (n = 12) makes it difficult to assign any true meaning to this pattern.

Food processing activities seem to be slightly less well represented within the Compound Locus than the Northern Locus, both in all contexts and only on floors. The range of activities represented within the Compound Locus seems to be more evenly distributed among pottery manufacture, and general percussion, grinding and scraping activities. Similarly, among Compound Locus and Northern Locus floor assemblages, food processing activities are better represented than any other activity.

The condition of the assemblage from the Compound Locus in comparison to that from the Northern Locus may be the result of shorter duration occupation. Fewer secondarily used artifacts may indicate that there was less of a need for conserving material by using a single tool in more than one activity and that there was less scavenging by the occupants from already abandoned areas of the settlement. Fewer burned artifacts may be representative of less trash accumulation in the structures or perhaps less structure burning upon abandonement.

Southwestern Locus

The assemblage from the Southwestern Locus is larger than those from the other two groups discussed here (Table 5.3). Less than half of the assemblage came from fill contexts. The proportion of the assemblage recovered from floors is the same as from Northern Locus structures and more than from Compound

Locus structures. More than half of the artifacts are whole and most are unburned (Table 5.3). Fewer artifacts from the Southwestern Locus were strategically designed than from the other two groups; however, more floor artifacts found in the Southwestern Locus were strategically designed than those from floor artifacts in the Northern Locus. The artifacts from the Southwestern Locus were less likely to have been used only in the activity for which they were designed than those from the other two groups (Table 5.3). Slightly more than half of those recovered from Southwestern Locus floors were used only in the activities for which they were designed. Of those secondarily used and recovered from floors, more were used sequentially than concomitantly. Perhaps the inhabitants of the Southwestern Locus lived in this area longer than the inhabitants of the other areas, or arrived later so that there were more abandoned artifacts to redesign and use in activities other than the one for which they were originally intended.

The artifacts recovered from the Southwestern Locus floors include higher percentages of food processing and general scraping tools than any other category. In general, the artifacts from all contexts have more activities represented. Thus, there may have been some activities that were not conducted within Southwestern Locus structures or many tools were removed upon structure abandonment.

Discussion

The Compound Locus structures have a sightly lower percentage of artifacts from floor contexts than structures in the Northern or Southwestern Loci (Table 5.3). The compound had fewer total ground stone artifacts, but there were also fewer structures. Far more of the floor artifacts in Compound Locus structures were whole and unburned than floor artifacts in the Northern and Southwestern Loci (Table 5.4). Perhaps fewer activities related to grinding technology were conducted within the compound. Higher percentages of Northern Locus artifacts, especially among the floor artifacts (Table 5.4), were broken and burned than from the Southwestern Locus or the Compound Locus. Perhaps this reflects the use of these structures as trash dumps, which may mean that they were abandoned while other areas of the settlement remained in use.

Appendix 5.A. Ground Stone Analysis Data.

Structure No.	Context	Artifact	Subtype	Condition	Burned	Length (in cm)	Width (in cm)	Thickness (in cm)
1	Unknown	Handstone	Flat	Fragment	No	0	9.4	2.0
2	Fill	Shaped	None	Whole		2.8	2.2	0.5
2	Roof/wall	Mortar	Indeterminate	Fragment		0	0	0
2	Floor	Polishing stone	None	Whole		7.7	7.7	4.3
2	Floor	Metate	Indeterminate	Fragment	No	0	0	0
2	Floor	Mano	Basin	Whole		12.8	12.8	3.7
2	Floor	Tabular tool	None	Fragment		0	0	0
2	Unknown	Tabular tool		Fragment	No	0	0	0
2	Unknown	Tabular tool		Fragment	No	0	0	0
2	Unknown	Nether stone	Indeterminate	Fragment	No	0	0	0
2	Unknown	Mano	Trough	Fragment	No	0	12.2	3.2
2	Unknown	Mano	Flat	Fragment		0	0	0
2	Unknown	Metate	Indeterminate trough	Fragment	No	0	0	5.3
2	Unknown	Tabular tool		Fragment	No	0	0	0
2	Unknown	Tabular tool		Fragment	No	0	0	0
2	Unknown	Tabular tool		Fragment	No	0	0	0
2	Unknown	Tabular tool		Fragment	No	0	0	0
2	Unknown	Tabular tool	Tool Fragment	Fragment	No	0	0	0
2	Unknown	Tabular tool		Fragment	No	0	0	0
3	Roof/wall	Metate	Open trough	Whole		38.3	29.0	20.0
3	Roof/wall	Tabular tool	Tool Fragment	Fragment	No	0	0	0
3	Floor fill	Handstone	None	Fragment	Heat cracked	0	0	0
4	Fill	Mano	Indeterminate	Broke	No	13.1	8.6	3.7
4	Fill	Tabular tool	Concave edge	Fragment	No	0	4.0	7.0
4	Fill	Whorl	Flat	Fragment	No	0	3.8	0.3
4	Fill	Tabular tool	Tool Fragment	Fragment	No	0	0	0
4	Fill	Tabular tool	Tool Fragment	Fragment	No	0	0	0
4	Fill	Tabular tool		Fragment	No	0	0	0
4	Fill	Polishing stone	None	Whole		2.4	2.2	1.5
4	Fill	Polishing stone	Pebbled surface	Whole	No	3	2.1	1.2
4	Fill	Tabular tool	Tool fragment	Fragment	No	0	0	0
4	Unknown	Mano	Indeterminate	Fragment	Heat cracked	0	0	0
4	Unknown	Pestle	Pebble	Whole	No	7.6	5.6	5.2
4	Unknown	Mano	Indeterminate	Fragment	No	0	0	0
4	Unknown	Mano	Indeterminate	Broke	No	16.3	8.1	2.9
4	Unknown	Mano	Trough	Fragment	No	0	10.5	3.2
5	Fill	Tabular tool		Fragment	No	0	0	0
5	Fill	Metate	Indeterminate trough	Fragment	No	0	0	0
5	Fill	Metate	Indeterminate trough	Fragment	No	0	0	0
6	Fill	Tabular tool	Shaped	Fragment	No	0	0	0
6	Fill	Tabular tool		Fragment	No	0	0	0
6	Fill	Handstone	Indeterminate	Fragment	No	0	0	0
6	Fill	Metate	Indeterminate trough	Fragment	No	0	0	0
6	Fill	Polishing stone	Pebbled surface	Whole	No	4.7	4.3	3.8
6	Floor	Tabular tool	None	Fragment		0	0	0
6	Floor	Pestle	Cobble	Whole	No	13.3	11.2	6.6
6	Unknown	Mano	Trough	Broke	No	13.6	8.4	3.7
6	Unknown	Mano	Concave	Fragment	No	9.3	9.0	4.1
6	Unknown	Tabular tool		Fragment	No	0	0	0
6	Unknown	Tabular tool		Fragment	No	0	0	0
7	Fill	Pestle	Cobble	Whole	No	18.6	10.1	5.7
7	Fill	Pot lid	None	Whole	Yes	9.1	6.5	1.3
7	Fill	Polishing stone	Pebbled surface	Whole	No	4.0	3.0	3.1
7	Roof/wall	Mano	Blank	Whole	No	17.4	8.7	5.2
7	Floor	Mano	Trough	Whole	No	14.4	9.0	4.6

Appendix 5.A. Ground Stone Analysis Data, cont'd.

Structure No.	Context	Artifact	Subtype	Condition	Burned	Length (in cm)	Width (in cm)	Thickness (in cm)
7	Floor	Metate	Open trough	Whole		36.0	25.0	13.0
7	Floor	Pecking stone	None	Whole	No	6.4	4.7	7.4
7	Unknown	Polishing stone	Pebbled surface	Whole	No	4.0	3.5	2.7
8	Fill	Mano	Trough	Fragment	No	0	0	0
8	Fill	Tabular tool	Tool fragment	Fragment	No	0	0	0
8	Fill	Pestle	Natural	Fragment	No	13.9	7.1	5.4
8	Fill	Mano	Indeterminate	Fragment	No	0	10.1	3.8
8	Fill	Pecking stone	None	Whole	No	7.7	9.0	7.0
8	Fill	Handstone	Indeterminate	Fragment	No	0	0	0
8	Fill	Pecking stone	None	Fragment	No	0	0	0
8	Fill	Mano	Trough	Fragment	No	0	10.4	4.3
8	Floor	Mano	Trough	Whole	No	14.4	8.5	3.0
8	Floor	Pestle	Cylindrical	Whole	No	10.8	6.8	4.1
8	Disturb	Metate	Open trough	Whole		41.0	23.0	16.0
8	Unknown	Mano	Indeterminate	Fragment	No	5.8	10.0	3.0
9	Fill	Pecking stone	None	Whole	No	6.6	4.8	5.2
9	Fill	Pecking stone	None	Whole	No	7.3	6.4	4.0
9	Fill	Mano	Concave	Whole	No	9.1	7.2	3.8
9	Fill	Tabular tool	None	Whole		10.3	8.2	0.6
9	Fill	Polishing stone	None	Whole		4.4	2.5	2.5
9	Fill	Tabular tool	Tool fragment	Fragment	No	0	0	0
9	Floor fill	Mano	Trough	Fragment	Heat cracked	0	0	0
9	Floor	Mano	Trough	Fragment	No	0	0	0
9	Floor	Tabular tool	Shaped	Whole	No	11.3	9.1	0.8
9	Floor	Pecking stone	None	Whole	No	8.9	5.9	4.0
9	Floor	Mano	Concave	Whole	No	8.9	6.9	3.8
9	Disturb	Handstone	Indeterminate	Fragment	No	0	0	0
9	Unknown	Pecking stone	None	Whole	No	6.8	7.1	6.3
9	Unknown	Mano	Indeterminate	Fragment	No	0	0	0
10	Modern surface	Disk	Biconical donut	Fragment	No	0	0	0
10	Fill	Tabular tool		Fragment	No	0	0	0
10	Fill	Tabular tool	None	Whole		21.0	9.9	1.1
10	Fill	Mano	Concave	Whole	Yes	14.6	8	4.2
10	Fill	Shaped	None	Whole	No	3.3	2.3	0.3
10	Floor	Tabular tool	Shaped	Fragment	No	0	0	0
10	Floor	Tabular tool		Whole	No	9.6	5.6	0.8
10	Floor	Tabular tool	Shaped	Fragment	No	0	0	0
10	Floor	Handstone	Flat	Whole	No	8.5	5.4	4.0
10	Floor	Mano	Trough	Broke	Yes	17.6	8.9	3.7
10	Floor	Polishing stone	Hand stone	Whole	No	10.7	4.3	5.3
10	Floor	Tabular tool	Shaped	Fragment	No	0	0	0
10	Floor	Tabular tool	Shaped	Fragment	No	0	0	0
10	Floor	Tabular tool	Shaped	Fragment	No	0	0	0
10	Floor	Mano	Blank	Broke	Yes	25.2	11.2	7.6
10	Floor	Metate	Open trough	Whole		57.0	43.0	19.0
10	Floor	Mano	Blank	Whole	No	25.1	10.6	3.6
10	Floor	Mano	Trough	Broke	Yes	18.1	9.6	3.6
10	Floor	Mano	Trough	Whole	Yes	19.1	10.5	3.3
10	Floor	Mano	Trough	Whole	No	21.8	9.8	8.2
10	Floor	Mano	Trough	Whole	Yes	18.8	11.9	3.0
10	Floor	Tabular tool	Shaped	Fragment	No	0	0	0
10	Unknown	Tabular tool	Tool fragment	Fragment	No	0	0	0
11	Fill	Pigment	None	Reused fragment	No	2.6	1.8	1.2
11	Fill	Mano	Trough	Fragment	No	0	0	0
11	Fill	Polishing stone	None	Whole	No	8.3	8.3	6.2

Appendix 5.A. Ground Stone Analysis Data, cont'd.

Structure No.	Context	Artifact	Subtype	Condition	Burned	Length (in cm)	Width (in cm)	Thickness (in cm)
11	Fill	Tabular tool		Fragment	No	0	0	0
11	Roof/wall	Tabular tool	Tool fragment	Fragment	No	0	0	0
11	Roof/wall	Mano	Trough	Whole	No	21.1	9.4	4.4
11	Roof/wall	Handstone	Indeterminate	Fragment	No	0	0	0
11	Floor	Lap stone	Flat	Whole	No	15.1	6.8	6.4
11	Floor	Pestle	Cylindrical	Whole	No	15.0	5.8	4.0
11	Floor	Mano	Trough	Fragment	No	0	0	0
11	Floor	Mano	Concave	Whole	No	8.3	9.9	4.5
11	Floor	Mano	Trough	Whole	No	18.2	10.7	5.3
11	Floor	Pestle	Shaped	Whole	No	15.6	10.1	6.4
11	Floor	Mano	Concave	Whole	No	14.1	7.9	4.4
11	Floor	Pot anvil	Grooved	Whole		9.6	9.6	5.2
11	Floor	Metate	Open trough	Whole		48.0	38.0	16.0
11	Floor	Mano	Trough	Whole	No	19.2	10.6	3.4
11	Floor	Tabular tool	None	Whole		8.9	5.3	0.6
11	Pit fill	Mano	Concave	Broke	No	15.7	10.9	6.0
11	Pit fill	Polishing stone	None	Whole		6.9	2.7	1.1
11	Unknown	Abrader	Flat	Fragment	No	0	0	0
11	Unknown	Mano	Trough	Fragment	No	0	8.1	3.1
11	Unknown	Mano	Trough	Fragment	No	0	7.8	2.6
11	Unknown	Handstone	Indeterminate	Fragment	No	0	0	0
11	Unknown	Tabular tool		Fragment	No	0	0	0
11 and 13	Unknown	Handstone	Flat	Whole	No	8.1	6.9	3.1
11 or 18	Modern surface	Mano	Indeterminate	Fragment	No	0	10.4	3.4
12	Fill	Mano	Indeterminate	Fragment		0	0	0
12	Fill	Mano	Indeterminate	Fragment		0	0	0
12	Fill	Mano	Trough	Whole	No	17.9	10.4	4.1
12	Fill	Shaped	None	Whole		11.1	3.7	1.1
12	Fill	Shaped	None	Whole		3.4	1.6	0.4
12	Fill	Tabular tool	Tool fragment	Fragment	No	0	0	0.5
12	Fill	Polishing stone	None	Whole		3.3	2.2	2.2
12	Fill	Mano	Indeterminate	Fragment		0	0	0
12	Fill	Ax	3/4 groove	Whole	No	10.1	4.4	5.9
12	Fill	Handstone	Indeterminate	Whole		14.9	9.5	6.4
12	Roof/wall	Mano	Concave	Whole	No	11.2	8.4	2.9
12	Roof/wall	Handstone	Indeterminate	Whole	No	13	10.2	4.3
12	Floor	Tabular tool	None	Whole		16.0	7.0	0.7
12	Floor	Mano	Indeterminate	Fragment		0	0	0
12	Floor	Tabular tool	None	Unknown	No	16.0	11.7	0
12	Floor	Polishing stone	Surface + edge	Whole	No	3.6	2.1	1.5
12	Floor	Tabular tool	None	Whole		21.5	10	0.7
12	Floor	Mano	Blank	Whole	No	23.0	10.9	5.2
12	Floor	Tabular tool	None	Fragment		0	0	0
12	Floor	Tabular tool	None	Whole		11.3	7.1	0.8
12	Floor	Metate	Indeterminate	Fragment	No	0	0	0
12	Floor	Handstone	None	Whole		13.2	9.7	4.2
12	Floor	Plane	None	Whole		18.0	9.7	1.2
12	Floor	Tabular tool	None	Whole		12.1	5.1	0.9
12	Floor	Mano	Indeterminate	Whole		21.0	10.5	4.3
12	Floor	Tabular tool	None	Whole		12.3	6.1	0.8
12	Floor	Mano	Indeterminate	Whole		14.5	8.4	3.3
12	Floor	Nether stone	Flat	Whole		29.0	26.0	4.8
12	Floor	Tabular tool	None	Whole	No	19.9	13.3	0
12	Floor	Tabular tool	None	Whole		16.0	8.5	1.0
12	Disturb	Mano	Trough	Whole		20.0	11.0	4.0
12	Disturb	Mano	Trough	Whole		17.5	10.7	7.5

Appendix 5.A. Ground Stone Analysis Data, cont'd.

Structure No.	Context	Artifact	Subtype	Condition	Burned	Length (in cm)	Width (in cm)	Thickness (in cm)
12	Disturb	Mano	Trough	Whole		19.7	11.1	3.8
12	Disturb	Mano	Trough	Whole		20.1	11.9	3.8
12	Unknown	Griddle	Flat	Whole	Yes	15.3	14.7	2.3
12	Unknown	Polishing stone	None	Whole	No	7.9	5.9	0
12	Unknown	Polishing stone	None	Whole	No	6.2	4.8	0
12	Unknown	Mano	Flat	Whole	No	19.3	10.8	2.4
12	Unknown	Mano	Trough	Whole	Yes	18.2	9.9	2.5
12	Unknown	Handstone	Basin	Whole	No	13.4	7.2	2.8
12	Unknown	Handstone	Multi	Whole	Indeterminate	9.5	3.6	3.3
12	Unknown	Mano	Concave	Whole	Yes	10.5	8.8	4.4
12	Unknown	Mano	Trough	Whole	No	18.8	10.9	3.3
12	Unknown	Mano	Trough	Whole	Yes	13.9	10.7	2.4
12	Unknown	Mano	Concave	Whole	Yes	11.2	8.7	5.3
12	Unknown	Polishing stone	None	Whole	No	4.7	3.7	0
12	Unknown	Polishing stone	None	Whole	No	6.3	5.1	0
13	Fill	Mano	Trough	Fragment	No	0	10.2	2.7
13	Fill	Lap stone	Flat	Whole	Yes	13	8.2	4.1
13	Floor fill	Lap stone	Flat	Whole	No	18.9	13.8	1.1
13	Floor	Mano	Concave	Whole	Yes	9.9	9.0	3.6
13	Floor	Mano	Trough	Fragment	No	0	0	0
13	Unknown	Griddle	Flat	Whole	Yes	15.8	12.4	3.0
13	Unknown	Mano	Concave	Whole	Yes	13.4	9.5	4.0
13	Unknown	Tabular tool	Tool fragment	Fragment	No	0	0	0
14	Fill	Lap stone	Flat	Whole	No	12.1	6.9	2.2
14	Fill	Metate	Indeterminate	Fragment	No	0	0	0
14	Fill	Ax	Full double bit	Whole	No	9.3	6.1	4.1
14	Fill	Mano	Trough	Fragment	No	0	0	3.3
14	Fill	Mano	Blank	Broke	No	21.0	11.0	7.2
14	Floor	Handstone	Indeterminate	Fragment	No	0	0	0
14	Floor	Mano	Trough	Whole	No	19.5	10.6	5.1
14	Unknown	Pestle	Cobble	Whole	No	12.9	11.2	6.6
15	Fill	Tabular tool	Tool fragment	Fragment	No	0	0	0
15	Fill	Tabular tool	Tool fragment	Fragment	No	0	0	0
15	Fill	Handstone	Flat	Whole	No	11.1	6.8	3.2
15	Fill	Shaped	None	Whole		8.0	3.7	0.8
15	Fill	Tabular tool	Tool fragment	Fragment	No	0	0	0
15	Floor	Metate	Flat/concave	Fragment	Yes	0	24.2	3.0
15	Unknown	Tabular tool	Tool fragment	Fragment	Yes	0	0	0.7
15	Unknown	Mano	Trough	Broke	No	0	3.8	2.7
15	Unknown	Tabular tool	Multiple surfaces	Fragment	No	0	0	0
16	Fill	Tabular tool	Tool fragment	Fragment	No	0	0	0.8
16	Fill	Polishing stone	None	Whole		2.8	2.3	1.9
16	Fill	Mano	Trough	Fragment	No	0	9.4	3.8
16	Fill	Handstone	Flat	Fragment	No	0	0	0
16	Fill	Mano	Trough	Whole	No	18.4	10.5	3.4
16	Fill	Lap stone	Flat	Fragment	No	0	7.1	0.9
16	Fill	Handstone	Flat	Whole	No	9.8	8.3	3.6
16	Fill	Tabular tool	Handled	Fragment	No	0	0	0.9
16	Fill	Mano	Trough	Fragment	Yes	0	9.6	2.8
16	Fill	Polishing stone	Flat	Whole		3.4	3.0	2.0
16	Floor	Tabular tool	Multiple surfaces	Fragment	No	0	0	0
16	Floor	Adze		Whole		13.0	7.0	1.6
16	Floor	Pestle	Pebble	Whole	No	4.8	4.2	3.9
16	Disturb	Mano	Trough	Fragment	No	0	10.0	2.9
16	Unknown		None	Fragment	No	0	0	0
17	Fill	Tabular tool	One concave edge	Fragment	No	0	0	0

Appendix 5.A. Ground Stone Analysis Data, cont'd.

Structure No.	Context	Artifact	Subtype	Condition	Burned	Length (in cm)	Width (in cm)	Thickness (in cm)
17	Fill	Nether stone	Indeterminate	Fragment	No	0	0	0
17	Fill	Handstone	Indeterminate	Fragment	No	0	0	0
17	Roof/wall	Lap stone	Flat	Fragment	Yes	0	0	1.7
17	Floor	Abrader	Single U	Whole		11.1	8.1	5.3
17	Floor	Nether stone	Flat	Whole	No	23.0	17.0	4.9
17	Floor	Nether stone	Flat/concave	Whole	No	29.0	13.2	8.4
17	Pit fill	Polishing stone	Pebbled surface	Broke	No	11.5	3.2	5.4
17	Unknown	Slab	Flat	Fragment	No	0	0	0
17	Unknown	Handstone	Flat	Whole	No	14.7	7.3	4.8
17	Unknown	Handstone	Other	Whole	No	6.1	5.4	1.8
18	Fill	Mano	Concave	Fragment	No	0	7.6	3.1
18	Fill	Mano	Trough	Fragment	No	0	11.0	3.0
18	Fill	Tabular tool	None	Whole		12.9	5.4	0.5
18	Fill	Lap stone	Flat	Whole	No	10.3	8.2	2.6
18	Fill	Mano	Trough	Broke	No	14.3	10.4	3.6
18	Floor	Mano	Trough	Whole	Yes	16.1	9.0	5.3
18	Floor	Tabular tool	None	Whole		10.7	7.1	0.9
18	Floor	Tabular tool	Handled	Whole	No	16.0	12.2	1.1
18	Floor	Mano	Concave	Whole	No	10.5	9.5	4.3
18	Floor	Mano	Trough	Whole	No	15.6	11.2	2.6
18	Floor	Mano	Concave	Whole	Yes	10.8	9.2	4.5
18	Unknown	Tabular tool	Tool fragment	Fragment	No	0	0	0
19	Floor	Ax	Ground	Fragment	No	0	0	0
19	Floor	Mano	Trough	Whole	No	18.8	9.3	1.8
19	Floor	Abrader	Single U	Whole	No	10.8	8.8	3.5
19	Floor	Lap stone	Flat	Whole	No	15.3	11.4	0.4
19	Floor	Pestle	Natural	Whole	No	12.5	5.3	3.2
23	Fill	Handstone	Concave	Whole	No	9.2	8.4	3.0
23	Fill	Mano	Concave	Fragment	No	0	7.5	3.2
23	Fill	Handstone	Indeterminate	Fragment	Yes	0	6.0	4.6
23	Fill	Shaped	None	Whole	No	3.3	3.0	0.3
23	Fill	Mano	Trough	Fragment	No	0	0	3.5
23	Fill	Tabular tool	Mixed	Whole	No	17.5	8.7	1.7
23	Fill	Lap stone	Flat	Fragment	No	0	7.2	1.8
23	Fill	Tabular tool	Tool fragment	Fragment	No	0	0	0.4
23	Fill	Handstone	Concave	Whole	No	8.8	6.3	4.0
23	Fill	Metate	Indeterminate	Fragment	No	0	0	0
23	Fill	Mano	Concave	Whole	No	9.2	6.7	3.4
23	Fill	Mano	Trough	Fragment	No	0	8.5	2.9
23	Fill	Mano	Indeterminate	Fragment	No	0	0	2.6
23	Fill	Mano	Indeterminate	Fragment	No	0	11.7	4.6
23	Fill	Mano	Blank	Fragment	No	0	11.3	7.2
23	Fill	Mano	Blank	Whole	No	21.0	11.5	5.9
23	Fill	Mano	Indeterminate	Fragment	No	0	9.2	3.2
23	Disturb	Polishing stone	Pebbled surface	Whole	No	3.6	4.3	2.5
23	Unknown	Handstone	Indeterminate	Fragment	No	0	9.3	2.9
23	Unknown	Metate	Indeterminate trough	Fragment	No	0	0	0
23	Unknown	Mano	Trough	Fragment	Heat cracked	0	0	0
23	Unknown	Mano	Trough	Fragment	No	0	9.7	3.9
24	Modern surface	Mano	Indeterminate	Fragment	No	0	0	3.8
24	Fill	Ax	Ground	Fragment	No	0	0	0
24	Fill	Mano	Indeterminate	Fragment	Heat cracked	0	0	4.0
24	Fill	Mano	Trough	Fragment	No	0	11.3	6.0
24	Fill	Polishing stone	Surface + edge	Whole	No	6.8	4.8	1.8
24	Fill	Handstone	Flat	Whole	Yes	7.5	8.1	2.7
24	Fill	Pestle	Cobble	Whole	No	18.7	11.3	6.1

Appendix 5.A. Ground Stone Analysis Data, cont'd.

Structure No.	Context	Artifact	Subtype	Condition	Burned	Length (in cm)	Width (in cm)	Thickness (in cm)
24	Fill	Handstone	Flat	Whole	Yes	9.7	7.2	3.4
24	Fill	Mano	Flat	Fragment	No	0	8.4	6.2
24	Fill	Handstone	Flat	Fragment	No	0	6.4	3.2
24	Fill	Tabular tool		Fragment	No	0	0	0
24	Fill	Mano	Concave	Fragment	No	0	8.2	5.0
24	Fill	Mano	Basin	Whole	No	10.7	10.3	4.7
24	Fill	Mano	Trough	Fragment	No	0	9.2	2.7
24	Fill	Pestle	Flat	Whole	No	11.1	6.7	4.3
24	Floor fill	Mano	Trough	Fragment	No	0	9.9	4.6
24	Floor fill	Pestle	Natural	Fragment	No	0	8.1	4.0
24	Floor	Mano	Trough	Fragment	No	0	9.7	3.9
24	Floor	Handstone	Indeterminate	Fragment	No	0	0	3.9
24	Floor	Shaped	None	Whole	No	11.3	8.7	1.8
24	Floor	Tabular tool	Unused material	Fragment	No	0	0	0
24	Sealed pit	Fire cracked rock	None	Fragment	Heat cracked	0	0	0
24	Sealed pit	Fire cracked rock	None	Fragment	Heat cracked	0	0	0
24	Disturbed	Mano	Trough	Fragment	Yes	0	10.2	2.6
24	Unknown	Handstone	Flat	Whole	No	5.9	4.6	3.4
24	Unknown	Abrader		Whole	No	7.2	6.9	2.1
24	Unknown	Polishing stone	Pebbled surface	Whole	No	2.9	2.8	2.1
24	Unknown	Mano	Trough	Fragment	Heat cracked	0	0	3.3
25	Fill	Mortar	Rock	Whole	Yes	14.4	11.6	7.5
25	Fill	Pestle	Block	Whole	Yes	20.8	7.0	6.0
25	Fill	Mano	Blank	Broke	Yes	26.3	10.3	3.8
25	Fill	Pestle	Cylindrical	Fragment	Yes	0	8.5	8.5
25	Fill	Pestle	Block	Whole	Yes	26.5	9.5	7.7
25	Fill	Tabular tool	Tool fragment	Fragment	No	0	5.7	0.5
25	Fill	Handstone	Flat	Whole	Yes	7.6	5.8	5.3
25	Fill	Handstone	Flat	Fragment	Yes	0	9.0	3.1
25	Fill	Mano	Trough	Broke	Heat cracked	18.0	10.0	3.2
25	Fill	Pestle	Cobble	Whole	No	16.9	15.2	8.8
25	Fill	Tabular tool	Mixed	Whole	Yes	16.0	8.4	1.0
25	Fill	Mano	Trough	Whole	No	20.0	9.6	3.4
25	Fill	Lap stone	Flat	Whole	No	16.0	14.3	3.2
25	Fill	Mano	Trough	Whole	Yes	16.0	10.8	3.2
25	Roof/wall	Mano	Trough	Fragment	Yes	0	10.6	4.6
25	Floor fill	Handstone	Indeterminate	Fragment	Yes	12.2	8.3	3.1
25	Floor fill	Handstone	Flat	Fragment	Yes	0	0	2.7
25	Floor fill	Mano	Trough	Whole	No	16.5	8.6	4.3
25	Floor	Tabular tool	Mixed	Fragment	Yes	0	9.9	1.0
25	Floor	Tabular tool	Mixed	Whole	No	15.2	7.1	0.9
25	Floor	Tabular tool	Mixed	Whole	No	12.4	8.7	1.3
25	Unknown	Mano	Trough	Fragment	No	0	0	3.3
25	Unknown	Abrader	Flat	Whole	Yes	15	5.4	3.1
25	Unknown	Mano	Trough	Whole	No	18.8	9.4	4.2
25	Unknown	Nether stone	Flat	Whole	No	32.6	19.4	5.3
25	Unknown	Pestle	Cobble	Whole	No	19.1	13.6	11.3
25	Unknown	Lap stone	Flat	Fragment	No	0	10.2	4.4
25	Unknown	Mano	Trough	Fragment	No	0	8.9	3.0
26	Fill	Mano	Blank	Broke	Yes	15.2	7.9	5.1
26	Fill	Mano	Trough	Fragment	No	0	9.3	3.2
26	Fill	Lap stone	Flat	Fragment	No	10.5	4.5	2.7
26	Fill	Handstone	Indeterminate	Fragment	No	0	0	0
26	Floor	Mano	Trough	Fragment	No	0	8.3	2.2

Appendix 5.A. Ground Stone Analysis Data, cont'd.

Structure No.	Context	Artifact	Subtype	Condition	Burned	Length (in cm)	Width (in cm)	Thickness (in cm)
28	Fill	Mano	Trough	Whole	Yes	21.0	8.9	1.8
28	Fill	Metate	Indeterminate	Fragment	No	0	0	0
28	Fill	Tabular tool	Hafted	Whole	No	7.6	7.1	0.7
28	Fill	Mano	Trough	Whole	No	19.0	11.5	5.4
28	Fill	Nether stone	Flat	Fragment	Yes	0	0	6.3
28	Fill	Pestle	Cobble	Whole	No	15.5	6.9	3.9
28	Floor	Mano	Trough	Fragment	No	0	10.1	3.1
28	Floor	Mano	Trough	Fragment	No	0	0	3.2
28	Unknown	Abrader		Whole	Yes	11.5	10.2	4.9
28	Unknown	Polishing stone	Pebbled surface	Whole	No	4.7	3.2	2.5
28	Unknown	Mano	Trough	Fragment	Yes	0	0	4.8
29	Fill	Disk	Flat donut	Fragment	No	0	0	0
29	Fill	Mano	Trough	Fragment	No	0	11.1	3.7
29	Fill	Lap stone	Flat	Whole	No	12.3	6.8	1.5
29	Fill	Lap stone	Flat	Fragment	No	0	0	1.3
29	Fill	Mano	Trough	Fragment	No	0	10.7	20.9
29	Fill	Metate	Indeterminate	Fragment	No	0	0	0
29	Fill	Mano	Trough	Fragment	Yes	0	9	2.2
29	Fill	Nether stone	Flat	Fragment	Yes	0	0	4.9
29	Fill	Mano	Trough	Whole	No	14.8	8.2	4.1
29	Fill	Mano	Trough	Fragment	No	0	9.8	4.5
29	Fill	Shaped	None	Whole	No	6.2	4.9	1.0
29	Roof/wall	Mano	Trough	Fragment	No	0	8.2	2.9
29	Floor fill	Mano	Trough	Fragment	No	0	9.6	3.8
29	Floor fill	Lap stone	Flat	Whole	No	14.5	8.7	5.7
29	Floor	Mano	Indeterminate	Fragment	Heat cracked	0	10.2	2.3
29	Floor	Tabular tool	One straight edge	Fragment	Yes	0	7.5	0.3
29	Floor	Tabular tool	Mixed	Whole	No	11.4	6.8	0.3
29	Floor	Tabular tool	Handled	Whole	No	10.1	8.1	0.7
29	Floor	Polishing stone	Pebbled surface	Whole	No	2.3	2.1	1.9
29	Floor	Mano	Basin	Whole	Yes	8.8	8.5	3.8
29	Floor	Tabular tool	One straight edge	Fragment	No	0	7.9	0.8
29	Floor	Lap stone	Flat	Whole	Yes	12.5	9.7	3.1
29	Floor	Polishing stone	Surface + edge	Whole	No	8.5	4.2	3.7
29	Floor	Abrader	Sing-u	Whole	Yes	8.0	7.1	4.4
29	Sealed pit	Pigment	None	Whole	No	5.5	4.5	3.2
29	Disturbance	Nether stone	Indeterminate	Fragment	Heat cracked	0	0	0
29	Unknown	Metate	Indeterminate trough	Fragment	No	0	0	0
30	Fill	Shaped	None	Whole	Yes	14.8	15.0	4.1
30	Fill	Shaped	None	Whole	No	2.9	2.7	1.1
30	Fill	Metate	Indeterminate trough	Fragment	No	0	0	0
30	Fill	Tabular tool		Fragment	No	0	0	0
30	Fill	Tabular tool	Tool fragment	Fragment	No	0	0	0
30	Fill	Tabular tool	Tool fragment	Fragment	No	0	0	0
30	Fill	Fergolith	None	Fragment	No	0	24.0	6.2
30	Fill	Tabular tool	Tool fragment	Fragment	No	0	0	0
30	Fill	Mano	Trough	Fragment	No	21.6	0	5.8
30	Fill	Mano	Concave	Broke	Yes	9.1	8.5	4.0
30	Fill	Mano	Concave	Fragment	No	0	8.3	4.4
30	Fill	Handstone	Indeterminate	Fragment	No	11.2	8.3	0
30	Fill	Mano	Indeterminate	Whole	No	17.2	10.3	3.6
30	Fill	Mano	Indeterminate	Fragment	Heat cracked	0	11.6	4.6
30	Fill	Mano	Indeterminate	Fragment	Heat cracked	0	0	4.1
30	Floor	Tabular tool	Concave edge	Whole	No	14.5	6.1	0.9
30	Floor	Tabular tool	Tool fragment	Fragment	No	0	0	0
27a	Fill	Mano	Concave	Whole	No	14.9	7.8	3.1

Appendix 5.A. Ground Stone Analysis Data, cont'd.

Structure No.	Context	Artifact	Subtype	Condition	Burned	Length (in cm)	Width (in cm)	Thickness (in cm)
27a	Fill	Mano	Trough	Fragment	No	0	9.8	3.5
27a	Fill	Polishing stone	Pebbled surface	Whole	No	6.1	5.5	2.6
27a	Fill	Handstone	Indeterminate	Fragment	Yes	0	9.5	4.9
27a	Floor	Mano	Concave	Whole	No	10.7	9.2	3.9
27a	Floor	Mano	Trough	Fragment	Yes	0	8.2	3.0
27a	Floor	Tabular tool		Fragment	No	0	0	0
27a	Floor	Mano	Trough	Fragment	Yes	0	8.8	2.8
27b	Fill	Polishing stone	Pebbled surface	Whole	No	2.8	2.2	2.2
27b	Fill	Tabular tool	One straight edge	Whole	No	9.5	6.0	0.8
27b	Fill	Mano	Trough	Fragment	No	0	10.1	4.8
27b	Fill	Tabular tool	Tool fragment	Fragment	No	0	0	0
27b	Fill	Polishing stone	Surface + edge	Fragment	No	0	3.0	2.5
27b	Fill	Handstone	Concave	Whole	No	7.2	6.8	2.5
27b	Fill	Mano	Concave	Whole	Yes	10.3	8.2	5.6
27b	Fill	Mano	Trough	Fragment	Yes	0	10.4	4.4
27b	Roof/wall	Tabular tool		Whole	No	11.4	8.0	0.7
27b	Floor	Ax	3/4 groove	Whole	Yes	11	5.0	6.7
27b	Floor	Tabular tool	One straight edge	Fragment	Yes	0	5.2	0.4
27b	Floor	Tabular tool	One straight edge	Fragment	No	11.6	6.3	0.7
27b	Floor	Mano	Trough	Whole	Yes	16	8.1	2.8
27b	Floor	Tabular tool	Tool fragment	Fragment	No	0	0	0
27b	Floor	Lap stone	Flat	Broke	Yes	12.3	6.4	2.1
27b	Floor	Mano	Trough	Whole	No	18.8	12.1	7.0
27b	Floor	Handstone	Flat	Whole	Yes	9.5	7.5	3.5
27b	Pit fill	Mano	Trough	Whole	Yes	17.9	10.5	5.8
27b	Pit fill	Mano	Concave	Whole	Yes	10.6	9	5.5
27b	Disturb	Nether stone	Flat	Fragment	Heat cracked	0	0	0
27b	Disturb	Mano	Indeterminate	Fragment	No	16.2	10.9	4.4
27b	Unknown	Ax	3/4 groove	Broke	Heat cracked	18.6	6.0	8.8
General site	Unknown	Pulping stone	None	Whole	No	5.0	8.2	2.5
General site	Unknown	Mano	Trough	Whole	No	22.2	11.5	3.2
Unknown	Fill	Pulping stone	None	Whole	No	9.0	10.7	2.2
Unknown	Unknown	Polishing stone	Pebbled surface	Whole	No	9.6	3.0	3.1
Unknown	Fill	Nether stone	Indeterminate	Fragment	No	0	0	0
Unknown	Fill	Tabular tool	Tool fragment	Fragment	No	0	0	0
Unknown	Fill	Mano	Indeterminate	Fragment	Yes	0	8.8	3.2
Unknown	Disturbance	Handstone	Flat	Fragment	No	0	0	3.4
Unknown	Disturbance	Tabular tool	Tool fragment	Fragment	No	0	0	0
Unknown	Disturbance	Handstone	Flat	Whole	No	4.1	3.5	2.7
Unknown	Disturbance	Polishing stone	Surface + edge	Fragment	No	0	4.3	2.7
Unknown	Disturbance	Polishing stone	Surface + edge	Whole	No	4.0	2.9	2.3
Unknown	Disturbance	Handstone	Flat	Whole	No	5.3	3.9	2.7
Unknown	Disturbance	Mano	Trough	Fragment	No	0	10.3	2.8
Unknown	Disturbance	Mano	Concave	Fragment	No	0	0	4.4
Unknown	Disturbance	Handstone	Flat	Fragment	Heat cracked	0	0	0
Unknown	Disturbance	Mano	Trough	Fragment	No	0	9	3.7
Unknown	Unknown	Tabular tool	Tool fragment	Fragment	Yes	0	0	0
Unknown	Unknown	Tabular tool	Tool fragment	Fragment	No	0	0	0
Unknown.	Pit fill	Pestle	Cobble	Broke	Yes	10.1	8.3	5.7
Unknown.	Pit fill	Handstone	Indeterminate	Fragment	Heat cracked	0	9.5	3.3
Unknown.	Pit fill	Handstone	Indeterminate	Fragment	Heat cracked	0	0	0
Unknown	Unknown	Metate	Indeterminate	Fragment	No	0	0	0

Chapter 6

Shell

Linda M. Gregonis
with contributions by Sharon F. Urban

The collection of shell from the Whiptail Ruin contains 164 specimens representing eight genera and one unknown category, as well as 11 artifact types. Within the genera three different habitats are represented: terrestrial, marine, and freshwater. Terrestrial shell is local; the freshwater shell may have come from the Agua Caliente springs or another semipermanent water source, such as the Tanque Verde Wash. The marine shell most likely came from the Gulf of California via the extensive Hohokam shell trade network (Brand 1938; McGuire and Howard 1987; Nelson 1991).

Shell artifacts were found in all loci of Whiptail. The shell artifacts analyzed for this report represent what was curated at the Arizona State Museum with the rest of the site's artifacts. Other shell exists in private collections, and some has been lost over time. The information in this chapter was prepared by Sharon F. Urban, who analyzed the shell and prepared the tables, descriptions, and definitions used.

Genera

Terrestrial and freshwater shells are represented by one genus each: *Succinea* and *Anodonta* respectively. *Succinea* sp., a genus of land snails (Bequaert and Miller 1973), is represented by two specimens. Three pieces of *Anodonta californiensis* were found. *Anodonta californiensis* is a freshwater clam found in fast, free-flowing streams and rivers (Bequaert and Miller 1973). Locations near the site that might have supported *Anodonta* during occupation include the Agua Caliente, Pantano, and Tanque Verde washes. Prehistorically, Pantano and Tanque Verde washes may have had water year round while Agua Caliente Wash was probably seasonal.

The remaining genera found at the site (159 pieces) are all marine taxa (Keen 1984; Morris 1966), of which only *Laevicardium elatum* (Giant Egg Cockle) is found in both the Pacific Ocean and the Gulf of California. The other genera are all from the gulf. These include, along with their counts, *Conus* sp. (cone shell; n = 4), *Glycymeris* sp. (clam, n = 117), *Laevicardium elatum* (n = 27), *Nassarius* sp. (basket shell; n = 1), *Olivella dama* (olive shell; n = 4), and *Pecten* sp. (scallop; n = 1). Five shells could not be classified because their characteristics have been obliterated, making identification impossible. They are listed in this chapter as "unknown." Table 6.1 presents the distribution of the various genera across the site.

Artifact Types

As mentioned earlier, the shell was classified into 11 artifact categories, following Gladwin et al. (1938) and Haury (1976). These categories are environmental, raw material, worked material, beads, bracelet, pendant, finger ring, frog, reworked bracelet, geometric, and tinkler. They are described briefly here.

Environmental Shell consists of terrestrial snails that occur naturally at the site. They could date from the time of occupation, but could also be more recent.

Raw Material consists of a piece of shell that shows no sign of human alteration.

Worked Material consists of shell that shows signs of human alteration such as cutting, grinding, drilling, or polishing. Some pieces in this category may be fragments discarded during shell manufacture; most are pieces from broken, finished artifacts.

Beads are, in general, small artifacts that have perforations through them so that they can be strung. Five types of beads were found at Whiptail: barrel, cap, disk, whole shell, and geometric. Barrel beads are made from gastropod shells and have both the spire and the canal end ground off. In cap beads, the body of the shell has been ground off, leaving only the spire, the tip of which has also been ground off. Disk beads are flat circles of material with a central perforation. In whole shell beads, the entire shape of the shell has been left, but an opening has been ground or cut into the artifact. Geometric beads are shaped and perforated—in the single case found at Whiptail the bead is tear-shaped.

Bracelet/Pendant. This category includes two forms and perhaps multiple uses. Bracelets are ornaments meant to be worn around the wrist, arm, or leg. At Whiptail all are made from *Glycymeris* sp. Three types (1, 2, and 3) were defined, based on band width, which changes over time (Haury 1976:313). No whole specimens were recovered from Whiptail.

In grinding a shell to form a bracelet, the beak sometimes was worn through, creating a perforation. This does not seem to have any special significance; instead, it is apparently just the end result of grinding. Perforations created in this way may not have been desired, but there were times when the perforation was deliberately enlarged (either into a conical or biconical hole). When that happened, the bracelet could have been suspended and used as an open center, circular pendant. A bracelet with an enlarged hole in the beak could also have had strings attached to dangle down and perhaps end in charms.

Broken bracelets could also be reworked into pendants. If the umbo or beak area remained, then the beak could be perforated, turning the broken bracelet into a serviceable

Table 6.1. Shell Genera and Species Represented by Location.

Provenience	Genus									Total No. Pieces
	Anodonta	*Conus*	*Glycymeris*	*Laevicardium*	*Nassarius*	*Olivella*	*Pecten*	*Succinea*	Unknown	
Compound Locus										
Structure 4			16				1		2	19
Structure 7			5							5
Structure 8			4						1	5
Structure 17			3	1						4
Compound			1	1						2
Central Locus										
Structure 5			1							1
Structure 15			1	1[a]						2
Structure 32			1							1
Structure 33			2							2
Cemetery 2				1						1
Cremation 19					1					1
Creamtion 20						2				2
Southwestern Locus										
Structure 2			5	1						6
Structure 9		1	4							5
Structure 10			2							2
Structure 11			3						1	4
Structure 12			2			1				3
Structure 13			1							1
Structure 16			5							5
Structure 18			1							1
Structure 23	2	1	8	1						12
Structure 24			4	2						6
Structure 25		1	14	2					1	18
Structure 26	1					1				2
Cremation 1			4	4						8
General area			3					1		4
Northern Locus										
Structure 3			2							2
Structure 21			1							1
Structure 27a			2							2
Structure 27b			2					1		3
Structure 28			1							1
Structure 29			1							1
Structure 30			1							1
Structure 31a			2							2
Structure 31b			2	1						3
Structure 31c			1							1
Northeastern Locus										
Structure 22				2						2
Southern Locus										
Structure 14			1	2						3
Structure 19		1	1	2						4
General Site			10	6						16
Totals	3	4	117	27	1	4	1	2	5	164

Note: a. This number represents 31 pieces of a single, burned *Laevicardium* shell.

piece of jewelry. In this case both arms were generally ground to rounded tips, creating a crescent-shaped pendant. This is probably one of the most common types of reworking.

Pendants are ornaments that are suspended. If in a string of beads, pendants hang below the line of beads.

Finger Rings are ornaments designed to fit around the finger.

Frog ornaments are single shells carved into the likenesses of frogs or toads.

Reworked Bracelets are broken bracelets that have been reworked into something else such as an awl, needle or pendant.

A geometric is a piece in a geometric shape whose use cannot be determined.

Tinklers are ornaments that, when strung with several others, produce a tinkling sound.

Findings by Provenience

Tables 6.2 and 6.3 list the shell found at the site by location. The artifacts are described by locus and provenience.

Compound Locus

Structure 4

Nineteen specimens were recovered from this structure, 16 of them were *Glycymeris*. Six *Glycymeris* pieces are bracelet fragments: one Type 1 with a perforated umbo; two medial Type 2 band fragments (Figure 6.1d), one of which has been acid burned; and three Type 3 medial band fragments, one of which has been burned (Table 6.4). Seven whole *Glycymeris* beads are represented; three have centers that have been broken through. There are two *Glycymeris* ring fragments. The sixteenth piece of *Glycymeris* found in Structure 4 is worked and burned; its original function could not be determined (Figure 6.1f). The three other shells found in the house are a whole shell bead of unknown genus (the perforation was broken through); a worked body fragment of unknown genus; and a body fragment from a *Pecten* (scallop).

Structure 7

All five specimens from this location are *Glycymeris,* of which three are bracelet fragments including one medial burned Type 2 band and two Type 3 medial bands that have one edge near the beak of the shell. The other two *Glycymeris* pieces are a large, juvenile whole shell bead and a juvenile shell carved into a frog.

Structure 8

This structure yielded five specimens, four of which are *Glycymeris* and one an unknown shell type. One piece of *Glycymeris* is worked and might have been a bracelet. Three others were bracelet fragments, all Type 3. One fragment has a reworked end; another is a slightly burned medial fragment. The third has a carved umbo and large, short arms (Figure 6.1m). This shell came from just outside of the structure. The final specimen from this provenience is a disk bead of an unknown species of shell. It is thin, with a large central perforation.

Structure 17

Three of the four specimens from this structure are *Glycymeris* including two finger ring fragments. The first is broken through the umbo, leaving one arm. The umbo had been perforated by grinding. The second ring is a medial band fragment. The third *Glycymeris*

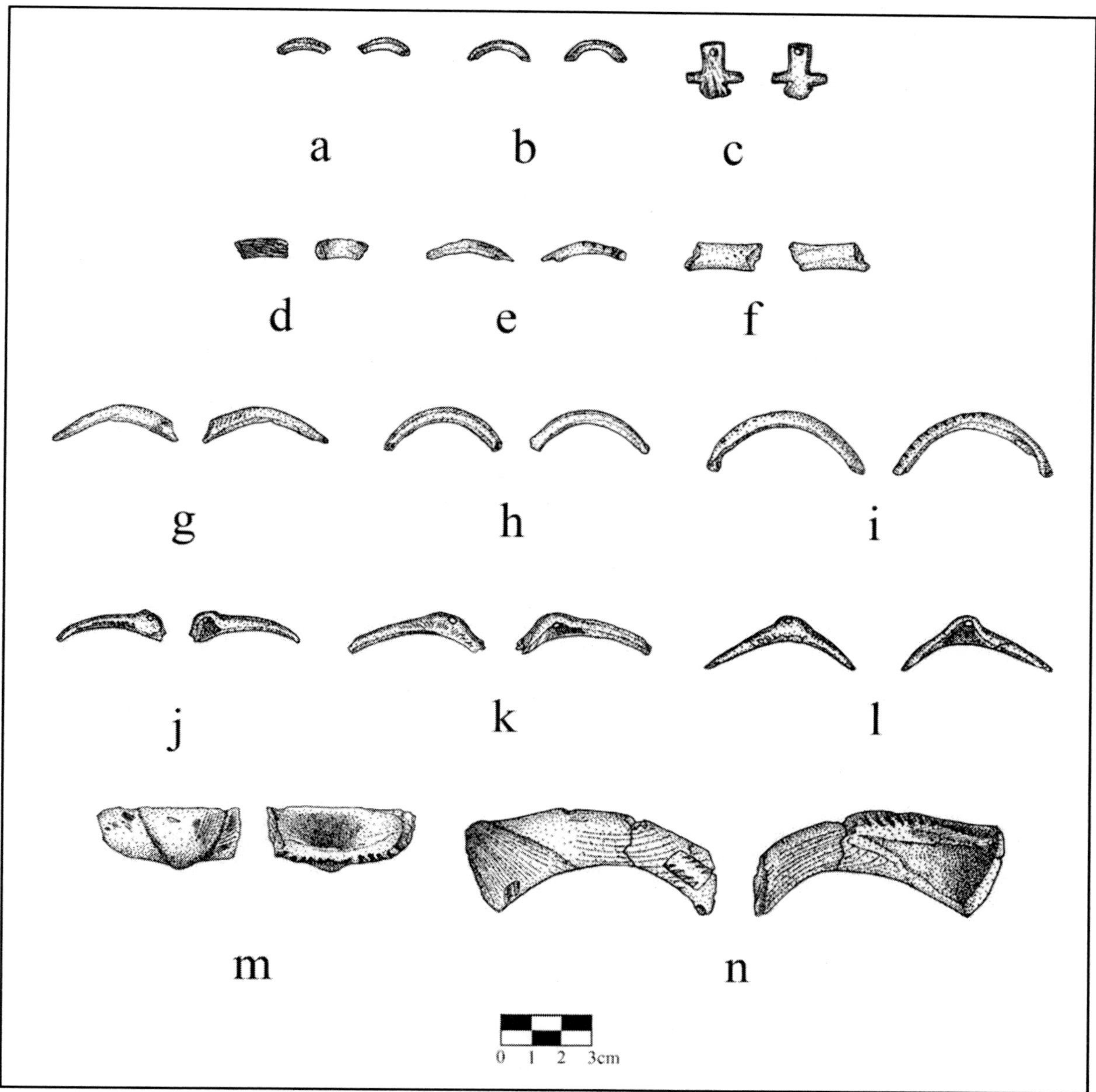

Figure 6.1. Various shell artifacts (Glycymeris unless otherwise indicated): (a) ring fragment made on a juvenile shell from Structure 10; (b) ring fragment from the fill of Structure 30; (c) Laevicardium pendant fragment, possibly part of a lizard, from Structure 19; (d) Type 2 fragment from the upper fill of Structure 4; (e) Type 1 small bracelet fragment from Structure 10; (f) worked and burned piece from Structure 4; (g) Type 2 bracelet fragment found in the compound; (h) reworked bracelet fragment found in Structure 21; (i) Type 2 bracelet found in Structure 13; (j) Type 1 bracelet/pendant with perforated umbo found in Structure 27a; (k) bracelet/pendant with perforated umbo found in Structure 11; (l) bracelet reworked into a crescent-shaped pendant found in Structure 29; (m) Type 3 bracelet with carved umbo, from area just outside of Structure 8; and (n) Type 3 bracelet fragment with carved umbo found on the floor of Structure 27b, can probably be associated with the burial on that floor.

Table 6.2. Distribution of Environmental Shell, Raw Material, and Worked Material.

Provenience	Environmental	Raw Material			Worked Material					Totals
	Succinea	*Glycymeris*	*Laevicardium*	*Pecten*	*Anodonta*	*Conus*	*Glycymeris*	*Laevicardium*	Unknown	
General Surface			2				1	4		7
Southwestern Locus										
Structure 2								1		1
Structure 16		1					1			2
Structure 23			1		2		1			4
Structure 24			1				1			2
Structure 25						1	1	1		3
Structure 26					1					1
Cremation 1 and Cemetery 1			1					3		4
General area	1						1			2
Compound Locus										
Structure 4				1			1		1	3
Structure 8							1			1
Structure 17			1							1
Compound								1		1
Central Locus										
Structure 15			1[a]							1
Northern Locus										
Structure 3		2								2
Structure 27a							1			1
Structure 27b	1									1
Structure 31b								1		1
Structure 31c							1			1
Northeastern Locus										
Structure 22			1					1		2
Southern Locus										
Structure 14		1						2		3
Structure 19								1		1
Totals	2	4	8	1	3	1	10	15	1	45

Note: a. This number represents 31 pieces of a single, burned *Laevicardium* shell.

piece is a Type 2 medial band bracelet fragment. The remaining specimen is an unworked triangular piece of *Laevicardium*

Compound

Two pieces of shell were found in the compound. One is a worked piece of *Laevicardium* consisting of a distal margin with a cut above it in the body. The other is a reworked Type 2 *Glycymeris* bracelet fragment that consists of part of the band that has been ground to a point (Figure 6.1g).

Central Locus

Structure 5

A single *Glycymeris* bracelet fragment was found in Structure 5. It is a Type 3 medial band that is well burned.

Structure 15

Two shell artifacts were found in this structure. One, a *Glycymeris* bracelet, was found in five pieces. It is a Type 2 medial band fragment. The other artifact is a burned *Laevicardium* valve that was shattered into 31 pieces.

Structure 32

One specimen of a *Glycymeris* finger ring was found in this structure. It is a medial band portion.

Structure 33

Two whole *Glycymeris* shell beads were found in this house. The beads were made from juvenile shells. They have perforated beaks and ground edges.

Cemetery 2

Four shell artifacts were found in Cemetery 2, one from the locality in general, one from Cremation 19, and two from Cremation 20. The specimen from the general locality is a carved pendant in the form of a stylized bird made from *Laevicardium* The specimen from Cremation 19 is a whole shell bead of *Nassarius*, the only one found at the site.

Two barrel beads of *Olivella dama* were found in Cremation 20. One is a typical specimen of this type of bead; the other has a very polished surface and a groove in the edge of the spire area, which may be use wear.

Southwestern Locus

Structure 2

Six shell artifacts were found in this house; five are *Glycymeris* and one is *Laevicardium* The *Glycymeris* artifacts include three bracelet fragments: one Type 1 medial band, one Type 2 medial band, and one Type 3 fragment including the umbo and arms. The other two *Glycymeris* pieces are a lizard-shaped pendant and roughly half of a finger ring. The worked *Laevicardium* piece is triangular in shape and might represent a lizard tail.

Structure 9

Five specimens were recovered from this location. One is a whole *Conus* tinkler. The remaining specimens are all *Glycymeris* Two are medial band portions of bracelets: one Type 1, the other Type 2. A third bracelet fragment—a Type 3 band—consists of the perforated umbo and arms. The final *Glycymeris* specimen is a whole juvenile shell bead.

Structure 10

Two items were found in this structure, both *Glycymeris.* One is a Type 1 medial band bracelet fragment (Figure 6.1e); the other a finger ring made from the medial band portion of a juvenile shell (Figure 6.1a).

Structure 11

Of the four specimens from this provenience, three are *Glycymeris* and one is of an unknown species. The single unknown shell is a very small disk bead. The remaining pieces of *Glycymeris* are two juvenile valves, of which one is a medial band making a finger ring, the other a lateral half of the valve in the shape of a frog. The final piece contains the umbo with a prepared hole, and arms to either side of a Type 2 bracelet (Figure 6.1k).

Structure 12

Three shell artifacts were found in this structure. One is whole barrel bead of *Olivella dama.* The other two specimens are Type 2 *Glycymeris* medial bracelet band fragments.

Structure 13

This structure contained only one small Type 2 *Glycymeris* medial band bracelet fragment (Figure 6.1i). Perhaps half of the bracelet is represented.

Table 6.3. Distribution of Shell Ornaments.

Provenience	Beads						Bracelet/ pendant	Pendant		Finger Ring	Frog	Reworked	Geometric	Tinkler	Totals
	Barrel	Cap	Disk	Whole Shell		Geometric									
	Olivella	*Conus*	Unknown	*Glycymeris*	*Nassarius*	Unknown	*Glycymeris*	*Glycymeris*	*Laevicardium*	*Glycymeris*	*Glycymeris*	*Glycymeris*	*Laevicardium*	*Conus*	
Compound Locus															
Structure 4				7		1	6			2					16
Structure 7				1			3				1				5
Structure 8			1				3								4
Structure 17							1			2					3
Compound												1			1
Central Locus															
Structure 5							1								1
Structure 15							1								1
Structure 32										1					1
Structure 33				2											2
Cemetery 2									1						1
Cremation 19					1										1
Cremation 20	2														2
Southwestern Locus															
Structure 2							3	1		1					5
Structure 9				1			3							1	5
Structure 10							1			1					2
Structure 11			1				1			1	1				4
Structure 12	1						2								3
Structure 13							1								1
Structure 16							3								3
Structure 18										1					1
Structure 23							5			2				1	8
Structure 24							3						1		4
Structure 25			1	9			4		1						15
Structure 26	1														1
Cemetery 1 & Cremation 1							4								4
General area							2								2
Northern Locus															
Structure 21												1			1
Structure 27a							1								1
Structure 27b							2								2
Structure 28							1								1
Structure 29								1							1
Structure 30										1					1
Structure 31a							1			1					2
Structure 31b							2								2
Southern Locus															
Structure 19		1		1					1						3
General Surface							6			3					9
Totals	4	1	3	21	1	1	60	2	3	15	2	2	1	2	119

Structure 18

One *Glycymeris* medial band finger ring fragment was recovered from this structure.

Structure 23

This structure contained 12 shell specimens including a variety of artifact types and species. Freshwater *Anodonta* is represented by two large pieces with cut edges. One *Conus* fragment was found. It is the longitudinal fragment of a body with a V-groove, probably a tinkler fragment. One piece of a worked juvenile *Glycymeris* valve with ground edges but missing the beak and umbo was found. Other *Glycymeris* specimens include two medial fragments of finger rings and five bracelet fragments of the same material. The bracelet fragments consisted of one medial Type 2 band, and two small medial Type 2 bands that had been burned, a Type 3 band that is broken through the umbo with one arm to the side, and a tiny medial Type 1 band that is very weathered. Also found in Structure 23 was an unworked, chunky lateral margin of *Laevicardium* from the portion containing the hinge teeth.

Structure 24

Six shell specimens were found in Structure 24. One is an unworked piece of *Laevicardium* from the lateral margin, with one hinge tooth. About half of a worked, juvenile *Glycymeris* valve that has rounded edges is also present. There are three *Glycymeris* bracelet fragments, two Type 3 and one Type 2. The Type 2 band contained part of the beak, which had been ground down. One Type 3 is a medial band; the other has two short arms of the band on either side of the beak, which was perforated but not enlarged. The sixth artifact is a geometric piece of *Laevicardium* from the medial part of the body of the valve. It is thick and elongated and may be a reworked lizard tail.

Structure 25

This structure contained 18 pieces of shell, representing three genera and one shell of unknown type. One worked *Glycymeris* juvenile valve has a ground distal margin and is missing its beak. A worked piece of *Conus* is a longitudinal fragment of the body. It may have been a tinkler. A third worked item is a long, cut rectangle of *Laevicardium.* Nine whole *Glycymeris* beads were found. Their beaks are perforated, and in some cases the surrounding edges are ground. The unknown shell is a disk bead with a biconical, centrally located perforation; it is wedge-shaped in cross section. There are four *Glycymeris* bracelet fragments. One is a medial Type 1 band, another band is Type 2, and the final two are Type 3. The final object is a *Laevicardium* pendant. It is square and comes from the medial body of the valve. It has a biconical perforation that is broken through due to wear friction.

Structure 26

Two specimens were found in Structure 26. One is a worked piece of *Anodonta*; it is thin and has V-shaped notches along one edge. The other specimen is a whole barrel bead of *Olivella.*

Cemetery 1 and Cremation 1

There are four specimens of *Glycymeris* and four of *Laevicardium* from Cemetery 1 and Cremation 1 in that cemetery. Three of the *Laevicardium* pieces are worked and one is raw material. They may have come from the same valve. The *Glycymeris* artifacts are all bracelet fragments, one of which, a Type 1 band, was made using a juvenile shell. It may

Table 6.4. Distribution of Bracelet Types.

Provenience	Bracelet Type 1	2	3	Total
Compound Locus				
Structure 4	1	2	3	6
Structure 7		1	2	3
Structure 8			3	3
Structure 17		1		1
Central Locus				
Structure 5			1	1
Structure 15		1		1
Southwestern Locus				
Structure 2	1	1	1	3
Structure 9	1	1	1	3
Structure 10	1			1
Structure 11		1		1
Structure 12		2		2
Structure 13		1		1
Structure 16		1	2	3
Structure 23	1	3	1	5
Structure 24		1	2	3
Structure 25	1	1	2	4
Cemetery 1 and Cremation 1	1	2	1	4
General area	2			2
Northern Locus				
Structure 27a	1			1
Structure 27b		1	1	2
Structure 28		1		1
Structure 31a		1		1
Structure 31b		1	1	2
General site		3	3	6
Totals	**10**	**26**	**24**	**60**

have been intended for a child. Two of the other bracelet fragments are Type 2 bands; the other is Type 3.

General Area

Three *Glycymeris* artifacts were found on the surface in the Southwestern Locus and one *Succinea* shell was found during stripping in the locus. The *Succinea* shell is a land snail that is part of the environment at the site. The *Glycymeris* pieces include one half of the outer ring of a juvenile valve that was perhaps intended for a finger ring (it is listed in Table 6.2 as worked material). The other two specimens are Type 1 bracelet fragments (Table 6.3).

Northern Locus

Structure 3

Two pieces of raw material, both *Glycymeris* body fragments, were found in this feature. One piece was burned.

Structure 21

A reworked bracelet fragment of *Glycymeris* was recovered from this structure (Figure 6.1h). It is a medial band, with one end beveled through wear. It also exhibits use polish.

Structure 27a

Glycymeris is represented here by two specimens, one a worked juvenile band, the other a Type 1 bracelet or pendant with a perforated umbo and one arm (Figure 6.1j).

Structure 27b

Three shell specimens came from this feature. Two are *Glycymeris* bracelet fragments. One is a medial Type 2 band; the other is the umbo and one arm of a Type 3 bracelet. The Type 3 bracelet fragment is carved on the exterior with a rectangular bordered design (Figure 6.1n). It was found on the floor of the structure and can probably be associated with the burial in this house. The third piece of shell is *Succinea,* a land snail and part of the site's natural environment.

Structure 29

The single specimen found in Structure 29 is a *Glycymeris* pendant (a reworked bracelet fragment) with a reworked perforation and one arm that has a rounded tip (Figure 6.1l).The piece is burned.

Structure 30

A *Glycymeris* finger ring fragment was recovered from this structure (Figure 6.1b). It is a segment of the medial band from a juvenile valve.

Structure 31a

Two specimens were recovered from Structure 31. Both are *Glycymeris*. One is a Type 2 bracelet fragment made from the medial band; the other is a finger ring fragment made from the medial body of a juvenile valve.

Structure 31b

Three shell artifacts were found in this feature. One is a piece of worked *Laevicardium* consisting of a medial section of the valve's body with a cut edge. The remaining two specimens were medial band bracelet fragments of *Glycymeris.* One Type 2 and one Type 3 are represented.

Structure 31c

This unit contained one reworked *Glycymeris* bracelet arm.

Northeastern Locus

Structure 22

Two specimens of *Laevicardium* were found in this feature. One is a burned piece of raw material that may have come from a cremation. The other is worked material; one end is rounded, smooth from polish, and, burned. It may also have come from a cremation.

Southern Locus

Structure 14

Three pieces of shell from this feature were analyzed. One is an unworked piece of a juvenile *Glycymeris* valve (in three, refittable pieces). The beak has been broken off. The other two specimens are two worked pieces of *Laevicardium.* One has a lateral margin with cut edges and much weathering; the other is the distal end of the shell. It is thick; its sculpture pattern is still present; and there are cut marks on the interior.

Structure 19

Four pieces of shell were found in Structure 19: a *Conus* cap bead, a *Glycymeris* bead made from a whole juvenile shell, a *Laevicardium* pendant fragment that is probably part of a lizard (Figure 6.1c), and a worked piece of *Laevicardium.*

General Site

Sixteen pieces of shell were collected from the surface of the site or from other, unspecified excavated locales. Ten are *Glycymeris* and six are *Laevicardium.*

Two of the *Laevicardium* pieces are raw material. One of these is burned and is the remains of the lateral margin with the hinge pit visible. The other raw material piece is from the hinge of a valve. The four other pieces of *Laevicardium* are worked fragments that contain the lateral margin with the center removed; another is a corner piece with the distal margin and two cut edges. The third is part of the lateral margin with a cut edge and the fourth piece, also a lateral margin, has been burned and has a ground edge.

The 10 *Glycymeris* pieces include worked material (n = 1), finger rings (n = 3), and bracelet fragments (n = 6). The worked material is a juvenile *Glycymeris* valve that may have been a finger ring in the making. One bracelet fragment is the size ideal for a child. Three bracelet fragments were Type 2 and three were Type 3.

Discussion

Glycymeris was by far the most abundant shell found at the site with 117 pieces or 71 percent of the total count. Artifacts made of this shell genus included the greatest variety of any genera at Whiptail, with artifact types including raw and worked material, whole shell beads, bracelets, pendants, finger rings, and reworked items. Two structures (7 and 11) produced *Glycymeris* frogs, in which the shell umbo was carved into the likeness of a frog. Both specimens were made from the juvenile form of the species, rather than a larger valve, which was more common. As seen in Table 6.1, *Glycymeris* shells were found in nearly every provenience at the site, indicating the genus was the most popular and desired material used for ornaments.

Laevicardium was the second most common shell with 27 pieces or 16 percent of the total. This large valve was used in many ways; at Whiptail the shells occur as raw (n = 8) and worked (n = 15) material, a geometric fragment (n = 1), and in pendant form (n = 3).

Olivella is often a common genus at sites, but at Whiptail it was poorly represented, with only four shells recovered. *Olivella* shells are most commonly used as whole shell beads (where the spires are ground off) and the shell strung longitudinally. At Whiptail, however, the four pieces were a more specialized type of bead where both the spire and canal ends were removed by grinding. This makes for a much shorter, more compact bead.

Only four pieces of *Conus* shell were recovered from the site. The genus *Conus* seemed to have two purposes, as whole shell pendants sewn on fabric as decoration or as sound makers. When several of these shells are strung together they tinkle when the wearer walks.

Two specimens that were represented by only one item each were a whole shell bead of *Nassarius* and a piece of *Pecten* in the raw material category.

Though raw and worked materials were found throughout the site, it cannot be said that shell manufacturing occurred at Whiptail. More likely, a piece broke and, on occasion, the pieces were salvaged for other ornaments. There were two reworked pieces of *Glycymeris* bracelet fragments found at the site, one in a trench in the compound and one in Structure 21 (where the fragment was reworked into a crescent-shaped pendant).

The *Anodonta* specimens may be the exception to the indication that Whiptail residents did not manufacture ornaments. *Anodonta* must be worked fresh as it is very fragile when dry, so it would have been worked where it was collected or immediately after it was taken back to a village. The three *Anodonta* specimens found at the site were finished pieces, however, so there is no direct evidence of manufacture.

Distribution Patterns

As mentioned previously, shell was found throughout the site (Table 6.1). Although some pieces were found on the surface and in various trenches and stripping areas, most items were recovered from structures. Many of the shell artifacts were found in the fill of structures and may represent trash fill. Three structures—4, 23, and 25—contained more than 10 pieces of shell. Structure 4, one of the earliest houses at the site, contained 19 pieces of shell, primarily *Glycymeris* pieces that are probably discards. The shell found in Structure 25, which is in the Southwestern Locus, resembles the collection from Structure 4 in that it consists primarily of *Glycymeris* fragments that were found in the upper fill. The lower fill, which may have been roof fill, contained a *Laevicardium* pendant and a *Conus* tinkler fragment. Structure 23 (also in the Southwestern Locus) was one of two structures that contained *Anodonta,* the local mussel that may have been used for food. This structure contained the most varied collection of shell. In addition to *Anodonta, Conus, Glycymeris,* and *Laevicardium* shells were found. The remaining structures contained one to six pieces of shell.

Cremations also yielded a number of shell artifacts. One piece of raw *Laevicardium* and four *Glycymeris* bracelet fragments were recovered from Cemetery 1 (one of those shell bracelets came from Cremation 1). Cemetery 2 yielded a pendant and pieces of worked *Laevicardium*. Two cremations in Cemetery 2, which was in the Central Locus, contained shell. Cremation 19 contained the only whole shell bead of *Nassarius* found at the site and Cremation 20 contained two *Olivella* barrel beads. The presence of shell artifacts in cremations is not unexpected, but it is interesting that two cremations (19 and 20) contained unusual shell artifacts—the *Nassarius* fragment and two *Olivella* barrel beads. This may mean that those individuals held a higher status in the village than others. Interestingly, according to Beck (Chapter 10), Cremation 19 may be a reburial. It contains the burned remains of only arm and leg bones, while Cremation 20 contains burned bone fragments from the entire body.

Landscape View

The Whiptail site, located in the northeast corner of the Tucson Basin, is close to Redington Pass, giving the site's inhabitants access to various sites in the San Pedro Valley to the east as well as to villages in the rest of the Tucson Basin. There are several sites of comparable age and configuration with which to compare shell assemblages. Here the shell collections of four sites are compared.

The first of these is Second Canyon Ruin (AZ BB:11:20 [ASM]). This village is located in the San Pedro Valley, on a terrace on the west side of the river, near the base of Redington Pass. The second site is Gibbon Springs (AZ BB:9:50[ASM]) located at the base of the Catalina Mountain foothills about three miles west of Whiptail. Gibbon Springs can be considered a "sister" site to Whiptail. It is very similar in its layout, location, and time of occupation. The third site is Rabid Ruin (AZ AA:12:16 [ASM]), located across the basin on a terrace west of the Santa Cruz River. The fourth site compared here is the Marana Platform Mound (AZ AA: 12:251[ASM]) an estimated distance of 30 miles to the west-northwest of Whiptail. Gibbon Springs and the Marana Platform Mound are contemporaneous with Whiptail. The other two sites have an early Classic period component but had a longer life than Whiptail. Second Canyon was occupied from the Colonial period through the late Classic period, while Rabid Ruin was used throughout the Classic period, unlike Whiptail, which was abandoned by A.D. 1300.

Second Canyon

Franklin (1980) reported on the shell (173 pieces) from Second Canyon, where artifacts were recovered from 18 structures, plazas, one use level, one test trench, trash areas, and the site's surface. *Glycymeris* was the best represented genus at the site with 98 examples of mostly bracelet fragments but with some reworked specimens. These items came from all parts of the site but mostly out of structures. Six *Glycymeris* ring fragments were analyzed. Nineteen *Olivella* whole beads were found in various parts of the site. Only three pieces of *Pecten* were recovered. *Conus* was well represented (18 pieces) in forms such as tinklers, wide finger rings, "shell ornaments formed from the perforated spire end [perhaps cap beads], and one whole shell with the spire end removed" (Franklin 1980:196). *Laevicardium* was represented by only eight pieces— four pendants and four fragments. Limited amounts of *Haliotis, Nassa, Anodonta, Neritina, Turritella, and Strombus* were recorded. The *Haliotis, Anodonta*, and *Strombus* specimens were fragments, while *Nassa, Neritina and Turritella* were whole shell beads. Ten disk beads of an unknown genus were also reported.

The shell was distributed unevenly at the site. Franklin (1980) reported that *Glycymeris* bracelet fragments were found in all parts of the site. Interestingly, as at Whiptail, no whole bracelets were recovered. *Olivella* shell was also found in all features of all time periods, although Franklin (1980:193) notes that the numbers recovered were "scarcely large enough to string one large necklace." The *Haliotis, Anodonta, Pecten, Conus, Neritina, Strombus, and Turritella* shell were all found in Classic period contexts, while the *Neritina* shell occurred in early contexts at the site.

Gibbon Springs

Shell from Gibbon Springs was analyzed by Arthur Vokes (1996) and although he does not indicate where every specimen was found, he does say that shell was scattered around the village and some pieces were found in structures, though no concentrations were noted. He reports 133 pieces representing 47 artifacts from the following genera: *Glycymeris* (n = 47 pieces representing 33 artifacts), *Laevicardium* (n = 73 pieces representing 7 artifacts), *Trachycardium* (n = 1), *Dosinia* (n = 1), *Mytella* (n = 1), *Conus* (n = 1), *Anodonta* (n = 1), and unknown (n = 10 pieces representing 4 artifacts). Artifact types comprised whole shell beads of *Glycymeris,* pendants made from *Glycymeris, Conus* tinklers, and *Laevicardium* valves. *Glycymeris* artifacts included two finger rings, one frog, and one reworked bracelet fragment. Three whole valves were recovered; one *Laevicardium* (reconstructed from 24 fragments) and two *Glycymeris* Both of these may have been acquired to be worked into items of adornment. Both raw and worked materials were found, indicating to Vokes that, unlike at Whiptail, people at Gibbon Springs were manufacturing shell beads and pendants.

Rabid Ruin

The features excavated at Rabid Ruin were primarily cremations, so most of the artifacts analyzed by Lisa Huckell (1976) were burned. Shell was found in 37 of the 56 cremation pits excavated at the site, as well as from one of the two excavated structures and from within stripping units. At least 1,809 pieces were found. Genera represented include *Glycymeris, Laevicardium, Anodonta, Olivella, Nassarius, Conus, Turritella, Haliotis*, and *Megathura. Glycymeris* came in the forms of frogs (n = 9), bracelets (n = 26), and whole shell beads (n = 437). *Laevicardium* valves found at the site were broken and warped in cremation fires and had no other indications of human alterations. Two small pieces of unworked *Anodonta* were found. *Olivella* was represented by 1,253 barrel beads; 17 whole shell *Nassarius* beads were also found. Four *Conus* specimens were found including one complete shell, one tinkler, one longitudinal fragment, and one wide finger ring fragment. *Turritella* came in the form of one whole shell bead. *Haliotis* was represented by four small fragments; what types of ornaments they were could not be determined. *Megathura,* a keyhole limpet, had its distal margin removed so all that remains is an oval of shell around the central opening. Fifty-four shells of an unknown genus were worked into tubular beads with a biconical perforation. Huckell (1976) referred to these as "long disk beads." She concludes that shell came to the site as nearly finished or completed artifacts.

Marana Platform Mound

Bayman (2007) analyzed the shell from the Marana Platform Mound. A technical report is not available for the shell, so the material presented here is gleaned from Bayman's article in *The Hohokam Millennium* (Fish and Fish 2007) and a photograph in the Marana Platform Mound volume (Fish et al. 1992). As a result, artifact types and genera can be described but not quantified. Bayman (2007:Figure 9.4) shows that *Conus, Glycymeris, Olivella, Columbella, Tevia, Chama, Cerithidea, Turritella*, and *Laevicardium* occur at the site. *Conus* is represented by raw material (whole specimen), a tinkler, a body bead, a cap bead, and a finger ring band fragment. *Glycymeris* occurs as whole juvenile valves in the form of two frogs, bracelet fragments (bands), and one reworked bracelet fragment. One large fragment of a distal end piece of *Laevicardium* is pictured but one cannot tell if lateral edges were cut or not, though the distal margin bears the natural crenulations of the species. One chunky piece of *Chama* was present; it appears to be worked material. In addition, there are several cut and ground pendants: one part of a spoked wheel, two lizards(?), one stylized bird, and a notched circle.

Summary

At Whiptail, *Glycymeris* was the most common type of shell found; most were in the form of bracelets and bracelet fragments. Although the bracelet fragments occur throughout the site, they are distributed in slightly different ways. Most (n = 8) of the 10 Type 1 bracelets found were in the Southwestern Locus; one each came from the Compound Locus and the Northern Locus (Table 6.4). Interestingly, one of the Type 1 bracelet fragments came from Structure 27b, which was one of the last features to be occupied at the site. Perhaps the bracelet had been kept as an heirloom.

The more numerous Type 2 (n = 26) and 3 (n = 24) bracelet fragments were evenly distributed in the Southwestern Locus, while more Type 3 bracelets (n = 8) were found in the Compound Locus than Type 2 fragments (n = 4) and there were more Type 2 bracelets (n = 4) than Type 3 (n = 2) pieces found in the Northern Locus. Because the time frame for Whiptail can include all three bracelet types, it was not unexpected that all three types would be found at the site. It is interesting, that the earlier Type 1 fragments did occur in one of the earliest known features at the site (Structure 4) as well as in the most densely occupied part of the site (the Southwestern Locus) and in one of the last features to be used (Structure 27a). Although the distribution of bracelet types at the site is enigmatic, the presence of Type 3 bracelets provides another indicator that the site was occupied into the mid- to late A.D. 1200s.

Laevicardium and *Glycymeris* were found at all of the sites discussed in this chapter. This is not unusual, as those shells are found on most Hohokam sites. The differences in the assemblages may be related to time differences or to function of the excavated portions of the sites. For example, the cremation burials at Rabid Ruin contained numerous *Olivella* beads, as well as tubular beads, a type not found elsewhere. The cremation offerings at Whiptail were not as specialized, although two of the four barrel beads found at the site came from a cremation.

Also interesting is the presence of *Anodonta* at Gibbon Springs, Rabid Ruin, Second Canyon, and Whiptail. Was *Anodonta* a substitute for the harder to get *Haliotis* shell? *Haliotis* was found at Second Canyon and Rabid Ruin in the same small, fragmented forms as the *Anodonta*.

Like *Glycymeris, Laevicardium* appears to be one type of shell that was valued by the residents of the Classic period sites just described. Found as whole valves (or, more commonly fragments that could be reconstructed into whole valves) or pendants, *Laevicardium* occurred in cremation burials as well as in household contexts.

With the exception of Rabid Ruin, the shell collections from these Classic contexts could be tossed together and be indistinguishable. Whiptail fits nicely with these other sites in quantity, genera, and artifact types.

Chapter 7

Miscellaneous Artifacts

Gayle Harrison Hartmann and Linda M. Gregonis

This chapter describes a variety of artifacts including chunks of daub or fired-clay, stone and mineral objects, and a few items of historical vintage. All were purposefully modified for human use or were affected by human use, with the exception of 11 samples of raw material that could have been collected for later use. Table 7.1 provides measurements and other information on these artifacts.

Daub or Fired-clay Artifacts

Daub clay is here defined as the clayey soil that was combined with caliche and small pebbles and was used to fill in chinks in walls, as well as to cover the roofs of structures. When structures burned, this material also burned and was, thus, preserved. Thirteen pieces of daub were collected from three different structures. The pieces collected from Structure 7 all exhibit semicircular impressions as does one of the two pieces from Structure 29. The impressions are the size that would have been left by the common reed, *Phragmites communis*. Pieces of daub with reed impressions were relatively common at Whiptail. They were noted in the description of six structures indicating the collapse of the roof after the structure burned. Lumps of daub (called "adobe" by the excavators of the site) were even more common, occurring in at least 20 structures.

Fired-clay objects are similar to daub, but do not seem to have the amount of caliche and small pebbles; and they do not seem to be structural in nature. For example, a globular piece of fired-clay from Structure 29 has no distinguishing features.

A pinched, flattened, semicircle of fired-clay with a central hole was collected from Structure 16. The outer edge is irregular indicating that this object is not a finished artifact such as a spindle whorl or clay bead. At one time, this piece was probably a complete circle

Table 7.1. Miscellaneous Stone and Mineral Objects.

Provenience	Artifact Type	Condition	Size	Comments
		Daub or Fired Clay		
Structure 7, Level 2A	Burned daub with impressions	8 fragments	Largest is 12 x 9 x 7 cm	Not catalogued; chunks have parallel semicircular impressions on one surface
Structure 7, south wall, west half	Burned daub with reed impressions	3 fragments	Largest is 3.5 x 3 x 3 cm	Not catalogued; two pieces have one reed impression, one has two impressions
Structure 16, lower fill	Pinch made semicircle of burned daub with central hole	Complete	2.3 x 1.7 x 1 cm	Not catalogued
Structure 29, SE 1/4, lower level	Flattened piece of burned daub with semicircular impression	Complete	5.4 x 5 x 2.7 cm	Not catalogued; piece has one flat, smooth surface and one with several semicircular impressions
Structure 29, SE 1/4, lower level	Globular piece of burned daub	Complete	5 x 3.8 x 3 cm	Not catalogued; piece has no impressions
		Turquoise, Chrysocolla, and Malachite		
Surface	Turquoise pendant or earbob	Complete	1.5 x 1.3 cm	ASM Catalog No. 38,025
Surface	Small piece of turquoise	Fragment	0.8 x 0.5 cm	ASM Catalog No. 38,229-x-1
Surface	Small piece of turquoise	Fragment	0.7 x 0.7 cm	ASM Catalog No. 38229-x-2
Compound, NE corner, 1 to 10 cm below surface	Possible pendant or earbob of turquoise or unidentified stone	Fragment	1.8 x 1.5 cm	ASM Catalog No. 38,024
Structure 2	Possible pendant or earbob of turquoise	Fragment	1.2 x 1.1cm	ASM Catalog No. 38,023
Structure 6, lower fill, near deer jaw	Worked piece of turquoise	Complete	Not measured	Not catalogued
Structure 10, lower fill	Turquoise pendant or earbob	Corner missing	1.3 x 1.0 cm	ASM Catalog No. 38,161
Structure 11, floor	Four-sided piece of turquoise	Complete	1.3 x 1.0 cm	ASM Catalog No. 38,185
Structure 11, floor	Small piece of turquoise	Complete	1.3 x 0.6 cm	ASM Catalog No. 38,173
Structure 17, lower fill	Triangular piece of turquoise	Complete	1.8 x 1.3 x 0.4 cm	Not catalogued; one edge and surfaces ground
Structure 27b, floor feature 6	Oval piece of turquoise	Complete	0.5 x 0.3 x 0.1cm	Not catalogued; polished
Structure 23, NE 1/4 lower fill	Rectangular piece of turquoise or chrysocolla	Complete	2.2 x 1.3 x 0.7 cm	Not catalogued; one ground side
Structure 31a, NE 1/4, middle fill	Turquoise chunk	Complete	0.5 x 0.4 x 0.2 cm	Not catalogued.
Structure 32, west-central post hole fill	Turquoise, chrysocolla chunk	Complete	2.4 x 1.7 x 1.4 cm	Not catalogued.
Structure 9, floor	Malachite, possible pigment source	Fragments	Largest: 1.2 x 0.8 x 0.4 cm	Not catalogued; many small, angular fragments
		Hematite, Magnetite, and Ocher		
No provenience	Flattened chunk of hematite-coated rock	Complete	5 x 4.7 x 1.4 cm	Not catalogued; has grooves on one surface.
Grid square J-16	Flattened chunk of hematite-coated rock	Complete	4.6 x 3.7 x 1.7 cm	Not catalogued; naturally flat chunk with surfaces ground to shape
Structure 2, lower fill	Hematite-coated rock	Complete	Not measured	Not catalogued; possible pigment source
Structure 12, wall fall	Hematite-coated rock	Complete	Not measured	Not catalogued; possible pigment source
Structure 12	Hematite-coated rock	Complete	4.5 x 4.5 x 3.7 cm	Not catalogued; ground surfaces; possible pigment source

Table 7.1. Miscellaneous Stone and Mineral Objects, cont'd.

Provenience	Artifact Type	Condition	Size	Comments
Structure 19a	Hematite-coated igneous rock	Complete	3.7 x 2.8 x 2.9 cm	Piece has polishing and striations; hematite is ground into surface (Figure 7.1f).
Structure 19a	Polished stone with hematite, rock type unknown	Complete	3.8 x 3.9 x 1 cm	
Structure 20	Hematite or magnetite	Complete	3 x 2.3 x 1.9 cm	Rock has one ground face and flaked surfaces; one face has clear crystals.
Structure 23, storage pit, floor B	Burned chunk of hematite	Complete	1 x 0.5 x 0.3 cm	
Structure 27b, inside Pot A	Hematite-coated igneous rock	Complete	1.7 x 1.6 x 1.4 cm	Ground facets with grooves and scratches; possible pigment source (Figure 7.1d)
Structure 27b, inside Pot A	Hematite-coated igneous rock	Complete	1.7 x 1.5 x 1.4 cm	Ground facets with grooves and scratches; possible pigment source (Figure 7.1b)
Structure 27b, inside Pot A	Hematite-coated igneous rock	Complete	1.4 x 1.3 x 1 cm	Ground facets with grooves and scratches; possible pigment source (Figure 7.1c)
Structure 27b, inside Bowl C	Hematite-coated rock	Complete	2.2 x 1.8 x 1.6 cm	Ground facets and grooved surfaces; possible pigment source (Figure 7.1e)
Structure 18	Magnetite hammer stone	Complete	11.7 x 11 x 7 cm	Not catalogued; very heavy river cobble
Structure 12, floor	Several chunks of prepared red ocher	Complete	Largest: 3.3 x 2.2 x 2.1 cm	Not catalogued
Structure 12, floor, contents of burned vessel	3 chunks of prepared red ocher	Complete	Largest: 7 x 6 x 4.5 cm	Not catalogued
		Quartzite		
Structure 3, roof fall, north end	Birdlike effigy	Complete	Not measured	Not catalogued
Structure 3	Phallus	Broken at tip	6.5 x 2.5 cm	ASM Catalog No. 38,209
Structure 12, lower fill	Polishing stone	Complete	3.3 x 2.2 cm	ASM Catalog No. 38,163
Structure 16, lower fill	Polishing stone blank	Nearly complete	2.8 x 2.3 cm	ASM Catalog No. 38,198
Structure 19a	Piece with ground corner	Complete	5 x 4.6 x 1.7 cm	Not catalogued; red color
Compound	Geode	Fragment	4 x 3.5 x 1.5 cm	Not catalogued; fine-grained band of quartzite surrounding a center of drusy quartz
		Mica, Slate, and Schist		
Structure 8, SE 1/4 floor	Worked piece of muscovite mica	Complete	Not measured	Not catalogued; has ground edges
Structure 9, upper fill, near surface	Worked piece of muscovite mica	Complete	Not measured	Not catalogued; has ground edges
Structure 13, SW corner, subfloor	Biotite mica flake	Complete	1.7 x 0.8 x 0.2 cm	Not catalogued
Structure 23, near hearth	3 sheets of biotite or muscovite	Complete	1.6 x 1.3 x 0.1 cm	Not catalogued
Structure 25, subfloor	Muscovite flake	Complete	1.7 x 1.3 x 0.4 cm	Not catalogued
Structure 7, floor	Schist spindle whorl	Small portion missing	6.1 cm diameter	ASM Catalog No. 38,026
Structure 10, floor	Schist spindle whorl	Complete	4.7 cm diameter	ASM Catalog No. 38,160
Structure 16, floor	Schist adze	Complete	13.0 x 7.0 cm	ASM Catalog No. 38,206
No provenience	Rectangular piece of schist	Complete	2.1 x 1.1 x 0.2 cm	Not catalogued; greenish color with saw-toothed lateral edges
Structure 24, NE 1/4, near east wall	Phyllite pendant	Fragment	3 x 5 x 0.1 cm	Not catalogued; about ½ represented

Table 7.1. Miscellaneous Stone and Mineral Objects, cont'd.

Provenience	Artifact Type	Condition	Size	Comments
Structure 13, SW corner, subfloor	Phyllite flake	Complete	2 x 1.1 x 0.1 cm	Not catalogued
Structure 23, NE 1/4, floor	Slate pendant	Fragment	2.8 x 3.2 x 0.3 cm	Not catalogued; about 1/4 represented
No provenience	Worked piece of slate	Nearly complete	2.1 x 1.6 x 0.3 cm	Not catalogued; has broken hole at one end
		Other Minerals and Rocks		
Surface near Structure 42	Argillite lip plug or ear spool	Complete	1.6 x 0.8 x 0.7cm	Not catalogued
Structure 16, lower fill	Basalt phallus	Complete	2.9 x 1.6 cm	ASM Catalog No. 38,222
Structure 28, SW 1/4, upper level	Carved piece of basalt	Fragment	5.8 x 1.6 x 1.5 cm	Not catalogued; elongated broken fragment; probably a handle or a tail; has scratches and a small groove; burned on one surface
Structure 10, floor	Bead of fine-grained siliceous stone	Complete	0.4 cm diameter	ASM Catalog No. 38,089
Structure 10, floor	Birdlike pendant of fine-grained siliceous stone	Complete	Not measured	Not catalogued
Structure 12, lower fill	Polishing stone of fine-grained siliceous stone	Incomplete	11.1 x 3.7 cm	ASM Catalog No. 38,087
Structure 17, floor	Arrowshaft straightener of metamorphosed limestone	Complete	11.1 x 8.1 cm	ASM Catalog No. 38,191
Surface, between Structures 9 and 10	Quartz crystal with worked ends	Complete	5.5 x 1.1 x 1 cm	
Structure 11, pot hole fill	Quartz crystal with worked surfaces	Complete	Not measured	
No provenience	Highly polished piece of plagioclase	Complete	2.8 x 2 x 0.5 cm	
Structure 12, floor	Kaolin piece with ground facets	Complete	Not measured	
Structure 27b, SW 1/4	Faceted polishing stone of unknown igneous rock	Complete	1.5 x 1.8 x 1 cm	Ground to shape (Figure 7.1a)
Cremation 4	Disk bead of unknown rock	Complete	0.3 cm diameter	Dark gray in color
Structure 22	Polished pebble, rock type unknown	Complete	1.1 x 1 x .09 cm	Red color

with a central hole, but as a result of its thinness it may never have been intended as a formal artifact.

Turquoise and Similar Minerals

Twelve examples of worked turquoise were recovered from Whiptail, three from the site's surface, one from the northeast corner of the compound, and eight from structures (Table 7.1). Two are complete or nearly complete small pendants or earbobs, two may be pendant or earbob fragments, eight small pieces have been worked in some way.

The only complete worked turquoise specimen is a small pendant or earbob of light blue stone, collected from the surface; it is somewhat circular in plan with a biconical perforation near one edge. One face is flat and other is rounded. A conical depression that may be incipient drilling for a second perforation is visible on one edge.

The second pendant or earbob, recovered from Structure 10, is also small and is of very light blue-green stone with some reddish markings on one face. Originally, the object was apparently trapezoidal with rounded corners, but one corner is now missing. One face is rounded and smooth while the other is flat. There is a biconical perforation through the narrow end of the pendant.

One specimen that appears to be a basal portion of a small pendant or earbob was recovered from the northeast corner of the compound, just below the surface. It is a piece of stone embedded with light-green turquoise and is roughly trapezoidal in plan with the broken end curved and narrower than the complete end. The complete end is notched in two places and the whole piece is elliptical in cross section.

The second fragmentary pendant or earbob, recovered from Structure 2, is green in color and also appears to represent the basal portion. It is rounded and beveled on the complete end and is elliptical in cross section.

The remaining eight small pieces of worked turquoise are relatively unremarkable. A small piece of worked turquoise was recovered from the lower fill of Structure 6, near a deer jaw. From the floor of Structure 11 two tiny pieces were recovered. One is described as flat and four-sided, blue-green in color, and with rounded ends and smooth faces. The other is described as light blue-green in color, irregular in shape, with one face and one edge smoothed, and almost rectangular in cross section. A triangular piece with one edge and both surfaces ground came from the lower fill of Structure 17. A rectangular piece of turquoise/chrysocolla with one side ground was recovered from the lower fill of Structure 23. A very small oval piece of polished turquoise came from the floor (or near the floor) of Structure 27b. Finally, there are two tiny fragments from the site's surface. Both specimens are blue-green in color. One is triangular in cross section with one smooth face and one rough face; the other has an irregular cross section with all faces smooth.

Several pieces of raw, turquoise-family pieces were also found at the site. Structure 31a yielded a tiny chunk of turquoise and Structure 32 yielded a larger, irregular chunk of turquoise or chrysocolla. Many tiny, angular fragments of malachite were recovered from the floor of Structure 9. These may have been used as pigment.

Hematite, Magnetite, and Ocher Artifacts

Among the most interesting artifacts found at Whiptail are several pieces of igneous stone that are coated and perhaps impregnated with hematite (Anna Domitrovic, Geologist Emeritus, Arizona-Sonora Desert Museum, personal communication 2008). The rocks have grooves and scratches on their surfaces; in addition, some have polished facets (Figure 7.1). Jenny Adams (personal communication 2008) suspects that the rocks are naturally hematite rich and that the grooves on them "were a way of loosening up the pigment on the 'stone/mineral' surface so that it could be directly applied and worked into a pliable to soft surface." She cleaned out the grooves and tested each piece to determine that the pigment is deeply embedded in each rock. Adams thinks that the rocks were used to color hides or human skin and that they were not used to burnish pottery, as polishing against the granular particles in the clay would not create the rounded and burnished surfaces seen on the artifacts.

The hematite-coated pieces were found in Structures 2, 12, 19a, and 27b. One piece was also recovered from the surface of the site and another from a grid square in the Southwestern Locus. Four of the pieces were found in two pots in Structure 27b, along with what looks like a wood or hide working kit of bifaces, drills, and utilized flakes (Figure 4.2). This supports Adams' idea that the pigment-bearing stones were used for coloring some kind of soft material.

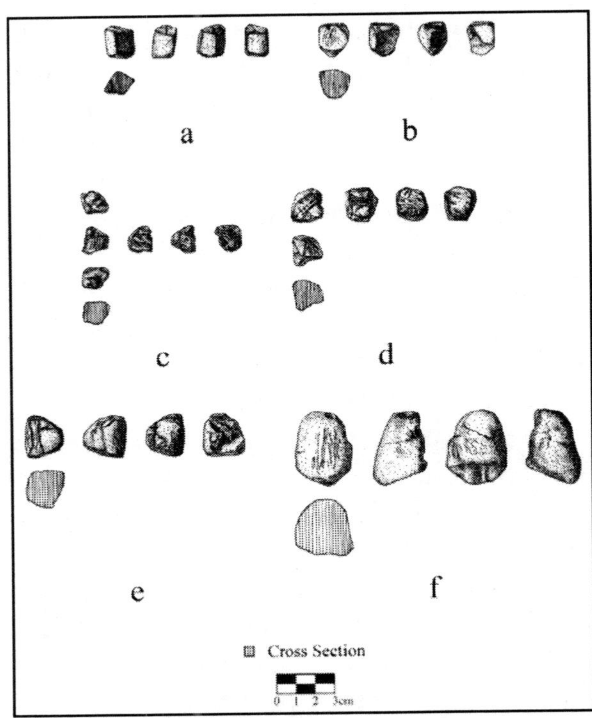

Figure 7.1. Faceted igneous and hematite-covered stones. The illustration shows facets on the stones that were polished and/or scratched. All stones but (a) have hematite on them; (a) is an igneous stone with polished facets. By its weight (c) appears to be a piece of hematite that has been grooved and polished. All of the hematite pieces have multiple facets and scratch marks. Stones a, b, c, d, and e are from pots in Structure 27b. Stone (f) is from Structure 19 (drawing by Gerry Crouse).

In addition to two hematite-coated rocks, several chunks of prepared red ocher were found in Structure 12 (Table 7.1). This structure also contained an unfired Tanque Verde Red-on-brown jar (Figure 2.14), indicating that the house was inhabited by a pottery maker. In this case, the hematite-coated rocks may have been used in the pottery decoration process.

Structure 19a contained one hematite-coated rock, as well as a rounded pebble-sized stone with hematite coloring on it. A burned chunk of hematite was found in a storage pit in Structure 23, and a dense piece of hematite or magnetite with polishing from grinding was found in Structure 20. A hematite or magnetite hammerstone was found in Structure 18 (Table 7.1).

Quartzite Artifacts

Six quartzite artifacts were found: two from Structure 3 and one each from Structures 12, 16, 19a, and the compound (Table 7.1). The objects from Structure 3 are an incomplete phallus and a birdlike effigy. The phallus is basically a flattened cylinder with a groove around the circumference near one end; it is broken at the tip. The birdlike effigy is gray and black in color.

A quartzite polishing stone and a quartzite polishing stone blank came from two structures, the lower fill of Structure 12 and the lower fill of Structure 16. The larger stone, from Structure 12, is light gray-brown in color and somewhat egg-shaped with a smooth surface; it is a complete specimen. Incipient facets suggest limited use. The slightly smaller stone, from Structure 16, is purple-brown in color; in shape it is a rounded cube with a smooth surface, except for a broken area at one corner. It has little if any evidence of use. The chunk of quartzite from Structure 19a is red in color with a ground corner.

About one-fourth of a small geode was recovered from the compound. The geode is fine-grained quartzite on the exterior and has crystalline (drusy) quartz in the center.

Mica, Schist, and Slate Objects

Given Whiptail's location at the base of the Santa Catalina Mountains, it is not surprising that mica flakes, sheets, and worked pieces were found at the site. Structures 13, 23, and 25 produced flakes and sheets of mica. Pieces of muscovite mica with ground edges were found in Structures 8 and 9 (one piece each). In addition, a phyllite pendant fragment was found in Structure 24 (Table 7.1).

Two schist spindle whorls were recovered, one from the floor of Structure 7 and one from the floor of Structure 10 (Table 7.1). Both objects are circular disks with biconical perforations in the center; the spindle whorl from Structure 7 is chipped along one edge, while the spindle whorl from Structure 10 is complete. Also of schist is a complete adze-like object from the floor of Structure 16. It is tapered-oval in plan with one squared-off end and one rounded end. It has two notches, presumably for lashing, about midway along its length. Structure 23 yielded a pendant fragment of slate. Two specimens lacked provenience information, one being a piece of worked slate with a broken hole at one end, and the other a rectangular piece of greenish schist with both lateral edges chipped into tiny sawteeth.

Other Minerals and Rocks

Other items from Whiptail include artifacts of argillite, kaolin, basalt, metamorphosed limestone, plagioclase, quartz, and a fine-grained siliceous stone (Table 7.1). Argillite is represented by a complete lip plug/ear spool. It was found on the site's surface near Structure 42.

A single specimen of kaolin with several ground facets was collected from Structure 12. The kaolin might have been part of the pottery making materials used by inhabitants of that structure.

A basalt phallus was recovered from the lower fill of Structure 16. The object is small, only 2.9 cm in length, carefully shaped, and well smoothed. Another basalt object was found in the upper fill of Structure 28. It is a carved piece that was probably a handle or tail.

A complete arrowshaft straightener of metamorphosed limestone was recovered from the floor of Structure 17. It is oval in shape with a single groove running perpendicular to the longitudinal axis; both ends of the artifact show signs of battering.

Plagioclase is represented by only one highly polished piece. The provenience of this artifact is unknown.

Two quartz crystals were found on the site: one from the surface between Structures 9 and 10 and one from Structure 11. The surface specimen is an elongated crystal with both ends ground. The specimen from Structure 11 is also a crystal, but in this case has ground surfaces.

Three artifacts were classified only as

fine-grained siliceous rock: a red disk bead and a bicolored birdlike pendant from the floor of Structure 10 and a polishing stone from the lower fill of Structure 12. The polishing stone is thin and roughly rectangular in shape.

In addition to the hematite-covered stones from Structure 27b, a faceted stone of unknown rock type was found. It has many of the same characteristics of the hematite-covered stones, but contains no hematite. Finally, a small, dark gray disk bead of unknown rock type was found in Cremation 4, and a red, polished pebble of unknown rock type was found in Structure 22.

Historical Objects

Immediately north of the portion of the Whiptail site described in this report lies the Agua Caliente Ranch (AZ BB:10:25 [ASM]). This ranch, named for the nearby springs, was occupied from the 1870s to the mid-1980s. In 1984 the ranch was purchased by Pima County and in July of that year it opened to the public as Roy P. Drachman Agua Caliente Regional Park. Its history has been described in detail by historical archaeologist James E. Ayres (2001:71-123).

During its long history the ranch property was owned by numerous families and served a variety of purposes. Primarily, it served as a cattle ranch, resort, citrus orchard, truck farm, and winter residence (Ayres 2001:122). In summarizing the history of the ranch, Ayres (2001:121) notes that in many ways, such as architecture, site layout, material culture, and the presence of livestock, it was similar to other small ranches in the Tucson area. It was distinct, however, in that it supported "an irrigated, commercial-sized orchard/citrus grove as early as the 1880s, and, at the same time, its hot springs were exploited to provide the first public resort outside of the city of Tucson."

Also, from 1875 to 1882, the ranch became part of the Fort Lowell Military Reservation. During that period, although the army did not occupy the ranch proper, soldiers probably visited the springs. As Ayres (2001:73) points out, there are no specific references to visits by army personnel, but it was likely used "as a pleasant place to camp, and even as a spot

Table 7.2. Historical Artifacts Collected during the Whiptail Excavations.

Provenience	Artifact Type	Condition	Size	Comment
Structure 8, outside S wall	Thin piece of metal	Fragment	3.4 x 3 cm	Not catalogued
Northeast corner of Structure 27b	Lapel pin	Complete	7.7 x 0.7 x 0.3 cm	Not catalogued; woman's decorative pin of pot metal with tiny rhinestones, ca. 1930s or 1940s (identified by Barbara Murphy, Nov. 30, 2005)
Compound, trench on south side north wall	.50-caliber rifle bullet	Complete	2 x 1.3 cm	Not catalogued; bullet belonged to a military type rifle and has been fired (identified by James E. Ayres, Nov. 28, 2005)
Structure 13	Stoneware jar	Fragments	Largest piece: 6.3 x 3.3 x 0.8 cm	Not catalogued; glazed, brown; larger piece is base and side; probably kitchenware (identified by James E. Ayres, Nov. 28, 2005)

at which to take a warm bath." Thus, it seems likely that three of the four historical objects described here were associated with the Agua Caliente Ranch. The fourth, a .50-caliber bullet, may have been associated with soldiers attached to Fort Lowell.

The four historical objects inventoried with the Whiptail collection are a thin piece of metal, a lapel pin, a bullet, and two pieces of a stoneware jar (Table 7.2). The thin piece of metal was recovered outside the south wall of Structure 8, above the prehistoric use level. The woman's decorative lapel pin of pot metal and tiny, faceted rhinestones, dated to the 1930s or 1940s; it was found in the northeastern corner of Structure 27b. The stoneware jar fragments came from Structure 13. The .50-caliber bullet was found in the compound. It was from a military-type rifle and the nose of the bullet is deformed indicating that it had struck a hard object after being fired.

In recent visits to the Whiptail site, we have noticed several historical trash dumps and artifacts scattered in and among the prehistoric features that still exist at the site. In addition, field notes make it clear that pot hunters' holes often included historical trash. We are not sure why, as a rule, the decision was made to not collect historical artifacts or why the four artifacts described were collected.

According to Bruce Bradley, Dale Berge excavated one of the historical middens, where he recovered "some 45-70 cartridges (one unfired with the powder still in it), a really nice Cienega jasper point and some historic pottery and glass" (Bradley email communication 2009). What happened to those artifacts and any report that Berge might have produced is unknown.

Chapter 8

Animal Remains

Linda M. Gregonis

Animal bone found during the excavations at Whiptail Ruin consisted primarily of six species: jackrabbit, cottontail, mule deer, white-tailed deer, pronghorn, and bighorn sheep. Other animals represented in the collection include Sonoran desert toad, colubrid snake, turtle, a variety of rodents, two different sizes of birds, and dog or coyote. Table 8.1 lists the orders, families, genera, and species of animals found by their scientific and common names. In this chapter, and elsewhere in the volume, we refer to animals by their common names.

Like the nearby Gibbon Springs site (Strand 1996), it appears that the people living at Whiptail Ruin procured a large number of hoofed animals: deer, pronghorn, and bighorn. These animals apparently were used for food and ritual, as evidenced by a number of jaws, skulls, and pelvic bones found in various features. There is also evidence for nonfood use of other species including rabbit or hare, turtle, and possibly golden eagle.

Analytic Methods

The animal bone was analyzed in the early 1980s by Arizona Archaeological and Historical Society volunteers. They used the Western Archeological and Conservation Center's National Park Service comparative skeletal collection, which is housed at the Arizona State Museum. The analysts counted and described each bone or bone fragment separately, and were conservative in identifying fragments to species and specific elements. Whole bones were identified by type of bone, side (if possible and applicable), and species or general size. The analysts made observations regarding the relative weathering of the bone, whether the bone was burned, charred, or calcined, and whether the bone had been worked. On occasion, they made remarks about the fusion of epiphyses to diaphyses, clarity of suture marks on skulls, and the like. They analyzed 3,093 bones and bone fragments.

Using the information recorded in the 1980s, I created a computerized database with the following information: provenience; species, genera, or general size of animal; element; side; whether the bone was fragmentary or whole; whether the bone was burned, charred, or calcined; whether the bone was weathered; whether it was worked; other notes on the condition of the bone; and the number of fragments or bones represented. (The information from this database is presented in Appendix 8.A.) It was difficult to tell from the analysis cards whether the analysts thought particular bones belonged to one or more individuals. In

Table 8.1. Scientific Names, Common Names, and General Categories of Animals Found at Whiptail.

Scientific Name or General Category	Common Name
Class: **Amphibia**	**Amphibians**
Family: Bufonidae	Toads
Bufo alvarius	Sonoran desert toad
Class: **Reptilia**	**Reptiles**
Family: Colubridae	Colubrid snake
Order: Testudines	Turtle or tortoise
Class: **Aves**	**Birds**
Family: Accipitridae	Hawks, Old World Vultures, and Harriers
cf. *Aquila chrysaëtos*	possible golden eagle
Medium-sized (passerine) bird	medium-sized song bird
Large bird	large bird—hawk sized or larger
Class: **Mammalia**	**Mammals**
Order: Artiodactyla	Artiodactyls (hoofed animals)
Family: Antilocapridae	Pronghorn
Antilocapra americana	pronghorn
Family: Bovidae	Cows, sheep, and allies
Ovis canadensis	bighorn sheep
Family: Cervidae	Deer and allies
Odocoileus hemionus	mule deer
Odocoileus virginianus	white-tailed deer
Odocoileus virginianus coues	Coues' white-tailed deer
Order: Carnivora	Carnivores
Family: Canidae	Dogs and allies
cf. *Canis latrans*	possible coyote
Canis sp.	dog or coyote
Order: Lagomorpha	Hares, rabbits, and pikas
Family: Leporidae	Hares and rabbits (lagomorphs)
Lepus alleni	antelope jackrabbit
Lepus californicus	black-tailed jackrabbit
Sylvilagus sp.	cottontail, desert or eastern
Order: Rodentia	Rodents
Family: Cricetidae	Native rats and mice
Neotoma albigua	white-throated wood rat
Family: Geomyidae	Pocket gophers
Thomomys sp.	pocket gopher, either valley or southern
Family: Heteromyidae	Kangaroo rats and pocket mice
Dipodomys spectabilis or *deserti*	banner-tailed or desert kangaroo rat
Perognathus sp.	pocket mouse
Family: Sciuridae	Squirrels and allies
Ammospermophilus harrisii	Harris' antelope squirrel
Spermophilus tereticaudus	round-tailed ground squirrel
Spermophilus variegatus	rock squirrel
Small mammal	rodent- to rabbit-sized mammal
Medium mammal	jackrabbit to coyote-sized mammal
Large mammal	larger than coyote-sized mammal

addition to the material analyzed in the 1980s, I used field notes and photograph labels to determine that animal bone had been found in Structure 19a. At the time of analysis, material from this feature was in the possession of Bruce Bradley and not available for study at the Arizona State Museum. Data gleaned from animal remains from Structure 19a were not included in the database, but are reported on in this chapter when I could confirm information through photographs and maps.

Because it was seldom clear how many animals might be represented by the collection of bones from any feature, I decided to use a presence-absence approach to recording the animals represented in each feature. Occasionally, it was clear that more than one animal was represented. For example, at least 16 rabbit or hare innominates (lain out as if they had been strung together), three and a half deer or pronghorn mandibles and four antlers were found on the floor Structure 19a. I chose not to try to determine either a lagomorph or artiodactyl index for the animal bone from Whiptail. This is because, in general, the bone was poorly preserved and it is not clear from the analysis cards whether any attempts were made to refit fragments. In addition, it was difficult to determine how much of the lagomorph bone had been burned. Finally, the depositional context (in house floor, floor fill, and roof proveniences) of much of the artiodactyl bone was indicative of ritual and storage rather than butchering, distribution, and consumption.

Results

Naturally Occurring Animals

A number of features contained the remains of animals that probably entered the structures after they were abandoned. They are listed in Table 8.2. Most of the identified bones were from rodents, but bones from one Sonoran desert toad were found in the fill of Structure 25 and colubrid snake bones were found in Structures 4 and 23. All of these animals can be found in burrows in the ground and they most likely found the relatively soft soil of the abandoned structures to their liking. One colubrid snake bone, a fragment of vertebra, found in Structure 4 was burned. It was found in the fill of the house, so its original context is not clear. Perhaps a snake was caught in the house when it burned, or its skeleton had been used in some way by the inhabitants of the house. Another snake vertebra found in the house was not burned.

Lagomorph Remains

As mentioned previously, lagomorphs (jackrabbit and cottontail) and artiodactyls (bighorn sheep, pronghorn, mule deer, and white-tail deer) make up the bulk of the bone found at Whiptail. Jackrabbit and cottontail rabbit bones were found in most of the features (Table 8.3), but it is not always clear whether the bones were naturally or culturally deposited. To try to determine whether the bones could have been used by the site's inhabitants, I looked at whether the bones were burned in some way (charred, burned, calcined) and whether the structure they were found in was burned. Burned bone found in a burned structure seems a good indicator of cultural deposition; that is, the bone burned at the same time as the feature and was part of the house "furniture" when the structure burned. Out of the 24 structures that contained cottontail or jackrabbit bone, only five (Structures 4, 8, 23, 27a, 31b) contained burned lagomorph bone. Four of the five structures were burned. One, Structure 27a, was not burned, but it was attached to two other rooms (27b and 28) that burned. Only three lagomorph bone fragments (one jackrabbit, two cottontail) were found in Structure 27a (Table 8.4), how-

Table 8.2. Animals that Probably Occurred Naturally in Site Features.

Provenience	Sonoran Desert toad	Colubrid snake	Pocket mouse	Harris antelope squirrel	Harris antelope squirrel or Round-tailed ground squirrel	Round-tailed ground squirrel	Rock squirrel	Banner-tailed or Desert kangaroo rat	White-throated wood rat	Gopher	Squirrel	Rodent	Total No. of Species
	Animal Species or Class												
Compound Locus													
Compound	--	--	--	--	--	--	--	--	--	--	--	1	1
Structure 4	--	1	--	1	--	--	--	--	--	--	--	--	2
Central Locus													
Structure 32b	--	--	--	--	--	--	--	--	--	--	--	1	1
Southwestern Locus													
Structure 10	--	--	--	--	--	1	--	--	1	--	--	--	2
Structure 12	--	--	--	1	--	--	--	--	--	--	--	--	1
Structure 13	--	--	--	--	--	--	--	--	--	--	1	--	1
Structure 16	--	--	--	1	--	--			--	--	--	--	1
Structure 18	--	--	--	--	1	--	--	--	--	--	--	--	1
Structure 23	--	1	1	1	1	--	1	1	--	1	--	1	8
Structure 25	1	--	--	1	1	--	--	--	--	--	--	--	3
Northern Locus													
Structure 27	--	--	--	1	--	--	--	--	--	--	--	--	1
Structure 27a	--	--	--	1	--	--	--	--	--	--	--	--	1
Structure 27b	--	--	--	--	--	--	--	--	--	--	--	--	1
Southern Locus													
Structure 19a	--	--	--	--	--	--	--	--	--	--	--	1	1
Total No. of Occurrences	1	2	1	7	3	1	1	1	1	1	1	4	25

Note: Numbers represent presence/absence of animals unless it is clear that more than one animal of a particular species was represented.

Table 8.3. Distribution of Cottontail and Jackrabbit.

Provenience	Antelope jackrabbit	Black-tailed jackrabbit	Jackrabbit	Cottontail	Rabbit or hare	Total No. of Occurrences	Burned bone	Burned Structure
	Species or Class							
Compound Locus								
Structure 4	1	--	--	1	--	2	+	+
Structure 6	--	1	--	1	--	2	--	+
Structure 7	--	--	1	1	--	2	--	+
Structure 8	--	1	--	1	--	2	+	+
Structure 17	--	--	1	--	--	1	--	--
Central Locus								
Structure 15	--	--	1	--	--	1	--	+
Southwestern Locus								
Structure 10	--	1	--	--	--	1	--	+
Structure 12	--	1	--	1	--	2	--	+
Structure 13	--	1	--	--	--	1	--	+
Structure 16	1	1	--	1	--	3	--	+
Structure 18	--	1	--	1	--	2	--	+
Structure 23	1	1	--	1	--	3	+	+
Structure 24	--	1	--	1	--	2	--	+
Structure 25	1	1	--	1	--	3	--	+
Northern Locus								
Structure 3	--	1	--	--	--	1	--	--
Structure 27a	--	1	--	1	--	2	+	--
Structure 27b	--	1	--	1	--	2	--	+
Structure 28	1	1	--	--	--	2	--	+
Structure 29	--	--	1	--	--	1	--	+
Structure 30	--	--	1	--	--	1	--	+
Structure 31b	--	1	--	1	--	2	+	+
Structure 31c	--	1	--	1	--	2	--	--
Southern Locus								
Structure 14	--	1	--	--	--	1	--	+
Structure 19a	--	--	--	--	1	1	--	+
Total No. of Occurrences	5	17	5	14	1	42		

Note: Numbers represent presence/absence of animals unless it is clear that more than one animal of a particular species was represented. Numbers from Structure 19a do not represent the actual totals for bones found in the feature as an unknown amount of bone was not available to analysts.

ever, which likely indicates that the bone was incidental to the structure.

Not all of the rabbit and hare bone found in the burned structures showed evidence of burning. For example, out of 97 lagomorph bones and bone fragments found in Structure 23, only 33 pieces (scapulae, leg, and foot bones) were burned. The bone elements found in Structure 23 also show the most variety; all parts of at least one black-tailed jackrabbit and most of at least one cottontail were found. These animals may have burrowed into the structure after its abandonment.

Szuter (1991) describes techniques of rabbit and hare preparation and bone disposal that were used in the Southwest. There are several ways that lagomorphs can be prepared for eating—e.g., spitting, roasting, or boiling. Not all of these food preparation techniques would result in burned bone, nor would the discard of bones from meals. As Table 8.4 shows, most of the bone recovered consisted of leg and foot bones, pieces that may have been discarded during food preparation (e.g., skinning the animal and discarding the feet), consumption (dropping the leg bones once the meat had been chewed off), or pelt preparation (keeping the feet as part of the pelt). The analysts did not record whether there was evidence that the bones had been broken for

Table 8.4. Rabbit and Hare Bone Elements by Provenience.

Provenience	Species or Class	Whole or Fragmentary	Bone Elements: Skull, mandible, teeth	Foot bones	Leg bones	Scapula	Pelvic bones	Ribs	Vertebrae	Sternum	Total Number of Bones and Bone Fragments
Compound Locus											
Structure 4	Black-tail jackrabbit	whole	--	1	--	--	---	--	--	--	1
	Black-tail jackrabbit	fragment	1	2	2	--	1	--	--	--	6
	Antelope jackrabbit	whole	--	4	3	--	--	--	--	--	7
	Antelope jackrabbit	fragment	--	--	3	1	--	--	--	--	4
	Jackrabbit	fragment	1	1	3	--	--	--	--	--	5
	Cottontail	fragment	--	--	1	--	1	--	--	--	2
Structure 4 totals			2	8	12	1	2	0	0	0	25
Structure 6	Black-tail jackrabbit	fragment	--	--	1	--	--	--	--	--	1
	Lepus	fragment	--	--	3	--	--	4	--	--	7
	Cottontail	whole	--	1	--	--	--	--	--	--	1
	Cottontail	fragment	--	--	1	--	--	--	--	--	1
Structure 6 totals			0	1	5	0	0	4	0	0	10
Structure 7	Lepus	fragment	--	--	--	--	--	1	--	--	1
	Cottontail	fragment	--	--	1	--	--	--	--	--	1
Structure 7 totals			0	0	1	0	0	1	0	--	2
Structure 8	Black-tail jackrabbit	whole	1	4	--	--	--	--	--	--	5
	Black-tail jackrabbit	fragment	13	2	7	1	--	--	--	--	23
	Jackrabbit	fragment	6	--	1	--	--	--	--	--	7
	Cottontail	whole	--	1	1	--	--	--	--	--	2
	Cottontail	fragment	--	--	1	--	1	--	--	--	2
Structure 8 totals			20	7	10	1	1	0	0	0	39
Central Locus											
Structure 15	Jackrabbit	whole	--	1	--	--	--	--	--	--	1
Structure 15 total			0	1	0	0	0	0	0	0	1
Structure 17	Jackrabbit	fragment	1	--	--	--	--	--	--	--	1
Structure 17 total			1	0	0	0	0	0	0	0	1
Southwestern Locus											
Structure 10	Black-tail jackrabbit	whole	--	16	1	--	--	--	--	--	17
	Black-tail jackrabbit	fragment	--	1	1	1	--	--	5	--	8
	Jackrabbit	fragment	--	--	--	--	--	--	3	--	3
Structure 10 totals			0	17	2	1	0	0	8	0	28
Structure 12	Black-tail jackrabbit	whole	--	2	--	--	--	--	2	--	4
	Black-tail jackrabbit	fragment	--	1	3	--	--	--	2	--	6
	Jackrabbit	whole	--	--	--	--	--	1	--	--	1

Table 8.4. Rabbit and Hare Bone Elements by Provenience, cont'd.

Provenience	Species or Class	Whole or Fragmentary	Bone Elements: Skull, mandible, teeth	Foot bones	Leg bones	Scapula	Pelvic bones	Ribs	Vertebrae	Sternum	Total Number of Bones and Bone Fragments
	Jackrabbit	fragment	--	--	2	--	--	6	6	--	14
	Cottontail	fragment	--	--	1	--	--	--	--	--	1
Structure 12 totals			0	3	6	0	0	7	10	0	26
Structure 13	Black-tail jackrabbit	fragment	--	1	--	--	--	--	--	--	1
Structure 13 total			0	1	0	0	0	0	0	0	1
Structure 16	Black-tail jackrabbit	whole	--	1	--	--	--	--	--	--	1
	Black-tail jackrabbit	fragment	--	1	--	--	--	--	--	--	1
	Antelope jackrabbit	fragment	--	--	--	--	1	--	--	--	1
	Jackrabbit	fragment	--	1	1	--	--	--	--	--	2
	Cottontail	fragment	--	1	--	--	1	--	--	--	2
Structure 16 totals			0	4	1	0	2	0	0	0	7
Structure 18	Black-tail jackrabbit	fragment	--	1	2	2	--	--	--	--	5
	Cottontail sp.	fragment	--	--	--	--	--	2	--	--	2
Structure 18 totals			0	1	2	2	0	2	0	0	7
Structure 23	Black-tail jackrabbit	whole	1	13	--	--	--	--	1	--	15
	Black-tail jackrabbit	fragment	--	5	13	1	1	1	3	--	24
	Antelope jackrabbit	fragment	--	--	1	--	--	--	--	--	1
	Jackrabbit	whole	2	4	--	--	--	--	--	1	7
	Jackrabbit	fragment	2	6	2	2	--	1	1	--	14
	Cottontail sp.	whole	--	11	--	--	--	--	--	--	11
	Cottontail sp.	fragment	1	5	10	2	--	1	--	--	19
	Leporidae	whole	--	1	--	--	--	1	--	--	2
	Leporidae	fragment	3	--	--	--	--	--	1	--	4
Structure 23 totals			9	45	26	5	1	4	6	1	97
Structure 24	Black-tail jackrabbit	fragment	--	1	--	1	--	--	--	--	2
	Jackrabbit	fragment	--	3	--	--	--	--	--	--	3
	Cottontail	fragment	--	1	--	--	1	--	--	--	2
Structure 24 totals			0	5	0	1	1	0	0	0	7
Structure 25	Black-tail jackrabbit	whole	--	4	--	--	--	--	--	--	4
	Black-tail jackrabbit	fragment	--	8	1	--	--	--	--	--	9
	Antelope jackrabbit	whole	--	3	--	--	--	--	--	--	3
	Antelope jackrabbit	fragment	--	1	4	--	1	--	--	--	6
	Jackrabbit	fragment	--	--	1	--	--	1	--	--	2
	Cottontail sp.	whole	--	1	--	--	--	--	--	--	1
	Cottontail sp.	fragment	--	1	2	--	--	--	--	--	3
Structure 25 totals			0	18	8	0	1	1	0	0	28

Table 8.4. Rabbit and Hare Bone Elements by Provenience, cont'd.

			Bone Elements								
Provenience	Species or Class	Whole or Fragmentary	Skull, mandible, teeth	Foot bones	Leg bones	Scapula	Pelvic bones	Ribs	Vertebrae	Sternum	Total Number of Bones and Bone Fragments
				Northern Locus							
Structure 27a	Black-tail jackrabbit	fragment	--	--	1	--	--	--	--	--	1
	Cottontail sp.	fragment	--	1	1	--	--	--	--	--	2
Structure 27a totals			0	1	2	0	0	0	0	0	3
Structure 27b	Black-tail jackrabbit	fragment	--	--	1	--	--	--	--	--	1
	Cottontail sp.	fragment	--	--	1	--	--	--	--	--	1
Structure 27b totals			0	0	2	0	0	0	0	0	2
Structure 28	Black-tail jackrabbit	whole	--	1	--	--	--	--	--	--	1
	Black-tail jackrabbit	fragment	--	1	--	--	--	--	--	--	1
	Antelope jackrabbit	whole	--	1	--	--	--	--	--	--	1
Structure 28 totals			0	3	0	0	0	0	0	0	3
Structure 29	Jackrabbit	fragment	--	--	1	--	--	--	--	--	1
Structure 29 total			0	0	1	0	0	0	0	0	1
Structure 30	Lepus	fragment	--	--	1	--	--	--	--	--	1
	Leporidae	fragment	--	1	--	--	--	--	--	--	1
Structure 30 totals			0	1	1	0	0	0	0	0	2
Structure 31b	Black-tail jackrabbit	whole	--	5	--	--	--	--	--	--	5
	Black-tail jackrabbit	fragment	--	1	3	1	--	--	--	--	5
	Jackrabbit	fragment	--	2	--	--	--	1	--	--	3
	Cottontail	whole	--	1	--	--	--	--	--	--	1
	Cottontail	fragment	2	--	1	--	--	--	--	--	3
Structure 31b totals			2	9	4	1	0	1	0	0	17
Structure 31c	Black-tail jackrabbit	fragment	--	--	1	--	--	--	--	--	1
	Lepus?	fragment	--	1	--	--	--	--	--	--	1
	Cottontail sp.	fragment	2	--	--	--	--	--	--	--	2
Structure 31c totals			2	1	1	0	0	0	0	0	4
				Southern Locus							
Structure 14	Black-tail jackrabbit	fragment	1	--	--	--	--	--	--	--	1
Structure 14 total			1	0	0	0	0	0	0	0	1
Grand totals			37	126	84	12	8	20	24	1	312

Note: Numbers do not reflect bone found in Structure 19a as those items were not available to analysts at the time of the study.

marrow extraction, an activity described by Szuter (1991), although many of the pieces recovered were fragments.

One clear example of cultural deposition was found in Structure 19a. There, at least 16 unburned rabbit or hare innominates were discovered. They were lined up as if they had been strung on a cord (Figure 8.1). They occurred in the same part of the house where a pile of artiodactyl bones (including several scapulae, mandibles, and a pronghorn skull) was found. Incidentally, the lagomorph innominates were misreported in Strand (1996:398) as artiodactyl pelves. The purpose of the pelvis string is unknown.

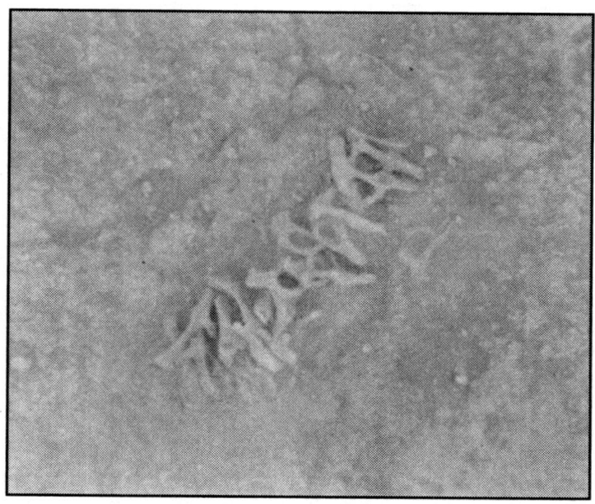

Figure 8.1. Rabbit or hare innominates found in Structure 19a (uncatalogued, Arizona State Museum, University of Arizona).

Artiodactyl Remains

Like the hare and rabbit bone, artiodactyl bones, bone fragments, and horn and antler parts were found in almost every structure. As Table 8.5 shows, they were found in all parts of the site except for the central locus that was immediately north of the compound. Coues' white-tailed deer seems to be the most common artiodactyl recovered. Identification of bone as white-tailed deer rather than mule deer was based on size, as the Coues' subspecies of white-tailed deer is distinctly smaller than mule deer. It is possible, however, that small mule deer bones were classified as Coues' white-tailed deer. Both species were found at the Gibbon Springs site (Strand 1996) and University Indian Ruin (Guo-qin 1983), so it is likely that many of the identifications are accurate.

Bones and horn material from bighorn and pronghorn were also found on the site. Bighorn remains were found in three features, Structures 8, 27b, and 30; pronghorn bones (including two skulls) were found in Structures 8, 16, 19a, and 30 (Table 8.5).

The presence of head elements (antler, horn, skull, jaw, teeth) and foot elements in various features may be an indication that the residents of Whiptail were using heads and hides in hunting and in ritual related to hunting. Leg bones may have been kept for use as tools. Szuter (1991:283) observes that head and foot elements are more common on lowland sites, perhaps because hunters brought back the meat, hide, and head, leaving the other bones at the hunting site. The presence of other elements—scapulae, pelves, ribs, and vertebrae—may be an indicator that the animals were hunted near the site, and that the entire animal was brought back to the site. The variety of artiodactyl bone elements at Whiptail is similar to that seen at Gibbon Springs, where Strand (1996:398) suggested that the presence of pelves, especially, may indicate the distribution of "gourmet" cuts of meat.

Ritual Deposition of Artiodactyls

Two features, Structures 8 and 27b, contained more artiodactyl remains than any other features on the site. Seventy-six percent (n = 496)

Table 8.5 Distribution of Bighorn Sheep, Pronghorn, Mule Deer, and White-tailed Deer.

Provenience	Bighorn sheep	Pronghorn	Mule deer	White-tailed deer	Cervidae	Artiodactyl	Total No. of Occurrences
			Compound Locus				
Structure 4	--	--	--	1	--	--	1
Structure 6	--	--	--	1	--	--	1
Structure 7	--	--	--	1	--	--	1
Structure 8	1	1	1	1	--	--	4
			Southwestern Locus				
Structure 10	--	--	--	1	--	--	1
Structure 11	--	--	--	1	--	--	1
Structure 16	--	1	--	1	--	--	2
Structure 23	--	--	--	1	--	--	1
Structure 25	--	--	1	--	--	--	1
			Northern Locus				
Structure 3	--	--	--	--	--	1	1
Structure 27	--	--	--	--	--	1	1
Structure 27a	--	--	--	1	--	--	1
Structure 27b	1	--	1	1	--	--	3
Structure 28	--	--	--	1	--	--	1
Structure 29	--	--	--	--	--	1	1
Structure 30	1	1	--	1	--	--	3
Structure 31b	--	--	--	--	1	--	1
			Southern Locus				
Structure 14	--	--	--	1	--	--	1
Structure 19a	--	1	--	--	--	--	1
Total No. of Occurrences	3	4	3	13	1	3	27

Note: Numbers represent presence/absence of animals unless it is clear that more than one animal of a particular species was represented. The numbers do not represent all of the bone found in Structure 19a as not all items were available to analysts at the time of the study.

of the identifiable artiodactyl bone, antler, and horn pieces were found in these two structures. The numbers of remains may be a bit misleading, as many of the pieces analyzed were skull, jaw, tooth, antler, and horn fragments, which together may make up only one individual of each species identified (Table 8.6).

The animal remains found in Structure 8 were from mule deer, white-tailed deer, pronghorn, and bighorn sheep. Skull, jaw, and tooth fragments from mule deer, bighorn sheep, and unspecified artiodactyls make up the majority of the bone from this feature (Table 8.6). Mule deer vertebrae and a scapula fragment were also found, as were a pronghorn scapula fragment, pronghorn rib fragments, and white-tailed deer leg and foot bones. All but vertebral fragments are represented among the unspecified artiodactyl bones. Much of the bone was found on the floor of the structure and 57 percent (n = 83) of the pieces were burned or calcined (Table 8.7).

Like the remains found in Structure 8, the artiodactyl bones found in Structure 27b consist primarily of skull, jaw, tooth, antler, and horn fragments, although pelvis fragments, scapulae, and ribs were also found. White-tailed deer remains include skull, jaw, tooth, scapula, pelvis, rib, leg, and foot bones; identified mule deer bone fragments represent every part of the body except the ribs; and bighorn horn core, skull, jaw, leg and foot bones were also found. One hundred fifty-four (44%) of the 350 pieces of bone from Structure 27b were antlers and antler fragments. Some of the antlers and at least one deer jaw were associated with a

Table 8.6. Distribution of Mule Deer, White-tailed Deer, Bighorn Sheep, and Pronghorn Bone Elements.

Provenience	Species or Class	Whole or Fragment	Bone Elements: Antler or horn	Skull, mandibles, teeth	Vertebrae	Scapula	Pelvis	Ribs	Leg	Foot and toe	Total No. of Bones and Bone Fragments
					Compound Locus						
Structure 4	Artiodactyl	fragment	--	1	1	--	--	--	3	2	7
	White-tailed deer	fragment	--	--	--	--	--	--	1	1	2
	White-tailed deer	whole	--	--	--	--	--	--		1	1
	Unspecified deer	fragment	1	--	--	--	--	--			1
Total, Structure 4			1	1	1	0	0	0	4	4	11
Structure 6	White-tailed deer	whole	--	--	--	--	--	--	--	1	1
	White-tailed deer or pronghorn	fragment	--	2	--	--	--	--	--		2
	Unspecified deer	fragment	--	19	--	--	--	--	--		19
	Artiodactyl	fragment	--	12	--	--	--	1	--	1	14
Total, Structure 6			0	33	0	0	0	1	0	2	36
Structure 7	White-tailed deer	whole	--	--	--	--	--	--	--	1	1
	Unspecified deer	fragment	--	--	--	--	1	--	--	--	1
Total, Structure 7			0	0	0	0	1	0	0	1	2
Structure 8	White-tailed deer	fragment	--	6	--	1	--	--	2	11	20
	White-tailed deer	whole	--	--	--	--	--	--	--	9	9
	Mule deer	fragment	--	28	4	1	--	--	--	--	33
	Unspecified deer	fragment	--	5	--	--	--	--	--	--	5
	Deer or pronghorn	fragment	--	1	--	--	--	1	--	--	2
	Pronghorn	fragment	--	--	--	1	--	1	--	--	2
	Bighorn sheep	fragment	4	1	--	--	--	--	--	--	5
	Artiodactyl	fragment	4	55	--	1	1	4	2	3	70
Total, Structure 8			8	96	4	4	1	6	4	23	146
					Southwestern Locus						
Structure 10	White-tailed deer	whole	--	--	--	--	--	--	--	1	1
Total, Structure 10			0	0	0	0	0	0	0	1	1
Structure 11	White-tailed deer (cf)	fragment	--	--	--	--	--	--	1	--	1
	White-tailed deer or pronghorn	fragment	--	--	--	--	--	--	--	1	1
	Unspecified deer	fragment	--	--	--	--	1	--	--	--	1
	Artiodactyl	fragment	--	--	--	--	--	--	1	--	1
Total, Structure 11			0	0	0	0	1	0	2	1	4
Structure 16	White-tailed deer	fragment	--	2	--	--	5	--	6	--	13
	Unspecified deer	fragment	--	--	--	--	1	--	--	--	1
	Pronghorn	fragment	--	--	--	--	--	--	--	2	2
	Artiodactyl	fragment	--	--	--	--	5	--	--	--	5
Total, Structure 16			0	2	0	0	11	0	6	2	21
Structure 23	White-tailed deer	fragment	--	1	--	--	--	--	--	--	1
Total, Structure 23			0	1	0	0	0	0	0	0	1
Structure 25	Mule deer	fragment	--	--	--	--	2	--	--	--	2
	Artiodactyl	fragment	--	--	--	--	--	2	--	--	2
Total, Structure 25			0	0	0	0	2	2	0	0	4
					Northern Locus						
Structure 3	Artiodactyl	fragment	--	--	1	--	--	--	--	--	1
Total, Structure 3			0	0	1	0	0	0	0	0	1
Structure 27a	White-tailed deer	fragment	--	--	--	--	--	--	--	1	1
	Artiodactyl	fragment	--	--	--	--	--	--	1	--	1
Total, Structure 27a			0	0	0	0	0	0	1	1	2

Table 8.6. Distribution of Mule Deer, White-tailed Deer, Bighorn Sheep, and Pronghorn Bone Elements, cont'd.

			Bone Elements								Total No. of Bones and Bone Fragments
Provenience	Species or Class	Whole or Fragment	Antler or horn	Skull, mandibles, teeth	Vertebrae	Scapula	Pelvis	Ribs	Leg	Foot and toe	
Structure 27b	White-tailed deer	fragment	--	8	--	2	4	--	1	7	22
	White-tailed deer	whole	--	--	--	--	--	--	--	4	4
	Mule deer	fragment	1	11	1	--	3	--	5	4	25
	Unspecified deer	fragment	43	18	--	--	1	--	--	1	63
	Cervidae	fragment	89	--	--	--	--	--	--	--	89
	White-tailed deer or pronghorn	fragment	--	1	--	4	1	--	--	2	8
	Bighorn sheep or pronghorn	fragment	--	12	--	--	--	--	--	1	13
	Bighorn sheep or mule deer	fragment	--	--	--	2	--	--	--	--	2
	Bighorn sheep	fragment	21	13	--	--	--	--	1	7	42
	Bighorn sheep	whole	--	1	--	--	--	--	--	3	4
	Artiodactyl	fragment	--	61	1	5	--	3	2	6	78
Total, Structure 27b			154	125	2	13	9	3	9	35	350
Structure 28	White-tailed deer	whole	--	--	--	--	--	--	--	1	1
Total, Structure 28			0	0	0	0	0	0	0	1	1
Structure 29	Artiodactyl	fragment	--	--	1	--	--	--	--	--	1
Total, Structure 29			0	0	1	0	0	0	0	0	1
Structure 30	White-tailed deer	fragment	--	--	--	--	3	--	1	2	6
	White-tailed deer	whole	--	--	--	--	--	--	--	1	1
	Unspecified deer	fragment	1	2	--	--	--	--	--	1	4
	Deer or elk	fragment	28	--	--	--	--	--	--	--	28
	White-tailed deer or pronghorn	fragment	--	--	--	--	--	--	--	1	1
	Pronghorn	fragment	--	--	--	--	--	--	2	--	2
	Bighorn sheep	fragment	--	--	--	--	--	--	--	1	1
	Artiodactyl	fragment	--	--	3	--	--	1	--	2	6
Total, Structure 30			29	2	3	0	3	1	3	8	49
Structure 31b	Unspecified deer	fragment	--	--	--	--	--	--	1	--	1
Total, Structure 31b			0	0	0	0	0	0	1	0	1
Southern Locus											
Structure 14	White-tailed deer	fragment	--	12	--	--	--	--	--	--	12
	Unspecified deer	fragment	--	2	--	--	--	--	--	--	2
	Artiodactyl	fragment	--	4	2	--	--	--	--	--	6
Total, Structure 14			0	18	2	0	0	0	0	0	20
Grand total			192	278	14	17	28	13	30	79	651

Note: Does not include bones found in Structure 19a as they were not part of detailed analysis.

human burial in the house. Based on locational information on analysis cards, the human bone that was bagged as animal bone, and drawings of a feature found on the floor and in the lower fill of the house, I suspect that most, if not all, of the bone was once in association with this burial. Most of the animal remains in this structure (artiodactyl and otherwise) exhibit some degree of burning, perhaps indicating that the structure was burned as part of a burial ritual.

The animal elements found with this burial indicate that whole carcasses may have been buried with the individual in Structure 27b. The animal remains and numerous other artifacts associated with the burial indicate that the individual was important. He may have been a great hunter or someone who could attract game.

Ritual deposition of artiodactyl remains was also evident in Structure 19a. In that structure, three and a half deer or pronghorn mandibles, an artiodactyl scapula, a pronghorn

Table 8.7. Burned Artiodactyl Bone.

Structure Number	Species or Category	Element	Number of Burned Pieces	Number of Calcined Pieces	Number of Charred Pieces	Total Number of Pieces
		Compound Locus				
4	White-tailed deer	tibia	1	--	--	1
		calcaneum	1	--	--	1
	Deer	antler tine	1	--	--	1
	Artiodactyl	skull fragment	1	--	--	1
		thoracic vertebrae	1	--	--	1
		tibia	1	--	--	1
Total, Structure 4			6	0	0	6
7	Deer	innominate	1	--	--	1
Total, Structure 7			1	0	0	1
8	Pronghorn	scapula	1	--		1
	Mule deer	mandible	7	--	1	8
		skull	21	--	--	21
		vertebrae	2	4	--	6
		scapula	1	--	--	1
	White-tailed deer	mandible	1	--	1	2
	Deer	maxilla or mandible	1	--	--	1
	Bighorn sheep	frontal	1	--	--	1
	Artiodactyl	skull	29	--	--	29
		mandible	1	--	2	3
		teeth	--	--	7	7
		scapula	--	1	--	1
		ischium	--	1	--	1
		tibia	--	--	1	1
Total, Structure 8			65	6	12	83
		Southwestern Locus				
11	Deer	ischium	--	--	1	1
Total, Structure 11			0	0	1	1
16	White-tailed deer	mandible	1	--	1	2
		innominate	2	--	1	3
	Deer	innominate	--	--	1	1
	Artiodactyl	innominate	1	--	2	3
Total, Structure 16			4	0	5	9
23	White-tailed deer	mandible	1	--	--	1
Total, Structure 23			1	0	0	1
25	Mule deer	sacrum	1	--	--	1
Total, Structure 25			1	0	0	1
		Northern Locus				
27	Artiodactyl	tibia	1	--	--	1
Total, Structure 27, Level 1			1	0	0	1
27a	White-tailed deer	calcaneum	1	--	--	1
Total, Structure 27a			1	0	0	1
27b	Pronghorn or White-tailed deer	innominate	1	--	--	1
		scapula	4	--	--	4
	White-tailed deer	scapula	1	--	--	1
		innominate	1	--	--	1
		foot bones	3	--	--	3
	Mule deer	antler	1	--	--	1
		cervical vertebrae	1	--	--	1
		pelvis	1	--	--	1

Table 8.7. Burned Artiodactyl Bone, cont'd.

Structure Number	Species or Category	Element	Number of Burned Pieces	Number of Calcined Pieces	Number of Charred Pieces	Total Number of Pieces
	Deer	antler	21	--	--	21
		metacarpal	1	--	--	1
	Cervid	antler	14	--	--	14
		undetermined	6	--	--	6
	Bighorn sheep or Mule deer	scapula	1	--	--	1
	Bighorn sheep	skull	7	--	--	7
		horn core	21	--	--	21
		proximal phalanx	1	--	--	1
	Artiodactyl	skull	7	--	--	7
		cervical vert #7	1	--	--	1
		scapula	3	--	--	3
		rib	1	1	--	2
		tibia	1	--	--	1
		foot bones	2	--	--	2
Total, Structure 27b			100	1	0	101
30	Pronghorn	humerus	1	--	--	1
		radius	1	--	--	1
	Pronghorn or White-tailed deer	metapodial	1	--	--	1
	White-tailed deer	radius	1	--	--	1
		innominate	3	--	--	3
		foot bones	3	--	--	3
	Deer	antler	1	--	--	1
		mandible	1	--	--	1
		metacarpal	1	--	--	1
	Cervid	antler	28	--	--	28
	Bighorn sheep	naviculo-cuboid	1	--	--	1
	Artiodactyl	lumbar vert	3	--	--	3
		rib	1	--	--	1
		foot bones	2	--	--	2
Total, Structure 30			48	--	0	48
Total Number of Pieces			228	7	18	253

skull, and assorted other bones of deer and pronghorn were found in one side of the house (Figures 8.2 to 8.4).

Other Animal Remains

Table 8.8 lists some of the less common animal remains found on the site. The turtle, bird, and canid bones may have been culturally deposited. Bird bones, found in four structures, include long bone fragments in Structures 10 and 31b, two long bone fragments from a large bird in Structure 16, and an ulna fragment from a medium-sized bird in Structure 25. One long bone from Structure 16 may have been from a golden eagle.

A turtle or tortoise carapace fragment was found on the floor of Structure 27b. The turtle or tortoise carapace fragment was burned, and may have been an artifact—a rattle or other tool—associated with the burial found in the house.

Bones from the dog family (Canidae) were found in three structures and in the compound. These are a metacarpal (foot bone) found in the fill of Structure 16; a fragment of a right humerus in the same feature that might have been from a coyote; a rib, possibly from a dog, found in a pit in Structure 18; and a burned left metacarpal and burned thoracic vertebral fragment found in Structure 27b.

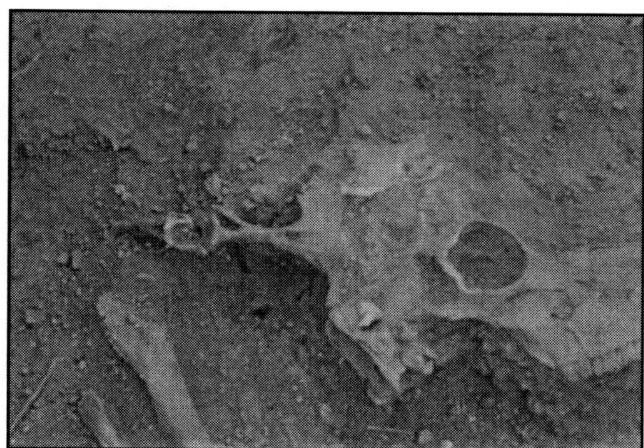

Figure 8.2. Pronghorn skull on floor of Structure 19a (photograph by Bruce Bradley).

Figure 8.3. Antlers on floor of Structure 19a (uncatalogued, courtesy Arizona State Museum, University of Arizona).

Figure 8.4. Deer or pronghorn jaws on floor of Structure 19a (uncatalogued, courtesy Arizona State Museum, University of Arizona).

Bone Tools and Ornaments

Whole and fragmentary bone tools or ornaments were found in nine houses. All but two of the tools or ornaments were made from medium-sized or large animals including deer, pronghorn, and other artiodactyls. Metapodials were a favored bone for producing tools. Many of the worked objects were grooved, indicating that craftsmen were creating tools using the "groove-and-snap" technique. In this technique, a groove is first incised into the bone. When deep enough, the bone is snapped in two along that groove. Most of the pieces appear to have been awls or hairpins. An antler tine flaking tool (from Structure 30), a possible weaving heddle (from Structure 19a), and a possible rasp (from Structure 16) were also found. In addition to artiodactyl bone, a small disk found in Cremation 4 appears to have been made from a human parietal. It is described further in Chapter 10. Brief descriptions of the nonhuman worked bone pieces are listed in Table 8.9.

Hunting and Hunting Ritual

Among the O'odham and the Zuni, who may be descendants of the Whiptail and Gibbon Springs residents, artiodactyl hunting, especially of deer, was done by specialists (Cushing 1988; Underhill 1946; Zuni People 1972). The Yuman tribes also engaged specialists to hunt artiodactyls (Spier 1970:69-70).

The Tohono O'odham considered deer, especially mule deer, to be dangerous animals. If treated incorrectly, they could send sickness to the village of the hunters (Rea 1998:240; Russell 1975). As a result, much care was taken in the hunt, with ceremonies before and after an animal was obtained (Underhill 1946:86).

When hunting in small groups, the Tohono O'odham used a deer-head disguise

Table 8.8. Distribution of Turtle or Tortoise, Bird, and Dog Family Bones and Bone Fragments.

Provenience	Turtle or Tortoise	Bird	Bird, medium songbird	Large bird	Large bird (golden eagle?)	Dog family	Possible coyote	Total No. of Occurrences
	Animal Species or Class							
Compound Locus								
Compound	--	--	--	--	--	1	--	1
Southwestern Locus								
Structure 10	--	1	--	--	--	--	--	1
Structure 16	--	--	--	1	1	1	1	4
Structure 18	--	--	--	--	--	1	--	1
Structure 25	--	--	1	--	--	--	--	1
Northern Locus								
Structure 27b	1	--	--	--	--	1	--	2
Structure 31b	--	1	--	--	--	--	--	1
Total No. of Occurrences	1	2	1	1	1	4	1	11

and accompanied their work with songs and dreams. Those who wore the deer head were called "headbearers." They went through extensive training to be able to wear the head. These professional hunters hunted year round, except in January when animals were thin and February "the month when deer smelled bad" (Underhill 1946:86). Successful hunters were able to supply enough meat for two to ten families (Underhill 1939:99). They considered 12 animals per year to be a good number (Underhill 1946:86).

The Tohono O'odham performed communal hunts in the winter season. Shamans would accompany these hunts, which could involve ritually smothering the animals after surrounding and clubbing them, or killing them with arrows, the stone points of which were described for Underhill (1946:87) as being "like the war arrows." The Zuni also reported smothering deer that were taken in communal hunting (Zuni People 1972). After butchering and distributing meat from a hunt, the bones were collected by shamans and "carefully put away where no dog could drag them about, and the horns [antlers] placed on the house roof or in some special repository" (Underhill 1946:86).

The O'odham and Yumans considered bighorn sheep to be sacred and, therefore, dangerous (Rea 1998:253-255; Spier 1970:69-70). The animals were hunted for meat and also for the hide, which was used, among other things, for sandals (Rea 1998:256). O'odham hunters killed the animals by waiting for them at waterholes. Rea's Gileño Piman informants indicated that bighorn sheep skulls, horns, and hides needed to be kept in a sacred place. If those remains were not kept "somewhere inside the house (usually) or in an undisturbed place outside" (Rea 1998:254), then a violent wind, severe rain, or a cold spell could result. Like the mule deer, bighorn sheep could also cause staying sickness. While the Gileños did not consider the remaining bones to be sacred or dangerous, Rea's Tohono O'odham informants indicated that bighorn sheep skulls and bones needed to be kept away from houses because of the danger of wind (Rea 1998:256, 258-259).

According to Rea (1998:250-251), pronghorns were regularly hunted by the O'odham, but were not considered sacred or dangerous.

Table 8.9. Worked Bone.

Provenience	Species/Class	Side	Bone	Descriptions	Number of Pieces
			Compound Locus		
Structure 7, fill	medium to large mammal	unknown	long bone	The awl or hairpin represented by this fragment was made by the groove and snap technique. No measurements were made.	1
			Southwestern Locus		
Structure 2, upper fill	Medium to large mammal	unknown	unidentified fragment, shaft	This 3-cm-long fragment may have been part of an awl or hair pin. It is calcined.	1
Structure 12, SE 1/4, lower fill	White-tailed deer	unknown	metacarpal	Burned fragment with a groove mark, possibly intended for groove and snap technique; ca. 2 cm by 2cm.	1
Structure 16, NW quad, lower fill	Large mammal	unknown	long bone	This burned fragment has series of incisions perpendicular to the length of the shaft; possible rasp? No measurements made.	1
Structure 23, SW 1/4 middle fill	Medium to large mammal	unknown	undetermined	Awl or hairpin fragment; no measurements made.	1
			Northern Locus		
Structure 27a, NE 1/4	Medium to large mammal	unknown	long bone	This burned fragment is part of an awl or hairpin made by the groove and snap technique. It has striations along and across the shaft; no measurements were made.	1
Structure 27a, NE 1/4 floor	Medium to large mammal	unknown	long bone	This fragment shows a groove and snap technique; it is polished on one side.	1
Structure 29, SE 1/4, Level 1A	Large mammal	unknown	cf. metapodial	This awl fragment consists of the distal end of the tool; the tip is shiny. No measurements were made.	1
Structure 29, SE 1/4, Level 1A	Medium to large mammal	unknown	undetermined	This fragment is part of an awl or hairpin fragment made with the groove and snap technique.	1
Structure 29, SE 1/4, level 1 A	Artiodactyl	unknown	metapodial	This awl tip fragment is polished and slightly weathered. It has a wide, blunt tip. No measurements were made.	1
Structure 30, NE 1/4, Level 3	White-tailed deer	right	metapodial	This burned fragment is from the proximal end of the bone. The fragment represents about one sixth of an awl or hairpin made through grooving.	1
Structure 30, SE 1/4 floor feature 5	Artiodactyl	unknown	metapodial	This burned fragment was grooved in preparation for grooving and snapping to make for awl and hairpin.	1
Structure 30, SW 1/4	Cervidae	unknown	antler tip	This tip was likely a flaking tool.	1
			Southern Locus		
Structure 19a	Large mammal	unknown	long bone	This possible weaving shuttle is 11.2 cm long and 1.2 cm in diameter at its widest. One end is pointed and awl-like; the other end is polished. The overall shape is a long, thin, curved, "kayak" shape. It has been shaped all along it, with polish heavier at each end.	1
Structure 19a	Large mammal	unknown	long bone	This tool is 6.8 cm long, 7 mm wide at one end, and 1 mm at pointed end. The wide end flattens out and has a couple of notches; it may have been a needle or an awl.	1
			Unprovenienced		
	Deer or pronghorn	left	metatarsal	This probable hairpin made with the groove and snap technique. The proximal end is polished; the tip is missing. It is about 15 cm long.	1
	Artiodactyl	unknown	metapodial	Complete hairpin or awl; no measurements given.	1
	Large mammal	unknown	metapodial	Fragment of an awl or hairpin; no measurements given.	1

Stalking them with the use of a pronghorn disguise would have been an effective hunting method for these curious animals.

At Whiptail, the presence of bone elements in "burned layers" (probably roof levels) and floors of various structures are suggestive of the ritual storage described by Underhill (1939, 1946) and Rea (1998). And the deer skulls, skull fragments, and bighorn sheep skull and horn core fragments found in various features, along with lower leg and toe bones of deer found in many of those same features are suggestive of "headbearer" disguises (Table 8.6). The complete pronghorn skull found in Structure 19a indicates that pronghorn may have had the same ritual importance to the inhabitants of Whiptail as deer and bighorn sheep.

Discussion and Summary

The faunal assemblage from Whiptail Ruin resembles other Classic period assemblages from the eastern Tucson Basin. Artiodactyl bone was more common than lagomorph bone at the Gibbon Springs site (Strand 1996) and University Indian Ruin (Guo-qin 1983) as it was at Whiptail. This abundance of hoofed animal bone in relation to rabbit and hare bone is seen at upland Hohokam sites (Bayham 1982; Szuter 1991; Szuter and Bayham 1989). This may simply be a factor in availability of game at these sites; why spend energy on rabbits when bigger game is immediately available?

Gibbon Springs and Whiptail Ruin were used as hunting areas since Archaic times, and University Indian Ruin is situated near a large mesquite bosque with perennial water—an ideal place for finding deer. The area east of Whiptail, approaching the base of Redington Pass is open and grassy—well-suited to pronghorn (as well as jackrabbit). The ridges above Whiptail and Gibbon Springs would have been prime bighorn territory. The low density of human habitation in the area compared to the area along the Santa Cruz to the west may have allowed a higher number of deer, pronghorn, and bighorn to flourish around Whiptail.

Artiodactyls may have been the most important animal food source for the inhabitants of Whiptail, but jackrabbit and cottontail were part of the diet. The numerous lagomorph bones found at the site likely represent some combination of naturally and culturally deposited remains, but it is certain that some of the bone represents the remnants of meals.

Artiodactyl antler and foot and leg bones were commonly used as tools at Whiptail. Awl or hairpin fragments were the most common tool found, but a possible rasp, weaving shuttle, and stone manufacturing tool (from an antler tine) were also found at the site.

Ritual use of bone is also evident at Whiptail. Among the bones that can be associated with ceremony are the "string" of lagomorph innominates, the pronghorn skull, and the artiodactyl scapula and leg and foot bones found in Structure 19a. A more obvious ritual association was found in Structure 27b, where remains of bighorn, white-tail deer, mule deer, turtle or tortoise carapace, and a burned canid vertebra and foot bone were found in association with a human burial. The artiodactyl offerings may indicate that the individual buried in the structure was an accomplished hunter.

Several structures contained artiodactyl skull and/or antler and horn parts (Table 8.6). This could indicate that skulls or, more likely, heads and skins, were a common part of household furniture for the people at Whiptail. If the Whiptail residents had the same ceremonial relationship with artiodactyls as the O'odham, then the animal items found in the structures would have been important parts of hunting ritual.

The bird bone found at the site may also be indicative of ritual, but the contexts are not clear. Long bone fragments from a large bird (possibly an eagle) were found in Structure 16, which also contained a right humeral fragment that may have been from a coyote. This possible association of a large bird and a coyote is intriguing. The pieces were found in the fill of the house, so they may have been from items that were hung from the ceiling of the house, or they could be trash fill.

The pattern of animal use seen at Whiptail is similar to that found at Gibbon Springs and other upland Hohokam sites, especially those dating to the Classic period. The emphasis on deer, bighorn, and pronghorn use over jackrabbit and rabbit use may be the natural result of the site's upland setting adjacent to permanent water sources. But there is also strong evidence that the artiodactyl remains in particular have a ritual association. The possible storage of artiodactyl bones in various features and the presence of skulls that could have been used in hunting disguises suggest that Whiptail housed hunting specialists.

Appendix 8.A. Data on Bone Recovered from Whiptail.

Provenience	Species or Class	Side	Bone	Burned, calcined, charred	Weathered	Whole or fragment	Total No. of Items
			Compound Locus				
Structure 4, pothole fill	*Lepus* sp.	right	radius		no	fragment	1
Structure 4, pothole fill	large mammal	undetermined	unidentified	burned	no	fragment	1
Structure 4, upper fill	*Ammospermophilus harrisii*	left	humerus		no	whole	1
Structure 4, upper fill	*Lepus californicus*	left	innominate		yes	fragment	1
Structure 4, upper fill	*Lepus californicus*	right	calcaneum		yes	whole	1
Structure 4, upper fill	*Sylvilagus* sp.	right	innominate		yes	fragment	1
Structure 4, upper fill	*Odocoileus virginianus*	right	astragalus		yes	whole	1
Structure 4, upper fill	Artiodactyl	right	metapodial		yes	fragment	1
Structure 4, upper fill	Artiodactyl	undetermined	humerus		no	fragment	1
Structure 4, upper fill	Artiodactyl	undetermined	humerus		yes	fragment	1
Structure 4, upper fill	Artiodactyl	undetermined	tibia	burned	no	fragment	1
Structure 4, upper fill	medium mammal	undetermined	long bone	burned	no	fragment	1
Structure 4, upper fill	medium to large mammal	undetermined	skull	burned	no	fragment	1
Structure 4, upper fill	medium to large mammal	undetermined	unidentified		no	fragment	2
Structure 4, upper fill	medium to large mammal	undetermined	unidentified	burned	no	fragment	1
Structure 4, upper fill	medium to large mammal	undetermined	unidentified	calcined	no	fragment	1
Structure 4, upper fill	medium to large mammal	undetermined	unidentified	charred	no	fragment	4
Structure 4, upper fill	large mammal	undetermined	rib		no	fragment	4
Structure 4, upper fill	large mammal	undetermined	unidentified		no	fragment	3
Structure 4, upper fill	large mammal	undetermined	unidentified	calcined	no	fragment	2
Structure 4, upper fill	indeterminate mammal	undetermined	unidentified	calcined	no	fragment	1
Structure 4, fill	Colubridae	not applicable	vertebra		yes	whole	1
Structure 4, fill	Colubridae	undetermined	vertebra	burned	no	fragment	1
Structure 4, fill	*Lepus alleni*	left	humerus		no	whole	3
Structure 4, fill	*Lepus alleni*	left	scapula		no	fragment	1
Structure 4, fill	*Lepus alleni*	left	ulna	calcined	no	fragment	1
Structure 4, fill	*Lepus alleni*	right	calcaneum		yes	whole	1
Structure 4, fill	*Lepus alleni*	undetermined	phalange		no	whole	1
Structure 4, fill	*Lepus californicus*	left	humerus		no	fragment	1
Structure 4, fill	*Sylvilagus* sp.	undetermined	humerus		no	fragment	1
Structure 4, fill	*Odocoileus* sp.	undetermined	antler tine	burned	no	fragment	1
Structure 4, fill	*Odocoileus virginianus*	left	tibia	burned	no	fragment	1
Structure 4, fill	Artiodactyl	right	skull	burned	no	fragment	1
Structure 4 fill	Artiodactyl	undetermined	thoracic vertebra	burned	no	fragment	1
Structure 4, fill	small to medium mammal	undetermined	long bone		no	fragment	3
Structure 4, fill	small to medium mammal	undetermined	unidentified		yes	fragment	3
Structure 4, fill	small to medium mammal	undetermined	unidentified	burned	no	fragment	1
Structure 4, fill	small to medium mammal	undetermined	vertebra		no	fragment	1
Structure 4 fill	medium to large mammal	undetermined	unidentified		no	fragment	2
Struture 4 fill	medium to large mammal	undetermined	skull	burned	no	fragment	1
Structure 4, fill	medium to large mammal	undetermined	unidentified	calcined	no	fragment	5
Structure 4 fill	medium to large mammal	undetermined	long bone	burned	no	fragment	2
Structure 4 fill	medium to large mammal	undetermined	unidentified		no	fragment	1
Structure 4 fill	small mammal	undetermined	long bone		no	fragment	1
Structure 4 fill	small mammal	undetermined	unidentified		no	fragment	1
Structure 4, lower fill	*Lepus californicus*	undetermined	phalange		no	fragment	2
Structure 4, lower fill	*Lepus* sp.	left	humerus		no	fragment	1
Structure 4, lower fill	*Lepus* sp.	undetermined	mandible		no	fragment	1
Structure 4, lower fill	*Lepus* sp.	undetermined	proximal phalange		no	fragment	1
Structure 4, lower fill	*Lepus* sp.	undetermined	radius		no	fragment	1
Structure 4, lower fill	*Odocoileus virginianus*	left	calcaneum	burned	no	fragment	1
Structure 4, lower fill	Artiodactyl	undetermined	metapodial		no	fragment	1
Structure 4, lower fill	medium to large mammal	undetermined	long bone		no	fragment	1
Structure 4, lower fill	medium to large mammal	undetermined	rib		no	fragment	1

Appendix 8.A. Data on Bone Recovered from Whiptail, cont'd.

Provenience	Species or Class	Side	Bone	Burned, calcined, charred	Weathered	Whole or fragment	Total No. of Items
Structure 4, lower fill	medium to large mammal	undetermined	unidentified		no	fragment	15
Structure 4, lower fill	large mammal	undetermined	tibia		no	fragment	1
Structure 4, lower fill	large mammal	undetermined	unidentified		no	fragment	5
Structure 4 floor fill	*Lepus californicus*	right	ulna	charred	no	fragment	1
Structure 4 floor	*Lepus alleni*	left	metacarpal		no	whole	2
Structure 4, hearth fill	*Lepus alleni*	left	femur		no	fragment	1
Structure 4, hearth fill	*Lepus alleni*	left	tibia		no	fragment	1
Structure 6, upper fill	*Odocoileus virginianus*	right	proximal phalange		yes	whole	1
Structure 6, upper fill	medium to large mammal	undetermined	unidentified		no	fragment	1
Structure 6, lower fill	Artiodactyl	undetermined	rib		no	fragment	1
Structure 6, lower fill	medium mammal	undetermined	rib?		no	fragment	3
Structure 6, lower fill, water washed area	*Lepus* sp.	left	long bone		no	fragment	3
Structure 6, lower fill, water washed area	*Lepus* sp.	undetermined	rib		no	fragment	4
Structure 6, lower fill, water washed area	large mammal	undetermined	unidentified		no	fragment	1
Structure 6, lower fill, water washed area	medium to small mammal	undetermined	unidentified		no	fragment	3
Structure 6, hard adobe layer	small mammal	undetermined	unidentified	calcined	no	fragment	1
Structure 6 SW corner	large mammal	undetermined	long bone		no	fragment	4
Structure 6 SW corner	large mammal	undetermined	rib		no	fragment	1
Structure 6, SW corner	Artiodactyl	undetermined	metapodial		no	fragment	1
Structure 6, SW corner	*Lepus californicus*	right	radius		no	fragment	1
Structure 6, SW corner	*Sylvilagus* sp.	right	tibia		no	fragment	1
Structure 6, SW corner	small mammal	undetermined	long bone		no	fragment	1
Structure 6, SW corner	small mammal	undetermined	unidentified		no	fragment	2
Structure 6, corner	*Sylvilagus* sp.	right	calcaneum		no	whole	1
Structure 6, floor fill	Artiodactyl	undetermined	tooth		no	fragment	12
Structure 6, floor fill	*Odocoileus* sp.	undetermined	mandible		yes	fragment	1
Structure 6, floor fill	*Odocoileus* sp.	undetermined	tooth fragments		no	fragment	18
Structure 6, floor fill	*Odocoileus virginianus* or *Antilocapra americana*	right	mandible		yes	fragment	1
Structure 6, floor fill	*Odocoileus virginianus* or *Antilocapra americana*	undetermined	mandible		yes	fragment	1
Structure 6, floor fill	indeterminate mammal	undetermined	unidentified		yes	fragment	15
Structure 6, floor fill	medium to large mammal	undetermined	unidentified		yes	fragment	22
Structure 7, top	medium to small mammal	undetermined	long bone		no	fragment	1
Structure 7, top	medium to small mammal	undetermined	unidentified	calcined	no	fragment	2
Structure 7, wall fall	medium to large mammal	undetermined	unidentified		no	fragment	1
Structure 7, SE 1/4 pollen column	*Odocoileus* sp.	right	innominate	burned	no	fragment	1
Structure 7 fill	medium mammal	undetermined	long bone	calcined	no	fragment	1
Structure 7 fill	medium mammal	undetermined	unidentified		no	fragment	1
Structure 7 fill	medium mammal	undetermined	unidentified	calcined	no	fragment	1
Structure 7, E 1/2 screened	medium mammal	undetermined	unidentified		no	fragment	2
Structure 7, E 1/2 screened	medium to large mammal	undetermined	unidentified	burned	no	fragment	1
Structure 7, E 1/2 level 3	*Sylvilagus* sp.	right	humerus		yes	fragment	1
Structure 7, E 1/2, level 3	medium to large mammal	undetermined	long bone		no	fragment	1
Structure 7, E 1/2, level 3	medium to large mammal	undetermined	unidentified		no	fragment	5
Structure 7, E 1/2, level 3	medium to large mammal	undetermined	unidentified	burned	no	fragment	3
Structure 7, E 1/4 fill	indeterminate	undetermined	unidentified		no	fragment	1
Structure 7, level 3	*Lepus* sp.	undetermined	rib		no	fragment	1
Structure 7, level 3	*Odocoileus virginianus*	left	mesial phalange		no	whole	1
Structure 7, level 3	medium mammal	undetermined	unidentified		no	fragment	4
Structure 7, level 3	medium to large mammal	undetermined	long bone	calcined	no	fragment	1
Structure 7, level 3	medium to large mammal	undetermined	unidentified		no	fragment	4
Structure 7, level 3	medium to large mammal	undetermined	unidentified	burned	no	fragment	3

Appendix 8.A. Data on Bone Recovered from Whiptail, cont'd.

Provenience	Species or Class	Side	Bone	Burned, calcined, charred	Weathered	Whole or fragment	Total No. of Items
Structure 7, level 3	medium to large mammal	undetermined	unidentified	calcined	no	fragment	1
Structure 7, level 3	indeterminate mammal	undetermined	unidentified		no	fragment	1
Structure 7, level 3 burned layer	jackrabbit-sized mammal	undetermined	tibia?		no	fragment	1
Structure 7, level 3 burned layer	jackrabbit-sized mammal	undetermined	unidentified		no	fragment	1
Structure 7, level 3 burned layer	medium to large mammal	undetermined	unidentified		no	fragment	1
Structure 7, level 3 burned layer	medium to large mammal	undetermined	unidentified	burned	no	fragment	1
Structure 7, level 3, burned layer	indeterminate	undetermined	unidentified		no	fragment	1
Structure 8, SW 1/4, outside, stripping	*Lepus californicus*	left	mandible		no	fragment	1
Structure 8, SW 1/4, outside, stripping	*Lepus californicus*	undetermined	cheek tooth		no	whole	1
Structure 8, NE 1/4, outside wall	large mammal	undetermined	long bone		yes	fragment	1
Structure 8, NE 1/4, outside wall	medium to large mammal	undetermined	unidentified	burned	no	fragment	1
Structure 8, NW 1/4 next to wall	medium to large mammal	undetermined	unidentified	burned	no	fragment	2
Structure 8, NW 1/4, outside wall	Artiodactyl	right	tibia	charred	no	fragment	1
Structure 8, outside wall, NE 1/4	mammal	undetermined	unidentified		no	fragment	1
Structure 8, outside south wall	large mammal	undetermined	long bone	calcined	no	fragment	1
Structure 8, stripping outside wall	small mammal	undetermined	long bone		no	fragment	1
Structure 8, stripping, NE 1/4	medium to large mammal	undetermined	unidentified		no	fragment	1
Structure 8, test pit fill	large mammal	undetermined	long bone	calcined	no	fragment	1
Structure 8, upper fill	*Odocoileus virginianus*	undetermined	proximal phalange		yes	fragment	1
Structure 8, upper fill	indeterminate mammal	undetermined	unidentified		no	fragment	8
Structure 8, upper fill	indeterminate mammal	undetermined	unidentified	burned	no	fragment	3
Structure 8, wall cleaning	large mammal	undetermined	long bone		no	fragment	1
Structure 8, E-W trench along N wall	Artiodactyl	left	scapula	calcined	no	fragment	1
Structure 8, E-W trench along N wall	small mammal	undetermined	unidentified		no	fragment	1
Structure 8, level 2 fill	*Odocoileus virginianus*	undetermined	mesial phalange		yes	whole	1
Structure 8, level 3	Artiodactyl	undetermined	rib		no	fragment	1
Structure 8, level 3	*Odocoileus virginianus*	right	proximal phalange		no	fragment	1
Structure 8, level 3	medium to large mammal	undetermined	unidentified		no	fragment	1
Structure 8, NW 1/4	*Antilocapra americana*	left	scapula	burned	no	fragment	1
Structure 8, NW 1/4	*Odocoileus virginianus*	undetermined	metapodial		yes	fragment	1
Structure 8, NW corner	Artiodactyl	undetermined	cheek teeth		yes	fragment	6
Structure 8, NW quad	Artiodactyl	left	occipital condyle	burned	no	fragment	12
Structure 8, NW quad	Artiodactyl	undetermined	mandible		no	fragment	10
Structure 8, NW quad	Artiodactyl	undetermined	mandible	burned	no	fragment	1
Structure 8, NW quad	Artiodactyl	undetermined	mandible	charred	no	fragment	2
Structure 8, NW quad	Artiodactyl	undetermined	skull	burned	no	fragment	6
Structure 8, NW quad	Artiodactyl	undetermined	teeth	charred	no	fragment	7
Structure 8, NW quad	Artiodactyl	undetermined	temporal	burned	no	fragment	11
Structure 8, NW 1/4	small mammal	undetermined	unidentified		no	fragment	1
Structure 8, NW 1/4	medium mammal	undetermined	flat bone		yes	fragment	1
Structure 8, NW 1/4	medium mammal	undetermined	long bone	calcined	no	fragment	2
Structure 8, NW 1/4	medium mammal	undetermined	skull	burned	no	fragment	10
Structure 8, NW 1/4	indeterminate mammal	undetermined	long bone		no	fragment	2
Structure 8, NW 1/4, level 4, burned layer	*Odocoileus virginianus*	undetermined	metapodial #5		yes	fragment	1
Structure 8, NW 1/4, level 4, burned layer	*Odocoileus hemionus*	left	mandible	burned	no	fragment	3
Structure 8, NW 1/4, level 4, burned layer	*Odocoileus hemionus*	right	mandible	burned	no	fragment	4
Structure 8, NW 1/4, level 4, burned layer	*Odocoileus hemionus*	right	skull	burned	no	fragment	9

Appendix 8.A. Data on Bone Recovered from Whiptail, cont'd.

Provenience	Species or Class	Side	Bone	Burned, calcined, charred	Weathered	Whole or fragment	Total No. of Items
Structure 8, NW 1/4, level 4, burned layer	*Odocoileus hemionus*	undetermined	auditory meatus	burned	no	fragment	2
Structure 8, NW 1/4, level 4, burned layer	*Odocoileus hemionus*	undetermined	skull	burned	no	fragment	10
Structure 8, NW 1/4, level 4, burned layer	*Odocoileus hemionus*	undetermined	vertebrae	calcined	no	fragment	4
Structure 8, NW 1/4 burned layer	*Odocoileus hemionus*	left	scapula	burned	no	fragment	1
Structure 8, NW 1/4 burned layer	*Odocoileus hemionus*	not applicable	spinus process	burned	no	fragment	2
Structure 8, NW 1/4, burn layer above floor	large mammal	undetermined	long bone		yes	fragment	9
Structure 8, NE 1/4	*Sylvilagus* sp.	right	femur		yes	whole	1
Structure 8, NE 1/4	*Odocoileus virginianus*	right	mandible		no	fragment	1
Structure 8, NE 1/4	medium to large mammal	undetermined	unidentified	burned	no	fragment	1
Structure 8, NE 1/4	small mammal	undetermined	unidentified		no	fragment	4
Structure 8, NE 1/4 outside	medium to large mammal	undetermined	unidentified		yes	fragment	1
Structure 8, SE 1/4	*Odocoileus virginianus* or *Antilocapra americana*	undetermined	rib		no	fragment	1
Structure 8, SE 1/4	*Odocoileus virginianus*	left	distal phalange		no	whole	1
Structure 8, SE 1/4	*Odocoileus virginianus*	left	proximal phalange		no	whole	1
Structure 8, SE 1/4	*Odocoileus virginianus*	right	calcaneum		no	fragment	2
Structure 8, SE 1/4	*Odocoileus virginianus*	right	distal phalange		no	whole	1
Structure 8, SE 1/4	*Odocoileus virginianus*	right	mesial phalange		no	whole	1
Structure 8, SE 1/4	*Odocoileus virginianus*	right	proximal phalange		no	whole	1
Structure 8, SE 1/4	*Odocoileus virginianus*	right	proximal phalange		no	whole	1
Structure 8, SE 1/4	large mammal	undetermined	long bone		no	fragment	2
Structure 8, NW 1/4, level 4	Artiodactyl	undetermined	antler		yes	fragment	1
Structure 8, NW 1/4, level 4	Artiodactyl	undetermined	ischium	calcined	no	fragment	1
Structure 8, NW 1/4, level 4	Artiodactyl	undetermined	metapodial		no	fragment	1
Structure 8, NW 1/4, level 4	Artiodactyl	undetermined	rib		no	fragment	1
Structure 8, NW 1/4, level 4	Cervidae	undetermined	antler		yes	fragment	1
Structure 8, NW 1/4, level 4	*Lepus californicus*	left	radius		no	fragment	1
Structure 8, NW 1/4, level 4	*Lepus californicus*	right	scapula		yes	fragment	1
Structure 8, NW 1/4, level 4	*Odocoileus virginianus*	left	proximal phalange		yes	fragment	1
Structure 8, NW 1/4, level 4	*Odocoileus virginianus*	left	proximal phalange		no	whole	1
Structure 8, NW 1/4, level 4	*Odocoileus virginianus*	left	radius		yes	fragment	1
Structure 8, NW 1/4, level 4	*Odocoileus virginianus*	right	ulna		yes	fragment	1
Structure 8, NW 1/4, level 4	large mammal	undetermined	flat bone		yes	fragment	2
Structure 8, NW 1/4, level 4	large mammal	undetermined	flat bone	burned	yes	fragment	2
Structure 8, NW 1/4, level 4	large mammal	undetermined	long bone	burned	no	fragment	1
Structure 8, NW 1/4, level 4	medium to large mammal	undetermined	unidentified		no	fragment	2
Structure 8, NW 1/4, level 4	small mammal	undetermined	unidentified		no	fragment	4
Structure 8, NE 1/4, level 4	*Lepus californicus*	left	metatarsal # 3		no	fragment	1
Structure 8, NE 1/4, level 4	*Lepus californicus*	right	humerus		no	fragment	2
Structure 8, NE 1/4, level 4	*Lepus californicus*	right	radius		no	fragment	1
Structure 8, NE 1/4, level 4	*Lepus californicus*	right	ulna		no	fragment	1
Structure 8, NE 1/4, level 4	*Lepus californicus*	undetermined	phalange		no	whole	1
Structure 8, NE 1/4, level 4	*Sylvilagus* sp.	right	calcaneum		no	whole	1
Structure 8, NE 1/4, level 4	*Odocoileus* sp.	undetermined	cheek teeth		no	fragment	4
Structure 8, NE 1/4, level 4	*Odocoileus* sp.	undetermined	maxilla or mandible	burned	no	fragment	1
Structure 8, NE 1/4,level 4	large mammal	undetermined	unidentified		no	fragment	1
Structure 8, NE 1/4,level 4	large mammal	undetermined	unientified	burned	no	fragment	3
Structure 8, SE 1/4, level 4	*Lepus* sp.	undetermined	tibia		no	fragment	1

Appendix 8.A. Data on Bone Recovered from Whiptail, cont'd.

Provenience	Species or Class	Side	Bone	Burned, calcined, charred	Weathered	Whole or fragment	Total No. of Items
Structure 8, SE 1/4, level 4	*Sylvilagus sp.*	undetermined	humerus		no	fragment	1
Structure 8, SE 1/4, level 4	*Odocoileus virginianus*	left	proximal phalange		no	fragment	1
Structure 8, SE 1/4, level 4	*Antilocapra americana*	undetermined	rib fragment		no	fragment	1
Structure 8, SE 1/4, level 4	Artiodactyl	undetermined	rib		no	fragment	2
Structure 8, SE 1/4, level 4	Artiodactyl	undetermined	ulna		yes	fragment	1
Structure 8, SE 1/4, level 4	large mammal	undetermined	unidentified		no	fragment	1
Structure 8, SE 1/4, level 4	medium to large mammal	undetermined	unidentified		no	fragment	13
Structure 8, SE 1/4, level 4	small mammal	undetermined	unidentified		no	fragment	7
Structure 8, SW 1/4, level 4	*Lepus californicus*	left	femur		no	fragment	1
Structure 8, SW 1/4, level 4	*Sylvilagus* sp.	left	innominate		no	fragment	1
Structure 8, SW 1/4, level 4	*Odocoileus* or *Antilocapra*	left	bulla tympanica		no	fragment	1
Structure 8, SW 1/4, level 4	*Odocoileus virginianus*	right	mesial phalange		no	fragment	2
Structure 8, SW 1/4, level 4	Artiodactyl	right	metacarpal		no	fragment	1
Structure 8, SW 1/4, level 4	small animal	undetermined	unidentified		no	fragment	1
Structure 8, W 1/3 of room, level 4	large mammal	undetermined	unidentified	burned	no	fragment	1
Structure 8, W 1/3 of room, level 4	medium to large mammal	undetermined	long bone	calcined	no	fragment	2
Structure 8, level 4	*Lepus* sp.	undetermined	mandible		no	fragment	2
Structure 8, level 4	*Lepus californicus*	left	mandible		no	fragment	1
Structure 8, level 4	*Lepus californicus*	right	mandible		no	fragment	2
Structure 8, level 4	*Lepus californicus*	right	tibia		yes	fragment	1
Structure 8, level 4	*Lepus californicus*	undetermined	incisor		no	fragment	8
Structure 8, level 4	*Odocoileus virginianus*	right	mesial phalange		no	fragment	1
Structure 8, level 4	*Odocoileus virginianus*	right	proximal phalange		no	whole	1
Structure 8, level 4 fill	indeterminate mammal	undetermined	unidentified		no	fragment	4
Structure 8, level 4 floor	large mammal	undetermined	long bone		no	fragment	1
Structure 8, NE 1/4, floor	medium to large mammal	undetermined	long bone		no	fragment	2
Structure 8, NE 1/4, floor	medium to large mammal	undetermined	skull	burned	no	fragment	14
Structure 8, NE 1/4, floor	medium to large mammal	undetermined	skull?		yes	fragment	1
Structure 8, NW 1/4 floor	*Lepus californicus*	left	mandible	burned	no	fragment	1
Structure 8 NW 1/4, floor next to N wall	*Lepus* sp.	undetermined	mandible	burned	no	fragment	4
Structure 8, NW 1/4 floor	*Odocoileus virginianus*	left	mandible		no	fragment	2
Structure 8, NW 1/4 floor	*Odocoileus virginianus*	left	scapula		no	fragment	1
Structure 8, NW 1/4 floor	*Odocoileus virginianus*	right	ascending ramus	burned	no	fragment	1
Structure 8, NW 1/4 floor	*Odocoileus virginianus*	right	mandible	charred	no	fragment	1
Structure 8, NW 1/4 floor	*Odocoileus virginianus*	undetermined	tooth		no	fragment	1
Structure 8, NW 1/4 floor	*Ovis canadensis*	left	horn core		no	fragment	1
Structure 8, NW 1/4 floor	*Ovis canadensis*	right	horn core		no	fragment	1
Structure 8, NW 1/4 floor	*Ovis canadensis*	undetermined	frontal	burned	no	fragment	1
Structure 8, NW 1/4 floor	*Ovis canadensis*	undetermined	horn core		no	fragment	2
Structure 8, NW 1/4 floor	Artiodactyl	undetermined	antler		yes	fragment	2
Structure 8, NW 1/4 floor	indeterminate mammal	undetermined	unidentified		no	fragment	3
Structure 8, NW 1/4 floor	indeterminate mammal	undetermined	unidentified	burned	no	fragment	5
Structure 8, NW 1/4, floor	Artiodactyl	undetermined	phalange		yes	fragment	1
Structure 8, NW 1/4, floor	medium to large mammal	undetermined	unidentified	burned	no	fragment	43
Structure 8, SE 1/4 floor	*Lepus californicus*	left	metatarsal #3		no	fragment	1
Structure 8, SE 1/4 floor	*Lepus californicus*	right	calcaneum		no	whole	1
Structure 8, SE 1/4 floor	*Lepus californicus*	undetermined	hind proximal phalange		no	whole	1
Structure 8, SE 1/4, floor	medium to large mammal	undetermined	unidentified		no	fragment	7
Structure 8, SW 1/4 level floor	large mammal	undetermined	long bone		no	fragment	14
Structure 8, floor along N wall	large mammal	undetermined	unidentified		no	fragment	1
Structure 8, main post hole	*Lepus californicus*	left	hind proximal phalange		no	whole	1
Structure 17, lower fill, test pit on east wall	*Lepus* sp.	undetermined	incisor		no	fragment	1

Appendix 8.A. Data on Bone Recovered from Whiptail, cont'd.

Provenience	Species or Class	Side	Bone	Burned, calcined, charred	Weathered	Whole or fragment	Total No. of Items
Structure 17, NW 1/4, lower fill	medium to large mammal	undetermined	unidentified	burned	no	fragment	1
Structure 17, SE 1/4, upper fill	medium to large mammal	undetermined	unidentified	calcined	no	fragment	1
Compound trench 3 along west wall	small mammal	undetermined	unidentified		no	fragment	3
Compound NE corner, level 2	Canid?	undetermined	proximal phalange		no	fragment	1
Compound NE corner, level 2	medium to large mammal	undetermined	unidentified		no	fragment	2
Compound, NE corner	cf. *Neotoma albigua*	not applicable	thoracic vertebra		no	whole	1
Compound, NE corner	medium to large mammal	undetermined	unidentified	calcined	no	fragment	1
		Central Locus					
Structure 15 NW 1/4	*Lepus* sp.	undetermined	proximal phalange		yes	whole	1
Structure 15, W & S wall, finding	large mammal	undetermined	long bone		yes	fragment	2
Structure 32 B SE quad, floor	rodent	undetermined	tibia		yes	whole	1
		Southwestern Locus					
Structure 2 fill	indeterminate mammal	undetermined	unidentified	calcined	no	fragment	1
Structure 2 fill	medium to large mammal	undetermined	unidentified	calcined	no	fragment	2
Structure 2 fill	small mammal	undetermined	unidentified	calcined	no	fragment	1
Structure 2,upper fill	indeterminate mammal	undetermined	unidentified	calcined	no	fragment	1
Structure 2,upper fill	medium to large mammal	undetermined	unidentified	calcined	no	fragment	2
Structure 2,upper fill	small mammal	undetermined	unidentified	calcined	no	fragment	1
Structure 2 lower fill	medium to large mammal	undetermined	unidentified		no	fragment	1
Structure 2,lower fill	medium to large mammal	undetermined	unidentified	calcined	no	fragment	1
Structure 9	large mammal	undetermined	unidentified	calcined	no	fragment	1
Structure 9	medium to large mammal	undetermined	unidentified		no	fragment	4
Structure 10, fill between 10 & 12	medium to large mammal	undetermined	radius?	calcined	no	fragment	1
Structure 10, fill between 10 & 12	medium to large mammal	undetermined	unidentified		no	fragment	1
Structure 10, N wall cleanup	medium to large mammal	undetermined	unidentified	calcined	no	fragment	1
Structure 10, SW 1/4 lower fill	*Lepus californicus*	undetermined	proximal phalange		no	whole	1
Structure 10, upper fill	bird	left	long bone		no	fragment	1
Structure 10, upper fill	*Neotoma albigua*	left	mandible		no	whole	1
Structure 10, upper fill	*Lepus californicus*	left	femur		no	fragment	1
Structure 10, upper fill	*Lepus californicus*	left	metatarsal # 3		no	whole	1
Structure 10, upper fill	*Lepus californicus*	left	metatarsal # 4		no	whole	1
Structure 10, upper fill	*Lepus californicus*	left	scapula		no	fragment	1
Structure 10, upper fill	*Lepus californicus*	right	metacarpal # 3		no	whole	1
Structure 10, upper fill	*Lepus californicus*	right	metatarsal # 2		no	whole	1
Structure 10, upper fill	*Lepus californicus*	right	metatarsal # 5		no	whole	1
Structure 10, upper fill	*Lepus californicus*	right	metatarsal #4		no	whole	1
Structure 10, upper fill	*Lepus californicus*	undetermined	distal phalange		no	whole	2
Structure 10, upper fill	*Lepus californicus*	undetermined	lumbar vert # 3		no	fragment	1
Structure 10, upper fill	*Lepus californicus*	undetermined	lumbar vert # 5		no	fragment	1
Structure 10, upper fill	*Lepus californicus*	undetermined	lumbar vert #6		no	fragment	1
Structure 10, upper fill	*Lepus californicus*	undetermined	lumbar vert #7		no	fragment	1
Structure 10, upper fill	*Lepus californicus*	undetermined	mesial phalange		no	whole	3
Structure 10, upper fill	*Lepus californicus*	undetermined	proximal phalange		no	whole	4
Structure 10, upper fill	*Lepus californicus*	undetermined	sacrum		no	fragment	1
Structure 10, upper fill	*Lepus* sp.	undetermined	vertebrae		no	fragment	3
Structure 10, upper fill	*Odocoileus virginianus coues*	left	astragalus		no	whole	1
Structure 10, upper fill	small mammal	undetermined	long bone	calcined	no	fragment	1
Structure 10, upper fill	small mammal	undetermined	unidentified		no	fragment	6
Structure 10, lower fill	*Neotoma albigua*	right	femur		no	whole	1
Structure 10, lower fill	*Lepus californicus*	left	metatarsal # 2		no	fragment	1
Structure 10, lower fill	*Lepus californicus*	right	humerus		no	whole	1

Appendix 8.A. Data on Bone Recovered from Whiptail, cont'd.

Provenience	Species or Class	Side	Bone	Burned, calcined, charred	Weathered	Whole or fragment	Total No. of Items
Structure 10, lower fill	*Ammosperm.* or *Spermoph.*	left	innominate		no	whole	1
Structure 10, lower fill	medium to large mammal	undetermined	unidentified		no	fragment	1
Structure 10, lower fill	medium to large mammal	undetermined	unidentified	burned	no	fragment	1
Structure 10, lower fill	small mammal	undetermined	unidentified	burned	no	fragment	1
Structure 10, wall cleanup	small mammal	undetermined	unidentified		no	fragment	1
Structure 11, wall stripping	medium to large mammal	undetermined	unidentified	burned	no	fragment	1
Structure 11, N wall trench	medium to large mammal	undetermined	unidentified	burned	no	fragment	2
Structure 11, middle fill, E end	large mammal	undetermined	unidentified		no	fragment	1
Structure 11, middle fill, E end	large mammal	undetermined	unidentified	burned	no	fragment	1
Structure 11, lower fill	*Odocoileus virginianus* or *Antilocapra americana*	undetermined	proximal phalange		no	fragment	1
Structure 11, W 1/2, lower fill	*Odocoileus* sp.	undetermined	ischium	charred	no	fragment	1
Structure 11, lower fill	Artiodactyl	left	humerus		no	fragment	1
Structure 11, W 1/2, lower fill	medium to large mammal	undetermined	unidentified		no	fragment	5
Structure 11, W 1/2, lower fill	medium to large mammal	undetermined	unidentified	calcined	no	fragment	2
Structure 11, W 1/2, lower fill	medium to large mammal	undetermined	unidentified	charred	no	fragment	2
Structure 11, lower fill	indeterminate mammal	undetermined	unidentified		no	fragment	3
Structure 11, lower fill	indeterminate mammal	undetermined	unidentified	charred	no	fragment	2
Structure 11, lower fill	medium to large mammal	left	humerus		no	fragment	1
Structure 11, lower fill	medium to large mammal	undetermined	unidentified	charred	no	fragment	1
Structure 11, lower fill	small mammal	undetermined	unidentified		no	fragment	1
Structure 11/16, NE 1/4, on floor	*Odocoileus virginianus* (cf)	undetermined	tibia		no	fragment	1
Structure 11, NE 1/4 floor, sherd cluster 5	medium to large mammal	undetermined	unidentified	calcined	no	fragment	1
Structure 11, floor	medium to large mammal	undetermined	unidentified	burned	no	fragment	1
Structure 11, floor	medium to large mammal	undetermined	unidentified	charred	no	fragment	1
Structure 12	*Lepus* sp.	left	tibia	calcined	no	fragment	1
Structure 12	*Lepus* sp.	undetermined	rib		no	fragment	1
Structure 12	*Lepus* sp.	undetermined	rib		no	whole	1
Structure 12, NE 1/4	*Lepus californicus*	left	tibia		no	fragment	1
Structure 12, NE 1/4	*Lepus* sp.	undetermined	rib		no	fragment	2
Structure 12, SE 1/4	*Lepus* sp.	undetermined	rib		no	fragment	1
Structure 12, upper fill	*Ammospermophilus harissii*	undetermined	lumbar vertebra		no	whole	1
Structure 12, upper fill	*Lepus californicus*	right	femur		no	fragment	1
Structure 12, upper fill	*Lepus californicus*	undetermined	vertebra #8		no	whole	1
Structure 12, upper fill	*Lepus californicus*	undetermined	lumbar vert. 3 or 4		no	fragment	1
Structure 12, upper fill	*Lepus californicus*	undetermined	lumbar vert. 3 or 4		no	whole	1
Structure 12, upper fill	*Lepus californicus*	undetermined	lumbar vert. 5 or 6		no	fragment	1
Structure 12, upper fill	*Lepus* sp.	undetermined	lumbar centrum		no	fragment	1
Structure 12, upper fill	*Lepus* sp.	undetermined	lumbar transverse		no	fragment	1
Structure 12, upper fill	Lepus sp.	undetermined	lumbar vertebra		no	fragment	1
Structure 12, upper fill	*Lepus* sp.	undetermined	rib		no	fragment	2
Structure 12, upper fill	*Lepus* sp.	undetermined	vertebrae		no	fragment	3
Structure 12, upper fill	*Sylvilagus* sp.	right	humerus		no	fragment	1
Structure 12, upper fill	medium to large mammal	undetermined	unidentified	calcined	no	fragment	1
Structure 12, upper fill	small mammal	undetermined	long bone		no	fragment	1
Structure 12, upper fill	small mammal	not applicable	vertebrae		no	fragment	4
Structure 12, NW 1/4, upper fill	small mammal	undetermined	tibia or radius		no	fragment	1
Structure 12, SE 1/4, lower fill	*Lepus californicus*	left	femur		no	fragment	1
Structure 12, SE 1/4, lower fill	*Lepus californicus*	left	metatarsal # 5		no	fragment	1
Structure 12, SE 1/4, lower fill	mammal?	undetermined	unidentified	calcined	no	fragment	1
Structure 12, SE 1/4, lower fill	small mammal	undetermined	long bone		no	fragment	5
Structure 12, NE 1/4, lower fill burned layer	small mammal	undetermined	unidentified		no	fragment	1

Appendix 8.A. Data on Bone Recovered from Whiptail, cont'd.

Provenience	Species or Class	Side	Bone	Burned, calcined, charred	Weathered	Whole or fragment	Total No. of Items
Structure 12, lower fill	*Lepus* sp.	undetermined	tibia		no	fragment	1
Structure 12, SE 1/4, lower fill	*Lepus californicus*	undetermined	phalange		no	whole	1
Structure 12, SE 1/4, lower fill	medium to large mammal	undetermined	unidentified		no	fragment	1
Structure 12, SE1/4, lower fill	medium to large mammal	undetermined	unidentified	calcined	no	fragment	2
Structure 12, lower fill, burned layer	*Lepus californicus*	right	metatarsal #4		no	whole	1
Structure 13, NE 1/4	*Lepus californicus*	undetermined	metapodium		yes	fragment	1
Structure 13, NW 1/4, lower fill	indeterminate	undetermined	unidentified	calcined	no	fragment	1
Structure 13, SE 1/4	indeterminate	undetermined	unidentified		yes	fragment	1
Structure 13, SE 1/4	indeterminate	undetermined	unidentified	calcined	no	fragment	4
Structure 13, SE 1/4	medium mammal	undetermined	unidentified	calcined	no	fragment	1
Structure 13, SW 1/4	indeterminate	undetermined	unidentified		yes	fragment	1
Structure 13, W 1/4, subfloor	large mammal	undetermined	rib	calcined	no	fragment	1
Structure 13, east posthole	indeterminate	undetermined	unidentified		yes	fragment	4
Structure 13, east posthole	medium to large mammal	undetermined	unidentified		yes	fragment	3
Structure 13, east posthole fill	Sciuridae	right	femur		no	fragment	1
Structure 16, upper fill	medium to large mammal	undetermined	long bone		yes	fragment	1
Structure 16, NW 1/4	*Odocoileus virginianus*	left	mandible	burned	no	fragment	1
Structure 16, NW 1/4	*Odocoileus virginianus*	undetermined	femur fragment		yes	fragment	5
Structure 16, NE 1/4, middle fill	*Canis* sp.	undetermined	metacarpal		no	whole	1
Structure 16, NE 1/4, middle fill	*Lepus* sp.	undetermined	metatarsal		no	fragment	1
Structure 16, NE 1/4, middle fill	*Odocoileus virginianus*	left	innominate	burned	no	fragment	1
Structure 16, SE 1/4, middle fill	Artiodactyl	right	innominate	burned	no	fragment	1
Structure 16, NE 1/4, lower fill	large bird (golden eagle?)	undetermined	long bone		no	fragment	1
Structure 16, NE 1/4, lower fill	large bird	undetermined	long bone		no	fragment	1
Structure 16, NW 1/4, lower fill	*Canis latrans*?	right	humerus		no	fragment	1
Structure 16, NW 1/4, lower fill	*Lepus alleni*	left	innominate		no	fragment	1
Structure 16, NW 1/4, lower fill	*Lepus* sp.	undetermined	humerus		no	fragment	1
Structure 16, NE 1/4, lower fill	*Sylvilagus* sp.	right	innominate		no	fragment	1
Structure 16, SE 1/4, lower fill	*Sylvilagus* sp.	right	metacarpal # 3		yes	fragment	1
Structure 16, NW 1/4, lower fill	*Odocoileus virginianus*	left	femur		no	fragment	1
Structure 16, NW 1/4, lower fill	*Odocoileus virginianus*	left	innominate		no	fragment	1
Structure 16, NW 1/4, lower fill	*Odocoileus virginianus*	left	mandible	charred	no	fragment	1
Structure 16, NE 1/4, lower fill	*Odocoileus virginianus*	right	innominate	charred	no	fragment	1
Structure 16, NE 1/4, lower fill	*Odocoileus* sp.	left	innominate	charred	no	fragment	1
Structure 16, NE 1/4, lower fill	Artiodactyl	right	innominate		no	fragment	1
Structure 16, NE 1/4, lower fill	Artiodactyl	right	innominate	charred	no	fragment	1
Structure 16, NE 1/4, lower fill	Artiodactyl	undetermined	innominate	charred	no	fragment	1
Structure 16, NE 1/4, lower fill	Artiodactyl	undetermined	pubis		no	fragment	1
Structure 16, NE 1/4, lower fill	indeterminate mammal	undetermined	unidentified	calcined	no	fragment	1
Structure 16, NW 1/4, lower fill	small mammal	undetermined	long bone		no	fragment	5
Structure 16, NW 1/4, lower fill	medium mammal	undetermined	long bone		yes	fragment	6
Structure 16, NW 1/4, lower fill	medium to large mammal	undetermined	unidentified		no	fragment	12
Structure 16, NW 1/4, lower fill	medium to large mammal	undetermined	unidentified	burned	no	fragment	9
Structure 16, NW 1/4, lower fill	medium to large mammal	undetermined	unidentified	calcined	no	fragment	2
Structure 16, NW 1/4, lower fill	large mammal	undetermined	long bone		no	fragment	4
Structure 16, NW 1/4, lower fill	large mammal	undetermined	long bone	charred	no	fragment	1
Structure 16, NW 1/4, lower fill	large mammal	undetermined	unidentified		no	fragment	30
Structure 16, NW 1/4, lower fill	large mammal	undetermined	unidentified	charred	no	fragment	2
Structure 16, NE 1/4, lower fill	large mammal	undetermined	unidentified		no	fragment	2
Structure 16, NE 1/4, lower fill	large mammal	undetermined	unidentified	charred	no	fragment	2
Structure 16, SW 1/4, lower fill	*Lepus californicus*	left	metatarsal # 3		no	whole	1
Structure 16, SW 1/4, lower fill	*Lepus californicus*	right	metatarsal # 4		yes	fragment	1
Structure 16, SW 1/4 lower fill	indeterminate mammal	undetermined	long bone	charred	no	fragment	1
Structure 16, SW 1/4, lower fill	small mammal	undetermined	long bone		no	fragment	2
Structure 16, SE 1/4, lower fill	medium to small mammal	undetermined	carpal or tarsal		no	whole	2
Structure 16, SE 1/4, lower fill	medium to small mammal	undetermined	carpal or tarsal		no	whole	3

Appendix 8.A. Data on Bone Recovered from Whiptail, cont'd.

Provenience	Species or Class	Side	Bone	Burned, calcined, charred	Weathered	Whole or fragment	Total No. of Items
Structure 16, SE 1/4, lower fill	medium to small mammal	undetermined	long bone		yes	fragment	1
Structure 16, SE 1/4, lower fill	medium to small mammal	undetermined	long bone		yes	fragment	1
Structure 16, NE 1/4, floor	*Antilocapra americana*	left	metapodial		yes	fragment	1
Structure 16, NE 1/4, floor	*Antilocapra americana*	right	metapodial		yes	fragment	1
Structure 16, NE 1/4, floor	*Odocoileus virginianus*	left	ilium		no	fragment	1
Structure 16, NE 1/4, floor	*Odocoileus virginianus*	right	ilium	burned	no	fragment	1
Structure 16, NE 1/4, floor	medium to large mammal	undetermined	unidentified		yes	fragment	3
Structure 16, south wall outside	*Ammospermophilus harrisii*	right	femur		yes	fragment	1
Structure 18, NE 1/4, upper fill	small mammal	undetermined	unidentified		no	fragment	11
Structure 18, NW 1/4 lower fill	indeterminate mammal	undetermined	unidentified		no	fragment	1
Structure 18, NW 1/4, lower fill	medium mammal	undetermined	unidentified		no	fragment	2
Structure 18, NW 1/4, floor	medium mammal	undetermined	long bone		no	fragment	1
Structure 18, SW 1/4 floor, sherd cluster	indeterminate mammal	undetermined	unidentified		no	fragment	5
Structure 18, SW 1/4, floor, sherd cluster	small mammal	undetermined	unidentified		no	fragment	1
Structure 18, SW 1/4, sherd cluster	*Lepus californicus*	left	scapula		no	fragment	2
Structure 18, NW 1/4, pit	*Ammo. harrisii* or *Spermoph.*	right	mandible		no	whole	1
Structure 18, NW 1/4, pit	*Lepus californicus*	left	metatarsal # 4		no	fragment	1
Structure 18, NW 1/4, pit	*Lepus californicus*	left	tibia		no	fragment	1
Structure 18, NW 1/4, pit	*Lepus californicus*	right	femur		no	fragment	1
Structure 18, NW 1/4, pit	*Sylvilagus* sp.	undetermined	rib		no	fragment	2
Structure 18, NW 1/4, pit	cf. *Canis* sp.	undetermined	rib		no	fragment	1
Structure 18, NW 1/4, pit	medium mammal	undetermined	rib		no	fragment	2
Structure 23, NE 1/4	indeterminate mammal	undetermined	unidentified		no	fragment	5
Structure 23, NE 1/4	medium to large mammal	undetermined	long bone		no	fragment	3
Structure 23, NE 1/4, upper fill	*Lepus* sp.	right	metatarsal #4		yes	fragment	1
Structure 23, NE 1/4, upper fill	*Lepus* sp.	undetermined	proximal phalange	calcined	no	fragment	2
Structure 23, SE 1/4, middle fill	*Lepus* sp.	right	metacarpal #4		no	whole	1
Structure 23, SE 1/4, middle fill	*Lepus* sp.	right	metapodial #2		no	whole	1
Structure 23, NE 1/4, middle fill	*Lepus californicus*	left	distal metatarsal		yes	fragment	1
Structure 23, NE 1/4, middle fill	*Lepus californicus*	undetermined	proximal phalange		yes	whole	1
Structure 23, NE 1/4, middle fill	*Lepus californicus*	left	ulna	burned	no	fragment	1
Structure 23, NE 1/4, middle fill	*Lepus californicus*	right	ulna		yes	fragment	1
Structure 23, NE 1/4, middle fill	*Lepus* sp.	undetermined	metatarsal		yes	fragment	1
Structure 23, NE 1/4, middle fill	*Lepus* sp.	undetermined	phalange		yes	whole	1
Structure 23, NE 1/4, middle fill	*Odocoileus virginianus*	left	mandible	burned	no	fragment	1
Structure 23, NE 1/4, middle fill	indeterminate mammal	undetermined	unidentified		no	fragment	1
Structure 23, NE 1/4, middle fill	indeterminate mammal	undetermined	unidentified	calcined	no	fragment	2
Structure 23, NE 1/4, middle fill	medium mammal	undetermined	unidentified	burned	no	fragment	2
Structure 23, NE 1/4, middle fill	medium mammal	undetermined	unidentified	calcined	no	fragment	2
Structure 23, NE 1/4, middle fill	medium to large mammal	undetermined	inidentified		no	fragment	1
Structure 23, NE 1/4, middle fill	medium to large mammal	undetermined	long bone		yes	fragment	1
Structure 23, NE 1/4, middle fill	medium to large mammal	undetermined	unidentified		no	fragment	1
Structure 23, NE 1/4, middle fill	small mammal	undetermined	unidentified		no	fragment	2
Structure 23, NE 1/4, middle fill	small to medium mammal	undetermined	long bone		yes	fragment	2
Structure 23, NE 1/4, middle fill	small to medium mammal	undetermined	long bone	calcined	no	fragment	5
Structure 23, NW 1/4, middle fill	*Dipodomys spectabilis* or *D. deserti*	right	tibia		no	whole	1
Structure 23, NW 1/4, middle fill	*Lepus californicus*	undetermined	humerus		yes	fragment	1
Structure 23, NW 1/4, middle fill	*Lepus* sp.	right	metatarsal #4		yes	fragment	1
Structure 23, NW 1/4, middle fill	*Lepus* sp.	undetermined	metatarsal		no	fragment	2
Structure 23, NW 1/4, middle fill	*Sylvilagus* sp.	left	tibia		yes	fragment	2
Structure 23, NW 1/4, middle fill	small mammal	undetermined	unidentified		no	fragment	23
Structure 23, NE 1/4, lower fill	*Lepus californicus*	left	humerus		yes	fragment	1

Appendix 8.A. Data on Bone Recovered from Whiptail, cont'd.

Provenience	Species or Class	Side	Bone	Burned, calcined, charred	Weathered	Whole or fragment	Total No. of Items
Structure 23, NE 1/4, lower fill	*Lepus californicus*	right	metatarsal # 2		yes	fragment	1
Structure 23, NE 1/4, lower fill	*Lepus californicus*	right	metatarsal # 3		yes	whole	1
Structure 23, NE 1/4, lower fill	*Lepus californicus*	right	ulna		no	fragment	1
Structure 23, NE 1/4, lower fill	*Lepus californicus*	right	ulna	burned	no	fragment	1
Structure 23, NE 1/4, lower fill	*Lepus californicus*	undetermined	proximal phalange		yes	whole	2
Structure 23, NE 1/4, lower fill	*Lepus californicus*	right	metatarsal #2		yes	fragment	1
Structure 23, NE 1/4, lower fill	*Lepus californicus*	undetermined	rib		no	fragment	1
Structure 23, NE 1/4, lower fill	*Lepus* sp.	undetermined	proximal phalange		no	whole	1
Structure 23, NE 1/4, lower fill	Sylvilagus sp.	left	metatarsal # 5	calcined	no	fragment	1
Structure 23, NE 1/4, lower fill	*Sylvilagus* sp.	left	scapula	burned	no	fragment	1
Structure 23, NE 1/4, lower fill	*Sylvilagus* sp.	undetermined	metacarpal #3-4		yes	whole	1
Structure 23 NE 1/4, lower fill	*Sylvilagus* sp.	left	metatarsal #2		yes	whole	1
Structure 23 NE 1/4, lower fill	*Sylvilagus* sp.	left	metatarsal #2	calcined	no	fragment	1
Structure 23 NE 1/4, lower fill	*Sylvilagus* sp.	left	metatarsal #4		no	whole	1
Structure 23 NE 1/4, lower fill	*Sylvilagus* sp.	left	scapula	burned	no	fragment	1
Structure 23 NE 1/4, lower fill	*Sylvilagus* sp.	right	metacarpal #3		no	fragment	2
Structure 23 NE 1/4, lower fill	*Sylvilagus* sp.	right	metatarsal #3		yes	fragment	1
Structure 23, NE 1/4, lower fill	small mammal	undetermined	unidentified		no	fragment	2
Structure 23, NE 1/4, lower fill	small mammal	undetermined	unidentified	calcined	no	fragment	6
Structure 23, NE 1/4, lower fill	small to medium mammal	undetermined	long bone		yes	fragment	1
Structure 23, NE 1/4, lower fill	medium to large mammal	undetermined	unidentified		no	fragment	2
Structure 23, NE 1/4, lower fill	medium to large mammal	undetermined	unidentified		no	fragment	4
Structure 23, NE 1/4, lower fill	medium to large mammal	undetermined	unidentified	calcined	no	fragment	1
Structure 23, NW 1/4, lower fill	*Amm. harrisii* or *Spermoph.*	left	tibia		no	whole	1
Structure 23, NW 1/4, lower fill	*Ammospermophilus harrisii*	left	tibia		no	whole	1
Structure 23, NW 1/4, lower fill	*Thomomys* sp.	undetermined	cheek tooth		no	whole	3
Structure 23, NW 1/4, lower fill	*Thomomys* sp.	undetermined	maxilla		no	fragment	1
Structure 23, NW 1/4, lower fill	*Dipodomys spectabilis* or *D. deserti*	right	maxilla		no	fragment	1
Structure 23, NW 1/4, lower fill	*Dipodomys spectabilis* or *D. deserti*	undetermined	cheek teeth		no	fragment	3
Structure 23, NW 1/4, lower fill	Rodentia	left	femur		no	fragment	1
Structure 23, NW 1/4, lower fill	*Lepus californicus*	left	metacarpal # 4		yes	whole	1
Structure 23, NW 1/4, lower fill	*Lepus californicus*	undetermined	vertebrae	calcined	no	fragment	2
Structure 23, NW 1/4, lower fill	*Lepus californicus*	left	humerus		yes	fragment	1
Structure 23, NW 1/4, lower fill	*Lepus californicus*	left	ulna		yes	fragment	2
Structure 23, NW 1/4, lower fill	*Lepus californicus*	right	metatarsal		no	whole	3
Structure 23, NW 1/4, lower fill	*Lepus californicus*	undetermined	phalanges		yes	whole	2
Structure 23 NW 1/4, lower fill	*Sylvilagus* sp.	left	metacarpal #3		yes	whole	1
Structure 23 NW 1/4, lower fill	*Sylvilagus* sp.	left	metacarpal #4		yes	whole	1
Structure 23 NW 1/4, lower fill	*Sylvilagus* sp.	left	metacarpal #5		no	whole	1
Structure 23 NW 1/4, lower fill	Sylvilagus sp.	left	metacarpal#2		yes	whole	1
Structure 23 NW 1/4, lower fill	*Sylvilagus* sp.	left	tarsal (cuboid?)		no	whole	1
Structure 23 NW 1/4, lower fill	*Sylvilagus* sp.	right	metapodial		no	whole	2
Structure 23 NW 1/4, lower fill	Leporidae	undetermined	rib		no	fragment	1
Structure 23, Balk B, lower fill	medium to large mammal	undetermined	unidentified		no	fragment	2
Structure 23, NE 1/4, lower fill	medium to large mammal	undetermined	rib		no	fragment	1
Structure 23 lower fill	medium to large mammal	undetermined	c.f. ulna		no	fragment	1
Structure 23 lower fill	medium to large mammal	undetermined	c.f. ulna	calcined	no	fragment	1
Structure 23 SE 1/4, floor fill	*Sylvilagus* sp.	left	ulna		yes	fragment	1
Structure 23 SE 1/4, floor fill	*Sylvilagus* sp.	right	femur		yes	fragment	1
Structure 23, SE 1/4, floor fill	medium to large mammal	undetermined	unidentified		no	fragment	5
Structure 23, SE 1/4, lower fill	*Lepus californicus*	right	calcaneum	burned	yes	fragment	1
Structure 23, SE 1/4, lower fill	*Sylvilagus* sp.	left	humerus		yes	fragment	1
Structure 23, SE 1/4, lower fill	*Sylvilagus* sp.	left	radius		yes	fragment	1

Appendix 8.A. Data on Bone Recovered from Whiptail, cont'd.

Provenience	Species or Class	Side	Bone	Burned, calcined, charred	Weathered	Whole or fragment	Total No. of Items
Structure 23, SE 1/4, lower fill	*Sylvilagus* sp.	right	femur		no	fragment	1
Structure 23, SE 1/4, lower fill	*Sylvilagus* sp.	right	radius		yes	fragment	1
Structure 23, SE 1/4, lower fill	medium mammal	undetermined	unidentified		no	fragment	1
Structure 23, SE 1/4, lower fill	small mammal	undetermined	long bone		no	fragment	3
Structure 23, SE 1/4, lower fill	small mammal	undetermined	long bone		yes	fragment	1
Structure 23, SE 1/4, lower fill	small mammal	undetermined	unidentified		no	fragment	2
Structure 23, NE 1/4 floor	*Sylvilagus* sp.	undetermined	hind proximal phalange		yes	whole	1
Structure 23, NE 1/4, floor B	*Lepus* sp.	undetermined	skull		no	fragment	1
Structure 23, NE 1/4, floor B	Leporidae	undetermined	proximal phalange		no	whole	1
Structure 23, NE 1/4, floor B	medium to large mammal	undetermined	unidentified		no	fragment	1
Structure 23, NE 1/4, floor B	small mammal	undetermined	long bone		no	fragment	1
Structure 23, NE 1/4, floor B	small mammal	undetermined	unidentified		no	fragment	1
Structure 23, NW 1/4, post hole fill	*Perognathus* sp.	right	tibia		no	whole	1
Structure 23, NW 1/4, post hole fill	*Lepus californicus*	undetermined	lower cheek tooth		no	whole	1
Structure 23, NE 1/4, pit fill	*Lepus* sp.	undetermined	tibia		no	fragment	1
Structure 23, NW 1/4, pit fill	Colubridae	undetermined	ribs		no	fragment	9
Structure 23, NW 1/4, pit fill	Colubridae	undetermined	ribs		no	whole	5
Structure 23, NW 1/4, pit fill	Colubridae	undetermined	vertebrae		no	fragment	10
Structure 23, NW 1/4, pit fill	Colubridae	undetermined	vertebrae		no	whole	2
Structure 23, NW 1/4, pit fill	*Lepus californicus*	undetermined	atlas		no	whole	1
Structure 23, NW 1/4, pit fill	*Lepus* sp. or *Urocyon cinereoargenteus*	undetermined	rib		no	fragment	1
Structure 23, NW 1/4, pit fill	*Perognathus* sp.	right	tibia		no	fragment	1
Structure 23, NW 1/4, pit fill	Rodentia	undetermined	incisor		no	whole	1
Structure 23, SE 1/4, middle fill	indeterminate mammal	undetermined	unidentified		no	fragment	1
Structure 23, SE 1/4, floor B	*Sylvilagus* sp.	undetermined	rib head		no	fragment	1
Structure 23, SE 1/4, floor fill	*Lepus californicus*	left	ulna		yes	fragment	1
Structure 23, SE 1/4, floor fill	*Spermophilus variegatus*	left	tibia		yes	fragment	1
Structure 23, SE 1/4, lower fill	unidentified	undetermined	unidentified		no	fragment	7
Structure 23, SW 1/4, lower fill	*Sylvilagus* sp.	left	mandible		yes	fragment	1
Structure 23, SW 1/4, lower fill	*Sylvilagus* sp.	right	humerus		yes	fragment	2
Structure 23, SW 1/4, lower fill	small mammal	undetermined	unidentified		no	fragment	11
Structure 23, SW 1/4, middle fill	*Lepus alleni*	left	tibia		yes	fragment	1
Structure 23, SW 1/4, middle fill	*Lepus* sp.	left	femur		no	fragment	1
Structure 23, SW 1/4, middle fill	*Lepus* sp.	undetermined	lower incisor		no	fragment	1
Structure 23, SW 1/4, upper fill	medium to large mammal	undetermined	unidentified		no	fragment	1
Structure 23, SW 1/4, lower fill	*Amm. harrisii* or *Spermoph.*	left	femur		no	whole	1
Structure 23, SW 1/4, lower fill	*Amm. harrisii* or *Spermoph.*	right	humerus		no	fragment	1
Structure 23, SW 1/4, lower fill	*Amm. harrisii* or *Spermoph.*	right	humerus		no	whole	1
Structure 23, SW 1/4, lower fill	*Amm. harrisii* or *Spermoph.*	right	innominate		no	whole	1
Structure 23, SW 1/4, lower fill	*Lepus californicus*	right	metacarpal #2		yes	whole	1
Structure 23, SW 1/4, lower fill	*Lepus californicus*	right	ulna		yes	fragment	1
Structure 23, SW 1/4, lower fill	*Lepus californicus*	undetermined	ulna		yes	fragment	1
Structure 23, SW 1/4, lower fill	small mammal	undetermined	unidentified		no	fragment	14
Structure 23, SW 1/4, middle fill	*Lepus californicus*	right	scapula		yes	fragment	1
Structure 23, SW 1/4, middle fill	medium to large mammal	undetermined	unidentified		no	fragment	1
Structure 23, storage pit, floor B	Leporidae	undetermined	vertebral process		no	fragment	1
Structure 23, balk, middle fill	small mammal	undetermined	unidentified		no	fragment	3
Structure 23, entry way	Leporidae	undetermined	tooth		yes	fragment	3
Structure 23, lower fill	*Ammospermophilus harrisii*	left	mandible		yes	fragment	1
Structure 23, lower fill	*Ammospermophilus harrisii*	right	radius		no	whole	1
Structure 23, lower fill	*Lepus* sp.	undetermined	cheek tooth		no	whole	2
Structure 23, lower fill	*Lepus* sp.	undetermined	rib head		no	fragment	1
Structure 23, lower fill	*Lepus* sp.	undetermined	scapula		no	fragment	1

Appendix 8.A. Data on Bone Recovered from Whiptail, cont'd.

Provenience	Species or Class	Side	Bone	Burned, calcined, charred	Weathered	Whole or fragment	Total No. of Items
Structure 23, lower fill	*Lepus* sp.	undetermined	scapula	burned	no	fragment	1
Structure 23, lower fill	*Lepus* sp.	undetermined	sternum		no	whole	1
Structure 23, lower fill	*Lepus* sp.	undetermined	vertebral fragment		no	fragment	1
Structure 23, lower fill	small to medium mammal	undetermined	c.f. ulna		no	fragment	3
Structure 23, post hole #2 fill	*Lepus* sp. or *Urocyon cinereoargenteus*	undetermined	rib		no	fragment	1
Structure 23, post hole #2 fill	small mammal	undetermined	unidentified		no	fragment	1
Structure 23, screened lower fill	*Lepus californicus*	left	metatarsal		no	whole	1
Structure 23, screened lower fill	*Lepus californicus*	left	metatarsal #3		no	whole	1
Structure 23, screened lower fill	*Lepus californicus*	right	radius	calcaneus	no	fragment	1
Structure 23, screened lower fill	*Lepus californicus*	undetermined	innominate		yes	fragment	1
Structure 23, NE 1/4, lower fill	indeterminate mammal	undetermined	unidentified		no	fragment	1
Structure 24, NE 1/4, floor fill	*Lepus californicus*	left	scapula		no	fragment	1
Structure 24, NE 1/4, floor fill	*Sylvilagus* sp.	right	calcaneum		no	fragment	1
Structure 24, NE 1/4, floor fill	*Sylvilagus* sp.	right	innominate		no	fragment	1
Structure 24, NE 1/4, floor fill	medium to large mammal	undetermined	unidentified		no	fragment	11
Structure 24, NE 1/4, floor fill	small mammal	undetermined	unidentified		no	fragment	4
Structure 24, NE 1/4, floor fill	small mammal	undetermined	unidentified	burned	no	fragment	1
Structure 24, NW 1/4, floor fill	*Lepus* sp.	undetermined	metapodial		no	fragment	3
Structure 24, NW 1/4, lower fill	*Lepus californicus*	undetermined	phalange		no	fragment	1
Structure 24, NW 1/4 lower fill	medium to large mammal	undetermined	unidentified		no	fragment	3
Structure 24, SE 1/4, floor fill	small mammal	undetermined	unidentified		no	fragment	1
Structure 24, strat column B	small mammal	undetermined	unidentified		no	fragment	1
Structure 25, NE 1/4, upper fill	*Lepus californicus*	undetermined	phalange		no	whole	1
Structure 25, SE 1/4, upper fill	medium to large mammal	undetermined	unidentified	calcined	no	fragment	1
Structure 25, upper fill	*Ammo. harrisii* or *Spermopholis* sp.	right	humerus		no	fragment	1
Structure 25, upper fill	*Lepus californicus*	undetermined	phalange		no	whole	1
Structure 25, NE 1/4, below floor	small mammal	undetermined	unidentified		no	fragment	2
Structure 25, NE1/4, below floor 1	*Lepus alleni*	left	metacarpal #2		no	fragment	1
Structure 25, NE1/4, below floor 1	*Lepus alleni*	left	metacarpal #3		no	whole	2
Structure 25, NE1/4, below floor 1	*Lepus alleni*	right	radius		no	fragment	3
Structure 25, NE1/4, below floor 1	*Lepus alleni*	right	ulna		no	fragment	1
Structure 25, NE1/4, below floor 1	*Lepus californicus*	left	humerus		no	fragment	1
Structure 25, NE1/4, below floor 1	*Lepus californicus*	left	metatarsal #4		no	whole	1
Structure 25, NE1/4, below floor 1	*Lepus californicus*	left	metatarsal #5		no	fragment	1
Structure 25, NE1/4, below floor 1	*Lepus californicus*	right	metatarsal #3		no	whole	1
Structure 25, NE 1/4, floor 1	*Lepus alleni*	right	metatarsal #2		no	whole	1
Structure 25, NE 1/4, floor 1 fill	*Sylvilagus* sp.	left	metatarsal #4		no	whole	1
Structure 25, NE 1/4, floor 2	*Lepus* sp.	undetermined	rib		no	fragment	1
Structure 25, NE 1/4, floor 2	*Sylvilagus* sp.	right	femur		no	fragment	1
Structure 25, NE 1/4, floor fill (floor 1)	*Bufo alverius*	undetermined	radio-ulna		no	whole	1
Structure 25, NE 1/4, lower fill	*Sylvilagus* sp.	left	tibia		no	fragment	1
Structure 25, NE 1/4, upper fill	*Bufo alverius*	undetermined	skeleton		no	fragment	1
Structure 25, NE 1/4, floor 2	*Sylvilagus* sp.	left	calcaneum		no	fragment	1
Structure 25, NW 1/4, upper fill	medium to large mammal	undetermined	unidentified	calcined	no	fragment	1
Structure 25, SE 1/4	Artiodactyl	undetermined	rib shaft		no	fragment	1
Structure 25, SE 1/4, below floor 1	*Lepus* sp.	undetermined	radius		no	fragment	1
Structure 25, SE 1/4, floor fill 1	Artiodactyl	undetermined	rib		no	fragment	1
Structure 25, SE 1/4, upper fill	*Lepus allenii*	right	innominate		no	fragment	1
Structure 25, SE 1/4, upper fill	*Odocoileus hemionus*	undetermined	sacrum		no	fragment	1
Structure 25, SE 1/4, upper fill	*Odocoileus hemionus*	undetermined	sacrum	burned	no	fragment	1
Structure 25, SW 1/4, below floor	small mammal	undetermined	long bone	calcined	no	fragment	2
Structure 25, SW 1/4, lower fill	*Amm. harrisii* or *Spermoph,*	right	tibia		no	fragment	1
Structure 25, SW 1/4, lower fill	*Lepus californicus*	left	metatarsal #4		no	fragment	1

Appendix 8.A. Data on Bone Recovered from Whiptail, cont'd.

Provenience	Species or Class	Side	Bone	Burned, calcined, charred	Weathered	Whole or fragment	Total No. of Items
Structure 25, SW corner	*Lepus californicus*	right	metatarsal #3		no	fragment	6
Structure 25, center of east wall	bird, medium passerine	undetermined	ulna shaft		no	fragment	1
Structure 25, center of east wall	indeterminate size mammal	undetermined	unidentified		no	fragment	3
Structure 25, center of east wall	medium to large mammal	undetermined	unidentified		no	fragment	1
Structure 25, center of east wall	small mammal	undetermined	long bone		no	fragment	5
Grids between Structures 9, 23, and 24	*Lepus alleni*	left	innominate		no	fragment	1
Grids between Structures 9, 23, and 24	large mammal	undetermined	long bone	calcined	no	fragment	1
Southern Locus							
Structure 14, SE 1/4, floor	*Odocoileus* sp.	right	temporal		yes	fragment	1
Structure 14, SE 1/4, floor	*Odocoileus* sp.	not applicable	basioccipital		yes	fragment	1
Structure 14, NW 1/4	Artiodactyl	not applicable	thoracic vertebra		no	fragment	1
Structure 14, NW 1/4	medium to large mammal	not applicable	thoracic vertebra	burned	no	fragment	1
Structure 14, NW 1/4	medium to large mammal	undetermined	unidentified		no	fragment	9
Structure 14, NW 1/4, lower fill	*Lepus californicus*	right	mandible		yes	fragment	1
Structure 14, NW 1/4, lower fill	Artiodactyl	undetermined	thoracic vertebra		no	fragment	1
Structure 14, SE 1/4	*Odocoileus virginianus*	left	mandible		yes	fragment	1
Structure 14, SE 1/4	*Odocoileus virginianus*	undetermined	mandible		no	fragment	3
Structure 14, SE 1/4	*Odocoileus virginianus*	undetermined	teeth		no	fragment	8
Structure 14, SE 1/4	*Odocoileus virginianus*	undetermined	tooth fragments		no	fragment	7
Structure 14, SE 1/4	small mammal	undetermined	unidentified		no	fragment	1
Structure 14, SE 1/4, east wall	medium to large mammal	undetermined	unidentified		no	fragment	55
Structure 14, SE 1/4, floor	Artiodactyl	undetermined	mandible		no	fragment	4
Northern Locus							
Structure 3, fill	Artiodactyl	undetermined	centrum		yes	whole	1
Structure 3, roof fall	*Lepus californicus*	right	mandible		no	fragment	1
Structure 27, back dirt	Artiodactyl	undetermined	tibia	burned	no	fragment	1
Structure 27, SE 1/4, lower fill	medium to large mammal	undetermined	unidentified		no	fragment	1
Structure 27, SW 1/4, fill	medium to large mammal	undetermined	unidentified		no	fragment	1
Structure 27, W & N wall trenches	medium mammal	left	tibia		no	fragment	1
Structure 27, level 2	*Ammospermophilus harrisii*	undetermined	skull		no	fragment	1
Structure 27, level 1	unidentified	undetermined	unidentified	burned	no	fragment	6
Structure 27a, NE 1/4	*Ammospermophilus harrisii*	right	innominate		no	whole	1
Structure 27a, NE 1/4	*Lepus californicus*	left	tibia	burned	no	fragment	1
Structure 27a, NE 1/4	indeterminate mammal	undetermined	unidentified	burned	no	fragment	5
Structure 27a, NE 1/4	indeterminate mammal	undetermined	unidentified		no	fragment	11
Structure 27a, NE 1/4	medium to large mammal	undetermined	long bone		no	fragment	4
Structure 27a, NE 1/4	medium to large mammal	undetermined	long bone	burned	no	fragment	1
Structure 27a, NE 1/4	medium to large mammal	undetermined	unidentified	burned	no	fragment	1
Structure 27a, NE 1/4, floor	*Sylvilagus* sp.	left	tibia		no	fragment	1
Structure 27a, NE 1/4, floor	medium to large mammal	undetermined	long bone	burned	no	fragment	1
Structure 27a, NW 1/4, ash layer	*Sylvilagus* sp.	undetermined	metapodial	burned	no	fragment	1
Structure 27a, SE 1/4, lower floor fill	medium to large mammal	undetermined	long bone		no	fragment	1
Structure 27a, SE 1/4, lower floor fill	medium to large mammal	undetermined	long bone ?		no	fragment	2
Structure 27A, SE 1/4, lower floor fill	medium to large mammal	undetermined	unidentified	calcined	no	fragment	1
Structure 27A, SE 1/4, lower floor fill	unidentified	undetermined	unidentified	calcined	no	fragment	1
Structure 27a, SW 1/4, level 3	*Odocoileus virginianus*	left	calcaneum	burned	yes	fragment	1
Structure 27b, level 4	large mammal	undetermined	unidentified		no	fragment	1
Structure 27b	*Canis* sp.	left	metacarpal # 2	burned	no	whole	1
Structure 27b	*Odocoileus* sp.	undetermined	antler tip	burned	no	fragment	1
Structure 27b	*Odocoileus virginianus*	left	metatarsal		no	fragment	1
Structure 27b	*Odocoileus virginianus*	right	distal phalange		yes	whole	1

Appendix 8.A. Data on Bone Recovered from Whiptail, cont'd.

Provenience	Species or Class	Side	Bone	Burned, calcined, charred	Weathered	Whole or fragment	Total No. of Items
Structure 27b	*Odocoileus virginianus*	right	proximal phalange	burned	yes	fragment	1
Structure 27b	*Odocoileus virginianus*	undetermined	metapodial	burned	yes	fragment	1
Structure 27b	*Ovis canadensis*	left	proximal phalange		yes	whole	1
Structure 27b	*Ovis canadensis*	left	proximal phalange	burned	yes	fragment	1
Structure 27b	*Ovis canadensis*	undetermined	skull		yes	fragment	1
Structure 27b	*Ovis canadensis*	undetermined	skull	burned	yes	fragment	1
Structure 27b	*Ovis canadensis*	right	mesial phalange		yes	fragment	1
Structure 27b	*Ovis canadensis*	right	skull	burned	no	fragment	1
Structure 27b	*Ovis canadensis*	undetermined	metapodial		yes	fragment	1
Structure 27b	*Ovis canadensis*	undetermined	occipital	burned	no	fragment	1
Structure 27b	*Ovis canadensis*	undetermined	skull		no	fragment	1
Structure 27b	*Ovis canadensis*	undetermined	skull	burned	no	fragment	1
Structure 27b	indeterminate mammal	undetermined	unidentified		no	fragment	2
Structure 27b	indeterminate mammal	undetermined	unidentified	burned	no	fragment	1
Structure 27b	indeterminate mammal	undetermined	unidentified	calcined	no	fragment	1
Structure 27b	medium to large mammal	undetermined	rib		no	fragment	1
Structure 27b	medium to large mammal	undetermined	skull	burned	no	fragment	1
Structure 27b	medium to large mammal	undetermined	unidentified		no	fragment	25
Structure 27b	medium to large mammal	undetermined	unidentified	burned	no	fragment	10
Structure 27b	medium to large mammal	undetermined	unidentified	calcined	no	fragment	3
Structure 27b	small to medium mammal	undetermined	unidentified		no	fragment	22
Structure 27b, Feature 6	medium to large mammal	undetermined	unidentified		no	fragment	6
Structure 27b, Feature 6	*Odocoileus hemionus*	left	antler	burned	no	fragment	1
Structure 27b, NE 1/4	medium to large mammal	undetermined	long bone	charred	no	fragment	2
Structure 27b, NE, level 4	large mammal	undetermined	long bone	burned	no	fragment	1
Structure 27b, NE, level 4	large mammal	undetermined	long bone	calcined	no	fragment	1
Structure 27b, NE, level 4	*Ovis canadensis*	left	proximal phalange		yes	fragment	1
Structure 27b, SW 1/4 Feature 6	*Canis* sp.	undetermined	thoracic vertebra	burned	no	fragment	1
Structure 27b, SW 1/4 Feature 6	large mammal	undetermined	long bone		yes	fragment	1
Structure 27b, SW 1/4 floor	medium to large mammal	undetermined	long bone		no	fragment	1
Structure 27b, SW 1/4 floor	medium to large mammal	undetermined	poss. long bone		yes	fragment	2
Structure 27b, SW 1/4 floor	medium to large mammal	undetermined	unidentified		no	fragment	30
Structure 27b, SW 1/4 floor	medium to large mammal	undetermined	unidentified	burned	no	fragment	19
Structure 27b, SW 1/4 floor	medium to large mammal	undetermined	unidentified	calcined	no	fragment	6
Structure 27b, SW 1/4 floor	medium to large mammal	undetermined	long bone	burned	no	fragment	1
Structure 27b, SW 1/4 floor	medium to large mammal	undetermined	unidentified	burned	no	fragment	17
Structure 27b, SW 1/4 floor	medium to large mammal	undetermined	unidentified	calcined	no	fragment	4
Structure 27b, SW 1/4, Feature 6	*Odocoileus hemionus*	undetermined	tooth		no	fragment	1
Structure 27b, SW 1/4, floor	mammal	undetermined	unidentified		no	fragment	29
Structure 27b, SW 1/4, floor	mammal	undetermined	unidentified	burned	no	fragment	7
Structure 27b, SW 1/4, floor	mammal	undetermined	unidentified	calcined	no	fragment	13
Structure 27b, SW 1/4, floor	Testuomata	undetermined	carapace	calcined	no	fragment	1
Structure 27b, W of Feature 6	medium to large mammal	undetermined	long bone		yes	fragment	3
Structure 27b, W of Feature 6	medium to large mammal	undetermined	unidentified		no	fragment	18
Structure 27b, W of Feature 6	medium to large mammal	undetermined	unidentified		yes	fragment	10
Structure 27b, W of Feature 6	medium to large mammal	undetermined	unidentified	burned	no	fragment	19
Structure 27b, W of Feature 6	medium to large mammal	undetermined	unidentified	burned	yes	fragment	2
Structure 27b, Feature 6, floor	medium to large mammal	undetermined	long bone		no	fragment	8
Structure 27b, Feature 6, floor	medium to large mammal	undetermined	long bone	burned	no	fragment	4
Structure 27b, Feature 6, floor	medium to large mammal	undetermined	unidentified		no	fragment	18
Structure 27b, Feature 6, floor	medium to large mammal	undetermined	unidentified	burned	no	fragment	2
Structure 27b, SW 1/4, floor	Artiodactyl	left	auditory meatus		yes	fragment	1
Structure 27b, SW 1/4, floor	*Odocoileus virginianus*	left	innominate	burned	no	fragment	1

Appendix 8.A. Data on Bone Recovered from Whiptail, cont'd.

Provenience	Species or Class	Side	Bone	Burned, calcined, charred	Weathered	Whole or fragment	Total No. of Items
Structure 27b, Feature 6	Artiodactyl	undetermined	skull		no	fragment	1
Structure 27b, Feature 6	Artiodactyl	undetermined	skull	burned	no	fragment	1
Structure 27b, Feature 6	indeterminate mammal	undetermined	unidentified		no	fragment	4
Structure 27b, Feature 6	large mammal	undetermined	rim		yes	fragment	1
Structure 27b, Feature 6	large mammal	undetermined	unidentified		no	fragment	5
Structure 27b, Feature 6	large mammal	undetermined	unidentified	burned	no	fragment	5
Structure 27b, Feature 6	medium to large mammal	undetermined	unidentified		no	fragment	25
Structure 27b, Feature 6	medium to large mammal	undetermined	unidentified	burned	no	fragment	12
Structure 27b, Feature 6	medium to large mammal	undetermined	unidentified		no	fragment	9
Structure 27b, Feature 6	medium to large mammal	undetermined	unidentified	burned	no	fragment	18
Structure 27b, Feature 6	*Odocoileus* sp.	right	antler	burned	no	fragment	1
Structure 27b, Feature 6	*Odocoileus* sp.	undetermined	antler		no	fragment	20
Structure 27b, Feature 6	*Odocoileus* sp.	undetermined	antler	burned	no	fragment	16
Structure 27b, Feature 6	*Ovis canadensis*	right	proximal phalange		yes	fragment	1
Structure 27b, Feature 6	*Ovis canadensis*	undetermined	horn core	burned	no	fragment	20
Structure 27b, SW 1/4, Feature 6	Artiodactyl	left	scaphoid		yes	fragment	1
Structure 27b, SW 1/4, Feature 6	Artiodactyl	right	tibia	burned	no	fragment	1
Structure 27b, SW 1/4, Feature 6	Artiodactyl	not applicable	cervical vert. #7	burned	no	fragment	1
Structure 27b, SW 1/4, Feature 6	Artiodactyl	undetermined	coracoid process	burned	no	fragment	1
Structure 27b, SW 1/4, Feature 6	Artiodactyl	undetermined	mandible		no	fragment	2
Structure 27b, SW 1/4, Feature 6	Artiodactyl	undetermined	mandible		yes	fragment	9
Structure 27b, SW 1/4, Feature 6	Artiodactyl	undetermined	metapodial		yes	fragment	3
Structure 27b, SW 1/4, Feature 6	Artiodactyl	undetermined	rib		no	fragment	1
Structure 27b, SW 1/4, Feature 6	Artiodactyl	undetermined	scapula	burned	no	fragment	1
Structure 27b, SW 1/4, Feature 6	Artiodactyl	undetermined	skull		yes	fragment	12
Structure 27b, SW 1/4, Feature 6	Artiodactyl	undetermined	skull	burned	yes	fragment	6
Structure 27b, SW 1/4, Feature 6	Artiodactyl	undetermined	tooth		no	fragment	13
Structure 27b, SW 1/4, Feature 6	Cervidae	undetermined	antler		no	fragment	45
Structure 27b, SW 1/4, Feature 6	Cervidae	undetermined	antler	burned	no	fragment	2
Structure 27b, SW 1/4, Feature 6	*Odocoileus virginianus*	left	pubis		yes	fragment	1
Structure 27b, SW 1/4, Feature 6	*Odocoileus hemionus*	right	metatarsal		yes	fragment	1
Structure 27b, SW 1/4, Feature 6	*Odocoileus hemionus*	right	pelvis	burned	no	fragment	1
Structure 27b, SW 1/4, Feature 6	*Odocoileus hemionus*	right	radius		yes	fragment	1
Structure 27b, SW 1/4, Feature 6	*Odocoileus hemionus*	right	tibia		no	fragment	1
Structure 27b, SW 1/4, Feature 6	*Odocoileus hemionus*	right	tibia		yes	fragment	1
Structure 27b, SW 1/4, Feature 6	*Odocoileus hemionus*	undetermined	cheek tooth		yes	fragment	3
Structure 27b, SW 1/4, Feature 6	*Odocoileus hemionus*	undetermined	skull		yes	fragment	3
Structure 27b, SW 1/4, Feature 6	*Odocoileus hemionus*	undetermined	tibia		yes	fragment	1
Structure 27b, SW 1/4, Feature 6	*Odocoileus* sp.	left	innominate		no	fragment	1
Structure 27b, SW 1/4, Feature 6	*Odocoileus* sp.	right	metacarpal	burned	no	fragment	1
Structure 27b, SW 1/4, Feature 6	*Odocoileus* sp.	undetermined	tooth		no	fragment	1
Structure 27b, SW 1/4, Feature 6	*Odocoileus virginianus*	left	scapula		yes	fragment	1
Structure 27b, SW 1/4, Feature 6	*Odocoileus virginianus*	right	calcaneum		yes	fragment	1
Structure 27b, SW 1/4, Feature 6	*Odocoileus virginianus*	right	ischium		no	fragment	1
Structure 27b, SW 1/4, Feature 6	*Odocoileus virginianus*	right	mandible		no	fragment	2
Structure 27b, SW 1/4, Feature 6	*Odocoileus virginianus*	right	pubis		yes	fragment	1
Structure 27b, SW 1/4, Feature 6	*Ovis canadensis*	right	radius		no	fragment	1
Structure 27b, SW 1/4, Feature 6	*Ovis canadensis*	undetermined	incisor		no	whole	1
Structure 27b, SW 1/4, Feature 6	small to medium mammal	undetermined	long bone		yes	fragment	2
Structure 27b, Level 1	*Ovis canadensis* or *Antilocapra americana*	undetermined	tooth		no	fragment	1
Structure 27b, Level 1	medium to large mammal	undetermined	long bone	burned	no	fragment	1
Structure 27b, Level 1	medium to large mammal	undetermined	possible long bone	burned	no	fragment	2
Structure 27b, Level 1	medium to large mammal	undetermined	unidentified		no	fragment	3
Structure 27b, Level 1	medium to large mammal	undetermined	unidentified	burned	no	fragment	7

Appendix 8.A. Data on Bone Recovered from Whiptail, cont'd.

Provenience	Species or Class	Side	Bone	Burned, calcined, charred	Weathered	Whole or fragment	Total No. of Items
Structure 27b, Level 1	small mammal	undetermined	unidentified		no	fragment	1
Structure 27b, Level 1	small mammal	undetermined	unidentified	burned	no	fragment	1
Structure 27b, Level 2	medium to large mammal	undetermined	unidentified	calcined	no	fragment	12
Structure 27b, Level 4, NE 1/4	small mammal	undetermined	unidentified	burned	no	fragment	1
Structure 27b, NE 1/4	Cervidae	undetermined	antler		no	fragment	1
Structure 27b, NE 1/4	*Odocoileus hemionus*	left	proximal phalanges		yes	fragment	1
Structure 27b, NE 1/4, level 4	Large mammal	undetermined	unidentified		no	fragment	1
Structure 27b, NE 1/4, level 4	large mammal	undetermined	1st cervical		no	fragment	1
Structure 27b, NE 1/4, level 4	large mammal	undetermined	metapodial	burned	no	fragment	1
Structure 27b, NE, level 4	large mammal	undetermined	unidentified		no	fragment	1
Structure 27b, NW 1/4	Artiodactyl	undetermined	rib	calcined	no	fragment	1
Structure 27b, NW 1/4, floor	Indeterminate mammal	undetermined	unidentified		no	fragment	2
Structure 27b, NW 1/4, floor	medium to large mammal	undetermined	unidentified	burned	no	fragment	6
Structure 27b, NW 1/4, level 2	Artiodactyl	undetermined	metatarsal	burned	no	fragment	1
Structure 27b, NW 1/4, level 2	Artiodactyl	undetermined	rib	burned	no	fragment	1
Structure 27b, NW 1/4, level 2	*Odocoileus* sp.	undetermined	antler tine	burned	no	fragment	1
Structure 27b, NW 1/4, level 2	indeterminate mammal	undetermined	unidentified		no	fragment	1
Structure 27b, NW 1/4, level 2	medium to large mammal	undetermined	unidentified		no	fragment	29
Structure 27b, NW 1/4, level 2	medium to large mammal	undetermined	unidentified	burned	no	fragment	29
Structure 27b, NW 1/4, level 2	medium to large mammal	undetermined	unidentified	calcined	no	fragment	9
Structure 27b, NW 1/4, level 3	*Lepus californicus*	right	humerus		yes	fragment	1
Structure 27b, NW 1/4, level 3	*Odocoileus* sp.	undetermined	tooth root		yes	fragment	1
Structure 27b, NW 1/4, level 3	*Ovis canadensis*	undetermined	horn core	burned	no	fragment	1
Structure 27b, NW 1/4, level 3	*Ovis canadensis*	undetermined	tooth		yes	fragment	1
Structure 27b, NW 1/4, first level	large mammal	undetermined	skull		no	fragment	1
Structure 27b, NW 1/4, level 2	*Odocoileus virginianus*	right	radius		yes	fragment	1
Structure 27b, NW 1/4, level 2	indeterminate mammal	undetermined	unidentified		no	fragment	1
Structure 27b, NW 1/4, level 2	indeterminate mammal	undetermined	unidentified	burned	no	fragment	2
Structure 27b, S wall trench	large mammal	undetermined	long bone shaft	burned	no	fragment	1
Structure 27b, SW 1/4	medium to large mammal	undetermined	long bone		yes	fragment	31
Structure 27b, SW 1/4	medium to large mammal	undetermined	long bone	calcined	no	fragment	7
Structure 27b, SW 1/4	medium to large mammal	undetermined	long bone	burned	no	fragment	12
Structure 27b, SW 1/4	medium to large mammal	undetermined	skull	burned	no	fragment	15
Structure 27b, SW 1/4	*Ovis canadensis* or *Antilocapra americana*	right	astragalus		yes	fragment	1
Structure 27b, SW 1/4	*Ovis canadensis* or *Antilocapra americana*	undetermined	tooth		no	fragment	2
Structure 27b, SW 1/4 Feature 6	medium to large mammal	undetermined	unidentified		no	fragment	73
Structure 27b, SW 1/4 Feature 6	medium to large mammal	undetermined	unidentified	burned	no	fragment	34
Structure 27b, SW 1/4 Feature 6	medium to large mammal	undetermined	vertebral fragments	burned	no	fragment	2
Structure 27b, SW 1/4 floor	*Antilocapra americana* or *Odocoileus virginianus*	undetermined	tooth		no	fragment	1
Structure 27b, SW 1/4 floor	medium to large mammal	undetermined	unidentified		no	fragment	52
Structure 27b, SW 1/4 floor	*Ovis canadensis or Antilocapra americana*	undetermined	tooth		no	fragment	3
Structure 27b, SW 1/4, Feature 6	*Antilocapra americana or O. virginianus*	right	innominate	burned	no	fragment	1
Structure 27b, SW 1/4, Feature 6	Cervidae	left	antler core		yes	fragment	1
Structure 27b, SW 1/4, Feature 6	Cervidae	right	antler core		yes	fragment	1
Structure 27b, SW 1/4, Feature 6	Cervidae	undetermined	antler		yes	fragment	12
Structure 27b, SW 1/4, Feature 6	Cervidae	undetermined	antler core frags.		yes	fragment	10
Structure 27b, SW 1/4, Feature 6	Cervidae	undetermined	antler frags.	burned	no	fragment	11
Structure 27b, SW 1/4, Feature 6	Cervidae	undetermined	unidentified	burned	no	fragment	6
Structure 27b, SW 1/4, Feature 6	indeterminate mammal	undetermined	unidentified		no	fragment	49
Structure 27b, SW 1/4, Feature 6	large mammal	undetermined	flat bone		yes	fragment	6
Structure 27b, SW 1/4, Feature 6	large mammal	undetermined	long bone		no	fragment	1

Appendix 8.A. Data on Bone Recovered from Whiptail, cont'd.

Provenience	Species or Class	Side	Bone	Burned, calcined, charred	Weathered	Whole or fragment	Total No. of Items
Structure 27b, SW 1/4, Feature 6	large mammal	undetermined	long bone		yes	fragment	7
Structure 27b, SW 1/4, Feature 6	large mammal	undetermined	skull		no	fragment	16
Structure 27b, SW 1/4, Feature 6	large mammal	undetermined	skull	burned	no	fragment	2
Structure 27b, SW 1/4, Feature 6	*Odocoileus hemionus*	left	acetabulum		no	fragment	1
Structure 27b, SW 1/4, Feature 6	*Odocoileus hemionus*	left	acetabulum		yes	fragment	1
Structure 27b, SW 1/4, Feature 6	*Odocoileus hemionus*	left	occipital condyle		yes	fragment	1
Structure 27b, SW 1/4, Feature 6	*Odocoileus hemionus*	left	otic bone		yes	fragment	1
Structure 27b, SW 1/4, Feature 6	*Odocoileus hemionus*	right	lambdoidal crest		yes	fragment	1
Structure 27b, SW 1/4, Feature 6	*Odocoileus hemionus*	right	otic bone		yes	fragment	1
Structure 27b, SW 1/4, Feature 6	*Odocoileus hemionus*	right	radius		yes	fragment	1
Structure 27b SW 1/4, Feature 6	*Odocoileus hemionus*	undetermined	metapodial		yes	fragment	2
Structure 27b, SW 1/4, Feature 6	*Odocoileus* sp.	right	teeth		no	fragment	1
Structure 27b, SW 1/4, Feature 6	*Odocoileus* sp.	undetermined	antler tip	burned	no	fragment	2
Structure 27b, SW 1/4, Feature 6	*Odocoileus* sp.	undetermined	antler tips		no	fragment	2
Structure 27b, SW 1/4, Feature 6	*Odocoileus* sp.	undetermined	tooth		no	fragment	15
Structure 27b, SW 1/4, Feature 6	*Odocoileus virginianus*	left	tooth		no	fragment	4
Structure 27b, SW 1/4, Feature 6	*Odocoileus virginianus*	right	mandible		no	fragment	1
Structure 27b, SW 1/4, Feature 6	*Odocoileus virginianus*	right	tooth		no	fragment	1
Structure 27b, SW 1/4, Feature 6, floor	*Odocoileus virginianus*	left	mesial phalange	burned	no	fragment	1
Structure 27b, SW 1/4, Feature 6, floor	*Odocoileus virginianus*	right	distal phalange		yes	whole	1
Structure 27b, SW 1/4, Feature 6, floor	*Odocoileus virginianus*	right	mesial phalange		yes	whole	1
Structure 27b, SW 1/4, Feature 6	Artiodactyl	left	coronoid		no	fragment	1
Structure 27b, SW 1/4, Feature 6	Artiodactyl	undetermined	tooth		no	fragment	15
Structure 27b, SW 1/4, Feature 6	mammal	undetermined	unidentified	burned	no	fragment	4
Structure 27b, SW 1/4, floor	large mammal	undetermined	long bone		no	fragment	8
Structure 27b, SW 1/4, floor	large mammal	undetermined	rib		no	fragment	2
Structure 27b, SW 1/4, floor	large mammal	undetermined	unidentified		no	fragment	1
Structure 27b, SW 1/4, floor	large mammal	undetermined	unidentified		no	fragment	1
Structure 27b, SW 1/4, Feature 6, floor	Artiodactyl	undetermined	proximal phalange		no	fragment	1
Structure 27b, SW 1/4, Feature 6, floor	Artiodactyl	right	tibia		no	fragment	1
Structure 27b, SW 1/4, Feature 6, floor	medium to large mammal	undetermined	long bone		no	fragment	24
Structure 27b, SW 1/4, Feature 6, floor	medium to large mammal	undetermined	long bone	burned	no	fragment	2
Structure 27b, SW 1/4, Feature 6, floor	medium to large mammal	undetermined	unidentified		no	fragment	40
Structure 27b, SW 1/4, Feature 6, floor	medium to large mammal	undetermined	unidentified	burned	no	fragment	1
Structure 27b, SW 1/4, Feature 6, floor	medium to large mammal	undetermined	vertebral process		no	fragment	1
Structure 27b, SW 1/4, Feature 6, floor	*Ovis canadensis*	left	metatarsal		yes	fragment	1
Structure 27b, SW 1/4, Feature 6, floor	*Ovis canadensis*	right	mesial phalange		yes	whole	1
Structure 27b, SW 1/4, Feature 6, floor	*Ovis canadensis*	right	proximal phalange		yes	fragment	1
Structure 27b, SW 1/4, level 2	medium to large mammal	undetermined	long bone	burned	no	fragment	1
Structure 27b, SW 1/4, level 2	medium to large mammal	undetermined	unidentified		no	fragment	3
Structure 27b, SW 1/4, level 2	medium to large mammal	undetermined	unidentified	burned	no	fragment	1
Structure 27b, SW1/4 Feature 6	medium to large mammal	undetermined	unidentified		no	fragment	50
Structure 27b, SW1/4 Feature 6	medium to large mammal	undetermined	unidentified		yes	fragment	6
Structure 27b, SW1/4 Feature 6	medium to large mammal	undetermined	unidentified	burned	no	fragment	12
Structure 27b, South wall trench	large mammal	undetermined	long bone shaft	burned	no	fragment	1

Appendix 8.A. Data on Bone Recovered from Whiptail, cont'd.

Provenience	Species or Class	Side	Bone	Burned, calcined, charred	Weathered	Whole or fragment	Total No. of Items
Structure 27b, backdirt	*Odocoileus virginianus*	right	scapula	burned	yes	fragment	1
Structure 27b, Feature 6	*Ovis canadensis* or *Antilocapra americana*	undetermined	tooth		yes	fragment	6
Structure 27b, Feature 6	mammal	undetermined	unidentified		no	fragment	2
Structure 27b, Feature 6	mammal	undetermined	unidentified	burned	no	fragment	5
Structure 27b, first level	large mammal	undetermined	flat bone	burned	no	fragment	1
Structure 27b, first level	large mammal	undetermined	unidentified		no	fragment	3
Structure 27b, floor	large mammal	undetermined	long bone		no	fragment	2
Structure 27b, floor	large mammal	undetermined	unidentified		no	fragment	2
Structure 27b, floor	mammal	undetermined	unidentified		no	fragment	1
Structure 27b, floor	mammal	undetermined	unidentified	burned	no	fragment	14
Structure 27b, floor	mammal	undetermined	unidentified	calcined	no	fragment	4
Structure 27b, SW 1/4, floor	Artiodactyl	left	temporal/parietal		no	fragment	1
Structure 27b, SW 1/4, floor	*Odocoileus virginianus*	right	proximal phalange		no	fragment	1
Structure 27b, SW 1/4, floor	*Ovis canadensis*	undetermined	metapodial		yes	whole	1
Structure 27b, SW 1/4, floor	*Ovis canadensis*	undetermined	skull		no	fragment	2
Structure 27b, SW 1/4, floor	*Ovis canadensis*	undetermined	skull		yes	fragment	1
Structure 27b, floor, SW 1/4	*Ovis canadensis*	undetermined	skull	burned	no	fragment	3
Structure 27b, floor, SW 1/4	*Sylvilagus* sp.	undetermined	femoral		yes	fragment	1
Structure 27b, wall trench, found in pot A	medium to large mammal	undetermined	unidentified	burned	no	fragment	1
Structure 27b, west of Feature 6	Artiodactyl	undetermined	metapodial	burned	yes	fragment	1
Structure 27b, west of Feature 6	Artiodactyl	undetermined	scapula	burned	no	fragment	1
Structure 27b, west of Feature 6	*Odocoileus hemionus*	undetermined	cervical vertebra	burned	no	fragment	1
Structure 27b, west of Feature 6	*Odocoileus virginianus* or *Antilocapra americana*	left	scapula	burned	no	fragment	2
Structure 27b, west of Feature 6	*Odocoileus virginianus or Antilocapra americana*	right	calcaneum		yes	fragment	1
Structure 27b, west of Feature 6	*Odocoileus virginianus* or *Antilocapra americana*	undetermined	metapodial		no	fragment	1
Structure 27b, west of Feature 6	*Odocoileus virginianus* or *Antilocapra americana*	undetermined	scapula	burned	no	fragment	2
Structure 27b, west of Feature 6	*Odocoileus virginianus*	left	calcaneum		yes	whole	1
Structure 27b, west of Feature 6	*Odocoileus virginianus*	undetermined	mesial phalange		yes	fragment	1
Structure 27b, west of Feature 6	*Ovis canadensis* or *Odocoileus hemionus*	left	scapula	burned	no	fragment	1
Structure 27b, west of Feature 6	*Ovis canadensis* or *Odocoileus hemionus*	undetermined	scapula		yes	fragment	1
Structure 27b-2, NE 1/4, level 4	Cervidae	undetermined	antler		no	fragment	5
Structure 27b-2, NE 1/4, level 4	Cervidae	undetermined	antler	burned	no	fragment	1
Structure 27b SW 1/4, floor	medium to large mammal	undetermined	long bone		no	fragment	1
Structure 27b SW 1/4, floor	medium to large mammal	undetermined	skull	burned	no	fragment	1
Structure 27b SW 1/4, floor	medium to large mammal	undetermined	unidentified		no	fragment	66
Structure 27b SW 1/4, floor	medium to large mammal	undetermined	unidentified	burned		fragment	1
Structure 28, NE 1/4, level 2	*Odocoileus virginianus*	left	mesial phalange		yes	whole	1
Structure 28, SE 1/4	medium to large mammal	undetermined	unidentified		no	fragment	7
Structure 28, SE 1/4	medium to large mammal	undetermined	unidentified	burned	no	fragment	3
Structure 28, SE 1/4	medium to large mammal	undetermined	unidentified	calcined	no	fragment	1
Structure 28, SE 1/4, level 2	*Lepus allenii*	right	metatarsal # 4		no	whole	1
Structure 28, SE 1/4, level 2	*Lepus californicus*	undetermined	hind proximal phalange		no	fragment	1
Structure 28, SE 1/4, level 2	medium to large mammal	undetermined	unidentified		no	fragment	31
Structure 28, SW 1/4, level 2	*Lepus californicus*	left	metatarsal		yes	whole	1
Structure 28, SW 1/4, level 2	medium to large mammal	undetermined	rib		no	fragment	1
Structure 28, SW 1/4, level 2	small mammal	undetermined	long bone	calcined	no	fragment	1
Structure 28, SW 1/4, level 2	small mammal	undetermined	unidentified	burned	no	fragment	1

Appendix 8.A. Data on Bone Recovered from Whiptail, cont'd.

Provenience	Species or Class	Side	Bone	Burned, calcined, charred	Weathered	Whole or fragment	Total No. of Items
Structure 29, E 1/2 major post hole	Artiodactyl	undetermined	vertebral epiphysis		yes	fragment	1
Structure 29, NE 1/4, level 1A	*Lepus* sp.	left	humerus		no	fragment	1
Structure 29, fire pit	medium to large mammal	undetermined	unidentified	burned	no	fragment	1
Structure 30, NE 1/4, level 3	medium to large mammal	undetermined	long bone	burned	no	fragment	12
Structure 30, NE 1/4, level 3	medium to large mammal	undetermined	unidentified	burned	no	fragment	1
Structure 30, NW 1/4, floor	*Odocoileus virginianus*	undetermined	innominate	burned	no	fragment	2
Structure 30, NW 1/4, floor	*Ovis canadensis*	right	naviculo-cuboid	burned	yes	fragment	1
Structure 30, NW 1/4, floor	*Odocoileus virginianus*	left	innominate	burned	no	fragment	1
Structure 30, NW 1/4, floor	*Odocoileus virginianus*	right	calcaneum	burned	yes	fragment	1
Structure 30, NW 1/4, floor	*Odocoileus virginianus*	right	metatarsal	burned	yes	fragment	1
Structure 30, SE 1/4 floor, Feature 5	*Odocoileus virginianus*	left	astragalus	burned	no	whole	1
Structure 30, SE 1/4 floor, Feature 5	*Odocoileus virginianus*	left	radius	burned	no	fragment	1
Structure 30, NE 1/4 floor 2-b	medium to large mammal	undetermined	temporal	burned	no	fragment	1
Structure 30, NE 1/4 floor 2-b	medium to large mammal	undetermined	unknown	burned	no	fragment	1
Structure 30, NE 1/4 level 2	medium to large mammal	undetermined	unknown	burned	no	fragment	10
Structure 30, NE 1/4 level 3	medium mammal	undetermined	tibia	burned	no	fragment	2
Structure 30, NE 1/4, level 3	*Antilocapra americana*	right	humerus	burned	no	fragment	1
Structure 30, NW 1/4, floor	Artiodactyl	right	naviculo-cuboid	burned	yes	fragment	1
Structure 30, NW 1/4, floor	*Odocoileus* sp.	undetermined	mandible	burned	no	fragment	1
Structure 30, NW 1/4, floor	Cervidae	undetermined	antler	burned	no	fragment	28
Structure 30, NW 1/4, floor	medium to large mammal	undetermined	unknown	burned	no	fragment	10
Structure 30, SE 1/4, floor, Feature 5	Artiodactyl	undetermined	lumbar vertebra	burned	no	fragment	2
Structure 30, SE 1/4 floor, Feature 5	Artiodactyl	undetermined	rib	burned	no	fragment	1
Structure 30, SE 1/4, floor, Feature 5	*Odocoileus* sp.	right	metacarpal	burned	no	fragment	1
Structure 30, SE 1/4, floor, Feature 5	medium to large mammal	undetermined	unidentified	burned	no	fragment	2
Structure 30, SW 1/4	*Antilocapra americana*	right	radius	burned	no	fragment	1
Structure 30, SW 1/4	*Odocoileus* sp.	undetermined	antler	burned	no	fragment	1
Structure 30, SW 1/4	*Odocoileus virginianus* or *Antilocapra americana*	undetermined	metapodial	burned	yes	fragment	1
Structure 30, SW 1/4, level 3	Artiodactyl	undetermined	lumbar	burned	no	fragment	1
Structure 30, SW 1/4, level 3	Artiodactyl	undetermined	proximal metapodial	burned	no	fragment	1
Structure 30, SW 1/4, level 3	*Odocoileus* sp.	undetermined	tooth		yes	fragment	1
Structure 30, SW 1/4, level 3	Large mammal	undetermined	long bone		yes	fragment	1
Structure 30, SW 1/4, level 3	Leporidae	undetermined	proximal phalange		yes	fragment	1
Structure 30, SW 1/4, level 3	*Lepus* sp.	left	humerus	burned	no	fragment	1
Structure 30, SW 1/4, level 3	medium to large mammal	undetermined	long bone		no	fragment	1
Structure 30, SW 1/4, level 3	medium to large mammal	undetermined	long bone	calcined	no	fragment	1
Structure 30, SW 1/4, level 3	medium to large mammal	undetermined	unidentified	burned	no	fragment	1
Structure 30, SW 1/4, level 3	medium mammal	undetermined	long bone	burned	no	fragment	1
Structure 31a, Feature 18, SW-NW balk	small mammal	undetermined	long bone	calcined		fragment	1
Structure 31a, Pot 3, floor	medium to large mammal	undetermined	unidentified	burned	no	fragment	1
Structure 31a, SE 1/4	indeterminate mammal	undetermined	unidentified			fragment	1
Structure 31a, SE 1/4	medium to large mammal	undetermined	unidentified	burned		fragment	1
Structure 31a, SW 1/4, level 3	medium to large mammal	undetermined	unidentified	calcined		fragment	1
Structure 31a, SW-SE balk	indeterminate mammal	undetermined	unidentified	calcined		fragment	1
Structure 31B	*Lepus californicus*	left	metatarsal # 5		no	whole	1
Structure 31B	*Lepus californicus*	right	metatarsal # 5		no	whole	1
Structure 31B	*Lepus sp.*	undetermined	metatarsal		no	fragment	1

Appendix 8.A. Data on Bone Recovered from Whiptail, cont'd.

Provenience	Species or Class	Side	Bone	Burned, calcined, charred	Weathered	Whole or fragment	Total No. of Items
Structure 31b	*Sylvilagus sp.*	left	radius	burned	no	fragment	1
Structure 31b	bird	undetermined	long bone		no	fragment	1
Structure 31b	small mammal	undetermined	unidentified		no	fragment	3
Structure 31b, level 3	*Lepus californicus*	undetermined	proximal phalange		no	whole	1
Structure 31b, NE 1/4, level 3	*Lepus californicus*	right	metatarsal # 5		no	whole	1
Structure 31b, NE 1/4, level 3	small mammal	undetermined	long bone		no	fragment	1
Structure 31b, NW 1/4, level 1	small mammal	undetermined	unidentified		no	fragment	1
Structure 31b, NW 1/4, level 3	indeterminate size mammal	undetermined	unidentified		no	fragment	3
Structure 31b, NW 1/4, level 3	medium to large mammal	undetermined	unidentified		no	fragment	3
Structure 31b, NW-SW balk, 1	medium to large mammal	undetermined	long bone		no	fragment	1
Structure 31b, SE 1/4, floor	*Lepus* sp.	undetermined	metacarpal	calcined	no	fragment	1
Structure 31b, SE 1/4, floor	*Lepus* sp.	undetermined	rib		no	fragment	1
Structure 31b, SE 1/4, floor	*Sylvilagus* sp.	left	metacarpal #2		no	whole	1
Structure 31b, SE 1/4, floor	*Sylvilagus* sp.?	undetermined	skull		no	fragment	2
Structure 31b, SE 1/4, level 3	medium to large mammal	undetermined	unidentified		no	fragment	2
Structure 31b, SE 1/4, floor	medium to large mammal	undetermined	unidentified		no	fragment	2
Structure 31b, SE 1/4, floor	medium to large mammal	undetermined	unidentified	calcined	no	fragment	1
Structure 31b, SE 1/4, floor	small mammal	undetermined	unidentified	calcined	no	fragment	1
Structure 31b, SE 1/4, level 1	small mammal	undetermined	unidentified	calcined	no	fragment	10
Structure 31b, SE 1/4, level 2	*Lepus californicus*	right	metacarpal # 2		no	whole	1
Structure 31b, SE 1/4, level 2	small mammal	undetermined	metapodial ?		no	fragment	1
Structure 31b, SE 1/4, level 2	small mammal	undetermined	unidentified		no	fragment	1
Structure 31b, SE 1/4, level 3	*Lepus californicus*	right	scapula		no	fragment	1
Structure 31b, SE 1/4, lower fill	*Odocoileus* sp.	left	femur		no	fragment	1
Structure 31b, SE balk, level 1	medium to large mammal	undetermined	unidentified		no	fragment	1
Structure 31b, SW 1/4	small mammal	undetermined	unidentified		no	fragment	4
Structure 31b, SW 1/4, lower fill	*Lepus californicus*	right	metatarsal # 3		no	fragment	1
Structure 31b, SW 1/4, sherd cluster	medium to large mammal	undetermined	unidentified		no	fragment	2
Structure 31b, SW 1/4, level 4	medium to large mammal	undetermined	unidentified		no	fragment	1
Structure 31b, SW 1/4, sherd cluster	small mammal	undetermined	unidentified	calcined	no	fragment	1
Structure 31b, SW-SE balk, levels 2 and 3	medium to large mammal	undetermined	unidentified		no	fragment	1
Structure 31b, SE 1/4, floor	*Lepus californicus*	left	femur		no	fragment	1
Structure 31b, SE 1/4, floor	*Lepus californicus*	right	radius		no	fragment	1
Structure 31b, SE 1/4, floor	*Lepus californicus*	undetermined	radius	calcined	no	fragment	1
Structure 31b, level 3	small mammal	undetermined	unidentified	burned	no	fragment	5
Structure 31b, wall trench	small mammal	undetermined	unidentified		no	fragment	1
Structure 31c, NE 1/4 floor, posthole	*Sylvilagus* sp.	right	mandible		no	fragment	1
Structure 31c, NE 1/4 floor, posthole	*Sylvilagus* sp.	undetermined	tooth		no	fragment	1
Structure 31c, NE 1/4 floor, posthole	small mammal	undetermined	tooth		no	fragment	3
Structure 31c, SW 1/4, level 3	*Lepus californicus*	undetermined	radius		no	fragment	1
Structure 31c, SW 1/4, level 3	indeterminate sized mammal	undetermined	unidentified	calcined		fragment	2
Structure 31c, SW 1/4, level 3	medium to large mammal	undetermined	long bone	burned		fragment	1
Structure 31c, SW 1/4, level 3	medium to large mammal	undetermined	unidentified	burned		fragment	5
Structure 31c, SW 1/4, level 4	*Lepus* ?	undetermined	metatarsal ?			fragment	1
Grand Total							3093

Chapter 9

Plant Remains

Linda M. Gregonis
with contributions by Lisa W. Huckell

Archaeobotanical remains recovered from the Whiptail excavations consisted of pollen, macrofossils, and wood. Pollen samples were obtained at two different times. The earliest samples were collected and processed in the early 1970s by Jamie Lytle-Webb (Lytle 1971; Lytle-Webb 1978) for her master's thesis. Pollen samples were also obtained from the Agua Caliente portion of the site during SWCA's investigations in 1995 and were processed by Richard Holloway (2001).

Macrofossils were obtained during the original Whiptail excavations and during SWCA's work at Agua Caliente Park. Some of the macrofossils collected during the earlier excavations were analyzed by Vorsila Bohrer in the 1970s; Lisa Huckell reanalyzed these pieces in the 1990s, as well as analyzing other items. Huckell prepared all but two of the tables in this chapter (although I have slightly modified others) and also photographed the corn kernels, beans, and cholla buds shown in Figures 9.1 through 9.3. Richard Holloway (2001) analyzed flotation samples collected from middens and roasting pits on the Agua Caliente Park property.

Wood samples were collected during the original Whiptail excavations, many as dendrochronological samples. The specimens were analyzed by Jeffrey Dean in the 1970s. He noticed that some of the pieces were datable and was able to develop a sequence, but at that time did not have an appropriate regional chronology with which to compare them. The datable pieces were reanalyzed by Dean and Dennie Bowden in the 1990s as an outgrowth of the Gibbon Springs project (Dean et al. 1996). A discussion of their successful analysis can be found in Chapter 11.

The plant remains recovered from Whiptail included cultivated species such as corn, beans, and agave; desert taxa such as saguaro, cholla, globe mallow, joint-fir, and various weedy species such as *Tidestromia lanuginosa*; wash-associated plants such as mesquite and net-leaf hackberry; water-loving species such as reed, knotweed or smartweed, cattail or bur reed, and willow; and mountain woodland species such as piñon pine, ponderosa pine, and juniper. Table 9.1 lists the taxa recovered from the site. Tables 9.2 and 9.3 provide provenience information on the specimens. The plants found in Whiptail excavations reflect usage of the varied habitats that were within easy walking distance for the Whiptail inhabitants.

Cultivated Plants

Maize (*Zea mays*) kernels and beans (*Phaseolus* sp.) were recovered from Structure 15, a storeroom in the Central Locus of the site. The charred seeds were found in vessels as well as the fill of the structure (Table 9.2). It is likely that the seeds originally were all in jars; the house was badly vandalized by pothunters.

Hundreds of burned maize kernels were found in Structure 15, some of which were bubbled and some fused into masses. The kernels are broad, but the original shapes are uncertain (Figure 9.1). The kernels were shelled prior to burning, probably for storage. They have coarse endosperm with exuding starch. Almost all of the analyzed kernels were missing their embryos.

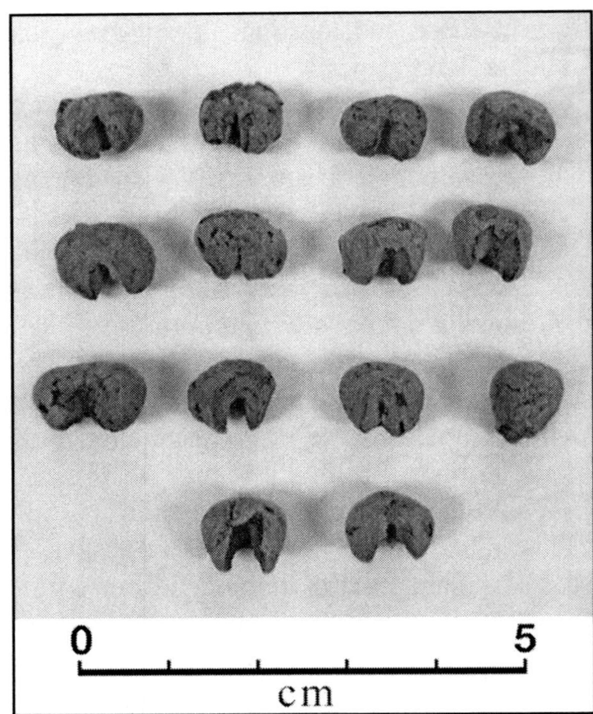

Figure 9.1. Charred maize kernels found in Structure 15 (photograph by Lisa W. Huckell).

Figure 9.2.Charred beans found in Structure 15 showing range of sizes (photograph by Lisa W. Huckell).

Table 9.4 lists measurements of 14 kernels. Huckell (analysis notes, 2009) thinks that some large kernels with a variety of endosperm types may be a mixture of flour and flint corn.

Maize kernels were also recovered from pit feature Number 47, in the Agua Caliente Park portion of the site (Holloway 2001). The kernels were used to radiocarbon date the feature, yielding historic period dates that seem

Table 9.1. Plant Taxa Recovered from Whiptail Ruin (AZ BB:10:30).

Taxon	Common Name	Part Recovered + Condition
Gymnospermae	**Gymnosperms**	
Cupressaceae	Cypress Family	
Juniperus sp.	Juniper	Branch/Stem—carbonized
Ephedraceae	Ephedra, Joint Fir Family	
Ephedra sp.	Joint-fir; Mormon tea	Pollen
Pinaceae	Pine Family	
Pinus discolor Bailey & Hawksworth	Piñon pine	Branch/Stem—carbonized
Pinus ponderosa Lawson	Ponderosa pine	Branch/Stem—carbonized
Pinus sp.	Pine	Pollen
Angiospermae	**Flowering Plants**	
Monocotyledonae	Monocots	
Agavaceae	Agave Family	
cf. *Agave* sp.	Agave; Mescal	Flower stalk—carbonized
Poaceae	Grass Family	Seeds—carbonized; Pollen
Phragmites australis (Cav.) Trin.	Reed	Culm—carbonized
Zea mays L.	Maize; Corn	Caryopsis—carbonized; Embryo—carbonized
Typhaceae/Sparganiaceae	Cattail Family/Bur Reed Family	
Sparganium type	Cattail or Bur reed	Pollen
Dicotyledonae	Dicots	Twig—carbonized
Asteraceae	Sunflower family	Pollen
Cactaceae	Cactus Family	
Carnegiea gigantea (Engelm.) B. & R.	Saguaro	Wood—carbonized; cf. Callus tissue—carbonized;
Cylindropuntia sp.	Cholla	Pollen; Buds—carbonized
Opuntia sp.	Prickly pear	Seeds—carbonized
Chenopodiaceae/Amaranthaceae	Chenopod Family/Amaranth Family	Pollen
Tidestromia languginosa	Tidestromia	Pollen
Compositae	Composite Family	Pollen
Artemisia	Sage	Pollen
Fabaceae	Bean Family	
Phaseolus vulgaris L.	Common bean	Seed—carbonized; Cotyledon—carbonized
cf. *Prosopis* sp.	Mesquite	Branch/Stem—carbonized
Malvaceae	Mallow Family	
Sphaeralcea	Globe mallow	Pollen
Polygonaceae	Buckwheat Family	
Polygonum	Knotweed, smartweed	Pollen
Salicaceae	Willow Family	
Salix sp.	Willow	Pollen
Ulmaceae	Elm Family	
Celtis reticulata Torr.	Netleaf Hackberry	Endocarp—uncarbonized

Note: Data from Lisa Huckell's analysis; Lytle-Webb 1978; Holloway 2001.

anomalous to the prehistoric artifacts found in the feature (Wellman and Grimm 2001:37).

Numerous beans and cotelydons (*Phaseolus* sp.) were also found in Structure 15 (Table 9.2; Figure 9.2). Table 9.5 lists measurements for some of the beans. Some of the beans were large, ranging from 10.15 mm to 11.8 mm in length and 6.1mm to 7.00 mm in width (Table 9.6). Despite their size, the beans fit the size range for the common bean (*Phaseolus vulgaris*) (Kaplan 1956; Karen Adams, email communication, September 2010).

Seven fragments of a blooming stalk from an agave (*Agave* sp.) or yucca (*Yucca* sp.) were found in the roof or wall fall of Structure 7. I grouped this material with cultivated plants, although the stalk could have come from either a cultivated or wild-gathered plant (and was certainly wild-gathered if it was yucca, rather than agave). We do not have direct evidence

Table 9.2. Whiptail Ruin Plant Macrofossils Curated at the Arizona State Museum.

LH Lot No.*	Provenience	Taxon	Common Name	Part	Quantity	Dimensions (mm)	Weight (gm)	Comments
17	Structure 7, SE corner of SE1/4, Layer 3, roof/wall	*Phragmites*	Reed	Culm	2			Internodes; Largest: 20.8 x 9.0
17	"	*Carnegiea*	Saguaro	Callus tissue	multiple	—	—	Boot and tabular tissue fragments
17	"	*Carnegiea*	Saguaro	Wood	3	—	—	Rib segments
17	"	cf. *Agave*	Agave	Stalk	7	—	—	
17	"	Dicot		Wood: twig	2	—	—	
12	Structure 10, from metate west of door	Pollen sample	—	—	—	—	—	"Shredded sample from metate west of door" - rebagged
8	Structure 11 (FN-29)	*Phragmites*	Reed	Culm	13	Diameter range: 3.9-8.1	0.6	Intact diam = 7, incomplete = 6; Longest = 32.5 mm
24	Structure 14, NW1/4, floor contact	*Phragmites*	Reed	Culm	5	—	—	1 intact: 14.5 x 8.0 mm
1	Structure 15	*Celtis*	Netleaf hackberry	Endocarp	2	—	—	2 valves, uncarbonized
1	"	*Phaseolus*	Bean	Bean	±30	(see Tables 9.5, 9.6)	—	Sample recorded + photographed (Figure 9.2); Includes 2 very large beans; Mixed maize + bean = 93.9 gm
1	"	*Phaseolus*	Bean	Cotyledon	>250	—	—	
1	"	*Zea*	Maize	Kernel	>250	(see Table 9.4)	—	Sample recorded + photographed (Figure 9.1)
1	"	*Cylindropuntia*	Cholla	Bud	2	13.5 x 5.5; 13.5 x 6.0	—	
1	"	Phragmites	Reed	Culm	1	10.0x6.0	—	Node
1	"	Unknown Wood	—	Branch/Stem	9	—	—	
2	Structure 15; SE1/4; In large jar on floor	*Cylindropuntia*	Cholla	Bud	150-200	(see Table 9.8)	23.0	Sample recorded + photographed (Figure 9.3)
2	"	*Phaseolus*	Bean	Bean + cotyledon	±100	—	6.8	
2	"	*Zea*	Maize	Kernel	±100	—	9.5	
3	Unlabeled bag	*Phragmites*	Reed	Culm node	2	21.0 x 9.0; 18.0 x 9.0	—	
3	"	*Phragmites*	Reed	Culm frag	7	—	—	
4	Structure 15, SE1/4; Lower fill #2	*Cylindropuntia*	Cholla	Bud	25	—	2.8	
5a	Unlabeled box: layer 1	*Zea*	Maize	Kernel	±100	—	6.8	
5b	Unlabeled box: layer 2	*Phaseolus*	Bean	Bean + cotyledon mixed	±100	—	9.5	Includes very large bean- 11.8x 6.3 x 2.8
6	Unlabeled bag	*Zea* *Phaseolus* *Cylindropuntia*	Maize Bean Cholla	Kernel Cotyledon Bud	multiple	—	5.2	Mixed, unsorted
6	"	*Cylindropuntia*	Cholla	Bud	11	—	—	>1/2 - complete

Table 9.2. Whiptail Ruin Plant Macrofossils Curated at the Arizona State Museum, cont'd.

LH Lot No.*	Provenience	Taxon	Common Name	Part	Quantity	Dimensions (mm)	Weight (gm)	Comments
7	Unprovenienced vial (Structure 15)	*Zea*	Maize	Kernel	23	—	2.6	"Measured by V. Bohrer"
7	"	*Zea*	Maize	Culm-fragment	6	longest: 32.5	—	
9	Lower fill #2, SE1/4	Cactaceae	Cereoid type	Epidermis/leaf ?	several	largest: 18.0 x 12.0	—	paper thin; singed= roasted or charred?
9	"	cf. Cactaceae		Epidermis	1	—	—	Superimposed strips
10	Structure 15, LF#1, SE1/4	*Phaseolus*	Bean	Bean + cotyledon	±100	—	4.9	
11	Structure 15, Lower fill #2; around manos 1+2 (bag with tag)	*Phaseolus*	Bean	Bean + cotyledon	multiple	—		Mixed maize + bean = 4.04 gm
11	"	*Zea*	Maize	Kernel	multiple	—	—	
11	"	*Cylindropuntia*	Cholla	Bud	1	—	—	
11	"	Wood			5	—	—	
13	Structure 15, lower fill #2; (bag with tag)	*Zea*	Maize	Kernel	multiple	—		Mixed maize + bean = 3.58 gm. 1 snail.
13	"	*Phaseolus*	Bean	Bean + cotyledon	multiple	—	—	
14a	Structure 15, Lower fill, NW1/4; screening (vial in glass bottle); 3/9/69	*Phaseolus*	Bean	Bean	1	—	—	
14a	"	*Zea*	Maize	Kernel	3	—	—	
14b	Small bag in glass bottle	2 bones, burned + 3 mica sheets	—	—	—	—	—	
15	Structure 15, NW1/4, 4-0 cm above floor	*Zea*	Maize	Kernel	25 comp+ 3 frags	—	1.96	
15	"	*Phaseolus*	Bean	Bean + Cotyledon	34 + 24 frgs	—	5.36	5 intact beans; Includes 2 very large beans: 11.2x7.0x6.0, 10.25x7.0x6.3
16	Structure 15, Misc Proveniences	*Zea*	Maize	Kernel	multiple	—		Mixed maize + bean = 19.1 gm
16	"	*Phaseolus*	Bean	Cotyledon	multiple	—	—	
17	Structure 15, SE1/4, Lower fill #2, 3/2/69	*Zea*	Maize	kernel	multiple	—		Kernel frags and sand
18	Structure 15, SE corner, lower fill #2	*Zea*	Maize	Kernel	multiple	—		Mixed maize +bean = 9.3 gm
18	"	*Phaseolus*	Bean	Cotyledon	multiple	—	—	
18	"	*Cylindropuntia*	Cholla	Bud	7	—	0.6	
18	"	Wood charcoal	Dicot	Branch/Stem	3	—	0.2	
19	Structure 15, Lower fill #1	*Zea*	Maize	Kernel	multiple	—	—	Mixed maize +bean fragments + bone, charcoal, and gravel
19	"	*Phaseolus*	Bean	Cotyledon	multiple	—	—	

Table 9.2. Whiptail Ruin Plant Macrofossils Curated at the Arizona State Museum, cont'd.

LH Lot No.*	Provenience	Taxon	Common Name	Part	Quantity	Dimensions (mm)	Weight (gm)	Comments
20	Structure 15, SE1/4, lower fill #2	*Zea*	Maize	Kernel	multiple	—		Mixed maize +bean = 16.1 gm; also charcoal, bone and gravel
20	"	*Phaseolus*	Bean	Cotyledon	multiple	—	—	
20	"	*Cylindropuntia*	Cholla	Bud	1	—	—	
20	"	*Celtis*	Hackberry	Endocarp	1	—	—	Complete; uncarbonized
21	Structure 15, SE1/4, lower fill #2	*Zea*	Maize	Kernel	multiple	—	—	Mixed maize + bean = 23.0 gm
21	"	*Phaseolus*	Bean	Cotyledon	multiple	—	—	
22	Structure 15, SE1/4; Lower fill #1	*Zea*	Maize	Kernel	multiple	—	7.7	
23	Structure 15, NE1/4, lower fill, 3/1/69	*Zea*	Maize	Kernel	multiple	—		Mixed maize + bean = 3.7 gm
23	"	*Phaseolus*	Bean	Bean + Cotyledon	multiple	—	—	

Note: All specimens are carbonized unless otherwise indicated.
* = Lot numbers used by Lisa Huckell.

that agave was being grown or roasted at Whiptail, but the abundance of tabular tools recovered from the site (Table 9.7) indicate that agaves or their relatives were being processed on or near the site. The stalk was probably part of the roofing for Structure 7; similar use of stalks for roofing have been noted at the Continental site, an early Classic period site at the southern edge of the Tucson Basin near Green Valley (Huckell 1997, 2005).

Desert Plants

Cholla (*Cylindropuntia* sp.) is another plant that could have been used as either a cultigen or a wild-gathered plant. Fish (1984:134-135; Bohrer 1991:229) has suggested that cholla were cultivated for their buds. Cholla pollen and buds are common in Hohokam sites in the Tucson Basin (e.g., Fish 1988). Species used by O'odham in southern Arizona include *Opuntia acanthocarpa, O. versicolor,* and *O. spinosior* (Rea 1997). At Whiptail, cholla buds were found in Structure 15 (many from the base of a jar) (Table 9.2) and cholla pollen was found in a vessel on the floor of Structure 19a (Lytle-Webb 1978). Figure 9.3 illustrates some of the buds found in Structure 15 and Table 9.8 lists measurements for a sample of the buds.

Prickly pear (*Opuntia* sp.) pollen and seeds were found in the Agua Caliente Park portion of the Whiptail site (Table 9.3). The pollen came from a midden (Feature 32) and the seeds from a pit (Feature 47) that also yielded charred grass seeds and grass pollen. Grass pollen was also recovered from a rock cluster (Feature 11), the midden (Feature 32), and a roasting pit (Feature 40) in the Agua Caliente Park area (Holloway 2001). The prickly pear pollen and seeds probably indicate that the Whiptail inhabitants were collecting and processing prickly pear fruit. Economically important wild grasses that occur in the

Table 9.3. Pollen and Flotation Data from 2001 Agua Caliente Park Investigations.

Feature No.	Feature Type	Sample No. and Type	Taxon	Common Name	Comments
6	roasting pit	1140–pollen	Cheno-am	Chenopod, amaranth	
		1140–pollen	low-spine Asteraceae	Sunflower family	
		1142–flotation	*Prosopis* or *Acacia*	Mesquite or Acacia	Wood charcoal
11	rock cluster	1164–pollen	*Pinus*	Pine	
			Poaceae	Grass family	
			Cheno-am	Chenopod, amaranth	
			low-spine Asteraceae	Sunflower family	
32	midden	825–pollen	*Pinus*	Pine	
			Poaceae	Grass	
			Cheno-am	Chenopod, amaranth	
			Artemisia	Sage	
			Polygonum	Knotweed, smartweed	
			Opuntia	Prickly pear	
40	roasting pit	909–pollen	Cheno-am	Chenopod, amaranth	
			low-spine Asteraceae	Sunflower family	
			Poaceae	Grass family	
44	midden	846–pollen	Cheno-am	Chenopod, amaranth	
			low-spine Asteraceae	Sunflower family	
47	pit	743, 754–pollen	Asteraceae	Sunflower family	low- and high-spine types
			Cheno-am	Chenopod, amaranth	
			Pinus	Pine	
			Poaceae	Grass family	
			Polygonum	Knotweed, smartweed	
			Ephedra	Joint-fir; Mormon tea	
47	pit	753, 748–flotation	*Opuntia*	Prickly pear	Seeds
			Poaceae	Grass family	Seeds
47	pit	not available	*Zea*	Corn	used for radiocarbon dating
72	roasting pit	2182–flotation	Conifer	Conifer	charcoal
72	roasting pit	2183–pollen	*Pinus*	Pine	
			Cheno-am	Chenopod, amaranth	
			Sphaeralcea	Globe mallow	

Source: Holloway 2001.

vicinity of Whiptail include Indian rice grass (*Oryzopsis* sp.) and dropseed (*Sporobolus* sp.). Although the seeds can be eaten raw, they are usually parched and then ground (Puseman 1996:452). Such activity would leave the kind of evidence found in pit Feature 47.

Saguaro (*Carnegiea gigantea*) rib segments and callus tissue were recovered from the roofing material of Structure 7 (Table 9.2). The callus tissue included a boot and several larger plates of tissue. Saguaro rib impressions in adobe were also found in the roofing material in Structure 12 (Figure 2.13).

Two fragments of a paper-thin cactus tissue with a conical shape (the largest is 12.0 by 18.0 mm) were found in Structure 15. According to Huckell's analysis, the tissue looks like a tubercle from a small ceroid cactus that had been roasted or charred. Some superimposed strips that were either cactus epidermis or leaf sections from another succulent were also found in the house (Table 9.2).

Samples from the Agua Caliente Park portion of Whiptail yielded pollen from two medicinally important desert plants—joint-fir (*Ephedra* sp.) and globe mallow (*Sphaeralcea* sp.) (Holloway 2001). The joint-fir pollen was found in pit Feature 47 and the globe mallow pollen was found in a roasting pit (Feature 72). Joint-fir, made into a tea, has been used as a diuretic, for venereal disease, and for kidney disease (Kay 1996:142-143). Globe mallow roots, mashed and made into a tea, have been used to treat diarrhea and sore throat (Kay 1996:259).

Composite, chenopod-amaranth, and *Artemisia* pollen occurred in Lytle-Webb's (1978) and Holloway's (2001) samples from the site. These pollen taxa are generally assumed to be from weedy species that would have been common in an active village, although some of these weeds have economic value as greens or as medicinal herbs.

One such plant is woolly tidestromia or woolly honeysweet (*Tidestromia languginosa*), a low-growing amaranth with fuzzy leaves. The Mayo make a tea from the leaves of this plant for use in alleviating the paint of ant bites (Yetman and Van Devender 2002:138). At Whiptail, pollen from the plant was found in samples from four vessels (two from Structure 17 and two from Structure 19a) (Lytle-Webb 1978). Although the pollen may have been deposited naturally along with composite and chenopod-amaranth pollen, it is possible that the presence of tidestromia is from medicinal use of the plant. The levels of *Tidestromia* pollen were particularly high in the Structure 19a samples. Incidentally, *Tidestromia* sp. pollen was also identified in samples from house floors at the Gibbon Springs site (Fish 1996).

Figure 9.3. Charred cholla buds found in Structure 15 (photograph by Lisa W. Huckell).

Wash-Associated Plants

Wash-associated plants found at Whiptail include mesquite (*Prosopis* sp.) and net-leaf hackberry (*Celtis reticulata*). Charred mesquite posts and wood were found in Structures 7, 8, 12, 13, and 15 (Table 9.9). In all of the houses except for Structure 13, the wood was used in conjunction with juniper and piñon pine poles.

Uncarbonized hackberry endocarps were found in Structure 15. Given that the other botanical materials in Structure 15 were charred and that uncharred plant materials rarely survive in an open site like Whiptail, it is likely that the endocarps were brought into the feature by a rodent or other small animal.

Water-Loving Plants

As might be expected, pollen and macrofossils from water-loving and water-dependent plants were found in Whiptail features. Lytle-Webb (1978) recovered cattail or bur reed pollen (*Typha* or *Spargium* sp.) from a vessel associated with Structure 17. Ethnographically, cattails have several economic uses, from food (roots and stalks), to weaving (leaves), to ceremonial scattering and body decoration (pollen) (Curtin 1949; Rea 1997:109).

Reeds (*Phragmites* sp.) were widely used in roofing and walls at Whiptail. Reed culms were recovered from four structures at Whiptail (Structures 7, 11, 14, and 15 (Table 9.2) and burned reeds were noted but not recovered from Structures 19a, 25, and 31a. Reed impressions were found in adobe roof and wall fall in Structures 7, 16, 27b, 31b, and 40 (Chapter 2).

Table 9.4. Structure 15 Maize Kernel Metric Data in Millimeters.

Kernel Number	Height	Width	Thickness
1	7.5	8.5	6.0
2	7.5	8.6	5.3
3	8.0	8.7	5.8
4	8.0	9.4	6.2
5	7.3	11.3	6.3
6	8.0	8.5	5.9
7	8.1	8.5	6.5
8	7.8	10.5	6.2
9	8.1	9.1	5.7
10	7.3	9.5	5.0
11	7.4	9.3	5.2
12	8.1	8.5	6.7
13	7.1	9.1	5.3
14	7.1	9.2	5.6
X (Mean)	7.67	9.19	5.84
St. Dev.	0.37	0.79	0.50
Extremes	7.1-8.1	8.5-11.3	5.0-6.7

Holloway (2001) found knotweed or smartweed (*Polygonum* sp.) pollen in samples from a midden (Feature 32) and a pit (Feature 47) in the Agua Caliente Park portion of Whiptail. *Polygonum* species plants have been used by the Acoma, Zuni, and Laguna for a variety of ailments relating to the digestive system (Stevenson 1915; Swank 1932).

Lytle-Webb (1978) found willow (*Salix* sp.) pollen in her samples from Whiptail. It is not clear if the pollen from this plant was the result of cultural activity or if it was deposited as part of the local environment.

Woods from the Mountains

The archaeologists working at Whiptail noticed early on that some houses contained charred posts and beams that were large for Hohokam sites. Rather than take a few samples for radiocarbon dating or archaeobotanical analysis, the excavators decided to collect the wood as dendrochronological samples. An initial analysis by Jeffrey Dean indicated that much of the wood was coniferous and that some of it was datable, although in the 1970s, he was unable to develop a sequence that could be tied to a master sequence (Dean et al. 1996). Dean's reanalysis and success in dating the woods is discussed in Chapter 11.

The species that Dean identified are piñon pine (*Pinus discolor*), ponderosa pine (*P. ponderosa*), and juniper (*Juniperus* sp.) (Table 9.9). They were found in structures in the Compound Locus (Structures 7, 8, and 17), the Southwestern Locus (Structures 10, 11, 12, 16, 18), the Central Locus (Structure 15), and the Southern Locus (Structures 14 and 19a). The Hohokam could have collected wood that washed down from the Santa Catalina Mountains. The cluster of dates in the A.D. 1230s and A.D. 1240s (Table 11.1) suggests, however, that the wood was all cut (or died) during a relatively short period of time. This implies that the Hohokam went into the Catalinas to procure the wood. A wider range of dates would imply that the Whiptail builders were scavenging older wood.

Summary

The range of botanical materials recovered from the Whiptail Ruin seems limited when compared with those from other early Classic period sites, such as nearby Gibbon Springs, the Continental site near Green Valley, and the San Xavier Bridge site near Mission San Xavier (Table 9.10). Rather than being a true indicator of the nature of botanical specimens at the site, the limited numbers of taxa recovered are likely due to the data recovery techniques and analysis procedures used in the 1970s, the problems in storing the materials over the decades, and the problems we ran into in accounting for and retrieving all of the materials from Whiptail as

Table 9.5 Structure 15 Bean Sample Metric Data in Millimeters.

Bean Number	Length (n = 28)	Length (n = 26)	Width (n = 28)	Width (n = 26)	Thickness (n = 28)	Thickness (n = 26)	Hilum Length	BL/HL
1	10.5	-----	6.1	-----	5.3	-----	-----	-----
2	9.5	9.5	5.3	5.3	5.0	5.0	2.8	3.39
3	7.8	7.8	4.6	4.6	3.9	3.9	-----	-----
4	9.3	9.3	5.9	5.9	4.8	4.8	-----	-----
5	8.2	8.2	4.7	4.7	4.0	4.0	-----	-----
6	7.7	7.7	4.3	4.3	3.0	3.0	-----	-----
7	9.2	9.2	5.8	5.8	3.5	3.5	-----	-----
8	11.0	-----	7.0	-----	5.8	-----	-----	-----
9	9.2	9.2	5.0	5.0	4.8	4.8	-----	-----
10	8.8	8.8	5.8	5.8	4.3	4.3	-----	-----
11	9.3	9.3	5.5	5.5	4.5	4.5	-----	-----
12	8.4	8.4	5.0	5.0	4.1	4.1	-----	-----
13	7.4	7.4	4.5	4.5	3.6	3.6	-----	-----
14	7.3	7.3	4.4	4.4	3.4	3.4	2.0	3.65
15	6.5	6.5	3.8	3.8	3.1	3.1	2.3	2.83
16	8.2	8.2	5.3	5.3	3.6	3.6	2.0	4.10
17	8.0	8.0	4.6	4.6	3.0	3.0	-----	-----
18	7.5	7.5	4.7	4.7	3.2	3.2	-----	-----
19	8.8	8.8	5.2	5.2	3.5	3.5	-----	-----
20	8.7	8.7	5.3	5.3	4.6	4.6	-----	-----
21	9.3	9.3	5.7	5.7	4.1	4.1	-----	-----
22	9.1	9.1	5.7	5.7	4.4	4.4	-----	-----
23	7.0	7.0	4.8	4.8	4.4	4.4	-----	-----
24	8.0	8.0	5.7	5.7	4.5	4.5	-----	-----
25	8.0	8.0	4.9	4.9	4.7	4.7	-----	-----
26	8.2	8.2	4.7	4.7	4.6	4.6	-----	-----
27	7.1	7.1	4.8	4.8	3.4	3.4	-----	-----
28	7.9	7.9	4.6	4.6	3.7	3.7	-----	-----
X (Mean)	8.43	8.25	5.13	5.02	4.1	4.0	2.28	3.70
St. Dev.	1.02	0.81	0.67	0.54	0.71	0.60	0.33	-----
Extremes	6.5-11.0	6.5 - 9.5	3.8-7.0	3.8-5.9	3.0-5.8	3.0-5.0	2.0-2.8	2.83-4.1

Key: BL/HL = Ratio of bean length divided by hilum length.

we proceeded on this project. These issues may be exemplified by comparing the earlier pollen and macrobotanical data with Holloway's data from features in the Agua Caliente Park portion of the site. In a relatively small number of samples, Holloway (2001) added five plant species, some of which are culturally significant, to the overall count (Table 9.3).

In terms of use, the Whiptail samples included edible, medicinal, and structural plants, as well as species that could have been used to make baskets, mats, and other utilitarian objects. Foods that occurred at Whiptail that are commonly found in other sites are corn, beans, and cholla (Table 9.10). Macrofossils of these plants were all found in Structure 15, a building that is thought to have been a storeroom.

Pollen and macrofossils from two other important food plants, agave and saguaro, have been found at the Continental and San Xavier Bridge sites (Table 9.10; Davis 1997; Fish 1987; Gasser 1987; Holloway 2005; Huckell 1997, 2005). Saguaro macrofossils and pollen were also recovered from the Gibbon Springs site (Table 9.10; Fish 1996; Puseman 1996;). Although food-related plant parts were not recovered from Whiptail, agave stalk fragments and saguaro wood and callus tissue (Table 9.2), indicate familiarity with these important economic plants. And the numerous tabular

Table 9.6. Structure 15 Large Bean Metric Data in Millimeters.

Large Bean Number	Length	Width	Thickness	LH Lot No.
1	10.50	6.10	5.30	1
2	11.00	7.00	5.80	1
3	11.80	6.30	2.80*	5b
4	11.20	7.00	6.00	15
5	10.25	7.00	6.30	15
X Mean	10.95	6.68	5.85	
St. Dev.	0.54	0.40	0.36	
Extremes	10.25-11.8	6.1-7.0	5.3-6.3	

Key: * = cotyledon.

tools found at Whiptail (Table 9.7) show that the site's residents were processing agave or similar plants.

Some of the weedy species recovered from Whiptail and other early Classic period sites may have been used as greens or for medicine. Among these are *Tidestromia* sp., *Sphaeralcea* sp., *Ephedra* sp., and *Polygonum* sp.

In addition to Whiptail, *Tidestromia* sp. pollen has been found at Gibbon Springs (Fish 1996) and the San Xavier Bridge site (Fish 1987). At Whiptail, the counts for *Tidestromia* were high in one feature (Structure 19a) and were found in vessels in Structure 19a and Structure 17, perhaps indicating that people collected the fuzzy leaves. At Gibbon Springs, the pollen occurred in samples from structure floors (Fish 1996), which seems to indicate material that was tracked in. The plant is a common weed in the Tucson area, but it also has medicinal value (Yetman and Van Devender 2002), so either environmental or cultural interpretations (or both) might apply. The same situation may be true for *Ephedra* sp., a wind-pollinated plant, and *Polygonum,* a water-associated plant, that occurred in the Agua Caliente Park portion of Whiptail (Table 9.3; Holloway 2002).

Sphaeralcea sp. pollen has been recovered from Whiptail (Holloway 2002), Gibbon Springs (Fish 1996), and the San Xavier Bridge site (Fish 1987); globe mallow macrofossils were recovered from the Continental site (Huckell 1997, 2005) and the San Xavier site (Gasser 1987). This insect-pollinated plant may have been collected on purpose at all of these sites, although the sticky stems and seed pods could have been incorporated accidentally into an archaeological setting.

Purposeful collection of cattail (*Typha* sp.) or bur reed (*Sparganium* sp.) is indicated by pollen found in a vessel in Structure 17 at Whiptail. Cattail pollen has also been found at Gibbon Springs (Fish 1996), the Continental site (Huckell 1997, 2005), and the San Xavier Bridge site (Fish 1987). Uses of cattail and bur reed range from medicinal and ceremonial (the pollen itself) to utilitarian (leaves used for baskets and mats).

Table 9.7. Distribution of Tabular Tools.

Structure No.	Whole Tool	Fragment	Number of Artifacts
Compound Locus			
4		5	5
6		5	5
8		1	1
17		1	1
Central Locus			
5		1	1
15		5	5
Southwestern Locus			
2		9	9
9	2	1	3
10	2	8	10
11	1	3	4
12	7	3	10
13		1	1
16		3	3
18	3	1	4
23	1	1	2
24		2	2
25	3	2	5
Northern Locus			
3		1	1
28	1		1
29	2	2	4
30	1	5	6
27a		1	1
27b	2	4	6
Total Number of Artifacts	25	65	90

Table 9.8. Structure 15 Cholla Bud Sample Metric Data in Millimeters.

Cholla Bud Number	Length	Diameter
1	10.8	5.8
2	11.0	6.8
3	15.5	5.8
4	15.0	6.3
5	15.3	5.8
6	11.3	5.0
7	11.5	5.0
8	10.8	5.5
9	10.8	5.3
10	10.8	5.5
11	11.0	4.5
12	11.0	6.8
X (mean)	12.1	5.7
St. Dev.	1.86	0.67
Extremes	10.8-15.5	4.5-6.8

The excavators of Whiptail and Gibbon Springs found numerous examples of plants used for construction of the houses at the two sites (Table 9.10). At Whiptail, the best example of the materials used for wall and roof construction were found in Structure 7. There, *Phragmites* culms and impressions, saguaro callus material and wood, agave stalk fragments, and mesquite and juniper wood were all recovered (Table 9.2; Table 9.9). The mesquite and juniper were probably used as posts and beams, with the other material being used as latillas (saguaro wood and agave stalks) and mats to cover the ceiling (*Phragmites* sp.).

The amount of coniferous wood recovered from Whiptail and Gibbon Springs shows intentional rather than casual use of juniper, piñon, ponderosa pine, and (at Gibbon Springs), Douglas fir (Dean and Bowden 1996; Dean et al. 1996). The cultural implications of conifer use by the Whiptail inhabitants are discussed in Chapter 11.

The botanical materials recovered indicate that the Whiptail inhabitants made good use of their local environment. The springs allowed them to harvest plants such as knotweed and cattail, as well as grow corn and beans. The desert foothills and washes provided a variety of wood and cactus. And the nearby mountains allowed the Whiptail residents to obtain woods that reminded some of them of their northern homelands.

Table 9.9. Structural Wood Identification Summary Data.

Sample No.	Structure	Provenience	Specimen No.	Taxon
1	7	SW corner, floor	WTR-4	cf. *Prosopis*
2	7	Floor along west wall	WTR-6	cf. *Prosopis*
3	7	SW quarter, level 3 + floor	WTR-18-1	cf. *Prosopis*
4	7	Floor	WTR-19	cf. *Prosopis*
5	7	SE quarter, floor	WTR-24	cf. *Prosopis*
6	7	West of center, level 3- lower fill	WTR-25	*Juniperus*
7	8	SW corner, floor	WTR-5	cf. *Prosopis*
8	8	SW quarter, level 4	WTR-29	*Pinus discolor*
9	8	Center along N-S axis, floor	WTR-15	*Juniperus*
10	8	SE quarter, floor	WTR-20	*Pinus ponderosa*
11	8	SE quarter, floor: Parallel to east wall	WTR-30	*P. ponderosa*
12	8	SE quarter, floor: 1 foot east of beam closest to hearth	WTR-31	*P. ponderosa*
13	8	SE quarter, floor: Parallel to east wall	WTR-32	*P. discolor**
14	8	SE quarter, floor: Near vertical beam	WTR-33	*P. discolor*
15	8	Level 4: over sherd cluster 4	WTR-27	*P. ponderosa*
16	8	Level 4	WTR-28	*P. ponderosa*
17	10	East wall, center	WTR-1	*P. ponderosa**
18	10	East wall, center	WTR-3	*P. ponderosa*
19	10	East posthole	WTR-14	*Juniperus*
20	10	East half support post	WTR-34	*Juniperus*
21	10	NE corner	WTR-36	*P. ponderosa*
22	10	West wall, center	WTR-2	*P. ponderosa*
23	10	West Wall	WTR-7	*Juniperus*
24	10	West end	WTR-8	*Juniperus*
25	10	Diagonal from west wall: SE-NW orientation	WTR-9	*P. ponderosa**
26	10	NW of hearth: SW-NE orientation	WTR-10	*P. ponderosa*
27	10	Halfway between west wall and hearth	WTR-11	*P. ponderosa*
28	10	Beam	WTR-35	*P. ponderosa**
29	11	South wall	WTR-12	*P. ponderosa*
30	11	NE corner	WTR-13	*P. ponderosa*
31	12	NE corner in lithic cluster	NA	cf. *Prosopis*
32	12	East posthole	NA	*Juniperus*
33	13	NW quarter, lower fill	WTR-22	cf. *Prosopis*
34	13	NW quarter, corner	WTR-26	cf. *Prosopis*
35	14	NE quarter, lower fill	WTR-37	*P. ponderosa*
36	14	NE quarter, floor: near north wall, center	WTR-38	*P. ponderosa*
37	14	NE quarter, floor	WTR-39	*P. ponderosa*
38	14	NW quarter, fill: 3 inches above floor	WTR-41	*P. ponderosa*
39	14	NW quarter, floor	WTR-40	*P. ponderosa*
40	14	SE quarter, lower fill	WTR-44	*P. ponderosa*
41	14	SE quarter, lower fill	WTR-45	*P. ponderosa*
42	14	SE quarter, floor	WTR-42	*P. ponderosa*
43	14	SE quarter, floor	WTR-43	*P. ponderosa*
44	14	SW quad, lower fill: along south wall	WTR-46	*P. ponderosa*
45	14	Center, 30 cm south of north wall	WTR-47	*P. ponderosa*
46	14	Center, 30 cm south of north wall	WTR-48	*P. ponderosa*
47	14	Center, 30 cm south of north wall	WTR-49	*P. ponderosa*
48	14	East end, lower fill	WTR-50	*P. ponderosa*
49	14	East end, lower fill	WTR-51	*P. ponderosa*
50	14	East end, lower fill	WTR-52	*P. ponderosa*
51	14	East end, lower fill	WTR-53	*P. ponderosa*
52	14	East end, lower fill	WTR-54	*P. ponderosa*
53	15	NE quarter, between entry and hearth	WTR-55	*Juniperus*
54	15	NE quarter, between entry and hearth	WTR-56	*P. discolor**
55	15	NE quarter, floor: near center of house	WTR-57	*P. discolor*
56	15	NW quarter, floor: near north wall, west of entry	WTR-58	*P. discolor*
57	15	NW quarter, floor: near north wall, west of entry	WTR-59	*Juniperus*
58	15	SE corner, lower fill 2: on top of sherd layer	WTR-61	*P. ponderosa*
59	15	SE quarter, lower fill 2	WTR-60	*P. discolor**

Table 9.9. Structural Wood Identification Summary Data, cont'd.

Sample No.	Structure	Provenience	Specimen No.	Taxon
60	15	SE quarter, floor	WTR-62	*P. discolor**
61	15	SE quarter, floor	WTR-63	*P. discolor*
62	15	SE quarter, lower fill 2	WTR-64	*P. discolor**
63	15	SE quarter, lower fill 2	WTR-23	cf. *Prosopis*
64	15	SE quarter, floor	WTR-65	*Juniperus*
65	16	NW quarter	WTR-66	*P. discolor*
66	16	NW quarter, floor	WTR-70	*P. discolor*
67	16	SE quarter, Beam 1	WTR-69	*P. discolor*
68	16	SE quarter floor, Beam 3: 90 cm from east wall along south wall	WTR-67	*P. discolor**
69	16	SE quarter, Beam 4: Middle of east wall, N-S orientation	WTR-68	*P. discolor*
70	16	Floor	WTR-16	*P. ponderosa*
71	16	Floor	WTR-17	*P. discolor**
72	17	NE quarter, lower fill	WTR-71	*P. ponderosa*
73	17	NE quarter, lower fill	WTR-72	*P. ponderosa*
74	17	NW quarter, lower fill	WTR-73	*P. ponderosa*
75	17	NW quarter, lower fill	WTR-74	*P. ponderosa*
76	17	NW quarter, lower fill	WTR-75	*P. ponderosa*
77	17	NW quarter, lower fill	WTR-76	*P. ponderosa*
78	17	NW quarter, lower fill	WTR-77	*P. ponderosa*
79	17	SE quarter, lower fill	WTR-78	*P. ponderosa*
80	17	SE quarter, lower fill	WTR-79	*P. ponderosa*
81	17	SE quarter, lower fill: Near south wall	WTR-80	*P. ponderosa*
82	17	SE quarter, lower fill: Between shaft straightener and wall	WTR-81	*P. ponderosa*
83	17	SE quarter, lower fill: along east wall	WTR-82	*P. ponderosa*
84	18	East posthole	WTR-83	*Juniperus*
85	18	Unknown	WTR-84	*Juniperus*
86	19	SW quarter	WTR-96	*P. ponderosa**
87	19	Beam	WTR-112	*P. ponderosa**
88	19	Beam	WTR-114	*P. ponderosa**
89	NA	Vessel 3	WTR-94	*P. ponderosa**
90	NA	Unknown	WTR-100	*P. ponderosa**
91	NA	Unknown	WTR-101	*P. ponderosa**

Key * = tree-ring date obtained.
Source: Adapted from Dean 1969, Dean et al. 1996:Table 2.

Table 9.10. Archaeobotanical Remains from Classic Period Hohokam Sites.

Taxon	Common name	Whiptail Ruin (AZ BB:10:3)	Gibbon Springs (AZ BB:9:50)	Continental Site (AZ EE:1:32)	San Xavier Bridge (AZ BB:13:14)
Zea	Maize	M	M, P	M/ P	M, P
Phaseolus	Bean	M	M	M	M
P. vulgaris	Common bean			M	
P. cf. *acutifolius*	Tepary bean			M	
Cucurbita	Squash			M	P
Gossypium	Cotton			M	M, P
Agave	Agave			M, P	M
Acacia	Acacia: unid species				M
Amaranthus	Amaranth				M
Apodanthera	Melon loco			M	
Artemisia	Sage	P			
Asteraceae	Sunflower Family: High spine	P	P	P	P
Asteraceae	Sunflower Family: Low spine	P	P	M, P	P
Astragalus	Vetch				M
Atriplex	Saltbush		M (cf.)	M	M
Boerhaavia	Spiderling		(P)	M, P	(P)
Brassicaceae	Mustard Family		P	M, P	M, P
Carnegiea	Saguaro		M, P	M, P	M, P
Cereoid cactus	Saguaro/Hedgehog type		P	P	
ChenoAm	Chenopod/Amaranth	P	P	M, P	M, P
Cercidium	Paloverde		P		P
Chenopodium	Goosefoot			M	M
Cycloloma	Winged pigweed			M	
Cylindropuntia	Cholla cactus	M, P	M, P	P	M, P
Cyperaceae	Sedge Family			P	P
Descurainia	Tansy mustard		M	M	
Echinocereus	Hedgehog cactus			M	M
Ephedra	Joint-fir, Mormon tea	P			
Eriogonum	Wild buckwheat		P	M, P	M, P
Euphorbia	Spurge		P	M	M, P
Fabaceae	Bean Familly				M
Kallstroemia	Caltrop, Arizona poppy		(P)	M	P
Lamiaceae	Mint Family			P	P
Larrea	Creosotebush		P	P	P
Mentzelia	Stickleaf			M	
Onagraceae	Primrose Family		P	P	P
Opuntia	Prickly pear cactus	M, P	M, P	P	M, P
Phragmites	Reedgrass	M	M (cf.)		
Poaceae	Grass Family	M, P	M, P	M, P	M, P
Polygonaceae	Buckwheat Family			P	
Polygonum	Knotweed, smartweed	P			
Portulaca	Purslane			M	
Prosopis	Mesquite		P	M	M, P
Quercus	Oak acorn		P	M/ P	P
cf. *Scirpus*	Bulrush				M
Solanaceae	Nightshade Family		P	M (cf.)	
Sphaeralcea	Globemallow	P	(P)	M	M, P
Sporobolus	Dropseed grass			M	
Tidestromia	Tidestromia	P	P		P
Trianthema	Horse purslane			M	M
Typha/Sparganium	Cattail/Bur-Reed	P	P	P	P
Wood:				NA	NA
Agave	Agave	X			
Carnegiea	Saguaro	X			
Cercidium	Paloverde		X		
Juniperus	Juniper	X	X		
Larrea	Creosotebush		X		

Table 9.10. Archaeobotanical Remains from Classic Period Hohokam Sites, cont'd.

Taxon	Common name	Whiptail Ruin (AZ BB:10:3)	Gibbon Springs (AZ BB:9:50)	Continental Site (AZ EE:1:32)	San Xavier Bridge (AZ BB:13:14)
Pinus discolor	Piñon pine	X	X		
Pinus ponderosa	Ponderosa pine	X	X		
Populus	Listed as poplar, probably cottonwood		X		
Prosopis	Mesquite	X	X		
Pseudotsuga	Douglas fir		X		
Salicaceae	Willow Family		X		

Key: M = macrofossil; P = Pollen; (P) = equivocal as economic plant (Fish 1996:478)
Sources: Whiptail: Huckell's analysis for this report, Lytle-Webb 1978; Holloway 2001;
Gibbon Springs: Dean and Bowden 1996; Fish 1996; Puseman 1996;
Continental Site: Huckell 1997, 2005; Davis 1997; Holloway 2005;
San Xavier Bridge, Gasser 1987; Fish 1987.

Chapter 10

Human Remains

Lane Anderson Beck

In the late 1960s and early 1970s, 24 cremations, three inhumations, and eight isolated pieces of human bone were encountered during excavations at the Whiptail Ruin. Remains from 20 of the cremations along with all three inhumations and the isolated finds were transferred to the Arizona State Museum. This chapter provides a general summary of those remains and of the field data located for each of these burials. Data for the cremations are discussed first with data on the inhumations following those sections.

Data on Cremations

Field Data

Search of the field records from the excavations at the Whiptail Ruin failed to discover systematic recording of the burial features. Burial data forms were located for only two features. A listing of artifacts from cremations was located for 12 features. Storage bags in the museum also had occasional references to field provenience or associations. No information as to either intrasite provenience, feature structure, or associations was located for a majority of the human remains. This lack of specificity in the field data seriously limits the extent of mortuary analysis that can be conducted for this site.

The field notes make reference to two cemeteries within the site. Cemetery 1 is on the southeastern edge of the Southwestern Locus, just west of compound Structure 8 (Figure 1.13). Cremations 1 through 13 were found in this area. Cremation 14 was found in Cemetery 2, which was situated west of the Central Locus. No locational information is provided for the other cremations. The presence of two cemeteries suggests that, like other sites of this period, interment of cremations was in clustered groups adjacent to clusters of structures.

From the limited field data available, it appears that there were three modes for interment of cremated remains. The notes that do exist identify Cremations 1, 5, 6, 9, and 12 as having been recovered from small pits. In each case, sherds are noted as having been present in these pits. Cremations 2 and 3 were reported to have been found in sherd concentrations and to have extremely little human bone present. No human remains from either of these cremations were turned over to the Arizona State Museum or could be located among any of the site collections. Cremations 4, 7, 8, and 10 are reported to have been found in pots.

Artifact listings were located for Cremations 1 through 10 and 12 and 13. Each of these listings stated that sherds were associated with the human remains. In addition, Cremation 1 had a fragment from a shell bracelet in association. Cremation 4 was the only other cremation of these 12 that included further associated materials. Five projectile points, a bone disk, and a bone awl were listed for this feature. The bone disk is roughly one inch in diameter and appears to be made from a human parietal, possibly that of a juvenile. (The bone thickness is less than would be expected for most adults.) Notes of the storage containers for Cremations 14 and 15 suggest that they were also associated with either sherds or reconstructible bowls. No further information on burial associations was discovered.

Biological Data

Bone from all cremations was gray to white in color. Extensive transverse cracking and warping was noted for each individual. Portions of most cremations were calcined with other fragments being more friable in texture. This pattern of burning is consistent with experimental studies on cremation. Cremation of a body is associated in many studies with transverse cracks and warpage while burning of dried bone yields a lesser degree of deformation of the bone. The burning of an intact body in a hot fire (500 to 800 degrees centigrade or higher) for an extended interval (greater than the few hours reported in most burning experiments) has been demonstrated to produce this pattern of burning (Baby 1954).

Of the 20 cremations available for observation, 18 were identified as adults, one as a child, and one was too fragmentary for evaluation. The adults ranged in age from young adults in their late teens or early twenties to individuals over forty years of age. Of the adults, sex could be identified for eight individuals, four males and four females (Table 10.1).

Bone weight for the cremations from Whiptail ranges from a low of 42 grams to a high of 1761 grams. Of the 20 cremations that were transferred to the museum, six had weights between 42 g and 100 g, ten had weights between 100 g and 1000 g, and four had weights over 1000 g. Size of fragments ranged from less than one centimeter in greatest dimension to over 20 cm in length. The cremations of greatest weight included the full range of size while those of lower weights were generally composed of only the smaller fragments. The cremations of greater weight were all recovered from pots, while those of lower weight, for which there are records, come from small pits mixed with scattered sherds.

Cremations in general do not allow for serious discussion of health and disease. The random nature of fragments that survive burning renders any effort at epidemiological analysis impossible. Aside from observations of arthritis among the older individuals, the only pathologies noted for the cremations from Whiptail were a mild periosteal reaction on the tibia of Cremation 10 and a possible healed

Table 10.1. Cremations.

Cremation No.	Structure	Associations	Weight in grams	Age	Sex	Comments
1	pit	sherds, shell bracelet	700	unknown	male	Cemetery 1
2	in sherds	sherds	unknown	unknown	unknown	Cemetery 1, field notes say very little bone
3	in sherds	sherds	unknown	unknown	unknown	Cemetery 1, field notes say very little bone
4	in pot	Tanque Verde Red-on-brown jar, 5 projectile points, bone disk, bone awl, sherds	1307	young adult to mature adult	unknown	Cemetery 1
5	pit	sherds	580	mature adult to old adult	unknown	Cemetery 1, sherd and bone cluster in SW corner of pit, pit 15 by 10 cm
6	pit	sherds	418	subadult to old adult	male	Cemetery 1
7	in pot	plain ware jar	1475	mature adult	male	Cemetery 1
8	in pot	Tularosa Black-on-white jar	205	child	unknown	Cemetery 1
9	pit	sherds	215	mature adult to old adult	male?	Cemetery 1
10	in pot	plain ware jar, San Carlos Plain bowl, Tanque Verde Red-on-brown cover sherd	1751	mature adult to old adult	female?	Cemetery 1
11	unknown	unknown	unknown	unknown	unknown	no field notes or remains located
12	pit	sherds	1057	mature adult	female	Cemetery 1
13	unknown	Tanque Verde Red-on-brown bowl sherd	unknown	unknown	unknown	
14	in pot?	bowl	252	young adult to mature adult	female?	Cemetery 2
15	in pot?	urn	747	young adult	female?	
16	unknown	warped plain ware bowl inverted over cremains	673	young adult to mature adult	unknown	
17	unknown	unknown	42	adult	unknown	
18	unknown	unknown	73	subadult to old adult	unknown	
18	unknown	unknown	89	unknown	unknown	
20	unknown	unknown	385	adult	unknown	
21	unknown	unknown	58	adult	unknown	
22	unknown	unknown	78	adult	unknown	
23	in pot?	Pinedale Black-on-white jar	98	adult	unknown	Cemetery 2?
24	unknown	unknown	425	young adult	unknown	

fracture of an unidentified metatarsal in the same individual.

Each set of cremated remains appeared to represent one individual. The exception to this is that the remains of the child, Cremation 8, included four fragments of bone from an adult. In the literature, when cremations containing multiple individuals are reported, they most often involved the combination of a child with an adult.

Interpretations

The weight of bone from modern cremations is reported to be roughly 1750 grams for the typical adult (Binford 1972). No modern weight range for the cremation of children is reported in the literature. Hohokam cremations are notorious for being well below the expected weight range. Often the average weight reported for a site is significantly less than 500 grams.

In general, three explanations have been offered for the low bone weight in Hohokam cremations: fragmentation via stirring of the pyre, careless or incomplete "gleaning" of the cremated remains prior to burial, and the division of cremated remains with multiple deposits being created to hold the remains of each individual. None of these explanations appears to fit the pattern of the data.

When one examines the distributions of bone weight within any Hohokam cremation cemetery, it becomes apparent that discussion of average weights is meaningless. For most sites, there are a few individuals in the low end of the weight range reported for modern cremations. The loss of some bone due to the open air burning process and passage through the archaeological record is to be expected. For most sites there is a bell-shaped distribution that runs from perhaps 400 g to 800 g and a second mode between 50 g and 100 g. This bimodal (or trimodal) distribution of bone weights raises the suggestion that distinctly varied processes were involved before the cremated remains entered the archaeological record.

As previously mentioned, bone weight for the cremations from Whiptail ranges from a low of 42 g to a high of 1716 g. Of the 20 cremations that were transferred to the museum, 10 had weights between 100 g and 1000 g, and four had weights over 1000 grams. The size of the bone fragments in the more complete cremations ranged from pieces less than 1 cm in length to pieces nearly 20 cm long. The size of fragments in the lower weight cremations tended to be smaller, averaging less than 5 cm in length. This overlap in fragment size suggests that archaeological recovery was comparable for all cremations and cannot explain the low weights. Similarly, the fact that the lightest weight cremations also tend to have generally smaller fragments argues against careless "gleaning" of the cremation pyre as the explanation.

Variation in age also cannot account for the lightest cremations. Only one child was identified in the 20 cremations examined and the remains of that child were slightly over 200 g in weight. In fact, the lightest weight cremations were all identified as the remains of adults. Similarly, sex cannot explain the weight differences. Although sex could not be determined for the most incomplete cremations, eight of the more complete adults were identified by sex. Of these eight, four were male and four female. The highest weight cremation (Cremation 10 at 1716 g) is that of an adult female.

Another explanation that has been proposed to account for the low bone weight is the practice of stirring the ashes (Birkby 1976; Dongoske 1986). The act of stirring might, in fact, produce greater fragmentation of the bone in a cremation, but would not serve to reduce its weight.

Rodent disturbance also must be eliminated as an explanation. When rodents disturb a cremation feature, their disturbance is random in form. They do not selectively remove the larger fragments. At other sites, features exhibiting the greatest degree of rodent disturbance were not necessarily those with either low bone weights or small fragment size (Beck 2000).

In the Snaketown report, Haury (1976) cited Spier (1970) as offering a possible explanation for the low bone quantity recovered from Hohokam cremations. The ethnographic report referred to describes a process where the ashes from a cremation are divided into four portions, which are each buried separately. Researchers reporting on Hohokam cremations since that date make frequent reference to this concept. Various refitting efforts have failed to find biological data to support this idea (Birkby 1976; Dongoske 1986; Reinhard and Fink 1982). The pattern reported by Spier is described as being highly unusual ethnologically. Furthermore, it would produce a patterning in the various deposits where each deposit held remains primarily from one quadrant of the individual's body. This distribution of body parts simply does not exist in Hohokam cremations. Furthermore, there is extensive duplication of specific elements among various cremations (see Beck 2000 for further discussion). Table 10.2 includes a listing of general areas of the body identified in each cremation from Whiptail.

Elsewhere (Beck 2000), I have argued that the medium to high weight cremation deposits

Table 10.2. Representation of Body in Cremations.

Cremation No.	Portions of body present
1	head, torso, arms, legs
2	unknown
3	unknown
4	head, torso, arms, legs
5	head, torso, arms, legs
6	head, torso, arms legs
7	head, torso, arms, legs
8	head, torso, arms, legs
9	head, torso, arms legs
10	head, torso, arms, legs
11	unknown
12	head, torso, arms, legs
13	unknown
14	head, torso, arms, legs
15	head, torso, arms legs
16	head, torso, arms, legs
17	arms, legs
18	head, arms, legs
19	arms, legs
20	head, torso, arms, legs
21	torso, arms, legs
22	torso, arms, legs
23	head, torso, arms, legs
24	head, torso arms, legs

from Hohokam sites represent the initial interment of cremated remains that were removed from the pyre, and that the lighter weight deposits may represent secondary interment of re-burnt remains following a mourning ceremony. The fact that, for those cremations with some field data, the highest weight cremations were all recovered from pots may suggest that interment in a pot represents the initial burial procedure at Whiptail. The medium weight cremations are described as coming from simple pits, and the lightest weight from scatters of sherds. It is possible that these are secondary burials. Without adequate field records, it is impossible to further test this concept at Whiptail.

Data on Inhumations

It appears from the human remains at the Arizona State Museum that three inhumations were recovered from Whiptail (Table 10.3). As with the cremations, the field data are largely incomplete. A burial record form was located only for Burial 1. A field sketch marked Burial 2 lists Structure 29 as the location. Figure 2.21 shows the location of Burial 3, which was found in Structure 27b.

Burial 1 is designated as being found in the southeast quad of Structure 28. The field notes describe the burial position as being flexed, but the field sketch of the burial suggests this is questionable. The remains are extremely incomplete and appear disorganized in the drawing. A shell bracelet, a shell ring, and a projectile point are described as associated with this individual. The remains are clearly those of an adult. Although the remains are fragmentary, the general robusticity of the bones suggest that this was a male.

Remains I have tentatively termed Burial 2 are identified on the storage bags as coming from Structure 29. These bones exhibit charring, but not substantial burning. This individual is most likely a young adult male, possibly between the ages of 20 and 40 at the

Table 10.3. Inhumations.

Burial No.	Location	Burnt or Not	Age	Sex	Condition
1	Structure 28, SE quad	no burning	young adult to old adult	male?	extremely fragmented
2	Structure 29	some charring of long bones	young adult to mature adult	male	extremely fragmented
3	Structure 27b, NE quad	no burning	mature adult	male	extremely fragmented

Table 10.4. Isolated Human Bone.

Location	Element	Burning	Age	Sex
Structure 27a, exterior, within pot 96	molar	burned	child	unknown
Structure 8, SW corner of floor	carpal phalanx	burned	adult	unknown
Structure 24, SW quad, center, upper fill	tibia	burned	unknown	unknown
Structure 4, general fill	rib	burned	unknown	unknown
Structure 25, NE half, lower fill, below floor	humerus	burned	adult	unknown
Structure 11, from fill used to cover step	incisor	burned	unknown	unknown
Cremation 4, in jar with remains	bone disk, human parietal	burned	unknown	unknown
Structure 17	long bone fragment	burned	unknown	unknown

time of death. No field data are available.

The final inhumation from Whiptail is listed as being found in Structure 27b in the northeast quad, and is listed on transfer documents as Burial 3. This individual is slightly more complete than the other two. The remains are those of a mature adult male, probably between the ages of 35 and 50 at the time of death. He has a healed fracture of his right clavicle.

Isolated Human Remains

Several pieces of isolated human bone were recovered from Whiptail. They are listed and described in Table 10.4. They include the bone disk previously described, one or more molars from a pot found just outside of Structure 27a, an incisor found in the fill of the entryway step in Structure 11, a long bone fragment from Structure 17, a humerus from Structure 25, a rib from Structure 4, a tibia from Structure 24, and a carpal phalanx from Structure 8. All of the pieces were burned, indicating a probable association with a cremation. The isolated bones and fragments may have washed into the various structures in which they were found. The incisor found in Structure 11 may have been accidentally incorporated into the entryway step, while the molar or molars seems likely to have been purposefully deposited into the pot.

Summary

Twenty-four cremations and three inhumations were reported for the Whiptail Ruin. The cremations include one child and at least 18 adults. Men and women are represented by these cremations. The three inhumations from Whiptail are all adult males. The incomplete nature of the field notes severely limits any analysis of mortuary patterns. It is suggested, by comparison to more complete data from other sites, that the cremations from Whiptail may include initial deposits of cremated remains as well as secondary deposits of reburnt remains following mourning ceremonies.

Chapter 11

Chronology, Ritual, and Migration: The Clues from Whiptail

Linda M. Gregonis

When Bruce Bradley and the Arizona Archaeological and Historical Society began excavating the Whiptail Ruin in the 1960s, the goals of research at the site were simple. Excavators were interested in determining when the site was occupied and how it fit into the culture history of the Tucson Basin and, perhaps, the nearby lower San Pedro Valley. By careful work and paying attention to opportunities, the excavators at Whiptail gathered data that can be used to address a number of current research themes, among them chronology, occupation sequencing, ritual use and abandonment of structures, and the thirteenth-century migration from the Mogollon highlands into Southern Arizona. These themes, along with a comparison of Whiptail with the nearby Gibbon Springs site and others in the eastern Tucson Basin, are addressed in this chapter.

Site Chronology

Dendrochronology

Whiptail Ruin is unusual in that it is one of a handful of Hohokam sites in the Tucson Basin to have yielded datable dendrochronological samples. When the site was excavated in the 1960s and 1970s care was taken to retrieve samples of burned beams and posts for tree-ring dating, even though desert sites were rarely known to yield datable wood. According to Dean et al. (1996:11), 117 samples of ponderosa and piñon pine, juniper, and nonconiferous woods were retrieved (Table 9.9 lists the majority of these samples). After examining 84 samples, Dean was able to develop a composite sequence of 122 rings using three ponderosa and seven piñon pine samples. Unfortunately, at the time of Dean's original analysis, the tree-ring sequence could not be anchored to a master sequence because the chronology for desert mountains had not been completed.

Work continued on developing the chronology for the southern desert mountains, and in the late 1980s, samples retrieved from dead wood from Black Mountain in southwestern New Mexico and Mt. Graham in southeastern Arizona allowed researchers to extend the tree-ring chronology for the region back into the late twelfth century (Dean et al. 1996:13).

When the Gibbon Springs site was excavated in the 1990s, archaeologists took samples of the many burned posts and beams found in structures at the site. The samples were submitted to the Laboratory of Tree-ring Research and dates were obtained from one structure, Feature 106, which was in the compound at that site. The datable wood came from piñon poles used in the structure's roof or in a platform that was on the structure's north wall. The dates revealed that the structure was built or remodeled shortly after A.D. 1249 (Ahlstrom and Slaughter 1996:483).

Spurred by the success of dating the feature at the Gibbon Springs site, Dean et al. (1996) reexamined the composite sequence from the Whiptail site. They were able to develop dates from 16 piñon and ponderosa pine samples that were found in six structures. The dates indicate that the wood used at Whiptail most likely was procured during the A.D. 1230s and 1240s (Dean et al. 1996:19; Table 11.1).

The earliest tree-ring dated feature at Whiptail was Structure 10, a detached adobe-walled room in the Southwestern Locus of the site. Three pieces of ponderosa pine found in that house yielded dates indicating that the structure was built after A.D. 1237 (Dean et al. 1996:16, 19). Dates compiled from samples of piñon pine found in the floor and fill of Structure 15 (in the Central Locus) suggest a construction date for that feature at some time after A.D. 1239.

Adjacent to the southwest corner of the compound was Structure 8, which yielded a datable piñon fragment from the floor. Like many of the samples from Whiptail, the piñon piece lacked an unknown number of exterior rings, but the date of the outermost surviving ring indicates that the house was built sometime after A.D. 1242.

Two features with contiguous walls, Structures 11 and 16, yielded piñon pine fragments that dated after A.D. 1246. The two dates from these structures are considered cutting dates (Dean et al. 1996:19), indicating that the two rooms (and probably Structure 18, the third room in this group of three contiguous rooms) were built at the same time.

The last set of tree ring dates from Whiptail came from six ponderosa pine beams and posts found in Structure 19a, a free-standing adobe-walled feature located in the wash that forms the southern boundary of the site. One of the samples yielded a probable cutting date of A.D. 1245 (Dean et al. 1996:19).

Archaeomagnetic Samples

Dates were also obtained from archaeomagnetic samples taken in the late 1960s. Table 11.2 lists the samples and derived dates. The information in this table was assembled from a handwritten note found in the Whiptail archives. The note records a conversation between Robert DuBois and the note taker, who may have been Laurence Hammack, as the note also includes information on the Rabid Ruin, a site Hammack was working on at the time. Alternatively, the note may have been made by Paul Grebinger (1976:43), who cites a personal communication with DuBois in a 1976 *Kiva* article in which he discusses Whiptail. According to the note, archaeomagnetic dates were derived from Structures 2, 5, 6, 10, 12, and 16. With the exception of a highly tentative date of A.D. 1350 +/- 44 from the hearth in Structure 5, the archaeomagnetic dates correlate fairly well with the dendrochronological dates, with dates clustering between A.D.1230 and 1250 (Table 11.3). The field notes and house report for Structure 5 indicate that the sampling of the hearth was unsuccessful. Because the raw data for the archaeomagnetic dates are not available, however, the dates discussed here should be considered as an interesting historical note, not as supporting or negating the dendrochronological dates.

Table 11.1. Dendrochronological Data.

Provenience	Specimen Number	Species	Form	Inner date (A.D.)	Symbol	Outer date (A.D.)	Symbol	Comment
Structure 8, SE 1/4, floor	WTR-32 (a-d)	Piñon pine	charcoal	1125		1242	vv	parallel to east wall, 115 rings
Structure 10, east wall, center	WTR-1	Ponderosa pine	charcoal	1196		1234	vv	38 rings; doubles
Structure 10, diagonal from west wall	WTR-9 (a, b)	Ponderosa pine	charcoal	1192		1237	r	SE-NW orientation, 45 rings; incomplete
Structure 10, beam	WTR-35	Ponderosa pine	charcoal	1184		1231	vv	34 rings, doubles
Structure 15, NE 1/4, between entry and hearth	WTR-56 (a-d)	Piñon pine	charcoal	1136		1226	++vv	same as WTR-57, 63
Structure 15, SE 1/4, lower fill #2	WTR-60	Piñon pine	charcoal	1160		1229	+vv	doubles
Structure 15, SE 1/4, floor	WTR-62	Piñon pine	charcoal	1178	p	1232	vv	
Structure 15, SW 1/4, lower fill #2	WTR-64	Piñon pine	charcoal	1159	p	1239	+vv	80 rings, erratic
Structure 16, floor	WTR-17 (a, b, c)	Piñon pine	charcoal	1180	p	1246	r	incomplete
Structure 16, SE 1/4, beam 3, floor	WTR-67	Piñon pine	charcoal	1170		1246	r	floor, 90 cm from east wall along south wall, 75 rings; incomplete
Structure 19a fill	WTR-96	Ponderosa pine		1164		1210	vv	
Structure 19a west beam	WTR-112	Ponderosa pine		1157		1233	vv	
Structure 19a, beam	WTR-114(a, b)	Ponderosa pine		1155	p	1239	vv	
Structure 19a floor	WTR-94	Ponderosa pine		1191		1236	vv	
Structure 19a floor fill	WTR-100	Ponderosa pine		1178		1234	vv	
Structure 19a floor fill	WTR-101	Ponderosa pine		1193		1245	v	complete

Source: Dean et al. 1996:16; letter to Paul Grebinger from Jeffrey S. Dean, dated August 29, 1969, in Whiptail archival material, ASM archives.

Key:
- p Pith
- \+ One or two rings may be missing near the end of the ring series.
- ++ Ring count near the end of the ring series; an unknown number of rings may be missing.
- vv Sample lacks the attributes of a cutting date; unknown number of rings gone from the exterior of the sample.
- v Considered by the analyst to be a cutting date although it lacks diagnostic attributes.
- r Outer ring is consistent around the arc of the circumference present on the sample; cutting date.

Occupation Sequence

Archaic and Pre-Classic Hohokam Use of the Site

While tree-ring and archaeomagnetic dates provide good information for the Tanque Verde phase occupation of the site, artifact types (projectile points and pottery) and radiocarbon dates obtained from SWCA's work at the Agua Caliente Park portion of the site provide information on earlier use of the site. The numerous Archaic points found across the Whiptail site (Chapter 4; Myers 2001) indicate that the Agua Caliente springs attracted hunters for thousands of years. No early features were found in the area of the site discussed in this report, but to my knowledge, no one actively searched for early components there. In the Agua Caliente Park portion of the site, an ash stain defined as a roasting area was found that was dated to the Early Ceramic or Early Pioneer period (A.D. 160 to A.D. 530) (Wellman and Grimm 2001:59).

Sherds dating to the Colonial and Sedentary periods (A.D. 700 to A.D. 1150) also occurred throughout the site including within the Agua Caliente Park portion, although most

Table 11.2. Archaeomagnetic Dates.

Sample No.	Structure No. and Provenience	Sampled by	Date	Comments
207	Structure 2	Robert DuBois	A.D. 1250 +/- 45	Date is tentative.
240	Structure 5 hearth	Allen Johnson	A.D. 1350 +/- 44	Date is highly tentative.
241	Hearth, no other provenience			No dates
248	Structure 6, adjacent to entry step	Allen Johnson	A.D. 1245 +/- 33	House was partially destroyed by pot hunters. Six samples, not tentative.
331	Structure 12, south entry	Jeff Eighmy	A.D. 1235 +/- 13	2 standard deviations at 95% confidence level.
332	Structure 12	Jeff Eighmy	A.D. 1225 +/- 18	
333	Structure 10	Jeff Eighmy	A.D. 1250 +/- 17	Not tentative, but has 1 standard deviation.
334	Structure 16	Jeff Eighmy	A.D. 1250 +/- 15	

were found in the Compound and Southwestern loci (Tables 3.3 and 3.4). The numbers of Colonial period sherds are small: three Rillito Red-on-brown and one Trincheras Purple-on-red from the excavated portion of Whiptail, and one Santa Cruz Red-on-buff sherd from the Agua Caliente portion of the site (Gregonis 2001b). These sherds and the lack of associated features and other artifacts indicate an incidental use of the site (probably for hunting and other resource procurement) during the Colonial period.

The numbers of Rincon Red-on-brown (n = 99), other Sedentary period sherds (three Rincon Polychrome, one Sahuarita Polychrome), and a few pieces of shell found at the site may indicate an actual occupation during the Sedentary period rather than temporary use of the area for hunting and gathering. At the excavated portion of Whiptail, Sedentary period sherds occurred primarily in the Compound and Southwestern loci of the site. The possible Sedentary period shell artifacts were found in the Compound, Southwestern, and Northern loci at the site.

Tanque Verde Phase Occupation

The tight cluster of tree-ring dates and correlating archaeomagnetic dates serve as an anchor dating the major occupation of Whiptail to the A.D. mid-1200s. The dates suggest that houses in the heart of the village were built during the A.D. 1240s. While the focus of occupation occurred in the mid-A.D. 1200s, architectural styles, superimposition of a few features, evidence of remodeling, pottery types, the presence of trash in several houses, and the presence of nonstructural features in house fill suggest that the Classic period presence at Whiptail might be extended to one hundred years or so. For example, Pit Structures 4 and 19b may date as early as A.D. 1150 and post-occupation fill in Structure 8 may date as late as A.D. 1300. Table 11.4 outlines a possible occupation sequence for Tanque Verde phase structures at the site.

As previously noted, based on their pit house architecture and stratigraphic placement, Structures 4 and 19b were the earliest houses at the site, dating perhaps as early as A.D. 1150. Although other pit structures may have existed, these two were the only ones identified during excavation. As mentioned previously, Structure 19b was built on the southern bank within a wash on the far southern edge of the site. It is a subrectangular pit structure with a bulbous entry that lies directly under Structure 19a, a free-standing adobe-walled structure. The walls of the later adobe-walled structure were built just outside of the outline of the pit house; it appears that the builders took care to frame the earlier feature. No artifacts could be associated directly with Structure 19b.

Structure 4, a subrectangular slant-walled pit house, was located just outside the east wall of the compound. Excavators noticed at least two plasterings of the structure's floor. Prior to

Table 11.3. Comparison of Dendrochronological and Archaeomagnetic Dates (features listed in roughly chronological order).

Provenience	Dendrochronological Dates	Archaeomagnetic Dates
Structure 12		A.D. 1225 +/- 18 to 1235 +/- 13
Structure 10	A.D. 1237r	A.D. 1250 +/- 17
Structure 15	A.D. 1239vv	
Structure 8	A.D. 1242vv	
Structure 6		A.D.1245 +/- 33
Structure 19a	A.D. 1245v	
Structure 16	A.D. 1246r	A.D. 1250 +/- 15
Structure 2		A.D. 1250 +/- 45
Structure 5		A.D. 1250 +/-45

Sources: Dean et al. 1996:16; letter to Paul Grebinger from Jeffrey S. Dean, dated August 29, 1969, in Whiptail archival material, ASM archives; summary of phone message, presumably between Laurence Hammack or Paul Grebinger and Robert DuBois, 1976, in Whiptail archival material, ASM archives.

Key: vv Sample lacks the attributes of a cutting date; unknown number of rings gone from the exterior of the sample.
v Considered by the analyst to be a cutting date although it lacks diagnostic attributes.
r Outer ring is consistent around the arc of the circumference present on the sample; cutting date.

one of the plasterings, it appears that a roughly made human figurine of clay was placed into a posthole. That posthole and another in the house were then plugged by the replastering. This purposeful remodeling occurred prior to the construction of the compound wall, as indicated by a stratigraphic test that showed the top of the pit house wall at the same level as the bottom of the compound wall. Corrugated sherds and a partially reconstructible Tanque Verde Red-on-brown bowl found in the lower fill of the structure indicate that the structure likely dates to the Tanque Verde phase. The house was filled with trash including more than 1,000 sherds, more than 1,000 pieces of flaked stone debitage, and 17 pieces of ground stone, as well as animal bones and bone fragments.

The next structures built at the site were adobe-and-cobble walled rooms found in the Southwestern Locus. Structure 10 was tree-ring dated to the late A.D. 1230s. Another feature, Structure 12, yielded an archaeomagnetic date in the A.D. 1230s. Structure 12 was remodeled during its use; its lower floor is slightly earlier in time. Stratigraphically, the lower floors of four other structures in the Southwestern Locus—Structures 9, 13, 23, and 25—likely date to the A.D. 1230s as well. The lower floors of these houses were separated from the upper floors by 5 cm to 10 cm of fill, and the hearths showed evidence of remodeling. Thus, the cluster of six structures in the Southwestern Locus appears to have been the core of the settlement at Whiptail. Structure 14 in the Southern Locus may also date to this time period, although its temporal placement is uncertain.

One house in the Northern Locus, Structure 20, may also have been one of the earlier features on the site. The lower, trash-filled layer, was full of gray to white, powdery ash. Excavators did not think the house had burned, so the ash apparently came from elsewhere. The upper layer, which may have been decomposed roofing (a reddish, gravelly material), also contained trash. The structure lies on the eastern edge of the Northern Locus and may have been a handy place for later builders to throw their trash.

The majority of building and site use likely occurred in the A.D. 1240s and A.D.

Table 11.4. Possible Sequence of Construction and Use of Various Structures.

Date Range	Compound	Central Locus	Northern Locus	Southwest Locus	Southern Locus
Post-abandonment use of structures	Structure 8 trash fill	Structure 33--hammerstones associated with rock clusters just above floor	Structure 27a--lithic manufacturing debris; burial in Structures 27b, 28, and 29 (Structure 29 contained 29 hammerstones)	Structure 24--15 hammerstones and 101 pieces of debitage	
A.D. 1240-1260	Compound, Structure 6 (after A.D. 1245 +/- 33) Structure 7 Structure 8 (after A.D. 1242) Structure 17	Structure 15 (after A.D.1239) Structure 32	Structures 27a-27b-28 ? Structures 31a-31b-31c ? Structure 20 Structure 28	Structure 2 (A.D. 1250 +/- 45) Structure 9 upper floor? Structure 13 upper floor? Structure 11-16-18 (11 and 16 are after A.D. 1246) Structure 10 (after 1237)	Structure 19a (after-A.D. 1245)
A.D. 1230-1240				Structure 9 (lower floor), Structure 12 (A.D. 1225-1235 +/1 18), Structure 13 (lower floors), Structure 23 Structure, 25 (lower floor?)	Structure 14?
ca. A.D. 1150-1200?	Structure 4				Structure 19b

Note: There are no chronological data for structures in the Northeastern Locus other than that they date to the Tanque Verde phase. Houses in other loci that are not included here were either vandalized, did not yield any dates, or did not have any distinctive artifacts or superposition to suggest their placement in a sequence.

1250s. The compound itself seems to have been built sometime in the A.D. 1240s, based on the construction of structures in and near that feature. Structure 8, adjacent to the compound, was built sometime after A.D. 1242, according to tree-ring dates. The other structures in the Compound Locus, Structures 6, 7, and 17, appear to be contemporaneous with Structure 8.

In the Southwestern Locus, the contiguous walled Structure 11-16-18 contained two samples of piñon pine that each yielded an A.D. 1246 cutting date. The tenuous archaeomagnetic dates for Structures 2 and 16 (ca. A.D. 1250) indicate contemporaneity with Structure 11-16-18. Structure 16 also yielded an archaeomagnetic date of A.D.1250 +/- 15 yrs. The upper floors of Structures 9 and 13 seem to be contemporaneous with the rest of the structures.

Structure 19a, in the Southern Locus, is the last feature at the site that can be dated with certainty to the A.D.1240s or A.D. 1250s. It contained a number of ponderosa pine beams, one of which had an A.D. 1245 cutting date (Table 11.1). Based on the ritual floor assemblage found in this house and relatively small amount of trash in the fill, it may have been one of the last structures to be used for habitation on the site.

It was not possible to define a particular occupation sequence for structures in the Northern, Northeastern, and Central loci. Based on architectural style and artifacts found in them, the structures date somewhere within the A.D. 1230s through A.D. 1250s. They can be considered roughly contemporaneous but there was some evidence of remodeling, suggesting that not all of the structures were occupied simultaneously. Remodeling evidence at the site included relocated and relined hearths (e.g., Structures 6, 11, 12, and 40), reworked and plugged entryways (Structures 12, 20), the presence of more than one floor in a house (e.g., Structures 6, 9, 13, 23, 25, 28), and the presence of replastering (e.g., Structure 9).

Wall construction also indicates sequential construction of houses. In the Northern Locus, for example, Structures 27a and 27b seem to have been built at the same time. Structure 28, a possible walled shade structure, was later abutted to the eastern wall of Structure 27a. In a second example, Structures 31a, b, and c abut one another, suggesting that they were built at different times. And in the Central Locus, Structure 32 opens directly into the back wall of Structure 33. This suggests that Structure 32 was abandoned before Structure 33 was built. Field notes indicate that in the three-room Structure 11-16-18, Structure 16 was added on to Structure 11-18. This may have happened when the feature was first built, however, as tree-ring dates from wood found in Structures 16 and 11 are identical (A.D. 1246).

Post-Habitation Use of Structures

In addition to remodeling and other architectural evidence of sequential use of houses, a number of houses had household trash in their fill. In some instances, such as the fill in Structure 6, the fill was washed in and reflects natural processes after site abandonment. But in other cases, the houses were used as trash pits or, perhaps, as food processing, craft production, and lithic production areas.

Field notes for Structure 33 (in the Central Locus) provide good evidence for post-habitation use of a structure. Excavators thought that the structure was abandoned; it then burned and subsequently collapsed. Artifacts found in a layer on or just above the floor indicate that the house was used as a craft production area of some type, perhaps just after abandonment and before the structure burned and collapsed. The artifacts include two clusters of unmodified rocks (there is no indication of type), hammerstones associated with the clusters, a bone awl, a tabular tool, a piece of worked slate with red pigment, a projectile point, a metate fragment, a fragment of a deer jaw, and three shell beads. Unfortunately, few of the artifacts from Structure 33 were analyzed.

Lithic production is suggested by quantities of lithic debitage in the fill of several features including Structures 23, 24, and 25 in the Southwestern Locus, Structure 33 in the Central Locus, and Structure 4 in the Compound Locus (Table 11.5). Structure 4 contained 14.4 percent (n = 1,100 out of 7,645) of the pieces of debitage analyzed from the site, as well as 17 hammerstones.

The numerous hammerstones associated with those features may have been used for lithic production, but they may also have been used in food processing, as suggested by the manos, handstones, metates, tabular tools, and pecking stones found in those same structures. For example, the fill of Structure 4 also contained one pestle, five manos, two polishing stones, and five tabular tools in addition to the chipped stone artifacts.

Jenny Adams (Chapter 5) suggested that some of the ground stone artifacts found in the fill of houses may have been stored there for future use. This may have been the case in Structure 24. The floor of this structure was covered with windblown soil, indicating a period of abandonment prior to its use as a storage or production area. In addition to 101 pieces of debitage, 9 unifaces, 15 hammerstones, an ax fragment, a mano, 10 mano fragments, 4 hand stones (one fragmentary), 2 pestles, and 2 tabular tool fragments, pieces from 18 small to large jars were found in the fill and floor fill of that house.

Burials in Abandoned Structures

Structure 29 is another house that may have been used for storage, food processing, or lithic production after abandonment. The floor and

Table 11.5. Structures with Concentrations of Chipped Stone, Hammerstones, and Ground Stone Artifacts.

Structure Number	Chipped Stone	Hammerstones	Ground Stone
		Compound Locus	
4	1100 flakes, 10 projectile points	17 hammerstones (not analyzed)	1 pestle, 5 manos, 2 polishing stones, 5 tabular tools
		Southwestern Locus	
9			2 tabular tools, 3 pecking stones, 1 hand stone, 1 polishing stone
12			Lots of manos (not analyzed)
23	336 flakes		1 metate, 25 pieces including manos, mano fragments, tabular tools, polishing stone
24	101 debitage pieces, 9 unifaces	15 hammerstones	1 ax fragment, 1 mano 10 mano fragments, 3 hand stones, 1 hand stone fragment, 2 pestles, 2 tabular tool fragments
25	275 flakes and debitage		23 pieces (unanalyzed)
		Northern Locus	
20		Cluster of hammerstones	3 manos
29	74 pieces of debitage, 2 cores, 1 projectile point, 2 unifaces	28 hammerstones	1 stone disk fragment, 3 lapstones, 1 lapstone fragment, 2 mano fragments, 5 mano fragments, 1 hammerstone and 1 hammerstone fragment, 2 tabular tools, 2 tabular tool fragments, 2 polishing stones, and a nether stone fragment.
31a			9 whole and fragmentary manos; metate

floor fill of this structure contained 74 pieces of debitage, two cores, one projectile point, two unifaces, 30 hammerstones and hammerstone fragments, a stone disk fragment, three lapstones, one lapstone fragment, seven mano fragments, two tabular tools and two tabular tool fragments, two polishing stones, and a nether stone. An inhumation burial was also found in a pit in this structure. The bones, which belonged to a young adult male, were charred but not burned indicating perhaps that the body was in the pit when the house burned above it. According to field notes (Chapter 2), this structure was badly vandalized, so it is difficult to determine whether the many artifacts found in the house were associated with the burial. It would be interesting if the burial preceded later use of the house for storage, craft production, or lithic manufacture.

Structure 29 was in the Northern Locus of the site and was located near two other structures that each contained an inhumation burial. These structures, 27b and 28, are part of a three-room contiguous feature that also included Structure 27a.

The burial in Structure 27b was the most elaborate and may be the remains of a respected hunter. Based on field notes and sketches, it appears that the body—a mature adult male between the ages of 35 and 50 at time of death (Chapter 10)—had been laid out on the floor of the structure and the remains of several artiodactyls (which may have included entire carcasses) placed next to and on top of the body (Table 8.6). Near the inhumation were four small ceramic vessels. Two of the vessels contained chipped stone debris and formal tools including a drill, end scraper, biface graver, and a Cienega point (Figures 4.2 and 4.3). The chipped stone debris and artifacts were made of chalcedony, chert, and jasper. Small igneous stones impregnated with hematite were also found in the jars. In one of the pots, the objects may have been in a leather bag. The assemblage of artifacts may have been a wood or hide-working kit. The animal bones and other objects in the burial were burned, but the inhumation itself was not. This may be because the animal carcasses protected the body when the house and its contents were set on fire, probably as part of a burial ceremony.

Sometime after the burning of the 27a-27b-28 structure, the third inhumation burial was placed in the fill of Structure 28. The burial was of a mature adult, probably a male, placed in a flexed position with a shell bracelet, shell ring, and projectile point found in association. Rocks were found on top of the body. Prior to the placement of the burial, the structure may have been reused as a cooking area: A circle of rocks was also found in one corner of the structure.

Loci Occupation Sequence and Estimating Site Population

Evidence for house remodeling and reuse of abandoned structures for trash deposition, food processing, lithic manufacture, and even burials makes it clear that the structures at Whiptail were not occupied simultaneously, and it is possible that not all loci at the site were occupied at the same time. As discussed previously, Structures 4 (in the Compound Locus) and 19 (in the Southern Locus) appear to have been the earliest houses built at the site and construction of the compound occurred after a remodeling and then reuse of Structure 4.

It is difficult to determine how the construction of the compound relates to use of the other loci at the site. Adams (Chapter 5) broadly addressed this issue, based on the condition of ground stone artifacts found in various features. She speculated that the compound was used for a shorter duration than other parts of the site because fewer secondarily used artifacts were found there. Tree-ring and archaeomagnetic dates indicate that two of the structures (6 and 8) were built in the A.D. 1240s or A.D. 1250s (Table 11.3); lack of superposition of features indicate that all four of the compound structures (6, 7, 8, 17) may have been used simultaneously during that time, although Structure 6 was remodeled at least once (Table 11.4). Trash fill in Structure 8 may indicate that the Compound Locus was abandoned while other loci at the site were in use. Or, perhaps, Structure 17, which contained very little trash, was the final structure occupied in the compound.

In regard to other loci, Adams (Chapter 5) found that higher percentages of floor-associated ground-stone artifacts in the Northern Locus were burned and broken in comparison to those in the Southwestern and Central Loci. Like Structure 8, this may indicate that structures in the Northern Locus were abandoned and used for trash dumping while those in other parts of the site were still occupied. As discussed previously, the final use of at least one set of structures—27a-27b-28—was as a burial site. Likewise, habitation of Structure 29 probably ended with a burial in the floor of that house, but it may have been used later for food processing or lithic production.

Adams (Chapter 5) also suggests that the Southwestern Locus was lived in longer than other loci because more redesigned and reused ground stone artifacts were found there than in other parts of the site. Tree-ring dates and feature remodeling indicate that at least half of the structures in the Southwestern Locus were occupied from the A.D. 1230s into the A.D. 1250s or later (Tables 11.1, 11.4).

It was not possible to determine where the other loci fit into the general occupation sequence, other than noting that Structure 15 in the Central Locus appears to date after A.D. 1239 and Structure 19a in the Southern Locus dates after A.D. 1245. And, based on superposition and feature type, it would appear that Structure 19b, a slant-walled pithouse, was one of two early structures on the site (Table 11.4). As mentioned previously, there is no good information on occupation sequence for the Northeastern Locus.

If the general occupation sequence is correct, then only about half of the structures identified at the site were inhabited at any given time during the site's history. Estimating the number of people who used those structures is tricky. According to Doelle (1981), historical data from the late 1600s and early 1700s in southern Arizona suggests that four to five people could be expected to use one house. Henry Wallace (personal communication, April 2009) uses this number to determine population of a typical ranchería-like Hohokam settlement, excluding store rooms and other nonresidential structures. Jeffery Clark (personal communication, April 2009) uses a slightly different formula, based on the contiguous-walled architecture found in southern Arizona during the early Classic period. He suggests using a three-person-per-room formula and counting every room, considering that there would have been one storage room for every two habitation rooms.

Because excavators were only able to define three storage structures at Whiptail and the use of the contiguous-room structures in relation to the free-standing structures is poorly understood, I decided to use three people per room in my estimate. If as few as 10 or as many as 25 structures were in use at any given time, then the population range for Whiptail would have been between 30 and 75 people. This range means that Whiptail may have been occupied by as few as three or as many as seven or eight extended families through its history.

Structure Use and Abandonment

When Classic period occupation of Whiptail began around A.D. 1150, it may have been as a hunting or other resource procurement camp that was occupied for a long enough period to warrant the construction of at least two houses—Structures 4 and 19b. Structure 4, a slant-walled pithouse was located about two-tenths of a mile south of the springs at Agua Caliente Park, a good location for a habitation that could make use of the wild resources at the springs and still be far enough away to not scare game off.

The Southern Locus

The location of Structure 19b, a slant-walled pithouse, is more suggestive of a house built to conceal the inhabitants from activities at and around the springs. The feature is built on a small bench within the banks of a shallow wash that defines the southern edge of the site. The house is situated in such a way that the entire structure would have been below the rim of the bank, hidden from view. To me, the location of Structure 19b alone suggests a ritual use for the feature.

Structure 19b was replaced after A.D. 1245 by Structure 19a, a rock-reinforced, adobe-walled structure. The builders of Structure 19a carefully encompassed the older house within the new walls (Figure 2.26), as if maintaining the substance of the older structure was important. According to field notes (Chapter 2), the floor of Structure 19a had been replastered several times, suggesting that the house was important enough to rejuvenate. And, when the feature was finally abandoned, artifacts were left on the floor in what looks like a staged arrangement (Figures 2.24 and 2.25). The map of the feature (Figure 2.24) shows only the pottery vessels and the bone concentration, but according to field notes there were a number of other artifacts placed on the floor including several projectile points, an ax fragment, a mano, an abrader, a lapstone, a pestle, two bone awls (one-double ended), a number of obsidian flakes, a polishing stone with red coloring on it, a piece of red quartzite with a ground corner, an igneous stone with polishing facets and striations, a piece of red ocher, and clusters of flakes.

The vessel arrangement is interesting. As shown in Figures 2.24 and 2.25, there are two groups of vessels, each including one smudged corrugated bowl. The bone cluster included a pronghorn skull and three and one-half deer or pronghorn mandibles as well as four antlers, at least two scapulae, teeth, a skull, and assorted other bones of deer, pronghorn, and rabbit (Figures 8.1 through 8.4). The rabbit bones consisted of at least 16 lagomorph innominates that look as if they had been hung together on a string (Figure 8.1). After the artifacts had been placed in the structure, it was burned, perhaps as a way to ritually close the feature.

The only other feature in the Southern Locus, Structure 14, also had an interesting floor assemblage and was also burned. The structure was built to the east of Structure 19b, on the same internal bench just above the bottom of the wash. Although it is difficult to know exactly when Structure 14 was built, I suspect that it was contemporaneous with or slightly predated the building of Structure 19a.The floor and wall adobe in Structure 14 was rougher than that found in Structure 19a; it included small pieces of weathered stone. The structure may have been used for a shorter period of time than Structure 19a, as no evidence of replastering or reworking was recorded by excavators. The floor assemblage found in Structure 14 included a white-tailed deer mandible, thoracic vertebrae from an artiodactyl (also found in the lower fill), four hammerstones, a mano, a handstone fragment, and a smudged red ware bowl.

I think that the two features in the Southern Locus primarily served a ceremonial function. Their location within the banks of a wash and out of view of the rest of the site gives them a subterranean aspect. The careful replacement of slant-walled pit house Structure 19b with the above-ground adobe-walled Structure 19a and subsequent replastering of floors in Structure 19a suggest renewal ritual of some kind. The isolation of the two features is curious, as is the fact that they represent one of the earliest (Structure 19b) and one of the latest (Structure 19a) features at the site. One would have expected a full blown segment of the site to have developed there, rather than only two structures. Finally, the staged floor assemblages and burning of the structures may indicate that closing rituals were conducted for the two houses.

Floor Assemblages and Room Closing Rituals

Is it presumptuous to interpret the presence of floor assemblages in burned houses as indicative of the ritual closing of structures? Perhaps, given that 29 structures at Whiptail had artifacts on their floors and all but 8 of those houses were burned (Table 11.6). But the nature of the assemblages on those floors including high quantities of artiodactyl bone, pottery making materials, and the distribution of corrugated vessels support that conclusion.

Rooms with Artiodactyl Remains

The most obvious of the houses that was ritually closed is Structure 27b and the rooms that were contiguous with it—Structures 27a and 28. As described previously, Structure 27b had an inhumation burial on its floor that was accompanied by bighorn sheep, white-tailed deer, pronghorn, and mule deer remains, as well as several vessels that contained lithic artifacts. Artifacts—a large metate, two hammerstones, and half of a Tanque Verde Red-on-brown bowl—were also found on the floor of Structure 27a. After burning, the three rooms were never used for habitation again. A second burial was placed in the fill of Structure 28.

Like Structure 27b and 19a, three other structures—6, 8, and 30—had considerable quantities of artiodactyl bone on their floors or in fill immediately above the floor, and two other structures—14 and 33—had one deer mandible apiece on the floor. The animal remains are most often skull and lower limb bones (Table 8.6; Appendix 8.A), indicating that the heads and hides of mule deer, white-tailed deer, bighorn, and pronghorn were preserved and valued. Pelvis, rib, and scapula fragments were found in Structure 8, indicating that at least one whole animal (or its bones) was left in the house. Pelvis and rib fragments were also found in Structure 30.

The bones in Structure 6 (in the Compound Locus) were primarily skull and foot bones from white-tailed deer and other artiodactyls. In addition to the bone, excavators found a tabular tool, a pestle, another unidentified piece of ground stone, a piece of turquoise, a deer jaw, and other artiodactyl bone fragments on the upper floor of the feature, which had probably been burned. The house had been vandalized, making it difficult to tell the original context of the floor artifacts in Structure 6.

Structure 8, located immediately southwest of the compound, contained four corrugated vessels—two jars and two bowls—on the floor, along with a handstone, two trivet stones (pot rests), a tabular tool, and mule deer, white-tailed deer, pronghorn, and bighorn sheep bones. The bones included skull, jaw, and tooth fragments, as well as a pronghorn rib and scapula, mule deer vertebrae and scapula, and white-tailed deer leg and foot bones. Pieces from a bighorn horn core were also found. The arrangement of artifacts on the floor would have made the structure difficult to use (Figure 2.5), a good indication that the objects on the floor were staged there prior to the house's burning.

The bone material found on the floor of Structure 30, in the Northern Locus, included an antler-tine flaking tool and two metapodial awl or hairpin fragments. Antler fragments made up the majority of animal remains found in the house; leg and toe bones were also found. Other items found on the floor included potsherds, a tabular tool, and a tabular tool fragment.

The artiodactyl bone, antler, and horn material found in the houses at Whiptail may have been part of hunting ritual. Historically, deer and pronghorn were considered to be sacred animals that had to be handled carefully in every aspect of killing, meat distribution, and disposal of the bone (Spier 1970; Underhill 1946; Zuni People 1972). If the Whiptail and Gibbon Springs villagers did what historical O'odham hunters did with artiodactyl bone, then the bones and antlers found in roof and floor contexts may have been stored in certain houses to protect the village. As discussed in Chapter 8, in her treatise on Tohono O'odham religion, Underhill (1946:86) states that "bones should be carefully put away where no dog could drag them about, and the horns placed on the house roof or in some special repository" such as a round house. Skulls, mandibles, and lower leg and foot bones that were part of a disguise would also have been carefully stored. Even the burial in Structure 27b reflected the importance of hunting in the way the deceased was interred with the remains of several animals.

Other Floor Assemblages

The floor assemblages of most structures did not have artiodactyl bone, but often had a variety of ground stone and pottery artifacts (Table 11.6). In one house, Structure 12, the floor assemblage looked like a craft workshop. In addition to an unfired Tanque Verde Red-on-brown jar (Figure 2.14), excavators found a pile of unfired clay in association with a large, flat sherd that had been made into plate, a Tanque Verde Red-on-brown bowl, a plain ware jar, chunks of prepared ocher (one of which was found in a vessel), a piece of kaolin with polishing facets, slate polishing stones, two spindle

Table 11.6. Floor Assemblages in Whiptail Structures.

Structure Number	House Burned?	Floor Assemblages
		Compound Locus
4	probably	Upper floor: 1 hammerstone, projectile point, mano, sherd, basalt flake, Tanque Verde Red-on-brown bowl Lower floor: sealed with figurine in post hole.
6	probably	1 tabular tool, 1 pestle, 1 unclassified piece of ground stone, piece of turquoise, 1 deer mandible, artiodactyl bone, spindle whorl.
7	probably	Sherds, cores, mano, Tanque Verde Red-on-brown bowl; most artifacts near north wall and west of entry
8	probably	Two corrugated jars; 2 corrugated bowls; burned animal bone including skulls and jaws of mule deer, bighorn sheep; mule deer vertebrae and scapula; pronghorn rib fragments, white-tailed deer fragments--more than half of bone is burned.
17	yes	Sherd clusters, 3 Tanque Verde Red-on-brown bowls; 1 McDonald Corrugated bowl; mano, arrowshaft straightener. 1 Tanque Verde Red--on-brown jar, 1 globular obliterated corrugated jar found in surface or pit outside door in possible roofed working area.
		Central Locus
5		Vandalized
15	yes	Store room with depressions that served as pot rests for 4 plain ware jars; also on floor were 11 corrugated vessels, 4 Tanque Verde Red-on-brown vessels; corn and beans in fill; one jar had cholla buds; 1 tabular tool, 2 shell pendants, 2 shell frogs.
32	no	None noted
33	yes	On floor or just above: 3 shell beads, 1 bone awl, 1 tabular tool, 1 piece of worked slate with red pigment, 1 metate fragment, 1 deer mandible fragment, 1 projectile point, hammerstones, projectile point. Hammerstones were found with two clusters of unmodified rocks.
		Northern Locus
3		None noted
20		3 manos and one cluster of hammerstones
21		Sherd clusters, mano cluster, partial plain ware storage jar; fire-cracked rock pit in floor of house
27a	yes	One large metate, half of a decorated bowl, two hammerstones.
27b	yes	Inhumation, chipped stone tools; manos; metate; 1 Tanque Verde Red-on-brown bowl; 1 indented obliterated corrugated handled jar; 4 Tanque Verde Red-on-brown vessels with chipped stone and other artifacts in them; engraved shell bracelet fragment; white-tailed deer skull, jaw, and limb bones; all but ribs of mule deer; bighorn horn core, skull, jaw, leg and foot bones; animal bones were burned; inhumation was not burned.
28		None noted
29		Three sherd clusters; 1 burial in floor pit. Possible floor assemblage (disturbed by vandalism) includes 74 pieces of debitage, 2 cores, 1 projectile point, 2 unifaces, 28 hammerstones, Stone disk fragment, 3 lapstones, 1 lapstone fragment, 2 mano fragments, 5 mano fragments, 1 hammerstone and 1 hammerstone fragment, 2 tabular tools, 2 tabular tool fragments, 2 polishing stones, and a nether stone fragment.
30	not noted	Pronghorn, white-tailed deer, bighorn sheep bone; one antler tine flaking tool; obliterated corrugated bowl
31a	yes	None noted
31b	yes	Trash including potsherds, chipped stone, jackrabbit and cottontail bone.
31c	yes	None noted
		Southwestern Locus
2	not noted	Polishing stone, flakes, pendant, cluster in Southwest corner, metate, Tanque Verde Red-on-brown bowl, projectile points
9	no	Upper floor: sherd clusters (not reconstructible), 1 metate fragment, 1 mano, 1 polishing stone, 1 hand stone, 1 tabular tool, 1 piece of *Glycymeris* shell, green pigment.
10	yes	Tanque Verde Red-on-brown bowl; grinding slab, tabular tool, bird-shaped stone, slate spindle whorl, 5 manos, metate propped on stacked manos.
11	yes	Tanque Verde Red-on-brown bowl; trough metate on floor, turquoise bead or blank, tabular tool, quartzite stone, shell ring; quartz crystal found in post hole.
12	yes	Tanque Verde Red-on-brown bowl; unfired Tanque Verde Red-on-brown jar; plain ware jar; spindle whorls; 8 tabular tools plus fragment, metate fragment; pottery working assemblage including ocher and slate polishing stones.
13	yes	None noted
16	yes	1 corrugated jar
18	yes	Three Tanque Verde Red-on-brown bowls; mano.
23	yes	3 projectile points on lower floor
24	yes	Not clear

Table 11.6. Floor Assemblages in Whiptail Structures, cont'd.

Structure Number	House Burned?	Floor Assemblages
25	yes	Roof: 1 jar, 7 shell beads, 13 manos, pestle-like implement. upper floor: Obliterated corrugated jar; 3 manos, tabular tool lower floor: t-shaped stone, spindle whorl, shell pendant
26	no	Not clear
		Southern Locus
14	yes	Deer mandible, 4 hammerstones, 1 mano, smudged plain ware bowl
19a	yes	7 Tanque Verde Red-on-brown bowls; two obliterated corrugated bowls; projectile points; arrowshaft smoother; slate slab; whetstone, polishing stone; hand stone; bone awls; obsidian flakes; ocher; deer or pronghorn mandibles; pronghorn skull; four antlers; artiodactyl teeth, scapula, and other bones; rabbit pelves.
19b	not clear	Not evident
		Northeastern Locus
1	no	Not evident
22	yes	Uncertain; possible bowl and sherd cluster
40	yes	Uncertain
41	uncertain	Green slate slab and jasper biface; vandalized with historic trash on floor
42	probably	Tanque Verde Red-on-brown jar, plain ware jar, obliterated corrugated jar, metate; Tanque Verde Red-on-brown bowl served as hearth

whorls, a metate fragment, a nether stone, eight tabular tools, and a tabular tool fragment on the floor. Other pottery working artifacts were found in the fill of the structure. They include a possible scraper made from a potsherd, two polishing stones, and three hematite coated rocks that may have been used as pigment sources. A fragment of a deer metacarpal with a groove was also found in the lower fill. These small tools may have been stored on a shelf or among the rafters of the house.

I suspect that the floor assemblage in Structure 12 was staged primarily because of the presence of the unfired clay and the poor manufacture of the unfired jar found on the floor. The jar was lopsided and thicker walled than most Tanque Verde Red-on-brown vessels from this site (Figure 2.14). Had the jar been one that was about to be fired, it would not have been sitting in the middle of the floor. It would have been in a more protected spot where it could dry slowly. In addition, when Structure 12 burned, the temperature of the fire was low enough that it did not affect either the unfired pot or the unfired clay.

Structure 12 was in the Southwestern Locus and was contiguous with Structure 10. Artifacts on the floor of that structure may also have been used in pottery making or other crafts. They include a grinding slab, a tabular tool, a metate propped on five manos, a bird-shaped stone, a slate spindle whorl, and a Tanque Verde Red-on-brown bowl.

Structure 15, in the Central Locus, was identified by excavators as a storage room. The feature had depressions in the floor that served as pot rests for vessels. In that structure, excavators found four large plain ware jars, 11 corrugated vessels, 4 Tanque Verde Red-on-brown vessels, 2 frog-shaped shell pendants, and a tabular knife. One of the jars contained cholla buds, and corn and beans were found in the fill of the house. The structure had burned.

One feature, Structure 17, did not have a huge floor assemblage, but did have a prepared surface immediately outside of the house. A Tanque Verde Red-on-brown jar and a corrugated jar were found on that surface. This area apparently burned when the house did, and the pottery was not retrieved as one might expect if the fire had been accidental. That, and the presence of a rare McDonald Corrugated bowl on the house floor, suggest staging and a ritual house closure. Structure 17 contained very little trash and may have been the last structure to be occupied in the Compound Locus.

One other floor assemblage is worth noting in regard to possible closure ritual. In this case, the assemblage might be interpreted as a closure-and-renewal ritual. Structure 25, in the Southwestern Locus, had two distinct floors, separated from one another by about 5 cm of fill. A T-shaped stone, a shell pendant, and a spindle whorl were left on the lower floor, which was sealed by 5 cm of fill and the plastering of the new floor above it.

Room Closing Rituals at Other Sites

The purposeful burning of structures at abandonment has been recognized in other Tucson Basin sites. The pattern of staged floor assemblages in association with burned houses has been identified at late Sedentary and Classic period sites such as Gibbon Springs, AZ BB:14:24 (ASM), University Indian Ruin, and AZ AA:12:77 (ASM) in the Saguaro Springs development.

Gibbon Springs

Sixteen of the 24 structures at the nearby, contemporaneous site of Gibbon Springs were burned and 13 of them had assemblages of floor artifacts that were similar to those found at Whiptail. Table 11.7 lists the floor artifacts found in Gibbon Springs houses.

Among the houses at Gibbon Springs, some apparently had trash on the floor (e.g., Features 125 and 126). This trash was found in floor fill and may have been left in a structure after it was abandoned and burned but, perhaps, before the roof collapsed.

Examples of rooms with intact floor assemblages include one store room (Feature 74) that catastrophically burned with a large variety of materials inside, a possible store room (Feature 15) that burned in a slow, smoldering fire, a room used as or staged as a ceramic workshop (Feature 42), and one room with several remodelings (Feature 106).

Feature 106 at Gibbon Springs had two floors. Like Structure 19 at Whiptail, the lower floor of Feature 106 was outlined by the upper superstructure (Slaughter 1996a:126, Figure 4.31). On the lower floor were a tabular tool and a lapstone. Like Structure 25 at Whiptail, which also had artifacts on a lower floor, the earlier floor was sealed by the upper floor, which had a Tanque Verde Red-on-brown platter, a corrugated bowl, and numerous deer and bighorn bones including pelvis bones from mule deer, white-tailed deer, and bighorn sheep (Strand 1996:390, Table 10.8). In fact, Feature 106 contained 47 percent of the faunal remains (NISP) found at Gibbon Springs. It is possible that this feature burned accidently, but its location in the compound, the careful remodeling with artifacts left on the earlier floor, and the presence of large amounts of artiodactyl bone suggest a ritual use and abandonment of this feature. Incidentally, Feature 106 was the structure at Gibbon Springs that had dateable wood. It was occupied sometime after A.D. 1249 (Dean et al.1996).

Feature 74 at Gibbon Springs was also located in the compound. It was clearly a storage room that burned catastrophically and perhaps accidentally, based on the positions of the vessels in this house, which were overturned and their contents scattered across the floor.

This differs from house Feature 15, which had storage jars with seeds as well as an assemblage resembling a craft workshop—polishing stones, hammerstones, paint-grinding stones, and two clumps of ocher. The distribution of vessels across the floor and the clustering of various lithic artifacts (Slaughter 1996a:85, Figure 4.10) are reminiscent of the distribution of the staged assemblage of artifacts in Structure 19a at Whiptail.

Finally, Feature 42 at Gibbon Springs is

Table 11.7. Floor Artifacts in Gibbon Springs Houses.

Structure Number	House Burned?	Floor Artifacts
		Compound Locus
8	yes	Tabular tool, lapstone, metate, 2 manos, t-shaped stone, 3 vessels on floor, 4 vessels in fill (probably had been on shelves)
21	?	Vandalized
74	yes	T-shaped stone fragment, biface, mortar, core, paint grinding stone, 20 to 24 reconstructible vessels (probably on shelves originally), faceted magnetite artifact, modeled spindle whorl; saguaro and tansy mustard seeds, corn, beans.
100	yes	Polishing stones; thinning flakes; 6 vessels; deer, bighorn and other artiodactyl bone
106	yes	Floor 2: Tabular tool, lapstone Floor 1: Tanque Verde Red-on-brown platter, corrugated bowl; deer, big horn and other artiodactyl bone
		Village Core
15	yes	3 polishing stones, metate, 4 manos, hammerstone, 2 paint grinding stones, 4 plain ware jars, 1 plain ware bowl, 1 corrugated jar, 1 Tanque Verde jar, 1 antler rasp, 2 clumps of ocher; saguaro, prickly pear, corn, tansy mustard seeds.
20	yes	None
25	yes	4 potsherds
26	?	Vandalized
31	?	Vandalized
32	?	Vandalized
34	yes	Artifacts removed prior to abandonment; in floor fill--hammerstone, groundstone, 1 Tanque Verde Red-on-brown jar, 1 corrugated jar, sherds
45	yes	Animal bone; vandalized
46	yes	1 corrugated bowl, 1 Tanque Verde Red-on-brown bowl, 1 corrugated bowl, 3 Mogollon brown ware bowls in floor fill; burned and calcined bone (½ of room excavated)
125	yes	Probably trash: 2 flakes, 1 core, ½ incised jar, 1/4 San Carlos Red bowl, 1 bone awl
		Northeastern Village Segment
5	yes	Bifaces, core, metate, 3/4-groove ax, 2 Tanque Verde Red-on-brown bowls, 1 Tanque Verde Red-on-brown jar
112	yes	2 projectile points, 1 clay figurine, 1 tabular tool, 7 vessels, shell ornament
		Western Village Segment
36	?	Vandalized
42	yes	Metate fragment, grinding slab, 5 Tanque Verde Red-on-brown bowls, pancake of unfired clay, ocher cake, *Glycymeris* valve, pottery scraper, whole *Laevicardium* valve.
126	yes	Probably trash: reused mano, mano, core; vessels in floor fill.

comparable to Structure 12 at Whiptail Ruin, with its pottery manufacturing materials and artifacts. A pancake of unfired clay was found on the floor of Feature 42.

AZ BB:14:24(ASM)

This is one of several small to medium-sized Tanque Verde phase sites situated on ridges above Rincon Creek, on the southern edge and just south of Saguaro National Monument East. Jack Zahniser (1966) excavated parts of AZ BB:14:24(ASM) in the 1960s. He described House 4 at that site as having been destroyed by fire as part of a burial ritual. In Zahniser's (1966:167) opinion, the pottery on the floor of the house had been purposefully smashed. In one instance he found a large storage jar that had been struck by a blow that left "a hole in the vessel wall similar to a 'kill' hole." In another instance, he found sherds from a Tanque Verde Red-on-brown jar that retained their original colors, unlike the rest of the jar. From that he inferred that the sherds had been protected from the fire by the rest of the already broken pot. In addition to the two jars just mentioned, 76 other artifacts were found in this structure, either on the floor or on a level that implied they had been stored on the roof. Sometime after the house was burned, a one- to three-year-old child was buried in the fill of the structure. It is not clear if Zahniser thinks the child was the person for whom the house was destroyed. Given that the house had an artifact assemblage that would have been used by an adult, and there were no grave goods associated with the child, it is likely that the house was destroyed as part of a mortuary ritual for an adult. Another structure at AZ BB:14:24(ASM), House 5, appears to have been destroyed in a similar manner.

University Indian Ruin

Julian Hayden (1957:50-51) excavated a Tanque Verde phase house at University Indian Ruin that had been destroyed by fire. The house, Room 5, D4, had two plain ware jars and a Tanque Verde Red-on-brown (identified by Hayden as Pantano Red-on-brown) dipper on the floor of the house. The house was full of black ash and pieces of charcoal. University Indian Ruin is about seven miles west of Whiptail, at the junction of the Pantano and Tanque Verde washes.

Saguaro Springs

A slightly earlier example of possible closing ritual was noted in Late Rincon contexts at site AZ AA:12:77 (ASM) in the Saguaro Springs development just west of the Tucson Mountains. There, Jones and Klune (2009) found two Late Rincon houses where material was left on the floors and the structure was then burned. The floor of one house—Feature 115—contained a reconstructible vessel, three polishing stones, a shell bracelet fragment, a metate, a nether stone, a hammerstone, a bone awl or hairpin, and fragments of a sheep or deer mandible. A quartz crystal was found in the entryway of the structure. The other structure at AZ AA:12:77—Feature 117—contained at least six vessels, five projectile points, two metates, a mano, and a large pestle. Above the burned debris from the roof of Feature 117, excavators found a bit of washed-in trash and also recovered "three quartz crystals, an obsidian projectile point, a disk bead, a shell bracelet fragment, and a stone censor" (Jones and Klune 2009). These objects may have been left as an offering.

Defining Room Closing Ritual

Rather than consider the floor assemblages and burned houses as evidence of closing ritual, the contexts just described might be attributed to accidental fires. There are, however, several reasons for suggesting that the contexts represent ritual activities.

First, excavators often made note of the unusual amount of artifacts on the floor and the burning of the structures. Zahniser (1966) mentioned, for example, that the adobe-walled houses were not particularly flammable, implying that a fire would have to have been set.

Second, although some of the house fires were catastrophic (e.g., those at BB:14:24 and University Indian Ruin), most appeared to have been slow, smoldering fires (Chapter 2; Hayden 1957; Slaughter 1996a; Zahniser 1966). This suggests that it may have been possible to retrieve important tools and artifacts before the roof collapsed or, in some cases roof beams may have charred but remained intact for a period of time after a fire.

Third, artifacts on the floors were positioned in ways that would have made it difficult to move around in some of the houses (Structures 8 and 19a at Whiptail and Feature 15 at Gibbon Springs). In at least one case, House 4 at BB:14:24, the artifacts were purposefully smashed before the fire (Zahniser 1966:130).

Fourth, some of the artifacts were odd or out of place—suggestive of offerings. For example, the unfired clay and pot left on the floor of Structure 12 at Whiptail seemed logical if the house was a craft workshop. But the jar was misshapen and crudely finished, as if it had been made in haste, and it was sitting in an unprotected spot on the floor—an odd place if one were letting the pot dry prior to firing. The unfired clay was also unprotected from drying. The pancake of unfired clay on the floor of Feature 42 at Gibbon Springs also seems odd (Slaughter 1996a). Unless the fire that destroyed that house occurred at the moment someone was starting to make a pot, the clay should have been in a pot or hole in the floor of the house—protected from drying, not laid out on the floor. And the presence of a quartz crystal in the entry of Feature 115 of AA:12:77 at Saguaro Springs is suggestive of an offering.

Fifth, the artiodactyl bone found on the floors of houses at Whiptail and the mass of artiodactyl bone found on the floor of Feature 106 at Gibbon Springs are, I think, particularly indicative of ritual. The bone elements left on the floor in Whiptail features consisted primarily of skull, mandible, and lower limb bones, but some innominates and scapulae were also found, suggesting that entire animals were deposited, either as offerings or as ways to store butchered bone, which could cause harm. The bone found in Feature 106 at Gibbon Springs also included artiodactyl innominates (Strand 1996:389).

Sixth, several of the features had been remodeled, sometimes repeatedly. Feature 106 at Gibbon Springs is one of those, where lower floors were carefully outlined by the upper, final structure (Slaughter 1996a:125). Structure 19a is the best example of that type of remodeling at Whiptail, although several of the houses described here had replastered floors or hearths and one, Structure 25, had artifacts sealed on a lower floor. Structure 6, within the compound at Whiptail, had also been remodeled at least once. This pattern of remodeling indicates that the structures were "renewed" periodically.

Finally, burials and offerings were sometimes found in the structures. Structure 27a-27b-28, with its burial on the floor of Structure 27b and burial in the fill of Structure 28 certainly represent a closing ritual. The case of the child burial in the fill of House 4 at AZ BB:14:24 is different because the destruction of House 4 may or may not have been directly related to the burial. The artifacts left in Feature 117 at AA:12:77 are characteristic of objects normally found in caches (Jones and Klune 2009).

In the Gibbon Springs report, Slaughter (1996a:87) suggests that houses in the entire village may have been burned simultaneously as a parting ritual. Although this is possible, I think that it is unlikely if the occupation pattern at Gibbon Springs is similar to that of Whiptail, where the abandonment sequence is complex. At Whiptail, houses were remodeled and reused or abandoned. At the end of habitation at Whiptail, perhaps 20 or fewer houses were actually in use. Some of these were cleaned out prior to abandonment while others, such as Structures 14 and 19a in the Southern Locus, were burned with artifact assemblages on their floors.

A Well-Established Custom

Room closing rituals including structure burning have been identified at Pre-Classic sites in Tucson, but the pattern of ritual differs somewhat from site to site. At Los Morteros (AZ AA:12:57 [ASM]), burned Rincon phase structures contained specially positioned ritual artifacts "such as censers and unusual vessels" (Wallace 1995:829). In one instance at that site, one ritually burned structure (Feature 3251) contained ceremonially associated artifacts including butchered rabbits in the fill; two badger penis bones, a tortoise shell fragment ground into a disk, and part of a bone hairpin in the lower fill; and miniature vessels on the floor. Like some of the structures at Whiptail, Feature 3251 continued to have ceremonial significance for the site's inhabitants.

The presence of ritually important artifacts in burned, abandoned houses has also been noted in Rillito phase contexts at the

Shell Man site (AZ EE:1:317 [ASM]) near Green Valley. One of the houses, Feature 45, contained 20 artiodactyl mandibles on the floor and an additional 25 in the floor fill. In this instance, Howell (2006:9.7) suggests that the placement of the mandibles and the abandonment of the structure may have been symbols of shamanic activities.

At the Rincon phase West Branch site, the structures were cleared of useful artifacts prior to the house being burned. Huntington (1986:343-346), in fact, thought that the lack of useable artifacts in a burned house was an important indicator of purposeful ritual burning rather than an accidental fire. This is because at the houses at the West Branch site, useful items were found in the most destroyed portion of a given structure, while objects were scavenged from areas that were less damaged. This is a pattern that is distinctly different from that seen in the structures at the late Sedentary and early Classic period sites just described.

Huntington (1986:343-344) proposed that the purposeful burning of the houses was specifically related to the death of the head of a household. Destroying that individual's home would allow his position to be reassigned to another individual. Greenleaf (1975:105) also associated the burning of houses in the Pre-Classic Punta de Agua project sites with mortuary ritual, suggesting that the custom was similar to that found historically among the O'odham and Opata of Sonora. There, in the 1700s, Father Joseph Och tried to prevent his parishioners from burning houses after a death. He succeeded in stopping people from burning the structures, but found that they instead remodeled the buildings so as to make them unrecognizable to the dead individual (Och 1965:129).

Ritual staging of artifacts, burning, ritual re-use, and remodeling of houses seems to have a long history in southern Arizona and northern Sonora. At Whiptail, house abandonment customs seem to have followed the regional pattern, from carefully placing artifacts in a house to ritually reusing structures after burning.

Structures without Floor Assemblages

According to field notes, 11 of the structures excavated at the Whiptail Ruin had no floor-associated artifacts. Five of those houses had burned. One of them, Structure 19b, was incorporated into the later Structure 19a, the floor of which was laid directly over the earlier room. Two others, Structures 31a and 31c, were attached to a room, Structure 31b, that contained a trash deposit on its floor. The three-room structure had burned, apparently after being cleared out, and then was used as a trash pit.

This type of room clearing may have occurred in Structure 28 as well. It was attached to Structures 27a and 27b. The reason for the room clearing in Structure 28 was likely related to the burial in Structure 27b. As previously mentioned, a burial was later placed in the fill of Structure 28.

Another structure without a floor assemblage—Structure 3—was described in field notes as a possible storage room. In the fill of the house were three manos, a phallus-shaped quartzite stone, two pieces of worked shell, and a bird-shaped quartzite effigy. According to field notes, there was a thick layer of sherds and discernable locations where vessels had rested on what may have been the roof. In Chapter 3, I estimated that the sherds represented at least four jars and four bowls. None of the jars or bowls was reconstructible, indicating that the sherds were deposited as trash rather than as vessels. I suspect the clusters of sherds represent different dumping episodes and that the structure was not, in fact, used for storage.

One final note on the floor assemblages: In Chapter 5, Jenny Adams noted that the floor-associated ground stone artifacts found in the Northern Locus did not represent all of the activities that took place in and around the houses. She suggests that the limited variety of ground stone means that important artifacts were removed from many of the structures as they were abandoned. I think a case can be made for this, with the exception of Structures 27a-27b-28 (the house with two burials); Structure 30 with its worked bone artifacts, antler and bone pieces, and other artifacts; and Structure 29 with its burial in a floor pit. As described previously, Structure 29 contained numerous pieces of ground and chipped stone that may have been part of a post-habitation lithic production, food processing, or storage area.

Role of the Compound

As discussed previously, the Whiptail compound and features associated with it were constructed and occupied sometime in the A.D. 1240s, towards the end of the use of Whiptail as a village. The compound is similar to the one found at Gibbon Springs (Slaughter and Roberts 1996a:504-508), in that it was the only one in the village and it was located adjacent to the most densely occupied part of the site. Rather than being strictly residential, the compounds at Gibbon Springs and Whiptail may have had a communal ritual purpose. The features were roughly contemporaneous; houses associated with them were tree-ring dated to the A.D. 1240s (Dean et al. 1996:16). Both compounds contained the largest structures at their respective sites: Structures 7 and 17 at Whiptail and Feature 8 at Gibbon Springs. The A.D. 1240s and 1250s structures associated with each of the compounds had floor assemblages and all had been burned. Houses in each of the compounds had been remodeled at least once (Feature 106 at Gibbon Springs, Structure 6 at Whiptail). And at least one of the houses at both the Gibbon Springs and Whiptail compounds had significant amounts of artiodactyl bone (Structure 8 at Whiptail and Feature 106 at Gibbon Springs).

Differences between the two compounds include the presence of at least one store room (Feature 74) in the Gibbon Springs compound. No structures were defined as such in the compound at Whiptail. According to site maps from Gibbon Springs, the western wall of the compound there was missing, although this could have been a result of recent disturbance at the site. Several cremation burials were found within the compound at Gibbon Springs (Roberts 1996a), while none were found in the Whiptail compound. The lack of cremations identified in the Whiptail compound may be due to limited excavation in that feature, although no bone or ash was noted. To my knowledge, no cremations or burials have ever been found in the compound, which today has a simple metal-bar corral on top of it.

Compounds are common at other mid-A.D.1200s sites in the Tucson Basin and in the adjacent lower San Pedro Valley. In most instances, the compounds appear to demarcate domestic courtyard space and there are usually several compounds on a site the physical size of Whiptail. At Sabino-Bear Canyon ruin, for example, remnants of at least four compounds have been mapped (Douglass and Leonard 1920-1921; reproduced in Welch 1997:3). Multiple residential compounds have also been found at the Marana Mound site on the northwest side of Tucson (Fish et al. 1992a), at sites such as Paloparado on the upper middle Santa Cruz (Di Peso 1956), and at numerous sites in the lower San Pedro Valley east of Whiptail (Clark and Lyons 2007; Clark et al. 2011).

Single compound sites like those at Gibbon Springs and Whiptail have been identified at a few sites in the region. According to Jeff Clark (personal communication, February 2009), the Twin Hawks site (AZ

BB:6:20[ASM]) near Oracle, possibly AZ BB:6:13(ASM) (also near Oracle), and the José Solas Ruin (AS BB:11:91[ASM]) along the San Pedro each has a single compound (or possible compound in the case of the José Solas Ruin) in association with detached and contiguous houses outside of compounds.

Closer to Whiptail, the Tanque Verde Ruin has a compound with two sets of contiguous- or abutted-wall houses inside it, as well as a house that was remodeled in ways similar to Structure 19a at Whiptail and Feature 106 at Gibbon Springs. Set on a narrow ridge, the site also has a house outside of the compound on either end of the ridge (Haury 1928; Zahniser 1966:120, Figure 4). At first glance, this compound looks residential, but the site may actually be a "center" for a cluster of hamlet or farmstead-sized sites on ridges in the area including AZ BB:14:24(ASM), the site that Zahniser (1966) excavated as a companion site to Tanque Verde Ruin. In other words, the topography of the area above Rincon Creek makes the spread-out pattern seen at Whiptail and Gibbon Springs impossible. Zahniser (1966:168-72) alludes to this in his discussion of the survey he conducted around AZ BB:14:24(ASM). If that is the case, the clustering of sites might be considered a village, with the compound at Tanque Verde Ruin being the communal center of that habitation.

Tanque Verde Ruin has some of the same characteristics of the compounds at Gibbon Springs and Whiptail: at least one remodeled house, houses burned with floor assemblages, and an earlier style pit house structure in or immediately adjacent to the compound (Structure 4 at Whiptail, House 1b at Tanque Verde Ruin, and Feature 100 at Gibbon Springs). The two earlier structures at Tanque Verde Ruin and Whiptail had been abandoned. Structures were superimposed over the top of House 1b at Tanque Verde Ruin, and the compound at Whiptail was clearly built after Structure 4 had been abandoned. Interestingly, the pit house at Gibbon Springs appears to have been contemporaneous with other structures in the compound. Like the compound at Gibbon Springs, the Tanque Verde Ruin compound contained burials. According to Henry Wallace (e-mail communication, 2009), pothunters digging in the compound exposed 30 or more burials, most likely cremations, along with between 30 and 40 decorated and plain ware pots. The pothunters took the vessels; what happened to the human remains is unknown.

At Whiptail, the construction of the compound at almost the exact spot of one of the earliest houses at the site, its apparent timing of construction during the last major phase of construction in the village, and its probable ritual abandonment argue for its communal orientation and use. Alternatively, the presence of the compound at Whiptail may represent a shift in village organization in the A.D. 1240s, and may have been the last construction at the site. The compound appears to have been built in the last "open" space in the core of the village (not counting the abandoned and filled-in Structure 4). If construction of the compound does represent such a shift, then compounds may be a good temporal marker for the later part of the Tanque Verde phase in the Tucson Basin, as well as a good marker for the end of the Soza phase, which is the lower San Pedro Valley's equivalent of the Tanque Verde phase.

The Soza Phase and Migration

Clark et al. (2011) and Clark and Lyons (2011) have noted that Gibbon Springs and Whiptail strongly resemble Soza phase sites in the lower San Pedro Valley. They define Soza phase sites as having cobble-reinforced adobe-walled houses that are often free-standing. During the phase, room forms changed from subrectangular to rectangular, with projecting entries being replaced by simple doorways. Compounds and wing-walls appear toward the end of the phase. Substantial amounts of artiodactyl bone were recovered from Soza phase contexts by the Center for Desert Archaeology's Lower San Pedro Valley project, so much so that Clark et al. (2011) suggested that the inhabitants of the San Pedro Valley exported bighorn, deer, and pronghorn meat. Finally, one of the most distinctive traits of the Soza phase in the San Pedro is the local production and use of brown corrugated pottery. Locally made decorated wares are notably rare or absent at Soza phase sites in the San Pedro Valley.

Corrugated Wares and Migration

Distribution of Corrugated Wares

Clark et al. (2011) use Soza phase traits and settlement patterns—especially the local production of corrugated pottery—to argue for migration of peoples from the Mogollon highlands into the San Pedro. They noticed that the distribution of corrugated wares in the San Pedro formed a corridor, with a high density (35 to 55 %) of the ceramic assemblage at three sites (Big Bell, Corrugated Ridge, and the 111 Ranch) in the San Manuel area, which is 15 to 20 miles northeast of Whiptail. An extension of the corridor forms a lobe that extends over Redington Pass to the sites of Whiptail and Gibbon Springs. The percentages of corrugated wares at those sites (13 and 15.3 percent respectively) is lower than the peak density in the San Manuel area, but corrugated wares still make up a significant part of the assemblages (Chapter 3; Gregonis 1996).

To the south and west of Whiptail and Gibbon Springs (excluding Sabino-Bear Canyon Ruin), the corrugated percentages drop off dramatically. At the cluster of sites around the Tanque Verde Ruin and AZ BB:14:24(ASM), 5 percent of the sherds recorded during a survey were corrugated, and corrugated sherds make up 2 percent of the sherds recovered from AZ BB:14:24(ASM) (Zahniser 1966). In a survey of Saguaro National Monument-Headquarters Division (Saguaro National Park East), Zahniser (1970) found one site—AZ BB:14:42—where 7 percent (16 out of 236) of the sherds he collected were corrugated. In a later survey of the park, Simpson and Wells (1983:57) found 61 sites with Classic period components. Forty-four of the sites had small numbers of corrugated sherds. At site SAGU 83A-101, they collected 11 corrugated sherds in their collected sample of 3,000 pieces (Simpson and Wells 1983:59). And in the 1990s, Kevin Wellman (1994) found two sites with corrugated pottery in his survey of a land acquisition for the park.

At the Classic period component of the Tanque Verde Wash site, which is about four miles southwest of Whiptail, only three corrugated sherds (out of 17,299) were recovered. Petrographic analysis of those sherds showed that two of the sherds were made using local Catalina petrofacies sands; the third was produced in the San Pedro River Valley (Heidke and Lavayen 2009). The vessels represented by these sherds could be indicators of exchange with the residents of Whiptail and Gibbon Springs.

Corrugated Wares at Gibbon Springs and Whiptail

One of the indicators that Clark (2001:6–9) uses to define the presence of a migrant population at a site is the local production of crafts in a style of the "home" region. In regard to the corrugated pottery, that home region is the Mogollon Highlands. Petrographic analyses of corrugated pottery at Whiptail and Gibbon Springs suggest that the wares were made using locally available sands for temper (Appendix B; Heidke 1996). Much of the Tanque Verde

Red-on-brown and plain ware ceramics made at Whiptail and Gibbon Springs have the same type of temper as those found in the corrugated wares, supporting the idea of local manufacture. Pottery-making tools and materials occur at both sites. They include pottery anvils, polishing stones, raw clay (found at Gibbon Springs), an unfired vessel (at Whiptail), temper sources (ground and burned schist and gneiss), pigment sources (hematite-coated rocks and ocher), and pigment grinding tools (Chapters 5 and 7; Fratt 1996).

If, as Clark et al. (2011; Clark and Lengyel 2002) suspect, the corrugated pottery at the two sites represents actual migrants at the villages, then corrugated wares should be unevenly distributed across the sites. That is, households with migrant potters should have higher percentages of corrugated wares relative to other types of pottery than households without migrants. There is differential distribution of corrugated wares at Gibbon Springs and Whiptail, but it is difficult to interpret the patterns.

Whiptail Distribution Pattern

At Whiptail, corrugated sherds and vessels were found throughout the site (Table 3.10), although the relative percentages varied. The highest relative percentage of corrugated sherds occurred in the Central Locus (25 % of the overall ceramic assemblage) and the lowest in the Southwestern Locus (7.6 %). Four structures at the site, Structures 4, 15, 22, and 31a had the highest percentage of corrugated sherds (Table 3.13). The sherds in Structure 4 appear to be dumped into the feature as trash; sherds from the other features represent vessels that were left in the structures. The corrugated sherds from Structures 22 and 31a represent approximately two vessels apiece, while those from Structure 15 represent at least 11 vessels (mostly jars). As discussed previously, Structure 15 was a store room in the Central Locus of the site.

Including Structures 15, 22, and 31a, complete, nearly complete, and reconstructible corrugated vessels were found in only ten structures at the site. Like the sherd distribution, the corrugated vessels were found in all loci, although features in the Compound and Central loci had higher numbers of whole and reconstructible vessels on their floors or in floor or roof fill. All but two of the features (Structures 22 and 31a) where reconstructible or whole corrugated vessels were identified had intact floor assemblages. As discussed previously, I think that at least some of these assemblages were staged (Table 11.6). In two of these features—Structures 17 and 19a—the corrugated wares seem to have had a special significance, based on the placement of the vessels (as in Structure 19a) and the presence of an imported corrugated ware (the McDonald Corrugated bowl in Structure 17). Two structures—8 and 15—had the highest number of corrugated vessels, with 6 in Structure 8 and, as mentioned previously, 11 in Structure 15. Those in Structure 15 appear to have been storage vessels, while those in Structure 8 included two bowls and four jars. One obliterated corrugated handled jar found outside of Structure 27a was used a cremation vessel. Of those vessels identifiable to shape, 45 were bowl forms and 46 were jars (Table 3.14).

At Whiptail, then, the pattern appears to be one where corrugated wares were distributed unevenly throughout the site, with a lower percentage found in the Southwestern Locus, the most densely occupied portion of the site. The distribution of the whole or reconstructible corrugated wares—in ten structures but in all loci and staged on the floor of at least two houses—suggests to me that corrugated vessels may have had symbolic importance. That is, all families at the site needed at least one corrugated pot in their assemblage. This, perhaps, indicates that the potters (possibly migrants) who made the corrugated wares were well integrated into the village society, or that they held a special social place in the village. True trade wares such as San Carlos Brown wares and Cibola White wares were evenly distributed throughout features at Whiptail (Table 3.14), suggesting that a single family either did not control contacts with those outside the basin or they distributed the trade wares in the same way they did the corrugated pottery.

Gibbon Springs Distribution Pattern

At Gibbon Springs, corrugated wares were found in all parts of the site except for the agricultural areas. The highest percentage was found in the Northeastern Village Segment, where 34.9 percent of the sherds were corrugated wares. Corrugated sherds in the other habitation segments of the village were 15 percent in the compound and 14 percent in the Village Core. In the Northeastern Village Segment one house (Feature 112) and an associated midden (Feature 108) contained the highest percentages of corrugated wares. In Feature 112 more than 54 percent of the sherds were corrugated wares; they represented at least six vessels. In Feature 108, 67 percent of the sherds were corrugated wares (Gregonis 1996).

Partially reconstructible, reconstructible, and whole corrugated vessels were found in 11 of the 24 houses. And, like those found at Whiptail, they were found in all of the habitation segments of Gibbon Springs. The biggest difference from Whiptail is that most of the vessels were found in fill and floor fill contexts rather than on the floor of houses. Given the small numbers of sherds associated with each pot, the vessels may represent primary trash deposits rather than pots that were abandoned in place. Corrugated bowls outnumbered jars at Gibbon Springs (Gregonis 1996).

In the Gibbon Springs site report Slaughter and I speculated in various chapters that the material left in house Feature 112 and midden Feature 108 represented a migrant household (Gregonis 1996; Slaughter 1996b). The house fits the criteria in that it is outside of the central part of the site. It is nearly 150 meters away from the compound and about 90 meters away from its nearest neighbor in the Village Core (Slaughter and Roberts 1996a). If Feature 112 does represent a migrant household, its residents may have had a special exchange relationship with other inhabitants of the village, as there are higher percentages of Tanque Verde Red-on-brown sherds (31.8%) in Feature 112 than occur elsewhere on the site.

Two other houses at Gibbon Springs had distinctive assemblages that are suggestive of migrant or migrant-associated households. Both of these houses are in the village core. One, Feature 46, was part of a two-room structure (along with Feature 45). Interestingly, the door of Feature 46 opened to the south, while the door to Feature 45 opened to the north. This structure is the only contiguous walled structure identified at the site; it was probably burned on purpose when it was abandoned. Although only half of Feature 46 was excavated, it appears to have had a staged floor and floor fill assemblage including two corrugated bowls, a Tanque Verde Red-on-brown bowl, three Mogollon-style brown ware bowls, and burned bone (Slaughter 1996:110).

Feature 125, a pit structure with an entry antechamber, contained five corrugated vessels, a small incised jar, two Mogollon-style brown ware bowls, numerous Tanque Verde Red-on-brown sherds, and San Carlos Red and Brown sherds (Slaughter 1996:135). Ten percent of the sherds from this house appear to have been made outside of the Tucson Basin, a high percentage for features on the site, where foreign sherds generally made up less than five percent of the assemblages. The ceramic assemblage in Feature 125 and the house architecture itself had a non-Tucson basin feel (Gregonis 1996:254).

At Gibbon Springs, then, the distribution of corrugated wares may be more suggestive of a migrant household in one house (Feature 112) and its associated midden (Feature 108). Two other houses—Features 45/46 and Feature 125—may also have been migrant-related structures, but instead of corrugated wares (which were present in both houses), the indicators were Mogollon-style brown ware bowls and the architecture of the structures themselves.

Other Indicators of Migration

Clark and colleagues (Clark and Lyons 2011; Clark and Lengyel 2002) effectively used the distribution of corrugated wares to make a case for migration of people from the Mogollon highlands into the San Pedro Valley during the Soza phase. As suggested previously, however, there are other indications of a migrant population in the archaeological record of the lower San Pedro and the neighboring northeastern Tucson Basin. These indicators include architecture, pottery, the use of conifer wood in house construction, the use of obsidian, perhaps the distinctive use of artiodactyls, and perhaps inhumation burial.

In his work on thirteenth- and fourteenth-century sites in the Tonto Basin, Clark (2001:6-9) developed four hypotheses of migration. These are exchange, emulation, ethnicity, and enculturation. Although Clark discussed these as competing hypotheses, I think that they are better considered as stages of migration, with exchange preceding or inspiring emulation, and (depending on the reasons and conditions for migration) emulation leading to enculturation and/or ethnogenesis. I agree with Clark (e-mail communication 2009) that the "mundane material culture reflecting enculturation is . . . the most reliable indicator of migration because it is typically not exchange and not easily emulated." At Whiptail Ruin there is evidence of exchange and emulation that led to enculturation and, perhaps ethnogenesis. I have treated enculturation and ethnicity as a single discussion here, because I'm not sure the two hypotheses can be separated in an archaeological context.

Exchange and Emulation

Exchange refers to short- or long-distance trade networks that were established prior to actual migration. Exchange can often lead to emulation of craft and other technologies, where locals manufacture of crafts in the style of the "home" region. The distribution and local manufacture of corrugated wares are an indicator of the strength of connections with areas outside of the Tucson Basin and the lower San Pedro Valley.

Local imitation of the black-on-white pottery, perhaps by migrants, is suggested by varieties of Tanque Verde Red-on-brown that were found at the site (Table 3.9). Nine sherds of a white-slipped, black-paint variant were found in the Whiptail compound. One hundred forty-three black paint variants of Tanque Verde Red-on-brown were also found. Although scattered throughout the site, more than half (n = 98) were found in the Southwestern Locus. White-slipped variants of Tanque Verde Red-on-brown were more common (n = 415 out of 24,776). They were found in the Compound, Central, Northern, and Southwestern loci.

Other ceramic indicators of exchange with the Mogollon area include the presence of Cibola White wares, White Mountain Red wares, and nonlocal corrugated wares at Whiptail. These sherds (n = 78) were found primarily in the Compound, Southwestern, and Northern loci of the site. A Tularosa Black-on-white jar was used as a crematory vessel (Cremation 8) and a Pinedale Black-on-white jar was found in one of the two cemeteries identified at the site, but not in direct association with cremated remains.

Other trade items found at Whiptail that might be connected with the migration into the lower San Pedro include San Carlos wares (probably made in the Aravaipa area) and small amounts of obsidian. The San Carlos sherds (n = 624) were found in all except the Southern Locus at Whiptail.

Obsidian artifacts are uncommon at the site. Fifteen projectile points including 14 Classic period points and 1 Archaic point were found. The tools including the Classic period points were recovered from the Compound and Southwestern loci. The obsidian flakes (n = 10) and core were found in the Compound, Southwestern, Central, and Northern loci. As described in Chapter 4, source analysis of three points by Shackley (2009) indicates that the items were made from Mule Creek obsidian, probably from the same nodule. According to Jane Sliva (email communication with Jeffery Clark 2009) two of the points were probably made by one person, while the other was made by another individual. The Mule Creek source ties nicely with the projected migration of Mogollon highlands people into the lower San Pedro (and eastern Tucson Basin) from the Safford area as nodules of Mule Creek obsidian are common in Gila River deposits in the Safford Valley. The indication that two people may have used a single obsidian nodule to produce artifacts suggests that obsidian was a highly valued, rare resource.

Gibbon Springs does not seem to have been as involved in exchange with the Mogollon highlands area as Whiptail. Only five Cibola White ware sherds were found. No White Mountain Red wares or pieces of obsidian were recovered (Gregonis 1996; Myers 1996). One hundred sixty-five San Carlos sherds were found; like the San Carlos wares at Whiptail, they occurred in most loci in fill contexts. As discussed previously, several Mogollon-style plain ware vessels were found in two houses at Gibbon Springs. The smaller numbers of exotic sherds and lithics from Gibbon Springs may be a factor of more intensive surface collection and a smaller sample size than Whiptail rather than a real difference in trade connections between the two sites.

Clark (2001:7–8) describes two categories of emulation: technological and ideological. Technological emulation is the spread of technological innovation, for example, the adoption of certain agricultural or construction techniques. Clark (2001:8) defines ideological emulation as the "appearance of artifacts and architecture associated with religion and other high-level ideologies."

The widespread focus on dry farming during the A.D. 1200s may have been a form of technological emulation, although the technology may have been a necessity due to climate change rather than adoption of a northern style of agriculture. If agricultural fields existed at Whiptail, they were destroyed during historical times by development of the springs into today's lakes at Agua Caliente Park. At Gibbon Springs, the agricultural systems near the springs are reminiscent of the check dam and spreader systems common on the Mogollon Rim and Colorado Plateau (Roberts 1996b).

The intensification of agave growing may have been a natural outgrowth of the expansion of dry farming systems. Clark and Lyons (2011) have shown that intense agave growing and use is associated with Soza phase contexts in the lower San Pedro. Considering that the Hohokam began growing agave long before the A.D. 1200s, it is possible that migrants enthusiastically adopted what to them was a new crop or a crop that they had only seen as a valued trade item in the past. At Whiptail, then, agave growing may have been one of the signatures of "Hohokamness," with the migrant families learning how to grow and process the plants.

The presence of tabular tools in nearly all contexts at Whiptail (Table 5.1) and the presence of agave remains at the site (Chapter 9) indicate that agave was an important resource. Because of the destruction of features around the Agua Caliente springs, it is not known if agave was grown or collected from the wild at Whiptail. The agricultural field systems (complete with rock piles) at Gibbon Springs suggest that agave was grown at that site, although no agave remains were identified in botanical samples from there (Puseman 1996).

In regard to technological emulation, the construction techniques used by early Classic period peoples throughout southern Arizona can be considered. The shift from subrectangular brush and puddled adobe houses-in-pits to rectangular cobble-reinforced structures that sometimes included contiguous rooms is dramatic and clearly visible on the landscape. Current research suggests that the new construction techniques are the result of Mogollon influence, although they could also have been an innovation inspired by interaction with northern Mexican populations.

The use of conifer wood in building may include technological and ideological emulation. One can argue that the sites near the base of the Santa Catalina Mountains were simply making use of available upland resources. The environments around Whiptail and Gibbon Springs were, however, rich in riparian resources and the sites' inhabitants made good use of them. Mesquite was an important building material at both sites and cottonwood and willow were used in structures at Gibbon Springs (Chapter 9; Puseman 1996).

That the inhabitants of the two sites thought it important enough to hike up into the mountains and bring down juniper, piñon, and ponderosa pine for their homes is significant. For some reason, they thought that conifer wood was the wood to use for beams. Or, at least, it was an important wood to use in certain structures.

At Whiptail, conifer wood was recovered from 11 of the houses including one contiguous walled house (Structures 11, 16, 18) and one where two rooms abutted one another (Structures 10 and 12) (Table 9.3). These two sets of rooms were located in the Southwestern Locus. Three structures in the Compound Locus—7, 8, and 17—had juniper, piñon, or ponderosa pine in them. Ponderosa pine, juniper, and piñon pine were recovered from Structure 15, the store room in the Central Locus. And ponderosa pine was the main structural wood used in Structures 14 and 19 in the Southern Locus. Datable wood in these structures ranged from the late A.D. 1230s (Structures 10 and 15) to the mid A.D. 1240s (Structures 8, 16, and 19). All of the structures had been burned and all of them had intact floor assemblages. As discussed previously, the houses in the Southern Locus probably served a ritual purpose; those associated with the compound may also have been important in communal activity. Perhaps the other structures also had a social significance that warranted the use of conifer wood.

Four features from Gibbon Springs yielded conifer wood: 42, 60, 106, and 125 (Slaughter 1996:523). Piñon post fragments found in Feature 106 were tree-ring dated to A.D. 1249. As previously described, this compound-associated feature had a floor assemblage and a substantial amount of artiodactyl bone. Feature 42, the ceramic workshop in the Western Village Segment, contained Douglas fir and ponderosa pine. Juniper was found in Feature 125, the pit structure with an antechamber and a Mogollon-like pottery assemblage. These three structures seemed to have been ritually closed, implying that they had some social significance to the villagers.

The fourth house with conifer wood was Feature 60. It was the sole habitation structure in the Western Agricultural Field. It contained ponderosa pine fragments. In his description of the feature, Slaughter (1996a:114-116) noted that the house had been cleaned out and intentionally burned.

Ethnicity and Enculturation

As a migrant population becomes more established in an area, the interacting groups move from an exchange and emulation relationship to one where ethnicities are defined and enculturation occurs. *Merriam-Webster's Collegiate Dictionary: Eleventh Edition* defines "ethnicity" as "a particular ethnic affiliation or group" and "ethnic" as "of or relating to large groups of people classed according to common racial, national, tribal, religious, linguistic, or cultural origin or background." That dictionary also defines "enculturation" as "the process by which an individual learns the traditional content of a culture and assimilates its practice and values." In regard to defining migration in an archaeological context, aspects of the two terms are intertwined.

Clark (2001:9) describes ethnicity as relating to a self-perceived group, one with common beliefs, a sense of historical continuity, and a common ancestry or place of origin. As migrant groups encounter local groups, as happened in the lower San Pedro Valley and the northeastern Tucson Basin, they develop new settlement histories and beliefs. As each group learns and assimilates another's culture, they adopt some aspects of culture and reject others. A new ethnicity develops as shared aspects develop. Clark (2001:9) defines these aspects as ecological (where to do), social (what to do), and utilitarian (how to do).

The ecological settings, village layouts, and material culture at Whiptail and Gibbon Springs illustrate an ethnicity (or ethnogenesis) that blended Tanque Verde phase, Tucson Basin Hohokam characteristics with Soza phase San Pedro migrant traits. During the early to mid-A.D. 1200s, hundreds of small villages were established in southern Arizona, often near secondary water sources, in areas where farming could be diversified, and where there was good access to wild resources.

Whiptail and Gibbon Springs were both established near springs at the base of a large mountain range in a setting that offered access to riparian, desert, and mountain resources. Although no Pre-Classic houses have been found at Whiptail, a roasting pit dating to the Pioneer period and small amounts of Pre-Classic Hohokam sherds have been recovered from the Agua Caliente Park portion of the site, and Colonial and Sedentary sherds do occur on the main portion of the site (Chapter 3; Gregonis 2001b; Wellman and Grimm 2001). Evidence for Pre-Classic occupation at Gibbon Springs is more limited. Only a few Rincon or Late Rincon Red-on-brown sherds were found at Gibbon Springs (Gregonis 1996). The presence of earlier Hohokam activity at the two sites probably means that the people establishing the villages were using part of a defined territory and not venturing into a previously unused, unowned area. Supporting that idea is the fact that there is no evidence of defensive structures at either site and neither is in a defendable location.

Potential home villages for the Whiptail and Gibbon Springs settlers could have been any number of villages that had pre-Classic occupations. Among them are Sabino-Bear Canyon Ruin (Welch 1989, 1997), the Tanque Verde Wash site (Elson 1986), an unexplored Pre-Classic site–AZ BB:10:16--located just west of Agua Caliente Wash from Whiptail, or one of several villages that are now in Saguaro National Park East (Simpson and Wells 1983, 1984). Second Canyon Ruin, on the east side of Redington Pass in the lower San Pedro Valley, may also have been a source for the families who founded Whiptail and Gibbon Springs. And it is possible, even probable, that the founding families came from both the Tucson Basin and the San Pedro, joining together to establish the new villages.

The people who established Whiptail and Gibbon Springs as permanent villages may have been trying to establish social and economic identities within the dynamic cultural framework created by the migrant populations moving into the lower San Pedro Valley and over the pass into the northeastern Tucson Basin. Specifically, the Whiptail and Gibbon Springs villagers may have been hunting specialists. As described in Chapter 8 and previously in this chapter, the nature of the artiodactyl remains at the two sites is suggestive of ritual that may have included the special deposition and storage of deer, bighorn, and pronghorn bone and antlers.

Clark and Lyons (2011) suggest that during the Classic period the lower San Pedro Valley inhabitants may have exported artiodactyl meat to neighboring areas where artiodactyls were scarce. If, as I suspect, some of the people at Whiptail and Gibbon Springs had social connections to the people in the San Pedro, they may have traded deer, pronghorn, and bighorn meat for products such as corn or cotton.

Archaeologically, the social aspects of enculturation (what to do) are tied to the utilitarian aspects (how to do). At Whiptail and Gibbon Springs, these two aspects can be seen in the architecture, craft manufacturing, and mortuary practices.

Like most other early Classic period sites in southern Arizona, Whiptail and Gibbon Springs has a combination of pit structures and cobble-reinforced adobe architecture. The pit structures at sites such as Whiptail, Gibbon Springs, and Tanque Verde Ruin seem to be the first houses built at the villages. They were then either abandoned and used for trash (for example, Structure 4 at Whiptail) or the houses were cleared out and essentially leveled, and cobble-reinforced adobe structures were carefully built on top of the outlines of the earlier houses (e.g. Structures 19a and 19b at Whiptail). The cobble-reinforced adobe rooms were either isolated or built with abutting or contiguous walls, a style that was foreign to the Hohokam but familiar to the Mogollon migrants in the lower San Pedro Valley. The use of conifer wood to build some of those structures may have been dictated by the migrant villagers.

The widespread adoption of compounds occurred during the mid-A.D. 1200s. Compounds at most sites in the region appear to define residential units, but those at Whiptail and Gibbon Springs seem to have had a village-wide communal use. The compound idea seems to have been foreign to the Hohokam, but the concept of dividing space with physical markers such as compound walls was common among ancestral Puebloans and Mogollon.

Burials at Whiptail and Gibbon Springs included Hohokam and Mogollon patterns. Following the Hohokam pattern, most of the burials found at both sites were cremations, which were found in pits and in urns, sometimes with grave goods, sometimes not. The amount of bone associated with the burials varied from a few pieces to 1,716 g, which is near the average of what is found in modern adult cremations (about 1,750 g) (Chapter 10). The pattern of cremation interment is similar to that seen at other Classic period sites in the region (Roberts 1996a:439-50). Beck (2000; Chapter 10) posits that the pattern was the result of a mourning ritual where cremations were periodically disinterred and reburied. At Whiptail and Gibbon Springs, the initial burial would have been in a pot, the reburial in a pit, with subsequent reburial appearing archaeologically as cremated bone fragments mixed with a cluster of sherds.

At Whiptail, the cremations included two instances where portions of one individual were buried with another. In Cremation 8, a child was buried with four fragments of bone from an adult. The bones were interred in a Tularosa Black-on-white jar. In the other instance (Cremation 4), a quarter-sized disk from a human temporal bone was buried in a Tanque Verde Red-on-brown jar with the cremated remains of a young to mature adult of unknown sex. The jar also held five chert projectile points, a bone awl, and sherds from another vessel (Table 10.1).

Inhumations at early Classic period sites in southern Arizona likely reflect a Mogollon influence. Three burials at Whiptail and two at Gibbon Springs were inhumations (Chapter 10; Roberts 1996a). One of the two inhumations at Gibbon Springs consisted only of the diaphyses of a tibia and humerus found in a pit. The second inhumation, of a 20- to 25-year-old female, was found in the Western Village Segment. Buried in a pit in an extended position, the burial had a cluster of rocks on top of it. As mentioned previously, one of the three inhumations at Whiptail also had rocks on top of it.

Several examples of this type of burial have been found in Classic period contexts at sites in the lower San Pedro Valley including Second Canyon and the Big Ditch site (Franklin 1980:207; Masse et al. 2009). The burial at Second Canyon may be slightly later in time than the burials at Whiptail and Gibbon Springs; it was semi-flexed and the skull had occipital deformation. The Big Ditch burial was found in a late Sedentary or Early Classic phase house. The body there was found sprawled face down on the floor of the house, with rocks on top of the body. Closer to Whiptail, a rock-covered infant burial was discovered at the University Indian Ruin (Hayden 1957:98). The purpose of the rocks on top of these burials is unclear, but the custom may have evolved into the crypt-like burials that occur occasionally in later Classic period sites in the San Pedro (Carpenter 1996:319) and perhaps into the historical O'odham system of burial that includes building a roof over the grave (Russell 1975:192). In any case, the gradual shift from cremation to inhumation in the region that occurred during the Classic period was part of the enculturation process for the inhabitants of southern Arizona.

The most straightforward evidence for enculturation is the production of pottery at Whiptail and Gibbon Springs. The villagers at both sites made Tanque Verde Red-on-brown and corrugated pottery. Tanque Verde Red-on-brown is a typical Tucson Basin pottery type and corrugated wares are associated with Mogollon migrants in the lower San Pedro Valley. Technologically, the corrugated wares are a blend of Hohokam and Mogollon technology. The pots were made by Mogollon coil-and-scrape methods and usually finished by paddling, a Hohokam technique.

The Blended Communities

The families who founded Whiptail and Gibbon Springs adopted traits from their Hohokam and lower San Pedro Valley migrant relatives to create their own social system. Like most people in southern Arizona at the time, they constructed cobble-reinforced adobe houses in a style that their Hohokam grandparents would not have recognized unless they had traveled north to the Mogollon Rim on a trading trip. Some villagers—possibly those with San Pedro migrant affinities—selected conifers to use as beams and pillars in their houses. For the most part the people at Whiptail and Gibbon Springs buried their dead in the old, traditional Hohokam style, performing mourning rituals and reburial of young and old. Grandmothers taught their granddaughters to make pottery in both the Hohokam and Mogollon style, but with a Hohokam-style paddled finish. Midway through the life of Whiptail and Gibbon Springs, villagers decided to add a new component, the compound. But instead of defining households with the adobe, cobble, and post walled enclosures, they used the compound to create a communal center. People performed hunting rituals; killed and butchered deer, bighorn, and pronghorn; grew corn and other crops; and processed agave, cholla, and saguaro fruit at the sites for two to three generations and then moved on. Whether they joined relatives in the Tucson Basin or the lower San Pedro Valley is impossible to say.

Whiptail's Role in the Northeastern Tucson Basin

Whiptail and its companion village Gibbon Springs were not the only small early Classic period sites in the northeastern Tucson Basin. During the early A.D. 1200s, people throughout southern Arizona spread out from older, well-established villages to create new homes on bajadas, ridges, and upland locations. But they also continued to live in already-established villages. In their survey of Saguaro National Park, Simpson and Wells (1983, 1984) found that although 43 percent (n = 61) of the sites they identified had Classic period pottery on them (44 sites had corrugated ware); many of them also had earlier pottery. In fact, the majority of sites identified by Simpson and Wells had Colonial and Sedentary period components. This is also true for sites in the immediate vicinity of Whiptail (ASM site survey file).

As mentioned previously, I think that the families who founded Whiptail may have come from one of the Pre-Classic villages at Saguaro National Park, from AZ BB:10:16 (a nearby, unexplored site), from the Tanque Verde Wash site, or from the Sabino-Bear Canyon Ruin. People from these well-established villages would have been aware of the springs at the base of the Catalinas and, like their predecessors, undoubtedly hunted big game and gathered other wild resources from those spots. They would have incorporated the springs into their territories.

In the late A.D. 1100s, the migrants from the Mogollon highlands began to establish themselves in the lower San Pedro Valley. As they developed social relationships, they explored the territory around them, coming into the Tucson Basin over Redington Pass. If, as Clark and Lyons (2011) have suggested, the Soza phase residents of the San Pedro were hunting specialists, then the permanent Agua Caliente Springs at Whiptail would have attracted them.

The original houses at Whiptail seem to have been built during the mid- to late A.D. 1100s, perhaps in response to interest in the area from lower San Pedro Valley people. As the villages grew, the local residents incorporated some migrants into their communities. The migrants' ideas about how to do things are most evident in the local manufacture of corrugated pottery and the use of conifer wood in house construction. But Hohokam identity remained strong, as evidenced by the local manufacture of Tanque Verde Red-on-brown pottery, the use of desert resources such as cholla and agave, and, most importantly, the continued use of cremation in mortuary rituals.

It is clear from the archaeological evidence that artiodactyl hunting was important to the people of Whiptail throughout its occupation. Projectile points were common on the site. Skulls, mandibles, antlers, horns, and lower leg bones were found in several features. Some of these may have been the remnants of carefully stored disguises used by hunting specialists. Other parts of the body found at the site—ribs, scapulae, and innominates—may have been the remnants of carcasses left as offerings (for example in Structure 8) or bones stored by shamans to protect the rest of the village (Underhill 1946).

When the inhabitants of Whiptail finally decided to live elsewhere, they apparently did not simply abandon the site. Hammerstones, chipped stone, and other artifacts in the fill of houses, as well as the inhumation burial in Structure 28 are all evidence that features at the site were revisited from time to time.

Based on the near absence of Roosevelt Red Wares and the low numbers of inhumations found at the site, it seems clear that Whiptail was abandoned as a village site before A.D. 1300. Apparently the entire northeastern Tucson Basin was vacated by that time. To date, there is no evidence that the northeastern Tucson Basin was occupied after A.D. 1300. The nearest Tucson phase sites are the University Indian Ruin at the confluence of the Tanque Verde and Pantano Washes to the west and Second Canyon Ruin in the lower San Pedro Valley to the east. That left almost all of the Tanque Verde and Rincon drainages free of occupation, although hunting and gathering activities probably continued there. The area may have been a buffer zone, a boundary, between the Tucson Basin folk along the Santa Cruz and their neighbors in the San Pedro. In historic times, the lack of occupation has been blamed on the presence of Apaches, but I wonder if the reasons for not using the seemingly abundant resources along the Tanque Verde Wash had a deeper history.

A Final Note

Although it was excavated by volunteers (many of whom were novice archaeologists) in the late 1960s and early 1970s, Whiptail yielded a surprising amount of usable data. The site was a testing ground for the then relatively new discipline of archaeomagnetic dating. By happenstance, the site yielded coniferous wood that can now be tree-ring dated (Dean et al. 1996). Petrographic analysis of pottery from the site provided some of the first evidence for local manufacture of corrugated pottery in this region (Appendix B). Jamie Lytle-Webb studied pollen collection methods at Whiptail for her master's thesis (Lytle 1971) and Paul Grebinger (1971) used data from his work at the site in his doctoral dissertation; both were from the University of Arizona. Summer excavations at the site became Pima College's first foray into excavation. Materials from the excavations were used for laboratory analysis classes by students at the University of Arizona and at Eisenhower College. Our final push to finish analyses and prepare a report has shown that the data gathered 40 years ago can be used to address today's research themes. And most importantly, people who own homes and property that include the Whiptail site (especially Ken and Mary Karrels) are today actively protecting the site, which still has great potential to yield information (Figure 11.1).

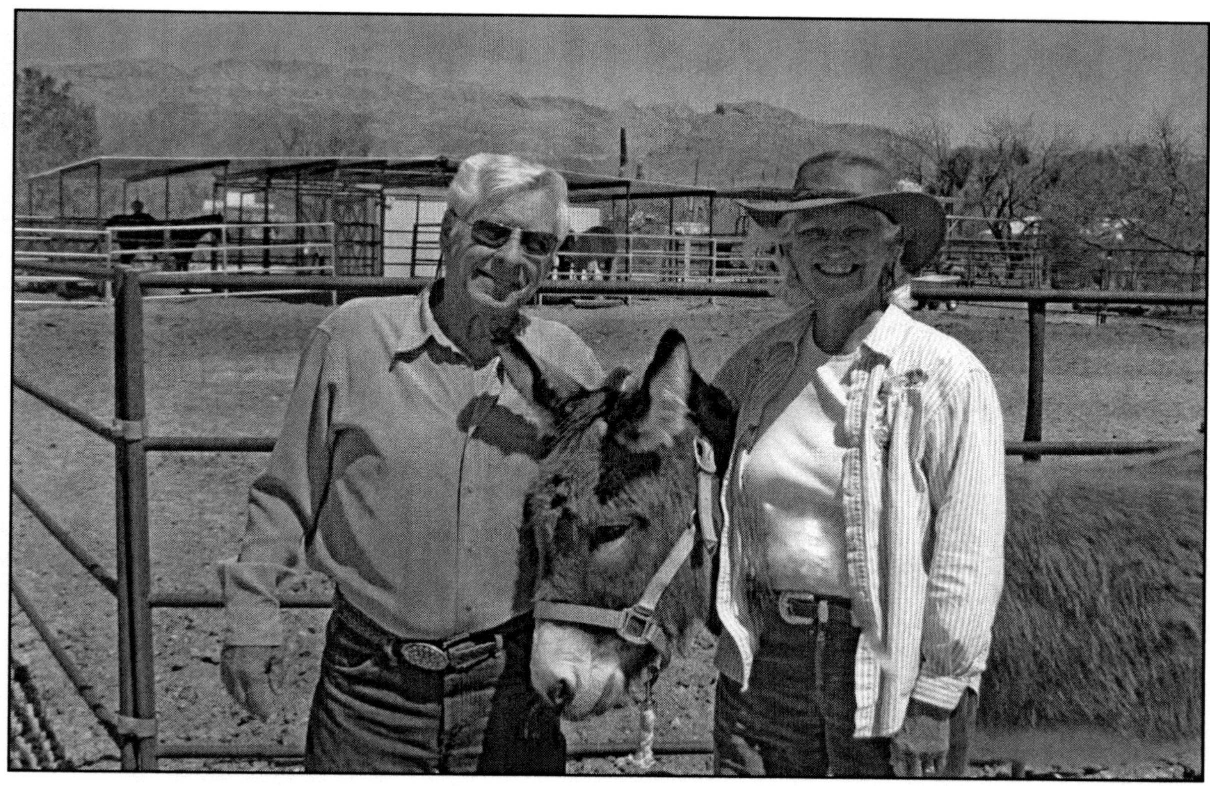

Figure 11.1. Ken and Mary Karrels, with their burro, Brighty. The corral where Brighty lives is on top of the compound.

Appendix A

Chemical Analysis of Pottery and Clay from Whiptail Ruin

Carl F. Aten
Emeritus Professor of Chemistry
Hobart and William Smith College
Geneva, New York

[Editorial note: This report is reproduced from a manuscript on file in Arizona State Museum archives, Whiptail Ruin collection. The report has been reformatted to fit into the style of this site report. Minor editorial changes have also been made.]

Samples of pottery and clay from Whiptail Ruin were studied to determine similarity of origin. A fairly standard approach to this kind of problem that has evolved is to make a set of measurements on each sample in order to create a pattern that represents the sample. The patterns are then classified or ranked according to some degree of similarity among them. For example, Simon et al. (1977) categorized paper samples on the basis of atomic composition of trace metals. Massart et al. (1982) classified iron meteorites according to trace element composition patterns. In this work the pottery and clay samples were analyzed for atomic composition in 10 elements and the resulting composition patterns were compared by a simple hierarchical clustering scheme.

Techniques for the determination of elemental composition of complex, solid materials fall into two main groups. The first, which includes methods such as X-ray fluorescence spectrometry and neutron activation, uses the solid material itself for the analysis (Giauque et al. 1977; Hancock 1976). The second requires that the sample material be digested chemically to produce a solution that is then analyzed by some instrumental technique. In this work most element determinations were effected with an inductively coupled plasma spectrometer similar to that described by Floyd et al. (1980). Digestion schemes for geologic solids are of two types, also. The sample material may be reacted with a strong base such as Na_2CO_3 (Jenke and Diebold 1982) or Na_3BO_3 (Sinex et al. 1980), or with a strong acid such as HNO_2, HF, $HClO_4$ (McQuaker et al. 1970) or H_3PO_4 (Lucas and Reprect 1971; Talvitie 1951). In this work two digestion schemes were compared, one using a mixture of HNO_3 and HF similar to that of McQuaker et al. (1970), and the other was a H_3PO_4 procedure similar to that of Lucas and Ruprect (1971). Most of our data were obtained with the latter digestion scheme.

Experimental Materials and Methods

All glassware and polyethylene bottles were rinsed with 1% HNO_3 and distilled water. All acids used were Reagent grade.

Samples were obtained from 13 pieces of pottery, 2 contemporary clays, and a standard reference material (SRM) (Table A.1). The chemical analytical scheme consisted of three steps:

1. Obtain a solid sample.
2. Digest the solid to produce a solution.
3. Determine the concentrations of selected elements in the solution.

Solid Sample Preparation

Each clay sample was ground in a mortar and sieved (100 mesh, passed particles with a diameter <149 Pm). Pottery samples were obtained by crumbling a small amount from broken edges of sherds into a mortar, where they were ground. These samples were not sieved. Specimen 12/P6 (Table A.1) was an intact bowl that was sampled by scraping it with a stainless steel knife blade. The masses of samples varied from 0.1 to 0.5 grams except for 12/P6, where the masses were 0.03 grams. Each specimen was sampled twice from different places and the samples were processed separately (one sample was lost for specimen 9B/P1).

Sample Digestion

For the chemical analysis it was necessary that each sample be in solution. Two different chemical treatments to achieve this were investigated. The first scheme was used in two forms only for preliminary work and provided data for comparison with the second scheme.

In the first scheme, the weighed sample of powder was digested in a perfluropolyethelyne-lined bomb in a solution containing equal volumes of hydrofluoric (HF) and nitric (HNO_3) acids, 1 to 3 mL volume depending on the mass of the sample. The bomb was heated in boiling water for four hours. After digestion, the solution was evaporated to dryness on a hot plate and the residue was redissolved in 50 to 150 mL 0.5M hydrochloric acid (HC). The samples were stored in polyethylene bottles. Dissolution was incomplete; a small residue of rust-colored material remained.

The sample was mixed with 1 to 3 mL HF in the bomb and was digested as previously described. After digestion, the resulting solution was diluted immediately with 50 to 150 mL 0.5M HCl. Dissolution was incomplete; a small amount of fine, black solid remained.

The second method was used for all 13 pottery samples, both clays, and the SRM. It provided the principal body of data. Samples were placed in platinum crucibles and were heated in a muffle furnace at 600°C for three hours. The samples were then digested in 15 mL 85% phosphoric acid (H_3PO_4) in the platinum crucibles on a hot plate for about two hours, until the mixtures looked like soft solids. The digested material was dissolved in 50 to 80 mL water and was stored in polyethylene bottles. A small amount of white residue remained in the solutions. The solutions were analyzed directly for the minor elements but were diluted five-fold for the determination of the major elements.

Elemental Analysis

The sample solutions were analyzed with an Instrumentation Laboratory Plasma-100

Table A.1. The Pottery and Clay Materials Sampled.

Laboratory Number (H_3PO_4)	Laboratory Number (HF)	Clustering Number	Sample Number and/or Description of Sample Source
1A,B	—	6. 7	H-C 109 wall, rim
2A,B	—	8. 9	H-C 131A base, rim
3A,B	—	10, 11	H-C 139 base, rim
4A,B	—	12, 13	H 699, base, rim
5A,B	—	14, ~~15~~[a]	H 731 wall, rim
6A,B	—	16, 17	H 796, wall rim
7A,B	—	18, 19	H 1767 wall, rim
8A,B	P3	20, 21	Structure 27b 110, 6-inch diameter Tanque Verde Red-on-brown, wall, rim
9B[b]	P1	22[b]	Structure 15, Southeast 1/4, lower fill, body sherd
10A,B	P2	23, 24	Structure 18 floor, NW 1/4, wall, rim
11A,B	P4	25, 26	Structure 27b 109, 8-inch diameter, Tanque Verde Red-on-brown, wall, rim
12A,B	P6	27, 28	Structure 27b 107, 10-inch bowl, Tanque Verde Red-on-brown, wall, rim
13A,B	P5	29, 30	Structure 27b 108, 9-inch bowl, nonlocal plain ware, wall, rim
Clay A	—	1, 2, 3	Collected 1/26/79, from north bank of wash running east-west along southern margin of Whiptail Ruin.
Clay B	—	4, 5	Collected 1/26/79 from western margin of saltbush flat northwest of Whiptail Ruin.
SRM97a			Flint clay from National Bureau of Standards.

Notes: a. Results for this sample were discarded (see text).
b. The duplicate of this sample was spilled and not replaced.

spectrometer. In this method the solution that contains the sample is aspirated into a standing plasma wherein chemical decomposition and electronic excitation occur. The intensity of radiation emitted at wavelengths characteristic of different elements is measured and is compared with intensities obtained from standard solutions. The method is relatively free of matrix effects. Each set of solutions was analyzed twice. The elements determined by this method were:

major elements: Al, Ca, Fe, Mg; and
minor elements: Sr, Ba, Ti, Mn, Zr, B, Zn, V, Cu.

Potassium, another major element, was determined by measuring the emission intensity at 766 nm from solutions aspirated into an acetylene-air flame to an atomic absorption spectrometer, Perkin-Elmer Model 305B.

Experimental Results

Comparison of the Digestion Schemes

In Table A.2, the two HF and the H_3PO_4 digestions are compared for samples P1 through P6 and the two clays. Data for potassium are omitted from the comparison because this element was determined only for the H_3PO_4 digests. Results are listed for the remaining nine elements that were used in the clustering analysis. The digestion using only HF gave low results for the alkaline earth elements, probably because the fluorides have low solubilities. In computing, the concentration rations for the HF digestions were not used for Ca, Mg, and Sr. The H_3PO_4 digests gave low values for the elements Ti (71%) and Zr (38%) relative to the HF and HF, HNO_3 digestions. For the other elements (Al, Ca, Fe Mg Sr, Mn, and V), the H_3PO_4 digestions agreed with the HF and/or HF, HNO_3 digestions with average ratios and standard deviation 0.99 ± 0.06. When Ti and Zr are included in the overall average, the ratio and standard deviation is 0.89 ± 0.22 (Table A.3). Since this uncertainty of about 25% was comparable to the heterogeneity and processing errors observed between duplicate samples of the same material, it was decided to use only the simpler H_3PO_4 digestion for the entire set of 13 pottery pieces. A further test of the H_3PO_4 digestion was carried out with a standard reference material. The results are shown in Table A.4. Compared with the certified values, the H_3PO_4 digestion results for the two samples gave an average error of -6%. The results for Ti and Zn are interesting: (1) Ti was found at 63% of the certified value, whereas the mean value in the H_3PO_4 digestions was 71% of the HF, HNO_3 digestions implying that our Ti values are 30 or 40% too low, and (2) Zr was found at 96% of the certified value in sharp contrast to the 38% ratio for the two digestion schemes. There is no clear answer to this latter discrepancy, but since the Zr values obtained for the SRM were satisfactory, it seemed reasonable to include the Zr concentrations for the pottery in the data analysis.

Table A.2. Comparison of HF/HNO_3, HF, and H_3PO_4 Digestions.

Lab No.	Digestion	Element Concentration								
		% (wt)				ppm				
		Al	Ca	Fe	Mg	Sr	Ti	Mn	Zr	V
Clay A	HF/HNO_3	7.53	4.55	3.40	1.960	688	2910	498	424	63
	HF	4.17	0.91	5.11	0.610	339	2670	681	310	48
	H_3PO_4	6.73	4.39	3.33	1.570	599	2330	470	210	68
	H_3PO_4	6.41	4.37	3.29	1.730	566	2270	452	131	67
	H_3PO_4	6.63	4.39	3.25	1.580	474	2020	476	191	72
Clay B	HF/HNO_3	6.74	7.14	2.75	1.260	508	2190	378	271	53
	HF	4.03	1.83	2.32	0.670	230	1830	262	193	59
	H_3PO_4	5.87	6.95	2.62	1.110	433	1680	394	87	58
	H_3PO_4	5.18	5.85	2.25	1.060	459	1740	372	89	59
P3	HF/HNO_3	9.73	0.81	4.62	0.711	307	4450	1214	183	72
	HF	9.11	0.24	3.70	0.133	176	2670	903	141	66
8A	H_3PO_4	7.95	1.06	3.39	0.423	271	1860	903	119	59
8B	H_3PO_4	8.30	0.67	3.39	0.521	252	1920	745	90	60
P1	HF/HNO_3	8.21	2.55	1.99	0.474	362	1300	854	404	21
	HF	7.83	0.51	1.61	0.240	154	1150	377	85	25
9B	H_3PO_4	7.05	2.49	1.64	0.372	292	670	793	49	24
P2	HF/HNO_3	6.99	2.26	1.44	0.475	338	1170	1186	107	21
	HF	7.74	0.53	2.18	0.241	185	1640	578	88	30
10A	H_3PO_4	6.74	2.27	1.50	0.378	348	840	441	41	23
10B		6.48	2.04	1.63	0.377	253	1000	643	33	24
P4	HF/HNO_3	4.32	0.73	3.13	0.000	42	3120	426	2144	61
	HF	10.20	0.41	3.86	0.424	216	2830	1116	154	62
11A	H_3PO_4	8.38	0.94	3.31	0.521	270	1920	758	77	61
11B	H_3PO_4	8.71	2.94	3.85	0.571	281	1970	1009	81	65
P6	HF/HNO_3	12.97	2.16	3.44	0.663	222	2260	1363	499	57
	HF	7.91	1.65	3.80	0.566	323	2350	723	434	51
12A	H_3PO_4	6.80	3.00	3.20	0.572	329	2130	497	186	61
12B	H_3PO_4	7.66	2.92	3.25	0.540	426	2400	507	309	55
P5	HF/HNO_3	8.94	0.76	4.85	0.969	230	4350	587	229	81
	HF	9.87	0.45	6.00	0.319	200	4680	665	172	89
13A	H_3PO_4	8.85	0.86	4.90	0.768	267	3040	788	77	83
13B	H_3PO_4	8.85	0.90	5.18	0.808	328	3210	613	80	93

Table A.3. Comparison of Digestion Schemes: Concentration Ratios of H_3PO_4 Digestion/HF, HNO_3 Digestion.

Laboratory Number	Ratio by Element								
	Al	Ca	Fe	Mg	Sr	Ti	Mn	Zr	V
Clay B	1.126	0.962	0.773	0.830	0.794	0.791	0.785	0.483	1.165
Clay A	1.026	0.896	0.960	1.124	0.878	0.851	1.161	0.379	1.045
P3/8	0.862	1.068	0.815	1.118	0.852	0.531	0.778	0.645	0.867
P1/9	0.879	0.976	0.911	1.042	0.807	0.547	1.288	0.200	1.043
P2/10	0.897	0.954	0.865	1.047	0.889	0.655	0.614	0.379	0.922
P4/11	1.170	2.658	1.024	—	—	0.654	1.146	0.069	1.024
P6/12	0.692	1.370	0.906	0.905	1.700	0.983	0.481	0.530	1.074
P5/13	0.941	1.158	0.929	1.224	1.293	0.692	1.119	0.392	1.035
Average	0.949	1.055	0.898	1.041	1.030	0.713	0.922	0.385	1.021
Φ	0.155	0.163	0.080	0.135	0.341	0.154	0.295	0.182	0.092

Note: For elements Al, Fe, Sr, Ti, Mn, Zr, and V, both the HF and HF,$HN0_3$ digestion results were used, but for Ca, Mg, and Sr, the HF digestion was discarded.
The ratio = the average H_3PO_4 result/average of HF and HF,HNO_3 result. The ratio is averaged over eight materials.
$\Sigma = 7$ 0.988 ± 0.63 (Ti, Zr omitted).

Table A.4. Comparison of Experimental and Certified Values of Concentrations in SRM 97a.

Samples	% (wt)						ppm		
	LOI[a]	Al	Ti	Fe	K	Sr	Mg	Ca	Zr
Sample 1	12.68	18.97	0.705	0.331	0.464	0.141	918	936	444
Sample 2	12.82	16.57	0.736	0.301	0.429	0.187	791	2112[c]	448
Certified	13.32	20.53	1.139	0.315	0.152	0.152	905		466
Average Relative Error (%)[b]	-4.28	-13.44	-36.740	+0.320	7.590	-11.840	-5.58	19.08[c]	-4.29

Note: The samples were digested in H_3PO_4.
Overall average relative error -5.5 ± 15.4. This is the average of all average relative errors with standard deviation.
a. LOI = loss on ignition in muffle furnace.
b. Average relative error =

$$\left[\frac{(\text{Sample 1} + \text{Sample 2})}{2 \times \text{Certified}} - 1\right] \times 100$$

c. The result 2112 ppm is apparently an error and was omitted from the calculation.

Table A.5. Data for 10 Elements in Each Pottery and Clay Sample.

Laboratory Number	Cluster Number	% (wt)					ppm				
		Al	Ca	Fe	K	Mg	Sr	Ti	Mn	Zr	V
Clay A I	1	6.734	4.385	3.331	2.159	1.571	599.0	2332	470.1	209.7	67.5
Clay A II	2	6.408	4.367	3.292	1.890	1.727	565.9	2270	451.8	131.0	66.8
Clay A III	3	6.632	4.374	3.254	1.979	1.581	474.4	2022	476.4	190.8	71.7
Clay B I	4	5.868	6.945	2.621	1.890	1.107	433.0	1684	394.2	86.6	58.1
Clay B II	5	5.182	5.849	2.254	1.710	1.062	459.1	1741	372.4	88.6	58.8
1A	6	7.418	3.104	2.898	2.543	0.685	469.2	2079	413.6	89.7	73
1B	7	8.179	3.831	3.168	2.684	0.698	465.3	2157	509.2	99.9	86.8
2A	8	6.186	3.344	3.238	2.178	0.818	371.6	2353	585.8	127.4	86.5
2B	9	7.056	3.219	3.388	2.641	0.827	428.3	2140	542.0	135.3	89.5
3A	10	5.994	1.922	2.776	2.296	0.636	322.8	2096	480.6	109.8	60.8
3B	11	6.467	2.434	2.826	2.841	0.592	336.4	1864	461.4	102.4	55.4
4A	12	6.796	2.088	3.093	2.847	0.709	391.4	2198	451.9	94.4	93.1
4B	13	7.303	2.892	3.210	2.266	0.801	453.2	2274	423.1	87.7	85.8
5A	14	6.990	2.439	3.097	2.944	0.756	366.9	2129	453.9	122.2	66.1
5B	15	14.708	2.742	3.195	2.728	0.813	436.8	2023	501.0	110.5	75.1
6A	16	5.880	5.248	2.216	1.908	0.672	377.6	2159	421.0	63.2	49.3
6B	17	4.954	4.039	2.085	2.078	0.629	312.4	1516	409.9	71.5	51.1
7A	18	8.138	1.183	3.538	2.547	0.536	239.2	2049	391.5	98.4	69.1
7B	19	7.513	1.166	3.315	2.630	0.563	311.9	2043	384.7	105.3	70.1
8A	20	7.950	1.060	3.394	3.233	0.423	270.6	1861	902.5	119.2	59.2
8B	21	8.298	0.670	3.392	3.314	0.521	252.4	1920	745.3	90.2	60.2
9B	22	7.050	2.493	1.637	2.549	0.372	291.7	667.8	293.4	49.0	24.2
10A	23	6.737	2.274	1.495	2.617	0.378	348.4	843.9	441.1	50.6	22.6
10B	24	6.484	2.043	1.632	2.012	0.372	252.7	999.6	642.8	32.9	23.6
11A	25	8.276	0.937	3.313	3.328	0.521	270.1	1923	757.6	76.9	61.4
11B	26	8.708	2.943	3.846	3.356	0.571	280.9	1968	1008.8	80.8	64.7
12A	27	6.801	3.004	3.204	2.089	0.572	328.7	2130	497.3	186.1	60.7
12B	28	7.662	2.922	3.254	2.979	0.540	426.3	2396	506.9	308.8	55.3
13A	29	8.849	0.862	4.401	2.583	0.768	267.2	3040	788.1	77.4	82.6
13B	30	8.847	0.901	5.180	2.459	0.808	328.4	3207	612.7	79.9	93.4

Elemental Analysis of the Samples

Data for 10 elements in each pottery and clay sample are listed in Table A.5. Measurements were made for the elements Ba, B, Zn, and Cu, also, but are not reported in Table A.5 because the concentrations were low and the agreement between duplicate samples was poor.

Data Processing and Discussion

The results shown in Table A.5 have been treated by a simple hierarchical clustering scheme. Each column of elemental concentrations was scaled with the Z-scaling procedure [$Z_{ij} = (C_{ij} - \overline{C}_{ii}) / \sigma_i$] where C_{ij} is the concentration of element *i* in sample material *j*, C_I is the mean value of *ii* and σ_i is the standard deviation of element *i*. The degree of independence of the variouis concentrations may be seen in the correlation matrix, Table A.6. The five major elements are practically uncorrelated while in the whole table only two correlations are apparent: the group Fe, Ti, and V, and the pair Mg and Sr have correlations of about 0.8. However, in the clustering analysis no use was made of these correlations. The scaled values were examined in two groups: (1) the 5 major elements only and (2) the entire group of 10 elements. The scaled values were used to calculate Euclidian distances between the various samples assuming complete independence of the analytical data for different elements (Massart and Kaufman 1983:17).

$$r_{ij} = \left[\sum \left(Z_{ik} - Z_{kj}\right)^2 \Big) n \right]$$

The matrix of intersample distances calcu-

Table A.6. Correlation Matrix of Elemental Concentrations in Pottery and Clay Materials.

	Al	Ca	Fe	K	Mg	Sr	Ti	Mn	Zr	V
Al	1									
Ca	-0.41	1								
Fe	0.44	-0.39	1							
K	0.49	-0.67	0.32	1						
Mg	-0.14	0.58	0.22	-0.52	1					
Sr	-0.10	0.67	-0.03	-0.45	0.79	1				
Ti	0.24	-0.14	0.88	0.05	0.35	0.22	1			
Mn	0.30	-0.47	0.29	0.61	-0.35	-0.53	-0.04	1		
Zr	0.02	0.16	0.28	0.01	0.37	0.45	0.39	-0.17	1	
V	0.30	-.08	0.77	0.11	0.35	0.31	0.83	-0.12	0.24	1

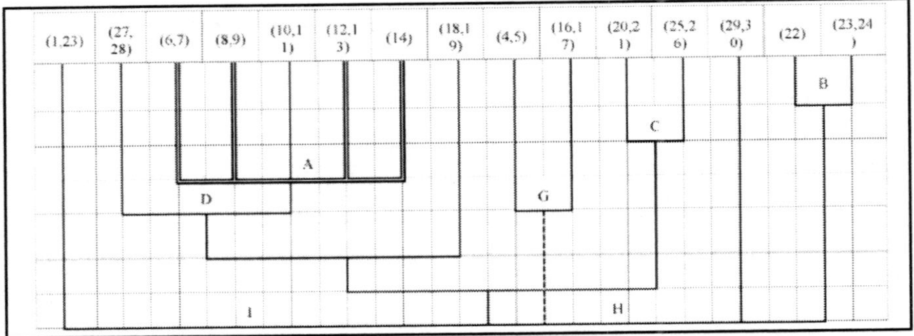

Figure A.1. Hierarchical clustering of samples. Sample clusters are in parentheses. Clusters that are hierarchically grouped (e.g., A, B, C, G) probably have a common geographical origin.

lated with the data for major elements is shown in Table A.7 and that calculated for all 10 elements is in Table A.8. These tables represent the analytical data and contain whatever information we have about sample similarity. The data have been compressed somewhat since results for replicate samples have been combined. The results for Sample 15 were discarded because there was an apparent error in the A1 determination. The A1 concentration was about twice that of the duplicate sample, No. 14, and was much higher than any other samples. The other elemental concentrations agreed closely with sample No. 14. As noted previously, the duplicate for No. 22 was spilled. Three samples of Clay A were processed as No. 1, No. 2, and No. 3. The diagonal terms in Tables A.7 and A.8 show the observed distances between duplicate samples (the average separation for No. 1, No. 2, and No. 3). The average value of the diagonal terms and standard deviation is:

<diagonal> = 1.03 ± 0.45 5-element distances
<diagonal> = 1.65 ± 0.59 10-element distances,

Table A.7. Paired Samples in Order of Increasing Total Euclidean Distance Sum.

	14	12, 13	10,11	6,7	27, 28	18, 19	8, 9	20, 21	22	25, 26	23, 24	16, 17	29, 30
14													
12, 13	0.930	1.413											
10, 11	1.160	1.172	1.252										
6, 7	1.160	1.122	1.438	0.788									
27, 28	1.388	1.317	1.450	1.238	1.974								
18, 19	1.430	1.382	1.528	1.673	1.594	0.496							
8, 9	1.372	1.084	1.452	1.140	1.389	1.860	1.131						
20, 21	1.682	2.202	2.274	2.382	2.274	1.542	2.801	0.464					
22	2.295	2.298	1.804	2.138	2.302	2.493	2.607	2.969					
25, 26	1.694	2.264	2.482	2.207	2.230	1.893	2.698	0.930	3.212	1.488			
23, 24	2.670	2.532	1.992	2.504	2.551	2.738	2.781	3.365	0.778	3.660	1.324		
16, 17	2.954	2.564	2.340	2.417	2.533	3.392	2.204	4.344	2.347	4.316	2.301	1.036	
29, 30	2.981	2.872	3.386	3.119	3.039	2.232	3.013	2.807	4.652	2.823	4.819	4.958	

Table A.8. Paired Samples in Order of Increasing Total Euclidean Distance Sum for all 10 Elements.

	14	10, 11	8, 9	6, 7	12, 13	18, 19	16, 17	20, 21	27, 28	25, 26	4, 5	23, 24	1,2,3	29, 30	22
14															
10, 11	1.545														
8, 9	1.964	2.250													
6, 7	1.887	2.530	1.834												
12, 13	1.922	2.507	1.751	1.515											
18, 19	1.880	2.016	2.797	2.823	2.484										
16, 17	3.382	2.731	3.478	3.403	3.664	3.804									
20, 21	3.141	3.122	3.951	4.161	4.147	3.198	5.236								
27, 28	2.988	3.169	3.113	3.609	3.784	5.543	4.386	4.474							
25, 26	3.457	3.551	4.043	4.185	4.277	3.705	5.378	2.479	4.896						
4, 5	4.154	3.979	3.706	3.627	4.061	4.964	2.416	6.441	5.013	6.391					
23, 24	4.684	3.784	5.471	5.165	5.457	4.652	3.606	4.948	5.792	5.329	5.113				
1, 2, 3	4.200	4.642	3.499	3.817	4.048	5.268	4.730	6.482	4.536	6.486	3.509	6.937			
29, 30	4.232	4.603	3.956	4.461	4.028	3.851	6.266	4.206	5.282	4.170	6.865	7.510	6.047		
22	5.003	4.142	5.663	5.489	5.863	5.150	4.342	4.425	5.994	4.703	5.673	2.023	7.254	7.565	

which may be taken as an estimate of the overall noise in the data. The samples are listed in Tables A.7 and A.8 in order of increasing total distance to all other samples. Thus, in Table A.7, No. 14 is nearest the other samples and No. 29,30 is farthest from the others.

The result of a hierarchical, agglomerative clustering of the data in Table A.7 is shown in Figure A.1 (Massart and Kaufman 1983:75). In this scheme the closest samples are grouped and regarded as a composite. The distance matrix is recalculated to show average distances from the composite point. This procedure is iterated until all samples have been combined. For our purposes, the samples that combine at or below the 1.6-distance level probably have a common geographical origin, while the other samples probably have different origins.

A similar treatment of the results using Euclidean distances calculated with data for ten elements gave the agglomeration shown in Figure A.2. Samples with intracluster separations less than 2.6 are probably significant whereas larger separations probably mean different physical origins of the samples.

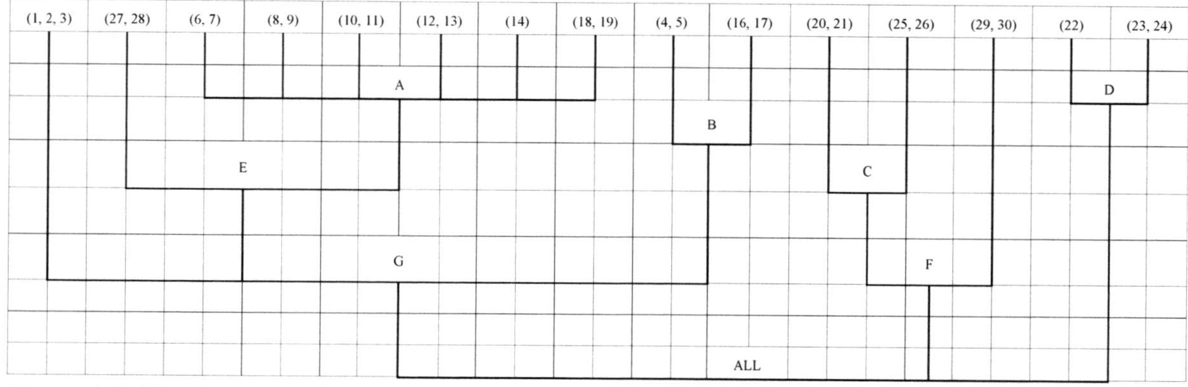

Figure A. 2. Ten-element agglomeration. Sample clusters are in parentheses. Clusters that are grouped (e.g., A, B, C, D) probably have common physical origins.

The samples apparently contain four clusters and several outliers. The principal cluster contains samples (6,7), (8,9), (10,11), (12,13), (14), and (18,19). The other clusters are (4,5), (16, 17), (20,21), (25,26), (22), and (23,24).

The large cluster suggests that one-third to one-half of the pottery came from a single source of clay. The pairing of samples (20,21) with (25,26) is interesting since they were found in the same house, but samples (27,28) and (29,30) were found in that same house and are outliers. Samples (22) and (23,24) are closely correlated, but different from the other clusters. Sample (16,17) is interesting because it pairs with the local clay, B. None of the samples correlate well with Clay A.

Experimental Errors

Errors in the chemical data arise from three principal sources. First, and most important, sample materials were obviously heterogeneous and contained grains of various minerals. We have no direct measure of this heterogeneity except the comparison of analyses of replicate samples. Second, the digestions were incomplete. The generally good agreement between the HNO_3/HF and H_3PO_4 digestions suggests, however, that the relative mass of residue was unimportant. Third, the values of concentrations measured by the ICP were uncertain by several percent because of drift of the instrument calibration.

Approximate numerical estimates of overall experimental precision are provided by:

1. The ratio of concentrations found in the H_3PO_4 digestions to those in HF/HNO_3 and HF digestions. These data were obtained from separate physical samples, different digestions, and different ICP runs. The range of concentration rations in Table A.3 (omitting Ti and Zr results that are systematically low) is 0.48 to 1.7. The average over seven elements and eight materials is:

$$\Sigma = 53$$
$$0.85 \pm 0.20.$$

2. The comparison of concentrations found in SRM 97a with the certified values provides a test of the H_3PO_4 digestion completeness and of the instrumental accuracy. (Omit Ti, include K). Average over two samples and seven elements:

$$\Sigma = 13$$
$$0.973 \text{ found} \pm 0.11.$$

3. Another estimate of overall uncertainty is provided by the Euclidean distance matrices. The diagonal terms show the separation of rep-

Table A.9. Error Rate in a Variety of Chemical Analyses.

Samples	Number of Elements	Error %	Reference
4 rocks	28	5	Giauque et al. 1977
3 SRM	35	5 to 10	Hancock 1976
10 SRM	26	5	Floyd et al. 1980
2 SRM, 2 ORE	11	2	Jenke and Diebold 1982
1 SRM, 1 mud	8	9 (SRM), 23(mud)	Sinex et al. 1980
2 soil	10	8	McQuaker et al. 1970
13 pottery, 2 clay, 1 SRM	10	20	this work

licate samples. For the five-element distances the mean separation of replicates is 1.03 ± 0.47 (Σ = 13) while the maximum separations that occur between samples is nearly five units. Similarly, for the 10-element distances, the mean separation of replicates is 1.65 ± 0.59, Σ= 13, and the maximum separations between samples are nearly 7.5. If we take the ratio of the mean separation of replicates to the maximum observed separation as a measure of overall experimental precision a value near 20% is obtained in each case, consistent with (1) and (2).

A mean value of 20% uncertainty is slightly higher than that reported in some other cases (Table A.9).

Appendix B

A Petrographic Analysis of Whiptail Site Ceramics

James P. Lombard

[Editorial Note: This report is reproduced from a manuscript in the Arizona State Museum Archives. It has been altered to meet formatting requirements and has been edited for grammar and style.]

This report summarizes the results of a petrographic analysis of 12 sherds from AZ BB:10:3.

Method

Point counts of all thin sections were made using a Carl Zeiss petrographic research microscope at the University of Arizona Laboratory of Geotectonics, and a Zeiss incremented mechanical stage with an 0.33-mm horizontal interval and a 1.98-mm interval between passes. Only grains greater than 0.03 mm in diameter were counted as temper; smaller material was counted as matrix. Only grains directly under the eyepiece cross hairs at equally spaced points along the grid superimposed on the thin section were counted. This method measures the area percentage of each grain type counted, which in turn approximates the volume percentages of each variable counted in the sample. The methods and assumptions of petrographic point counting are discussed in Chayes (1956).

Standard petrographic thin sections were prepared by Ray Lund in Tucson, Arizona, by first impregnating the sherds with epoxy and then grinding them in water. All slides were then stained with sodium cobaltinitrate solution to render potassium feldspar more easily identifiable.

Data

Detailed results of point counting are presented in tabular form in Table B.1. The tables are of percentages calculated from counted frequencies. Percentages are used because total counts per slide varied.

Four plain ware thin sections from AZ

Table B.1. Point Counting Results.

	Sample Number											
	7	8	9	10	11	12	1	2	3	4	5	6
Feature Number	11	27	17	11	27	17	11	27	17	7	18	31
Pottery Type or Ware	Plain ware	Plain ware	Plain ware	Tanque Verde Red-on-brown	Tanque Verde Red-on-brown	Tanque Verde Red-on-brown	Corrugated	Corrugated	Corrugated	Corrugated	Corrugated	Corrugated
	Granitic Temper Constituents											
MAG	0.00	0.25	0.24	0.00	0.00	0.00	1.26	0.85	0.46	0.42	0.24	0.00
PLAG	5.54	5.15	7.30	8.74	10.82	12.37	1.83	5.77	6.62	0.50	5.54	4.49
UNID	2.65	5.64	2.43	3.87	4.09	3.09	4.92	4.51	3.20	2.73	1.93	2.49
QTZT	0.00	1.23	2.68	1.21	1.92	1.80	5.62	7.61	5.25	5.66	0.72	3.74
KSPAR	6.99	11.53	7.06	7.51	9.86	15.21	8.99	14.08	10.73	8.39	6.75	5.74
EPI	0.48	0.12	0.24	0.24	0.72	0.25	0.14	0.28	0.46	0.21	0.24	0.25
MICR	0.00	3.56	0.00	0.00	0.00	0.00	0.70	0.42	0.23	0.00	0.72	0.25
ANDES	0.00	1.23	0.00	0.24	0.00	0.00	1.54	0.00	0.00	0.00	0.96	0.25
PLUT	12.53	9.82	9.49	8.23	12.02	16.24	8.29	2.11	7.08	1.11	14.22	10.72
MAT	51.33	44.42	55.47	55.69	45.19	36.60	51.83	44.23	50.46	55.97	53.01	64.34
PORE	6.27	2.70	5.35	3.63	1.20	1.29	3.09	0.14	3.65	1.05	2.41	0.75
MYL	0.48	0.25	0.24	0.00	0.24	0.25	2.11	8.73	0.91	1.68	1.20	0.00
MUSC	1.45	1.96	0.48	0.24	0.72	3.09	0.84	0.42	1.37	1.05	0.48	0.00
SLTS	0.24	0.12	0.00	0.00	0.00	0.00	0.56	2.11	0.00	0.00	0.00	0.00
MQTZ	0.00	0.00	0.24	0.00	0.00	0.25	0.28	0.00	0.68	0.00	0.24	0.00
PQTZ	0.53	7.12	7.54	8.47	6.97	7.73	7.16	6.76	3.65	3.78	8.67	6.98
BIOT	0.96	3.07	0.48	1.45	3.61	1.29	0.28	0.00	2.28	1.28	1.93	0.00
HEM	0.00	1.84	0.00	0.00	0.00	0.00	0.14	0.42	0.00	0.00	0.72	0.00
GAR	0.00	0.00	0.24	0.00	0.96	0.00	0.42	0.00	0.00	0.00	0.00	0.00
CARB	4.82	0.00	0.48	0.73	1.68	0.52	0.00	1.13	2.51	0.00	0.00	0.00

Key: MAG = magnetite; PLAG = plagioclase; UNID = unidentified; QTZT = quartzite; KSPAR = potassium feldspar; EPI = epidote; MICR = microcline; ANDES = volcanic (?) rock; PLUT = rock with plutonic textures and granitic composition; MAT = matrix; PORE = pore spaces in thin sections; MYL = mylonitic rock; MUSC = muscovite mineral; SLTS = siltstone; MQTZ = metamorphic quartz; PQTZ = plutonic quartz; BIOT = biotite; HEM = hematite; GAR = garnet; CARB = carbonate.

BB:10:3 that were already available were not counted because they were not stained and already had cover slips glued onto them. Point count results from unstained slides are not readily comparable to data from stained slides due to discrepancies in identification of quartz, K feldspar, and plagioclase. Qualitatively, these four samples had similar temper sand to the 12 stained slides with 1 exception. One uncounted plain ware had about 1% rhyolite grains, an occurrence not seen in any of the other sherds from AZ BB:10:3.

All 12 sherds were tempered with granitic sand of fairly uniform composition. A plot of the mean and standard deviation for each ware type taken as a group of total K-feldspar, plagioclase, total quartz, biotite, and granitic plutonic rock fragments shows this similarity (Figure B.1). These constituents are the most abundant sand grain types in the temper. The nearest geologic source for the main temper sand found in these sherds is the Agua Caliente Hills and Milagrosa Canyon area. The composition of the temper sands suggest derivation from a mixture of Oracle and Wilderness type granites, which are mapped in that area (Dickinson 1983). General remarks pertaining to each counted category are included here.

Granitic Temper Constituents

KSPAR Untwinned potassium feldspar, probably orthoclase, lightly stained when fresh to heavily stained when weathered. Unaltered to severely altered to kaolinite. Found as large, single grains up to 1.5-mm diameter and as large phenocrysts in plutonic rock fragments. Sometimes occurs as shattered aggregates of 0.02-mm diameter crystals.

PLAG Plagioclase, albite twinned, average composition of Oligoclase from Michel-Levy method. Unaltered to severely altered to sericite. Unweathered to severely weathered to brown spongy brown material. Found as large, single grains up to 1.2 mm and as phenocrysts in plutonic rock fragments. Some albitization of plagioclase was evident in grains showing albite twinning being replaced by stained, untwinned feldspar.

MAG Magnetite(?). Opaque oxide found as equant crystals in matrix about 0.03 mm to 1.0 mm in diameter. Also found in mylonite and plutonic rock fragments in trace amounts.

UNID Unidentified. Usually small rock fragments partly obscured by matrix or highly altered grains.

QTZT Quartzite. Stretched metamorphic quartzite with quartz recrystallized to 0.03 mm or smaller grains with sutured boundaries and parallel elongation.

EPI Epidote mineral. Single grains between 0.03 mm and 0.1 mm in matrix, and as a replacement mineral in plutonic rock fragments and ANDES rock fragments. One angular grain larger than 1.0 mm was observed with a small k-feldspar inclusion. A few small, possibly zoisite grains with anomalous blue intereference colors were seen in the large epidote grain.

MICR Microcline. Polysynthetic twinned variety of potassium feldspar. Identified only when fresh to moderately altered. Found as large grains 0.3 mm to 1.0 mm in diameter.

ANDES Fine-grained volcanic(?) rock fragment consisting of plagioclase feldspar laths and opaque oxides. These grains often have a yellowish brown color in plain light. Fresh to severely altered. No phenocrysts were observed in these grains. One grain was seen with epidote attached. This rock may correspond to a microdiorite described by Benson (1981).

PLUT Rock fragments with plutonic textures and granitic composition. K-feldspar, plagioclase, quartz, microcline, biotite, muscovite, epidote, opaque oxides, and garnet may be found in these rock fragments in order of decreasing frequency.

MAT Matrix. All material smaller than 0.03 mm in diameter. Mostly clay and quartz-feldspar silt, with up to 1% of total matrix composed of identifiable micas. Clay has oriented appearance, especially around sand-sized temper grains. Color and degree of siltiness and micaceousness vary slightly and were qualitatively observed. Composition of matrix cannot be determined with the petrographic microscope.

PORE Pore spaces in the thin sections. Either original porosity or material removed from the thin section during the grinding process. A few pore spaces have unusual shapes suggestive of burned-out organic matter.

MYL Mylonitic rock fragments characterized by parallel micaceous minerals, ductilely deformed quartz, and cataclastically deformed feldspars.

MUSC Muscovite mineral. Pale green in plain light, sometimes slightly pleochroic. Less than 0.03 mm to 1.0 mm in length. About half of the large (0.5-1 mm) muscovites are parallel to the surface of the thin section and show anomalous interference colors and undulatory extinction. One large grain consisted of an aggregate of 0.015-mm to 0.03-mm-sized muscovite crystals.

SLTS Siltstone. Hematite cemented arkosic siltstone rock fragments.

MQTZ Metamorphic quartz. Mosaic textured 0.1 mm to 0.5 mm quartz crystal aggregates with strong undulatory extinction. They do not show parallel elongation as in QTZT, but do not have plutonic textures, either.

PQTZ Plutonic quartz. Quartz crystal aggregates with typical plutonic textures or single grain large equant grains. Size ranges from 0.3 mm to 1.5 mm. A few large PQTZ grain appear to be partially altered to sericite.

BIOT Biotite. Single crystals. Usually smaller than 0.1 mm, but up to 1.4 mm long. Three pleochroic color schemes occur: yellowish-brown to dark yellowish-brown, greenish brown to dark greenish brown, and reddish brown. Some alteration to chlorite observed.

HEM Hematite single grains. Translucent grains showing deep red color. Up to 1.1 mm in size. Contain inclusions of quartz, feldspar, and muscovite.

GAR Garnet single crystals. Mostly euhedral pinkish(?) garnet crystals, about 1.2 mm to 0.5 mm in diameter. Several are broken.

CARB Carbonate. Angular to rounded dirty cryptocrystalline carbonate grains 0.1-mm to 1.5-mm diameter with occasional quartz, feldspar, biotite, and clean cryptocrystalline carbonate inclusions.

Temper sands in all samples are very poorly sorted coarse silt to coarse sand (0.03 mm to 2.0 mm) in size. Most grains are subangular to angular, with only a few rounded grains. No bimodal distribution of sizes was observed qualitatively, and quantitative study of texture is not effectively determined using the point counting method (Middleton et al. 1985).

Discussion and Summary

Point count results were combined for each ceramic type rather than plotted individually because of the accuracy of the data obtained. A test of the variation of each variable at 100-count intervals up to a total of 800 counts was made on two samples to determine when the percentages for each variable begin to be consistent. Between 400 and 600 counts the variability became reasonably stabilized for major temper components. Minor components required greater than 800 counts to stabilize. Chayes (1956) suggests counts of greater than 1000 for reproducible results in sedimentary rocks. Total counts made on AZ BB:10:3 samples were between 400 and 450 except on Samples A and H, which were counted to 800 +. Time is the major factor in determining the number of counts per slide. The accuracy of 400 counts per slide did not warrant comparison of individual samples with one another, so they were grouped according to type and averaged for comparative purposes.

No analyses of sand samples were made in this study. Several possible sources of temper sand are hypothesized, requiring a more comprehensive sampling plan than previously thought necessary. These sources include (1) sand included naturally in argillic horizons of older soils developed on bajada or pediment surfaces in the vicinity of AZ BB:10:3 and (2) sand interbedded naturally with argillaceous (silt and clay-rich) Tertiary sedimentary deposits, Rillito I Beds (Pashley 1966), found less than a kilometer away along Ft. Lowell Road to the south of AZ BB:10:3.

The unusually high frequency of plutonic rock fragments and low frequency of mylonite rock fragments compared to expected frequencies in modern washes draining the predominantly mylonitic granitic terrains in the adjacent mountains suggests that wash sands were not exclusively exploited and added artificially as temper sand. Rather, clay-rich material naturally mixed with nonmylonitic sand characteristic of the Rillito I Beds at that locality (Pashley 1966) may have been used for the raw material of ceramic manufacture, possibly with some wash sand artificially admixed. This hypothesis can only be tested by comparing sands from the Rillito Beds and modern washes. Argillic horizon sources are hypothesized because they are clay rich and contain abundant sand-sized inclusions. The composition of argillic horizon sands depends on the parent material on which they are developed. All three of these possible sand sources should be samples and analyzed before the origin of the ceramic temper sands can be determined.

In sum,

1. The mean temper sand compositions of each ceramic type are nearly identical.

2. The closest sources to compositionally and texturally similar parent rocks are in the Agua Caliente Hills and Milagrosa Canyon area, and the Rillito I Beds outcropping less than 1 kilometer south of the site.

References Cited

Adams, Jenny L.

1993 Mechanisms of Wear on Ground Stone Surfaces. *Pacific Coast Archaeological Society Quarterly* 29(4):60-73.

1994 *The Development of Prehistoric Grinding Technology at Point of Pines, East-Central Arizona.* Ph.D. dissertation, University of Arizona, Tucson. University Microfilms, Ann Arbor.

1995 Life History as a Framework for the Analysis of Ground Stone Artifacts. Paper presented at the 60th Annual Meeting of the Society for American Archaeology, Minneapolis.

1996 *Manual for a Technological Approach to Ground Stone Analysis.* Center for Desert Archaeology, Tucson.

2002 *Ground Stone Analysis: A Technological Approach.* University of Utah Press, Salt Lake City.

Ahler, Stanley A.

1979 Functional Analysis of Non Obsidian Chipped Stone Artifacts: Terms, Variable, and Quantification. In *Lithic Use-Wear Analysis*, edited by Brian Hayden, pp. 301-328. Academic Press, New York.

Ahlstrom, Richard V.N., and Mark C. Slaughter

1996 Site Chronology. In *Excavation of the Gibbon Springs Site: A Classic Period Village in the Northeastern Tucson Basin,* edited by Mark C. Slaughter and Heidi Roberts, pp. 481-489. Archaeological Report No. 94-87. SWCA Environmental Consultants, Tucson.

Ayres, James

2001 Agua Caliente: Life of a Tucson-Area Ranch. In *Archaeological Investigations at Roy P. Drachman Agua Caliente Park: The Whiptail Site and Agua Caliente Ranch,* prepared by Kevin D. Wellman and Mark C. Slaughter, pp. 71-123. Cultural Resource Report No. 00-03. SWCA Environmental Consultants, Tucson.

Baby, Raymond S.

1954 Hopewell Cremation Practices. *Papers in Archaeology* No. 1. Ohio Historical Society.

Bayham, Frank

1982 *A Diachronic Analysis of Prehistoric Animal Exploitation at Ventana Cave.* Unpublished Ph.D. dissertation, Department of Anthropology, Arizona State University, Tempe.

Bayman, James M.

2007 Artisans and Their Crafts in Hohokam Society. In *The Hohokam Millennium,* edited by Suzanne K. Fish and Paul R. Fish, pp. 75-82. School for Advanced Research Press, Santa Fe.

Beck, Lane Anderson

2000 Cremation Deposits from Sunset Mesa. In *Excavations at Sunset Mesa Ruin*, edited by Michael Lindeman, pp. 215-228. Technical Report No. 2000-02. Desert Archaeology, Tucson.

Benson, G. S.
1981 *Structural Investigations of the Italian Trap Allocthon, Redington Pass, Pima County, Arizona.* Unpublished master's thesis, Department of Geosciences, University of Arizona, Tucson.

Bequaert, Joseph C., and Walter B. Miller
1973 *The Mollusks of the Arid Southwest, with an Arizona Check List.* University of Arizona Press, Tucson.

Bettison, Cynthia Ann
1998 Descriptions of Mimbres Mogollon Pottery and Other Common Pottery Found in Various Parts of the Mogollon Area. Ms. on file, Western New Mexico University Museum, Silver City.

Binford, Lewis R.
1963 An Analysis of Cremations from Three Michigan Sites. *Wisconsin Archaeologist* 44:98-110.

1972 Analysis of a Cremated Burial from the Riverside Cemetery, Menominee County, Michigan. In *An Archaeological Perspective,* by Lewis R. Binford, pp. 383-389. Seminar Press, New York.

Birkby, Walter H.
1976 Cremated Human Remains. Appendix 9 in *The Hohokam, Desert Farmers and Craftsmen: Excavations at Snaketown, 1964-1965*, by Emil W. Haury, pp. 380-384. University of Arizona Press, Tucson.

Bohrer, Vorsila L.
1991 Recently Recognized Cultivated and Encouraged Plants. *Kiva* 56(3):227-235.

Bradley, Bruce
n.d. Whiptail Ceramics. Ms. in Whiptail paper files. Arizona State Museum Archives, University of Arizona, Tucson.

Brand, Donald
1938 *Aboriginal Trade Routes for Sea Shells in the Southwest.* Association of Pacific Coast Geographers Yearbook 4-10.

Callahan, Errett
1979 The Basics of Biface Knapping in the Eastern Fluted Point Tradition: A Manual for Flintknappers and Lithic Analysis. *Archaeology of Eastern North America* 7:1-180.

Carpenter, Alice H.
1996 The Feather Prince: A Personal Narrative of Southeastern Arizona Prehistory. In *Alice Hubbard Carpenter: The Legacy and Context of a Southwestern Avocational Archaeologist,* edited by Linda M. Gregonis and W. Bruce Masse, pp. 299-342. Journal of the Southwest 38(3).

Carr, Christopher
1982 *Handbook on Soil Resistivity Surveying: Interpretation of Data from Earthen Archaeological Sites.* Research Series No. 2. Center for American Archaeology Press, Northwestern University, Evanston, Illinois.

Chapman, Richard C.
1977 Analysis of the Lithic Assemblages. In *Settlement and Subsistence along the Lower Chaco River*, edited by Charles A. Reher, pp. 371-452. University of New Mexico Press, Albuquerque.

Chayes, F.
1956 *Petrographic Modal Analysis: An Elementary Statistical Appraisal*. John Wiley and Sons, New York.

Clark, Jeffery J.
2001 *Tracking Prehistoric Migrations: Pueblo Settlers among the Tonto Basin Hohokam.* Anthropological Papers No. 65. University of Arizona Press, Tucson.

Clark, Jeffery J., J. Brett Hill, Patrick D. Lyons, and Stacey Lengyel
2011 Of Migrants and Mounds. In *Migrants and Mounds: Classic Period Archaeology of the Lower San Pedro Valley* (draft), edited by Jeffery Clark and Patrick Lyons. Anthropological Papers No. 45. Center for Desert Archaeology, Tucson (in press).

Clark, Jeffery, and Stacey Lengyel
2002 "Mogollon" Migrations into Southeastern Arizona. Paper presented at the 12th Mogollon Conference, Las Cruces, New Mexico.

Clark, Jeffery J., and Patrick D. Lyons
2011 How, Where, and What We Excavated. In *Migrants and Mounds: Classic Period Archaeology of the Lower San Pedro Valley* (draft), edited by Jeffery Clark and Patrick Lyons. Anthropological Papers No. 45. Center for Desert Archaeology, Tucson (in press).

Collins, Michael B., and Jason M. Fenwick
1974 Heat Treating of Chert: Methods of Interpretation and Their Application. *Plains Anthropologist.* Vol. 19:64.

Colton, Harold S., and Lyndon Lane Hargrave
1937 *Handbook of Northern Arizona Pottery Wares.* Museum of Northern Arizona Bulletin 11. Northern Arizona Society of Science and Art, Flagstaff.

Crabtree, Donald E., and B. Robert Butler
1964 Notes on Experiments in Flintknapping, 1: Heat Treatment of Silica Minerals. *Tebiwa* 7:1-6.

Curtin, Leonora S. M.
1949 *By the Prophet of the Earth: Ethnobotany of the Pima.* San Vincente Foundation, Santa Fe. Reprinted, 1984, University of Arizona Press, Tucson.

Cushing, Frank Hamilton
1988 *Zuñi Folktales.* University of Arizona Press, Tucson. Reprint of 1931 publication by Knopf, New York.

Davis, Owen
1997 Pollen Analysis In *Archaeological Excavations at the Continental Site in Green Valley, Pima County, Arizona, in 1995: An Investigation of the Portion of Site AZ EE:1:32(ASM) within Tucson Electric Power Company's Substation Expansion Zone,* by Jeffrey T. Jones, pp. 179-182. Archaeology Report No. 9. Old Pueblo Archaeology Center, Tucson.

Dean, Jeffrey S.
1969 Letter to Paul Grebinger discussing dendrochronological samples from Whiptail. In Whiptail paper materials, Arizona State Museum Library, University of Arizona, Tucson.

Dean, Jeffrey S., and Dennie O. Bowden III
1996 Laboratory of Tree-Ring Research Data. In *Excavation of the Gibbon Springs Site: A Classic Period Village in the Northeastern Tucson Basin,* edited by Mark C. Slaughter and Heidi Roberts, pp. C.1-C.4. Archaeological Report No. 94-87. SWCA Environmental Consultants, Tucson.

Dean, Jeffrey S., Mark C. Slaughter, and Dennie O. Bowden III

1996 Desert Dendrochronology: Tree-ring Dating Prehistoric Sites in the Tucson Basin. *Kiva* 62(1):7-26.

Deaver, William L.

1984 Pottery. In *Hohokam Habitation Sites in the Northern Santa Rita Mountains,* by Alan Ferg, Kenneth C. Rozen, William L. Deaver, Martyn D. Tagg, David A. Phillips, Jr., and David A. Gregory, pp. 237-419. Archaeological Series No. 147. Arizona State Museum, University of Arizona, Tucson.

Dickinson, W. R.

1983 Reconnaissance Compilation Geologic Map of the Bellota Ranch Quadrangle. Unpublished map on file, Department of Geosciences, University of Arizona, Tucson.

DiPeso, Charles C.

1956 The Upper Pima of San Cayetano del Tumacacori: An Archaeological Reconstruction of the Ootam of Pimeria Alta. Amerind Foundations Papers No. 7. Amerind Foundation, Dragoon, Arizona.

1958 *The Reeve Ruin of Southeastern Arizona: A Study of a Prehistoric Western Pueblo Migration into the Middle San Pedro Valley.* Amerind Foundation Papers No. 8. Amerind Foundation, Dragoon, Arizona.

Doelle, William H.

1981 The Gila Pima in the Late Seventeenth Century. In *The Protohistoric Period in the North American Southwest, AD 1450-1700,* edited by David R. Willcox and W. Bruce Masse, pp. 57-70. Anthropological Research Papers No. 24. Arizona State University, Tempe.

Dongoske, Kurt

1986 Human Skeletal Remains. Appendix A in *Archaeological Investigations at the Tanque Verde Wash Site, a Middle Rincon Settlement in the Eastern Tucson Basin,* by Mark D. Elson, pp. 467-472. Anthropological Papers No. 7. Institute for American Research, Tucson.

Douglass, A. E., and H. B. Leonard

1920-1921 "Map of the Bear-Sabino Canyon Ruin." On file in the Arizona State Museum, University of Arizona, Tucson.

Elson, Mark D.

1986 *Archaeological Investigations at the Tanque Verde Wash Site, a Middle Rincon Settlement in the Eastern Tucson Basin.* Anthropological Papers No. 7. Institute for American Research, Tucson.

Fish, Suzanne K.

1984 Agriculture and Subsistence Implications of the Salt-Gila Aqueduct Pollen Analysis. In *Environment and Subsistence,* pp. 111-138. Hohokam Archaeology Along the Salt-Gila Aqueduct Central Arizona Project, vol. 7, edited by Lynn S. Teague and Patricia L. Crown. Archaeological Series No. 150. Arizona State Museum, University of Arizona, Tucson.

1987 Pollen Analysis. In *The Archaeology of the San Xavier Bridge Site (AZ BB:13:14), Tucson Basin, Southern Arizona,* edited by John Ravesloot, pp. 319-334. Archaeological Series No. 171. Arizona State Museum, University of Arizona, Tucson.

1988 Environment and Subsistence: The Pollen Evidence. In *Recent Research on Tucson Basin Prehistory: Proceedings of the Second Tucson Basin Conference,* edited by William H. Doelle and Paul R. Fish, pp. 31-37. Anthropological Papers No. 10. Institute for American Research, Tucson.

Fish, Suzanne K., cont'd.
1996 Pollen Results from the Gibbon Springs Site. In *Excavation of the Gibbon Springs Site: A Classic Period Village in the Northeastern Tucson Basin,* edited by Mark C. Slaughter and Heidi Roberts, pp. 473-480. Archaeological Report No. 94-87. SWCA Environmental Consultants, Tucson.

Fish, Suzanne K., and Paul R. Fish (editors)
2007 *The Hohokam Millennium*. School for Advanced Research Press, Santa Fe.

Fish, Suzanne K., Paul R. Fish, and John H. Madsen
1992a Evolution and Structure of the Classic Period Marana Community. In *The Marana Community in the Hohokam World,* edited by Suzanne K. Fish, Paul R. Fish, and John H. Madsen, pp. 20-40. Anthropological Papers of the University of Arizona No. 56. University of Arizona Press, Tucson.

Fish, Suzanne K., Paul R. Fish, and John H. Madsen (editors)
1992b *The Marana Community in the Hohokam World.* Anthropological Papers of the University of Arizona No. 56. University of Arizona Press, Tucson.

Flenniken, Jeffrey, and Ervan Garrison
1975 Thermally Altered Novaculite and Stone Tool Manufacturing Techniques. *Journal of Field Archaeology* 2:125-131.

Floyd, M. A. V. A. Fassel, A. P. D'Silva
1980 Computer-controlled Scanning Monochromator for the Determination of 50 Elements in Geochemical and Environmental Samples by Inductively Coupled Plasma—Atomic Emission Spectrometry. *Analytical Chemistry* 52:2168-2173.

Franklin, Hayward H.
1980 *Excavations at Second Canyon Ruin, San Pedro Valley, Arizona.* Contribution to Highway Salvage Archaeology in Arizona No. 60. Arizona State Museum, University of Arizona, Tucson.

Fratt, Lee
1996 Ground Stone Tools and Other Stone Artifacts from the Gibbon Springs Site (AZ BB:9:50[ASM]). In *Excavation of the Gibbon Springs Site, a Classic Period Village in the Northeastern Tucson Basin,* edited by Mark C. Slaughter and Heidi Roberts, pp. 267-329. Archaeological Report 94-87. SWCA Environmental Consultants, Tucson.

Frison, George
1968 A Functional Analysis of Certain Chipped Stone Tools. *American Antiquity* 33(2): 149-155.

Gasser, Robert
1987 Macrofloral Analysis. In *The Archaeology of the San Xavier Bridge Site (AZ BB:13:14) Tucson Basin, Southern Arizona,* edited by John C. Ravesloot, pp. 303-318. Archaeological Series No. 171, University of Arizona, Tucson

Giauque, D., R. B. Garrett, and L. Y. Goda
1977 Energy Dispersive X-ray Fluorescence Spectrometry for Determination of Twenty-six Trace and Two Major Elements in Geochemical Specimens. *Analytical Chemistry* 49:62-67.

Gladwin, Winifred, and Harold S. Gladwin
1933 *Some Southwestern Pottery Types, Series III.* Medallion Papers No. 13. Gila Pueblo, Globe, Arizona.

Gladwin, Harold S., Emil W. Haury, E. B. Sayles, and Nora Gladwin
1938 *Excavations at Snaketown: Material Culture*. Medallion Papers No. 25. Gila Pueblo, Globe. Reprinted, 1965, by the University of Arizona Press, Tucson.

Gould, R.A., D.A. Koster, and A.H. Sontz
1971 The Lithic Assemblage of the Western Desert Aborigines of Australia. *American Antiquity* 36:149-169.

Govindaraju, K.
1994 Compilation of Working Values and Sample Description for 383 Geostandards. *Geostandards Newsletter* 18 (special issue).

Grebinger, Paul F.
1971 *Hohokam Cultural Developments in the Middle Santa Cruz River Valley, Arizona.* PhD. dissertation, University of Arizona, Tucson. University Microfilms, Ann Arbor.

1976 Salado—Perspectives from the Middle Santa Cruz Valley. *Kiva* 42(1).

Greenleaf, J. Cameron
1975 *Excavations at Punta de Agua in the Santa Cruz River Basin, Southeastern Arizona.* Anthropological Papers No. 26. University of Arizona Press, Tucson.

Gregg, Michael L., and Richard Greybush
1976 Thermally Altered Siliceous Stone from Prehistoric Contexts: Intentional Versus Unintentional Alterations. *American Antiquity* 2:189-192.

Gregonis, Linda M.
1996 Cultural Interaction in the Northeastern Tucson Basin: The Gibbon Springs Ceramic Assemblage. In *Excavation of the Gibbon Springs Site, a Classic Period Village in the Northeastern Tucson Basin,* edited by Mark C. Slaughter and Heidi Roberts, pp. 183-257. Archaeological Report No. 94-87. SWCA Environmental Consultants, Tucson.

2001a Ceramics. In *The 1997-1998 Archaeological Excavations at the Torres Blancas Village Site, AZ EE:1:194(ASM), in Block 5 of the Santa Rita Springs Development Property, Green Valley, Arizona,* by Jeffrey T. Jones, pp. 73-100. Archaeology Report No. 18. Old Pueblo Archaeology Center, Tucson.

2001b Indigenous Ceramics Analysis. In *Archaeological Investigations at Roy P. Drachman Agua Caliente Park: The Whiptail Site and Agua Caliente Ranch,* prepared by Kevin D. Wellman and Mark C. Slaughter, pp. 149-60. Cultural Resource Report No. 00-03. SWCA Environmental Consultants, Tucson.

Gregonis, Linda M., and Mark C. Slaughter
1993 Artifacts, Features, and Agave Use: An Aspect of Technological Organization at La Ciudad de Los Hornos. Paper presented at the 58th annual meeting of the Society for American Archaeology, St. Louis.

Guo-qin, Qi
1983 The Analysis of Faunal Remains from the University Indian Ruin. *The Kiva* 49(1-2):81-103.

Hancock, R. G. V.
1976 Cow Flux Multielement Instrumental Neutron Activation Analysis in Archaeometry. *Analytical Chemistry* 48:1443-1445.

Haury, Emil W.

1928 *The Succession of House Types in the Pueblo Area.* Master's thesis, University of Arizona, Tucson.

1945 *The Excavation of Los Muertos and Neighboring Ruins in the Salt River Valley, Southern Arizona.* Papers of the Peabody Museum of American Archaeology and Ethnology 24(1). Harvard University, Cambridge.

1976 *The Hohokam, Desert Farmers & Craftsmen: Snaketown, 1964-1965.* University of Arizona Press, Tucson.

Hawley, Florence

1936 *Field Manual of Prehistoric Southwestern Pottery Types.* Bulletin, Anthropological Series 1(4). University of New Mexico, Albuquerque.

Hayden, Julian D.

1957 *Excavations 1940, at the University Indian Ruin.* Technical Series No. 5. Southwestern Monuments Association, Globe, Arizona.

Hays-Gilpin, Kelley (compiler)

1998 Identifying and Classifying Prehistoric Ceramics of the Puerco Valley. In *Prehistoric Ceramics of the Puerco Valley: The 1995 Chambers-Sanders Trust Lands Ceramic Conference,* edited by Kelley Hays-Gilpin and Eric van Hartesveldt, pp. 53-180. Ceramic Series No. 7. Museum of Northern Arizona, Flagstaff.

Heckman, Robert A.

2000 The Trincheras Tradition. In *Prehistoric Painted Pottery of Southeastern Arizona,* by Robert A. Heckman, Barbara K. Montgomery, and Stephanie M. Whittlesey, pp. 75-81. Technical Series No. 77. Statistical Research, Inc., Tucson.

Heidke, James M.

1995 Ceramic Analysis. In *Archaeological Investigations at Los Morteros, a Prehistoric Settlement in the Northern Tucson Basin,* edited by Henry D. Wallace, pp. 263-422. Anthropological Papers No. 17. Center for Desert Archaeology, Tucson.

1996 Qualitative Temper Characterization of Potsherds from the Gibbon Springs Site. In *Excavation of the Gibbon Springs Site, a Classic Period Village in the Northeastern Tucson Basin,* edited by Mark C. Slaughter and Heidi Roberts, pp. 259-266. Archaeological Report 94-87. SWCA Environmental Consultants, Tucson.

Heidke, James, and Mark D. Elson

1988 Tucson Basin Stucco-Coated Plain Ware: A Technological Assessment. *The Kiva* 53:273-85.

Heidke, James M., and Carlos P. Lavayen

2009 Prehistoric Pottery from the Tanque Verde Wash Site: Dating, Provenance, and Function. In *The Tanque Verde Wash Site Revisited: Excavations in the Northwest Locus*, edited by Mark D. Elson and Patricia Cook. Technical Report No. 2007-01. Desert Archaeology, Tucson.

Hester, Thomas

1972 Ethnographic Evidence for the Thermal Alteration of Siliceous Stone. *Tebiwa* 12:63-65.

Hoffman, Marshall C.

1988 Lithic Technology and Tool Production at Casa Buena. In *Excavations at Casa Buena: Changing Hohokam Land Use Along the Squaw Peak Parkway*, Vol. 1, edited by Jerry B. Howard, pp. 359-457. Soil Systems Publications in Archaeology No. 11.

Holloway, Richard G.

2001 Pollen and Flotation Analyses. In *Archaeological Investigations at Roy P. Drachman Agua Caliente Park: The Whiptail Site and Agua Caliente Ranch,* prepared by Kevin D. Wellman and Mark C. Slaughter, pp. 211-223. Cultural Resource Report No. 00-03. SWCA Environmental Consultants, Tucson.

2005 Pollen Analysis. In *Archaeological Excavations at the Continental Site in 2000: Hohokam Classic Period Features at Site AZ EE:1:32 (ASM) in Lots 5 and 7 of the Park Centre Subdivision, Pima County, Arizona,* by Jeffrey T. Jones, pp. 87-95. Archaeology Report No. 26. Old Pueblo Archaeology Center, Tucson.

Howell, Joseph

2006 Ritual at AZ EE:1:317(ASM): Abandonment and Material Culture. In *The Cultural Resources of Quail Creek: Archaeological Excavations at AZ EE:1:317 (ShellMan), AZ EE:1:275, AZ EE:1:175, AZ EE:1:176, and AZ EE:1:302(ASM)*, edited by Michael D. Cook. Cultural Resource Report No. 2006-42. WestLand Resources, Inc., Tucson.

Huckell, Bruce B.

1988a Flaked Stone. In *Hohokam Archaeology Along Phase B of the Tucson Aqueduct Central Arizona Project*, edited by Jon. S. Czaplicki and John C. Ravesloot pp. 175-200. Archaeological Series No. 178. Arizona State Museum, University of Arizona, Tucson.

1988b Late Archaic Archaeology of the Tucson Basin: A Status Report. In *Recent Research on Tucson Basin Prehistory: Proceedings of the Second Tucson Basin Conference,* edited by William H. Doelle and Paul R. Fish, pp. 56-76. Anthropological Papers No. 10. Institute for American Research, Tucson.

Huckell, Lisa W.

1976 Analysis of the Shell Remains from the Rabid Ruin, Arizona. Unpublished manuscript on file, Arizona State Museum Archives, University of Arizona, Tucson.

1997 Plant Remains. In *Archaeological Excavations at the Continental Site in Green Valley, Pima County, Arizona, in 1995: An Investigation of the Portion of Site AZ EE:1:32(ASM) within Tucson Electric Power Company's Substation Expansion Zone,* by Jeffrey T. Jones, pp. 159-178. Archaeology Report No. 9. Old Pueblo Archaeology Center, Tucson.

2005 Additional Plant Remains from AZ EE:1:32 (ASM), the Continental Site, Pima County, Arizona. In *Archaeological Excavations at the Continental Site in 2000: Hohokam Classic Period Features at Site AZ EE:1:32 (ASM) in Lots 5 and 7 of the Park Centre Subdivision, Pima County, Arizona,* by Jeffrey T. Jones, pp. 97-112. Archaeology Report No. 26. Old Pueblo Archaeology Center, Tucson.

Huckleberry, Gary

2001 Geomorphic Context and Stratigraphy. In *Archaeological Investigations at Roy P. Drachman Agua Caliente Park: The Whiptail Site and Agua Caliente Ranch,* prepared by Kevin D. Wellman and Mark C. Slaughter, pp. 5-7. Report No. 00-03. SWCA Environmental Consultants, Tucson.

Huntington, Frederick W.

1986 *Archaeological Investigations at the West Branch Site: Early and Middle Rincon Occupation in the Southern Tucson Basin.* Anthropology Papers No. 5. Institute for American Research, Tucson.

Jenke, D. R., and F. E. Diebold

1982 Characterization of Phosphite Ores. *Analytical Chemistry* 54:1008-1011.

Johnson, J. K.
1981 Yellow Creek Archaeological Project. *Archaeological Papers of the Center for Archaeological Research* No. 2. University of Mississippi, Jackson.

Jones, Jeffrey T.
1999 *A Cultural Resources Survey of Two Parcels Totaling 64.92 Acres near the Whiptail Ruin at the East End of Roger Road in Pima County, Arizona.* Technical Report No. 9901. Old Pueblo Archaeology Center, Tucson.

Jones, Jeffrey T., and Ingrid Klune
2009 Excavation Results. In *Archaeological Investigations at AZ AA:12:77(ASM), AA:12:327(ASM), AA:12:328(ASM), and AA:12:965(ASM) within the Saguaro Springs Residential Development in Marana, Pima County, Arizona,* edited by Barbara K. Montgomery and Jeffrey J. Jones. Tierra Archaeological Research Series. Tierra Right of Way Services (draft).

Kaplan, Lawrence
1956 The Cultivated Beans of the Prehistoric Southwest. *Annals of the Missouri Botanical Garden* 43:189-251.

Kay, Margarita A.
1996 *Healing with Plants in the American and Mexican West.* University of Arizona Press, Tucson.

Keeley, Lawrence H.
1980 *Experimental Determination of Stone Tool Uses.* University of Chicago Press, Chicago.

Keen, A. Myra
1984 *Sea Shells of Tropical West America: Marine Mollusks from Baja California to Peru,* second edition. Stanford University Press, Palo Alto.

Kelly, Isabel T.
1978 *The Hodges Ruin: A Hohokam Community in the Tucson Basin.* Anthropological Papers No. 30. University of Arizona Press, Tucson.

King, Mary E.
1974 Medio Period Perishable Artifacts: Textiles and Basketry. In *Casas Grandes: A Fallen Trading Center of the Gran Chichimeca,* edited by Charles C. Di Peso, John B. Rinaldo, and Gloria J. Fenner. Publication No. 9. Amerind Foundation, Dragoon, Arizona.

Lange, Charles H., and Carroll L. Riley
1970 *The Southwest Journals of Adolph F. Bandelier 1883-1884.* University of New Mexico Press, Albuquerque.

Lucas, R. P., and B. C. Reprect
1971 Analysis of Chrome Ores and Chrome-Magnesite Refractory Samples by Atomic Absorption Spectrometry. *Analytical Chemistry* 43:1013-1016.

Lytle, Jamie
1971 *A Microenvironmental Study of an Archaeological Site, Arizona BB;10:3, Whiptail Ruin.* Master's thesis, Department of Geochronology, University of Arizona, Tucson.

Lytle-Webb, Jamie
1978 Pollen Analysis in Southwestern Archaeology. In *Discovering Past Behavior: Experiments in the Archaeology of the American Southwest,* edited by Paul Grebinger, pp. 13-28. Gordon and Breach, New York.

McGuire, Randall H., and Ann Valdo Howard
1987 The Structure and Organization of Hohokam Shell Exchange. *Kiva* 52(2):113-146.

McGuire, Randall H., and María Elisa Villalpando C. (editors)
1993 *An Archaeological Survey of the Altar Valley, Sonora, Mexico.* Arizona State Museum Archaeological Series No. 184. University of Arizona, Tucson.

McQuaker, N. R., D. F. Brown, and P. D. Kluckner
1970 Digestion of Environmental Materials for Analysis by Inductively Coupled Plasma-Atomic Emission Spectrometry. *Analytical Chemistry* 51:1082-1084.

Mandeville, M. D., and J. Jeffrey Flenniken
1974 A Comparison of Flaking Qualities of Nehawka Chert Before and After Thermal Pretreatment. *Plains Anthropologist* 19:146-148.

Massart, D. L., and L. Kaufman
1983 *The Interpretation of Analytical Chemical Data by the Use of Cluster Analysis.* John Wiley & Sons, New York.

Massart, D. L., L. Kaufman, and K. H. Esbensen
1982 Hierarchical Nonhierarchical Clustering Strategy and Application to Classification of Iron Meteorites According to Their Trace Element Patterns. *Analytical Chemistry* 54:911-971.

Masse, W. Bruce, Linda M. Gregonis, and Mark C. Slaughter
2009 Corridor, Frontier, Melting Pot, or Autonomous Systems: The Lower San Pedro Valley, A.D. 600-1200. In *Between Mimbres and Hohokam: Exploring the Archaeology and History of Southeastern Arizona and Southwestern New Mexico,* edited by Henry D. Wallace (draft).

Middleton, A. P., I. C. Freestone, and M. N. Leese
1985 Textural Analysis of Ceramic Thin Sections: Evaluation of Grain Sampling Procedures. *Archaeometry* 27(1):64-74.

Morris, Percy A.
1966 *A Field Guide to Shells of the Pacific Coast and Hawaii: Including Shells of the Gulf of California.* Houghton Mifflin, Boston.

Myers, Laural
1996 Lithics. In *Excavation of the Gibbon Springs Site: A Classic Period Village in the Northeastern Tucson Basin,* edited by Mark C. Slaughter and Heidi Roberts, pp. 331-372. SWCA Archaeological Report No. 94-87. Tucson.

2001 Lithic Artifacts. In *Archaeological Investigations at Roy P. Drachman Agua Caliente Park: The Whiptail Site and Agua Caliente Ranch,* prepared by Kevin D. Wellman and Mark C. Slaughter, pp. 161-207. Cultural Resource Report No. 00-03. SWCA Environmental Consultants, Tucson.

Nelson, Richard S.
1991 *Hohokam Marine Shell Exchange and Artifacts.* Arizona State Museum Archaeological Series No. 179. University of Arizona, Tucson.

Och, Joseph

1965 *Missionary in Sonora: The Travel Reports of Joseph Och, S.J., 1755-1767,* translated and annotated by Theodore E. Treutlein. California Historical Society, San Francisco.

Odell, George H.

1981 The Mechanics of Use-Breakage of Stone Tools: Some Testable Hypotheses. *Journal of Field Archaeology* 8:197-209.

Pashley, E. F., Jr.

1966 *Structure and Stratigraphy of the Central, Northern, and Eastern Parts of the Tucson Basin, Arizona.* Open-file report. USDI, U.S. Geological Survey, Washington, D.C.

Patterson, Leland

1979 Replication and Classification of Small Sized Debitage. *Plain Anthropologist* 23:103-172.

1982 The Importance of Flake Size Distribution. *Contract Abstracts and Cultural Resources Management Archaeology* 3(1):70-72.

1990 Characteristics of Bifacial Reduction Flake-Size Distribution. *American Antiquity* 55:550-558.

Purdy, Barbara Ann

1974 Investigations Concerning the Thermal Alteration of Silica Minerals. *Tebiwa* Vol. 17:1

Puseman, Kathryn

1996 Macrofloral Analysis. In *Excavation of the Gibbon Springs Site: A Classic Period Village in the Northeastern Tucson Basin,* edited by Mark C. Slaughter and Heidi Roberts, pp. 449-472. Archaeological Report No. 94-87. SWCA Environmental Consultants, Tucson.

Rea, Amadeo M.

1997 *At the Desert's Green Edge: An Ethnobotany of the Gila River Pima.* University of Arizona Press, Tucson.

1998 *Folk Mammalogy of the Northern Pimans.* University of Arizona Press, Tucson.

Roberts, Heidi

1996a Human Remains from the Gibbon Springs Site and Other Classic-Period Sites in the Tucson Basin. In *Excavation of the Gibbon Springs Site: A Classic Period Village in the Northeastern Tucson Basin,* edited by Mark C. Slaughter and Heidi Roberts, pp. 413-448. Archaeological Report No. 94-87. SWCA Environmental Consultants, Tucson.

1996b Nonarchitectural Features. In *Excavation of the Gibbon Springs Site: A Classic Period Village in the Northeastern Tucson Basin,* edited by Mark C. Slaughter and Heidi Roberts, pp. 141-182. Archaeological Report No. 94-87. SWCA Environmental Consultants, Tucson.

Roth, Barbara J., and Bruce B. Huckell

1992 Cortaro Points and the Archaic of Southern Arizona. *Kiva* 57(4):353-70.

Russell, Frank

1975 *The Pima Indians.* University of Arizona Press, Tucson. Originally published 1908, Twenty-sixth Annual Report of the Bureau of American Ethnology, 1904-1905, U.S. Government Printing Office, Washington, D.C.

Sauer, Carl, and Donald Brand
1931 *Prehistoric Settlements in Sonora with Special References to Cerros de Trincheras.* Publications in Geography 5(3). University of California, Berkeley.

Scantling, Frederick H.
1940 *Excavations at the Jackrabbit Ruin, Papago Indian Reservation, Arizona.* Unpublished Master's thesis, Department of Anthropology, University of Arizona, Tucson.

Schiffer, Michael B.
1987 *Formation Processes of the Archaeological Record.* University of New Mexico Press, Albuquerque.

Schlanger, Sarah H.
1990 Artifact Assemblage Composition and Site Occupation Duration. In *Perspectives on Southwestern Prehistory*, edited by P. E. Minnis and C. L. Redman, pp. 103-121. Westview Press, Boulder.

Shackley, M. Steven
1995 Sources of Archaeological Obsidian in the Greater American Southwest: An Update and Quantitative Analysis. *American Antiquity* 60:531-551.

2005 *Obsidian: Geology and Archaeology in the North American Southwest.* University of Arizona Press, Tucson.

2009 An Energy Dispersive X-ray Fluorescence Analysis of Obsidian Artifacts from the Whiptail Site (AZ BB:10:3 [ASM]), Tucson Basin, Arizona. Letter Report, Berkeley Archaeological XRF Lab, Department of Anthropology, University of California, Berkeley.

Simon, P. J., B. C. Glessen, and T. R. Copeland
1977 Categorization of Papers by Trace Metal Content Using Atomic Absorption Spectrometric and Pattern Recognition Techniques. *Analytical Chemistry* 48:2285-2288.

Simpson, Kay, and Susan J. Wells
1983 *Archaeological Survey in the Eastern Tucson Basin, Saguaro National Monument, Rincon Mountain Unit, Tanque Verde Ridge, Rincon Creek, Mica Mountain Areas.* Publications in Anthropology No. 22(1). Western Archeological and Conservation Center, National Park Service, Tucson.

1984 *Archeological Survey in the Eastern Tucson Basin, Saguaro National Monument, Rincon Mountain Unit, Tanque Verde Ridge, Rincon Creek, Mica Mountain Areas.* Publications in Anthropology No. 22(3). Western Archeological and Conservation Center, National Park Service, Tucson.

Sinex, S. A., A. Y. Cantillo, and G. R. Helz
1980 Accuracy of Acid Extraction Methods for Trace Metals in Sediments. *Analytical Chemistry* 53:2342-2346.

Slaughter, Mark C.
1996a Architectural Features. In *Excavation of the Gibbon Springs Site: A Classic Period Village in the Northeastern Tucson Basin,* edited by Mark C. Slaughter and Heidi Roberts, pp. 69-140. Archaeological Report No. 94-87. SWCA Environmental Consultants, Tucson.

1996b Summary and Concluding Thoughts. In *Excavation of the Gibbon Springs Site: A Classic Period Village in the Northeastern Tucson Basin,* edited by Mark C. Slaughter and Heidi Roberts, pp. 523-534. Archaeological Report No. 94-87. SWCA Environmental Consultants, Tucson.

Slaughter, Mark C., and Heidi Roberts
1996a Land Use Patterns and Site Structure: Social Organization at the Gibbon Springs Site. In *Excavation of the Gibbon Springs Site: A Classic Period Village in the Northeastern Tucson Basin*, edited by Mark C. Slaughter and Heidi Roberts, pp. 503-522. Archaeological Report No. 94-87. SWCA Environmental Consultants, Tucson.

Slaughter, Mark C., and Heidi Roberts (editors)
1996b *Excavation of the Gibbon Springs Site: A Classic Period Village in the Northeastern Tucson Basin.* Archaeological Report No. 94-87. SWCA Environmental Consultants, Tucson.

Slaughter, Mark C., Susan B. Bierer, Linda M. Gregonis, and William Grimm
1995 *Archaeological Monitoring of Tree Holes at the Roy P. Drachman Agua Caliente Park: The Whiptail Site and Agua Caliente Ranch Site, Pima County, Arizona.* Archaeological Report No. 95-46. SWCA Environmental Consultants, Tucson.

Sliva, Jane
1996 Flaked Stone Artifacts. In *Archaeology Investigations of the Early Agricultural Period Settlement at the Base of A-Mountain, Tucson, Arizona,* edited by Michael W. Diehl. Technical Report No. 96-21. Center for Desert Archaeology, Tucson.

1997 Flaked Stone. In *Archaeological Investigations at the Wetlands Site, AZ AA:12:90 (ASM),* edited by Andrea Freeman. Technical Report No. 97-5. Center for Desert Archaeology, Tucson.

1999 Cienega Points and Late Archaic Period Chronology in the Southern Southwest. *Kiva* 64(3):339-67.

2001 Flake Stone Artifacts. In *Excavations in the Santa Cruz River Flood Plain: The Early Agricultural Period Component at Los Pozos.* Anthropological Papers No. 21. Center for Desert Archaeology, Tucson.

Spencer, Jon E.
2000 Possible Origin and Significance of Extension-Parallel Drainages in Arizona's Metamorphic Core Complexes. *Geological Society of America Bulletin* 112(5):727-735.

Spier, Leslie
1970 *Yuman Tribes of the Gila River, Chicago.* Cooper Square Publishers, New York. Originally published in 1993, University of Chicago Press, Chicago.

Steen, Charlie, Lloyd M. Pierson, Vorsila L. Bohrer, and Kate Peck Kent
1962 *Archaeological Studies in Tonto National Monument.* Technical Series Vol. 2. Southwest Monuments Association, Globe, Arizona.

Steere, Peter L.
1987 Lithics. In *Archaeological Investigations at the Classic Period Continental Site AZ EE:1:32*, edited by Laurie Slawson, David C. Hanna, Peter L. Steere, and Skip Miller, pp. 94-130. Southwest Cultural Series No. 5. Cultural & Environmental Systems, Tucson.

Stevenson, Matilda Coxe
1915 *Ethnobotany of the Zuni Indians.* Annual Report No. 30. Bureau of American Ethnology, Smithsonian Institution, Washington, D.C.

Strand, Jennifer G.
1996 An Analysis of Vertebrate Remains from the Gibbon Springs Site. In *Excavation of the Gibbon Springs Site: A Classic Period Village in the Northeastern Tucson Basin,* edited by Mark C. Slaughter and Heidi Roberts, pp. 373-399. Archaeological Report No. 94-87. SWCA Environmental Consultants, Tucson.

Sullivan, Allan P., and Kenneth C. Rozen
1985 Debitage Analysis and Archaeological Interpretation. *American Antiquity* 50(4):755-779.

Swank, George R.
1932 *The Ethnobotany of the Acoma and Laguna Indians*. Master's thesis. Department of Anthropology, University of New Mexico, Albuquerque.

Szuter, Christine R.
1991 Hunting by Hohokam Desert Farmers. *Kiva* 56(3):277-91.

Szuter, Christine R., and Frank Bayham
1989 Sedentism and Animal Procurement Among Desert Horticulturalists of the North American Southwest. In *Farmers as Hunters: The Implications of Sedentism,* edited by Susan Kent, pp. 80-95. Cambridge University Press, Cambridge.

Talvitie, N. A.
1951 Determination of Quartz in Presence of Silicates Using Phosphoric Acid. *Analytical Chemistry* 23:623-626.

Teague, Lynn S.
1998 *Textiles in Southwestern Prehistory.* University of New Mexico Press, Albuquerque.

Thomas, D.H.
1971 *Prehistoric Subsistence-Settlement Patterns of the Resse River Valley, Central Nevada.* Unpublished Ph.D. dissertation, University of California, Davis.

Twilling, Shannon D., Jenna L. Bray, David B. Tucker, and Melissa Keane
2002 *The Eternal Spring: A Cultural Resource Survey of Roy P. Drachman Agua Caliente Park, Pima County, Arizona*. Cultural Resources Report No. 02-22. SWCA Environmental Consultants, Tucson.

Underhill, Ruth
1939 *Social Organization of the Papago Indians.* Columbia University Press, New York.

1946 *Papago Indian Religion.* Columbia University Press, New York.

Vokes, Arthur W.
1996 Shell Material from the Gibbon Springs Site. In *Excavation of the Gibbon Springs Site: A Classic Period Village in the Northeastern Tucson Basin,* edited by Mark C. Slaughter and Heidi Roberts, pp. 401-412. Archaeological Report No. 94-87. SWCA Environmental Consultants, Tucson.

Wallace, Henry D.
1986a Decorated Ceramics. In *Archaeological Investigations at the Tanque Verde Wash Site, a Middle Rincon Settlement in the Eastern Tucson Basin,* by Mark D. Elson, pp. 126-180. Anthropological Papers No. 7. Institute for American Research, Tucson.

1986b *Rincon Phase Decorated Ceramics in the Tucson Basin: A Focus on the West Branch Site.* Anthropological Papers No. 1. Institute for American Research, Tucson.

Wallace, Henry D., cont'd.
1995 Summary and Concluding Remarks. In *Archaeological Investigations at Los Morteros, a Prehistoric Settlement in the Northern Tucson Basin,* part II, by Henry D. Wallace, pp. 801-835. Anthropological Papers No. 17. Center for Desert Archaeology, Tucson.

Waters, Michael R.
1982 The Lowland Patayan Ceramic Typology. In *Hohokam and Patayan: Prehistory of Southwestern Arizona,* edited by Randall H. McGuire and Michael B. Schiffer, pp. 537-590. Academic Press, New York.

Welch, John R.
1989 Early Investigations at the Sabino Canyon Ruin. *Archaeology in Tucson Newsletter* 3(3):4-6. Institute for American Research, Tucson.

1997 Did Archaeoastronomy Begin at the Sabino Canyon Ruin? The Earliest Studies of Archaeological Site AZ BB:9:32 (ASM). *Old Pueblo Archaeology* 10:1-5.

Wellman, Kevin D.
1994 *Archaeological Survey of Saguaro National Monument 1994: The Saguaro Land Acquisition and Trails Inventory.* Publications in Anthropology No. 65. Western Archeological and Conservation Center. National Park Service, U.S. Department of the Interior, Tucson.

Wellman, Kevin D., and William Grimm
2001 Data Recovery Methods and Results. In *Archaeological Investigations at Roy P. Drachman Agua Caliente Park: The Whiptail Site and Agua Caliente Ranch,* prepared by Kevin D. Wellman and Mark C. Slaughter, pp. 27-70. Cultural Resource Report No. 00-03. SWCA Environmental Consultants, Tucson.

Wellman, Kevin D., and Mark C. Slaughter
2001 *Archaeological Investigations at Roy P. Drachman Agua Caliente Park: The Whiptail Site and Agua Caliente Ranch.* Cultural Resource Report No. 00-03. SWCA Environmental Consultants, Tucson.

Whittlesey, Stephanie M., and Robert A. Heckman
2000 Other Painted Ceramics of Southeastern Arizona. In *Prehistoric Painted Pottery of Southeastern Arizona,* by Robert A. Heckman, Barbara K. Montgomery, and Stephanie M. Whittlesey, pp. 95-114. Technical Series No. 77. Statistical Research, Inc., Tucson.

Wilmsen, Edwin N.
1970 *Lithic Analysis and Cultural Inferences: A Paleo-Indian Case.* Anthropological Papers of the University of Arizona No. 16. University of Arizona Press, Tucson.

Withers, Arnold
1941 *Excavations at Valshni Village, Papago Indian Reservation, Arizona.* Master's thesis, Department of Anthropology, University of Arizona, Tucson.

Yarborough, Clare
1986 The Chipped Stone Assemblage. In *The 1985 Excavation at the Hodges Site, Pima County, Arizona,* edited by Robert W. Layhe, pp. 127-165. Archaeological Series No. 170. Arizona State Museum, University of Arizona, Tucson.

Yetman, David, and Thomas R. Van Devender
2002 *Mayo Ethnobotany: Land, History, and Traditional Knowledge in Northwest Mexico.* University of California Press, Berkeley.

Zahniser, Jack L.
1966 Late Prehistoric Villages Southeast of Tucson, Arizona and the Archaeology of the Tanque Verde Phase. *The Kiva* 31(3):102-204.

1970 The Archaeological Resources of Saguaro National Monument. *The Kiva* 35(3):105-120.

Zuni People
1972 *The Zunis: Self-Portrayal,* translated by Alvina Quan. University of New Mexico Press, Albuquerque.

CPSIA information can be obtained at www.ICGtesting.com
232622LV00003B/1/P

9 781889 747880